Conte KU-520-668

List of Tables and Illustrations	ix
Preface	xiii
Foreword to the Sixth Edition, Ramesh Thakur	xxiv
Foreword to the Fifth Edition, Richard Jolly	xxvii
Foreword to the Fourth Edition, James O. C. Jonah	xxxi
Foreword to the Third Edition, Leon Gordenker	xxxvi
Foreword to the Second Edition, Inis L. Claude Jr.	xxxix
Acronyms	xli
Introduction	**xlvi**
The Legal Foundations of Sovereignty	l
State Sovereignty	li
Changing *Raisons d'État*	lvi
The United Nations: Actor or Institutional Framework?	lviii
UN Politics	lxii
Notes	lxv
PART ONE	
INTERNATIONAL PEACE AND SECURITY	**1**
1 The Theory of UN Collective Security	**3**
Collective Security in General	4
The United Nations and Security: Some Basics	7
Regional Arrangements	18
Straying from the Course	24
Notes	24
2 UN Security Efforts During the Cold War	**29**
The Early Years: Palestine, Korea, Suez, the Congo	29

Understanding Peacekeeping   34
"Chapter Six and a Half" on Hold, 1978–1988   41
Economic Sanctions   42
Notes   44

3 UN Security Operations After the Cold War (1988–1998)   47

The First UN Military Operations After the End of the Cold War,
    1988–1993   48
The Rebirth of Peacekeeping   48
Moving Toward the Next Generation   52
Moving Toward Enforcement   54
Nonforcible Sanctions in the Post–Cold War Era:
    Humanitarian Dilemmas   59
Operational Quandaries: Cambodia, the Former Yugoslavia, Somalia,
    Rwanda, and Haiti   61
Conclusion   75
Notes   76

4 Evolving Security Operations: Kosovo, East Timor, Sierra Leone,
   Lebanon, and Sudan   81

Using Military Force for Human Protection Purposes   82
Implications for the UN's Security Efforts   84
The Crisis in the Balkans   90
Turmoil in Timor-Leste (East Timor)   94
Reestablishing Stability in Sierra Leone   95
Lebanon—Again   97
Darfur, Sudan   100
Conclusion: The Responsibility to Protect   103
Notes   106

5 The Challenges of the Twenty-First Century   111

After September 11, What's New?   111
Political Challenges   120
Institutional Challenges   123
The World Summit 2005   131
Strengthening the Secretariat   135
Explaining Change   139
Notes   141

PART TWO
HUMAN RIGHTS AND HUMANITARIAN AFFAIRS   147

6   The United Nations, Human Rights, and
    Humanitarian Affairs   149
    The Theory   150
    Understanding Rights   152
    Basic Norms in the UN Era   158
    Core Norms Beyond the Charter   161
    Supplementing the Core   166
    Notes   172

7   The United Nations and Applying Human Rights Standards 177
    Security Council   178
    General Assembly   186
    International Criminal Court   188
    Office of the Secretary-General   191
    High Commissioner for Human Rights   194
    Commission on Human Rights (1946–2006)   197
    Human Rights Council (2006–)   201
    Supplemental Human Rights Bodies   204
    Human Rights and Development   211
    Emergency Assistance   214
    Notes   220

8   Change, the United Nations, and Human Rights   227
    More on Raisons d'État   229
    State Coalitions   233
    Nonstate Actors   235
    Theories of Change   239
    Final Thoughts   246
    Notes   247

PART THREE
SUSTAINABLE HUMAN DEVELOPMENT   251

9   Theories of Development at the United Nations   253
    The Politics of Changing Theories   253
    Notes   275

10   Sustainable Development as Process: UN Organizations and Norms   279

    Understanding the Organizational Chart: Coordination, Again   280
    Particular Contributions to Sustainable Development   284
    The World Bank, IMF, and WTO   296
    Norm Creation and Coherence: A History of Ideas   302
    The UN's Sustainable Human Development Model   314
    Notes   317

11   The UN, Development, and Globalization   323

    Globalization and Global Governance   324
    The MDG Strategy   326
    Implementing the MDGs   329
    A Global Partnership for Development   344
    Explaining Change   353
    Notes   357

    Conclusion: Learning from Change   363

    Measuring Change   364
    Learning Lessons?   367
    Articulation and Aggregation of Interests   369
    Rule-Making   376
    Rule Enforcement   380
    Some Final Thoughts   386
    Notes   391

Appendix A: The United Nations System   395
Appendix B: Concise List of Internet Sites Relevant to the United Nations   396
Appendix C: Charter of the United Nations   397
Appendix D: United Nations Universal Declaration of Human Rights   416
About the Book and Authors   420
Index   422

Tables and Illustrations

Tables

2.1	UN Peacekeeping Operations During the Cold War and During the Initial Thaw	37
3.1	UN Peace and Security Operations, 1988–2000	49
4.1	UN Peace and Security Operations, 1999–Present	87
4.2	UN Peace and Security Operations: Completed as of December 2008	88
6.1	UN Human Rights Conventions	168
7.1	Controversial Human Freedom Index	213
7.2	Human Development Index, 2008	213
7.3	Top Financial Contributors to the International Committee of the Red Cross, 2007	217
9.1	UN Development Milestones with a Strong Economic Flavor, 1943–1980	255
9.2	UN Development Milestones with a Strong Ecological Flavor, 1948–1982	263
10.1	Chronology of Selected Development-Related Conferences, 1990–2005	308
11.1	Millennium Development Goals and Targets	327

Figures

7.1	UN Human Rights Organizational Structure	178

Photographs

Intro.1	A view of the United Nations headquarters in Manhattan as seen from the southwest. The headquarters site covers approximately sixteen acres, from 42nd to 48th streets between First Avenue and the East River.	lxi

1.1 Edward R. Stettinius Jr., chairman of the U.S. delegation, signs the
    UN Charter in San Francisco on June 26, 1945. President Harry S.
    Truman stands by.   8

2.1 Prisoners guarded by a South Korean soldier wait to be taken to a
    POW camp near Inchon in October 1950.   32

2.2 Congolese refugees uprooted from their homes by fighting in
    Katanga Province wait for water at a refugee camp in September 1961.   33

2.3 Brian E. Urquhart, under-secretary-general for special political
    affairs, answers questions in June 1985 about his mission to the
    Middle East to free soldiers of the UN Interim Force in Lebanon.   40

3.1 Medical personnel from the multinational forces carry an Iraqi
    refugee into a camp near Safwan, Iraq, in March 1991.   57

3.2 Participants in an UNTAC demining course learn to cope with
    trip wires near Siem Reap Town, Cambodia, 1993.   63

3.3 UNPROFOR soldiers in Stari Vitez, Yugoslavia.   64

3.4 Somalian children receiving food in 1992.   68

3.5 Members of the Jordanian battalion of the United Nations
    Stabilization Mission in Haiti (MINUSTAH) rescue children from
    an orphanage destroyed by Hurricane Ike.   73

4.1 Secretary-General Kofi Annan holds the Nobel Peace Prize awarded
    in December 2000 to the United Nations and to him, as the
    organization's Secretary-General.   82

4.2 Ana Vaz (second from right), a Formed Police Unit officer of the
    United Nations Mission in Timor-Leste from Portugal, speaks to a Rapid
    Intervention Unit officer of the Timor-Leste Police about protecting
    the trucks distributing food with the help of the International
    Organization for Migration and the World Food Programme, by
    providing security for the camps of the internally displaced persons
    in his area of responsibility.   95

4.3 United Nations Interim Force in Lebanon (UNIFIL) troops observe
    Section 83 near the Blue Line on the border between Lebanon and Israel. 99

4.4 Chinese engineers working for the United Nations/African Union
    Mission in Darfur (UNAMID) unload their equipment kits upon arrival
    in Nyala, Sudan.   103

5.1 President George W. Bush and Secretary-General Kofi Annan at
    Ground Zero in New York City.   114

5.2 Secretary-General Ban Ki-moon addresses the staff members of the
    United Nations High Commissioner for Refugees.   121

6.1 Eleanor Roosevelt holding a Universal Declaration of Human
     Rights poster.   162

6.2 The Palais des Nations, UN Office at Geneva.   166

7.1 Haitians take to the streets of Port-au-Prince to celebrate
     Jean-Bertrand Aristide's election in 1990.   183

7.2 Secretary-General Ban Ki-moon unveils the artistic new ceiling of a
     conference room of the United Nations Human Rights Council.   203

7.3 Despite the best efforts of Operation Lifeline Sudan, millions of
     displaced people endured famine in the country even in areas that
     did not directly experience military clashes.   210

8.1 The Peace Palace, seat of the International Court of Justice.   228

8.2 Navanethem Pillay, United Nations high commissioner for human
     rights, addresses a plenary meeting of the General Assembly on the
     promotion and protection of human rights, on the sixtieth anniversary
     of the adoption of the Universal Declaration of Human Rights.   230

8.3 The rubble of United Nations headquarters in Baghdad following a
     suicide bomber attack on August 19, 2003, that killed twenty-two,
     including the Secretary-General's special representative for Iraq,
     Sergio Vieira de Mello.   231

8.4 At the "Killing Fields" memorial near Phnom Penh, shelves filled
     with skulls testify to Cambodia's tragic past.   234

9.1 Housewives cut and sew traditional farmers' cotton shirts to be sold
     in local markets and the women's cooperative shop in Mung Mo,
     Thailand.   260

9.2 A slum in São Paulo, Brazil, illustrates the shortage of adequate
     housing as rural settlements are abandoned by people moving to
     the cities.   265

9.3 UNICEF supplies the Zarghuna Girls School with educational supplies,
     provides teachers' training, and assists in repairing the infrastructure. 269

9.4 With UNDP and ILO support, the Rural Artisan Training Centre
     in Dakar, Senegal, instructs rural artisans, such as this potter. 274

10.1 A female work crew builds a road in Lesotho, 1969.   281

10.2 Brazilian president Collor de Mello acknowledges the applause of
     world leaders after he formally closes the UN Conference on
     Environment and Development in June 1992.   304

10.3 Scene at the Non-Governmental Organizations Forum held in
     Huairou, China, as part of the Fourth UN World Conference on
     Women held in Beijing, September 4–15, 1995.   310

10.4 Refugees returning to Cambodia in 1992 under the oversight of the
     UN Transitional Authority in Cambodia were offered different forms
     of UNHCR assistance, including a house plot and house kit.   311

10.5 A visiting foreign official inspects a solar cooker at a research facility
     in Gansu Province in China. The Natural Energy Research Institute
     focuses on new forms of energy-producing products.   314

10.6 A water pump powered by solar energy at Thies, Senegal.   315

11.1 Miguel d'Escoto Brockmann, president of the sixty-third session of
     the General Assembly, joined by Secretary-General Ban Ki-moon,
     addresses a high-level event of world leaders, private sector
     representatives, and civil society partners to discuss specific ways to
     energize collaboration to achieve the Millennium Development
     Goals (MDGs).   329

12.1 A group photo of the High-level Plenary Meeting of the sixtieth
     session of the General Assembly (2005 World Summit).   390

Preface

The United Nations and Changing World Politics is about the role of the UN and its associated family of organizations and specialized agencies in contemporary global governance. The UN is in an extraordinary period of transition, which is part and parcel of change in world politics. The three substantive sections of this text—international peace and security, human rights and humanitarian action, and sustainable human development—continue to be at the center of world politics. How the UN, with its 192 member states, responds to the related challenges, both old and new, is the substance of this book.

In September 2005, the world organization hosted the World Summit on the occasion of its sixtieth anniversary, somewhat hyperbolically dubbed "San Francisco II," (the UN was created at a diplomatic conference in San Francisco in 1945). The 2005 meeting was an ambitious effort designed to reform the United Nations, correcting for shortcomings and positioning the organization to meet ongoing and future challenges. "A once-in-a-generation opportunity to reform and revive the United Nations has been squandered," read the opening line of the lead editorial from the *New York Times*.[1] Once seen as a window of opportunity to revisit UN structure and roles in light of changes in world politics, instead negotiations exposed the very debilitating political and bureaucratic conflicts that regularly paralyze the organization. Ironically, the negotiations displayed in the limelight the state indecisiveness and pettiness that the summit was supposedly convened to address.

The UN has been on a roller-coaster ride since the end of the Cold War, especially in the area of peace and security, which is why Ramesh Thakur in his "Foreword" comments that we could have switched our book's title to *World Politics and the Changing United Nations*. Sometimes states call on the world organization to play central roles, especially concerning peacekeeping, and sometimes states bypass it and resort to their own version of enforcement—which some others call aggression or breach of the peace. By the 2005 World Summit, there was a consensus that the record of the UN Commission on Human Rights was so disappointing that it ought to be replaced altogether. Debate continued about whether the World Bank and International Monetary Fund, officially part of the

UN system, had helped or hurt developing countries since the late 1940s. Some reform has taken place. The General Assembly has since created the Human Rights Council and the Peacebuilding Commission. This sixth edition assesses the efficacy of these new bodies, highlighting their strengths and weaknesses, along with the rest of the family's members that have been around since 1945.

The UN continues to teeter on the verge of financial insolvency. Its chronic financial difficulties are not new and represent continuity rather than change in the organization's operation. Threats from the United States to hold up the UN's operating budget in exchange for managerial reforms also reflect the continuity of U.S. policy toward the world organization. The election of President Barack Obama holds promise that the UN might become more central to U.S. diplomacy; however, Obama has stressed that financing will continue to be tied to effective reform of the world body.[2] While it might be tempting for some to lay the blame for the UN's shortcomings squarely at the feet of the United States, the challenges facing the world organization defy such a neat explanation. Its shortcomings involve politics entrenched in state rivalries, between the haves and have-nots, and bureaucratic infighting involving control of agendas and resources. We have endeavored first and foremost to capture the essence of the United Nations as a political organization caught in the struggle to make public policy through the exercise of power. We stress how representatives of member states and other actors such as international civil servants seek to use UN symbols and procedures to shape policy. Clearly states do not approach the UN only or even primarily in terms of peace, security, and justice. They may give some attention to these abstract values, but they are primarily driven by their own values, needs, and interests. Indeed, a classic study of the UN and the great powers concluded that conceptions of immediate interests, not long-term and abstract concerns for peace and justice, have been the most important factors in shaping UN activities.[3]

Policymaking always involves power, understood as a synonym for influence. We also observe how UN structure and processes constrain the exercise of power. Hard power is coercion through manipulation of economic resources and through military force. Soft power is persuasion and pressure through words and symbolic acts. The central question for those interested in the United Nations is: Who seeks what policy objective, using what power, and with what outcome? What occurs at the UN, to paraphrase Harold Lasswell, is about who governs across national boundaries and who gets what, when, how, and why.[4]

The United Nations is about global governance without a world government, or attempts to collectively manage transnational problems in the absence of the "normal" attributes of government.[5] These attributes include a true legislature, a single executive branch, an integrated court system, and, above all, a legitimate monopoly on the exercise of force. Our primary objective is to get students to understand the UN as part of the fabric of world politics and its presumed centrality in managing complicated problems involving war, reconstruction, protection and promotion of human dignity, development, and environmental protection. We construct a balance sheet of achievements and shortcomings, and we seriously address the UN's role relative to regional organizations, unilateral undertakings, and ad hoc arrangements.

We also wanted to capture the essence of public international law as an institution that exerts real influence on real political struggles. We emphasize that, like all public law, international law is not a technical subject independent of politics but rather part and parcel of world politics. International law is formulated through a political process, frequently centering on the United Nations. Consequently, international law interacts with world politics, sometimes shaping it greatly and sometimes only slightly or not at all.

Whatever its ultimate impact on a given policy or situation, international law is influential in UN proceedings. Indeed, the world organization is a construction of public international law because the UN Charter is a multilateral treaty. The ever-present, often subtle influence of international law is perhaps better understood by those who practice politics at the UN than by many academics observing the process from the outside. We want readers to understand how international law interacts with "pure" politics; how attention to international legal rules (reflecting formalized policy) interacts with subsequent considerations of policy and power.

We also stress the importance of history. The present and the future have a history. When seemingly new issues arise, there is almost always a background to the issue that affects its management or disposition. When U.S. Secretary of State Colin Powell spoke at the UN Security Council in early 2003 about whether Iraq had complied with previous council resolutions demanding disarmament, many commentators referred back to the council of 1962. Then, U.S. permanent representative Adlai Stevenson dramatically confronted the Soviet Union over the issue of Soviet missiles in Cuba. In 2003 the United States did not have the kind of compelling evidence—the "smoking gun"—of denied weapons activity presented some forty years earlier. Still, UN history was part of the drama for Powell's presentation.

History does not necessarily determine the future, but history often affects the future in that it provides insights, lessons, and even prescriptions for policy. The history of such issues as using force, coordinating humanitarian assistance, or promoting sustainable development affects new policy decisions. It is essential for understanding UN politics. We want readers to know the political and legal history of the UN so that present and future choices can be analyzed and debated against that background.

The notion of change has long bedeviled social scientists. We have found it easier to chart the past than to understand the full implications of current issues, or where policy decisions on those issues may take us in the future. Nevertheless, we want to try to say as much as we can about change in world politics and what this might mean for the future of the United Nations. In *Taming the Sovereigns*,

Kalevi Holsti wrestles with the question and provides several alternative ways of measuring it—trends, great events, and significant social and technological innovations.[6] Ultimately, as in many debates, we are attempting to gauge the nature and extent of continuity versus change.

Certainly the fundamental units of the international legal order, sovereign states, are still organized to pursue their perceived national interests in a world without a single powerful central authority. International relations remains what Hedley Bull aptly called "the anarchical society."[7] Any thought that the UN will become a world government before the next edition of this textbook is simply not worth discussing. Sovereignty, as Stephen Krasner aptly put it, is still the same "organized hypocrisy" that it always was, in that powerful states still regularly violate the independence and autonomy of weaker states, whatever the UN Charter might proscribe.[8] In spite of the construction of a seemingly ever-denser web of international institutions, what Harold K. Jacobson called "networks of interdependence,"[9] there is nothing like a world government in the offing. This is because states do not want to create an independent power center that they might not be able to control or greatly influence. Nevertheless, various international regimes, often involving parts of the UN system, provide multiple forms of global governance even if not global government.

In short, diplomats following UN debates in New York as well as politicians back home face the same constraints today as they have confronted since the dawn of modern efforts at multilateral cooperation in the nineteenth century. Nothing has altered the pithy evaluation by Adam Roberts and Benedict Kingsbury in their aptly titled overview in *United Nations: Divided World*: "international society has been modified, but not totally transformed."[10]

While this overwhelming continuity of the state, or as some would prefer, the Westphalian, system pervades this book, it would be hard to argue that substantial changes have not also permeated most facets of international relations. Hence, readers will discover that we also emphasize how change in the United Nations can affect the future of world politics. We stress this interactive process as being part and parcel of the development of international relations. We also stress that individuals do matter. Since the fifth edition of this book, the United Nations has new leadership. Ban Ki-moon, a soft-spoken South Korean diplomat, was elected as the eighth Secretary-General, replacing the more charismatic Kofi Annan, who served from 1997 to 2006. The differences between the two are evident. Annan was an active Secretary-General who was vocal and visible in upholding UN ideals and was instrumental in developing relatively new principles such as the "responsibility to protect." Despite being widely perceived as "in the pocket of the Americans," he often was at odds with the United States, especially with the Bush administration's decision to go to war in Iraq without Security Council authorization. He also refused to commit the UN to helping Iraq (and other states as well) develop domestic criminal legal systems that envisioned the death penalty as a possible sentence. As with any leader, his record was mixed; however, he did make important and substantive contributions to the United Nations. Secretary-General Ban has a very different style. Although still early in his tenure, he has demonstrated a commitment to quiet diplomacy and avoided actions that might offend important member-states; his use of the bully pulpit is unlikely to be a prominent feature of his tenure. He has had some success getting the new Peacebuilding Commission off the ground and in creating and launching a peacekeeping mission with the African Union for the Darfur region of Sudan. Managerial and organizational reform, progress on climate change, and ensuring that the new Human Rights Council lives up to its responsibilities appear to be priorities. In this text, we outline and assess Ban's initial record.

Another important leadership development is the election of Barack Obama as president of the United States. We have made no secret that we think that the administration of George W. Bush did great harm to the United Nations and to the United States. After September 11, 2001, Washington did pay its past dues and sought Security Council assistance and approval for its counterterrorism activities and war with Afghanistan; however, beginning with the U.S. decision to invade Iraq, U.S.-UN relations went downhill. The Bush administration often sought to systematically undermine the world organization. Only a few weeks before the 2005 World Summit, Bush used a recess appointment to permit unilateralist firebrand John R. Bolton to represent the United States in New York. During the summit's preparations, he promptly proposed some 750 amendments and deletions to the "draft outcome document" that had been through several diplomatic refinements. Bolton's actions were disruptive and meant to derail the summit. While relations improved somewhat after Bolton's departure, the Bush administration worked to keep the UN at the margins on many issues in world politics. Bolton was not the only official in the Bush administration who took a dim view of international law and organization.

Obama's election holds considerable promise as he pledged during the campaign to work constructively and multilaterally with the UN. As a senator, for example, he sponsored the Global Poverty Act in 2008, which would increase U.S. overseas development assistance to .7 percent of GDP—a goal reached by the Nordic countries years ago—with much of that aid being devoted toward the Millennium Development Goals (MDGs). The appointment of Susan Rice as the U.S. representative to the United Nations and the elevation of that position once again to cabinet status sent positive signals of a change in Washington's policy toward the United Nations, especially with regard to such a pressing topic as climate change.[11] At the same time, this initial optimism should be balanced by caution. The Obama administration will need to face the "diminished power of American diplomacy" at the UN and constructively deal with the Third World voting blocs that "have been radicalized by eight years of confrontation with the Bush administration."[12] Moreover, the Obama administration might show more continuity with some Bush policies than some had forecast. Like Bush, Obama refused to participate in Durban II, the second UN conference on racism and xenophobia, mostly because the April 2009 meeting, like its predecessor in 2001, continued to criticize Israel more than Washington liked.

In analyzing past, present, and future actions of the UN, we have intentionally kept discussion of social science theories to a minimum. One can certainly use UN affairs to test some of the major schools of thought that seek a shortcut to, or a parsimonious understanding of, the essentials of international relations. For a different audience we could discuss whether realism, liberalism, constructivism, neoconservatism, Marxism, or some other "ism" helped explain developments at the United Nations. But to test the validity of any theory, one needs a detailed knowledge of UN debates, resolutions, and field operations. We wanted to present an analytical summary of the detailed UN record here, unencumbered by devotion to one theoretical preference or a survey of all. Moreover, the number of theoretical options is great, encompassing, in addition to the above, others such as feminism and functionalism. Furthermore, there is much debate about the boundary between realism and liberalism.

Some users of our previous editions thought that we showed great sensitivity to power politics, which would seem to make us collectively some type of realist. But other users saw our work as reflecting some type of institutional and state-centered liberalism. When the United States utilized the UN in 2002 regarding Afghanistan, was this an example of realism—because the UN was used to maximize state power? Or did U.S. policy reflect liberalism—because there was attention to international law and the Security Council provided approval for the U.S. military actions there? We have consciously chosen to avoid much of this theoretical debate with our eclectic and atheoretical approach. Already we use some "middle-range" theories in this book—for example, how knowledge affects power and policy, whether one can get to peace by the "back door" of functional cooperation, and whether democracies compose a peaceful security community. We also pay attention to economic theory as it relates to sustainable development as models of development are embedded in and informed by economics.

We have endeavored to design this book so that it can be used in at least two ways. First, we want it to serve as a core text in college courses on international organization and the United Nations, and we also are immodest enough to believe that many graduate students and even diplomats could learn a great deal from these pages. Second, we want it to be useful as supplemental reading in other courses, such as international relations and international law. Thus we have sought to present the essentials of politics at the UN in three central arenas: security, human rights, and sustainable human development. We selected these areas not only because of their intrinsic importance in world politics but also because the United Nations has had significant normative and operational impacts in all three; in addition, the 2005 World Summit used these three pillars to organize decisions about the UN's future. We have brought our collective experiences and judgment to bear on analyses of these issues.

Four outside reviewers read the original manuscript of the first edition in 1993. Craig Murphy of Wellesley College and Lawrence Finkelstein, then at Northern Illinois University, are both recognized scholars of international organization and world politics; they provided comments through the cooperation of the International Organization Section of the International Studies Association (ISA). Two other readers, unknown to us, were provided by Westview Press. A discussion group focused on this manuscript at the annual meeting of the Academic Council on the United Nations System (ACUNS) in Montreal during June 1993. Another ISA panel focused on the book at the 2002 conference in New Orleans. Thus, this book is in some ways a product of the International Studies Association and ACUNS. Although only the authors are responsible for the final version, we acknowledge with gratitude the time and effort that others put into improving our work.

We would like to express our special gratitude to those staff members of our respective academic institutions who—with good humor and professionalism—assisted in the preparation of the various versions of the manuscript. Quite simply, this sixth edition would not have appeared as quickly or been as incisive without the essential contributions from Danielle Zach and Janet Reilly at the Ralph Bunche Institute for International Studies of the Graduate Center of The City University of New York. Without the help of Susan Costa, Mary Lhowe, Melissa Phillips, Fred Fullerton, and Laura Sadovnikoff at Brown University's Watson Institute, and of Elisa Athonvarangkul at the Bunche Institute, earlier texts (upon which this one draws substantially) would have been considerably slower in appearing and certainly less well presented. Another word of appreciation goes to those younger researchers who have helped at one stage or another in framing arguments, checking facts and endnotes, and prodding their mentors: Peter Breil, Christopher Brodhead, Cindy Collins, Paula L'Ecuyer, Jean Garrison, Mutuma Ruteere, Barbara Ann Rieffer, Lekesha Harris, Peter Söderholm, and Corinne Jiminez.

We four authors are sympathetic to multilateral organizations in general, and to the United Nations in particular. We believe that the UN fits into a complicated world that less and less often favors unilateral undertakings. We believe that the first Clinton administration recognized this reality when initially describing its foreign policy as one that pursued "assertive multilateralism." Although it retreated from this rhetoric, it was reluctant to act without collective approval and support. Madeleine Albright, secretary of state for the second Clinton administration, stated clearly in 1993, when she was U.S. permanent representative to the United Nations, what remains valid today: "There will be many occasions when we need to bring pressure to bear on the belligerents of the post–Cold War period and use our influence to prevent ethnic and other regional conflicts from erupting. But usually we will not want to act alone—our stake will be limited and direct U.S. intervention unwise."[13] This orientation was much in evidence in 1999 when the Clinton administration led the bombing of

Serbia over the issue of Kosovo, even when its multilateralism was to be found in NATO rather than the UN.

Even more to the point, when the Republican administration of George W. Bush responded to world affairs after the attacks of September 11, 2001, Washington found that multilateralism was important to the success of its policies in the war on terrorism.[14] It then went to the Security Council in November 2002 to put pressure on Iraq but subsequently abandoned the council when it could not obtain its primary objective, nine votes of support. It was striking that after the major combat in Iraq in 2003, the United States went back to the council to get collective approval for its plans for occupation and post-conflict policies. Whether state foreign policy was embedded in the Security Council or some regional organization or some "coalition of the willing," multilateralism remained a key element of legitimacy and support.[15]

We have indicated our cautious optimism regarding a possible sea change in U.S. attitudes toward multilateralism under the Obama administration. A little over a month before the November 2008 presidential election, CNN's Christiane Amanpour interviewed five former secretaries of state.[16] They did not agree on much. But after the disastrous past eight years, they all stressed the necessity to cultivate friends, find new partners, and even do the "unthinkable" and engage Teheran and Pyongyang. They at least gave lip service to the role of international institutions. In both style and substance, there are many solid signs in the initial months after the inauguration of the forty-fourth president, but clearly we will have to await the seventh edition of this textbook to make a firmer judgment.

The current global financial crisis poses significant challenges to the international community of states as it requires a coordinated international response and significant reforms of international financial institutions in order to manage the economic fallout.[17] Perhaps as much as any recent event, the global financial and economic meltdown—which the late John Kenneth Galbraith might well have dubbed "the great crash of 2008"[18]—made even clearer what less serious previous crises had not, namely the risks, problems, and costs of a global economy without adequate international institutions, democratic decision-making, and powers to bring order and ensure compliance with collective decisions. "The global financial and political crises are, in fact, closely related," wrote no less an observer than Henry Kissinger on Inauguration Day, and the financial collapse "made evident the absence of global institutions to cushion the shock."[19] In all societies, what is legal or legitimate is, most often, collectively approved. So it is in modern world politics. This central fact mandates attention to the role of the United Nations and other international organizations, regimes, and arrangements.

We do not subscribe to "Wilsonian idealism," and so we approach the subject pragmatically, reflecting critically on the UN system. A preference for multilateral diplomacy is not idealistic at the start of the twenty-first century. On the contrary, unilateralists promoting an image of unbridled state control over events are the real utopians of the twenty-first century. Richard Haass—who was president of the Council on Foreign Relations and was director of the National Security Council during the first administration of George W. Bush—puts it this way: "No single country, no matter how powerful, can contend successfully on its own with transnational challenges. . . . The United States can only achieve what it seeks in the world if others work with it as opposed to against it or not at all."[20] Or, as former British Prime Minister Tony Blair noted, "We are all internationalists now, whether we like it or not."[21] British Prime Minister Gordon Brown, who followed Blair, has called for a complete overhaul of the existing architecture through a global "new deal." With the financial crisis looming on the horizon, Brown stated that "we must summon up the best instincts and efforts of humanity in a cooperative effort to build new rules and institutions for a global era."[22]

In principle we believe that collectively endorsed policies within the confines of the UN Charter stand a better chance of being successful than others agreed in less-than-universal forums. The UN's universal membership provides legitimacy and is a unique asset. We usually are suspicious of unilateral actions; we believe in the beneficial effects of channeling perceptions of national interests through the process of collective evaluation. Thus we do not endorse the view that states should use the UN framework only as a last resort. We believe that much damage has been done to world affairs by states that disregard the UN Charter and shun serious multilateral consultation, whether during the Cold War or after. Multilateral diplomacy can be complicated and messy, but too much unilateral action can be dangerous and destructive.

As John Ruggie, American academic and sometime UN official, has noted, all states resort to unilateral action from time to time. That is normal, especially with regard to their homeland security. But, he argues, increasingly it is clear that a doctrinaire unilateralism that bypasses the multilateral approach represented by the United Nations can be sustained in a globalized world only with great cost and difficulty.[23]

Nevertheless, we point out the weaknesses of the UN system. We do not hesitate to discuss places where the organization has not measured up to reasonable expectations. After all, the UN is not a religion and should be not worshipped but critically analyzed. Our text is not hagiography but presents the world organization warts and all. It is basically a political organization, even if it is affected by international law. And it is primarily affected by the foreign policies of member states, even if independent international civil servants like the UN Secretary-General and supportive nongovernmental organizations (NGOs) have important roles to play. We believe that constructive criticism of the United Nations is essential for a more peaceful, just, and prosperous world. Parts of the UN are clearly badly designed. We do not shy away from this reality. Officials representing the UN have made some terrible decisions. We do not shrink from recognizing this either. But unlike John Bolton and the American neocons, we do not regard the United Nations simply as an instrument of various foreign Lilliputians who would tie down a virtuous and powerful United States. One paradox of American power, increasingly recognized by initial unilateralists such as Ronald Reagan and George W. Bush, is that despite all of its hard power, the United States often needs an effective United Nations.

If we can get students to better understand the United Nations as a political organization, affected by international law, with its own history; if we can accurately portray the UN as greatly affected by basic changes in its political milieu; and if we can provide insights about what the UN has done and how these efforts might be improved in the future, we will have succeeded.

Each of the three substantive parts starts with an overview of basic ideas about the UN and that issue area (security, human rights, and sustainable human development). Each follows with a historical overview of how the UN has been involved and a discussion on changes that might lead to improved UN performance. Each part situates the broader political changes driving events at the UN; the nature of these political changes appears prominently in both the introduction and the conclusion.

Thomas G. Weiss
David P. Forsythe
Roger A. Coate
Kelly-Kate Pease
March 2009

NOTES

1. "The Lost U.N. Summit Meeting," *New York Times*, September 14, 2005.

2. "Obama, UN Chief Discuss reform while US Rededicates itself to the World Organizations," *Chicago Tribune*, November 20, 2008.

3. John G. Stoessinger, *The United Nations and the Superpowers* (New York: Random House, 1966), 176.

4. Harold D. Lasswell, Politics: *Who Gets What, When, How* (New York: McGraw-Hill, 1936).

5. For a brief discussion, see Thomas G. Weiss, "What Happened to the Idea of World Government?" *International Studies Quarterly* 53, no. 2 (2009): 253–271.

6. Kalevi J. Holsti, *Taming the Sovereigns: Institutional Change in International Politics* (Cambridge: Cambridge University Press, 2004), Chapter 1.

7. Hedley Bull, *The Anarchical Society: A Study* (New York: Columbia University Press, 1977). A more recent treatment is Robert Jackson, *The Global Covenant: Human Conduct in a World of States* (Oxford: Oxford University Press, 2000).

8. Stephen J. Krasner, *Sovereignty: Organized Hypocrisy* (Princeton, N.J.: Princeton University Press, 1999).

9. Harold K. Jacobson, *Networks of Interdependence: International Organizations and the Global Political System* (New York: McGraw-Hill, 1979).

10. Adam Roberts and Benedict Kingsbury, "Introduction: The UN's Roles in International Society since 1945," in *United Nations: Divided World*, 2nd ed., eds. Roberts and Kingsbury (Oxford: Oxford University Press, 1993), 1.

11. For commentary and speculation, see Thomas G. Weiss, "Toward a Third Generation of International Institutions: Obama's UN Policy," *Washington Quarterly* 32, 3 (2009): 343–364.

12. Colum Lynch, "With Rivals in Key Posts, U.S. Faces Hurdles at U.N.," *Washington Post,* February 22, 2009.

13. Quoted in the *Washington Post*, National Weekly Edition, June 21–27, 1993.

14. See, for example, Jane Boulden and Thomas G. Weiss, eds., *Terrorism and the UN: Before and After September 11* (Bloomington: Indiana University Press, 2004).

15. Ian Hurd, *After Anarchy: Legitimacy and Power in the United Nations Security Council* (Princeton, N.J.: Princeton University Press, 2007).

16. *The Next President: A World of Challenges*, aired September 20, 2008, transcript available at http://transcripts.cnn.com/TRANSCRIPTS/0809/20/se.01.html.

17. See Keith Bradsher, "Leaders of Europe and Asia Call for Joint Economic Action," *New York Times,* October 26, 2008, and Mark Landler, "Financial Chill May Hit Developing," *New York Times*, September 26, 2008.

18. John Kenneth Galbraith, *The Great Crash, 1929* (Boston: Houghton Mifflin, 1954).

19. Henry Kissinger, "The World Must Forge a New Order or Retreat into Chaos," *The Independent*, January 20, 2009.

20. Richard N. Haass, *The Opportunity: America's Moment to Alter History's Course* (New York: PublicAffairs, 2005), 26–27.

21. Speech delivered at the Economic Club of Chicago on April 24, 1999, available at www.number10.gov.uk/output/Page1297.asp.

22. Katie Zezima, "Brown Urges Global Push to Solve Global Problems," *New York Times,* April 19, 2008.

23. See John Gerard Ruggie, "Doctrinal Unilateralism and Its Limits: America and Global Governance in the New Century," in *American Foreign Policy in a Globalized World*, eds. David P. Forsythe, Patrice C. McMahon, and Andrew Wedeman (New York: Routledge, 2006), 31–50.

Foreword to the Sixth Edition

RAMESH THAKUR

*Foundation Director, Balsillie School of
International Affairs, Waterloo, Ontario,
and former Senior Vice Rector, UN University
and UN Assistant Secretary-General*

International organizations are among the most prominent features of contemporary world affairs. The United Nations lies at their center, touching our daily lives in numerous ways that would surprise most people if they were made aware of it. The organization is a mirror to the world; its history has been inseparable from human history since 1945, so much so that the title of this admirable book could just as easily have been transposed to *World Politics and the Changing United Nations.*

The United Nations was created from the ashes of the Second World War. Not surprisingly, therefore, its primary responsibility was the maintenance of international peace and security.

The war was a catalyst also to the destruction of the worldwide empires of the major European powers. The large numbers of countries coming out of the colonial experience eagerly embraced the values and ideals enshrined in the United Nations Charter and applied for membership in the international organization as the final imprimatur of sovereign independence. The rapid expansion in UN membership altered the dynamics of the international organization's internal relations and policy agenda. The newer countries were interested primarily in national integration, state-building, and economic development. Since at least the 1960s, therefore, development has been the second great normative mandate of the United Nations.

While the European powers lost their far-flung empires across the world's oceans in the aftershocks of the Second World War, the land-based Soviet empire crumbled in the wake of the collapse of the Soviet Union at the end of the 1980s. The end of the Cold War had a triple impact on world affairs, including, of course, the United Nations. First, it terminated the power rivalry between the United States and the Soviet Union to leave the former as the world's only re- maining superpower. Second, it marked the triumph of the market over the command economy. And third, but by no means the last in importance, it marked the victory of liberal democracy over totalitarian communism. Between them, they led to a markedly improved atmosphere of cooperation and collabo- ration at the United Nations, culminating in the UN-authorized grand coalition assembled to defeat and reverse Iraq's invasion and conquest of Kuwait in 1990–1991. The spirit of solidarity and cooperation was evident also in the unanimous and spontaneous bursts of sympathy and support for the United States after the horrific terrorist attacks of September 11, 2001. Yet a mere two years later, that sense of optimism, goodwill, and working together already seemed a distant memory. The tremors from the Iraq war launched in 2003 con- tinue to roil the United Nations as much as the world.

The last of the three changes ushered in by the end of the Cold War opened up space for the rise of human rights as a truly universal norm, albeit with local interpretations and applications in the different parts of the world. The world is better for the Cold War having been fought, for the manner in which it was fought, and for the side that eventually triumphed. Likewise, on balance the world is a better and safer place for all of us because the United Nations exists, because of what it does, and because of how it does it. The last two Secretaries- General, Boutros Boutros-Ghali and Kofi Annan, were the first chief executives of the United Nations to operate in a unipolar world, navigating their way through the thicket of intrigues, manipulations, demands, and expectations. Annan also was the first explicitly to elevate human rights, alongside security and development, as the third co-equal normative mandate of the international organization. He did this in his landmark 2005 report, *In Larger Freedom*.

The authors of this book are to be commended for organizing their chapters in the same three broad categories of international peace and security, human rights and humanitarian affairs, and sustainable human development. Well- known students of world affairs, of the United Nations, and of the place and role of the organization in world affairs, they deserve credit also for distinguishing the three United Nations: the world of member-states, the Secretariat, and inter- national civil society or the oft-forgotten and neglected "We the peoples." Their writing is as clear and accessible as their understanding of the subject matter is comprehensive and sophisticated. They instruct, inform, and occasionally enter- tain. They share an appreciation of the work that the United Nations does on a 24/7 basis but are not blind to its many flaws and shortcomings. Three of the four are personal friends as well as professional colleagues for whom my respect and admiration has grown only stronger over the course of the past decade.

That decade is history. Now there is a new Secretary-General at the helm of the United Nations, a new American president elected on the twin promises of change and hope, and new leaders also in France and the United Kingdom. The changing of the guard in Washington took place at a time when the great American nation was at war, the planet was in peril of irreversible damage from global climate change, and the great financial crisis seemed to herald a new constitutional moment in the history of international governance. Many of the great challenges and problems have proven to be remarkably obdurate and resistant to national solutions. It is easy and tempting to engage in finger-pointing and subvert UN diplomacy into waging warfare by other means. It will be far more difficult but commensurately more rewarding to engage with other nations in the one common forum dedicated to serving humanity to look for solutions across borders to problems without passports: from international terrorism to nuclear arms, proliferation, and warfare, from poverty and financial meltdowns to global pandemics, from desertification and global warming to food shortages and water scarcity, and from armed conflict to genocide and other atrocity crimes.

To solve a problem, we must first understand it. To use the United Nations to its fullest potential, deploy its assets to maximum effect, and exploit its strengths most effectively, we must study it, appreciate it, change it, and improve it as necessary, but also work with it as the international organization of choice. And there are few better guides to its inner workings and lofty ambitions within the constraints of human imperfections and foibles than this book.

Foreword to the Fifth Edition

RICHARD JOLLY

Honorary Professorial Fellow,
Institute of Development Studies, University of Sussex;
Senior Fellow, Ralph Bunche Institute for International Studies;
Co-Director, United Nations Intellectual History Project

As this fifth edition of *The United Nations and Changing World Politics* was going to press, one of the most eventful years in the UN's life had just closed. The 2005 vintage opened with the UN's being asked to lead action to cope with the gigantic human tragedy of the tsunami, which hit in the same month, December 2004, as the collective thoughts about moving ahead to confront terrorism and other new threats to the planet came from the High-level Panel on Threats, Challenges and Change.[1] This was followed in March by the publication of *Investing in Development*—the report to the UN Secretary-General on how to achieve the Millennium Development Goals for global poverty reduction;[2] and in the same month, Secretary-General Kofi Annan issued his own draft proposals for UN reform, adopted later after negotiation as *In Larger Freedom: Towards Development, Security and Human Rights for All.*[3] In September came the 2005 World Summit, the largest-ever gathering of heads of state—153 sovereigns, presidents, prime ministers, and representatives.[4] Against these largely positive advances, there were also a succession of attacks and doubts expressed about the Secretary-General and the UN's authority, from the neoconservatives and the Bush administration in the United States and right-wing sympathizers in other countries. All this meant that there was scarcely a day when the UN was not prominently on the TV or on the front page of the more serious press around the world.

Notwithstanding this high profile, ignorance about the United Nations remains widespread. Confusion reigns in many countries about its structure and capacity, its decision-making mechanisms, and its political and economic constraints.

Such confusion and ignorance come at a high cost—for the world organization itself and for the national interests of countries around the world. Like it or not, the UN (including the World Bank, the IMF, and related bodies such as the World Trade Organization) provides the main institutions of our fledgling efforts at international cooperation and global governance. Its mandates and operations bring oversight and coordination to a vast area of international activities: security, human rights, health and disease control, support for development and poverty reduction in poorer countries, conventions to eliminate discrimination against women and to promote concern for children, recognition and protection of world heritage sights—and a host of other important but less emphasized areas, such as oversight and coordination of international air transport, shipping, telecommunications, postal services, patents and intellectual property rights, global statistics, crime, illicit drugs, and terrorism. The UN also takes the international lead on key environmental issues: climate change and global warming, biodiversity, pollution and overfishing, nuclear safety, and the protection of water resources and the marine environment.

The UN's operations in these areas are often (though perhaps not quite as often as some countries argue) partial, weak, inefficient, and even biased. In the words of the Secretary-General, there is "a democracy deficit" in the UN's structures of decision-making.[5] Nonetheless, in many of these areas of global governance, the UN is the only show in town—and certainly the only one with recognized legitimacy and a universal mandate for action.

For all these reasons, citizens of all countries need to be better informed about the world organization—and certainly more than surveys suggest is the case at present. Citizens of the richer more developed countries have a particular obligation to be better informed, since their countries exercise dominant power and influence within the UN, especially those that are the permanent members of the Security Council—the United States, France, the United Kingdom, Russia, and China. Not only do these countries have disproportionate power and influence within the UN today, three of them—the United States, United Kingdom, and Russia—were overwhelmingly responsible for the creation of the current generation of international organizations. And two of them, the United States and the United Kingdom, were the main architects of the system when it was created at the end of World War II. Over the past sixty years, these countries have continued to exercise dominant, but not overwhelming, power in modifying the UN's structure and operations. The industrial countries provide the largest share of the UN's finance—of its regular budget, peacekeeping budget, and international aid and development assistance. Although within each of these totals, the United States makes the largest absolute contribution to the UN's resources, its per-capita share is less than that of Europe or of Asia taken as a whole.

In spite of this dominance by the major powers, there are limits to their control, set not only by other governments but by what can be seen as the "other parts of the UN." One can indeed refer to three United Nations: the first being the UN comprised of its member states; the second, of the Secretary-General and other international officials; and the third, of the NGOs closely associated with the UN. All three UNs have influence, and in explaining what happens within the world organization, an analyst needs to take account of all three. For example, a number of recent advances, such as the adoption of the international land mines convention or the establishment of the International Criminal Court, are the result of mobilization of action and support from the third UN.

At any time, the above reasons would add up to a compelling case for all people to know more about the United Nations—not only decision-makers, diplomats, and international activists but even more especially students, the decision-makers and diplomats of the future. The case is even stronger when UN reform is so high on the international agenda.

There is a particular priority for citizens of the United States to be better informed and engaged. As the world's only superpower, at the top of the world in terms of trade, technology, economic clout, and military power, Washington is often the leader in supporting or opposing action by the world organization. Ironically, the United States has led the charge in calling for UN reform but is then one of the least willing to negotiate with other governments in shaping collective decisions on reform. Of course, multinational decision-making among 192 countries is bound to seem tiresome and inefficient for any superpower in comparison with simply going it alone and then leaning on others or pressuring them to go along with its lead. Alternatives such as "coalitions of the willing" are an option, but they have their own costs and limitations, as is increasingly shown by events in Iraq.

In short, citizens of every country need to be better informed about the UN and how its operations and objectives relate to contemporary and future global challenges. Now in its fifth edition, *The United Nations and Changing World Politics* provides an admirable and well-proven introduction to the subject. Weiss, Forsythe, Coate, and Pease are a truly knowledgeable team, and they have once again assembled a comprehensive, up-to-date, and accessible text. Read it, study it, debate it—and enjoy. There are special rewards for those who debate and discuss it with those from other countries and who may have different views and perspectives. The book will then serve as a true introduction to the difficulties and dilemmas—but ultimately the opportunities—of reaching international agreement on the problems that the world faces and the role that the world organization can play in helping to resolve them.

NOTES

1. *Report of the High-level Panel on Threats, Challenges and Change, A More Secure World: Our Shared Responsibility* (New York: United Nations, 2004).

2. Millennium Project, *Investing in Development: A Practical Plan to Achieve the Millennium Development Goals* (New York: UNDP, 2005).

3. Kofi Annan, *In Larger Freedom: Towards Development, Security and Human Rights for All*, UN document A/59/2005, March 21, 2005.

4. United Nations, *2005 World Summit Outcome*, UN document A/60/1, September 15, 2005.

5. Kofi Annan, Speech to UNA-UK, London, UN document SG/SM/10332, January 31, 2006.

Foreword to the Fourth Edition

JAMES O. C. JONAH

Senior Fellow, Ralph Bunche
Institute for International Studies;
UN Under-Secretary-General (ret.)

Supporters and defenders of the United Nations system have often bemoaned the fact that despite the commendable contribution that it continues to make in the alleviation of human suffering and the promotion of social and economic development and human rights, the UN is often dismissed as a failure or irrelevant due to its perceived shortcomings in maintaining international peace and security. Although this concern is unfortunate, it is understandable that the general public should measure the success or relevance of the world organization in terms of its political and security preoccupation. After all, the UN Charter proclaims loudly that its central goal is to prevent succeeding generations from the scourge of war. The gloom surrounding the UN's future is particularly noticeable in the aftermath of the war in Iraq as this book goes to press in January 2004.

The fact that this is the fourth edition of *The United Nations and Changing World Politics* speaks volumes about why the book has been so successful. It presents an unusually well-informed and comprehensive analysis of what the UN has undertaken and achieved in the past fifty-seven years. The authors have not shied away from the failures by both parts of what they label "the two United Nations," the arena where states make decisions and the secretariat that executes many of them. The three authors—Thomas G. Weiss, David P. Forsythe, and Roger A. Coate—include a former UN staff member, and they are all keen observers of the UN system. Their title is apt, for they have presented a clear and thoughtful analysis of the manner in which changing world politics has had an impact on the performance, problems, and prospects of the world organization. The publication of this new edition provides a wealth of knowledge to enable scholars, students, and commentators to better understand the factors that account for the present dilemma with which the United Nations is confronted.

While the end of the Cold War has resulted in the emergence of a sole superpower with a predisposition to project military power, preemptively or otherwise, the fundamentals for understanding the UN have not changed. No matter what one's ideological views, the willingness and determination of major powers to change regimes that they do not like is nothing new. The United States and the then Soviet Union, with varying justifications, successfully conducted regime changes without much concern for the UN Charter. The only difference is that what was once done covertly is now pronounced publicly. Students of history know that the implication of the Yalta Agreements, as reflected in the Charter, placed the five permanent members (P-5) virtually above the provisions of the organization's constitution. Accordingly, only a naive observer could believe that the Security Council could prevent one of the permanent members from pursuing what it considered to be of supreme importance to its national interests. You do not have to be the hyperpower to ignore the Security Council, you only have to be one of the five.

Inis Claude, in justifying the useful role of the veto in the Security Council, observed that its use is an indication of a deadlock in the council that requires serious negotiations among the permanent members.[1] What has been hoped for over the years was that the P-5 would exercise maximum restraint, refrain from excessive use of the veto, and respect the decent and clearly expressed opinion of humankind. Even though Charter principles limit the use of force, they do permit it under certain circumstances, especially as set out in Article 51. But as was evident in the case of the first Gulf War of 1991, the council authorized the use of force to remove Iraqi forces from Kuwait. The Security Council took this action not because of the overwhelming influence of the only superpower—at the time, U.S. primacy had already become clear—but because of the unprecedented behavior of Iraq. For the first time since the Charter was agreed to in San Francisco in 1945, a sovereign member of the organization (Kuwait) was wiped off the map. Therefore, even the natural allies of Iraq were critical of its action and called for intervention by the Security Council. It was this unanimous international revulsion against Baghdad's behavior that may have led President George H. W. Bush to declare, somewhat prematurely, the existence of the "new world order."

The painful debate in the Security Council in the winter of 2003 over the use of force in Iraq, or more precisely over the issue of preemption and regime change, should draw our attention to the reality that nothing fundamentally has changed. Despite its status as the only superpower, the United States could not override concerns of the other members of the Security Council over its policy in Iraq. Apart from the United Kingdom and Spain, which were the other cosponsors of the draft resolution, other members of the council were prepared to give more time to the UN inspectors to determine the existence of weapons of mass destruction (WMD) in Iraq. It is unrealistic to argue that the only super-power could compel the United Nations to do what the majority of the member states did not wish to undertake. Even the way and manner in which Washington projects its power should be placed in context. Would the United States have suc-ceeded in changing the regime in Afghanistan without the full cooperation of Pakistan and other states in the periphery of Afghanistan? Or would the U.S.-UK coalition have succeeded in Iraq without the cooperation of states in the area that allowed the deployment of coalition forces in their countries in preparation for the commencement of the campaign?

With the view of implementing their policy on oil-for-food as well as the modalities of their administration of post-war Iraq, both Washington and Lon-don understood that they had to bring along other members of the Security Council in order to obtain its blessing.[2] This is a good illustration that the Secu-rity Council is not dead.[3] The obituaries have been premature. It has always been the case that member states, particularly the P-5, will willingly resort to the Se-curity Council or other organs of the United Nations if they believe that they can obtain support for their policies.

The disagreement in the council over Iraq further raises three issues that are discussed in the book and need further emphasis here. The first is the nature of international politics. Whether one likes it or not, balance of power still func-tions in international politics. U.S. preponderance of power will certainly pro-voke the creation of a coalition to balance that superpower. It should, therefore, come as no surprise that three permanent members, France, Russia, and China, together with Germany, have made serious attempts to restrain U.S. power by using the Security Council. This should only surprise those who have argued that the concept of balance of power is dead. This natural tendency could not be stopped by threats or insults—it is inevitable. For Washington to win support for its position and policy, it should be mindful of what the prominent historian Louis J. Halle once referred to as the "economy of power." The United States has to come to grips with the reality that "the consent enjoyed by a great power tends to diminish when its force is used in ways that are regarded as illegitimate whether against a small or another great power."[4]

The second issue that needs further elucidation is the role of the Secretariat and its head, the Secretary-General. Too often, commentators of the United Na-tions have played down the role of the Secretariat, forgetting that it is one of the six main organs of the United Nations. Although the Secretary-General is its head, the Secretariat has its own esprit de corps and is grounded in the concept of an international civil service. What was clear in the Security Council debate over the implementation of resolution 1441 in November 2002, which created a legal-diplomatic framework for dealing with Iraq, was the role of the inspectors. Under the new dispensation of the UN Monitoring, Verification and Inspection Commission (UNMOVIC), they were bona fide international civil servants. They stood in stark contrast to the earlier inspection units, the UN Special Commission

(UNSCOM), which was based on the concept of "loaned officers."[5] The majority of the council's members displayed confidence in UNMOVIC inspectors and was prepared to rely on their judgment before deciding whether the use of force was necessary. Here was a case where war and peace were to be determined by the independence of the world organization's civil servants. And it is to the credit of UNMOVIC that despite threats and browbeating, the inspectors stood their ground and informed the council that while they had not obtained full cooperation of the Iraqi officials, they were not prepared to make a definitive judgment that there existed material breach that justified war.

Moreover, the leadership of the Secretary-General is crucial. Regrettably, we have reached a stage where some commentators and officials are saying that because of the existence of one superpower, the Secretary-General should accommodate himself to that new reality. Such comments take little cognizance of the history of the United Nations. At the most acute stage of the Cold War, within the halls of the General Assembly, Secretary-General Dag Hammarskjöld was publicly challenged by Soviet premier Nikita Khrushchev, the leader of the era's second superpower. Hammarskjöld did not bend to the threat and insults but rose in defense of his office and the necessary independence of the international civil service. Accordingly, at that crucial stage of the UN's history, Moscow was promoting the concept of a three-headed monster, a troika, instead of a single leader. This would have definitely destroyed the United Nations. It was the courageous leadership of Hammarskjöld in his opposition to that proposal that ensured the United Nations' survival.

During the conflict in Iraq, it was unusual that the Secretary-General, although he had indicated his opposition to the war, kept quiet during the period of intense bombing when civilian lives were lost. While the archbishop of Canterbury and the pope were outspoken, nothing was heard from the thirty-eighth floor of UN headquarters. When the Secretary-General did finally speak, it was too late. Is it too much to expect to have a truly independent Secretary-General? One major obstacle is the practice of campaigning for the office. Undoubtedly, this has changed the nature of the position and has made it vulnerable to great-power control and influence. To prevent such an outcome, the proposal has often been made to limit an individual to hold one term of seven years.

The third issue that is not explicitly discussed in the book but is implied in many of its sections is the availability of accurate and independent information for the Security Council to make wise decisions. Mention has already been made of the council's reliance on UNMOVIC inspectors. Within the Secretariat there were attempts to obtain reliable and timely information by independent channels by establishing the Office for Research and the Collection of Information (ORCI) in 1987, but there was no linkage with the Security Council except for the responsibility of the Secretary-General under Article 99 of the Charter. The topic that has now resurfaced is the prominence and accuracy of information provided by member states.

The art of "spinning" has developed to such an extent that it is becoming increasingly difficult to discern facts from fiction, and the council has become victim to this. It is in this sense that members were reluctant to take at face value U.S. Secretary of State Colin Powell's presentation to the council in February 2003. In this context one must not forget what British Prime Minister Winston Churchill said during World War II: "In wartime, truth is so precious that she should always be attended by a bodyguard of lies."[6]

The authors of this volume have done a commendable service by providing the crucial ingredients for a better appreciation of the United Nations in all its diverse aspects and phases. Unlike most textbooks, this collaboration by Weiss, Forsythe, and Coate provides a theoretically and conceptually rich text that is also readable and informed by concrete activities by the world organization. This is "must" reading for anyone interested in the United Nations.

Among other things, and I stress this in concluding, the United Nations has gone through several phases when it was alternatively embraced warmly, viewed with profound skepticism and disenchantment, and viewed as the convenient punching bag by ill-informed critics. There is, therefore, no need for panic or despair concerning the travail of the world body after the U.S.-led invasion of Iraq. Nevertheless, the process of realistic reforms of the institution should proceed, particularly with respect to the Security Council. We now know that there is urgent need to revisit the use of the veto and the expansion of the Security Council to bring in Japan, Germany, and representatives of Africa, Asia, and Latin America. The financing of the organization should be on firmer ground, aimed at making the assessment of contribution more fair and equitable. For a greater part of the history of the United Nations, there was a struggle for universality; now we have obtained universality of membership. The difficult task ahead is to convince the general membership that this valuable institution belongs to all of its members and not just those that are powerful and affluent.

NOTES

1. Inis L. Claude Jr., *Power and International Relations* (New York: Random House, 1962), 158–165.

2. UN document S/PV.4644, 2002.

3. See, for example, Michael Glennon, "Why the Security Council Failed," *Foreign Affairs* 82, no. 3 (2003): 16–35.

4. Louis J. Halle, *Civilization and Foreign Policy* (New York: Harper Brothers Publishers, 1955), 81.

5. For a discussion, see Jean E. Krasno and James S. Sutterlin, *The United Nations and Iraq: Defanging the Viper* (Westport, Conn.: Praeger, 2003).

6. Quoted by Anthony Cave Brown, *Bodyguard of Lies*, vol. I (New York: Harper & Row, 1975), 11.

Foreword to the Third Edition

LEON GORDENKER

Professor Emeritus, Princeton University,
Center of International Studies

As this is written, soldiers wearing patches indicating participation in a mission for the United Nations have been taken captive in Sierra Leone. From Lebanon, where the Israeli military has just withdrawn from its so-called security zone, voices call for a strengthened presence by the United Nations to ensure tranquillity. Ironically, for more than forty years, spokesmen on both sides of that border have often vilified UN activities, and on many occasions actions rendered peacekeeping ineffective. In New York, the five main nuclear powers complemented an existing nonproliferation treaty, worked out thirty years ago by the United Nations, by pledging to eliminate nuclear weapons. In Washington, renewed obstacles in the U.S. Senate to paying a financial obligation for UN membership ensure continuing penury for the organization to which almost every country of every conceivable size and capacity belongs. In Geneva, in meeting rooms that date back to the League of Nations, a gathering of experts on human rights pores over reports to the United Nations. The intrusiveness of their discussion into national domains would have made the nationalistic hair of old-school diplomats stand up in shock. A covey of representatives from nongovernmental organizations intensely follows the proceedings for which they provide information. In East Timor, a UN mission offers help with the construction of a government.

On many a day during the last fifty-five years such a paragraph about UN activities could have been written. And, as now, it would have ignored more than it disclosed.

The United Nations, then, is a fact of our global life. To say so is not a defense of the organization, a claim about its worthiness, or a denunciation. It rather signals a need to understand this fact, to explain its boundaries, to fit it with other facts of contemporary life. This book, by three authors who have been close observers and students of, and participants in, several UN activities, fills that need.

The authors do not pretend to relate everything that could be known about the UN system. To begin with, UN history, spanning more than half a century, has been anything but fully compiled. And it is as complex as the world around it. Other parts of the story remain cloistered in inaccessible governmental and organizational archives.

The UN decision-making process includes some of the best and worst practices of international diplomacy and parliamentary procedure. Much of it consists of painstaking searches for agreement on texts on which representatives of many governments can agree. This effort involves speech-making that can be incomprehensible to the untutored onlooker. Some of the keys to understanding can be found in the usually bland published documents prepared by international civil servants in the name of the UN Secretary-General. Outside the meeting rooms, guarded informal encounters, instructions from national capitals that remain secret, and sometimes flamboyant nationalistic demands complement the public proceedings.

The words that set out what is agreed, encoded in diplomatic language and the catchphrases of international law, themselves guarantee little. They have to be applied by governments, most of which, it is sad to admit, either routinely avoid giving the words the fullest execution or do not have the means to do so. But words, as the Universal Declaration of Human Rights illustrates, can have lasting and even profound effects on what governments and their subjects do.

As the book suggests, no single theory provides a shortcut to understanding all of this. Some of the simpler theoretical approaches, much loved by muscle flexers, simply fail to explain much. Nor do analytical frameworks that concentrate on claims of national interests as seen from the perspectives of national capitals. Beyond the UN institutions, moreover, lies an increasingly complex, intertwined set of extragovernmental practices, organizations, and communications channels that help shape the UN agenda.

Instead of an encyclopedic approach or an abstract sketch, this book highlights three of the most important sectors of UN concern—peace and security, human rights, and sustainable development and environmental protection. As a result of digging deeply in those sectors, some of the main historical developments also emerge. Policy issues are clearly posed, the nature of the UN process comes into view. Some nuanced judgments about success and failure are drawn.

At the same time, the demand for a third edition of this book makes clear that as a totality the book admirably introduces its subject. Moreover, it opens doors to more inquiry. Why is the UN system so complex? How does it match and diverge from the actual world around it? Is it paralyzed by its own diplomatic culture? Can it be counted on to continue to develop? Can it, and should it, have a

greater influence on international relations generally? What encourages that development and what holds it back? For that matter, is the institution's form, built
around the concept of national sovereignty and parliamentary and diplomatic
procedures, increasingly obsolete in a world that each day less resembles that of
1945, when the United Nations was created?

If the responses to such questions remain uncertain, cause controversy, and
seem beyond terse summaries, avoiding them will not make them disappear.
They challenge imagination, bedevil statesmen, intrigue scholars, and ultimately
condition our future as they have affected our past. In providing an analytical
and historical framework for understanding where the United Nations has been,
Weiss, Forsythe, and Coate provide the foundation for understanding where its
future may lie.

Foreword to the Second Edition

INIS L. CLAUDE JR.
Professor Emeritus, University of Virginia

Since the end of the Cold War, the United Nations has enjoyed—and suffered—a burst of unaccustomed prominence. The organization initially gained attention as sponsor of the successful effort to roll back Iraq's conquest of Kuwait. Euphoric expectations of a global collective security apparatus soon gave way to disillusionment as the United Nations became conspicuously involved in disasters in Somalia and Bosnia. In any case, the United Nations is no longer ignored and neglected; whether it is regarded with utopian idealism or with cynical disdain, it has achieved notable visibility.

The organization's revived prominence has continued largely because of the role it has undertaken in dealing with many of the crises that have erupted within states. We no longer hear the United Nations praised or scorned as a talkshop. Rather, evaluations of the organization now relate mainly to what it does, tries to do, or should do or to what it should be equipped to do as an operating agency in the field. The focus of international relations is no longer exclusively interstate but has become predominantly intrastate, and the most significant activity of the United Nations is no longer that occurring at headquarters but that taking place in trouble spots around the globe.

These changes intensify the need for serious study of the United Nations with a view to development of realistic and sophisticated understanding of the nature of the organization, its possibilities and limitations, its merits and defects, the promise that it holds, and the dangers that it poses. Above all, we need to examine the United Nations in its political context, regarding it as essentially an institutional framework within which states make decisions and allocate resources, arranging to do a variety of things with, to, for, and against each other. Americans, in particular, need to escape the illusion that the world organization is some gigantic "it," beneficent or sinister, and to realize that the United Nations is instead a "we"—ourselves and other states. States acting jointly as well as singly are primary members of the cast in the drama of international politics.

The authors of this volume are keenly aware of this reality. Whether they are writing about the use of the United Nations in operations relating to peace and security, or its role in protecting human rights and responding to humanitarian needs, or its programs in economic and environmental fields, they emphasize its political character. Wisely forgoing the effort to present a comprehensive history of the United Nations and related agencies, they concentrate on the areas in which the United Nations has recently been most actively engaged. In so doing, they illuminate the changes that are sweeping the world in the post–Cold War era and the corresponding changes in the character of the United Nations and in its agenda. Students who seek a thoughtful analysis of the multilateral aspects of today's international relations will find it here. The book effectively conveys the thoughts of three well-qualified scholars; even better, it informs and stimulates the reader to develop his or her own thinking on the subject. I stand by the proposition that I enunciated a generation ago: The United Nations has too many supporters and opponents and too few students. May their tribe increase!

Acronyms

ASEAN	Association of Southeast Asian Nations
AU	African Union
CAT	Committee Against Torture
CEB	United Nations System Chief Executives Board for Coordination
CEDAW	Committee on the Elimination of Discrimination Against Women
CERD	Committee on the Elimination of Racial Discrimination
CIS	Commonwealth of Independent States
CHR	Commission on Human Rights
CRC	Committee on the Rights of the Child
CSCE	Conference on Security and Co-operation in Europe
CSD	Commission on Sustainable Development
DESA	United Nations Department for Economic and Social Affairs
DPA	Department of Political Affairs
DPKO	Department of Peacekeeping Operations
DSP	Dispute Settlement Panel
EC	European Community
EC-ESA	Economic and Social Affairs Executive Committee
ECA	Economic Commission for Africa
ECAFE	Economic Commission for Asia and the Far East
ECE	Economic Commission for Europe
ECHA	Executive Committee for Humanitarian Affairs
ECLAC	Economic Commission for Latin America and the Caribbean
ECOMOG	Military Observer Group of the Economic Community of West African States
ECOSOC	Economic and Social Council
ECOWAS	Economic Community of West African States
EPTA	Expanded Programme of Technical Assistance
ERC	emergency relief coordinator
ESCAP	Economic and Social Commission for Asia and the Pacific
ESCWA	Economic and Social Commission for Western Asia
EU	European Union
FAO	Food and Agriculture Organization

FMLN   Frente Farabundo Martí para la Liberación Nacional (Farabundo
          Martí National Liberation Front)
G7   Group of Seven
G8   Group of Eight
G77   Group of 77
GATT   General Agreement on Tariffs and Trade
GCC   Gulf Cooperation Council
GDP   gross domestic product
GEF   Global Environment Facility
GEI   Green Economic Initiative
HABITAT   UN Conference on Human Settlements
HIPC   Heavily Indebted Poor Countries Initiative
HIV/AIDS Human Immunodeficiency Virus/Acquired Immunodeficiency
          Syndrome
HLP   High-level Panel on Threats, Challenges and Change
HRC   Human Rights Council
IAEA   International Atomic Energy Agency
IASC   Inter-Agency Standing Committee
IBP   International Biological Programme
IBRD   International Bank for Reconstruction and Development
ICC   International Criminal Court
ICISS   International Commission on Intervention and State Sovereignty
ICJ   International Court of Justice
ICRC   International Committee of the Red Cross
ICSU   International Council of Scientific Unions
ICT   Information and Communications Technology
IDA   International Development Association
IDP   internally displaced person
IFI   international financial institution
IFOR   Implementation Force (in the former Yugoslavia)
IGBP   International Geosphere-Biosphere Programme
IGO   intergovernmental organization
IHL   international humanitarian law
ILO   International Labour Organization
IMF   International Monetary Fund
IMO   International Maritime Organization
INTERFET International Force in East Timor
IOC   International Oceanographic Commission
IPCC   Intergovernmental Panel on Climate Change
ISAF   International Security Assistance Force
ITO   International Trade Organization
ITU   International Telecommunications Union
ITUC   International Trade Union Confederation

IUCN	International Union for the Conservation of Nature and National Resources
KLA	Kosovo Liberation Army
LDCs	least developed countries
LLDCs	landlocked developing countries
MCA	Millennium Challenge Account
MDA	Magen David Adom Israeli aid society
MDG	Millennium Development Goal
MDGR	Millennium Development Goal Report
MINURCAT	United Nations Mission in the Central African Republic and Chad
MINUSTAH	United Nations Stabilization Mission in Haiti
MNF	Multinational Force
MONUC	United Nations Observer Mission in the Democratic Republic of the Congo
MSC	Military Staff Committee
NAM	Non-Aligned Movement
NATO	North Atlantic Treaty Organization
NGLS	Non-Governmental Liaison Service
NGO	nongovernmental organization
NIEO	New International Economic Order
NSA	nonstate actor
NTB	nontariff barrier
OAS	Organization of American States
OAU	Organization of African Unity
OCHA	Office for the Coordination of Humanitarian Affairs
ODA	overseas development assistance
ODC	Overseas Development Council
OECD	Organisation for Economic Co-operation and Development
OEF	Operation Enduring Freedom
OHCHR	Office of the High Commissioner for Human Rights
ONUB	United Nations Operation in Burundi
ONUC	United Nations Operation in the Congo
ONUCA	United Nations Observer Group in Central America
ONUSAL	United Nations Observer Mission in El Salvador
ONUVEH	United Nations Observer Mission to Verify the Electoral Process in Haiti
ONUVEN	United Nations Observer Mission to Verify the Electoral Process in Nicaragua
OPEC	Organization of Petroleum Exporting Countries
OSCE	Organization on Security and Co-operation in Europe
PBC	Peacebuilding Commission
PEPFAR	President's Emergency Plan for AIDS Relief
PLO	Palestine Liberation Organization
PMC	Permanent Mandates Commission

PVO   private voluntary organization
RUF   Revolutionary United Front
SAARC   South Asian Association for Regional Cooperation
SADCC   Southern African Development Coordination Conference
SARS   severe acute respiratory syndrome
SCOPE   Scientific Committee on Problems of the Environment
SIDS   small island developing states
SMG   Senior Management Group
SUNFED Special United Nations Fund for Economic Development
SWAPO   South-West Africa People's Organization
TDB   Trade and Development Board
TNC   transnational corporation
TRIMS   trade-related investment measures
TRIPS   Trade-Related Aspects of Intellectual Property Rights
UDHR   Universal Declaration of Human Rights
UNAMA   United Nations Assistance Mission for Afghanistan
UNAMET United Nations Mission in East Timor
UNAMID African Union/United Nations Hybrid Mission in Darfur
UNAMIR United Nations Assistance Mission in Rwanda
UNAMSIL United Nations Mission for Sierra Leone
UNAVEM United Nations Angola Verification Mission
UNCDF   United Nations Capital Development Fund
UNCED   United Nations Conference on Environment and Development
UNCHE   United Nations Conference on the Human Environment
UNCHS   United Nations Center for Human Settlements (Habitat)
UNCTAD United Nations Conference on Trade and Development
UNDOF   United Nations Disengagement Observer Force
UNDP   United Nations Development Programme
UNDRO   United Nations Disaster Relief Office
UNEF   United Nations Emergency Force
UNEP   United Nations Environment Programme
UNESCO United Nations Educational, Scientific and Cultural Organization
UNFICYP United Nations Peacekeeping Force in Cyprus
UNGOMAP United Nations Good Offices Mission in Afghanistan and Pakistan
UNHCR   United Nations High Commissioner for Refugees
UNICEF United Nations Children's Fund
UNIFEM United Nations Development Fund for Women
UNIFIL United Nations Interim Force in Lebanon
UNIIMOG United Nations Iran-Iraq Military Observer Group
UNITA   National Union for the Total Independence of Angola
UNITAF Unified Task Force (in Somalia)
UNMEE   United Nations Mission Ethiopia and Eritreas
UNMIH   United Nations Mission in Haiti
UNMIK   United Nations Interim Administration Mission in Kosovo

UNMIL	United Nations Mission in Liberia
UNMIS	United Nations Mission in the Sudan
UNMISET	United Nations Mission of Support in East Timor
UNMIT	United Nations Integrated Mission in Timor-Leste
UNMOGIP	United Nations Military Observer Group in India and Pakistan
UNMOVIC	United Nations Monitoring, Verification and Inspection Commission
UNOCI	United Nations Operation in Cote d'Ivoire (UNOCI)
UNOMSIL	United Nations Observer Mission in Sierra Leone
UNOSOM	United Nations Operation in Somalia
UNPROFOR	United Nations Protection Force (in the former Yugoslavia)
UNSMIH	United Nations Support Mission in Haiti
UNTAC	United Nations Transitional Authority in Cambodia
UNTAET	United Nations Transitional Administration in East Timor
UNTAG	United Nations Transition Assistance Group in Namibia
UNTSO	United Nations Truce Supervision Organization
UPU	Universal Postal Union
USSR	Union of Soviet Socialist Republics
VOLAG	volunteer agency
WACAP	World Alliance of Cities Against Poverty
WCRP	World Climate Research Programme
WFP	World Food Programme
WHO	World Health Organization
WMD	weapon of mass destruction
WMO	World Meteorological Organization
WTO	World Trade Organization

Introduction

The most casual observer of the international scene can see that the problem of world order has not been solved.

—Inis L. Claude Jr., *Swords into Plowshares*

The twentieth century was an era of bold transition. When the century began, global multilateral relations and international organizations were in their infancy. Experiments with international unions, conference diplomacy, and the expansion of multilateral relations beyond Europe remained fledgling. As the decades unfolded, so did universal multilateralism, albeit on the European state-system model. First, the League of Nations was created to meet the challenges posed by the increasing lethality of warfare and the associated evolving norm of the "illegality" of aggressive war. Although this first great experiment failed, it laid the foundation for its successor, the United Nations. When the second great European war of the century became a global conflict, national governmental leaders once again began to search for a way to prevent global conflicts. Under the leadership of officials from the United States and Great Britain, the United Nation's allies launched this second great experiment in universal international organization. This time, however, the collective security agreement was seen as part of a more comprehensive global arrangement in which the guarantees of collective security were linked to a series of international institutions aimed at promoting and fostering the social and economic conditions necessary for peace to prevail.

The UN system was born plural and decentralized and was never intended to approximate a centralized unitary system that would have resembled a government. It also was born from pragmatism. A great war against fascism and irrationalism was being fought and won; the price of a third great war was viewed as too great—this realization seemed even more striking when the nuclear era began in Hiroshima barely six weeks after the ink dried on the Charter in San Francisco. The founders saw the UN as the harnessing of state power for the management of pressing problems—in the words of one analyst, "Its wartime architects bequeathed us this system as a realist necessity vital in times of trial, not as a liberal accessory to be discarded when the going gets rough."[1] This was hardly wide-eyed idealism or utopianism run amok.

It bears emphasizing that even the UN's socioeconomic agencies were seen not as part of altruism but as an indirect attack on war as well as a means of promoting economic prosperity at home as well as abroad. Franklin Delano Roosevelt believed strongly that the origins of World War II lay in the economic and social misery of the 1920s. In his view, it was those conditions that had given rise to aggressive fascism in Europe. So even as the Second World War continued, the U.S.-led United Nations alliance began putting in place a broad UN system that included the Food and Agricultural Organization (1943), United Nations Rehabilitation and Relief Administration (1943), International Bank for Reconstruction and Development/World Bank (1944), International Monetary Fund (1944), and other economic and social agencies.[2]

Given that the primary purpose of the UN was to deal with international peace and security, most observers no doubt think in terms of a traditional management of the use of force rather than an indirect approach to peace through economic and social development. In viewing the record of the former concern, one can say that the history of the United Nations illustrates the trials and tribulations of collective security since World War II.[3] UN officials managed more than 20,000 troops in the old Belgian Congo in the 1960s (later Zaire and more recently once again the Congo). Secretary-General Dag Hammarskjöld died while coping with that crisis, which almost caused the collapse of the world organization. UN diplomatic and military personnel were deeply involved in Middle Eastern politics since the late 1940s in Palestine but especially in the 1956 Suez crisis and the 1967 Arab-Israeli War.

At times the United Nations was placed on the back burner. For much of the 1970s and even more in the 1980s, major states bypassed the world organization on international security issues. Some developing countries continued to look upon the UN as central to world politics, but both the United States and the Soviet Union mostly favored action outside it. Circles of opinion in Washington, both public and private, were particularly harsh in their criticisms of the organization in the 1980s. The first administration of Ronald Reagan, and related think tanks like the Heritage Foundation, manifested a deep distrust of multilateral diplomacy. One Reagan official, Charles Lichenstein, assigned to the UN, spoke publicly of "waving . . . a fond farewell as [the UN] sailed into the sunset."[4] Several U.S. allies also shied away from an organization whose "automatic" voting majorities had shifted over the decades from being controlled by the United States to being dominated by developing countries. They, like the United States, appeared at times to despair of an organization whose resolutions were not followed by commitment to action. That the world organization, at least as embodied in the rules and procedures of the Security Council, was not supposed to act unless there existed a concert of the major powers—the Permanent 5—became lost in the critique of those who normatively wished otherwise.

A marked change came over the organization in the wake of the collapse of European communism from 1985 to 1991. Mikhail Gorbachev, then the first secretary of the Communist Party of the Soviet Union, called upon the world organization in a September 1987 article in *Pravda* to play a more central role in world politics as a cornerstone of global security. Then boldly, more boldly than any previous leader of a superpower, Gorbachev embraced the UN and its collective security mechanism as a cornerstone of Soviet security policy. The Reagan administration, the most unilateralist in modern American political history up to that point, responded cautiously. Nonetheless, by the end of the George H. W. Bush administration in 1993, the United States had used the UN to a great extent in dealing with such major issues as the Iraqi invasion of Kuwait in 1990,[5] although earlier it had bypassed the UN on other matters such as the invasion of Panama in 1989. By the mid-1990s, the UN was back on the front pages and in the headlines—and on CNN and the BBC as well.

Many developing states constituting the Global South were cautious as the Soviet Union (and subsequently Russia) and the United States—"two elephants," to paraphrase a popularly used image during that period—and their three Security Council permanent-member counterparts danced the dance of consensus, which led to an unprecedented use of the Security Council as a global security mechanism. In the years immediately after the Cold War, UN peacekeeping and enforcement activities underwent a tremendous surge. From 1988 to 1993, more UN military operations—over twenty new operations—were launched than during the entire first four decades of the world organization. Great euphoria reigned in pro-internationalist circles in the United States just as great concern reigned in many smaller member states.

The roller-coaster ride continued as the UN's peacekeeping and peace-enforcement profile once again changed. The scope of the Security Council's business slowed after 1993.[6] In the next five years, sixteen peacekeeping operations were authorized; however, that number is misleading because seven were offshoots of previous missions. Of the remaining new operations, only the third UN Angola Verification Mission (UNAVEM III) was of significant size (with 6,500 troops) and duration. Both the total number of UN blue helmets and the peacekeeping budget fell by two-thirds from 1994 to 1998, reflecting disillusionment with the results from controversial involvement in Somalia, Rwanda, and the Balkans.

In 1999, change set in again, effectively more than doubling the number of personnel involved in UN security operations. Major new missions were launched in Sierra Leone (6,260 military troops and observers), East Timor (9,150 troops and observers), and Kosovo (approximately 4,500 UN and partner organization personnel and civilian police). But the numbers of operations and personnel tell only part of the story. The missions in Kosovo, East Timor, and another new operation, the UN Observer Mission in the Democratic Republic of the Congo (MONUC), represented a qualitatively different kind of exceedingly complex and multidimensional operation. The missions were tasked with creating viable political and social institutions, rebuilding basic social and economic infrastructures, strengthening the rule of law as well as protecting human rights, and demobilizing former combatants and reintegrating them into society. Greatly expanding on earlier multidimensional operations, especially in El Salvador and Cambodia, the new efforts aimed at reconstituting viable states, an ambitious effort that critics referred to as "neocolonialism" but that one observer, Jarat Chopra, has dubbed "peace-maintenance."[7] Still others referred to "nation-building" or "state-building," while some military establishments talked of "post-combat reconstruction."

This intense involvement in post-conflict situations took a new form following the attacks on the United States on September 11, 2001. The overthrow of the Taliban regime in Afghanistan led to a new type of UN involvement, a so-called light footprint by the UN so that Afghans played a prominent role rather than foreigners. In Iraq in 2003, the UN made almost no footprint for a time. After the government of Saddam Hussein was removed, the Security Council, despite not approving the U.S.-led invasion, approved the administrative control by the United States and a small coalition of states, the most important of which was the United Kingdom. Later the council approved a scheme for the development of post-Saddam Iraq, but in reality the fate of Iraq largely rested with the United States.

Sometimes the administration of George W. Bush surpassed the vitriol of the Reagan administration in its criticism of the United Nations and willingness to resort to unilateralism. The National Security Strategy of the United States of America, unveiled by the president in September 2002, colored discussions about using force.[8] Many regarded the new doctrine, with its emphasis on preventive intervention, as a threat to the principle of nonintervention.

Yet the Bush administration pursued a variety of other unilateral measures in other spheres, from "unsigning" the statute on the International Criminal Court (ICC) to opting out of the antiballistic missile treaty to treating with disdain efforts to mitigate climate change through the Kyoto Protocol. The administration seemed oblivious to what Joseph Nye calls the "paradox of American power"[9]—the inability of the world's strongest state to secure some of its major goals alone. Bush's rampant unilateralism prompted a former Reagan official, conservative economist Clyde Prestowitz, to label the United States a "rogue nation."[10]

Unless Washington is prepared to bend on occasion, governments are unlikely to sign on when their help is needed for U.S. priorities. As in a poker game, a player should not want to win every hand, because then the other players will drop out. As well as pursuing elections, weapons inspections, and a host of other tasks in Iraq, other obvious examples where U.S. interests would be fostered more through cooperation than going it alone include fighting terrorism (intelligence sharing and anti–money laundering efforts), confronting the global specter of infectious diseases (HIV/AIDS, Ebola, and SARS), and the monitoring of human rights and supporting criminal tribunals. Humanitarian intervention is a quintessentially multilateral task because of the desirability of both collective approval and cost sharing.[11] Ironically, as John Ikenberry aptly notes in echoing Nye, "There are limits on American imperial pretensions even in a unipolar era."[12]

As occurred in Reagan's second term, there was some increased pragmatism in George W. Bush's second term, including occasionally a more positive evaluation of multilateralism. That administration, having rejected NATO's offer of help for Afghanistan in 2001, sought a greater NATO role there several years later—indeed, it lamented that some NATO partners were not pulling their weight, a criticism that became quite public in 2008. Having tried to kill the ICC, the Bush administration later did not veto a Security Council resolution asking the ICC prosecutor to investigate relevant crimes in the Darfur region of Sudan. The administration took a multilateral approach to the issue of North Korea and nuclear weapons, albeit one largely outside the United Nations. And the organization's peace operations budget ballooned to some $8 billion by early 2009. The financial and economic meltdown that began in 2008 was the occasion to begin multilateral conversations, but action remained primarily national and uncoordinated.

In the peacekeeping arena, the character of UN operations has been changing. Fewer than 20 percent of the UN missions launched since 1988 have been in response to interstate conflict, the type for which the UN founders had originally planned. The majority of UN operations have been in response to intrastate conflict. Security Council responses to domestic armed conflicts in the post–Cold War era fundamentally called into question antiquated notions of the inviolability and absolute character of state sovereignty as well as the sanctity of the notion of noninterference in the internal affairs of states. After all, once human rights became codified in international law, the state's treatment of its citizens was no longer a matter of purely domestic jurisdiction shielded by state sovereignty.

So, world politics has been in constant change leading to ups and downs in UN responses to major issues. These ups and downs mostly depend on the policies of member states. Overall, the UN continues to be centrally involved in many if not most important situations, although on some issues, whether human rights in the Darfur region of Sudan or ecological protection via the Kyoto Protocol, states like China, Russia, the United States, and India may not be supportive of an important role for the United Nations. Despite all the problems and challenges, however, its peacekeeping business grew, with 2008 witnessing by far the largest number of UN uniformed forces in the field—some 100,000, a number that promised to continue to grow in 2009.

THE LEGAL FOUNDATIONS OF SOVEREIGNTY

When the Peace of Westphalia essentially ended European religious wars in 1648, powerful political circles accepted that the world should be divided into territorial states. Before that time, dynastic empires, city-states, feudalistic orders, clans and tribes, churches, and a variety of other arrangements organized persons into groupings for personal identity and problem solving. From about the middle of the fifteenth century to the middle of the seventeenth, the territorial state emerged, first in Europe and then elsewhere, as the basic unit of social organization that supposedly commanded primary loyalty and was responsible for order, and eventually for justice and prosperity, within a state's territorial boundaries. European rulers found the institution of the state useful and perpetuated its image; then politically aware persons outside the West adopted the notion of the state to resist domination by European states.

However, other groupings persisted. In nineteenth-century Europe, Napoleon sought to substitute a French empire for several states, and European imperialism thrived and colonialism persisted in Africa until the 1970s. Despite these exceptions and the persistence of clan, ethnic, and religious identities, most of those exercising power increasingly promoted the perception that the basic political-legal unit of world affairs was the state: an administrative apparatus with a supposed monopoly on the legitimate use of force over a specific geographical area, with a stable (non-nomadic) population. Frequently, the territorial state is referred to as the "nation-state." This label is not totally false, but it can be misleading because nations and states are not the same. A nation is a people (a group of persons professing solidarity on the basis of language, religion, history, or some other bonding element) linked to a state. Legally speaking, where there is a state there is a nation, but there may be several peoples within a state. For example, in Switzerland (officially the Helvetian Confederation), by legal definition there is the Swiss nation, but in social reality there are four peoples linked to that state: the Swiss-Germans, the Swiss-French, the Swiss-Italians, and the Swiss-Romanisch. The confusing notion of a multinational state also has arisen alongside a divided nation (East and West Germany between 1945 and 1989, and North and South Korea today) and states with irredentist claims (Serbia). The members of the United Nations are territorial states (with the exception of the Vatican), but this only begs the question of who is a national people entitled to a state. Many persons in existing states, from Belgium to Sri Lanka, have not settled this issue.

STATE SOVEREIGNTY

The emergence of the territorial state was accompanied by the notion that the state was sovereign. Accordingly, the sovereignty of all other social groupings was legally subordinated to the state's sovereignty. Political and legal theorists argued that sovereignty resided in territorial states' rulers and they had ultimate authority to make policy within a state's borders. Those who negotiated the two treaties making up the Peace of Westphalia wanted to stop the religious wars that had brought so much destruction to Europe. They specified that whoever ruled a certain territory could determine the religion of that territory. Europeans further developed the ideas about state sovereignty. Jean Bodin, a sixteenth-century French jurist, thought the notion of sovereignty a useful argument on behalf of the monarchs of new states who were trying to suppress the power of feudal officials contesting the power of the emerging monarchs.

State sovereignty was thus an idea that arose in a particular place at a particular time. But it came to be widely accepted as European political influence spread around the world. The argument was about legal rights, but it was intended to affect power. All states were said to be sovereign equals, regardless of their actual "power"—meaning capability to influence outcomes. They had the right to control policy within their jurisdictions even if they did not have the power to do it. Framed in the language of the abstract state, sovereignty enhanced the power of those persons making up the government that represented the state.

Sovereignty arose as an idea designed to produce order, legitimate existing power arrangements, and stop violence between and within states over religious questions. But did state sovereignty become, on balance, an idea that guaranteed international disorder? Was it necessary to think of relations between and among states as anarchical—not in the sense of chaos but in the sense of interactions among equal sovereigns recognizing no higher rules and organizations?

The original versions of state sovereignty, coming as they did out of a Europe that was nominally Christian, emphasized external limits on monarchs by virtue of the "higher" norms of natural law. These monarchs were the highest secular authorities, but they still were inferior to an external set of rules—at least from the viewpoint of political and religious theorists. But as Europe became more and more secular—which is to say, as the Catholic Church in Rome gave up its pretenses at territorial empire and increasingly emphasized the spiritual domain, at least in church dogma—the presumed restraints of natural law theory fell away. Thus the notion of state sovereignty came to represent supreme secular authority.

Political duplicity was part of all of this. The more powerful states, while agreeing that all states were equally sovereign, repeatedly violated the national jurisdiction of the weaker states. As we noted earlier, Stephen Krasner has pointed to the evolution and entrenchment of state sovereignty in international relations as a reflection of hypocrisy.[13]

State sovereignty, originally designed to produce order and to buttress central authority within the state, led to negative external consequences, the main one being that central authority over global society and interstate relations was undermined. All territorial states came to be seen as equal in the sense of having ultimate authority to prescribe what "should be" in their jurisdictions. No outside rules and organizations were held to be superior to the state. Only those rules consented to, and only those organizations voluntarily accepted, could exist in interstate relations with the logic of the Westphalian system of world politics.[14] Thus states were legally free to make war, violate human rights, neglect the welfare of citizens, and damage the ecology. However, state sovereignty is not a physical fact, like energy or a doorknob. It becomes a social fact only when it is widely accepted and becomes part of the dominant psychology. This process of "socially constructing" the notion of sovereignty means that it has evolved to mean different things in different eras. At one time, sovereignty meant a state had the ultimate and absolute right to govern, even if that meant practicing slavery or systematically persecuting a minority. Today, such state behavior invites international opprobrium and sometimes intervention.

Who should govern and by what means are the kinds of questions being raised at the UN. For example, by 1992 the state had disintegrated in the geographical area known as Somalia, which is to say that the governing system for the territory did not function. With no effective government to represent the state, should the UN be the organization ultimately responsible for ending disorder and starvation and helping to reestablish the state? If disputes within a state—such as was the case in Bosnia and Herzegovina and between Bosnia and Herzegovina and a smaller Yugoslavia (Serbia and Montenegro)—lead to mass murder, mass migration, and mass misery, should the UN be ultimately responsible? Or, as was the controversial case in Kosovo, should another multilateral organization—to wit, NATO (the North Atlantic Treaty Organization)—override claims to sovereignty by Serbia if the Security Council is paralyzed? If states fail to take proper action in relation to major violations of international criminal law (genocide, major war crimes, crimes against humanity), should the International Criminal Court have the right to prosecute and convict the individuals responsible?

Governments act in the name of states to determine how to manage certain transnational problems. On occasion they have agreed to let an international organization have the ultimate say as to what should be done. For example, more than forty states in the Council of Europe have created the European Convention on Human Rights. Under this treaty, the European Court of Human Rights has the ultimate say as to the correct interpretation of the convention, and the court regularly issues judgments to states concerning the legality of their policies. If one starts, as do European governments, with the notion that their states are sovereign, then these states have used their sovereignty to create international bodies that restrict the authority of the state. Among these states, the protection of human rights on a transnational basis is valued more highly than complete state independence. States have used their freedom to make policies that reduce their freedom. Initial sovereignty, linked to territory, has been used to restrict that sovereignty by an international body acting primarily on the basis of nonterritorial considerations.

This European situation is not typical of interstate relations and the latter is not likely to change in the foreseeable future. A few other examples of what is called supranational authority in world politics are apparent. Although much noise arises in the United States about the right of the World Trade Organization's (WTO) dispute panels to dictate policy to states, this authority is modest. States ultimately decide whether to apply sanctions for violations of WTO rules.

Power, especially economic power, affects the efficacy of sanctions authorized under such rules. So when the WTO's Dispute Settlement Board (DSB) rules that U.S. policy violates WTO strictures, sometimes the United States changes its policy, sometimes it does not, and sometimes Washington engages in protracted negotiations with other states that make it difficult to decide whether the United States is complying with the DSB ruling. But in any case, the purportedly most powerful state has agreed to abide by rules agreed by an international organization.

Most states, especially the newer ones that have achieved formal independence since the 1950s, value state sovereignty more than supranational cooperation to improve security, protect human rights, or pursue sustainable development. For many, it is a matter of protection against large bully or "rogue" states. Indeed, several older states also highly value state sovereignty. Edward Luck has pointed to American "exceptionalism" and traditional skepticism about inroads on its authority within the UN that is every bit as ferocious as any Third World state.[15] Or as Richard Haass puts it, "Americans have traditionally guarded their sovereignty with more than a little ferocity."[16] Jack Goldsmith, an official in George W. Bush's Justice Department, and afterward a member of the Harvard Law School faculty, regards most international law and organization, including the concept of war crimes, with great skepticism, seeing them as limits on what a president thinks is needed to protect American homeland security.[17] China, too, argues that only the state, not outside parties, can determine what is best for the Chinese people, whether in the realm of security, human rights, or sustainable human development. In short, considerable international cooperation exists but usually falls short of being supranational and of giving an international organization the legal right to override state independence.

Nevertheless, as the peoples and states of the world become more interconnected and interdependent, materially and morally, demands increase for more effective international management even at the expense of state sovereignty. Because interdependence involves sensitive relations, some issues that were formerly considered domestic or inconsequential have come to be redefined as international or significant because of the strength of transnational concern—of either a material or a moral nature. Still, even in the context of interdependence, most states are reluctant to transfer supranational authority to an international organization, including the UN. While the Security Council appears to exercise supranational authority, it is state representatives who most often make the key decisions. The Security Council determined that human rights repression in Iraq in 1991 threatened international peace and security, that the breakdown of order within Somalia in 1992 was a proper area for UN enforcement action, and that the humanitarian situation in Bosnia from 1992 was such that all states and other actors were entitled to use "all measures necessary" to provide humanitarian assistance. Situations similar to these used to be considered within the domestic jurisdiction of states. But the situations inside Iraq, Somalia, and Bosnia—and more recently in Rwanda, Haiti, Albania, Kosovo, and East Timor—came to be redefined as proper international concerns, subject to action by the United Nations and other external actors. In these cases the principle of state sovereignty yielded to a transnational demand for the effective treatment of pressing humanitarian problems.

Indeed, the responsibility to protect civilians emerged as a mainstream concern.[18] Hence the demand is growing for global governance, not in the sense of a unified world government, but in the sense of effective transnational management of pressing problems—in this case, of humanitarian disasters.[19] Yet in all the cases mentioned above, state authorities remained the most important, even if meeting in the Security Council or other international bodies. Even in these cases, the dominant pattern showed little desire by major states to let an independent UN official like the Secretary-General make the key decisions about use of force or other important responses.[20] Legally speaking, the Security Council or NATO may have taken a decision to use force or levy sanctions over matters essentially inside a state, but in political reality it was certain member states taking that decision and backing it with resources.

In many parts of the world, existing states are under pressure from within because a variety of groups—usually loosely called "ethnic," although they often are based on religious, linguistic, or other cultural characteristics—demand some form of sovereignty and self-determination. Many demands cause problems, but conflict is particularly pronounced when self-determination takes the form of a demand for a people's right to construct a new state. In these cases, the idea of accepting the territorial state as the basic unit of world politics is not at issue, at least in principle. What is at issue, and unfortunately fought over frequently, is which states and nations should be recognized.

State legitimacy may be questioned by armed elements or neighbors, as Russia's invasion of Georgia in 2008 aptly demonstrated. It also may be irrelevant to, for example, the managers of transnational corporations who have a global vision, doing what is best for their firms without much thought about state boundaries. They are bolstered by the globalization of finance capital and the meshing of the perspectives of corporate executives, regardless of nationality.[21] Yet, state sovereignty persists in the perceptions of most political elites. It is reaffirmed in principle at each annual meeting of the UN General Assembly. But state sovereignty, linked to the power and independence of those who govern in the name of the state, is not the only value in world politics. Other values can challenge state sovereignty and include enhanced security, human rights, and sustainable human development.

World politics consists, in large part, of managing the contradictions between conceptions of state sovereignty, on the one hand, and the desire for improved security, human rights, and sustainable human development, on the other. These contradictions are not the only ones in world politics, and managing them is not the only pressing need, but they constitute a fault line that permeates much debate at the United Nations. Sovereignty versus other considerations is one of the leading issues—if not the leading issue—in changing world politics at the beginning of the twenty-first century. Some time ago Lawrence Finkelstein observed that "although the picture is blurred and in many places hard to decipher, there has been movement away from the decentralized system of respect for sovereignty and toward a more centralized system of decision that in some respects approaches being international governance."[22] Most of the time, the UN is very much part of this trend while remaining far short of a global government.

CHANGING *RAISONS D'ÉTAT*

Those who rule in the name of the state, basing their views on the principle of state sovereignty, have claimed the right to determine what norms and actions are needed in the "national interest," which is perhaps better captured by what French speakers call *raisons d'état* (reasons of state). Whether those who rule are primarily concerned about the interests of the nation, meaning the people, or the interests of the state, meaning the government of the state, or their own interests is fair to ask. Nomenclature aside, individuals acting in the name of a state display a variety of interests. State interests may, because of necessity, come down on the side of state power and independence. From a self-interested point of view, this may be rational. If we assume an anarchical international society without effective governing arrangements, it may seem rational to protect the independent power of the state. That power can then be used to secure "good things" for those who rule. Indeed, members of the English School of international relations would argue that the state is the only accountable entity.[23]

Whether states—at least some of them, some of the time—may be coming to see their interests in fundamentally different ways is a provocative question. The belief that democratic states have a long-run interest in multilateralism was christened "good international citizenship" by Gareth Evans, Australia's foreign minister in the 1990s and now president of the International Crisis Group.[24] A similarly broad vision often underpins Canada's human security agenda.[25] No single national government, for example, is able unilaterally to solve the problem of the thinning ozone layer. In regard to this issue, states can secure their long-term interests in a healthy environment only through multilateral action. Such situations can lead to the adoption of shared norms, such as the 1987 Montreal Protocol, or to concrete action by an international organization such as the United Nations Environment Programme (UNEP). The result can create important legal and organizational restrictions on states.

States remain sovereign as an abstract principle, at least in the eyes of those who rule. But the operational application of sovereignty is another matter. Perceptions of raisons d'état cause state actors to sometimes subordinate state authority and independence to multilateral norms and procedures, especially when it is in the perceived national interest to do so.[26] In order to manage problems, state officials may increasingly agree to important principles, rules, and decision-making procedures, giving authority to a cluster of different actors.

The notion of an international regime has come into vogue as a way of describing this reality. An international regime is a set of shared principles, norms, rules, and procedures for "governing," or managing, an issue. The norms (principles and rules) can be legal, diplomatic, informal, or even tacit. The procedures frequently include nongovernmental (NGOs) and intergovernmental organizations (IGOs) as well as states. World politics is frequently characterized by a network of different actors, all focusing on the same problem. Not infrequently, several parts of the UN system are involved in problem solving.

Take, for example, the problem of forced migration and the international refugee regime. The norms of managing refugee problems derive from international law and from UN General Assembly resolutions as well as from daily practice. The various actors involved in trying to apply these norms in concrete situations are states, NGOs such as the American Refugee Committee, and different parts of the UN system such as the office of the UN High Commissioner for Refugees (UNHCR). States have determined that it is in their interest to coordinate policies to manage refugee problems, and they have constructed norms and organizations to pursue this goal. At the same time, the most numerous victims displaced by wars are internally displaced persons (IDPs), who in 2005 outnumbered refugees by 2.5 to 1 but for whom states have not yet agreed to a convention or established a dedicated UN agency. This is partly because IDPs remain inside states, thus presenting clear challenges to state authority and control when outside actors seek to help them.

This application of raisons d'état may stem from moral or practical concerns—or most likely from some combination of the two. In the case of Cuban refugees, for instance, U.S. officials may want the UN to help because they are human beings victimized by what U.S. officials see as the abuses of communism, and because the United States has wanted to keep Fidel Castro (and now his brother Raúl) from, as some American pundits crudely put it, "dumping mental patients and other undesirables on U.S. shores." Both viewpoints lead to use of the UNHCR to screen and interview Cuban immigrants to determine if individuals have a well-founded fear of persecution or mental health problems or a criminal background.

Many states appear to be "learning" a new concept of raisons d'état—one that is conducive to an expansion in the authority, resources, and tasks of the United Nations. Given the impact of communications and other technologies, states may be in the process of learning that their own interests would be better served by greater international cooperation. Many state leaders learned from World War I that there was a need for the League of Nations to institute a cooling-off period so that states would not rush blindly into hugely destructive wars. State actors learned from World War II that a stronger world organization was needed, one with a security council that had the authority to make binding decisions when the major powers agreed to oppose calculated aggression and cope with other threats to the peace. Some state leaders subsequently learned and promoted the notion that peacekeeping was needed to respond to security crises during the

Cold War so that armed disputes could be managed without triggering another world war. Similarly, even the most powerful states have learned that even they cannot "go it alone" in securing their broad security interests.

States progressively adjusted their policies on security affairs, based on perceptions of interests, in ways that increased the importance of international organizations. The process was not a zero-sum game in which the state lost and the United Nations won. Rather, states won in the sense of obtaining greater barriers against armed attacks on them, and the UN won in the sense of being given more authority and tasks than the League of Nations once had.

For about a century leading up to 1919, traditional international law considered resorting to war to be within the sovereign competence of states.[27] If state officials perceived that their interests justified force, it was used. But increasingly state authorities, not ivory-tower academics or pacifists, have agreed that changing patterns of warfare require international attempts to avoid or constrain force. Interest in peace and security has been combined with an interest in state authority, power, and independence. The result is international norms and organizations that continue to depend on state authority and power even as those norms and organizations try to restrain illegal uses or threats of force.

State actors originally thought that their best interests were served by absolute sovereignty and complete freedom in the choice of policy. Many if not most learned that this was a dangerous and frequently destructive situation. From the viewpoint of their own interests, limiting the recourse to and the process of force was highly desirable. That led to the part of international law called *jus ad bellum* (law regulating recourse to war) and also *jus in bello* (law regulating the process of war). International laws and organizations were developed to contribute to state welfare even as they limited state freedom.[28]

Central questions now are: How far are state actors willing to go in this process of international cooperation? How far can they be nudged by IGOs, NGOs, and public opinion? Are state actors willing to do more than create modern versions of the League of Nations—international organizations without the authority and resources to play decisive roles in world politics? Are they willing to cede significant authority and resources, as in the European Union, so that international organizations can act somewhat apart from state control in ways that really make a difference across borders? Can the UN be more than a debating society and a set of passive procedures?

THE UNITED NATIONS:
ACTOR OR INSTITUTIONAL FRAMEWORK?

Many journalists and not a few other observers use phrases like "the UN failed" (to stop ethnic cleansing in the Balkans) or "the UN was successful" (in checking Iraqi aggression against Kuwait). This phraseology obscures a complex reality.

The UN is most fundamentally an intergovernmental organization in which key decisions are made by governments representing states. The UN Charter may say initially, "We the peoples," but the members of the UN are states. This is the "first UN."

However, the UN is also a broad and complex system of policymaking and administration in which some decisions are made by individuals who are not instructed by states. The Secretary-General and the international civil service constitute the "second UN."

On occasion, NGOs and independent experts and commissions are active and sometimes influential in their interactions with the intergovernmental system; they could even be considered a "third UN."[29] Indeed, an increasing number of observers such as Kerstin Martens find this area a fruitful research agenda, and both scholars and practitioners are increasingly preoccupied with nonstate involvement in world politics.[30] It is no longer disputed that NGOs play a prominent role on the world stage and that we are unable to fully understand contemporary international relations without looking at these nonstate actors. What is insufficiently known is that their rate of growth has surpassed intergovernmental organizations. In 2004, international NGOs had grown to 6,600 while IGOs had shrunk to 238 (down from a peak of over 300 at the outset of the 1980s),[31] which means that over a quarter of a century "the ratio of NGOs to IGOs stood at 15:1, whereas today the relation is 28:1."[32] Increasingly, there is a global or transnational civil society.

This book, however, is essentially concerned with the nuts and bolts of the first and the second United Nations, the world organization as an arena for state decision-making and as a group of officials working for those who pay their salaries. If we return to the first UN, made up of states, we note that when it is said that the Security Council decided to authorize force in Somalia or the Balkans, in reality representatives of fifteen states made the decision, acting as the Security Council according to the UN Charter. This first UN may have been influenced by reports from the Secretary-General and his staff, and this second UN in theory and often in practice is independent from state control and is responsible only to the Charter.[33] Nevertheless, state representatives decide. Moreover, to the extent that UN decisions involve force or economic resources, or considerable diplomatic pressure, these elements of UN action are, in effect, borrowed from member states. Moreover, in the context of the Security Council the concert of major powers—the P-5—is required. This is the way it was intended to be by the institution's founders, and it is embodied in the Charter. The General Assembly and other official UN bodies are also made up of states. States make most of the important decisions taken in the name of the United Nations, however much they may be influenced, pressured, or educated by independent UN personnel or NGOs.

But authority—and influence flowing from it—may be delegated by intergovernmental bodies to independent UN personnel. And the Charter confers some independent authority on the Secretary-General, who may address the Security Council and makes an annual report on the UN's work to the General Assembly, focusing attention on certain problems and solutions. Moreover, certain

UN organs are made up of independent persons, not state officials. UN agencies have independent secretariats. Within the broad system, UN personnel may come to exercise some influence as independent actors not controlled by states. Their authority is not supranational, but their influence may be significant. Hence, they cannot tell states how to act, but they may be able to induce states to behave in certain ways.

The United Nations is primarily an institutional framework through which member states may pursue or channel their foreign policies. The UN Charter is the closest thing we have to a global constitution. When state actors comply with the Charter and use UN procedures, their policies acquire the legitimacy that stems from adherence to international law. They also acquire the legitimacy that stems from collective political approval. Normally, policies that are seen as legal and collectively approved are more likely than not to be successful. The weight of collective political approval may induce recalcitrant political authorities to accept a UN policy or program. It is better to have UN approval than otherwise. Indeed, the importance of the United Nations and other intergovernmental organizations is often missed in thinking too statically about the nature of international law. "To the extent international lawyers or others acknowledge that IOs [international organizations] have an impact on what is regarded as 'real' international law—usually defined narrowly to embrace only norms governing states in their relations," writes José Alvarez, "we continue to pour an increasingly rich normative output into old bottles labeled 'treaty,' 'custom,' (or much more rarely) 'general principles.'"[34]

The question of legitimacy in world politics is a complicated matter.[35] In Iraq in 2003, as in Kosovo in 1999, or for that matter in Grenada in 1982, the United States used military force in another state without Security Council approval. It sought to create legitimacy for its action by obtaining collective support. Regarding Kosovo, for example, legitimacy was enhanced because the nineteen liberal democracies, representing all of NATO's member states at the time, responded to gross violations of human rights by unanimously approving the use of force. Legitimacy in the first use of force is a subjective matter. What may not be fully legal in international law may still be legitimate in moral or political terms, which in fact was the characterization by an independent group of human rights experts who studied the case.[36] Hence, the safest ground on which to rest military action is prior approval by the Security Council, but in exceptional circumstances ignoring UN Charter Article 42—hence, acting "illegally" according to the law of the UN constitution—may be justified.

In the pages that follow we speak mostly of decisions at the United Nations. We write of politics at or through the UN. We are careful to distinguish the "first UN," which is a framework through which states act from the "second UN" as actor. At times "the UN" is phraseology that refers to important behavior by independent persons representing the world organization, such as the Secretary-General. The "third UN" is obvious in much of the discussion as well.

A view of the United Nations headquarters in Manhattan as seen from the southwest. The headquarters site covers approximately sixteen acres, from 42nd to 48th streets between First Avenue and the East River. (UN Photo 165054/L)

One of the more interesting questions in the twenty-first century is whether the growing demand for UN management of transnational problems will lead to greater or reduced willingness by member states to confer authority on the world organization's personnel and to transfer the resources necessary to resolve problems effectively. The options and processes are complex. The global economic and financial crisis that began in late 2008 and the severity of violent conflict demand a coordinated, effective, multilateral response. With what Paul Collier termed the "bottom billion"—who are at immediate risk from war, violence, poverty, disease, and bad governance—multilateral agencies need resources, talent, and even the authority to respond.[37] Moreover, state decisions outside the United Nations affect what "the UN" is allowed to do, or how UN procedures and symbols are employed. The willingness of states to commit forces and/or resources is necessary before the Security Council can proceed to authorize force or a peacekeeping operation.

In terms of a fundamental generalization, political factors outside the UN are primary and factors inside the UN are secondary. The end of the Cold War, indeed the end of the Soviet Union, primarily explained the renaissance of UN security activities that began in the late 1980s. The Security Council did not end the Cold War. Rather, the end of the Cold War allowed the Security Council to act with renewed consensus, commitment, and vigor.

Once allowed to act, UN personnel and organs may independently influence states and other actors. What was once a secondary factor, dependent on state approval, may come to be a primary factor in the ongoing process to make and implement policy. Once member states decided to create an environmental program, UNEP came to exert some relatively independent influence—both in cleaning up the Mediterranean Sea and in coordinating scientific evidence about the need to protect the ozone layer.

State decisions about power and policy constitute the primary force driving events at the UN. When important states show a convergence in policy, the UN may be allowed to act. Without that political agreement, the members of the UN system will be severely restricted in what they can accomplish. This was the case in 1945, and since then it has not been altered in any fundamental way. As such, one prominent group of scholars noted that "the UN is simultaneously in crisis and in demand." [38]

UN POLITICS

In the exercise of power needed to make and implement policy through the United Nations, states naturally seek allies. Academic and diplomatic observers have usually adopted generalizations about different political alliances, coalitions, or blocs within the United Nations. The countries of the West—that is, the Western industrialized democracies that are members of the Organisation for Economic Co-operation and Development (OECD), sometimes joined by Israel—frequently have been grouped as the First World. The "developing countries," basically all of the countries of Asia, Africa, and Latin America, have been examined under the rubric of the Third World, the South, the Non-Aligned Movement (NAM), or the Group of 77 (or G77, for the original constellation of 77 states, which has now grown to some 130 members). The "socialist countries," when the Soviet Union and its bloc existed, were also called the East and the Second World. The West and the East, in a curious bit of mathematical geography, were added together to constitute the North, or the developed countries, in juxtaposition to the South, or the developing countries.

Although these distinctions roughly correspond to the bulk of voting patterns during the Cold War, they have become less useful over time. Not only has the bloc of European socialist states and the Soviet Union ceased to exist, but also some of this terminology was in fact never accurate: Cuba was hardly nonaligned, and the socialist countries were not nearly as economically developed as the West, with some at levels comparable to the Third World.

The end of the Cold War has allowed scholars, and especially diplomats, to begin to look more objectively at various kinds of coalitions within the United Nations, although many of the labels from the former era remain. For example, it is now quite common to point out that developing countries consist of a series of cross-cutting alignments reflecting the heterogeneous character of their economies and ideologies.[39] In the past, it was politically more correct to speak of the Third World as if it were homogeneous, with little hesitation in grouping Singapore's and Chad's economies or Costa Rica's and North Korea's ideologies.

Only on a few issues—such as emphasizing the importance of the General Assembly, where each state has one vote—do developing countries show truly common interests. In such instances, and in some other international forums, the North-South divide continues to be salient. This was true, for example, in negotiations over a new Human Rights Council in 2006, as a classic North-South divide could be observed on many questions. Frequently, however, developing countries subdivide according to the issue before the UN: between radicals and moderates, between Islamic and non-Islamic, between those in the region and outside, between maritime and landlocked, between those achieving significant economic growth and otherwise. Even within the Western group, there have always been numerous differences, which have come more to the fore with the abrupt disappearance of East-West tensions. Divisions among and within all groups over the pursuit of war against Iraq in 2003 were clear examples of this phenomenon.

Given the changing nature of world politics and ongoing learning processes that can shape views toward state sovereignty and raisons d'état, new alignments and coalitions should be anticipated. Indeed, as world politics changes, so does the United Nations. In 1991 the General Assembly, whose majority of developing countries normally reflects concern for traditional notions of state sovereignty, voted by consensus to condemn the military coup in (briefly) democratic Haiti. Subsequently, many of these same countries supported the imposition of economic sanctions—first at the regional level through the Organization of American States and afterward through the UN—and eventually military enforcement action authorized by the Security Council to restore the elected government. The nature of government as democratic or authoritarian, a subject that had mostly been considered a domestic affair protected by the principle of state sovereignty, came to be seen by all states as a legitimate subject for diplomatic action through the UN.

In the following pages we inquire more systematically into changing world politics, and what it portends for the United Nations as the world organization gropes with the twenty-first century's most pressing challenges of insecurity, abuses of human rights, and lack of sustainable human development. These three issues encompass the central challenges to improving the human condition and hence the central tests for international organization.[40]

Part One of this book introduces the evolving efforts of the United Nations to combat threats to international peace and security. Because it is impossible to understand the nature of international cooperation without a grasp of the Charter's provisions for pacific settlement of disputes, enforcement, and regional arrangements, we first cover the theory of collective security in Chapter 1. Chapter 2 deals with UN security efforts during the Cold War and then turns to economic sanctions and the creation of the peacekeeping function. Although not mentioned in the Charter, peacekeeping is a distinctive contribution of the UN and has been its main activity in the security field for some forty years. In Chapter 3, "UN Security Operations After the Cold War (1988–1998)," and in Chapter 4, "Evolving Security Operations: Kosovo, East Timor, Sierra Leone, Lebanon, and Sudan," we explain the renaissance in UN activities, including peacekeeping, enforcement, and a series of other actions in virtually all of the world's most troubled regions. Chapter 5, "The Challenges of the Twenty-First Century," discusses current political dynamics and proposed changes in the UN to make it better able to address security challenges in the current century, including terrorism and WMDs.

Part Two introduces UN efforts to protect human rights and humanitarian values in conflicts. Chapter 6 briefly traces the origins of international action on human rights, indicating what the UN contributed to principles on human rights. Chapter 7 focuses on UN activity to help implement the human rights principles that member states have formally accepted or that constitute emerging norms, including the responsibility to protect. Finally, there is a balance sheet in Chapter 8 on UN developments in the field of human rights, exploring some of the dynamics that drive events and what they portend for the future.

Part Three introduces efforts by the United Nations to build sustainable human development. Chapter 9 examines the evolution of international attempts to build a humane capitalist world order and explores the progression of various theoretical frameworks for promoting development. Chapter 10 focuses on UN institutions and activity to build sustainable human security and presents some information about how the UN is structured for economic and environmental policymaking. In Chapter 11, we explore the role of the United Nations in promoting development and human security in the context of the forces and tensions of globalization. Our concluding chapter is about "Learning from Change."

NOTES

1. Dan Plesch, "How the United Nations Beat Hitler and Prepared the Peace," *Global Society* 22, no. 1 (2008): 137–158.

2. Doris Kearns Goodwin, *No Ordinary Time: Franklin and Eleanor Roosevelt* (New York: Touchstone Books, 1994), and Cass R. Sunstein, *The Second Bill of Rights: FDR's Unfinished Revolution and Why We Need It More Than Ever* (New York: Basic Books, 2004).

3. See Vaughan Lowe, Adam Roberts, Jennifer Welsh, and Dominik Zaum, eds., *The United Nations Security Council and War: The Evolution of Thought and Practice since 1946* (Oxford: Oxford University Press, 2008).

4. Quoted in Robert Gregg, *About Face? The United States and the United Nations* (Boulder, Colo.: Lynne Rienner, 1993), 68.

5. See David M. Malone, *The International Struggle Over Iraq: Politics in the UN Security Council 1980–2005* (Oxford: Oxford University Press, 2007).

6. For an overview, see David M. Malone, ed., *The UN Security Council: From Cold War to the 21st Century* (Boulder, Colo.: Lynne Rienner, 2004).

7. Jarat Chopra, *Peace-Maintenance: The Evolution of International Political Authority* (London: Routledge, 1999).

8. *National Security Strategy of the United States of America*, September 2002, available at http://georgewbush-whitehouse.archives.gov/nsc/nss/2002/, March 1, 2004.

9. Joseph S. Nye Jr., "U.S. Power and Strategy After Iraq," *Foreign Affairs* 82, no. 4 (2003): 60–73.

10. Clyde Prestowitz, *Rogue Nation: American Unilateralism and the Failure of Good Intentions* (New York: Basic Books, 2003).

11. See Andrew Cottey, "Beyond Humanitarian Intervention: The New Politics of Peacekeeping and Intervention," *Contemporary Politics* 14, no. 4 (2008): 429–446.

12. G. John Ikenberry, "Illusions of Empire: Defining the New American Order," *Foreign Affairs* 83, no. 2 (2004): 154.

13. See also Thomas J. Bierstecker and Cynthia Weber, eds., *State Sovereignty as Social Construct* (Cambridge: Cambridge University Press, 1996), and Daniel Philpott, *Revolutions in Sovereignty: How Ideas Shaped Modern International Relations* (Princeton, N.J.: Princeton University Press, 2001).

14. In the history of international relations, and despite the notion of the sovereign equality of states, all sorts of unequal relations have existed and have even been formally approved sometimes. In this sense the unequal relations in the UN, such as the five permanent members of the Security Council possessing the veto, follow many examples of inequality—despite the centrality of sovereignty. See the chapter by Jack Donnelly in David P. Forsythe, Patrice C. McMahon, and Andy Wedeman, eds., *American Foreign Policy in a Globalized World* (New York: Routledge, 2006).

15. Edward Luck, *Mixed Messages: American Politics and International Organization, 1919–1999* (Washington, D.C.: Brookings Institution, 1999).

16. Richard N. Haass, *The Opportunity: America's Moment to Alter History's Course* (New York: PublicAffairs, 2005), 41.

17. Jack Goldsmith, *The Terror Presidency* (New York: Norton, 2008).

18. International Commission on Intervention and State Sovereignty, *The Responsibility to Protect* (Ottawa: ICISS, 2001). See also Gareth Evans, *The Responsibility to Protect*

(Washington, D.C.: Brookings Institution, 2008); Alex Bellamy, *Responsibility to Protect: The Global Effort to End Mass Atrocities* (Cambridge, UK: Polity, 2009); Thomas G. Weiss, *Humanitarian Intervention: Ideas in Action* (Cambridge, UK: Polity, 2007); Ramesh Thakur, *The United Nations, Peace and Security: From Collective Security to the Responsibility to Protect* (Cambridge: Cambridge University Press, 2006); and J. L. Holzgrefe and Robert O. Keohane, eds., *Humanitarian Intervention: Ethical, Legal, and Political Dilemmas* (Cambridge: Cambridge University Press, 2003).

19. For a discussion, see Thomas G. Weiss, *Military-Civilian Interactions: Humanitarian Crises and the Responsibility to Protect*, 2nd ed. (Lanham, Md.: Rowman & Littlefield, 2005).

20. In later pages we will show the extent of independent policymaking by UN officials with regard to places like the Balkans and Somalia. For discussion on the Office of the Secretary-General, see Leon Gordenker, *The Secretary-General and the Secretariat*, 2nd ed. (London: Routledge, 2010), and Edward Newman, *The UN Secretary-General from the Cold War to the New Era: A Global Peace and Security Mandate?* (London: Macmillan, 1998).

21. For collections of essays on these topics, see Rorden Wilkinson and Steve Hughes, eds., *Global Governance: Critical Perspectives* (London: Routledge, 2002), and Gary P. Sampson, ed., *The Role of the World Trade Organization in Global Governance* (Tokyo: UN University Press, 2001).

22. Lawrence S. Finkelstein, ed., *Politics in the United Nations System* (Durham, N.C.: Duke University Press, 1988), 30.

23. Christopher Bickerton, Philip Cunliffe, and Alexander Gourevitch, eds., *Politics without Sovereignty: A Critique of Contemporary International Relations* (London: Routledge, 2007).

24. See Nicholas J. Wheeler and Tim Dunne, "Good International Citizenship: A Third Way for British Foreign Policy," *International Affairs* 74, no. 4 (1998): 847–870.

25. Lloyd Axworthy, "Human Security and Global Governance," *Global Governance* 7, no. 1 (2001): 19–23. See further Edward Newman and Oliver P. Richmond, eds., *The United Nations and Human Security* (New York: Palgrave, 2001), and Rob McRae and Don Hubert, eds., *Human Security and the New Diplomacy: Protecting People, Promoting Peace* (Montreal and Kingston: McGill-Queen's University Press, 2001).

26. On the subject of whether UN and other officials for international organizations can get states to change their perceptions of national interest, see especially Michael Barnett and Martha Finnemore, *Rules for the World: International Organizations in Global Politics* (Ithaca, N.Y.: Cornell University Press, 2004).

27. For an insightful and readable overview, see Stephen C. Neff, *War and the Law of Nations: A General History* (Cambridge: Cambridge University Press, 2005).

28. See Adam Roberts and Richard Guelff, eds., *Documents on the Laws of War*, 3rd ed. (Oxford: Oxford University Press, 2000).

29. For a discussion, see Thomas G. Weiss, Tatiana Carayannis, and Richard Jolly, "The 'Third' United Nations," *Global Governance* 15, no. 1 (2009): 123–142. This is a major theme in the capstone volume from the United Nations Intellectual History Project by Richard Jolly, Louis Emmerij, and Thomas G. Weiss, *UN Ideas That Changed the World* (Bloomington: Indiana University Press, 2009).

30. Kerstin Martens, *NGOs and the United Nations: Institutionalization, Professionalization and Adaptation* (Houndmills, Basingstoke, UK: Palgrave Macmillan, 2005), 2.

31. Union of International Associations, *Yearbook of International Organisations*, vol. 40 (Brussels: UIA, 2004).

32. Martens, *NGOs and the United Nations*, 2.

33. During the early and middle part of the Cold War, members of the UN Secretariat from the USSR, and perhaps its allies, were widely seen as taking orders from, and reporting back to, Moscow. Since the end of the Cold War, the independence of the UN Secretariat has generally increased.

34. José E. Alvarez, *International Organizations as Law-makers* (Oxford: Oxford University Press, 2005), x. See also J. Martin Rochester, *Between Peril and Promise: The Politics of International Law* (Washington, D.C.: CQ Press, 2006).

35. See Ian Hurd, *After Anarchy: Legitimacy and Power in the United Nations Security Council* (Princeton, N.J.: Princeton University Press, 2007).

36. Independent International Commission on Kosovo, *Kosovo Report: Conflict, International Response, Lessons Learned* (Oxford: Oxford University Press, 2000).

37. Paul Collier, *The Bottom Billion: Why the Poorest Countries are Failing and What Can Be Done About It* (New York: Oxford University Press, 2007).

38. Quoted in the Princeton Project on National Security, *Forging a World of Liberty Under Law* (Princeton, N.J.: Princeton University Press, 2006), 7.

39. Soo Yeon Kim and Bruce Russett, "The New Politics of Voting Alignments in the United Nations General Assembly," *International Organization* 50, no. 4 (1996): 629–652. See also Evan Luard, *A History of the United Nations: The Years of Western Domination* (London: Macmillan, 1982).

40. For in-depth treatments of most of the topics and institutional entities, see Thomas G. Weiss and Sam Daws, eds., *The Oxford Handbook on the United Nations* (Oxford: Oxford University Press, 2007).

PART ONE

INTERNATIONAL PEACE
AND SECURITY

CHAPTER 1

The Theory of
UN Collective Security

THE END OF THE Cold War in 1989 ushered in a period of rapid change in world politics. External political events spurred fundamental changes within the United Nations and many citizens and diplomats expressed optimism about the role of UN multilateralism in a "new world order." Yet, the U.S.-led attack on Iraq beginning in March 2003, without Security Council authorization, demonstrates that the UN has always been dependent on states and the status of international affairs. The UN is part and parcel of world politics. It influences and is influenced by international events and outcomes.

The UN remains largely dependent on the nature and quality of state foreign policy; however, organizational arrangements matter and UN officials have maneuvering room in carrying out the organization's tasks, especially relating to maintaining international peace and security. In the wake of the attacks on the United States by Al Qaeda on September 11, 2001, in wanting to obtain multilateral endorsement of its security policies, Washington quickly paid off most of its assessed UN dues, which totaled $862 million. The United States sought and received the Security Council's blessing for several of its security objectives, such as military attacks on the Taliban government in Afghanistan that was sheltering Al Qaeda and shutting down financing for "terrorism." A year later, the United States returned to the UN seeking legitimacy in invading Iraq. Washington was successful in securing from the UN a renewed inspections regime for weapons of mass destruction (WMD). While Washington was subsequently rebuffed in seeking a specific authorization to use military force against Iraq, these events demonstrate how the UN continues to play an important role and how change outside the UN drives developments within. The institution, principally the Security Council, is often thrust into important roles.

The UN system was designed during World War II. The international community of states undertook a new experiment to control war when the Charter was signed and came into effect in 1945, thereby creating the United Nations

Organization (UNO). The maintenance of international peace and security is the primary task of the UNO, or more simply the UN. Two world wars within two decades, the Holocaust, and the advent of the nuclear age produced the political will to improve on the League of Nations, to safeguard the peace that had been won at great cost. In the inspiring words of the Charter's preamble, the UN's role was to save "succeeding generations from the scourge of war, which twice in our lifetime has brought untold sorrow to mankind."

The League of Nations, although technically not outlawing war, had established a set of procedures constituting a cooling-off period for states contemplating the use of force. This approach to peace was conditioned by the judgment that the advent of World War I had been caused by emotionalism and mistaken perceptions. Time was needed for rationality to prevail. This approach to peace had clearly been inadequate to stop Adolf Hitler's premeditated aggressions, which in some ways were not only rational but also astute (for example, his anticipation of early appeasement on the part of the Western democracies). Equally deficient was the legalistic approach to peace reflected in the Kellogg-Briand Pact in 1928, which outlawed war as an instrument of foreign policy but failed to provide enforcement measures, thus nullifying its contribution to international order. It did nothing to change the nature of world politics. It did not provide peaceful means of conflict resolution. It just made war illegal.

In San Francisco, where the United Nations Conference on International Organization drafted the Charter in late spring 1945, diplomats made the threat or use of force illegal except in self-defense, or unless authorized by the Security Council. Unlike during the League period, they gave the United Nations the authority to enforce the peace through diplomatic, economic, and even military action in response to "threats to the peace . . . acts of aggression or . . . breaches of the peace." State power, or perhaps even independent UN power backed by the most important states, was to be put at the service of the Security Council to protect the peace.

Even a novice of world politics is aware that the reality of the past half century has diverged dramatically from these ideals. Since the end of the Cold War, about thirty-five "major" wars occurred.[1] Some of these continue today. At the same time, the United Nations remains present in many armed conflicts around the world. If catastrophic wars among nuclear and other great powers have not occurred, this has been attributed more to international interdependence and restraint among national policymakers rather than to singular features of the UN Security Council.

COLLECTIVE SECURITY IN GENERAL

The idea of collective security can be traced through a long history of proposals to deal with war and peace.[2] The central thread remains the same: All states would join forces to prevent one of their number from using coercion to gain advantage. Under such a system, no government could conquer another or otherwise disturb the peace for fear of retribution from all other governments. An attack on one would be treated as an attack on all. The notion of self-defense, universally agreed on as a right of sovereign states, was expanded to include the international community's right to prevent war.

The apparent common sense and appealing simplicity of the logic of collective security contrasts with the difficulties of its application. Indeed, some have come to question whether collective security can be relied upon with confidence to protect or restore the peace. Skeptics ask: In a world with a large number of states (192 UN member states in 2009), will states not defect from the collective enterprise, in pursuit of their own narrow national interests, and thereby undermine the collective effort? This is the old problem of the hunters and the stag. As the hunters encircle the stag, one hunter defects to chase a rabbit he will not have to share with the others. Another does the same. Soon the stag escapes through the gaps in the collective effort.[3]

Experience with collective security indicates considerable "gaps." First, some states have refused to join a collective-sanctioning effort because they have already defined their friends and enemies. The United States would not have joined in a UN effort at collective security against one of its NATO allies, nor would the Soviet Union have done so against its Warsaw Pact allies. In an exceptional move, the United States did oppose the British, French, and Israeli invasion of Egypt in 1956 and eventually helped to roll it back by diplomacy. But the United States never seriously considered UN sanctions against its allies in 1956, precisely because it wanted to maintain their cooperation in the Cold War. Under true collective security, all aggressors have to be treated the same. All threats to and breaches of the peace have to be firmly and automatically opposed. This requirement seems beyond the realm of most great powers in history, which have always had their cultural and strategic friends. A military alliance is incompatible with the logic of global collective security. In the contemporary world, then, alliances exist and collective security does not.

Second, there is the fundamental problem of power. Since 1945 the international community of states has had major and probably insurmountable problems in applying collective security against a nuclear state, especially the United States, the USSR (now Russia), Britain, France, or China.[4] Of course, in the case of these five—the P-5—the Security Council was constrained procedurally from intervening. By design, the Security Council was supposed to act only when there was concurrence among the P-5. Moreover, how could one justify the massive destruction that could result from trying to apply forcible collective security against such a state, even if clear-cut aggression had occurred? The nuclear problem extends to India, Israel, Pakistan, and North Korea, although they are not permanent members of the Security Council. Iran may be next.

But the problem of regulating powerful potential aggressors goes beyond the nuclear question. Many states control sufficient conventional forces, or biological and chemical weapons of mass destruction, or economic resources, so that collective security against them would be highly disruptive to international society. For this reason, the vast majority of states have had to content themselves with diplomatic opposition to such acts as the U.S. invasions of Grenada and Panama in the 1980s or the Soviet invasions of Hungary and Czechoslovakia in the 1950s and 1960s, knowing full well that any attempt at military or economic sanctioning would be disruptive and ineffectual. The great powers are not the only ones difficult to manage. South Africa, Saudi Arabia, Vietnam, and other lesser powers also have considerable economic and military strength that can make them important actors depending upon issues and timing.

Third, collective security can be costly to those supporting it. Sanctions cut both ways, affecting not only the aggressor but the defenders. Communist Bulgaria voted in the UN for sanctions against white-minority rule in South Africa in the 1980s but also sold arms to South Africa under the table. Bulgaria did not want to miss out on profits from the arms trade despite its formal support for economic collective security against the white-minority government in Pretoria. It was one thing for states to accept that apartheid constituted a threat to the peace. It was another for states to engage collectively against apartheid at a cost to their own narrow national interests. Similarly, UN sanctions against Iraq in the 1990s and in Sudan were undermined by their major trading partners.

Fourth, the concept of collective security is based on the assumption that all victims are equally important—that the international community of states will respond in the same way to an attack on Bosnia or Armenia as to an attack on Kuwait or Germany. Even aside from the issue of standing alliances, this, too, is a very high standard. Historical evidence shows that most states have differentiated between countries worth defending and otherwise. In 1991 the United States was willing to disrupt its home front by putting almost half a million military personnel into the liberation of oil-rich Kuwait, but in 1994 it dithered about taking action and failed to halt the genocide in Rwanda. As a result, decisive and forcible collective security occurred through Desert Storm in 1991. But indecisive and mostly nonforcible collective-security efforts were tried in Rwanda as 800,000 people were murdered in three months.

Collective security is a halfway house between world government and the pure state system. It is a process that could make the state system more humane by making it more secure. Forms of collective security have worked at times. Iraqi aggression against Kuwait was rolled back in 1991 through collective force authorized by the UN, as was a military coup in Haiti after UN-sponsored economic sanctions fell short. But these tend to be the exceptional examples proving the general rule that collective security, either military or economic, is exceedingly difficult to organize and enforce. States have numerous narrow national interests that they are reluctant to see overridden in the name of peace or justice. They therefore tend to defect from inconvenient collective-security efforts. Member states of the Security Council may also genuinely disagree as to when economic and military enforcement measures are justified. Such was the case in 2002 and 2003 when the council was divided over how to enforce disarmament measures in Iraq. If agreement on international enforcement issues were easier, one might aspire to world government, not just collective security.[5]

THE UNITED NATIONS AND SECURITY: SOME BASICS

In theory, successful collective security depends upon three factors: consensus, commitment, and organization.[6] Consensus refers to the recognition by members that a threat to international peace and security exists. Does genocide in Rwanda really threaten international peace, especially when the conflict occurs largely within the territorial borders of Rwanda itself? Similarly, does a dictator like Saddam Hussein present a gathering threat to international peace, especially when his military forces are contained and his regime isolated? The answers to these questions are not clear-cut and are influenced by the politics of the day. Members of a collective security arrangement, especially the most powerful members, must agree that a threat to the peace or a breach of the peace has occurred or at least stand aside (i.e., abstain) when others wish to act.

Once that obstacle has been overcome, member states must then agree about what to do about the threat. Should economic sanctions be used, military force, or a combination of both? Once a course of action has been decided upon, then states must be committed to that course of action and have contingency plans if it falters. They must be willing to bear the costs and sacrifice their national interests for the collective good.

Finally, if the first two conditions can be met, then there must be organization. That is, agreed-upon mechanisms, rules, and procedures must exist for carrying out a course of action. If sanctions are imposed, how will member states detect cheating, enforce sanctions, or evaluate their political and social impact? If military force is approved, which states will conduct the operations and how will they be monitored? These kinds of policy choices are complicated and represent the kind of questions member states wrestle with at the UN. The record of the world organization in collective security is determined in large part by its ability to meet the conditions of consensus, commitment, and organization in practice.

The Institutional Basics

The two central bodies to directly safeguard the peace are the Security Council and the General Assembly.[7] Chapter V of the UN Charter designates the Security Council as the organ primarily responsible for maintaining international peace and security. The Charter originally specified that the Security Council have eleven members, but in 1965 its membership was increased to fifteen to better reflect the expanded UN after decolonization. The most powerful states assumed special roles. As mentioned, the United States, Russia (formerly the Soviet

Edward R. Stettinius Jr., chairman of the U.S. delegation, signs the UN Charter in San Francisco on June 26, 1945. President Harry S. Truman stands by. (UNICO Photo 2463)

Union), France, China, and Great Britain are permanent members, each with a veto over decisions. The remaining ten members are elected to two-year terms by the General Assembly. When electing the nonpermanent members, the assembly tries to maintain a geographical balance by including representatives of the four major regions of the world: usually three from Africa, two from Asia, three from Europe, and two from Latin America. The Security Council, whose permanent members were arguably the most powerful military states in 1945, is vested with the duty of maintaining international peace and security. Unlike in the League of Nations, all UN member states are legally required to abide by Security Council "decisions."

The permanent members are accorded special responsibilities and privileges in the collective-security schema. They pay more of the bills, and no decision can be made on nonprocedural questions unless they concur or at least agree to abstain. The veto power ensures that no enforcement action takes place against one of the great powers of the international system in order to avoid starting a major war—the very thing that the United Nations was established to forestall. By preventing action against a permanent member, the veto saved the organization from wrecking itself in operations against its most powerful members. Enforcement actions can be undertaken only with great-power consensus, the first key element for collective security.

After expanding in 1965, the Security Council altered its decision-making process. Enlargement of the council has reduced the mathematical weight that the permanent members hold in the voting. Nine affirmative votes are now needed to pass a resolution. Barring permanent member vetoes, all permanent members and one nonpermanent member could theoretically abstain from a vote without jeopardizing the passage of a resolution, although some unity among the five permanent members is practically indispensable.

Disagreement during the formal voting process has been reduced by efforts to gain a consensus during informal consultations before any vote. During the Cold War, 279 vetoes were cast, but not one was cast from May 1990 until May 1993, and only a few have been used since.[8] With or without vetoes, the need for more flexibility for multilateral diplomacy remained. So instead of the formal sessions riddled with vetoes that characterized the early years, crucial discussions now occur informally under the aegis of the president until the Security Council is ready either to make a decision or to vote formally. During the Cold War, the United States pressed for many formal votes, knowing that the Soviet Union would use its veto, thus allowing Washington to paint Moscow as obstructionist. After the Cold War, there was less game playing and more interest in trying to negotiate among the P-5.

The presidency of the council revolves monthly among council members and plays a critical role in setting the agenda and smoothing the way to a vote. The president meets with the Secretary-General to identify the parties to a dispute, negotiates with the permanent members to ensure that the veto will not be used, and consults with the nonaligned members of the Security Council and other relevant groups or actors. Accordingly, unified decision-making is facilitated and disunity in the council can be reduced.[9] Sometimes a president decides to push a particular theme for a month—for example, protection of civilians or peace-building.

The General Assembly, where every member state is represented, serves as a more open forum for discussion. Duties include election of heads of other UN organs and the judges of the International Court of Justice (ICJ), budgetary and administrative decisions, and joint control of decisions on Charter amendments and admission of new members to the organization. The assembly also elects the Secretary-General upon a recommendation from the Security Council. But this vote is pro forma, with the real decision made among the P-5.

The General Assembly's role in relation to international peace and security increased for a time with the passage of the Uniting for Peace Resolution in 1950. In circumstances in which the Security Council is unable to act, the General Assembly has taken measures in accordance with the purpose and spirit of the world organization's Charter. The assembly has played a role over the years in debating actions against such pariahs as South Africa and Israel. It is worth repeating, however, that the General Assembly makes "recommendations" whereas the Security Council can make binding "decisions"—some council resolutions, however, constitute recommendations. The Uniting for Peace procedure obscured the distinctions between the Security Council and the General Assembly. Whether this procedure is illegal, represents a de facto alteration of the Charter, or constitutes a new legal rule is in dispute. Supporters of the resolution argued that the Security Council's formal responsibility for maintaining peace was "primary" but not "exclusive." The importance of the resolution was political, symbolic, and psychological, if not legal. This transfer of matters from council to assembly has declined with time but could be resurrected.

This resolution, which can be initiated either by the General Assembly or Security Council, was first enacted in 1950 to allow the assembly to address North Korean aggression in South Korea amidst Security Council inaction after its initial condemnation of aggression and approval of assistance to South Korea. The absence by the boycotting Soviet Union (protesting Taiwan's occupation of the "Chinese seat" on the council in spite of the victory by the Chinese communists under Mao Zedong) had permitted the initial call for assistance and linked the UN to the subsequent military action against North Korea and its allies. But once Moscow ended its boycott and entered the fray, the Security Council was paralyzed by the Soviet veto.

The Uniting for Peace Resolution was not used again until 1956, when permanent members were involved in two crises. The General Assembly approved UN actions in the Suez crisis because effective action in the Security Council had been blocked by France and Britain; earlier that year, the assembly had censured Moscow's use of armed force in Hungary.[10] Another use was in 1960, after the Security Council became deadlocked over the Congo operation because the Soviet Union and the United States supported different sides in the conflict. In total the Uniting for Peace Resolution has been invoked ten times, the last being against Israel in 1997 for its policies in the occupied territories. Several NGOs such as Greenpeace and the Center for Constitutional Rights called upon the General Assembly to invoke the resolution in response to the U.S. invasion of Iraq in 2003. Yet, no state on the Security Council or in the General Assembly has formally called for its consideration in recent years. Given its sporadic use, the efficacy of the Uniting for Peace Resolution for enhancing the General Assembly's role in international security is subject to considerable skepticism.

The Charter spells out other important actors in collective security: the executive head of the organization (the Secretary-General) and the professional staff (the secretariat). Selected by the General Assembly upon the recommendation of the Security Council, the Secretary-General is the chief executive officer. Today's professional and support staff number approximately 55,000 in the UN proper and an additional 20,000 in the specialized agencies. This number excludes temporary staff in peace operations (about 100,000 in 2009) and the staff of the International Monetary Fund and the World Bank Group (another 15,000). These figures represent substantial growth from the 500 employees in the UN's first year at Lake Success and the peak total of 700 staff employed by the League of Nations.[11] In matters of peace and security, several departments are involved including the under-secretaries-general for political affairs, humanitarian affairs, and peacekeeping operations. Depending on the number of peace operations under way at any moment over the past two decades, somewhere between 10,000 and 100,000 UN soldiers, police, and other special personnel also have served under the Secretary-General.

Beyond organizing and directing staff, the Secretary-General plays an instrumental role in the mediation of disputes, negotiations between or among warring parties, and deployment of UN-sponsored forces. This role reaches beyond that assigned to any other international official. An important mechanism in this regard is the appointment of special and personal representatives or envoys of the Secretary-General, who undertake missions in conflict areas.[12] Article 99 of the UN Charter makes it possible for the Secretary-General to "bring to the attention of the Security Council any matter which in his opinion may threaten the maintenance of international peace and security." Even without formally invoking Article 99, the Secretary-General can still press his views behind the scenes with small and great powers. His personal judgment and readiness to run risks and take initiatives are crucial to accomplishing his duties.

Article 99 has been used only three times in the UN's history. Secretaries-General know that it is fairly pointless, as well as embarrassing, to invoke the article if P-5 support for their position will not be forthcoming. As one former Secretariat official said off the record to one of the authors, "There is no point diving into an empty swimming pool."[13] But the role of the Secretary-General and the possible resort to Article 99 provide the basis for less dramatic but potentially useful activities.[14] "Quiet diplomacy" was Secretary-General Dag Hammarskjöld's description, although sometimes the displeasure of target governments became noisy.[15]

Whether Article 99 is invoked or not, the Secretary-General's actions are closely scrutinized by governments. Depending upon the political climate, criticism can be scathing, and it certainly affects the UN Secretariat. Secretary-General U Thant was stridently criticized by the West for pulling UN troops from the Sinai in 1967, just as Trygve Lie, the first Secretary-General, and Hammarskjöld had been criticized by the Soviet bloc for their respective actions in Korea and the Congo. U Thant was also criticized by Washington for his clear opposition to the U.S. presence in Vietnam. More recently, Secretaries-General Pérez de Cuéllar, Boutros Boutros-Ghali, and Kofi Annan have been criticized for their actions in the Persian Gulf, Bosnia, Somalia, and Iraq. The eighth occupant of the job, Ban Ki-moon, assumed office in January 2007 and has proceeded gingerly on issues of international peace and security and thus has not yet taken criticism for his leadership in this arena although his lack of visible leadership has led to widespread discontent. As with all visible policy positions, criticism goes with the territory of this job. However, since the time of Trygve Lie and the Korean War, the Secretary-General has rarely issued a harsh public judgment concerning armed conflict for the very good reason that he is not effective if he loses the confidence of important states.

The Secretary-General walks a tightrope, needing to appear independent and not simply a pawn of any or all of the P-5 states, but at the same time, he must maintain the confidence and support of those same states. So from time to time he must speak out in a critical way, but not to the point that he becomes persona non grata.

The Legal Basics

The core of the UN Charter concerning security questions is Article 2, paragraph 4: All states shall refrain from the threat or use of force in their international relations. This language, rather remarkably, was written initially by the United States. At that time it had primacy of power compared to the other leading states, which were exhausted by World War II. Why then Washington would choose to apparently limit its own exercise of force by this legal language is not clear.[16]

On the one hand, Article 2 (4) is visionary, even idealistic. States have engaged in the threat or use of force repeatedly in the history of world politics. How could it be otherwise when there are few procedures to guarantee peaceful change? That being so, it is quite remarkable that Article 2 (4) has not completely withered away under the pressures of a violent world.

On the other hand, a world without the threat or use of force continues to be the primary objective of the United Nations. When Iraq invaded Kuwait in 1990, the Security Council immediately labeled the action impermissible under the Charter. The same process has occurred in numerous other situations, although the language and form of international responses vary. The General Assembly opposed not only Iraq's invasion of Kuwait but also the U.S. invasions of Grenada and Panama, Vietnam's invasion of Cambodia, the Soviet Union's invasion of Afghanistan, India's invasion of East Pakistan, and so on.

Article 2 (4) is not a dead letter. After the Cold War, a state contemplating the use of force to resolve a dispute, especially if not a great power, cannot be certain that its action will not result in some type of condemnation and punishment. To be sure, the process is not automatic; UN resolutions may be worded in a soft way, and actual sanctions can vary. The functioning of collective security frequently shows one political bias or another. Nevertheless, Article 2 (4) is alive and reasonably well as a general standard of achievement.[17]

According to the General Assembly in the 1970s, if a state engages in the first use of force, it has probably committed aggression. That is, the first use of force will normally be regarded as aggressive and non-defensive unless the Security Council holds otherwise. Individual or collective self-defense under Article 51 remains the only clearly legal use of force. Anticipatory self-defense, in which the purported defender state uses force first, in the face of an imminent armed attack, is not completely ruled out, but it is not explicitly endorsed either. The UN Security Council never did fully and clearly evaluate the Israeli first use of force in 1967 in the face of various Arab threats. The Bush doctrine of preventive war, what the U.S. administration labeled "pre-emption" in its 2002 National Security Strategy, reawakened debate over the legitimate first use of force. Given the dangerous nature of the logic of striking first on the basis of a purely national judgment, especially when the alleged threat is not imminent, great controversy greeted this aspect of U.S. security policy.[18] The Bush doctrine was the main reason that France and other countries in "old Europe" and elsewhere would not support the use of force against Iraq in March 2003. In the past, similar claims met a similar response, as when Israel claimed the right to strike first to take out an Iraqi nuclear reactor in Osirak in 1981 and was unanimously condemned by the council. But when Israel attacked a Syrian facility in 2007, suspecting it of being part of a nuclear weapons program, the Security Council and most states were silent about how to evaluate that complex situation. The Israelis did not proclaim "pre-emption" as a principle, and many states did not want to see Syria with nuclear weapons.

Inherent in this discussion is that force means military action. A number of developing countries wanted force to include economic coercion, but this view has not prevailed in General Assembly debates. Analytical clarity requires keeping in mind the continuum from outside military intervention to the everyday exercise of political influence to the unconscious impact of such "soft power" as culture and language.[19] International relations frequently involve states' affecting the internal affairs of other countries, although most diplomats prefer to avoid "intervention," which implies the forceful action by outsiders, in favor of "involvement" or "intrusion" or "interference."[20]

In addition to dealing with aggression entailing first use of force, Article 42 specifies that there can be threats to and breaches of the peace. Neither the Security Council nor the World Court has ever clarified the difference between "aggression" and a "breach of the peace." However, a situation can create a threat to the peace without necessarily consisting of armed attack by one state on another. In the spring of 1991, for example, the Security Council declared that the consequences of the human rights situation in Iraq constituted a threat to the peace. At that time the government of Saddam Hussein was engaged in such repression that hundreds of thousands of persons were being displaced within Iraq or were fleeing into Turkey or Iran.

Thus, not only interstate force but also other actions constituting a threat to the peace can violate the Charter. In the mid-1960s the UN authorized economic sanctions against Rhodesia. That territory had announced a unilateral declaration of independence from the United Kingdom, denied internationally recognized human rights, and was the scene for growing violence between the white-minority government and the Patriotic Front. The Organization of African Unity (OAU) and eventually the General Assembly called the Patriotic Front a "national liberation movement." While no armed attack by one state on another took place, the Security Council said that there was no peace and that binding economic sanctions were in order. This is another example of the Security Council reaching consensus and then committing to a course of action. Sometimes in this pursuit the council will "fuzz" legal categories. After all, the council is both a political and a legal organ. To gain votes for a council resolution, vague language may be necessary.

When the Security Council finds a situation of aggression, or threat to or breach of the peace, it can impose binding sanctions. In effect, the council can make international law. Chapter VII of the Charter, containing Articles 39 to 51, gives far more legal authority than the council of the League of Nations ever did. During the Cold War, the Security Council imposed binding sanctions on only two targets: the Ian Smith government in Rhodesia (now Zimbabwe) and the apartheid government in South Africa. Since the end of the Cold War, the Security Council has authorized mandatory economic sanctions on a variety of parties in Iraq, Haiti, Yugoslavia, and elsewhere. It imposed a binding arms embargo on all parties fighting in the Balkans—to such an extent that the 1990s were labeled "the sanctions decade."[21] It did not impose but did authorize military action for the liberation of Kuwait. Likewise, it did not require but did authorize all necessary means for delivering humanitarian assistance in both Somalia and Bosnia. All this occurred under Chapter VII of the Charter, leading to legally binding decisions by the Security Council. These decisions were not recommendations; they were mandatory from the viewpoint of international law. In effect, countries breaking sanctions were breaking international law.

Most Security Council resolutions, and all General Assembly resolutions except for those setting the budget, constitute recommendations, legally speaking. When dealing with peace and security issues, the council usually acts under Chapter VI, not Chapter VII. Chapter VI deals with the pacific settlement of disputes. Under this part of the Charter the council suggests to parties how they might resolve their disputes. Traditional peacekeeping, even though UN personnel may be lightly armed, takes place under Chapter VI. As we will see in some depth in the next few chapters, UN peacekeepers do not shoot their way into situations; they proceed with the consent of the parties, usually to supervise some cease-fire or other agreement. But the theory of the Charter's operation always entailed the notion that persuasion under Chapter VI should be seen against the more coercive possibilities under Chapter VII. If the parties cannot agree, upon pacific urging of the Security Council under the purview of Chapter VI, they might face sanctions under Chapter VII.

One of the great complexities facing the world organization in the twenty-first century is that although the Charter was written for states, much political instability and violence arise today either from violence within states or from violence across state boundaries by nonstate actors (NSAs). The problems in Somalia and Liberia, to name just two, arose from the absence of a functioning state and a government capable of speaking in the name of the state. In the legal vacuum, various armed factions exercise as much power as they can. In Bosnia, the problems stemmed not just from Serbian and Croatian foreign policies but from the actions of Bosnian Serbs and Bosnian Croats who were, in effect, unrecognized or quasi-recognized rebels in an internationalized internal armed conflict. In Cambodia, four groups vied for power. In Sri Lanka, armed Tamils have long sought to violently carve a new state out of that island to the north. Particularly after September 11, 2001, the importance of transnational NSAs, such as Al Qaeda and other terrorist groups, seems obvious.

These forms of violent conflict have been dubbed the "new wars."[22] Whether they are truly new has been the subject of much scholarly debate.[23] Among the "new war" implications are the contemporary meanings of Article 2 (7) of the UN Charter, which prohibits the UN from intervening in the domestic jurisdiction of a state. In the context of failed states or humanitarian crises generated by state and nonstate actors, can the UN, and presumably also member states, intervene in matters previously considered to be part of domestic jurisdiction? If the consequences of repression by the Iraqi government against Iraqis, including those who remain physically within Iraq, constitute a threat to international peace and security—as the council determined in 1991—then what is left to constitute domestic jurisdiction? If the UN and its member states are entitled to use all necessary means to provide a secure environment for humanitarian assistance inside Somalia—as the council stated in 1992—in a situation in which there were few if any consequences for other states, then domestic jurisdiction means very little. If the restoration of a deposed but duly elected government is the basis for a Chapter VII intervention in Haiti—as the council decided in 1994—then what is the difference between domestic and international affairs? If the bombing of Belgrade over its repressive actions in its former province of Kosovo is condoned, what actions can be considered purely domestic?

The Permanent Court of International Justice said in the 1920s that the dividing line between domestic and international jurisdictions was a changing one, depending on the nature of international relations. The realm of international action has been expanding. The Security Council, driven by the foreign policies of its members, is attempting to deal more with the causes of violence even if they arise from conditions within states than just with conditions between states. Legal notions follow from these political facts. Human security inside states may be as important at times to the Security Council as traditional notions of security between states.

Power matters. If the United Kingdom says that the situation in Northern Ireland is a domestic matter, this view may carry the day because of the power of the UK and its friends, just as Russia's characterization of its war against Chechnya or China's against Xinjiang are less likely to confront open international opprobrium than would similar actions by a less powerful state. Surely some matters clearly remain a part of domestic jurisdiction. Elections to the legislature in Nebraska, New York, South Carolina, or Missouri are internal or domestic and are not going to be supervised by the United Nations—although national elections in El Salvador, Nicaragua, Haiti, Angola, and Cambodia have been.

Increasingly the United Nations, especially through Security Council action, has undertaken all sorts of deeply intrusive actions pertaining to human rights and economic affairs inside states in an effort to resolve security problems. Security issues do not separate so easily from these other concerns in many contemporary conflicts. In Cambodia, in theory if not fully in practice, UN personnel were in charge of governmental ministries. In theory at least, the UN governed Cambodia on an interim basis. The limits to UN action, respecting Article 2 (7) and domestic jurisdiction, are first and foremost political. If the international community of states wants to act in Somalia or Cambodia or Iraq, via the UN, this article will be redefined to fit a particular situation. States have ratified the UN Charter, which conveys powers of auto-interpretation on the Security Council. What the international political traffic will bear determines the meaning of this article.

The precise boundaries of state sovereignty are elusive. If sovereignty means that a national government sets policy in its domestic jurisdiction, evolving international standards suggest that this remains true only as long as a national government adheres to international law. Perhaps the best example was Saddam Hussein's government after the 1991 Gulf War. He set policy in Iraq only as long as his government did not engage in aggression or in gross violations of internationally recognized human rights. When his government engaged in aggression, as against Kuwait, the United Nations put Iraq into a type of "receivership" in which it forfeited many attributes of a sovereign state—for example, it was no longer free to fashion its national security policy as it thought best, and it had to forgo using certain weapons. When it engaged in gross human rights violations, it had to tolerate UN protection of some threatened groups on Iraqi soil—for example, the Iraqi Kurds. When inspections for weapons of mass destruction resumed in November 2002, the extent of the outside intrusion was unprecedented.

The Secretary-General was referring to such trends when he wrote in 1992 that the time of absolute sovereignty had passed. Boutros-Ghali wrote in *Foreign Affairs*, "The centuries-old doctrine of absolute and exclusive sovereignty no longer stands, and was in fact never so absolute as it was conceived to be in theory. A major intellectual requirement of our time is to rethink the question of sovereignty."[24]

The seventh Secretary-General, Kofi Annan, has been even more outspoken on the subject:

State sovereignty, in its most basic sense, is being redefined—not least by the forces of globalization and international cooperation. States are now widely understood to be instruments at the service of their peoples, and not vice versa. At the same time individual sovereignty—by which I mean the fundamental freedom of each individual, enshrined in the charter of the UN and subsequent international treaties—has been enhanced by a renewed and spreading consciousness of individual rights. . . . This developing international norm in favour of intervention to protect civilians from wholesale slaughter will no doubt continue to pose profound challenges to the international community. In some quarters it will arouse distrust, skepticism, even hostility. But I believe on balance we should welcome it.[25]

Much of what was supposedly agreed remains undone. Under Article 43 of the Charter, all states are obligated to conclude an agreement with the Military Staff Committee (MSC), a subsidiary of the Security Council, whereby military forces are made available to the UN. No state has ever concluded such an agreement. In the past the great powers simply could not agree among themselves about how to construct Article 43 agreements. Some observers thought that during the Cold War neither Washington nor Moscow was seriously interested in these agreements. And in the United States, the question of Article 43 agreements got entangled in the controversy over "war powers," and whether the president alone was entitled to use various types of force pursuant to a Security Council resolution under Chapter VII. So this important matter remains unfinished over half a century after the Charter was signed.[26]

In 2004 the High-level Panel on Threats, Challenges and Change (HLP), and in 2005 Secretary-General Annan in his *In Larger Freedom*, recommended that the MSC be abolished. At the 2005 World Summit, the General Assembly recommended that the Security Council review the composition and mandate of the MSC. Hence, the body exists in theory, but in practice the council and Secretary-General are left with the task of constructing military forces mostly de novo for each security crisis in which a UN military presence is contemplated. It is amazing that large-scale UN peacekeeping, which after all started in 1956, remains on such shaky organizational ground.[27]

The UN has had to resort to the "sheriff's posse"[28] approach to a number of security crises—as in Korea, Iraq, Somalia, Haiti, and East Timor. In effect, the UN enters into a "contract" with the United States or other major powers to enforce UN policy in countering either aggression or threats to the peace. In the former Yugoslavia following the Dayton accords, NATO became the UN's agent. This is not so different from the Rhodesian situation in the 1960s and 1970s, when the Security Council authorized the British navy to enforce the mandatory embargo in Mozambican territorial waters. This approach has the advantage of efficiency, which is no small matter when lives are on the line. But it has the drawback of the loss of UN control over its own policies, entailing loss of accountability for precisely what is done in the UN's name. In other words, effective institutionalization—the final component for successful collective security—is still evolving for the world organization.

Chapter VIII of the Charter lays out a theory for UN linkage with regional organizations. This subject is important enough for extended analysis, particularly in light of calls to expand regional organizations' roles in the international security arena.

REGIONAL ARRANGEMENTS

Is it more appropriate to deal with local conflict through multilateral organizations whose scope is regional (for instance, the European Union or NATO) or universal (for instance, the United Nations)?[29] The preference for regional management of regional conflict was enshrined in Chapter VIII of the UN Charter at the urging of the United States, based on the insistence of its Latin American allies. The Persian Gulf War produced a strong sense that the original security provisions of the Charter, including a renewed interest in regional organizations, could sometimes be implemented. At the 2005 World Summit, the UN reiterated its commitment to Chapter VIII by strengthening the links between the world body and regional organizations.

Regional organizations, when and where they exist effectively, are often an appropriate locus for action because instability poses a greater threat to regional actors than those farther away. At the outset of the present Charter regime, the preference for peaceful settlement was clearly articulated. Even Article 21 of the Covenant of the League of Nations noted the validity of regional understandings as a basis for maintaining peace. However, one of the most controversial aspects at the San Francisco conference was the relative balance between regionalism and universalism.[30] While the creation of the Security Council, with its enforcement power, gave globalism a significant edge over regionalism, Chapter VIII, "Regional Arrangements," was also considered essential. The basic idea, called "subsidiarity," is that the organization closest to the conflict take action, if possible, before asking the universal UN to get involved. That way, the Security Council remains an option if regional efforts fall short. Chapter VIII was designed to limit Security Council deliberations to the most severe and intractable disputes.

Article 52 of Chapter VIII declares, "Nothing in the present Charter precludes the existence of regional arrangements or agencies dealing with matters relating to the maintenance of international peace and security" under the condition that "their activities are consistent with the Purposes and Principles of the United Nations." This article encourages states to use regional organizations before directing their conflicts to the Security Council and also recommends that the council make use of regional arrangements. Articles 53 and 54 define relations between the UN and regional organizations by prohibiting the latter from taking peace and security measures without Security Council authorization and by insisting that regional organizations inform the council of their activities.

The active use of the veto throughout the Cold War not only prevented the use of the Security Council but also meant that regional organizations sometimes provided the United States and the Soviet Union with convenient pretexts for containing disputes within organizations that were themselves under superpower control. Crises in Guatemala, Cuba, Panama, and the Dominican Republic were relegated to the Organization of American States, dominated by the United States. Hungary and Czechoslovakia were in the jurisdiction of the "socialist community" of the Warsaw Pact, dominated by the Soviet Union.

The supposed deficiencies of universal international organizations and the resulting apparent strengths of regional ones should be examined in light of the ambiguity of region as a concept, the overstretched capacities of the UN in international peace and security, and the purported better familiarity with local crises by the member states of regional organizations. The framers deliberately avoided precision in the language in Chapter VIII, thereby allowing governments the flexibility to fashion instruments to foster international peace and security. Although the commonsensical notion of region is related to geography, the ambiguity of the Charter means that a region can also be conceived of geopolitically, culturally, ideologically, and economically. Such groups could include treaty-based organizations that pre- or postdate the United Nations or ad hoc mechanisms created to deal with a specific concern. In addition to including such geographic entities as the African Union (AU) or the OAS, the Charter's definition of a regional organization might also include NATO, the Islamic Conference, and the OECD. Recent research points to the emergence of such "subregional" units as the Gulf Cooperation Council (GCC) and the Southern African Development Coordination Conference (SADCC) as potentially significant.[31] The concept of regionalism remains a conundrum.

A second issue concerns institutional resources. The United Nations continues to experience grave financial difficulties and sorely lacks sufficient and qualified staff. The great powers appear reluctant to pay for any substantial expansion of UN conflict management. The end of East-West tensions diminishes the perceived Western interests in many regional conflicts. Moreover, the war on terrorism introduced other priorities, not just in the United States but throughout the Western world. Governing elites and publics sought to divert expenditure from foreign policy to postponed domestic economic and social needs. Smaller powers traditionally active in peacekeeping are unlikely to continue to pick up more of the tab. They share the economic problems of the larger states. The 2005 World Summit failed to approve any significant additional resources for the UN, and it even stumbled over giving the Secretary-General more authority for budget and management decisions. Such a change would have implied reducing the control by the General Assembly, where developing countries are the majority, in favor of the UN's central administration, where the perception is that Western donors (and especially Washington) are in control.

In this context, regional approaches to crisis management and conflict resolution seem attractive. States near a country in conflict suffer most from the destabilizing consequences of war in their area. They receive the refugees and bear the political, social, and economic consequences, willingly or unwillingly, of combatants from neighboring countries seeking sanctuary. They face the choice of pacifying and repatriating combatant and noncombatant aliens on their territory or of resisting hot pursuit by those from whom these refugees have fled. Local conflict and the consequent perceptions of regional instability dampen investment flows and retard growth. They divert public resources into defense expenditures.

States from a region at war appear to be well suited to mediating local conflicts. They understand the dynamics of the strife and of the cultures involved more intimately than outsiders do. Leaders are far more likely to have personal connections to the involved parties, and these connections may be used as a basis for mediation. Involvement by other regional powers or organizations is less likely to be perceived by the international community as illegitimate interference than would involvement by extra-regional organizations. Finally, issues of local conflict are far more likely to be given full and urgent consideration in regional gatherings than in global ones, as the latter have more extensive agendas.

The apparent advantages of regional institutions exist more in theory than in practice. In reality, most of these organizations are far less capable than the United Nations. The comparative advantage of organizations in the actual region in conflict is more than offset by such practical disadvantages as partisanship, resource shortages, and local rivalries. Apart from very unusual cases (such as NATO), regional organizations have neither sufficient military capacity nor diplomatic leverage. Furthermore, regional organizations are also plagued by the same problems of achieving consensus, commitment, and organization.

Many of the factors favoring regional organizations are questionable. Regional actors do tend to suffer most from the destructive consequences of conflict among their neighbors. At the same time, they frequently have stakes in these conflicts, are committed to one side or another, and stand to benefit by influencing the outcome. Sometimes they even are active participants. In this sense, their interests are more complex than many proponents of regional organizations suggest. Their shared interest in the public good of regional stability is often accompanied by unilateral interest in obtaining specific favorable outcomes. Despite President Barack Obama's commitment to add 17,000 American soldiers to the 50,000 NATO troops in Afghanistan in 2009, the Western Alliance was finding it difficult to sustain long-term engagements because of political pressures on domestic fronts.

A favorable result for one regional power is likely to enhance its regional position at the expense of other countries, which are likely to oppose such initiatives. In the terminology of international relations theory, we have simultaneous considerations of absolute gain (stability) and relative gain (power). There is no certainty that stability will predominate. Indeed, the recent literature provides compelling arguments to the effect that cooperation and regime maintenance are particularly difficult where questions of power are prominent, as in national security.[32] Such issues are far more likely to be prominent in regional international relations than they are at the global level.

Situating crises in their regional historical and political contexts enhances the overall argument considerably. In Africa, the paralysis and bankruptcy of the OAU—now renamed the African Union—in curbing intervention and in managing the civil war in Angola reflected deep disagreement among its own members about the desirable outcome of the process of liberation. With its headquarters in Addis Ababa, the OAU appeared particularly inept in helping to end the Ethiopian civil war. The lack of any substantial OAU initiative also arose from the fact that other African states were deeply implicated in the conflict in pursuit of diverging national interests. Similar difficulties were evident in OAU efforts to cope with crises in Chad, Somalia, Liberia, and Sierra Leone during the Cold War. The modern African Union proved irrelevant to the bloodletting in the Congo (2003) and has been slow to respond to the crisis in Darfur (in 2004 termed "genocide" by U.S. Secretary of State Colin Powell and the U.S. House of Representatives by a vote of 422–0).[33] In an effort to institute a friendly order in Somalia in 2007–2008, the United States relied primarily on an informal ally, Ethiopia, not on the African Union, but Ethiopia withdrew in 2009, thereby leaving the country pretty much in the same failed-state condition as when it entered but with piracy in the adjoining seas even more acute.

In South Asia, it is hard to see how any regionally based initiative to settle the Afghan civil war might have succeeded, not only because of the presence of Soviet forces but also because India had no interest in seeing a pro-Pakistani or Islamic fundamentalist regime in Kabul. To take a more extreme case, the capacity of the South Asian Association for Regional Cooperation (SAARC) to act as a neutral mediator of conflict between India and Pakistan over Kashmir is extremely problematic; the two principal members of the organization are the very states involved. Elsewhere on the continent, efforts by the Association of Southeast Asian Nations (ASEAN) to resolve the Cambodian conflict were handicapped by differing conceptions of Chinese and Vietnamese threats to the region. More recently, the UN Security Council authorized the Australian-led International Force in East Timor (INTERFET) to restore peace and security on the island, an action taken with the acquiescence of the Indonesian government.

In Central America, the ability of the OAS to deal effectively with civil wars in Nicaragua and El Salvador during the 1980s was inhibited greatly by the U.S. failure to abide by the essential norm of nonintervention in its pursuit of a unilateral agenda to prevent revolution in El Salvador and reverse it in Nicaragua. The capacity of the European Community, now the EU, to come up with an effective response to the civil war in Croatia was significantly constrained by deep differences of opinion between France and Germany, and a number of disagreements among NATO members hampered military humanitarianism in Bosnia and Herzegovina. In short, regional organizations replicate regional power imbalances. They may be used by the more powerful to expand their influence at the expense of the weak. This problem has appeared, or is likely to appear, in regions where power imbalances are so substantial that it is not possible for weaker states in coalition to balance against the strong. Cases in point include South Africa in southern Africa, Nigeria in West Africa, India in South Asia, Indonesia in Southeast Asia, and the United States in the Americas.

A further concrete problem with regional organizations as managers of conflict is that frequently their membership is not inclusive and their coverage is partial. OAU conflict management in southern Africa was inhibited by the organization's exclusion of the region's major military and economic power—South Africa. The same might be said of ASEAN's role, given the exclusion of Vietnam, Laos, and Cambodia. In light of the vast differences in their levels of economic development, this situation is unlikely to change once these anomalous exclusions are rectified. The Arab League excludes one of the three major regional powers (Iran). The Gulf Cooperation Council excludes two of three (Iraq and Iran). In a number of these instances (the OAU in southern Africa, the GCC in the Gulf, and ASEAN), the consciousness of the organization is defined in large part by its members' opposition to the threat posed by the excluded parties. The premise of these organizations has been partiality, hardly a capacity for neutral intervention and security management.

Moreover, these organizations have traditionally demonstrated their greatest structural weaknesses in dealing with civil war, the main growth industry for international conflict managers. This shortcoming follows in part from the international legal impediments associated with the doctrine of noninterference in internal affairs. These impediments have proven even more acute for many countries in the Third World, preoccupied with exerting control over their own tenuous bases of power.[34]

The reluctance to become involved in civil conflict reflects the sensitivity of regional powers to creating precedents that might later be used to justify intervention in their own countries. In Africa, for example, many governments are themselves threatened by the possibility of civil conflict, which leads to caution about fostering norms that would legitimize regional involvement in such conflicts. Curiously, the challenge to the sovereignty of colonial powers facilitated decolonization. But newly independent countries immediately became staunch defenders of state sovereignty, a sentiment that is also prevalent in central Europe and the former Soviet republics. Respect for conventional definitions of sovereignty has verged on slavishness—including the license to murder and repress. This weakness was shared during the Cold War by the United Nations; it is likely to play out more strongly at the regional level. For all of the above reasons, the general case for reliance on regional organizations is weak, as was very much in evidence in Zimbabwe, where the African Union stood on the sidelines in the face of Robert Mugabe's destructive repression.

At the same time, an overstretched United Nations has resorted to creative measures. The Gulf War in 1991 and the creation of safe havens for Iraqi Kurds are clear and successful illustrations of military "subcontracting" to the Allied Coalition, as was NATO's presence in Bosnia from 1995 until December 2004, when it handed over the military reins to the EU. A more controversial and less successful example was Somalia, where a U.S.-led effort was mounted to break the back of warlord-induced famine. Moreover, three Security Council decisions in July 1994 indicated the relevance of military intervention by major powers in regions of their traditional spheres of influence: a Russian plan to deploy its troops in Georgia to end the three-year-old civil war; the French intervention in Rwanda, supposedly to cope with genocidal conflict; and the U.S. plan to spearhead a military invasion to reverse the military coup in Haiti.

Regional organizations have also turned to subcontracting. In 1994, the then Conference (now Organization) on Security and Co-operation in Europe (CSCE and OSCE) authorized troops from the Commonwealth of Independent States (CIS) and other OSCE member states after a definitive agreement regarding Nagorno-Karabakh. Similarly, the Economic Community of West African States (ECOWAS) authorized a contingent of largely Nigerian troops to stabilize Liberia and Sierra Leone.

The results from these arrangements have not been consistently superior to the UN's record. Yet the evident gap between the UN's capacities and persistent demands for help could be filled by regional powers, or even hegemons, operating under the scrutiny of a wider community of states.[35] The argument has become stronger in light of the experience in Kosovo and more especially the smooth handover in Timor from the Australian-led force to the UN one in February 2000.

In attempting to determine a possible division of labor between global and regional organizations to meet the exigencies of particular conflicts, distinctions should be made between Europe and developing countries as well as between the use of outside military forces to keep the peace and diplomatic measures for negotiations. In Europe, UN diplomacy could well be combined with the use of NATO forces under a UN flag in regional disputes, as throughout the former Yugoslavia. Also, the EU has taken a series of steps to create its own military capacity, which leads Andrew Moravcsik, for one, to propose a division of labor between American enforcement and European peacekeeping.[36] In developing countries, the division of labor could be different. In crises of manageable size (for example, in Guatemala), the UN could deploy its troops and work closely with regional partners in diplomatic arm-twisting. In more dangerous conflicts like the ones in Somalia and the Congo, UN diplomacy could be teamed with the troops of countries willing to run risks in a coalition.

In short, the will and the capacity of regional organizations to outperform the UN in the management of conflict within their areas are in doubt, with the notable exception of Europe. The end of the Cold War has done little to change this conclusion. The potential of regional organizations needs to be tempered with the reality of recent efforts.

STRAYING FROM THE COURSE

Since 1945, untold numbers of wars have broken out and tens of millions of people have perished.[37] According to the logic of the Charter, the leadership for the UN's peace and security duties rests on the shoulders of a small segment of the international community of states, notably the great powers on the Security Council. Conflict between the United States and the Soviet Union poisoned the atmosphere and prevented their working together on most security issues during the Cold War. World politics often made it impossible to act collectively, and states often chose to disobey or ignore the prohibitions and restrictions on the use of force to pursue raisons d'état.

In place of the ideal collective-security system, the UN developed alternate means to mitigate certain conflicts: peacekeeping. We now turn to this story.

NOTES

1. Some have argued that there has been an upswing in the number, intensity, and duration of civil wars, particularly since 1989. However, data indicate that the quantity of overall conflicts decreased while negotiated settlements increased over the 1990s. See Swedish International Peace Research Institute, *SIPRI Yearbook 1998: Armaments, Disarmament, and International Security* (Oxford: Oxford University Press, 1998), 17. This work is shortened and updated annually by Peter Wallensteen and Margareta Sollenberg in the *Journal of Peace Research*. An even more optimistic interpretation is found in Andrew Mack, ed., *Human Security Report 2005* (Vancouver: Human Security Centre, 2005), and in subsequent updated *Briefings* available at www.humansecuritybrief.info. See also Human Security Project Report and World Bank's Mini-atlas of Human Security, available at www.miniatlasofhuman security.info.

2. For a discussion, see F. H. Hinsley, *Power and the Pursuit of Peace* (Cambridge: Cambridge University Press, 1963); S. J. Hambleben, *Plans for World Peace Through Six Centuries* (Chicago: University of Chicago Press, 1943); F. P. Walters, *A History of the League of Nations*, 2 vols. (London: Oxford University Press, 1952).

3. Lynn H. Miller, *Global Order: Values and Power in International Politics*, 2nd ed. (Boulder, Colo.: Westview Press, 1990), 46–50.

4. See Jane Boulden, Ramesh Thakur, and Thomas G. Weiss, eds., *The United Nations and Nuclear Orders* (Tokyo: UN University Press, 2009).

5. Chapter 12 of Claude, *Swords into Plowshares*, is still the best single treatment of collective security. The interested reader is also referred to Inis L. Claude Jr., *Power and International Relations* (New York: Random House, 1962); Ernst B. Haas, "Types of Collective Security: An Examination of Operational Concepts," *American Political Science Review* 49,

no. 1 (1955): 40–62; Thomas G. Weiss, ed., *Collective Security in a Changing World* (Boulder, Colo.: Lynne Rienner, 1993); and George W. Downs, ed., *Collective Security Beyond the Cold War* (Ann Arbor: University of Michigan Press, 1994). For a statistical view, see John Mearsheimer, "The False Promise of International Institutions," *International Security* 19, no. 3 (1994–1995): 5–49.

6. See Robert Riggs and Jack Plano, *The United Nations: International Organization and World Politics*, 2nd ed. (Belmont, Calif.: Wadsworth, 1994), 100.

7. For discussions, see Edward C. Luck, *UN Security Council: Practice and Promise* (London: Routledge, 2006), and M. J. Peterson, *The UN General Assembly* (London: Routledge, 2005).

8. See Peter Wallensteen and Patrik Johansson, "Security Council Decisions in Perspective," in *The UN Security Council: From the Cold War to the 21st Century*, ed. David Malone (Boulder, Colo.: Lynne Rienner, 2004), 17–33.

9. Johan Kaufmann, *United Nations Decision-Making* (Rockville, Md.: Sijthoff and Noordhoff, 1980), 43–52. See also Sydney D. Bailey and Sam Daws, *The Procedure of the UN Security Council*, 3rd ed. (Oxford: Oxford University Press, 1998); and James P. Muldoon et al., *Multilateral Diplomacy and the United Nations Today* (Boulder, Colo.: Westview Press, 1999).

10. See M. J. Peterson, *The General Assembly* (London: Routledge, 2005). For a discussion of formal and informal processes, see Johan Kaufmann, *Conference Diplomacy: An Introductory Analysis*, rev. ed. (Dordrecht, Netherlands: Martinus Nijhoff, 1988).

11. Thant Myint-U and Amy Scott, *The UN Secretariat: A Brief History (1945–2006)* (New York: International Peace Academy, 2007), 126–128.

12. See Cyrus R. Vance and David A. Hamburg, *Pathfinders for Peace: A Report to the UN Secretary-General on the Role of Special Representatives and Personal Envoys* (New York: Carnegie Commission on Preventing Deadly Conflict, 1997).

13. Confidential interview, November 2004.

14. The best sources for the Charter are Leland Goodrich, Edvard Hambro, and Anne Patricia Simons, *Charter of the United Nations* (New York: Columbia University Press, 1969); and Bruno Simma, *The Charter of the United Nations: A Commentary* (Oxford: Oxford University Press, 2002).

15. See Kent Kille, ed., *The Moral Authority of the UN Secretary-General* (Washington, D.C.: Georgetown University Press, 2007); and Benjamin Rivlin and Leon Gordenker, eds., *The Challenging Role of the UN Secretary-General* (Westport, Conn.: Praeger, 1993). For recent autobiographies, see Javier Pérez de Cuéllar, *Pilgrimage for Peace: A Secretary-General's Memoirs* (New York: St. Martin's Press, 1997); and Boutros Boutros-Ghali, *Unvanquished: A U.S.-U.N. Saga* (Mississauga, Ontario: Random House of Canada, 1999).

16. Edward C. Luck reviews the possible reasons for this in David P. Forsythe, Patrice C. McMahon, and Andrew Wedeman, eds., *American Foreign Policy in a Globalized World* (New York: Routledge, 2006). He concludes that it is impossible to say whether the United States really expected this language to be effective. See also Stephen C. Schlesinger, *Act of Creation: The Founding of the United Nations* (Boulder, Colo.: Westview Press, 2003); Townsend Hoopes and Douglas Brinkley, *FDR and the Creation of the U.N.* (New Haven, Conn.: Yale University Press, 1997).

17. For a different view, see Michael Glennon, "The UN vs. U.S. Power," *Foreign Affairs* 82, no. 3 (2003): 16–35.

18. See Lee Feinstein and Anne-Marie Slaughter, "A Duty to Prevent," *Foreign Affairs* 83, no. 1 (2004): 136–150; and Allan Buchanan and Robert O. Keohane, "The Preventive Use of

Force: A Cosmopolitan Institutional Proposal," *Ethics & International Affairs* 18, no. 1 (2004): 1–22.

19. For discussion, see Joseph P. Nye Jr., *Bound to Lead: The Changing Nature of American Power* (New York: Basic Books, 1990) and *The Paradox of American Power: Why the World's Only Superpower Can't Go It Alone* (Oxford: Oxford University Press, 2002).

20. See Stanley Hoffmann, "The Problem of Intervention," in *Intervention in World Politics*, ed. Hedley Bull (New York: Oxford University Press, 1984), 7–28.

21. David Cortright and George A. Lopez, *The Sanctions Decade: Assessing UN Strategies in the 1990s* (Boulder, Colo.: Lynne Rienner, 2000).

22. See, for example, Mary Kaldor, *New and Old Wars: Organized Violence in a Global Era* (Stanford, Calif.: Stanford University Press, 1999); and Mark Duffield, *Global Governance and the New Wars: The Merging of Development and Security* (London: Zed Books, 2001).

23. See Peter J. Hoffman and Thomas G. Weiss, *Sword & Salve: Confronting New Wars and Humanitarian Crises* (Lanham, Md.: Rowman & Littlefield, 2006); Stathis N. Kalyvas, "'New' and 'Old' Civil Wars: A Valid Distinction?," *World Politics* 54, no. 1 (2001): 99–118.

24. Boutros Boutros-Ghali, "Empowering the United Nations," *Foreign Affairs* 72, no. 5 (1992–1993): 98–99.

25. Kofi Annan, "Two Concepts of Sovereignty," *The Economist* (September 18, 1999).

26. See Eric Grove, "UN Armed Forces and the Military Staff Committee: A Look Back," *International Security* 17, no. 4 (1993): 172–181.

27. See Michael W. Doyle and Nicholas Sambanis, *Making War and Building Peace: United Nations Peace Operations* (Princeton, N.J.: Princeton University Press, 2006).

28. See Brian Urquhart, "Beyond the 'Sheriff's Posse,'" *Survival* 32, no. 3 (1990): 196–205.

29. See S. Neil MacFarlane and Thomas G. Weiss, "Regional Organizations and Regional Security," *Security Studies* 2, no. 1 (1992): 6–37.

30. See Francis O. Wilcox, "Regionalism and the United Nations," *International Organization* 19, no. 3 (1965): 789–811; and Tom J. Farer, "The Role of Regional Collective Security Arrangements," in *Collective Security in a Changing World*, ed. Thomas G. Weiss (Boulder, Colo.: Lynne Rienner, 1993), 153–189.

31. See William T. Tow, *Subregional Security Cooperation in the Third World* (Boulder, Colo.: Lynne Rienner, 1990).

32. On this point, see Joseph Grieco, "Anarchy and the Limits of Cooperation: A Realist Critique of the Newest Liberal Institutionalism," *International Organization* 62, no. 3 (1988): 488–507; and John Mearsheimer, "Instability in Europe After the Cold War," *International Security* 15, no. 1 (1990): 44.

33. See William G. O'Neill and Violette Cassis, *Protecting Two Million Internally Displaced: The Successes and Shortcomings of the African Union in Darfur* (Washington, D.C.: Brookings Institution–University of Bern Project on Internal Displacement, 2005). For broader discussion, see Jane Boulden, ed., *Dealing with Conflict in Africa: The United Nations and Regional Organizations* (London: Palgrave, 2003).

34. See Mohammed Ayoob, *The Third World Security Predicament: State Making, Regional Conflict, and the International System* (Boulder, Colo.: Lynne Rienner, 1995); and Brian Job, ed., *The Insecurity Dilemma: National Security of Third World States* (Boulder, Colo.: Lynne Rienner, 1992).

35. The discussion about the components of accountability was first made in relationship to Russia by Jarat Chopra and Thomas G. Weiss, "Prospects for Containing Conflict in the

Former Second World," *Security Studies* 4, no. 3 (1995): 552–583; see also Lena Jonson and Clive Archer, eds., *Peacekeeping and the Role of Russia in Eurasia* (Boulder, Colo.: Westview Press, 1996). For an extended argument about a "partnership" between the UN and regional organizations, see Alan K. Henrikson, "The Growth of Regional Organizations and the Role of the United Nations," in *Regionalism in World Politics: Regional Organizations and World Order*, eds. Louise Fawcett and Andrew Hurrell (Oxford: Oxford University Press, 1995), 122–168.

36. Andrew Moravcsik, "Striking a New Transatlantic Bargain," *Foreign Affairs* 82, no. 4 (2003): 74–89. See also Bastian Giegrich and William Wallace, "Not Such a Soft Power: The External Deployment of European Forces," *Survival* 46, no. 2 (2004): 163–182.

37. For a discussion of the unsettling numbers, see the annual publications of the International Institute for Strategic Studies, *Strategic Survey 2008/2009* and the *Military Balance 2008–2009* (Oxford: Oxford University Press, 2008).

CHAPTER 2

UN Security Efforts
During the Cold War

THE UN CHARTER'S requirement for unanimity among the permanent members of the Security Council reflected the realities of the power politics of the day and historical norms of European interstate relations in that regard. The council was created less out of naive idealism and more out of a hardheaded effort to mesh state power with international law, a necessary link for effective enforcement. However, the underlying requirement that members would agree was not borne out with any frequency until after the Cold War. The veto held by the P-5 was not the real problem; disagreement among those with power was.

THE EARLY YEARS:
PALESTINE, KOREA, SUEZ, THE CONGO

The onset of the Cold War ended the big-power cooperation on which the postwar order had been predicated. Nonetheless, the UN became involved in four major security crises: Palestine (1948), Korea (1950), Suez (1956), and the Congo (1962). After Israel declared its independence in 1948, war broke out between it and its four neighbors—Egypt, Jordan, Lebanon, and Syria. Soon thereafter, the Security Council ordered a cease-fire under Chapter VII and ultimately created an observer team, the United Nations Truce Supervision Organization (UNTSO) under Chapter VI to supervise it. UNTSO observer groups were deployed, unarmed, along the borders of Israel and its neighbors and operated with the consent of the parties involved. Close to 600 observers were eventually deployed, including army units from Belgium, France, the United States, and Sweden. Troops had no enforcement mandate or capability, but their presence did deter truce violations. To exercise their mandates without relying upon military might, they relied on the moral authority of the United Nations. Also, warring parties knew that their truce violations would be objectively reported to UN headquarters in New York for possible further action. Although observers wore the uniforms of their respective national armies, their first allegiance theoretically was to the world organization, symbolized by UN armbands. Later, blue helmets and berets became the trademark of UN peacekeepers. The observers were paid by their national armies and granted a stipend by the world organization. UNTSO's activities continue to be financed from the UN's regular operating budget.

UNTSO has performed a variety of important tasks. UNTSO observers set up demilitarized zones along the Israeli-Egyptian and Israeli-Syrian borders, established Mixed Armistice Commissions along each border to investigate complaints and allegations of truce violations, and verified compliance with the General Armistice Agreements. If a truce violation occurred, the chief of staff of UNTSO attempted to deal with the matter locally, negotiating cease-fires when necessary. De-escalating crises before they blossom into significant threats to the peace has been a chief function of the operation. UNTSO also became a training ground and resource center for other peacekeeping operations; its observers and administrators were consistently redeployed in other parts of the world. UNTSO's experience over the years has been integrated into other operations to improve their functioning.

UNTSO did, unfortunately, contribute to a freezing of the conflict. From 1949 to 1956 and then to 1967, the main parties to the conflict were unwilling to use major force to break apart the stalemate. UNTSO was there to police the status quo. Being freed from major military violence, the parties lacked the necessary motivation to make concessions for a more genuine peace. This problem of successful UN peacekeeping contributing to freezing but not solving a conflict was to reappear in Cyprus and elsewhere.

The first coercive action taken in the name of the United Nations concerned the Korean peninsula.[1] UN involvement in this crisis merits careful attention because arguably the UN engaged in a type of collective security there between 1950 and 1953. World War II left Korea divided, with Soviet forces occupying the North and U.S. forces the South. The UN call for withdrawal of foreign troops and elections throughout a unified Korea was opposed by communist governments, leading to elections only in the South and the withdrawal of most U.S. troops. In 1950, forces from North Korea (the Democratic Republic of Korea), which was informally allied with the Soviet Union and China, attacked South Korea (the Republic of Korea). The United States then moved to resist this attack.

At the UN, the USSR was boycotting the Security Council to protest the seating of the Chinese government in Taiwan as the permanent member instead of the Chinese communist government on the mainland. The United States knew the Security Council would not be stymied by a Soviet veto and could adopt some type of resolution on Korea. So Washington referred the Korean situation to the council. The Truman administration ordered U.S. military forces to Korea, albeit before the Security Council approved a course of action. The council passed a resolution under Chapter VII declaring that North Korea had committed a breach of the peace. Before the council recommended, but did not require, that UN members furnish all appropriate assistance (including military assistance) to South Korea, the USSR abandoned its boycott and returned to its council seat. The General Assembly improvised, through the Uniting for Peace Resolution, to continue support for the South in the name of the United Nations.

In essence, Security Council resolutions on Korea provided international legitimacy to U.S. decisions. The Truman administration was determined to stop communist expansion in East Asia. It proceeded without a congressional declaration of war or any other specific authorizing measure, and it was prepared to proceed without UN authorization—although once this was obtained, the Truman administration emphasized UN approval in its search for support both at home and abroad.

The UN's symbol and reputation were therefore thrust into a security dilemma of major proportions, even though the permanent members of the council, and the communist government of China outside the council, were definitely not in complete agreement. Once the USSR returned to council deliberations, direct military actions being taken in the UN's name became impossible. Absent the USSR, a unified UN command had been established. In reality, however, the UN deputized the United States to lead the defense of South Korea in the name of the United Nations. When the early tide of the contest turned in favor of the South, Truman decided to carry the war all the way to the Chinese border. This was a fateful decision that prolonged war by bringing Chinese forces into the fight in major proportions—and thus continued the war until 1953, when stalemate restored the status quo ante. All important strategic and tactical decisions pertaining to Korea that carried the UN's name were in fact made by the United States. Other states, such as Australia and Turkey, fought for the defense of South Korea, but that military operation was, in fact, a U.S. operation behind the UN flag.

The defense of South Korea was not a classic example of collective security. A truncated Security Council clearly labeled the situation a breach of the peace and authorized the use of military force, something that would not occur again during the Cold War. The council in effect authorized military support for the South, but it did not mandate it, a form of council action that would be repeated in the 1990s concerning Iraq, Somalia, and Bosnia. However, neither the council nor its Military Staff Committee really controlled the use of UN symbols. No Article 43 agreements transferring national military units to the UN were concluded. And the Secretary-General, Trygve Lie of Norway, played almost no role in the situation once he came out clearly against the North Korean invasion. The Soviet Union stopped treating him as Secretary-General. Given that power play, he was eventually forced to resign because of his ineffectiveness. He was legally correct to take a public stand against aggression, but doing so then left him without the necessary political support of a major power, Moscow. Subsequent Secretaries-General tried to learn from his difficulties, representing Charter

Prisoners guarded by a South Korean soldier wait to be taken to a POW camp near Inchon in October 1950. (UN Photo 32240)

values but, they hoped, without antagonizing the permanent members whose support was necessary for successful UN action.

The 1956 Suez Canal crisis resulted in the first use of what became known as "peacekeepers" to separate warring parties. France, Britain, and Israel had attacked Soviet-backed Egypt against the wishes of the United States, claiming a right to use force to keep the Suez Canal open after Egyptian president Gamel Abdel Nasser had closed it. Britain and France used their vetoes, blocking action by the Security Council. The General Assembly resorted to the Uniting for Peace Resolution—this time for peacekeeping, not enforcement—and directed Secretary-General Dag Hammarskjöld (of Sweden) to create a force to supervise the cease-fire between Israel and Egypt once it had been arranged. The first UN Emergency Force (UNEF I) oversaw the disengagement of forces and served as a buffer between Israel and Egypt. In this instance, the United States and Soviet

Congolese refugees uprooted from their homes by fighting in Katanga Province wait for water at a refugee camp in September 1961. (UN Photo 71906)

Union were not so far apart. U.S. President Dwight D. Eisenhower acted in the spirit of collective security by preventing traditional U.S. allies from proceeding with what he regarded as aggression. UN peacekeeping in 1956 and for a decade thereafter was hailed as a success.

The efforts by the world organization to deal with one of the most traumatic decolonizations, in the former Belgian Congo (then Zaire and more recently the Democratic Republic of Congo), illustrated the limits of peacekeeping. The ONUC (or the French acronym United Nations Operation in the Congo)[2] almost bankrupted the world organization and also threatened its political life, and Secretary-General Hammarskjöld lost his own life in a suspicious plane crash in the country.

This armed conflict was both international (caused by Belgium's intervention in its former colony) and domestic (caused by a province's secession within the new state). The nearly total absence of a government infrastructure led to a massive involvement of UN civilian administrators in addition to 20,000 UN soldiers. After having used his Article 99 powers to get the world organization involved, the Secretary-General became embroiled in a situation in which the Soviet Union, its allies, and many nonaligned countries supported the national prime minister, who was subsequently murdered while under arrest; the Western powers and the UN organization supported the president. At one point the president fired the prime minister, and the prime minister fired the president, leaving no clear central authority in place. The political vacuum created enormous problems for the United Nations as well as opportunities for action.

Instead of neutral peacekeepers, UN forces became an enforcement army for the central government, which the UN Secretariat created with Western support. This role was not mandated by the assembly or council, and in this process the world organization could not count on cooperation from the warring parties within the Congo. Some troop contributors resisted UN command and control; others removed their soldiers to register their objections. The Soviet Union, and later France, refused to pay assessments for the field operation. This phase of the dispute almost destroyed the UN, and the General Assembly had to suspend voting for a time to dodge the question of who was in arrears on payments and thus who could vote. The USSR went further in trying to destroy Hammarskjöld's independence by suggesting the replacement of the Secretary-General with a troika (or a three-person administrative structure at the top of the organization). Four years later, the UN departed from a unified Congo, an accomplishment. However, it had also acquired an operational black eye in Africa because of its perceived partisan stance. No UN troops were sent again to Africa until the end of the Cold War (to Namibia). The UN also incurred a large budgetary deficit and developed a hesitancy to become involved in internal wars. Questions about funding lay unresolved, to arise again in later controversies.

The 1973 Arab-Israeli War ended with the creation of the second United Nations Emergency Force (UNEF II). This lightly armed interpositional force became the blueprint for other traditional peacekeeping operations. UNEF II was composed of troops from Austria, Finland, Ireland, Sweden, Canada, Ghana, Indonesia, Nepal, Panama, Peru, Poland, and Senegal—countries representing each of the world's four major regions. The operation consisted of over 7,000 persons at its peak. UNEF II's original mandate was for six months, but the Security Council renewed it continually until 1979, when the U.S.-brokered Israeli-Egyptian peace accord was signed. UNEF II functioned as an impartial force designed to establish a demilitarized zone, supervise it, and safeguard other provisions of the truce. Small-scale force was used to stop those who tried to breach international lines. The presence of UNEF II had a calming influence on the region by ensuring that Israel and Egypt were kept apart. The success of both UNEF I and II, and the problems with the operation in the Congo, catalyzed traditional peacekeeping, the subject to which we now turn.

UNDERSTANDING PEACEKEEPING

The effective projection of military power under international control to enforce international decisions against aggressors was supposed to distinguish the United Nations from the League of Nations. The onset of the Cold War made this impossible on a systematic basis. A new means of peace maintenance was necessary, one that would permit the world organization to act within carefully defined limits when the major powers agreed or at least acquiesced.

UN peacekeeping proved capable of navigating the turbulent waters of the Cold War through its neutral stance and limited range of activities. Again, global politics determined the nature of UN activities. Although peacekeeping is not specifically mentioned in the Charter, it became the organization's primary function in the domain of peace and security. The use of troop contingents for this purpose is widely recognized as having begun during the 1956 crisis in Suez. Contemporary accounts credit Lester B. Pearson, then Canada's secretary of state for external affairs and later prime minister, with proposing to the General Assembly that Secretary-General Hammarskjöld organize an "international police force that would step in until a political settlement could be reached."[3]

Close to 500,000 military, police, and civilian personnel—distinguished from national soldiers by their trademark powder-blue helmets and berets—served in UN peacekeeping forces during the Cold War, and some 700 lost their lives in UN service during this period. Alfred Nobel hardly intended to honor soldiers when he created the peace prize that bears his name, and no military organization had received the prize throughout its eighty-seven-year history. This changed in December 1988, when UN peacekeepers received the prestigious award. This date serves as the turning point in the following discussion to distinguish UN security activities during and after the Cold War.

The Cold War and the Birth of Peacekeeping, 1948–1988

The lack of any specific reference to peacekeeping in the Charter led Hammarskjöld to coin the poetic and apt expression "Chapter six and a half," which referred to stretching the original meaning of Chapter VI. And certainly peacekeeping "can rightly be called the invention of the United Nations," as then Secretary-General Boutros Boutros-Ghali claimed in *An Agenda for Peace*.[4] The lack of a clear international constitutional basis makes a consensus definition of peacekeeping difficult, particularly because peacekeeping operations have been improvised in response to the specific requirements of individual conflicts. Despite the lack of consensus and the multiplicity of sources,[5] former UN under-secretary-general Marrack Goulding provided a sensible definition of peacekeeping: "United Nations field operations in which international personnel, civilian and/or military, are deployed with the consent of the parties and under United Nations command to help control and resolve actual or potential international conflicts or internal conflicts which have a clear international dimension."[6]

The first thirteen UN peacekeeping and military observer operations deployed during the Cold War are listed in Table 2.1.[7] Five were still in the field in December 2008. From 1948 to 1988, peacekeepers typically served two functions: observing the peace (that is, monitoring and reporting on the maintenance of cease-fires) and keeping the peace (that is, providing an interpositional buffer between belligerents and establishing zones of disengagement). The forces were normally composed of troops from small or nonaligned states, with permanent members of the Security Council and other major powers making troop contributions only under exceptional circumstances. Lightly armed, these neutral troops were symbolically deployed between belligerents who had agreed to stop fighting; they rarely used force and then only in self-defense and as a last resort. Rather than being based on any military prowess, the influence of UN peacekeepers in this period resulted from the cooperation of belligerents mixed with the moral weight of the international community of states.[8]

Peacekeeping operations essentially defended the status quo. They helped suspend a conflict and gain time so that belligerents could be brought closer to the negotiating table. However, these operations do not by themselves guarantee the successful pursuit of negotiations. They are often easier to institute than to dismantle, as the case of over four decades of this activity in Cyprus demonstrates. The termination of peacekeeping operations creates a vacuum and may have serious consequences for the stability of a region, as happened in 1967 at the outbreak of the Arab-Israeli War following the withdrawal of UNEF I at Egypt's request.

Detailed histories of the first decades of peacekeeping are readily available. One illustration of the UN's handling of conflict in this period of East-West tensions helps to set the stage for a discussion of general principles that will bring in other UN operations. The UN Disengagement Observer Force (UNDOF) represents a classic example of international compromise during the Cold War. This operation was designed as a microcosm of geopolitics, with a NATO member and a neutral on the pro-Western Israeli side of the line of separation, and a member of the Warsaw Pact and a neutral on the pro-Soviet Syrian side. UNDOF was established on May 31, 1974, upon the conclusion of disengagement agreements between Israel and Syria that called for an Israeli withdrawal from all areas it occupied within Syria, the establishment of a buffer zone to separate the Syrian and Israeli armies, and the creation of areas of restricted armaments on either side of the buffer zone. UNDOF was charged with verifying Israel's withdrawal, establishing the buffer zones, and monitoring levels of militarization in the restricted zones.

UNDOF employed 1,250 armed soldiers, including ninety military observers. Troop deployment emphasized equal contributions by countries that were either politically neutral or sympathetic to the West or East. Originally, Peru, Canada, Poland, and Austria provided troops for the operation. (The Peruvian troops were replaced by Iranians in 1975 and by Finns in 1979.) Canadian and Peruvian forces operate along the Israeli side; Polish and Austrian troops operate in Syrian territory.

Despite the declared hostility between Israel and Syria, UNDOF proved instrumental in maintaining peace in the Golan Heights between the two longtime foes. From 1977 through 2005, no major incidents have occurred in areas under UNDOF's jurisdiction. Success is attributable to several factors: the details of the operation were thoroughly defined before its implementation, leaving little

TABLE 2.1   UN Peacekeeping Operations During the Cold War and During the
Initial Thaw

Years Active	Operation
1948–Present	United Nations Truce Supervision Organization (UNTSO, based in Jerusalem)
1949–Present	United Nations Military Observer Group in India and Pakistan (UNMOGIP)
1956–1967	United Nations Emergency Force (UNEF I, Suez Canal)
1958	United Nations Observation Group in Lebanon (UNOGIL)
1960–1964	United Nations Operation in the Congo (ONUC)
1962–1963	United Nations Force in New West Guinea (UNSF, in West Irian)
1963–1964	United Nations Yemen Observation Mission (UNYOM)
1964–Present	United Nations Peacekeeping Force in Cyprus (UNFICYP)
1965–1966	United Nations India-Pakistan Observation Mission (UNIPOM)
1965–1966	Mission of the Representative of the Secretary-General in the Dominican Republic (DOMREP)
1973–1979	Second United Nations Emergency Force (UNEF II, Suez Canal and later the Sinai Peninsula)
1974–Present	United Nations Disengagement Observer Force (UNDOF, Golan Heights)
1978–Present	United Nations Interim Force in Lebanon (UNIFL)
1988–1990	United Nations Good Offices Mission in Afghanistan and Pakistan (UNGOMAP)
1988–1991	United Nations Iran-Iraq Military Observer Group (UNIIMOG)
1989–1990	United Nations Transition Assistance Group (UNTAG, in Namibia)
1989–1991	United Nations Angola Verification Mission (UNAVEM I)
1989–1992	United Nations Observer Group in Central America (ONUCA)

room for disagreement; Israel and Syria cooperated with UNDOF; and the Security Council supported the operation fully.

Principles of Traditional Peacekeeping

The man who helped give operational meaning to "peacekeeping," Sir Brian Urquhart, has summarized the characteristics of UN operations—which can be gleaned inductively from the case of UNDOF—during the Cold War as follows: consent of the parties, continuing strong support of the Security Council, a clear and practicable mandate, nonuse of force except in the last resort and in self-defense, the willingness of troop contributors to furnish military forces, and the willingness of member states to make available requisite financing.[9] Developing each of the characteristics serves as a bridge to our subsequent discussion of subsequent UN efforts that extend beyond traditional limitations because many of these traditional standard operating procedures would need to be set aside or seriously modified to confront the challenges of many post–Cold War peace operations.

Consent Is Imperative Before Operations Begin. In many ways, consent is the keystone of traditional peacekeeping, for two reasons. First, it helps to insulate the UN decision-making process against great-power dissent. For example, in Cyprus and Lebanon the Soviet Union's desire to obstruct was overcome because the parties themselves had asked for UN help.

Second, consent greatly reduces the likelihood that peacekeepers will encounter resistance while carrying out their duties. Peacekeepers are physically in no position to challenge the authority of belligerents (either states or opposition groups), and so they assume a nonconfrontational stance toward local authorities. Traditional peacekeepers do not impinge on sovereignty. In fact, it is imperative to achieve consent before operations begin.

The emphasis that traditional missions place on consent does have drawbacks, as two observers have noted: "Peacekeeping forces cannot often create conditions for their own success."[10] For example, belligerents will normally consent to a peacekeeping mission once wartime goals have been achieved or losses have made belligerents war-weary. In instances where neither of these conditions has been met, it becomes necessary to find alternate ways to induce warring parties to achieve and maintain consent. Moreover, major powers need to pressure their clients not only to consent but also to negotiate. When political will is lacking, wars either continue unaddressed by the organization, or UN peacekeepers become inextricably tied down in conflict—neither able to bring peace to the area nor able to withdraw from it. For example, the United Nations Peacekeeping Force in Cyprus (UNFICYP), originally deployed in 1964 to separate warring Turkish and Greek Cypriot communities and then given a new mandate in 1974, remains in the field because consent for deployment has not been matched by a willingness to negotiate the peace. Likewise, the United Nations Military Observer Group in India and Pakistan (UNMOGIP), established in 1949; UNDOF, created in 1974; and the United Nations Interim Force in Lebanon (UNIFIL), deployed in 1978—all continue to operate because of the absence of political conditions allowing for their removal.

Peacekeeping Operations Need Full Support from the Security Council. The council's support is necessary not only in the beginning stages of the mission, when decisions regarding budgets, troop allotments, and other strategic priorities are made, but also in its later stages, when mandates come up for renewal. The host of problems in the Congo illustrates the dangers of proceeding without the support of the major powers in the Security Council. Backing by both the United States and the Soviet Union of UNEF I in the General Assembly was the only case in which the United States and the Soviet Union abandoned the Security Council and then resorted to the General Assembly to get around a veto. A practice has developed for the Security Council to renew the mandate of missions several times—frequently semiannually for years on end—in order to keep pressure on parties who may be threatened with the possible withdrawal of peacekeepers. Full Security Council support also enhances the symbolic power of an operation.

Participating Nations Need to Provide Troops and to Accept Risks. Successful peacekeeping missions require the self-sustained presence of individual peacekeeping battalions, each of which is independent but also functions under UN command. Frequently they deploy in areas of heavy militarization. Mortal danger exists for peacekeepers. Democratic governments in particular that provide troops must be willing to accept the risks inherent in a given mission, and they also must be able to defend such expenditures and losses before their parliaments.

Permanent members do not normally contribute troops except for logistical support. Providing logistical support has become a specialty of the United States, which during the Cold War essentially airlifted most start-up troops and provisions for UN operations. Keeping major powers from an active role in peacekeeping was imperative for the neutrality that successful peacekeeping strives to attain. Washington and Moscow were thought to be especially tainted by the causes that they supported worldwide.

The experience with exceptions to this rule has been mixed. Because of the special circumstances involved in Britain's possession of extraterritorial bases on the island of Cyprus, the United Kingdom was involved in UN operations there from the outset; that effort has been worthwhile. The experience of French peacekeepers deployed in UNIFIL in Lebanon was a source of problems because of France's perceived involvement as an ex-colonial power on the Christian side of the conflict. Consequently, French troops came under attack by local factions and were forced to withdraw from the zone of operations and to remain in the UN compound in Naquora. This experience was a smaller-scale indication of the problems that would be incurred later by both the United States and France in the non-UN operation in Beirut in 1984, when some 300 soldiers were killed.[11]

A Clear and Precise Mandate Is Desirable. The goals of the mission should be clear, obtainable, and known to all parties involved. Enunciation of the mission's objectives reduces local suspicion. Yet a certain degree of flexibility is desirable so that the peacekeepers may adapt their operating strategies to better fit changing circumstances. The goals of the operation may be expanded or reduced as the situation warrants. In fact, diplomatic vagueness may at times be necessary in Security Council voting to secure support or to keep future options open.

Force Is Used Only in Self-Defense and as a Last Resort. Peacekeepers derive their influence from the diplomatic support of the international community, and therefore they use force only as a last resort and in self-defense. The Peacekeeper's Handbook states this wisdom: "The degree of force (used) must only be

Brian E. Urquhart, under-secretary-general for special political affairs, answers questions in June 1985 about his mission to the Middle East to free soldiers of the UN Interim Force in Lebanon. (UN Photo 165579/Y. Nagata)

sufficient to achieve the mission on hand and to prevent, as far as possible, loss of human life and/or serious injury. Force should not be initiated, except possibly after continuous harassment when it becomes necessary to restore a situation so that the United Nations can fulfill its responsibilities."[12]

Peacekeeping techniques differ greatly from those taught to most soldiers and officers by their national training authorities. However, in the past only the Scandinavian states and Canada have trained large numbers of their recruits and officers specifically for the peacekeeping method. Soldiers from other countries have often found themselves unprepared for peacekeeping situations where the prohibition against the use of force contradicts their standard military training.

Using minimal force affords several advantages.[13] With limited military capability, peacekeepers have insufficient firepower to threaten belligerents, who are apt to treat peacekeepers with less suspicion than they direct toward regular forces. Peacekeepers are often able to mediate and forestall local flare-ups of violence.

Traditionally, peacekeeping forces have had the luxury of operating without enemies. The need to operate at peak military efficiency has not been as great as it would have been if "enemies," in the normal sense of the term, had existed. As a result, the administrative, technological, and strategic structures that sustain peacekeeping have reflected the need for professional diplomatic and political expertise more than the need for professional soldiers.

"CHAPTER SIX AND A HALF" ON HOLD, 1978–1988

From 1948 to 1978 thirteen UN peacekeeping operations took place. In the ten years after 1978, however, no new operations materialized, even as a rash of regional conflicts involving the superpowers or their proxies sprang up around the globe.[14]

The last operation approved before the decade-long hiatus highlights the difficulties the UN encountered during this period. UNIFIL in Lebanon was beset with problems similar to those experienced in the Congo during the 1960s, where domestic conflict and an absence of government structures had given the world organization an operational black eye.[15] UNIFIL's difficulties illustrate the dangers inherent in operations that lack both clear mandates and the effective cooperation of belligerents and that exist amidst political chaos and great-power disagreement.

UNIFIL was established at the Security Council's request on March 19, 1978, following Israel's military incursion into southern Lebanon. Israel claimed that military raids and shellings by members of the Palestine Liberation Organization (PLO) who were based in southern Lebanon threatened Israeli peace and security. Israel's response embarrassed its primary ally, the United States. Washington used its influence in the Security Council to create UNIFIL as a face-saving means for Israel to withdraw. The operation's duties included confirming the Israeli withdrawal; establishing and maintaining an area of operations; preventing renewed fighting among the PLO, Israel, and the Southern Lebanese Army (Christian militia backed by Israel and led by Major Saad Haddad); and restoring Lebanese sovereignty over southern Lebanon.

At UNIFIL's maximum strength, over 7,000 soldiers were deployed, including contingents from Canada, Fiji, France, Ghana, Iran, Ireland, Nepal, the Netherlands, Nigeria, Norway, and Senegal. UNIFIL encountered significant problems due to the conflicting interests of the major parties involved in southern Lebanon. Israel refused to cede control of the South to UNIFIL, choosing instead to rely upon Major Haddad's Southern Lebanese Army, which resisted UNIFIL's efforts to gain control in the area. The PLO demanded that it be allowed to operate freely in the South to continue its resistance against Israel. The Lebanese government insisted that UNIFIL assume control of the entire region, including areas Haddad controlled. Consequently, UNIFIL found itself sandwiched between the PLO and Haddad's forces; its contingents routinely came under fire. The PLO continued its military maneuverings against Israel, and Haddad's forces continued their attacks on the PLO. In 1982, as Israel reinvaded Lebanon and marched to Beirut, UNIFIL stood by, powerless, in the face of Israel's superior firepower and the unwillingness of troop contributors or the UN membership to resist. UNIFIL's refusal to stand its ground echoed Egypt's 1967 request to withdraw UNEF I; once UN troops were pulled out, war ensued.

The lack of political will among the regional participants and troop contributors was matched by the incapacity of the Lebanese government's army and police.

Yet, UNIFIL became part of the local infrastructure,[16] and its withdrawal would be disruptive. It would have resulted in greater instances of fighting between the PLO, Israel, and Haddad's army, and a probable third Israeli intervention would almost certainly have been countered by direct Syrian opposition.

Much of the impetus for the increased tension between East and West and for the end of new UN deployments came from the United States after the Reagan administration assumed power in 1981. Elected on a platform of anticommunism, the rebuilding of the national defense system, and fiscal conservatism, the administration was determined to roll back Soviet gains in the Third World. Washington scorned the world organization and cast it aside as a bastion of Third World nationalism and procommunism. The UN's peacekeeping operations were tarred with the same brush. The Reagan administration also refused to pay its assessed dues (including a portion of the assessment for UNIFIL, which Washington had originally insisted upon).[17] The organization was in near bankruptcy at the same time that U.S. respect for international law seemed to evaporate and unilateral action gained favor.[18] Intervening in Grenada, bombing Libya, and supporting insurgencies in Nicaragua, Angola, Afghanistan, and Cambodia attested to U.S. preferences. The Soviet Union countered these initiatives. Central America, the Horn of Africa, much of southern Africa, and parts of Asia became battlegrounds for the superpowers or their proxies. This situation changed only with the Gorbachev regime in the Soviet Union and the advent of glasnost and perestroika, which figure in the next chapter.

ECONOMIC SANCTIONS

Short of sending international forces, a group of states may attempt to isolate an aggressor by cutting off diplomatic or economic relations with a view toward altering offensive behavior. These are coercive, albeit nonforcible, actions—the first step in Chapter VII's enforcement progression. Diplomatic and economic sanctions are significantly more emphatic than the political influence that makes up the everyday stuff of foreign policy, even if less emphatic than the dispatch of troops.

On a spectrum ranging from political influence to outside military intervention, economic sanctions are a form of nonforcible enforcement. For the same reasons that real collective security was not possible during the Cold War, these milder forms of enforcement were also largely underused. The exceptions were the cases of two pariahs, Rhodesia and South Africa, whose domestic racist policies were widely condemned. As a reaction to Rhodesia's unilateral declaration of independence (UDI) from the United Kingdom in 1965, the Security Council in 1966 ordered limited economic sanctions under Chapter VII of the Charter for the first time in UN history.[19] Whether the trigger was more due to the UDI or the human rights situation for Africans is debatable, but the result was that the council characterized the domestic situation as a "threat to the peace." The council toughened the stance against the white-minority government by banning all exports and imports (except for some foodstuffs, educational materials, and medicines). These sanctions became "comprehensive" in 1968.

The sanctions initially extracted some costs from the government of Rhodesian prime minister Ian Smith. But, ironically, they eventually helped immunize the country against outside pressure in the form of nonforcible sanctions because they prompted a successful program of import substitution. In short, Rhodesia diversified its economy. Although most members of the UN complied, some of those who counted did not. The United States, for example, openly violated sanctions after the Byrd amendment by Congress allowed trade with Rhodesia, even though the United States had voted for sanctions in the Security Council. According to U.S. judicial doctrine, if Congress uses its statutory authority to violate international law intentionally, domestic courts will defer to congressional action in U.S. jurisdiction. Many private firms as well as some other African countries also traded with Rhodesia, including the neighboring countries of Mozambique (a Portuguese colony) and the Republic of South Africa.

Although the Security Council authorized a forceful blockade to interrupt supplies of oil and the British navy did halt a few tankers, there was insufficient political will to effectively blockade the ports and coastlines of Mozambique and South Africa. Hence, the Security Council helped but can hardly be credited with the establishment of an independent Zimbabwe in 1979. The UN's use of economic sanctions in this case was more important as legal and diplomatic precedent than as effective power on the ground.

UN-imposed sanctions against South Africa reflected the judgment that legally approved racial separation (apartheid) within the country also was considered a threat to the peace. Limited economic sanctions, an embargo on arms sales to South Africa, boycotts against South African athletic teams, and selective divestment were all part of a visible campaign to isolate South Africa. These acts exerted pressure; however, it is difficult to quantify their impact. Initially, South Africa's high-cost industry thrived by trying to replace missing imports (as had Rhodesia's), and it even managed to produce a variety of sophisticated arms that eventually became a major export. The transition to democracy (and the end of white rule) probably resulted more from the dynamics of the internal struggle by the black majority and the end of the Cold War than from nonforcible sanctions. Sanctions no doubt contributed to altering the domestic balance by demonstrating the risks and the costs of being isolated, but measuring their precise impact requires greater empirical work.[20] As in Rhodesia, some major states were slow to endorse sanctions on South Africa, and others participated in trade under the table that lessened sanctions' impact.

The Rhodesian and South African experiences show how the UN, through the Security Council, can link the domestic policies of states to threats to international peace and security and thereby justify Chapter VII action. Earlier, we pointed out the power of self-definition, and thus the council expanded the definition of a threat by the use of sanctions as enforcement tools for a domestic issue and thereby set an important precedent. UN sanctions are analytically distinct from bilateral economic sanctions or those imposed by treaty (for example, the Montreal Protocol to protect the ozone). The UN Charter never uses the word "sanctions" in Chapter VII, but Article 41 speaks of "measures not involving the use of armed force," which "are to be employed to give effect to its decisions." The continued use of partial or comprehensive sanctions has come under increased criticism because of their impact on vulnerable populations within targeted countries, a subject to which we return at the end of Chapter 3.

NOTES

1. See Leon Gordenker, *The UN Secretary-General and the Maintenance of Peace* (New York: Columbia University Press, 1967); and Leland M. Goodrich, *Korea: A Study of U.S. Policy* (New York: Council on Foreign Relations, 1956).

2. The tradition of acronyms in English was set aside as operations in Spanish- and French-speaking countries became more widespread beginning in the late 1980s.

3. Max Harrelson, *Fires All Around the Horizon: The UN's Uphill Battle to Preserve the Peace* (New York: Praeger, 1989), 89.

4. Boutros Boutros-Ghali, *An Agenda for Peace: Preventive Diplomacy, Peacemaking and Peace-keeping* (New York: United Nations, 1992), para. 46.

5. Other definitions can be found in United Nations, *The Blue Helmets: A Review of United Nations Peace-keeping* (New York: UNDPI, 1990), 4; Alan James, *Peacekeeping in International Politics* (London: Macmillan, 1990), 1; and Boutros-Ghali, *Agenda*, para. 20.

6. Marrack Goulding, "The Changing Role of the United Nations in Conflict Resolution and Peace-keeping," speech given at the Singapore Institute of Policy Studies, March 13, 1991, 9. See also Marrack Goulding, "The Evolution of Peacekeeping," *International Affairs* 69, no. 3 (1993): 451–464. See also his *Peacemonger* (London: John Murray, 2002).

7. For further analyses of peacekeeping during the Cold War, see Thomas G. Weiss and Jarat Chopra, *Peacekeeping: An ACUNS Teaching Text* (Hanover, N.H.: Academic Council on the United Nations System, 1992), 1–20. For a discussion of operations during the Cold War but with an emphasis on transferring lessons to the present, see Sally Morphet, "UN Peacekeeping and Election-Monitoring," in *United Nations, Divided World: The UN's Roles in International Relations*, eds. Adam Roberts and Benedict Kingsbury (Oxford: Clarendon Press, 1993), 183–239. The United Nations published its own volume, *The Blue Helmets* (New York: United Nations, 1985), which was revised in 1990 and 1996. Updates are now on the United Nations website at www.un.org. See also Rosalyn Higgins, *United Nations Peacekeeping, Documents and Commentary*, vols. 1–4 (Oxford: Oxford University Press, 1969, 1970, 1980, 1981).

8. For a discussion of UN and non-UN operations in a comparative military perspective in this period, see John Mackinlay, *The Peacekeepers* (London: Unwin Hyman, 1989). See also Augustus Richard Norton and Thomas G. Weiss, *UN Peacekeepers, Soldiers with a Difference* (New York: Foreign Policy Association, 1990); William J. Durch, ed., *The Evolution of UN Peacekeeping* (New York: St. Martin's Press, 1993); and Paul Diehl, *International Peacekeeping* (Baltimore: Johns Hopkins University Press, 1993).

9. Brian Urquhart, "Beyond the 'Sheriff's Posse,'" *Survival* 32, no. 3 (1990): 198; see also his autobiography, *A Life in Peace and War* (New York: Harper and Row, 1987).

10. John Mackinlay and Jarat Chopra, "Second Generation Multinational Operations," *Washington Quarterly* 15, no. 3 (1992): 114.

11. For a discussion of these issues, see Mackinlay, *Peacekeepers*; and Pierre Le Peillet, *Les berets bleus de l'ONU* (Paris: Editions France-Empire, 1988).

12. International Peace Academy, *Peacekeeper's Handbook* (New York: Pergamon, 1984), 56.

13. See F. T. Liu, *United Nations Peacekeeping and the Non-Use of Force* (Boulder, Colo.: Lynne Rienner, 1992).

14. For a discussion of this period, see S. Neil MacFarlane, *Superpower Rivalry and Third World Radicalism* (Baltimore: Johns Hopkins University Press, 1985); Elizabeth Valkenier, *The Soviet Union and the Third World* (New York: Praeger, 1985); and Jerry Hough, *The Struggle for the Third World* (Washington, D.C.: Brookings Institution, 1986).

15. For a discussion, see Bjorn Skogmo, *UNIFIL: International Peacekeeping in Lebanon* (Boulder, Colo.: Lynne Rienner, 1989); and E. A. Erskine, *Mission with UNIFIL* (London: Hurst, 1989).

16. See Marianne Heiberg, "Peacekeepers and Local Populations: Some Comments on UNIFIL," in *The United Nations and Peacekeeping*, eds. Indar Jit Rikhye and Kjell Skjelsback (London: Macmillan, 1990), 147–169.

17. See Jeffrey Harrod and Nico Shrijver, eds., *The UN Under Attack* (London: Gower, 1988).

18. See David P. Forsythe, *The Politics of International Law: U.S. Foreign Policy Reconsidered* (Boulder, Colo.: Lynne Rienner, 1990).

19. See Henry Wiseman and Alistair M. Taylor, *From Rhodesia to Zimbabwe* (New York: Pergamon, 1981); and Stephen John Stedman, *Peacemaking in Civil War: International Mediation in Zimbabwe, 1974–1980* (Boulder, Colo.: Lynne Rienner, 1991). The League of Nations had previously tried limited sanctions against Franco's Spain.

20. Audie Klotz and Neta C. Crawford, *How Sanctions Work: Lessons from South Africa* (New York: Palgrave Macmillan, 1999).

CHAPTER 3

UN Security Operations After the Cold War (1988–1998)

T HE DECLINE OF THE Cold War marked an important period of transition for the United Nations. Soviet leader Mikhail Gorbachev sought to reduce East-West tensions by reinvigorating multilateralism generally and UN peacekeeping more particularly.[1] The USSR made payments on its UN debt of over $200 million in 1987, generating renewed international interest in the United Nations and collective security. Gorbachev officially redefined the Soviet Union's relationship with the UN in 1988 at the General Assembly by calling for an extension of his domestic "new thinking" to apply to the management of international conflicts. In particular, UN peacekeeping provided a face-saving means to withdraw from what Gorbachev described as the "bleeding wound" of Afghanistan.

Changes in the Soviet Union's attitude toward the UN influenced the international climate and more particularly the U.S. approach to the world organization. In 1988, President Ronald Reagan abruptly altered his public stance and praised the work of the organization, the Secretary-General, and UN peacekeepers.[2] After helping to spearhead attacks that had led to almost a decade of UN-bashing, he declared at the General Assembly that "the United Nations has the opportunity to live and breathe and work as never before" and vowed to repay U.S. debts to the organization. This orientation was continued by President George H. W. Bush, a former U.S. permanent representative to the world body. Great-power cooperation grew, allowing the Security Council to resume part of its role as a guarantor of international peace and security. The UN also provided a convenient way for France, Great Britain, and Russia[3] to maintain international preeminence despite their declining economic, political, and military significance. The UN also enabled the United States to proceed as a hegemonic rather than dominant power, allowing it to act through the UN on the basis of cooperation rather than having to coerce other states into compliance.

THE FIRST UN MILITARY OPERATIONS
AFTER THE END OF THE COLD WAR, 1988–1993

From 1988, collegiality and regular collaboration among great powers in the Security Council were politically possible. After a ten-year gap in deploying new UN security operations, five post–Cold War operations (listed at the top of Table 3.1) were launched—in Afghanistan and Pakistan, astride the Iran-Iraq border, and in Angola, Namibia, and Central America (for Nicaragua).

These were largely traditional peacekeeping operations, but they also incorporated some improvisations characteristic of the evolution of UN peacekeeping. For example, there were large numbers of civilians working in tandem with soldiers in Namibia and Central America. The first supervision of domestic elections as well as the collection of weapons from insurgents took place in Nicaragua. These precedents illustrated clearly the UN's capacity for growth in the new era, just as improvisation and task expansion had been present in earlier UN activities. At the same time, these new operations were essentially extensions of the time-tested recipe for UN peacekeeping. In particular, all enjoyed the consent of fighting parties and relied upon defensive concepts of force employed by modestly equipped UN soldiers, few of whom came from armies of the major powers. Peace operations begun between 1988 and 1998 are listed in Table 3.1. Two of the operations also fall into the traditional peacekeeping category—the follow-up operation in Angola and the one in the Western Sahara.[4]

Three operations begun during this period are so different in scope and mandate that to characterize them as "peacekeeping" stretches analytical categories to the breaking point. UN operations in Cambodia, the former Yugoslavia, and Somalia indicated the new challenges for the UN. The evolution of these and two subsequent operations (Rwanda and Haiti) illustrates the limits of UN military operations, which is where we conclude this chapter. Another UN operation in the Iraq-Kuwait war merits a separate discussion because its deployment followed the first UN collective security action of the post–Cold War era.

The distinction between traditional peacekeeping and the operations beginning with Somalia will become clear by the end of this chapter. However, before we analyze precisely how the new field operations illustrate challenges for the future, we need to examine in more detail a few cases of post–Cold War cooperation that cemented big-power collaboration and made possible the movement toward bolder UN operations. At a maximum, these cases suggest the revival of collective security as a possible policy option for governments.

THE REBIRTH OF PEACEKEEPING

The UN Good Offices Mission in Afghanistan and Pakistan (UNGOMAP), the UN Iran-Iraq Military Observer Group (UNIIMOG), the first UN Angola Verification Mission, and the UN Transition Assistance Group in Namibia (UNTAG)

TABLE 3.1   UN Peace and Security Operations, 1988–2000

Years Active	Operation
1988–1990	United Nations Good Offices Mission in Afghanistan and Pakistan (UNGOMAP)
1988–1991	United Nations Iran-Iraq Military Observer Group (UNIIMOG)
1989–1990	United Nations Transition Assistance Group (UNTAG, in Namibia)
1989–1991	United Nations Angola Verification Mission (UNAVEM I)
1989–1992	United Nations Observer Group in Central America (ONUCA)
1991–1992	United Nations Advance Mission in Cambodia (UNAMIC)
1991–1995	United Nations Observer Mission in El Salvador (ONUSAL)
1991–1995	United Nations Angola Verification Mission II (UNAVEM II)
1991–Present	United Nations Mission for the Referendum in Western Sahara (MINURSO)
1991–2003	United Nations Iraq-Kuwait Observer Mission (UNIKOM)
1992–1993	United Nations Transitional Authority in Cambodia (UNTAC)
1992–1993	United Nations Operation in Somalia I (UNOSOM I)
1992–1994	United Nations Operation in Mozambique (ONUMOZ)
1992–1995	United Nations Protection Force, former Yugoslavia (UNPROFOR)
1993–1994	United Nations Mission Uganda-Rwanda (UNOMUR)
1993–1995	United Nations Mission in Somalia II (UNOSOM II)
1993–1996	United Nations Mission in Haiti (UNMIH)
1993–1996	United Nations Assistance Mission for Rwanda (UNAMIR)
1993–1997	United Nations Observer Mission in Liberia (UNOMIL)
1993–Present	United Nations Observer Mission in Georgia (UNOMIG)
1994–1994	United Nations Aouzou Strip Observer Group (UNASOG, Chad/Libya)
1994–2000	United Nations Mission in Tajikistan (UNMOT)
1995–1996	United Nations Confidence Restoration Operation, Croatia (UNCRO)
1995–1997	United Nations Angola Verification Mission III (UNAVEM III)
1995–1999	United Nations Preventive Deployment Force, former Yugoslav Republic of Macedonia (UNPREDEP)
1995–2002	United Nations Mission in Bosnia and Herzegovina (UNMIBH)
1996–1997	United Nations Support Mission in Haiti (UNSMIH)
1996–1998	United Nations Transitional Administration for Eastern Slavonia, Baranja and Western Sirmium (UNTAES)
1996–2002	United Nations Mission of Observers in Prevlaka (UNMOP)
1997–1997	United Nations Verification Mission in Guatemala (MINUGUA)
1997–1999	United Nations Observer Mission in Angola (MONUA)
1997–1997	United Nations Transition Mission in Haiti (UNTMIH)
1997–2000	United Nations Civilian Police Mission in Haiti (MIPONUH)
1998–1998	United Nations Civilian Police Support Group (UNCPSG)
1998–2000	United Nations Mission in the Central African Republic (MINURCA)
1998–1999	United Nations Observer Mission in Sierra Leone (UNOMSIL)

were missions that renewed peacekeeping's visibility and perceived workability in the international arena of conflict resolution. UNGOMAP, UNIIMOG, and UNTAG are also significant because they afforded the UN the opportunity to demonstrate its usefulness in war zones, a capacity that had been frozen from 1978 to 1988. Successes built confidence and allowed the UN to move back toward center stage, and the operations provided the space to experiment with innovations beyond the scope of previous deployments.

These operations are examples of "observation," a diverse set of tasks that occupies the least controversial part of the peacekeeping spectrum. Traditionally, observation has meant investigation, armistice supervision, maintenance of a cease-fire, supervision of plebiscites, oversight of the cessation of fighting, and reports to headquarters. It has been expanded to include the verification of troop withdrawal, the organization and observation of elections, the voluntary surrender of weapons, and human rights verification. These operations are distinct from the other traditional task: interposition—placing peacekeepers between belligerents along a cease-fire line.

UNGOMAP verified the withdrawal of Soviet troops from Afghanistan after 1988. The USSR had entered the country in 1979 to ensure a friendly Afghan government in Kabul. By the early 1980s Afghanistan had become Moscow's Vietnam. The Soviets had become inextricably tied down in an unwinnable conflict against the *mujahideen*, armed local groups backed by Pakistan and the United States—and a few others like Saudi Arabia. The Gorbachev administration sought a face-saving device to extricate itself. The 1988 Geneva Accords provided the means to achieve Soviet withdrawal, mutual noninterference and nonintervention pledges between Pakistan and Afghanistan, the return of refugees, and noninterference pledges from the United States and the Soviet Union. These accords had been brokered by the United Nations and the indefatigable efforts of under-secretary-general Diego Cordovez.

The deployment of UNGOMAP was not accompanied by the political will needed to implement the international agreements concerning peace, elections, and disarmament. The symbolic size of the operation—fifty officers divided between Islamabad and Kabul—attested to its inability to independently perform tasks other than reporting on the Soviet withdrawal after the fact. The operation paved the way to a potential peace by reducing the direct East-West character of the conflict; however, the power vacuum left by the Soviet withdrawal also set the stage for the rise of the Taliban, which provided sanctuary to Al Qaeda.

In 1988, the Iran-Iraq War drew to a close with over one million lives lost. The Security Council ordered a cease-fire in 1987 with the compulsory intent provided for under Chapter VII to set up UNIIMOG in 1988 to maintain the cease-fire astride the international border. It established cease-fire lines between Iranian and Iraqi troops, observed the maintenance of the cease-fire, and investigated complaints to defuse minor truce violations before they escalated into peace-threatening situations.

Composed of only 350 unarmed observers from some twenty-five states, UNIIMOG nonetheless played a useful role in preserving the cease-fire between Iran and Iraq, two countries whose mutual antagonism continued after hostilities ceased. In its first five months alone, UNIIMOG investigated some 2,000 complaints of truce infractions. Although UNIIMOG was instrumental in stopping the situation from deteriorating, it was more Iraq's diminished position after the 1991 Persian Gulf War that kept the peace than any diplomatic effort.

In Africa, Angola, Cuba, and South Africa signed a trilateral agreement on December 22, 1988. This provided for the simultaneous withdrawal of Cuban troops from Angola and of South African troops and administrators from Namibia. This diplomatic breakthrough was monitored successfully by the first United Nations Angola Verification Mission, which led the way for the UN-sponsored peace process that brought Namibian independence on March 21, 1990, from South Africa's illegal colonial rule. The second UNAVEM was more problematic because civil war returned despite UN-supervised elections at the end of 1992; the difficulties faced by this group are discussed with other more problematic operations later in this chapter.

UNTAG was established to facilitate and monitor South Africa's withdrawal from Namibia, to set up free and fair elections, and to determine the future government and constitution of Namibia. This was one of the last major decolonization efforts under UN auspices. UNTAG was tasked with monitoring and facilitating the departure of South Africa's army and the withdrawal and confinement of the South-West Africa People's Organization's (SWAPO) fighters to base camps in Angola, monitor the southwest African police force controlled by South Africa to prevent meddling in elections, oversee the repeal of discriminatory laws that threatened the fairness of the election, help ensure the respect for amnesty to political prisoners, and provide for the return of all Namibian refugees. UNTAG also registered voters and facilitated information about the election process.

At its maximum deployment, nearly 8,000 persons were involved in UNTAG—about 4,500 military personnel, 2,000 civilian personnel, and 1,000 police officers. It was the first sizable operation in Africa since the contested one in the Congo almost three decades earlier. The operation was rushed into the field in order to respect an April deadline. Hundreds of SWAPO fighters crossed the border on the first day after the UN's deployment in violation of the agreement, although they claimed that they had interpreted the text otherwise. In any event, South Africa–supported defense forces killed several hundred SWAPO guerrillas, the heaviest casualties in two decades of armed conflict.

But the parties to the conflict, in particular South Africa, were committed to making the operation work. UNTAG is generally considered a success, and Secretary-General Javier Pérez de Cuéllar viewed it as one of his better accomplishments. Virtually the entire population was registered to vote. SWAPO won forty-one of seventy-two seats in the Constitutional Constituents Assembly and was duly empowered to lead the formation of the Namibian government. On March 21, 1990—ahead of schedule and under budget—UN Secretary-General Javier Pérez de Cuéllar swore in Sam Nujoma as president of Namibia.

UNTAG provides a helpful analytical hinge between the old and new types of UN security operations. It went smoothly because traditional rules were followed—especially consent and minimal use of force. At the same time, it undertook several new tasks related to civil administration, elections, and police activities. These tasks foreshadowed new UN activities that would more routinely intrude into the affairs of sovereign states.

MOVING TOWARD THE NEXT GENERATION

The work of the United Nations in Central America during the late 1980s and early 1990s provides a transition in our discussion of the progressive movement toward a new generation of peacekeeping and peace-enforcement operations.[5] World politics was changing and so were the possibilities for UN action. Governments removed political obstacles that had previously blocked or impeded UN activities. Although not at all comparable in most ways, the UN's efforts in Central America were similar to the Afghanistan operation in that the world organization was helping a superpower move beyond an unwinnable confrontation in its own backyard.

An analysis of the United Nations Observer Group in Central America (ONUCA), the United Nations Observer Mission to Verify the Electoral Process in Nicaragua (ONUVEN), and the United Nations Observer Mission in El Salvador (ONUSAL) illustrates the complex transition process that the UN's peace and security functions began to undergo. These also set the stage for analysis of the UN-sponsored Chapter VII enforcement action against Iraq. ONUSAL in particular shows the independent nature of UN action when states give the world organization some political room to maneuver. All of this was made possible not only by the rise of Gorbachev in the Soviet Union but also by the replacement of Reagan with President George H. W. Bush (father of President George W. Bush).

In the late 1980s, the conclusion of the so-called Esquipulas II agreements between the countries of Central America—Nicaragua, Costa Rica, El Salvador, Guatemala, and Honduras—began the peace process that ended a decade of civil war and instability in the region. The cornerstone of the agreements involved setting up free and fair elections in Nicaragua. In addition to calling for elections, the Esquipulas II agreements prohibited aid to rebel groups and the use of a state's territory for guerrilla operations in another. ONUCA (1989–1992) was established to ensure that these provisions were respected. Although ONUCA was officially an "observer" mission, duties were far-reaching. They included verifying that all forms of military assistance to insurgent forces had ceased and preventing states from sponsoring such activity for infiltration into neighboring countries. ONUCA observers made spot checks and random investigations of areas prone to guerrilla activity along the borders of Nicaragua, El Salvador, Guatemala, Honduras, and Costa Rica. Although the signatories to Esquipulas II were expected to cooperate with ONUCA, the participation of the Nicaraguan resistance movement, the Contras, was not ensured until after the electoral defeat of the Sandinista government in February 1990. ONUCA military observers operated in a tense, potentially dangerous situation where armed attacks were possible.

ONUCA's mandate expanded after the Nicaraguan election to include demobilizing the Contras. Bases were set up inside the borders of Nicaragua, where many rebel soldiers came and handed over some of their weapons and military equipment to ONUCA soldiers, who destroyed them and helped to advance demilitarization. In spite of the continued existence of arms among disgruntled partisans of both the Contra and Sandinista causes, this was the first instance of UN involvement in demilitarization through the physical collection and destruction of armaments. This task is important for conflict resolution in areas where heavily armed regular as well as irregular forces need to be drastically reduced before any meaningful consultative process can occur. The collection of arms has been integrated into numerous subsequent UN peacekeeping operations and has been made even more rigorous.[6] The importance of such a task was recognized by the United Kingdom as part of its efforts to end direct rule over Northern Ireland in 1999–2000.

ONUVEN was created to ensure the fairness of elections in Nicaragua and is the first example of UN observation of elections inside a recognized state, an extraordinary intrusion according to conventional notions of domestic jurisdiction. It operated in tandem with ONUCA's soldiers, but ONUVEN consisted of some 120 civilian observers who monitored the election process, from start to finish, to ensure that it was free and fair. They verified that political parties were equitably represented in the Supreme Electoral Council; that there was political, organizational, and operational freedom for all political parties; that all political parties had equal access to state television and radio broadcasts; and that the electoral rolls were drawn up fairly. It also reported any perceived unfairness to the Supreme Electoral Council, made recommendations about possible remedial action, and reported to the Secretary-General.

One unusual development was the extent to which the UN operations were linked with supporting efforts from regional and nongovernmental organizations. The UN and the Organization of American States—in particular, the secretaries-general of the UN and the OAS—cooperated closely in diplomacy and in civilian observation. During the Nicaraguan elections, a host of such nongovernmental groups as former U.S. president Jimmy Carter's (the Council of Freely Elected Heads of Government) provided additional outside observers as part of a large international network.

The operation began in August 1989 and ended in February 1990 with the surprising electoral defeat of the Sandinista government. ONUVEN's success—

which was fortified by its links to the OAS and private groups—enhanced the prospects of UN election-monitoring teams working within the boundaries of states. This practice has gained wider international acceptance even when no armed conflict has taken place. For instance, from June 1990 to January 1991, the United Nations Observer Mission to Verify the Electoral Process in Haiti (ONUVEH) performed tasks similar to the missions in Nicaragua, which set the stage for subsequent UN action when the duly elected government of Jean-Bertrand Aristide was overthrown. ONUVEN's civilian composition changed the content of peacekeeping's definition by blurring the distinction between civilian and military operations and between security and human rights.

In neighboring El Salvador, ONUSAL was an essential element in helping to move beyond a decade of brutal civil war in which over 75,000 persons had been killed and serious human rights abuses had taken place. The government and rebel sides, and their foreign backers, came to a stalemate. This created the conditions for successful and creative UN mediation. Negotiations under the good offices of the UN Secretary-General led to a detailed agreement on January 1, 1992, which was actually initialed a few hours after Javier Pérez de Cuéllar had completed his second five-year term.

An essential component of moving beyond the war was the use of UN civilian and military personnel in what, by historical standards, would have been seen as unacceptable outside interference in purely domestic affairs. Ongoing human rights abuses were to be prevented through an elaborate observation and monitoring system that began before an official cease-fire. Previous violations by both the army and the government as well as by the armed opposition, the FMLN, were to be investigated by a truth commission. The highly controversial findings—including the documentation of a former president's approval of a dissident archbishop's assassination and the incrimination of a sitting defense minister in other murders—served to clear the air, although the exact impact of the political processes within the country took time to have effects. There was also a second commission to identify those military personnel who had committed major human rights violations.

In addition, ONUSAL personnel collected and destroyed many insurgents' weapons and helped oversee the creation of a new national army staff college, where students included former members of the armed opposition in addition to new recruits and members of the national army. Some of the early UN involvement on the ground in El Salvador took place even before the cease-fire was signed, thus putting UN observers at some risk.

MOVING TOWARD ENFORCEMENT

The creative adaptations by the UN's member states and civil servants have proved to be as important as the grand visions and long-term plans for international organizations. Political changes and crises occur, and then governments and the United Nations react. Precedents are created that circumscribe what can be possible later. UN actions in the Persian Gulf beginning in 1990 set important precedents relating to collective security, humanitarian actions, and sanctions.

On August 2, 1990, Iraqi armed forces swept past the border of neighboring Kuwait and quickly gained control of the tiny, oil-rich country. The invasion met with uniform condemnation in the United Nations, including the Security Council's first unequivocal statement about a breach of the peace since 1950 and the Korean War. From early August until the end of the year, the Security Council passed twelve resolutions directed at securing Iraq's withdrawal from Kuwait. The council invoked Chapter VII, Articles 39 through 41, to lay the guidelines for the first post–Cold War enforcement action. Resolutions 661 of August 6 and 665 of August 25 called upon member states to establish economic sanctions against Iraq and to use force to police them. Resolution 678 of November 29 authorized member states to use "all necessary means" to expel Iraq from Kuwait and thus represented a major shift in strategy. The organization's experience during the Persian Gulf War contains valuable lessons about the needs of a workable collective-security system for the future.

At Washington's insistence the date of January 15, 1991, was negotiated as the deadline for the use of military force. Iraq remained in Kuwait past this date, and the U.S.-led coalition of twenty-eight states began military operations two days later.[7] A bombing campaign against Iraq and its troops commenced, followed by a ground war one month later with about half a million U.S. military personnel. The coalition's victory reversed the Iraqi invasion and occupation at minimal cost in blood and treasure. It placed the United Nations at the center of the international security stage.

Members of the Allied Coalition lost relatively few lives, but tens of thousands of Iraqi civilians and perhaps many more soldiers were killed, so questions were raised about the proportionality of UN-sponsored actions.[8] The Security Council's process of decision-making and the conduct of the war have led some critics to be skeptical about the precise value of the Gulf War as a precedent for subsequent Chapter VII enforcement action.[9] Dominance by the United States, the decision to replace nonforcible sanctions with force as the dominant means of ensuring Iraq's compliance with the organization's wishes, the extensive use of military means that ensued, and the UN's inability to command and control the operation are also concerns. Each of these criticisms raises serious questions about the ability of the UN's collective-security apparatus to function in a variety of contexts.

Strengths and Weaknesses of UN Involvement in the 1991 Gulf War

The first criticism of the Persian Gulf War—that the United States too easily used the United Nations to rubber-stamp its own agenda—was a general criticism of geopolitics after the disappearance of the Soviet Union as a superpower. Washington used its influence to foster perceived national interests, creating and maintaining a diverse coalition against Iraq. The process by which the coalition was created illustrated the extent to which the UN had become a reflection of U.S. influence. The UN had never been a completely neutral forum—Western dominance in the early years had been partially replaced beginning in the 1960s by the Third World's "automatic majority" in the General Assembly, but not in the Security Council. This Third World majority had contributed to a new popular sport, UN-bashing, for two Republican administrations. Yet the United States was able to use its considerable political and economic clout in the Security Council to ensure that its Persian Gulf agenda was approved. Political concessions were provided to the Soviet Union to gain its approval for enforcement and to China for its abstentions (instead of vetoes). The United States promised financial aid and debt relief to a number of developing countries for their votes and withdrew aid commitments to Yemen in retribution for its opposing the use of force. This is precisely the way a hegemonic power is supposed to operate, making the "side payments" necessary to get many other states to consent to what the hegemon desires.[10] Moreover, Kuwait, a member state of the UN, had been attacked by traditional means; the question of aggression or breach of the peace was reasonably clear.

A second criticism centers on how the nonforcible sanctions mandated by the Security Council were overtaken by forcible ones after only three months. According to Article 42, the Security Council may authorize force after all other means of settlement, and economic sanctions in particular, have proven inadequate. Yet the Security Council chose to use military force before the sanctions leveled against Iraq had had a chance to take full effect. Critics pointed out that in South Africa, by contrast, partial sanctions had not been discarded in favor of military force even though that country's racist policy had been condemned for decades. They also noted that Israel's expansion and continued occupation of territories from 1967 had not been met with either economic or military sanctions.

At the same time, sanctions can take a long time to take effect—and some doubt their efficacy as violence often continues and can even increase. The use of sanctions became so widespread that David Cortright and George Lopez called the 1990s the "sanctions decade."[11] When economic sanctions were applied later to Haiti, some observers said military force should have been used earlier and would have caused less suffering. The record regarding the use of nonforcible sanctions and military force suggests that the politics of the day play a large part in determining a course of action and, ultimately, the sequence in which action is taken. The UN continued to use economic sanctions against Iraq after the end of the formal military operations, and they were removed with UN approval after the U.S. invasion in 2003.

The third criticism of the handling of the 1991 Persian Gulf War is that no limits on the use of force were enacted and that the organization exerted no control over the U.S. military operation. According to the Charter, military enforcement operations are to be directed and controlled by the Military Staff

Medical personnel from the multinational forces carry an Iraqi refugee into a camp near Safwan, Iraq, in March 1991. (UN Photo 158302/J. Isaac)

Committee so that the UN can exercise control and military forces can be held accountable to the international community for their actions. As in Korea forty years earlier, command and control of the Gulf War was in the hands of the U.S.-led coalition forces. Only this time, in the Persian Gulf, there was no blue flag and no decision specifically authorizing the preponderant U.S. role. The Security Council was essentially a spectator, but U.S. control appeared necessary for reasons of efficiency as well as political support.

Resolution 678 authorized "all necessary means" and made no restrictions on what kind of, how much, and how long force could be used. According to critics, the United States had left with a blank check to pursue the expulsion of Iraq. Authorizations of this kind may run contrary to the spirit of the world organization's Charter, especially in this case because there was extensive civilian injury and damage inside Iraq. Logistically, however, it may be the only feasible way for the UN to enforce its decisions.

These doubts and criticisms about the handling of the Persian Gulf War are pertinent to the UN's future security operations not because they are necessarily accurate but because they are widespread. The Persian Gulf War provides the first example of the existing security apparatus in an enforcement action in the post–Cold War era. Although the organization proved successful in achieving its stated objective—expelling Iraq from Kuwait—the way that this goal was achieved continues to be debated by diplomats, lawyers, and scholars. There was simply no alternative but to "subcontract" to the twenty-eight members of the U.S.-led coalition. In view of the UN's limited capacities, such a procedure for enforcement operations seems inevitable for the foreseeable future.

As former Secretary-General Boutros-Ghali points out, the UN will "perhaps never be sufficiently large or well enough equipped to deal with a threat from a major army equipped with sophisticated weapons."[12] The organization was ill prepared to handle the test posed by the 1991 Persian Gulf War. Thus, the role of the council regarding collective security and military enforcement remains that of collective legitimization rather than operational control of combat forces. And if the council fails to agree, major powers may well proceed with what they perceive as legitimate use of military force, as illustrated by the war to oust Saddam Hussein in 2003.

Forceful Action in Northern Iraq on Behalf of Humanitarian Values

On April 5, 1991, the Security Council passed resolution 688. It declared that the international repercussions of Saddam Hussein's repression of Kurdish and Shiite populations constituted a threat to international peace and security. It insisted that Iraq allow access to international relief organizations so that they could care for the beleaguered groups. Elite troops from the United States, the United Kingdom, France, and the Netherlands moved into Iraq—without explicit approval from the Security Council—and carved out a safe haven above the thirty-sixth parallel, which they guarded to ensure the security of UN relief operations. The council had already taken a broad view of its duty to protect human rights in Rhodesia and South Africa, but this resolution was a dramatic and straightforward linkage between human rights and international peace and security. The notion of human security inside states was much discussed in the corridors of the UN. In Iraq, the Hussein government eventually agreed to the presence of UN guards providing security to agencies working with Iraqi Kurds, but obviously under Western military pressure.

Many in the West applauded resolution 688 as a vigorous step toward enforcing human rights protection,[13] but others feared the precedent. "Who decides?" became a rallying cry for those, particularly in the global South, who opposed granting the Security Council, dominated by Western foreign policy interests, the authority of Chapter VII to intervene for arguably humanitarian reasons. Later military responses with a humanitarian justification—in Somalia, Bosnia and Herzegovina, Rwanda, Haiti, Kosovo, and East Timor—served to keep the debate alive about the weight to be given state sovereignty relative to the international community's duty to protect human rights. The theme of humanitarian intervention reappears in later humanitarian crises, as does its reformulation as the "responsibility to protect,"[14] a subject to which we return later.

The effort under UN auspices in northern Iraq actually continued the efforts of outside actors to help persons in dire straits that had been attempted in the late 1960s in the Nigerian civil war, and which had led two scholars to write about "an extraordinary remedy, an exception to the postulates of State sovereignty and territorial inviolability that are fundamental to the traditional theory if not actual practice of international law."[15] These events suggest a double standard. Certain humanitarian crises and widespread media coverage create a domestic and international political climate that fosters action by the United States, sometimes towing the United Nations in its wake. Similar if not greater humanitarian emergencies in other parts of the world (for example, in Liberia, Angola, Sudan, or Democratic Congo) are ignored for long periods. Moreover, events in the spring of 1991 created a controversial reference point for later decisions also pertaining to Iraq. In 2003 the United States, the United Kingdom, and certain lesser powers decided to use force pursuant to earlier council resolutions demanding widespread disarmament by the Saddam Hussein government. Once again, the council had not explicitly authorized military force, but the United States and its allies claimed a right to interpret previous resolutions as they saw fit.

NONFORCIBLE SANCTIONS IN THE POST–COLD WAR ERA: HUMANITARIAN DILEMMAS

Economic sanctions have long been seen as a policy option to give teeth to certain international decisions. We have discussed the Cold War pattern and its two notable exceptions (UN-approved sanctions on Rhodesia and South Africa). But the Security Council resorted to them more than a dozen times during the 1990s. Partial or comprehensive sanctions were decided on by the Security Council against various countries: Iraq, the states of the former Yugoslavia, Libya, Liberia, Somalia, Haiti, and Rwanda. Moreover, the council also imposed them on several nonstate actors, including the Khmer Rouge in Cambodia (when it was called Kampuchea), the National Union for the Total Independence of Angola (UNITA), and the Afghan faction known as the Taliban, which also called itself the Islamic Emirate of Afghanistan. More needs to be known about their precise impact, in particular about their negative and sometimes dire humanitarian consequences.[16]

Research reveals three pertinent challenges. The first results from the nature of modern warfare as exemplified by the 1991 Persian Gulf War.[17] The Gulf crisis dramatizes the extent to which the international responses in modern armed conflicts can themselves do serious harm to innocent and powerless civilians. The political strategies adopted, the economic sanctions imposed, and the military force authorized by the Security Council not only created additional hardships but also complicated the ability of the UN's own humanitarian agencies to help civilians caught in the throes of conflict. OAS and UN economic sanctions may have harmed as many as 100,000 people in Haiti in 1993, most of whom were children.

A range of sanctions is available to the UN when a state refuses to respect a decision made by the Security Council. Before the council decides on enforcement action with potentially major humanitarian consequences, organizations with humanitarian competence and responsibilities could be consulted. Whether the impact is upon citizens in the pariah country or elsewhere, the staff of the United Nations Children's Fund (UNICEF), the United Nations High Commissioner for Refugees (UNHCR), the World Health Organization (WHO), and the World Food Programme (WFP) are well situated to warn against, anticipate, and monitor such consequences. There are also private humanitarian agencies that consult regularly with UN bodies and can provide detailed and specialized information on the humane impact of sanctions. Among these, the International Committee of the Red Cross (ICRC) usually has personnel on the ground as well as a reputation for accurate reporting.

In Iraq, the decision to use economic sanctions to force compliance with weapons inspections had damaging effects on women and children in Iraq. The ICRC and a few other agencies reported on the looming crisis in the first half of the 1990s. UNICEF in 1998 found that 90,000 deaths occurred yearly in Iraq as a result of sanctions, and 5,000 children a month were dying. The gender dimensions of sanctions are often overlooked, as women (and female children) tend to bear the brunt as they sacrifice their food rations for the male members of their families.

If the Security Council decides to proceed, governments could provide resources to the UN system so that it could respond fully to the immediate and longer-term human consequences of sanctions.[18] These options clearly were not explored during the 1991 Persian Gulf crisis. UN planning in 2003 in anticipation of a coalition attack on Iraq, while improved, was also insufficient.

The second challenge is an eminently practical one. How does the UN provide humanitarian sustenance after the initial outpouring of international concern has subsided and humanitarian interests are left to vie with other causes for the international spotlight? Resolution 688 insisted that Iraq provide the United Nations with humanitarian access to its people, a watershed for the UN.[19] Yet, the exact impact of sanctions on the behavior of the Iraqi government is not well understood. Iraq reacted negatively against UN assertive humanitarianism, creating havoc for UN and NGO efforts. The Iraqi regime, whose human rights abuses against its own population and brinkmanship tactics were well documented, still had understandable reactions against the Security Council's treatment of Iraq. International assistance flowed more easily to minority populations in revolt against Baghdad than to civilians in equal need in parts of the country under the central government's control. Eventually, the Security Council approved a program of allowing Iraq to sell oil in order to pay for food and other civilian needs, which in turn led to numerous abuses.

The third challenge relates to timing the deployment of UN military forces in conjunction with economic sanctions. The UN Charter assumes that nonforcible sanctions should be tried first; only when they fail should collective military action ensue. The suffering civilian populations of the former Yugoslavia and Haiti provided compelling reasons to rethink the conventional wisdom. In the former Yugoslavia, vigorous and earlier preventive deployment of UN soldiers to Bosnia and Herzegovina (rather than just to Croatia, with a symbolic administrative presence in Sarajevo) might have obviated the later need for sanctions to pressure Belgrade and Serbian irregulars and might have prevented that grisly war. This reasoning justified in part the preventive positioning of UN observers as part of the United Nations Protection Force (UNPROFOR) in Macedonia in December 1992. In Haiti, some observers, with considerable reason, queried whether an earlier military enforcement action to restore an elected government would have entailed far less civilian suffering than extended economic sanctions did, particularly because the willingness to use such overwhelming force was visible in September 1994. In short, the reluctance to use force may not always be a good thing, if delay means that civilians suffer and aid agencies are projected into conflict as a substitute for needed military intervention.

OPERATIONAL QUANDARIES: CAMBODIA, THE FORMER YUGOSLAVIA, SOMALIA, RWANDA, AND HAITI

Several UN operations during the 1990s serve to highlight the inadequacy of the principles of traditional peacekeeping to meet the challenges of the new world disorder. In order to deal with the kinds of challenges the United Nations faces in operations such as the UN Transitional Authority in Cambodia (UNTAC), the second and third UN Angola Verification Missions (UNAVEM II and UNAVEM III), the UN Protection Force in the former Yugoslavia, the first and second UN Operations in Somalia (UNOSOM), the UN Assistance Mission in Rwanda (UNAMIR), and the UN Mission in Haiti (UNMIH), the world organization sought new ways of responding to conflict.

These operations were qualitatively and quantitatively different from UN operations during the Cold War. The formal consent of the parties simply could not be assumed to mean very much on the ground. Also, the military effectiveness required from, and the dangers faced by, UN military forces went far beyond the parameters of traditional lightly armed peacekeepers. Moreover, these operations suggest the magnitude of the new demands on the UN for services that threatened to overwhelm troop contributors and to break the bank. If classic peacekeeping was said to be based on Chapter "VI.5," these new field operations could be considered part of Chapter "VI.9"—that is, very close to the war-fighting orientation of Chapter VII. Indeed, a criticism waged later by David Rieff was that the gentle vocabulary—especially the "h" word of "humanitarian"—obfuscated the reality that these efforts were ugly and resembled war.[20]

After stable levels of about 10,000 troops and a budget of a few hundred million dollars in the early post–Cold War period, the numbers jumped rapidly. In the mid-1990s, 70,000 to 80,000 blue-helmeted soldiers were authorized by the UN's annualized peacekeeping budget, which approached $4 billion in 1995.

Accumulated total arrears in these years hovered around $3.5 billion—that is, almost equal to this budget and approaching three times the regular UN budget. The roller-coaster ride continued between 1996 and 1998, when both the number of soldiers and the budget dropped precipitously by two-thirds, at least partially reflecting the world organization's overextension and administrative indigestion. It changed again in the new millennium as police efforts in Kosovo and military ones in Timor and the Congo began. Throughout, arrears remained at a critical level, and the world organization's cash reserves often covered barely one month's expenditures.

As the 1990s came to a close, significant cash-flow problems continued—former UN under-secretary-general for administration Richard Thornburgh earlier had referred to the situation as a "financial bungee jump"—even if the amount of money appeared almost trivial or a "bargain" according to a prominent group of bankers.[21] Compared with the U.S. Defense Department's budget of close to half a trillion dollars after the invasion of Afghanistan and occupation of Iraq—more than the rest of the world's militaries combined—UN peacekeeping is a bargain indeed.[22] The UN's annual budget for security operations during that same period would represent only a few days of Operation Desert Storm in 1991 or about the annual budget of the New York City police and fire departments. The assessed U.S. contribution to these operations, about 30 percent of the total bill, was only about .05 percent of the U.S. defense budget. The cost of a few weeks of fighting in Iraq in 2003 or of occupation thereafter, estimated at some $1 billion per week, dwarfs either the annual UN administrative budget of about $1.8 billion or the annual total spending of the UN system of some $10 billion.

What exactly were the operational quandaries? The Cambodian operation amounted to the UN's taking over all of the important civilian administration of the country while simultaneously disarming guerrillas and governmental armed forces. The UN registered most of the nation for the first democratic election in the country's history. The UNTAC deployment was based—as are most UN undertakings—on national budgetary projections out of touch with real military requirements. These estimates were based on best-case scenarios; the situation on the ground was closer to worst-case ones.

Japan's desire—sustained in part by U.S. and other pressures—to make a large contribution to this operation in "its own region" was important—especially given the later desire by Washington to "pick and choose" among complicated field operations. Despite many problems and sometimes fatal attacks on its personnel, Japan stayed the course in Cambodia—in part because it was urged to do so by Yasushi Akashi, a Japanese national who was head of the UN operation in that country. Also, Japan wanted to prove that it deserved a seat on an expanded Security Council, which provided another reason for its larger role in UN security policy.

Years of internal conflict had left Cambodia's infrastructure devastated and its population displaced. In response, the United Nations invested over $1.6 billion

Participants in an UNTAC demining course learn to cope with trip wires near Siem Reap Town, Cambodia, 1993. (UNHCR Photo/I. Guest)

and over 22,000 military and civilian personnel. Yet UNTAC's success was hardly a foregone conclusion, particularly in light of the Khmer Rouge's unwillingness to respect key elements of agreements and Prince Norodom Sihanouk's stated position that the peace process and elections should continue with or without the Khmer Rouge. Failure here could have seriously undermined the confidence of member states attempting an undertaking of this scale or complexity elsewhere.

The May 1993 elections were a turning point. A Khmer Rouge attack on a UN fuel and ammunition dump three weeks before the elections exposed how inadequately prepared UN soldiers were to resist even symbolic military maneuvers, let alone a return to full-scale civil war. However, the elections were held and returned Prince Sihanouk to power as the head of a coalition that included the former government and part of the opposition—but excluded the Khmer Rouge. The UN's achievement was that the Cambodian people struggled for power for the first time by means of a secret ballot. The relative lack of violence—the Khmer Rouge had demonstrated that it could attack with impunity—happened in spite of UNTAC, not because of it. However, the United Nations began to pull out its personnel as quickly as possible, raising concerns that a larger civil war might erupt. The uneasy internal peace managed to hold, the Khmer Rouge continued to weaken, and the UN stayed heavily involved in diplomacy—mainly trying to liberalize the Heng Sen government, as in discussions about what to do about past and present violations of human rights.[23]

In the former Yugoslavia, the UN began its first military operation on European soil after many years in which regional conflicts were assumed to be a monopoly

UNPROFOR soldiers in Stari Vitez, Yugoslavia. (UN Photo 186716/J. Isaac)

of developing countries. The Balkans and some former Soviet republics soon emerged as the possible scene of increased demand for UN security operations.[24] The dissolution of the former Yugoslavia entailed violence and displacement of a magnitude not seen in Europe since World War II. In addition to violence between the warring factions, the region was plagued by ethnic cleansing, detention camps, refugees, killing, systematic rape, and other atrocities committed by all sides. The UN's initial security involvement in Croatia, with close to 14,000 peacekeepers, achieved some objectives such as implementing the cease-fire between Croatia and the Yugoslav Federation. The UNPROFOR mandate was expanded to neighboring Bosnia and Herzegovina in part to alleviate the human suffering and ensure the delivery of humanitarian assistance to Muslims and Croats under siege from Serbia and Serbian irregulars.

The 1,500 UN soldiers initially assigned to the Sarajevo area quickly proved inadequate. The Security Council later authorized adding 8,000 soldiers to protect humanitarian convoys and to escort detainees in Bosnia and Herzegovina. The United Nations also asked NATO to enforce a no-fly zone for Serbian aircraft. In an approach reminiscent of the voluntary financing of the United Nations Peacekeeping Force in Cyprus, the Secretary-General insisted that these additional humanitarian soldiers be provided at no cost to the world organization, and NATO countries responded affirmatively. Later, U.S. airdrops of food to isolated and ravaged Muslim communities were seen mostly as a symbolic gesture by the Clinton administration, but they helped save lives. These efforts were insufficient to halt the bloodshed or inhibit the carving up of Bosnia and Herzegovina by the Serbs and Croats.

After months of efforts by the UN special envoy, former U.S. secretary of state Cyrus Vance, and the European Community's mediator, former British foreign minister David Owen, a tenuous plan to create a "Swiss-like" set of ten semi-autonomous ethnic enclaves within Bosnia and Herzegovina was finally agreed upon by the belligerents. NATO was approached to help make sure that the agreement—however unacceptable to critics who argued that the arrangements rewarded Serbian aggression—would stick.

The Vance-Owen plan was undermined almost immediately by renewed Serbian and Croatian military offensives. When former Norwegian foreign minister Thorvald Stoltenberg took over from Vance in May 1993, it was clear that Bosnia would be partitioned. Serbian war efforts had left Serbia in control of 70 percent of the territory, and Croatia held 20 percent. The Bosnian Muslims were left with what were ironically called UN safe areas. These were anything but safe, as these areas were systematically attacked.

The situation in the Balkans deteriorated and demonstrated that the United Nations also can provide the means for governments to pretend to do something without really doing very much. There was a shift from Chapter VI to Chapter VII operations, but without the necessary political will to make the shift work. The half measures in Bosnia can be considered worse than no action at all. Given their traditional operating procedures and constraints, UN soldiers were not strong enough to deter the Serbs. But they deterred the international community of states from more assertive political and military intervention under Chapter VII because the troops, along with humanitarian workers, were vulnerable targets. Although assistance to refugees saved lives, it also helped foster ethnic cleansing by cooperating in the forced movement of unwanted populations. Airdrops of food made it seem as if people salved consciences while massive and unspeakable human rights abuses continued unabated. Thus, inadequate UN military and humanitarian action constituted a powerful palliative.[25] Then high commissioner for refugees Sadako Ogata articulated what was all too clear: "There are no humanitarian solutions to humanitarian problems."[26] She, and others like the International Committee of the Red Cross, called for political solutions to the root causes of human suffering in the Balkans.

The initial UN response was followed by a steadily growing number of additional UN troops that, although mainly from NATO countries, were equally feeble. No-fly zones were imposed but not fully enforced; other forms of saber rattling, including low-altitude sorties over Serbian positions and warnings about possible retaliatory air strikes, were tried; and the Security Council passed what *The Economist* called "the confetti of paper resolutions."[27] As Lawrence Freedman observed, the Security Council "experimented with almost every available form of coercion short of war."[28] UN token measures did little to halt

Serbian irredentism and consolidation of territory in either Croatia or Bosnia; nor did these measures prevent the initial expansion of Croatian claims in Bosnia. The UN mandatory arms embargo instituted in September 1991 had benefited primarily the Serbs, who controlled the bulk of the military hardware of the former Yugoslav army. Given their traditional operating procedures and constraints—not to mention their small numbers and inadequate equipment— UN soldiers were powerless to deter the Serbs. The vulnerability of UN "protectors" was regularly invoked by Europeans as a rationale against more forceful military measures.

The key dynamic once again involved calculation outside the UN, which then affected decisions taken inside the Security Council. Powerful Western states, especially the United States, did not see in the early 1990s that their traditional vital national interests were at stake. Moreover, they feared "sticky" involvement, as in Southeast Asia in the past and as in Somalia and Rwanda then unfolding. Russia, for its part, viewed the Balkans through the lens of Slavic solidarity rather than more general concern for nonaggression and human rights. China was distant and detached.

The idea of "safe areas" brought derision because, with only slight hyperbole, one could say that the least safe places in the Balkans were under UN control. The ultimate ignominy arrived in summer 1995 when two of these enclaves in eastern Bosnia were overrun by Bosnian Serbs. Srebrenica, a Muslim enclave, was the scene of the largest massacre in Europe since 1945 where some 7,000–8,000 men and boys were systematically executed. Srebrenica had been designated a UN safe haven after the UN brokered an agreement between Muslims and Serbs to disarm the enclave in return for UN protection against Serb forces. The agreement provided a modicum of safety for a time, but as the political and military situation in Bosnia deteriorated, the Serbs moved against the "safe haven." It should also be noted that Bosnian Muslim fighters used Srebrenica as a base for staging attacks on Serb forces outside. The outgunned UN peacekeeping unit withdrew from Srebrenica (after the death of one Dutch soldier) leaving its inhabitants vulnerable to the advancing Serb forces, whose known tactics included mass execution, systematic rape, and forced expulsion. Shortly before this horrific incident, Serbs had chained UN blue helmets to strategic targets and thereby prevented NATO air raids.[29] Srebrenica became a conversation stopper in UN circles. UN peacekeepers in Croatia were unable to implement their mandate because they received no cooperation from the Croats or Krajina Serbs. In Bosnia, UN forces were under Chapter VII but lacked the capability to apply coercive force across a wide front. Shortly before resigning in January 1994 from a soldier's nightmare as UN commander in Bosnia, Lt. Gen. Francis Briquemont lamented the disparity between rhetoric and reality: "There is a fantastic gap between the resolutions of the Security Council, the will to execute those resolutions, and the means available to commanders in the field."[30]

The "UN" in this case was the first UN of governments that were simply unwilling to react militarily in the former Yugoslavia until August 1995, and this provides a case study of what not to do. This inaction left many of the inhabitants of the region mistrustful of the United Nations and lent a new and disgraceful connotation to the word "peacekeeping." Bound by the traditional rules of engagement (fire only in self-defense and only after being fired upon), UN troops never fought a single battle with any of the factions in Bosnia that routinely disrupted relief convoys. The rules of engagement led to the appeasement of local forces rather than to the enforcement of UN mandates.

A much heavier dose of NATO's bombing and U.S. arm-twisting proved necessary to compel the belligerents, sequestered at Ohio's Wright-Patterson Air Force Base in November 1995, to attempt to reach a political settlement. The Dayton peace agreements laid the groundwork for military deployment by almost 60,000 NATO soldiers, one-third from the United States, in the International Force (IFOR). Although the numbers of soldiers in the successive NATO operations diminished over time, still many observers wondered why UN peacekeepers—poorly equipped and without a mandate—were deployed when there was no peace to keep and why NATO war-fighters appeared when there was. Observers usually point to the "Somalia syndrome" as the turning point in soured public attitudes toward the world organization (a case that we will come to next). But Richard Holbrooke, the former U.S. assistant secretary of state who became UN ambassador in 1999 and is generally credited with having engineered the Dayton accords, suggests, "The damage that Bosnia did to the U.N. was incalculable."[31]

The Dayton Peace Accord led to the deployment of 60,000 NATO-led peacekeepers and the creation of a police force that served to stabilize Bosnia-Herzegovina. However, such a large military deployment is accompanied by additional problems. Bosnia-Herzegovina has become the center of human trafficking into Western Europe and the locus of a very active sex industry. UN officials have been accused of corruption, facilitating the trafficking, and looking the other way regarding the behavior of many peacekeepers. The sexual behavior of peacekeepers has become one of the more serious problems facing current UN peacekeeping efforts.[32] In fact, a trio of former staff members exposed stunning details of several operations.[33]

Somalia provided another complicated challenge for UN involvement in internal wars and a breakdown in governance, or "complex emergencies." Like Bosnia, Somalia was an example of violent fragmentation, yet, unlike Bosnia, one without an ethnic logic. In Somalia, a single ethnic group sharing the same religion, history, and language split into heavily armed clans. Somalia had no government in any meaningful sense, and one-third of the population risked death from starvation because the violence prevented humanitarian aid workers from reaching the needy.

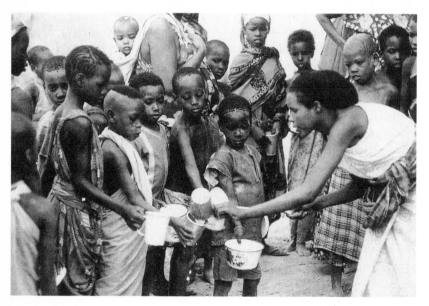

Somalian children receiving food in 1992. (UN Photo 146504/J. Isaac)

The Security Council at the end of August 1992 authorized 3,000 to 4,000 UN soldiers (UNOSOM I) to protect the delivery of humanitarian assistance under Chapter VII. While the council made formal reference to Chapter VII, quiet diplomacy obtained the consent of the leading clans for deployment of UN force. That force was directed initially not against clan leaders but against bandits interfering with relief. The most important delivery point for relief was not a UN agency, but rather the private International Committee of the Red Cross. UNHCR in particular had retired to the sidelines in Kenya.

In December 1992 President George H. W. Bush moved vigorously to propose a U.S.-led humanitarian intervention. Within days of the passage of Security Council resolution 794, the first of what would become over 27,000 U.S. troops arrived to provide a modicum of security to help sustain civilians. They were augmented by 10,000 soldiers from twenty-two other countries. This effort was labeled Operation Restore Hope from the American side, or the Unified Task Force (UNITAF), an acronym that reflected the Security Council's authorization to use force to ensure the delivery of humanitarian relief. UNITAF was always under U.S. operational command. With virtually no casualties, humanitarian space was created and modest disarming of local bandits began.

UNITAF ceased operations in April 1993, when the second phase of the UN Operation in Somalia began as authorized by Security Council resolution 814. The Secretary-General, for the second time, directly commanded a military force deployed under Chapter VII. The Security Council authorized UNOSOM II under Chapter VII to use whatever force was necessary to disarm Somali warlords who refused to surrender their arms and to ensure access to suffering civilians. At its maximum strength, some 20,000 soldiers and 8,000 logistical troops from thirty-three countries were deployed.

As in Cambodia, almost 3,000 civilian officials were expected to take over the administration of a country, only this time a country that was totally without a functioning government. Significantly, the United States initially remained on the ground with logistics troops for the first time under the command of a UN general—who was an officer from a NATO country, Turkey. Another 1,300 soldiers, including 400 Army Rangers, were held in reserve as a "rapid-reaction force" in boats offshore. These U.S. units were under strictly U.S. command.

In retaliation against attacks on UN peacekeepers and aid personnel, U.S. Cobra helicopter gunships were called in by the UN command in June and July 1993 against the armed supporters of one of the main belligerents, General Mohammed Aideed. These attacks were followed by the arrival of U.S. Army Rangers later in the summer. These violent flare-ups put the UN in the awkward position of retaliation, which elicited more violence. The assassination of foreign journalists and aid workers and further attacks on U.S. troops—including the ugly scene in October 1993 when the body of a dead Ranger was dragged by crowds through the streets of Mogadishu in front of television cameras—further inflamed the situation.

The shift from Chapter VI to Chapter VII, and along with it a significant expansion of objectives from humanitarian relief to coercive nation- and state-building, constituted one set of problems. The absence of political commitment and staying power was yet another. The approval of presidential decision directive 25 in May 1994 marked the official end to the Clinton administration's attitude of assertive multilateralism. This phrase became a liability to the Democrats in American domestic politics, as Republicans attacked a supposed U.S. subservience to the United Nations. The Clinton administration had left itself open to this attack by misrepresenting the situation in Somalia, trying to blame UN officials for the decisions made by U.S. military personnel. Given the virtual necessity for U.S. participation in major multilateral military operations, the unseemly images of eighteen dead troops in October 1993 were considerably more costly than the tragic loss of these individuals. The "Somalia syndrome" was linked to its predecessor, the "Vietnam syndrome," as a call for caution, and military multilateralism was put in abeyance.

The U.S. military involvement in the Horn of Africa is criticized on numerous grounds. First, the military was obsessed with the capture of Aideed, which resembled a Wild West hunt, complete with a wanted poster. Hunting a single individual in a foreign and unforgiving land can be demoralizing for troops. Second, the United States was slow to engage in disarmament and nation-building. A striking disequilibrium between the military and humanitarian components existed as the costs of Operation Restore Hope alone, at $1 billion, amounted to three times the U.S. total aid contribution to Somalia since independence. Seven months of UNOSOM II in 1993 were estimated to cost $1.5 billion, of which the lowest estimate for humanitarian aid was 0.7 percent of the total and the highest, 10 percent.[34] Also, as UN objectives expanded, resources were actually reduced.

When the last UN soldiers pulled out of Somalia in March 1995, the impact of military and humanitarian help was unclear. Three years and some $4 billion had left the warring parties better armed, rested, and poised to resume civil war. But the worst of starvation had been brought under control. In 2006 Somalia still remained without a viable national government, although concerted diplomatic efforts continued to improve the situation.

An even worse horror story had developed simultaneously in East Africa, where long-standing social tensions in Rwanda led to the genocide of some 800,000 of Rwanda's Tutsi minority by the government manipulating the Hutu majority. UN peacekeeping forces (UNAMIR) had actually been on the scene during this time. UNAMIR had been present in Kigali for about eight months, to facilitate the Arusha Peace Accords between Rwandan Hutu and Tutsi elements when the genocide commenced on April 6, 1994. The Security Council reduced these UN military forces a few days later, at the behest of Belgium, after a small number of Belgian peacekeepers had been abused and killed. This reduction came in spite of the previous request of the Canadian commander of the blue helmets for an augmented force and a warning that genocide was planned by Hutu extremists. As the UN withdrew, the Hutu extremists committed genocide unimpeded, even slaughtering the Tutsis under UN protection. As the scale of the killings became more widely known, the Security Council wrestled with whether the killings constituted genocide. Members refrained from calling it genocide because such a designation might have a corresponding legal obligation to act. Ironically, Rwanda was seated on the Security Council as one of the nonpermanent members, and sadly, no other members asked Rwanda to explain the killings. The genocide ended as the rebel Tutsi army invaded from neighboring Burundi and overthrew the Hutu government.

The Security Council now found itself "gravely concerned" as two million persons were displaced within Rwanda, while another two million refugees, mostly Hutus, fled into neighboring states. The council authorized two stand-alone initiatives. First, it issued resolution 929 under Chapter VII authorizing the French-led Opération Turquoise from June to August to stabilize the southwestern part of the country. One effect was that the French used their presence to protect their Hutu allies and their families (who were now refugees in dire need of international assistance) from the invading Tutsi army, despite Hutu participation in the genocide. Second, the UN authorized a massive two-month logistics effort through the U.S. Operation Support Hope in July and August to provide relief to the Hutu refugees in the Goma region of Zaire. Numerous national contingents also deployed to this region in support of the assistance efforts by the UNHCR.

Fostering a secure environment—a task in which the military has the clear, comparative advantage—was the least visible operation. The military's cautious standard operating procedures accompanied by the widespread concerns among governments about a possible quagmire paralyzed international military responses for two months while as many as 10 percent of Rwanda's population were murdered. Arguably, Opération Turquoise prevented another refugee crisis of the record-setting magnitude of the one in May in Goma, where almost a million Rwandan refugees appeared virtually overnight. The first crisis was accompanied by a cholera epidemic that is estimated to have killed between 50,000 and 80,000 people.[35] Ironically, these efforts also served to aid and protect the perpetrators of the genocide and their families.

Massive amounts of food, clothing, medicine, shelter, and water were delivered. Outside armed forces thus made essential contributions by using their unexcelled logistical and organizational resources, but only after the genocide had occurred. Rapid military action in April proved totally unfeasible, but the costs of the genocide, massive displacement, and a ruined economy (including decades of wasted development assistance and outside investment) were borne almost immediately afterward by the same governments that had refused to respond militarily a few weeks earlier.

The role of the media in provoking international responses continues to be controversial.[36] Rwanda illustrates probably better than the other cases that such coverage may generate adequate support for humanitarian assistance even if it is insufficient for timely and robust military action. Even when humanitarian assistance does arrive, however, it may ironically exacerbate the problems of affected populations. The refugee camps established by the UNHCR in Goma and elsewhere after the genocide were taken over by the Hutu extremists who had found sanctuary there and used them as military bases to launch attacks against Tutsis in Rwanda. The inability of the UN to control the refugee camps and the repeated attacks by Hutu extremists from the Congo prompted Rwanda to invade the Congo, sparking an African "world war" involving nine nations and more than 3.5 million deaths.[37]

The UN's response to the Rwandan genocide stands as one of its greatest acknowledged failures, just as previous development efforts are now acknowledged to have exacerbated tensions.[38] Several years later, Secretary-General Kofi Annan, who had been in charge of the UN's peacekeeping department in New York during the crisis, felt compelled during a visit to Kigali to confess, "We must and we do acknowledge that the world failed Rwanda at that time of evil. The international community and the United Nations could not muster the political will to confront it."[39] In a later statement he continued, "There was a United Nations force in the country at the time, but it was neither mandated nor equipped for the kind of forceful action which would have been needed to prevent or halt the genocide. On behalf of the United Nations, I acknowledge this failure and express my deep remorse."[40] It was Annan who had "buried" the cable from the Canadian commander, General Roméo Dallaire, asking for a proactive role to head off the 1994 genocide.[41]

Meanwhile in the Caribbean, nine months after the United Nations had overseen the first democratic elections in Haiti, the populist priest Jean-Bertrand Aristide was overthrown by a military junta led by General Raoul Cédras. The inclusion of Haiti in our discussion is of interest for a number of reasons. Although Haiti had not really endured a civil war, it had all the attributes of a failed state—in particular, political instability, widespread poverty, massive migration, and human rights abuses. It also became the target of international coercive actions—that is, both nonforcible and forcible sanctions under Chapter VII of the UN Charter similar to those in the other war-torn countries analyzed earlier. Moreover, the basis for outside intervention was the restoration of a democratically elected government; this precedent has widespread potential implications because of its relevance for other countries in crisis.

Multilateral military forces were essential to the solution that ultimately resulted in late 1994. First, however, came the embarrassing performance of the initial UN Mission in Haiti (UNMIH I), including the ignominious retreat by the USS *Harlan County*, which carried unarmed American and Canadian military observers, in September 1993 following a rowdy demonstration on the docks in Port-au-Prince. In September 1994, the first soldiers of the UN-authorized and U.S.-led Multinational Force (MNF) landed in Haiti on the basis of Security Council resolution 940. What Pentagon wordsmiths labeled Operation Uphold Democracy grew quickly to 21,000 troops—almost all American except for 1,000 police and soldiers from twenty-nine countries, mostly from the eastern Caribbean. This operation ensured the departure of the illegal military regime and the restoration of the elected government.

Most important for this analysis, the MNF used overwhelming military force—although there was only a single military person killed in action and the local population was almost universally supportive—to accomplish two important tasks with clear humanitarian impacts. First and most immediately, the MNF brought an end to the punishing economic sanctions that had crippled the local economy and penalized Haiti's most vulnerable groups because the programs of humanitarian and development agencies were paralyzed. Second, the MNF established a secure and stable environment that stemmed the tide of asylum seekers, facilitated the rather expeditious repatriation of about 370,000 of them, and immediately stopped the worst human rights abuses.

The United States provided about $1 billion for troops—of which only one-fifth was over and above what normal Department of Defense expenditures would have been had the troops been at their home base—and another $325 million on assistance in the first half year, only a small part of which was administered by American soldiers directly. Once the MNF achieved its goals, it was en-

Members of the Jordanian battalion of the United Nations Stabilization Mission in
Haiti (MINUSTAH) rescue children from an orphanage destroyed by Hurricane Ike.
(UN Photo 192376/Marco Dormino)

trusted at the end of March 1995 with the next UN Mission in Haiti (UNMIH
II). The 6,000 soldiers from over a dozen countries had an annual budget of
about $350 million. The continued involvement of a substantial number of U.S.
Special Forces (2,500) and an American force commander for the UN follow-on
operation demonstrated concretely Washington's commitment through the end
of February 1996. UNMIH was extended for four additional months at about
half its former size (without American soldiers) before it was replaced by the even
smaller UN Support Mission in Haiti (UNSMIH) in July for a period of twelve
months. A small UN presence was continued for the remainder of the decade,
working with the government of Haiti to professionalize the Haitian National
Police. These latter periods of UN involvement were characterized by Canadian
financial, political, and military leadership.

Haiti provides a relatively straightforward and positive balance sheet—at least
in the short term. The longer-term evaluation was a very different matter. A decade after the initial intervention and in spite of subsequent stabilization missions, Haiti was still characterized by political instability, violence, kidnapping,
and widespread poverty. The United Nations returned to the island nation in
2004, in response to armed conflict between Aristide and his opponents, who
after taking control of the northern part of the country threatened to march on
the capital, Port-au-Prince. With Aristide's flight into exile in Africa in February

2004, and following the interim president's request, the Security Council authorized a Multinational Force led by the United States, which was followed up by the 7,500-strong UN Stabilization Mission in Haiti (MINUSTAH). Armed gangs, probably working in tandem with certain political factions, actually killed some blue helmets. Under the stress of the action, their Brazilian commander apparently took his own life.

As of 2009, the stabilization mission had done little to improve the police and judiciary and nothing to alter the fundamental economic situation. The disparity in the distribution of wealth and power between a tiny elite and the vast majority of the population made Haiti one of the world's most polarized societies; this inequality had led to the rise and fall of Aristide.

As in other military interventions for humanitarian or other purposes, the perception that the interests of key states were threatened spurred leadership and risk-taking. The geography of the crisis brought into prominence not just the United States but also Canada and several Caribbean countries. Washington was and is particularly anxious to end the perceived "flood" of boat people upsetting the demographics and politics of places like south Florida and Louisiana. The success of the military deployment was dramatic, notwithstanding that it was authorized to restore democracy rather than respond to a complex emergency. Both the U.S. Congress and the Pentagon were initially lukewarm about what turned out to be a successful operation in the short term. The effective use of military force and the resulting humanitarian benefits have led some observers to question the chronology and logic of the UN Charter's calling for nonforcible economic sanctions before forcible military action.

A swifter military intervention undoubtedly would have proved more humanitarian than a tightening of the screws through economic sanctions. It would have accomplished the major goal of replacing the de facto regime with the constitutional authorities but would have avoided the massive suffering and dislocations from sanctions. "Sanctions, as is generally recognized, are a blunt instrument," wrote Boutros-Ghali. "They raise the ethical question of whether suffering inflicted on vulnerable groups in the target country is a legitimate means of exerting pressure on political leaders whose behaviour is unlikely to be affected by the plight of their subjects."[42]

The most significant feature of the international responses just discussed has been the willingness to address, rather than ignore, fundamental problems within the borders of war-torn states—at least at times. As the UN Development Programme calculated, eighty-two armed conflicts broke out in the first half-decade following the collapse of the Berlin Wall, and seventy-nine were intrastate wars; in fact, two of the three remaining ones (Nagorno-Karabakh and Bosnia) also could legitimately have been categorized as civil wars.[43] But trying to put a lid on civil wars is not the same as a persistent effort to deal with their root causes. As regards Haiti, the administration of George W. Bush became preoccupied with Afghanistan, Iraq, Iran, North Korea, and Palestine, and so Washington's interest in UN involvement in Haiti drifted.

Having gone from famine to feast in the mid-1990s, the United Nations had a bad case of institutional indigestion. The climate had changed so much that Secretary-General Boutros Boutros-Ghali was obliged to write a follow-up, *Supplement to An Agenda for Peace*, to his earlier agenda document. In this January 1995 report he noted, "This increased volume of activity would have strained the Organization even if the nature of the activity had remained unchanged."[44] This observation would become common knowledge spelled out in the so-called Brahimi report, named after its chair, Lakhdar Brahimi.[45]

CONCLUSION

What lessons emerged for the United Nations from security operations after the Cold War, from 1988 to 1998? These operations represent a qualitatively different kind of peace mission from the world organization's previous experiments. UN efforts in Cambodia and El Salvador were ambitious, complex, and multidisciplinary. They represent the first UN attempts at creating or re-creating civil order and respecting the rule of law where governance and stability had either broken down or been nonexistent. They entail reconstructing the social and economic infrastructure, building democratic political institutions, providing humanitarian assistance, and much more. This task expansion changed the character of the humanitarian agencies and led to much soul-searching.[46]

"Learning by doing" seems the order of the day. Not to act seems to many unthinkable, especially in light of Srebenica and Rwanda. But how to "act" remains uncertain in an ever-evolving international environment. These kinds of challenges lie ahead for UN peacekeepers in the twenty-first century. Hence we can conceive of traditional peacekeeping and complex peacekeeping, both operating under Chapter VI of the Charter. The former involves primarily neutral interposition to supervise cease-fire lines and other military demarcations. The latter involves a complex range of tasks mostly intended to move postconflict or failed states toward a liberal democratic order.[47] In places like the Balkans, the UN has attempted no less than to change an illiberal region into a liberal one—on a stable, permanent basis.

Observers continue to debate the extent to which the dynamics of contemporary civil wars are new,[48] but the two dominant norms of world politics during the Cold War—namely, that borders were sacrosanct and that secession was unthinkable—no longer generate the enthusiasm that they once did, even among states. At the same time, an almost visceral respect for nonintervention in the internal affairs of states has made way for a more subtle interpretation, according to which on occasion the rights of individuals take precedence over the rights of repressive governments and the sovereign states that they represent.

Until early in 1993, the dominant perception of outside intervention under UN auspices was largely positive. Rolling back Iraq's aggression against Kuwait along with the dramatic life-saving activities by the U.S.-led coalitions in northern Iraq and initially in Somalia had led to high hopes. There was undoubted success for the UN in Central America, especially El Salvador. In spite of the lack of resolve in Bosnia, it seemed possible that we were entering an era when governments and insurgents would no longer be allowed to commit abuses with impunity. Some analysts even worried then about "the new interventionists."[49] The new emphasis on protecting persons inside states led to a focus on human security. This new focus coexisted alongside the older notion of traditional interstate military security.[50] In the next chapter, we analyze more recent UN security operations to illustrate the links between traditional peacekeeping, peace enforcement, and peacebuilding activities.

NOTES

1. For a discussion of this historical period, see Thomas G. Weiss and Meryl A. Kessler, "Moscow's U.N. Policy," *Foreign Policy* no. 79 (Summer 1990): 94–112. For a series of essays about the initial impact of these changes, see Thomas G. Weiss and Meryl A. Kessler, eds., *Third World Security in the Post–Cold War Era* (Boulder, Colo.: Lynne Rienner, 1991); Thomas G. Weiss and James G. Blight, eds., *The Suffering Grass: Superpowers and Regional Conflict in Southern Africa and the Caribbean* (Boulder, Colo.: Lynne Rienner, 1992); and G. R. Berridge, *Return to the UN* (London: Macmillan, 1991).

2. Many observers credit first lady Nancy Reagan for encouraging this policy shift, as she did not wish her husband to go down in history as the president who destroyed the UN.

3. When the Soviet Union dissolved, Russia was its successor state. As such, it assumed the permanent seat on the Security Council beginning in 1991.

4. An indication of the growing importance of this phenomenon is found in a new annual publication from the Center on International Cooperation. An overview of all UN operations—including costs, mandates, and troop levels—can be found in Ian Johnstone, ed., *Annual Review of Global Peace Operations 2006* (Boulder, Colo.: Lynne Rienner, 2006).

5. See Tom J. Farer, ed., *Beyond Sovereignty: Collectively Defending Democracy in the Americas* (Baltimore: Johns Hopkins University Press, 1996). For an overview of complex or second-generation peacekeeping, involving especially human rights roles, see David P. Forsythe, "Human Rights and International Security: United Nations Field Operations Redux," in *The Role of the Nation-State in the 21st Century: Human Rights, International Organizations and Foreign Policy*, eds. Monique Castermans-Holleman, Fried van Hoof, and Jacqueline Smiths (The Hague: Kluwer, 1998), 265–276. On the issue of democracy, see Fareed Zakaria, *The Future of Freedom: Illiberal Democracy at Home and Abroad* (New York: W.W. Norton, 2003).

6. See Mats R. Berdal, *Disarmament and Demobilisation After Civil Wars* (Oxford: Oxford University Press, 1996).

7. Washington's shift to forcible liberation occurred just after U.S. congressional elections. The Senate approved of the new strategy by only five votes, which almost led to a constitutional crisis in the United States over "war powers."

8. For a discussion of the legitimacy of the Persian Gulf War, see Oscar Schachter, "United Nations Law in the Gulf Conflict," and Burns H. Weston, "Security Council Resolution 678 and Persian Gulf Decision Making: Precarious Legitimacy," both in *American Journal of International Law* 85, no. 3 (1991).

9. For a series of skeptical views, see essays by Stephen Lewis, Clovis Maksoud, and Robert C. Johansen, "The United Nations After the Gulf War," *World Policy Journal* 8, no. 3 (1991): 539–574.

10. For discussions of the Gramscian notion of hegemonic power compared to dominant power, see Robert J. Lieber, ed., *Eagle Rules: Foreign Policy and American Primacy in the Twenty-First Century* (Upper Saddle River, N.J.: Prentice-Hall, 2002), chapter 1.

11. See David Cortright and George A. Lopez, eds., *The Sanctions Decade*; and *Sanctions and the Search for Security* (Boulder, Colo.: Lynne Rienner, 2002).

12. Boutros Boutros-Ghali, *An Agenda for Peace: Preventive Diplomacy, Peacemaking and Peace-keeping* (New York: United Nations, 1992), para. 43.

13. This controversial subject was launched by the French government, especially by Mario Bettati and Bernard Kouchner, *Le Devoir d'ingérence* (Paris: DeNoël, 1987).

14. International Commission on Intervention and State Sovereignty, *The Responsibility to Protect* (Ottawa: ICISS, 2001). For a view about the dangers from such an approach, see Robert Jackson, *The Global Covenant: Human Conduct in a World of States* (Oxford: Oxford University Press, 1998).

15. Michael Reisman and Myres S. McDougal, "Humanitarian Intervention to Protect the Ibos," in *Humanitarian Intervention and the United Nations*, ed. Richard Lillich (Charlottesville: University of Virginia Press, 1973), 168.

16. See David Cortright and George A. Lopez, eds., *Economic Sanctions: Panacea or Peacebuilding in a Post–Cold War World?* (Boulder, Colo.: Westview Press, 1995); and *The Sanctions Decade*. Previous research had concentrated largely upon the utility of sanctions as a foreign policy tool of the United States. See Gary Clyde Hufbauer, Jeffrey J. Schott, and Kimberly Ann Elliott, *Economic Sanctions Reconsidered: History and Current Policy*, and *Economic Sanctions Reconsidered: Supplemental Case Histories* (Washington, D.C.: Institute for International Economics, 1990), which updated *Economic Sanctions in Pursuit of Foreign Policy Goals* (Washington, D.C.: Institute for International Economics, 1983). See also David A. Baldwin, *Economic Statecraft* (Princeton, N.J.: Princeton University Press, 1985); Theodore Goldi and Robert Shuey, *U.S. Economic Sanctions Imposed Against Specific Countries: 1979 to the Present* (Washington, D.C.: Congressional Research Service, 1992); and Lisa Martin, *Coercive Cooperation: Explaining Multilateral Economic Sanctions* (Princeton, N.J.: Princeton University Press, 1992). For a discussion of the humanitarian consequences, see David Cortright, George A. Lopez, Larry Minear, and Thomas G. Weiss, *Political Gain and Civilian Pain: The Humanitarian Impact of Economic Sanctions* (Boulder, Colo.: Westview Press, 1997).

17. For a discussion of these issues, see Larry Minear and Thomas G. Weiss, "Groping and Coping in the Gulf Crisis: Discerning the Shape of a New Humanitarian Order," *World Policy Journal* 9, no. 4 (1992): 755–777.

18. In many ways, the call to make provisions for vulnerable populations in the wake of sanctions is analogous to efforts to mitigate structural adjustment policies. For a discussion, see Richard Jolly and Ralph van der Hoeven, eds., "Adjustment with a Human Face—Record and Relevance," *World Development* (special issue) 19, no. 12 (1991). For general discussions

of this issue, see Lori Fisler Damrosch, "The Civilian Impact of Economic Sanctions," in *Enforcing Restraint: Collective Intervention in Internal Conflicts*, ed. Damrosch (New York: Council on Foreign Relations, 1993), 274–315; and Patrick Clawson, "Sanctions as Punishment, Enforcement, and Prelude to Further Action," *Ethics and International Affairs* 7 (1993): 17–37.

19. See Jarat Chopra and Thomas G. Weiss, "Sovereignty Is No Longer Sacrosanct: Codifying Humanitarian Intervention," *Ethics and International Affairs* 6 (1992): 95–117; and David J. Scheffer, "Toward a Modern Doctrine of Humanitarian Intervention," *University of Toledo Law Review* 23, no. 2 (1992): 253–293.

20. David Rieff, *At the Point of a Gun: Democratic Dreams and Armed Intervention* (New York: Simon & Schuster, 2006).

21. See *Financing an Effective United Nations* (New York: Ford Foundation, 1993), a report of an expert group chaired by Paul Volker and Shijuro Ogata.

22. See "Last of the Big Time Spenders: U.S. Military Budget Still the World's Largest, and Growing," Center for Defense Information Table on "Fiscal Year 2004 Budget," available at www.cdi.org/budget/2004/world-military-spending.cfm. This information is based on data from the U.S. Department of Defense and the International Institute for Strategic Studies.

23. See Stephen R. Rather, *The New UN Peacekeeping* (New York: St. Martin's Press, 1995); and Michael W. Doyle, Ian Johnstone, and Robert C. Orr, eds., *Keeping the Peace: Multidimensional UN Operations in Cambodia and El Salvador* (Cambridge: Cambridge University Press, 1997).

24. For a discussion of these possibilities before the UN's involvement in the former Soviet bloc, see Thomas G. Weiss and Kurt M. Campbell, "The United Nations and Eastern Europe," *World Policy Journal* 7, no. 3 (1990): 575–592. For another treatment, see Jarat Chopra and Thomas G. Weiss, "Prospects for Containing Conflict in the Former Second World," *Security Studies* 4, no. 3 (1995): 552–583.

25. See Richard H. Ullman, *The World and Yugoslavia's Wars* (New York: Council on Foreign Relations, 1996), 59–96. For a comparative look at this period, see William J. Durch, *UN Peacekeeping, American Policy, and the Uncivil Wars of the 1990s* (New York: St. Martin's Press, 1997). See also James S. Sutterlin, *The United Nations and the Maintenance of International Security: A Challenge to be Met* (Westport, Conn.: Praeger, 1995); Muthia Alagappa and Takashi Inoguchi, eds., *International Security Management and the United Nations* (Tokyo: United Nations University Press, 1998); Donald C. F. Daniel and Bradd C. Hayes, eds., *Beyond Traditional Peacekeeping* (London: Macmillan, 1995); and Olara A. Otunnu and Michael W. Doyle, eds., foreword by Nelson Mandela, *Peacemaking and Peacekeeping for the New Century* (Lanham, Md.: Rowman & Littlefield, 1998).

26. Sadako Ogata, *The Turbulent Decade: Confronting the Refugee Crises of the 1990s* (New York: W.W. Norton, 2005), 25.

27. "In Bosnia's Fog," *The Economist*, April 23, 1994, 16.

28. Lawrence Freedman, "Why the West Failed," Foreign Policy 97 (Winter 1994–1995): 59.

29. For a report from an official inquiry, see Netherlands Institute for War Documentation, *Srebenica, a "Safe" Area: Reconstruction, Background, Consequences, and Analyses of the Fall of a Safe Area* (Amsterdam: Boom Publishers, 2002), also available at www.srebenica.nl/en/. See further, from a growing literature, Jan Willem Honig and Norbert Both, *Srebrenica: Record of a War Crime* (London: Penguin, 1996), and David Rohde, *Endgame: The Betrayal and Fall of Srebrenica* (Boulder, Colo.: Westview Press, 1998).

30. "U.N. Bosnia Commander Wants More Troops, Fewer Resolutions," *New York Times*, December 31, 1993.

31. Quoted by Alison Mitchell, "Clinton's About-Face," *New York Times*, September 24, 1996. For a discussion of the impact of Somalia, see Tom J. Farer, "Intervention in Unnatural Humanitarian Emergencies: Lessons of the First Phase," *Human Rights Quarterly* 18, no. 1 (1996): 1–22; and Thomas G. Weiss, "Overcoming the Somalia Syndrome—'Operation Rekindle Hope'?" *Global Governance* 1, no. 2 (1995): 171–187.

32. UN General Assembly, *A Comprehensive Strategy to Eliminate Future Sexual Exploitation and Abuse in United Nations Peacekeeping Operations*, UN document A/59/710, March 24, 2005.

33. See Kenneth Cain, Heidi Postlewait, and Andrew Thomson, *Emergency Sex and Other Desperate Measures: A True Story from Hell on Earth* (New York: Hyperion, 2004).

34. See Debarati G. Sapir and Hedwig Deconinck, "The Paradox of Humanitarian Assistance and Military Intervention in Somalia," in *The United Nations and Civil Wars*, ed. Thomas G. Weiss (Boulder, Colo.: Lynne Rienner, 1995), 168.

35. See Larry Minear and Philippe Guillot, *Soldiers to the Rescue: Humanitarian Lessons from Rwanda* (Paris: OECD, 1996); Gérard Prunier, *The Rwanda Crisis: History of a Genocide* (New York: Columbia University Press, 1995); Joint Evaluation of Emergency Assistance to Rwanda, *The International Response to Conflict and Genocide: Lessons from the Rwandan Experience*, 5 vols. (Copenhagen: Joint Evaluation of Emergency Assistance to Rwanda, March 1995).

36. For discussions of this phenomenon in relationship to this crisis, see Robert I. Rotberg and Thomas G. Weiss, eds., *From Massacres to Genocide: The Media, Public Policy, and Humanitarian Crises* (Washington, D.C.: Brookings Institution, 1996); Larry Minear, Colin Scott, and Thomas G. Weiss, *The News Media, Civil War, and Humanitarian Action* (Boulder, Colo.: Lynne Rienner, 1996); Charles C. Moskos and Thomas E. Ricks, *Reporting War When There Is No War* (Chicago: McCormick Tribune Foundation, 1996); Edward Girardet, ed., *Somalia, Rwanda, and Beyond: The Role of the International Media in Wars and Humanitarian Crises* (Dublin: Crosslines Communications, 1995); Johanna Newman, *Lights, Camera, War* (New York: St. Martin's Press, 1996); Nik Gowing, *Real-Time Television Coverage of Armed Conflicts and Diplomatic Crises* (Cambridge, MA: Harvard Shorenstein Center, 1994) and *Media Coverage: Help or Hindrance in Conflict Prevention* (New York: Carnegie Commission on Preventing Deadly Conflict, 1997); and Warren P. Stroble, *Late-Breaking Foreign Policy: The News Media's Influence on Peace Operations* (Washington, D.C.: U.S. Institute of Peace Press, 1997).

37. Sadako Ogata, head of the UN refugee office, asked the Security Council to control the Hutu militia in the refugee camps, but the state members of the council lacked the necessary fortitude for a proper response. Ogata then contracted with Zaire, as it then was, to provide some security in the camps, but this proved less than an ideal solution. See *Turbulent Decade*, Chapter 3.

38. See Peter Uvin, *Aiding Violence: The Development Enterprise in Rwanda* (West Hartford, Conn.: Kumarian, 1998).

39. Kofi Annan, *Address to the Parliament of Rwanda*, Kigali, May 7, 1998, document SG/SM/6552.

40. Kofi Annan, "Statement on Receiving the Report of the Independent Inquiry into the Actions of the United Nations During the 1994 Genocide in Rwanda," United Nations, New York, December 16, 1999.

41. For his own recollections, see Roméo Dallaire, *Shake Hands with the Devil: The Failure of Humanity in Rwanda* (Toronto: Brent Beardsley, 2004). See further, Michael N. Barnett, *Eyewitness to a Genocide: The United Nations and Rwanda* (Ithaca, N.Y.: Cornell University Press, 2002). Barnett faults the culture of the UN bureaucracy in New York for not responding better to the clear signs of genocide evident for a long time in Rwanda. For the UN's own hard-hitting report, see www.un.org/News/ossg/rwanda_report.htm.

42. Boutros Boutros-Ghali, *Supplement to An Agenda for Peace*, document A/50/60-S/1995, January 5, 1995, para. 70, reprinted in *An Agenda for Peace 1995* (New York: United Nations, 1995) along with the 1992 *An Agenda for Peace*. Paragraph numbers are the same in the original.

43. United Nations Development Programme, *Human Development Report 1994* (New York: Oxford University Press, 1994), 47.

44. Boutros-Ghali, Supplement, para. 77.

45. *Report of the Panel on United Nations Peace Operations*, UN document A/55/305-S/2000/809, August 21, 2000. For a discussion, see David M. Malone and Ramesh Thakur, "UN Peacekeeping: Lessons Learned?" *Global Governance* 7, no. 1 (2001): 11–17.

46. See Michael Barnett, "Humanitarianism Transformed," *Perspectives on Politics* 3, no. 4 (2005): 723–740; and Janice Stein, "Humanitarianism as Political Fusion," *Perspectives on Politics* 3, no. 4 (2005): 740–744.

47. Forsythe, "Human Rights and International Security."

48. See Mohammed Ayoob, "The New-Old Disorder in the Third World," in *Collective Security in a Changing World*, ed. Thomas G. Weiss (Boulder, Colo.: Lynne Rienner, 1993), 13–30.

49. Stephen John Stedman, "The New Interventionists," *Foreign Affairs* 72, no. 1 (1993): 1–16. For an exhaustive review of the literature, see Oliver Ramsbotham and Tom Woodhouse, *Humanitarian Intervention in Contemporary Conflict* (Oxford: Polity Press, 1996). See also John Harriss, ed., *The Politics of Humanitarian Intervention* (London: Pinter, 1995); James Mayall, ed., *The New Interventionism: United Nations Experience in Cambodia, Former Yugoslavia, and Somalia* (New York: Cambridge University Press, 1996); and Jan Neederveen Pieterse, ed., *World Orders in the Making: Humanitarian Intervention and Beyond* (London: Macmillan, 1998).

50. See Rob McRae and Don Hubert, eds., *Human Security and the New Diplomacy: Protecting People, Promoting Peace* (Montreal & Kingston: McGill-Queen's University Press, 2001). See also S. Neil MacFarlane and Yuen Foong Khong, *Human Security and the UN: A Critical History* (Bloomington: Indiana University Press, 2006).

CHAPTER 4

Evolving Security Operations: Kosovo, East Timor, Sierra Leone, Lebanon, and Sudan

A N INTERESTING LENS through which to examine normative and operational change emerging from ongoing UN security operations is the International Commission on Intervention and State Sovereignty (ICISS). The commission's 2001 report, *The Responsibility to Protect*, provides a snapshot of issues surrounding nonconsensual international military action to foster values.[1] The ICISS responded to two sets of events. The first were several moral pleas in 1999 from the future (in 2001) Nobel Laureate UN Secretary-General Annan, who argued that human rights concerns transcended claims of sovereignty, a theme that he put forward more delicately a year later at the Millennium Summit.[2] The reaction was loud, bitter, and predictable, especially from China, Russia, and much of the Third World. "Intervention"—for whatever reasons, including humanitarian—was taboo.[3] The second set of events concerned the weak, untimely, and inadequate reactions by the Security Council in Rwanda and Kosovo. In Rwanda, although a traditional UN peacekeeping mission was on the ground, meaningful intervention through enforcement action proved politically impossible and the UN presence failed to halt or even slow the murder of as many as 800,000 people in the Great Lakes region of Africa. In 1999, the formidable NATO finessed the council and waged war for the first time in its history in Kosovo. But many observers saw the bombing campaign as being too much and too soon, perhaps creating as much human suffering as it relieved.

In both cases, the Security Council was unable to act expeditiously and authorize the use of deadly force to protect vulnerable populations. The role of humanitarian concerns in justifying outside military force was the most salient new dimension of UN security operations in the 1990s, which is the story for much of this chapter.

Secretary-General Kofi Annan holds the Nobel Peace Prize awarded in December 2000 to the United Nations and to him, as the organization's Secretary-General. (UN/DPI Photo by S. Bermeniev)

USING MILITARY FORCE FOR
HUMAN PROTECTION PURPOSES

The justifications for UN involvement often involved a substantial element of pulling humanitarian heartstrings. For students of politics, the ICISS and its report encapsulated four conceptual developments.

First, and most critically, the responsibility to protect (R2P) infused state sovereignty with a human rights dimension—that is, sovereignty was not a license to do as state authorities wished but was contingent on respecting minimal human rights standards. The standards may not have been that high—not committing mass atrocity crimes—but sovereignty was contingent instead of absolute and this clearly represents a substantial change in international relations.

Second, R2P reformulates the conceptual basis for humanitarian intervention. It calls for moving away from the rights of interveners (outsiders) toward the rights of victims (insiders) and the obligations of outsiders to act. The responsibility to protect includes action not only to intervene when large-scale loss of life occurs but also to prevent armed conflicts and to help mend societies.

Third, the ICISS proposes a new international default setting—a modified just-war doctrine for future interventions to sustain humanitarian values or human rights. As such, just cause, proportionality, likelihood of success, and right authority (ideally, the Security Council) are seen as essential elements of a responsible decision to act.

Why was this such a sea change? As a result of the Cold War, the Security Council was largely missing in action regarding humanitarian matters. There was a tabula rasa—no resolution mentioned the humanitarian aspects of any conflict from 1945 until the Six-Day War of 1967.[4] The first mention of the ICRC was not until 1978. And in the 1970s and 1980s, "the Security Council gave humanitarian aspects of armed conflict limited priority . . . but the early nineteen-nineties can be seen as a watershed."[5] During the first half of the decade, twice as many resolutions were passed as during the first forty-five years of UN history. They contained repeated references, in the context of Chapter VII, to humanitarian crises amounting to threats to international peace and security, and repeated demands for parties to have respect for the principles of international humanitarian law.

The ICISS reiterates the central role of the Security Council, reformed and enlarged or not, and urges it to act. But if it does not, humanitarians and victims are left where the Secretary-General himself was in September 1999, when he queried his diplomatic audience about their reactions had there been a state or a group of states willing to act in April 1994 even without a Security Council imprimatur. "Should such a coalition have stood aside," he asked rhetorically, "and allowed the horror to unfold?"[6] The answer by any of the 800,000 dead Rwandans would be clear even if in UN circles it remains cloudy.

In short, enthusiasm for UN helping hands must be tempered with the realities of UN operations. There certainly is no evidence of a diminishing number of "complex political emergencies"—a new phenomenon to depict a "humanitarian crisis in a country, region or society where there is a total or considerable breakdown of authority resulting from internal or external conflict and which requires an international response that goes beyond the mandate or capacity of any single agency and/or the ongoing UN country programme."[7] It is within this context that the military might help quell ethnic violence, create humanitarian space, and protect fundamental human rights. One is not obliged to agree with Robert Kaplan's apocalyptic visions[8] to recognize a distressing fragmentation of societies that may require outside military intervention if various groups are not to be subjugated or annihilated—which of course is also an option, although states are loath to admit as much publicly. And as long as these threats to human security exist, a role for the United Nations will be debated, given the weaknesses of regional options and the reluctance of any one state to become the world's policeman. This latter point is all the more obvious after the United States became bogged down in Iraq after spring 2003, while still being entrapped in Afghanistan after late 2001.

However, coercive military intervention necessitates a revision of conventional wisdom regarding the lack of consent for Chapter VII operations. Legally speaking, intervention as authorized by the Security Council does not require "consent" from the targeted authorities, *de jure* or de facto. Politically speaking, however, intervention normally requires the support of the domestic constituencies in troop-contributing countries and from affected local populations—or there may be debilitating blowback, as was the case in Somalia on both fronts.

Thus a progression of three steps underlies this lesson. First, the chances for a successful intervention are improved when preceded by establishing and maintaining the consent of the publics that send their sons and daughters into hostile environments. For example, Americans were prepared for possible casualties prior to Washington's involvement on the ground in Kuwait and Iraq, but they were not prepared, nor was their consent sought, in Somalia, which ended up inhibiting U.S. action in Rwanda, for example, because of the fierce negative reaction—in Mogadishu and in the United States. Second, although consent by definition is not necessary from local belligerents for Chapter VII, the consent of local populations should be sought and nurtured. Somalia illustrates the neglect by third-party interveners of local populations manipulated easily by belligerents into believing that those who come to assist them are contributing to their pain. Third and finally, with legitimacy established for possible deaths in action of soldiers and for the presence of "outsiders," there should be no compromises made in robustly making all requisite military efforts to quickly establish a secure environment.

Without a commitment to satisfying all three steps, an intervention is risky and may backfire. The "messiness" of intervention comes from both lack of legitimacy and lack of efficiency, which the first lesson addresses. A well-planned, systematic response is required, but only after consent has been garnered from local populations in both troop-contributing states and the area of conflict. Outsiders need to reestablish security quickly and credibly in part of a disputed territory even if subsequently additional reinforcements are sent or another strategy evolves. This is the opposite of a slowly-turning-the-screws approach in the hopes that either political will or a meaningful strategy will appear over time. If there is no clarity about mission and little commitment to equipping the UN to act responsibly, "then the U.N. and the world at large," in John Ruggie's words, "are better off by lowering the organization's military profile and not muddling in the strategic calculus of states."[9]

IMPLICATIONS FOR THE UN'S SECURITY EFFORTS

And what about the UN as something of an independent variable, the semi-independent actor staffed with a semi-autonomous civil service? Without putting too fine a point on it, we maintain that the history of security operations after the Cold War indicates that the United Nations is incapable of exercising command and control over combat operations. The capacity to plan, support, and command peacekeeping, let alone peace-enforcement, missions is scarcely greater now than during the Cold War. And this situation will not change in the foreseeable future. Powerful member states simply do not want the world body to possess such autonomous military capabilities.

At the same time, however, states have made modest improvements to augment the UN Secretariat's anemic military expertise and intelligence capacities—for example, a round-the-clock situation room and satellite telephones—and still others are feasible and desirable. The Canadians and Dutch were joined by twenty-two other countries as "the friends of rapid reaction," and they proposed in 1996 a mobile military headquarters capable of fielding command teams within hours of a Security Council decision. Seven states (Austria, Canada, Denmark, the Netherlands, Norway, Poland, and Sweden) signed an agreement to set up a 4,000-member UN Standby High Readiness Brigade, which could be used by the Security Council for peacekeeping or preventive operations. Although its existence would perhaps be helpful in exercising a restraining effect on combatants, the real problem is the reluctance of states to move quickly and to authorize forces large enough to do the job. This reality became perfectly clear when Canada offered to lead a UN effort in eastern Zaire in autumn 1995, and no one volunteered. In short there is no chance that states will empower the world organization with the wherewithal to contradict Michael Mandelbaum's harsh judgment that "the U.N. itself can no more conduct military operations on a large scale on its own than a trade association of hospitals can conduct heart surgery."[10]

Taking advantage of experience over the 1990s and the demonstrated need for change, Secretary-General Annan appointed a high-level international panel to examine critically the UN's handling of peace operations. Led by Lakhdar Brahimi,[11] the panel found a great deal to criticize, as shown in its August 2000 report. The blunt language focused on getting states to take their responsibilities seriously, on creating clear mandates and reasonable goals, and on providing well-trained and -equipped troops. None of the prescriptions offered would surprise the readers of these pages, nor would the absence of consensus that has followed and the accompanying lack of implementation.

The United Nations as actor should distance itself from actually exercising coercion for two reasons. First, states are unwilling to provide the Secretary-General with the necessary tools for Chapter VII. Standby troops and funds, independent intelligence, and appropriate systems for command and control along with professional personnel are simply not forthcoming. The Secretary-General simply does not have the capacity of independent action in this regard.

Second, and perhaps more important, the strength of the office of the Secretary-General lies in its neutrality, which is derived from the lack of vested interests. Giandomenico Picco, a former senior official who negotiated the release of hostages in Lebanon, has argued persuasively that "transforming the institution of the Secretary-General into a pale imitation of a state" in order "to manage the use of force may well be a suicidal embrace."[12] When the security situation has somewhat stabilized, the Secretary-General should be prepared to facilitate the administration of collapsed states, but after the warring parties themselves are exhausted or cleansed from a territory or following a humanitarian intervention. Proceeding in these ways requires separating military intervention from civilian administration in order to break a cycle of violence and to create both a respite and the preconditions for an interim government to return. Moreover, in order to maintain credibility as a third party, the United Nations—insofar as it is separate from states—should refrain from taking sides. Fen Hampson concluded his comprehensive study on the UN's negotiating the end to five ethnic conflicts with the suggestion, "Enforcement is therefore best left to others."[13] The Security Council should still authorize enforcement on selected occasions, but such efforts should be subcontracted to regional arrangements or coalitions of the willing. The UN's comparative advantage—certainly in comparison with the United States—seems to be in post-conflict peace-building, according to a massive study by the Rand Corporation led by an experienced former U.S. government official.[14]

The failure to distinguish between the military operations that the United Nations Secretariat can manage (traditional and even slightly muscular peace-keeping) and those that it cannot and should not (enforcement) has led to obfuscation. The latter are problematic under any circumstances, but they have given governments that are unable and unwilling to act decisively the opportunity to treat the United Nations as scapegoat. One is reminded of the third UN Secretary-General, U Thant, who commented wryly, "It is not surprising that the organization should often be blamed for failing to solve problems that have already been found to be insoluble by governments."[15]

With Richard Holbrooke of the United States presiding in the Security Council in January 2000, the focus was on Africa's woes. Everyone agreed that a peacekeeping force in the Democratic Republic of the Congo (MONUC) was desirable. Yet, with what is somewhat hyperbolically called "Africa's World War," the initial force of some 5,000 soldiers was way too small when there was no peace to keep. Subsequent increases in troop levels alongside continued chaos in the Congo only confirmed the accuracy of the original skepticism. The UN field presence there remains largely symbolic, although approaching 20,000 international soldiers and political staff, because the physical size of the country and its political challenges compound the lack of political will in New York and elsewhere to make a greater practical impact. In regions (especially to the East in Ituri), the UN's presence has nonetheless been helpful in tamping down violence.[16]

At the same time, a positive development within the UN has been the ability, on occasion, to call a spade a spade. The UN Secretary-General's 1999 report on Srebrenica and the Ingmar Carlsson report on Rwanda contained plenty of blame to go around and were followed by another remarkably frank document—about the failings of sanctions against Angola—by a group under Robert Fowler.[17] States should be held accountable for a lack of political will, but also important is to hold senior UN officials' feet to the fire because they are capable of choices, of doing the right or the wrong thing. State political will, or the lack thereof, matters. But UN officials matter as well.

TABLE 4.1   UN Peace and Security Operations, 1999–Present

Years Active	Operation
1999–Present	United Nations Interim Administration Mission in Kosovo (UNMIK)
1999–Present	United Nations Mission in Sierra Leone (UNAMSIL)
1999–2002	United Nations Transitional Administration in East Timor (UNTAET)
1999–Present	United Nations Organization Mission in the Democratic Republic of the Congo (MONUC)
2000–Present	United Nations Mission in Ethiopia and Eritrea (UNMEE)
2002–2005	United Nations Mission of Support in East Timor (UNMISET)
2003–Present	United Nations Mission in Liberia (UNMIL)
2004–Present	United Nations Operation in Cote d'Ivoire (UNOCI)
2004–Present	United Nations Stabilization Mission in Haiti (MINUSTAH)
2004–Present	United Nations Operation in Burundi (ONUB)
2005–Present	United Nations Mission in the Sudan (UNMIS)
2006–Present	United Nations Integrated Mission in Timor-Leste (UNMIT)
2006–Present	United Nations Interim Force in Lebanon (UNIFIL)
2007–Present	African Union/United Nations Hybrid Mission in Darfur (UNAMID)
2007–Present	United Nations Mission in the Central African Republic and Chad (MINURCAT)

Note: UNIFIL was created in 1978 to monitor an Israeli withdrawal from Lebanon; however, the mission was significantly enhanced following the outbreak of violence between Israel and Lebanon in July 2006.

Regardless of the challenges, the UN's security activities continue and the demand for action remains as great as ever. It is important to keep in mind that states and other actors often seek to involve the UN or "hide behind a blue skirt" to buy time or because they cannot or will not undertake action alone. In the last few years, the Security Council held sessions on the situations in Kosovo, Sierra Leone, Western Sahara, Ethiopia/Eritrea, Somalia, Guinea-Bissau, Congo, Burundi, Macedonia, Croatia, Bosnia and Herzegovina, Central African Republic, Georgia, Tajikistan, Afghanistan, Iraq and Kuwait, Haiti, Cyprus, Lebanon, Syria, Israel, Iran, Libya, and Sudan.

In the face of these crises, the critical question confronting the UN was how to respond effectively when demand so clearly outstripped supply—in short, how to "muddle through." The answer to this question emerged on a case-by-case basis, yet with each new response seemingly informed by and building on the last. Table 4.1 illustrates peace and security operations since 1999 and Table 4.2 lists completed operations. The following discussion illustrates the evolution in UN security operations, many with a humanitarian dimension and with robust military requirements.

TABLE 4.2   UN Peace and Security Operations: Completed as of December 2008

Location	Acronym/Name	Duration
Middle East	UNEF I/First United Nations Emergency Force	November 1956–June 1967
Lebanon	UNOGIL/United Nations Observation Group in Lebanon	June 1958–December 1958
Congo	ONUC/United Nations Operation in the Congo	July 1960–June 1964
West New Guinea	UNSF/United Nations Security Force in West Guinea (West Irian)	October 1962–April 1963
Yemen	UNYOM/United Nations Yemen Observation Mission	July 1963–September 1964
Dominican Republic	DOMREP/Mission of the Representative of the Secretary-General in the Dominican Republic	May 1965–October 1966
India and Pakistan	UNIPOM/United Nations India-Pakistan Observation Mission	September 1965–March 1966
Middle East	UNEFII/Second United Nations Emergency Force	October 1973– July 1979
Afghanistan and Pakistan	UNGOMAP/United Nations Good Offices Mission in Afghanistan and Pakistan	April 1988–March 1990
Iran and Iraq	UNIIMOG/United Nations Iran-Iraq Military Observer Group	August 1988–February 1991
Angola	UNAVEM I/United Nations Angola Verification Mission I	January 1989–June 1991
Namibia	UNTAG/United Nations Transition Assistance Group	April 1989–March 1990
Central America	ONUCA/United Nations Observer Group in Central America	November 1989–January 1992
Iraq and Kuwait	UNIKOM/ United Nations Iraq-Kuwait Observer Mission	April 1991–October 2003
Angola	UNAVEM II/ Angola Verification Mission II	June 1991–February 1995
El Salvador	ONUSAL/United Nations Observer Mission in El Salvador	July 1991–April 1995
Cambodia	UNAMIC/United Nations Advance Mission in Cambodia	October 1991–March 1992
Cambodia	UNTAC/United Nations Transitional Authority in Cambodia	March 1992–September 1993
Former Yugoslavia	UNPROFOR/United Nations Protection Force	March 1992–December 1995
Somalia	UNOSOM I/United Nations Operation in Somalia I	April 1992–March 1993
Mozambique	ONUMOZ/United Nations Operation in Mozambique	December 1992–December 1994
Somalia	UNSOM II/United Nations Operation in Somalia II	March 1993–March 1995
Rwanda and Uganda	UNOMUR/United Nations Observer Mission Uganda-Rwanda	June 1993–September 1994

TABLE 4.2 (*continued*)

Location	Acronym/Name	Duration
Haiti	UNMIH/United Nations Mission in Haiti	September 1993–June 1996
Liberia	UNOMIL/United Nations Observer Mission in Liberia	September 1993–September 1997
Rwanda	UNAMIR/United Nations Assistance Mission for Rwanda	October 1993–March 1996
Chad and Libya	UNASOG/United Nations Aousou Strip Observer Group	May 1994–June 1994
Rwanda	Operation Turquoise	June 1994
Angola	UNAVEM III/United Nations Angola Verification Mission III	February 1995–June 1997
Croatia	UNCRO/United Nations Confidence Restoration Organization	March 1995–January 1996
Former Yugoslav Republic of Macedonia	UNPREDEP/United Nations Preventive Deployment Force	March 1995–February 1999
Croatia	UNTAES/United Nations Transitional Administration for Eastern Slavonia, Balanja and Western Sirmium	January 1996–January 1998
Haiti	UNSMIH/United Nations Support Mission in Haiti	July 1996–July 1997
Guatemala	MINUGUA/United Nations Verification Mission in Guatemala	January 1997–May 1997
Angola	MONUA/United Nations Observer Mission in Angola	July 1997–February 1999
Sierra Leone	UNAMSIL/United Nations Assistance Mission in Sierra Leone	October 1999–December 2005
Haiti	UNTMIH/United Nations Transition Mission in Haiti	August 1997–November 1997
Croatia	United Nations Civilian Police Support Group	January 1998–October 1998
Sierra Leone	UNOMSIL/United Nations Mission of Observers in Sierra Leone	July 1988–October 1999
Central African Republic	MINURCA/United Nations Mission in Central African Republic	April 1998–February 2000
Haiti	MIPONUH/United Nations Civilian Police Mission in Haiti	December 1997–March 2000
East Timor	UNTAET/United Nations Transitional Administration in East Timor	October 1999–May 2002
Tajikistan	UNMOT/United Nations Mission in Tajikistan	December 1994–May 2000
Bosnia and Herzegovina	UNMIBH/United Nations Mission in Bosnia and Herzegovina	December 1995–December 2002
Prevlaka Province, Croatia/Federal Republic of Yugoslavia	UNMOP/United Nations Mission of Observers in Prevlaka	February 1996–December 2002

TABLE 4.2   (*continued*)

Location	Acronym/Name	Duration
East Timor	UNMISET/United Nations Mission of Support in East Timor	May 2002–May 2005
Ethiopea-Eritrea	UNMEE/United Nations Mission Ethiopia and Eritrea	July 2000–July 2008
Burundi	UNUB/United Nations Operations Burundi	June 2004–December 2006

Note: Although authorized by the UN Security Council, Operation Turquoise was commanded and financed by France.

THE CRISIS IN THE BALKANS

The 1991 Gulf War and the creation of internal safe havens for Kurds in Iraq illustrate what we referred to in Chapter 1 as military "subcontracting." That is, the "job" of exercising coercion is subcontracted to others. Other examples include IFOR and SFOR (the Implementation Force and the Stabilization Force, respectively, in the former Yugoslavia) and the more controversial case of UNITAF in Somalia. The growing relevance of military intervention by major powers in regions of their traditional interests had become obvious; however, the gap between UN capacities and demands for action remains. This has led almost inevitably to calls for action by various states with the blessing of the larger community of states through either the explicit or the implicit approval of the Security Council.[18]

The NATO action in Kosovo in spring 1999 is a dramatic case in point. Depending on how one reads the script of diplomatic code embedded in Security Council resolutions, the action by NATO could be argued to represent a breach of international law or to have been launched with the council's implicit approval. The Independent Commission on Kosovo, composed largely of human rights proponents, called it "illegal but legitimate"—that is, without the Security Council's blessing but justified in human terms.[19] The secretary-general of NATO, Javier Solana, of course, chose the latter interpretation of Security Council resolution 1199. On the other hand, both Russia and China condemned the action as illegal.[20] Russia weakened its own position and made a tactical blunder by introducing a resolution criticizing the NATO bombing and asking that it be halted. The resolution's defeat by a wide margin (12–3) enhanced the status of NATO's action. In any case, UN Secretary-General Kofi Annan drew considerable fire for his speech at the opening of the General Assembly in September 1999. Although he wished the Security Council had been able to give explicit approval to the bombing, he nonetheless could not condone idleness in the face of Serb atrocities.[21]

Diplomacy had failed to change Serbian policy. Time and again Yugoslav president Slobodan Milošević demonstrated his blatant disregard for negotiated agreements. In late January 1999, U.S. officials shifted away from a diplomatic approach and threatened military action. The Secretary-General had apparently arrived at a similar conclusion. In a statement before NATO leaders in Brussels, he indicated that indeed force might be necessary. In doing so, he praised past UN-NATO collaboration in Bosnia and suggested that a NATO-led mission under UN auspices might well be what was needed. He concluded:

> The bloody wars of the last decade have left us with no illusions about the difficulty of halting internal conflicts by reason or by force particularly against the wishes of the government of a sovereign state. Nor have they left us with any illusions about the need to use force, when all other means have failed. We may be reaching that limit, once again, in the former Yugoslavia.[22]

But neither NATO nor the UN was willing to give up totally on diplomacy. The so-called contact group—the United States, France, Germany, Italy, Russia, and the United Kingdom—hosted a peace conference in Rambouillet, France, in February 1999, which sought to broker a solution between Yugoslavia and an Albanian Kosovar delegation. But Belgrade was unwilling to yield on key points, and the talks floundered. The situation in Kosovo deteriorated even further.

On March 24, NATO began a seventy-seven-day aerial bombardment of Serbian targets. Soon after the bombing started, Serbian security forces launched an all-out campaign to exorcise Kosovo of its predominant ethnic-Albanian population. Within weeks a huge segment of Kosovo's 1.8 million ethnic Albanians had been displaced from their houses and villages. That is, initially the intervention accelerated flight and humanitarian suffering. However, as the NATO intervention progressed, air strikes intensified until finally, in the context of a Russian mediated settlement, Milosevic agreed on June 3 to an immediate and verifiable end to the violence and repression and to the withdrawal of all Serbian security forces.

Other aspects of the agreement included the deployment under UN auspices of an effective international civilian and security presence with substantial NATO participation, the establishment of an interim administration, safe return of all refugees and displaced persons, demilitarization of the Kosovo Liberation Army (KLA), and a substantially self-governing Kosovo.

On June 10, 1999, the council, in a 14–0–1 vote (China abstained), adopted resolution 1244 authorizing an international civil and security presence in Kosovo under UN auspices. NATO's preceding "humanitarian war" had been unusual to say the least, and many aid agencies had trouble pronouncing those two words together, and choked trying to say "humanitarian bombing."[23] But the new UN peace mission, the UN Interim Administration Mission in Kosovo (UNMIK), was unprecedented in its nature and scope. NATO authorized 49,000 troops (KFOR) to maintain order and security and UNMIK was to assume authority over all the territory and people of Kosovo, including judicial, legislative, and executive powers. It was to move the region toward self-governance; perform all normal civilian administrative functions; provide humanitarian relief, including the safe return of refugees and displaced persons; maintain law and order and establish the rule of law; promote human rights; assist in reconstructing basic social and economic infrastructure; and facilitate the development of a democratic political order.

The mission was path-breaking in integrating several non-UN international organizations under a unified UN leadership. It was organized around four substantive pillars: civil administration (UN-led); humanitarian affairs (UNHCR-led); reconstruction (European Union–led); and democratic institution-building (OSCE-led). The scope was mind-boggling. Civil administration, for example, was to be comprehensive, including health, education, energy and public utilities, post and telecommunications, judicial, legal, public finance, trade, science, agriculture, environment, and democratization. Over 800,000 people had to be repatriated. Over 120,000 houses had been damaged or destroyed. Schools needed to be reestablished; food, medical aid, and other humanitarian assistance provided; electrical power, sanitation, and clean water restored; land mines cleared and security ensured; and so on.

Although the initial UNMIK mandate was twelve months, it remains in Kosovo today. Military forces have been reduced, elections held, and the rebuilding of a society begun. Serious problems persist regarding continued ethnic violence, the status of the Serb minority, widespread unemployment, and the thriving sex trade. In 2004, ethnic Albanians rioted and attacked ethnic Serbs in the volatile and ethnically mixed city of Mitrovica, killing nineteen people. Both NATO and UNMIK were criticized for not protecting Serbian enclaves or confronting the rioters.[24] This outbreak of ethnic violence, and UNMIK and NATO's inability to prevent it, has plagued the negotiations on the most serious and intractable of Kosovo problems—the final status of the mostly Albanian province.

The UN set several deadlines for negotiating the final status of Kosovo with all the relevant parties. The initial negotiations were launched in 2005 by Special Envoy Marti Ahtisaari, the former Finnish president, who presented a plan that called for Kosovo's formal independence from Serbia. The plan was immediately rejected by Serbia with the backing of Russia and China. These states said such a plan would inspire other separatist movements and set a dangerous precedent. The negotiations were then turned over to the so-called troika of the European Union, the United States, and Russia and another deadline was set for December 10, 2007. The troika was responsible for mediating the final status agreement between Serbia and Kosovo. Backed by Russia, Serbia offered Kosovo the autonomous status it enjoyed under the former Yugoslavia prior to the rise of Milosevic; however, Serbia would retain sovereignty over the province. Kosovo, backed by the United States and the European Union, wanted formal independence with special political protection for the Serb minority in Kosovo. In the view of these actors, Serbia had, in effect, lost its sovereign right to govern the province because of its mistreatment of the Albanian minority, which led to the NATO intervention and eventual UN administration. Moreover, the Albanian majority overwhelmingly voted for independence. The December 2007 deadline passed again without an agreement because neither Serbia nor Kosovo was willing to cede its position on sovereignty.[25]

Kosovo represents an important challenge for the UN and the European Union. Without a final negotiated agreement, Kosovo was unlikely to receive the foreign and domestic investment necessary for generating economic growth and to deal with the chronic unemployment. Furthermore, the unresolved status continued to exacerbate ethnic tensions and created distrust of the UN and European Union among the ethnic Albanian majority. The UN is in a difficult position in that Security Council resolution 1244 reaffirms the sovereignty and territorial integrity of the Federal Republic of Yugoslavia, of which Kosovo was a part. With Serbia as the internationally recognized successor state, Kosovo falls under Serbia's sovereignty. With the specter of a unilateral declaration of independence by Kosovo, the UN and its member states, as in 1999, were faced with a choice of reaffirming the principles of sovereignty and territorial integrity or supporting the collective right of individuals to self-determination. Opting for the latter opens a Pandora's box for other separatists, including Serbs in Kosovo and Bosnia. Kosovo is a watershed for the UN as it pits the rights of individuals against the rights of states. It also pits the West, albeit a somewhat divided West, against Russia, China, and many states in the developing world.[26]

The situation came to a head with the declaration of independence in February 2008 by Kosovo, basically a UN protectorate since 1999. The secession of a former part of a sovereign state (Serbia) with international assistance was particularly problematic for Moscow because it faced its own tensions in Chechnya. While Albanians celebrated in the streets in the new capital, Pristina, Serbs in their enclave to the north confronted NATO troops, and Serbs in Belgrade burned the U.S. embassy as Washington and several Western states recognized a sovereign Kosovo. The outcome will profoundly affect the legal status of humanitarian intervention and the future of self-determination in a world with evolving notions of the rights and responsibilities associated with state sovereignty.

The international community of states remains sharply divided. While 48 states (including 22 EU countries and the United States) have recognized Kosovo, 144 states have not.[27] In October 2008, the General Assembly voted to approve Serbia's bid to the International Court of Justice (ICJ) to review the legality of Kosovo's unilateral declaration of independence. The ICJ's ruling is expected to have a profound impact on the legal rules associated with recognizing new states.

TURMOIL IN TIMOR-LESTE (EAST TIMOR)

After over a decade and a half of UN-mediated efforts to resolve the status of East Timor, an agreement was reached on May 5, 1999, between Indonesia and Portugal (the last colonial power) regarding a process to determine the future of that long-troubled territory.[28] The two states agreed that the UN Secretary-General would be responsible for organizing and conducting a popular consultation to determine whether the people of East Timor would accept or reject a special autonomous status within the unitary Republic of Indonesia. A rejection of such special status meant the UN would be responsible for administering the territory during its transition to independence. Security Council resolution 1246 established the UN Mission in East Timor (UNAMET) with the mandate of conducting such a consultation and, after several postponements, the popular vote was held and the special autonomy status option was overwhelmingly rejected in favor of independence.

News of the outcome stirred pro-integration forces backed by armed militias to violence. Within a matter of weeks nearly a half million East Timorese were displaced from their homes and villages. Indonesian military troops and police were either unwilling or unable to restore order, and the security situation deteriorated. In September, the Security Council, in resolution 1264, authorized the creation of a multilateral force to restore order and protect and support UNAMET. Member states were welcomed to lead, organize, and contribute troops to such a force. Sitting in the wings ready to act, an Australian-led force began arriving in East Timor less than a week later. Numerous arms had been twisted in Jakarta so that Indonesia "requested" the coalition force. In less than a month general order was restored, and the Indonesian People's Consultative Assembly voted on October 19 to formally recognize the results of the popular consultation. The following week the Security Council unanimously approved resolution 1272, establishing the UN Transitional Administration in East Timor (UNTAET).

As in the case of UNMIK, the nature and scope of the UNTAET mission was exceedingly ambitious and wide-ranging.[29] As in the case of Cambodia, a country with substantial interests and motivation (in this case, Australia, not Japan) took the military lead. It was empowered to exercise all legislative and executive powers and judicial authority; establish an effective civil administration; assist in developing civil and social services; provide security and maintain law and order; ensure the coordination and delivery of humanitarian assistance, rehabilitation, and development assistance; promote sustainable development; and build the foundation for a stable liberal democracy. To carry out this mandate, authorization was given for a military component of 8,950 troops and 200 observers and a civilian police component of up to 1,640 personnel. By 2000, the processes of reconstruction and state-building were well under way and in 2002 East Timor became the 191st member of the United Nations with its new name—Timor-Leste.

Ana Vaz (second from right), a Formed Police Unit officer of the United Nations Mission in Timor-Leste from Portugal, speaks to a Rapid Intervention Unit officer of the Timor-Leste Police about protecting the trucks distributing food with the help of the International Organization for Migration and the World Food Programme, by providing security for the camps of the internally displaced persons in his area of responsibility. (UN Photo 186422/ Martine Perret)

Any evaluation of this effort at UN "trusteeship" awaits the passage of time. In mid-2006, skeptics' fears were confirmed with the explosion of violence in Dili and the hurried return of Australian soldiers to restore order and security. The violence was sparked by former soldiers who rebelled against the newly elected civilian government. In August 2006, the Security Council created the United Nations Integrated Mission in Timor-Leste (UNMIT) through resolution 1704 with a mandate to help the current government to consolidate stability and keep the peace. Continued violence (and the emergency return of Australian troops in 2007) and instability suggest that the UNMIT mandate may need to be extended for some time by the Security Council.

REESTABLISHING STABILITY IN SIERRA LEONE

The year 1999 brought both great sorrow and hope to the people of Sierra Leone, who were reeling from over eight years of civil war. The bloody civil conflict that had intensified during 1998 turned even bloodier in January 1999, when rebel forces once again captured the capital, Freetown, and launched a four-day spree of killing and destruction. Judges, journalists, human rights workers, government officials, civil servants, churches, hospitals, prisons, UN offices, and others were targets of the rebel alliance, comprising forces of the former junta and the Revolutionary United Front (RUF). Over 6,000 were killed, and about 20 percent of the total stock of dwellings was destroyed. The UN Observer Mission in Sierra Leone (UNOMSIL), which had been established in June 1998, was evacuated.[30]

Fighting continued throughout the spring and early summer, uprooting more than a million people, about 450,000 of whom fled to neighboring Guinea. The issue remained on the Security Council agenda, and the council kept extending UNOMSIL's mandate several months at a time. Finally, on July 7, 1999, a peace agreement, called the Lomé Peace Agreement, was negotiated between the government and the RUF. The Security Council responded positively to this move and on August 20 unanimously adopted resolution 1260, extending and expanding the UNOMSIL mandate. The UN presence was further expanded in October when the council adopted resolution 1270, creating a new mission, the UN Mission for Sierra Leone (UNAMSIL), which mandated the tasks of: establishing a presence at key locations throughout the country to assist the government of Sierra Leone in implementing the disarmament, demobilization, and reintegration of rebel troops; ensuring the security and freedom of movement of UN personnel; monitoring adherence to the cease-fire agreement of May 18; encouraging the parties to create confidence-building mechanisms and support their functioning; facilitating the delivery of humanitarian assistance; supporting the operations of UN civilian officials, including the special representative of the Secretary-General and his staff, human rights officers, and civil affairs officers; and providing support, as requested, for the elections, which are to be held in accordance with the present constitution of Sierra Leone.

Initially, the UN mission did not go very well, in part because member states predictably did not follow through on the UNAMSIL mandate with the necessary resources. The force of 6,000 soldiers (from Nigeria, Kenya, and Guinea) was authorized under Chapter VII to use force if necessary to protect UN personnel and civilians threatened with imminent physical violence. However, the security situation was unstable as 45,000 combatants remained armed and in control of the diamond mines. In May 2000, nearly 500 UNAMSIL peacekeepers were kidnapped and held hostage by rebels. At the same time, the United Kingdom sent heavily armed forces to protect and extricate its nationals from the deteriorating security situation in the capital, Freetown.[31] Although unplanned, events on the ground played out such that UNAMSIL and UK forces worked together to stabilize Freetown and restore order to outlying regions. As the British began to draw down troops in 2001, the Security Council, in resolution 1346, expanded the peacekeeping force to 17,500 soldiers.

UNAMSIL and UK military forces were successful in establishing a "negative peace" in that they were able to lock down Sierra Leone militarily and also deter rebel groups from pursuing violence as a political strategy.[32] However, militaries and soldiers are often ill-suited for the other necessary elements of peacekeeping, such as humanitarian activities and post-conflict reconciliation.[33] Part of the problem centers on how to square the militarized masculinity associated with being a soldier in war-fighting situations with the requirements of maintaining peace.[34] Soldiers are trained for war-fighting, not for post-conflict reconstruction. On the other hand, properly trained civilian corps can make important progress in deepening political integration, reaching compromises among multiple and competing parties, and building the institutions of civil society. Sierra Leone, as well as other cases discussed thus far, represents the informal and often ill-defined relationship between state military power and UN peacekeeping and peacebuilding capacities.

To create a "positive peace" in Sierra Leone, the newly created Peacebuilding Commission (PBC, discussed in more detail in the next chapter) decided in 2006 to undertake missions in Sierra Leone and Burundi as pilots for the new and more concentrated UN efforts in so-called post-conflict countries. By selecting Sierra Leone and Burundi, two of the more troubled African countries, the PBC took on some exceptional challenges. The commission's mandate is to "marshal resources at the disposal of the international community to advise and propose integrated strategies for post-conflict recovery, focusing attention on reconstruction, institution-building and sustainable development, in countries emerging from conflict." In its report on Sierra Leone, it notes that while important political progress has been made, "the majority of the population remains extremely insecure because of poverty, lack of access to justice, lack of employment opportunities, high crime rates and corruption. The situation is even more difficult for young people and women, who face additional marginalization and discrimination. Many of the root causes of conflict, such as lack of employment for the large youth population, the proliferation of small arms, inadequate State capacity to deliver basic services, corruption and instability in the region, persist today."[35] In 2007, the UN Peacebuilding Fund (PBF), which supports PBC missions, allocated $35 million for youth employment, good governance, justice and security, and capacity building for public administrations. Sierra Leone remains an important test for the nascent Peacebuilding Commission and the Peacebuilding Fund.

LEBANON—AGAIN

On July 12, 2006, Hezbollah, an Iranian-backed militia based in Lebanon, conducted a raid into Israel kidnapping and later executing two Israel Defense Forces (IDF) soldiers. In the past, such raids have been used against Israel as a negotiating tactic to secure the release of Islamic militants held in Israeli prisons. Israel responded by launching a large-scale war against Hezbollah, beginning with air strikes on Hezbollah strongholds in southern Lebanon. Hezbollah responded by launching rockets into the Israeli cities of Kiryat Shmona and Haifa, leading to further escalation by Israel. IDF forces in massive attacks, including the use of cluster bombs, destroyed a substantial part of the economic infrastructure of Lebanon and eventually entered southern Lebanon to create a buffer zone between Hezbollah rockets and Israeli territory. After nearly a month of intense fighting where more than 1,200 civilians were killed and more than 4,000 wounded, the UN Security Council, in resolution 1701, called for a cease-fire and the deployment of UNIFIL into southern Lebanon. Recall from Chapter 3 that UNIFIL was created in 1978 to deal with earlier crises in Lebanon. Before the 2006 deployment, UNIFIL forces would need to be increased from some 2,000 to a more robust 15,000 soldiers. Its mandate also had to be expanded.

According to resolution 1701, UNIFIL's mandate is to monitor the cease-fire; assist the Lebanese government in deploying its troops into southern Lebanon; and assist in the delivery of humanitarian assistance or the safe return of displaced persons. Most important, 1701 calls for UNIFIL to create a zone along the Israeli-Lebanon border where the only armed personnel are members of the Lebanese military or UNIFIL. Finally, the Security Council authorized UNIFIL to use appropriate military force as necessary to carry out its mandate.

Beefing up UNIFIL and its mandate was not without its problems. Two issues generated considerable media attention and debate at the UN. The first issue centered on rules of engagement for UNIFIL. Although UNIFIL was authorized to use military force, questions remained about whether it should attempt to disarm Hezbollah or engage Hezbollah directly. The answers to these questions would directly affect the second issue of the composition of UNIFIL forces. France, which helped broker the cease-fire, was widely expected to contribute the bulk of the military forces and to lead UNIFIL. However, Paris announced on August 16 that it would contribute only 200 soldiers and provide some logistical support.[36] After a few days of widespread criticism, France offered to contribute 400 soldiers, generating even more criticism that such a paltry contribution would harm UN peacekeeping recruiting efforts for UNIFIL. Only after Italy offered to contribute 2,000 troops and lead UNIFIL did France agree to increase its troops to 2,000.

By the end of 2009, UNIFIL had 12,158 military troops from twenty-seven countries and an annual operating budget of $681 million.[37] By most accounts, the mission has been successful in that it has deterred violence in the border region, observed the Israeli withdrawal, and assisted with the deployment of Lebanese troops. The mixture of local armed forces with UN military forces was yet another departure for peace operations. The problems of command and control seemingly have been overcome, largely because the combined forces have not yet encountered serious challenge. The deterrence capacity of UNIFIL is due in large part to its military strength, which includes significant naval as well as land forces.[38] Although UNIFIL is a more traditional peacekeeping operation, it is unique in that it is more "robust," meaning that it is heavily armed and allowed

United Nations Interim Force in Lebanon (UNIFIL) troops observe Section 83 near the Blue Line on the border between Lebanon and Israel. (UN Photo 123914/Mark Garten)

to use military force "beyond self-defense." UNIFIL lacks the capacity as well as the mandate to undertake post-conflict peacebuilding, which is desperately needed in the war-ravaged country once again.

UNIFIL faces several challenges in the months and years ahead. The first centers on the sustainability of the mission. Fielding such a large and well-equipped military force indefinitely, especially in the absence of a political solution regarding the leadership of the Lebanese government, will test UN peacekeeping resolve. Resolution 1701 extended the newly enhanced UNIFIL mandate until August 2007 and resolution 1773 extended the mission until August 2008. Israel is especially concerned that European countries will begin to draw down their UNIFIL commitments in 2008, weakening its ability to deter Hezbollah should serious violence return.[39] A second concern centers on balancing the security of UNIFIL forces with the security of civilians in the border region. UNIFIL has had a remarkable record in that only six peacekeepers have lost their lives, all in a single June 2007 suicide car bombing. UNIFIL has been criticized for spending more time protecting itself than preventing Hezbollah rocket attacks in Israel, raising questions of whether it has become a victim of "soldier safety first," or the so-called UN peacekeeping syndrome.[40] At the same time, UNIFIL has done some remarkable work in clearing land mines and other weapons, including cluster bombs, making civilians' lives considerably safer. Finally, to date, neither Hezbollah nor Israel has really challenged the resolve to UNIFIL. Hezbollah sporadically fires rockets at Israel and Israel occasionally violates Lebanese airspace by conducting air patrols; however, these incidents have not posed a significant impediment to UNIFIL operations. Given that Hezbollah is not adverse to terrorist attacks against UN personnel and in the past Israel has ignored UNIFIL and in the 1980s invaded Lebanon, questions remain about what will happen if or when UNIFIL comes into violent conflict with the well-armed Hezbollah or Israel or both.

The future of Lebanon, and by extension UNIFIL, will depend in large part on the prospect of a peaceful settlement to the current political leadership vacuum in Lebanon. A series of political murders has decimated the leadership of pro-Western forces in Lebanon, while Hezbollah, backed by Iran and Syria, has increased its political influence. The odds of another Lebanese civil war have increased, which complicates the UN mission to keep the peace and protect civilians from threats of imminent violence. Also complicating the issue is the UN's involvement in the use of an international judicial response to the murder of former prime minister Rafik Hariri. Using Chapter VII, the Security Council created an international tribunal in 2005 to investigate and try suspects in the assassination. The work of the tribunal is slow in large part because of the controversy surrounding its creation, the lack of sufficient funding, and the minimal cooperation of the Lebanese government, now heavily influenced by Hezbollah.

DARFUR, SUDAN

The gravest humanitarian crisis currently facing the international community is in the Darfur region of Sudan.[41] The Darfur crisis is the culmination of a series of unresolved conflicts resulting from Sudan's decolonization in 1956. After Sudan gained independence from the United Kingdom, it descended into an almost continuous civil war,[42] which has pitted the government of Sudan in the North against rebel groups in the South, East, and West. Darfur, in the western part of Sudan, is home to two insurgencies, the Sudan Liberation Army and the Justice Equality Movement. Intense fighting erupted in 2003 between Sudanese government forces and the Sudan Liberation Army, creating a humanitarian crisis for civilians in the area. After sustaining attacks in the North, Sudanese government forces along with Arab militias, known as the *Janjaweed*, attacked towns and villages in Darfur with little regard for civilians. Claiming that the civilian population was harboring the insurgents, government and Janjaweed forces razed entire communities and pursued a scorched-earth policy. Although estimates vary, it is commonly thought that since 2003 at least 300,000 people have lost their lives and over 2.5 million people been displaced.

In the case of Darfur, the relative effectiveness of regional versus universal organizations comes back into focus as a major theme. Both the African Union and the UN have been involved in efforts to resolve this very complicated conflict and to protect the civilian population. The African Union until recently had been at the forefront by mediating peace talks and successfully brokering an important cease-fire in 2004. It also deployed its first peacekeeping mission, the African Union Mission in Sudan (AMIS) to monitor the cease-fire in 2004 and to help build a secure environment for delivering humanitarian assistance. Originally consisting of 150 troops, AMIS expanded over the next few years to include 7,000 troops. AMIS was plagued by poor funding, poor equipment, and poor training—in short, nothing like the force that would be necessary to improve conditions in an area the size of France. Moreover, its mandate did not include disarmament or the use of force to protect civilians. The cease-fire brokered in 2004 did not hold and neither did a series of cease-fires in 2006 and 2007. Attacks on civilians continued. To complicate matters even more, AMIS peacekeepers and humanitarian aid workers also became targets of government, Janjaweed, and insurgent forces.

The UN initially played a supporting role to the African Union by highlighting human rights abuses and keeping pressure on the Sudanese government. UN agencies and personnel, such as the UN coordinator for Sudan and the UN high commissioner for human rights, reported that gross violations and ethnic cleansing were occurring in Sudan as early as 2004. In September 2004, Secretary of State Colin Powell used the term "genocide" to describe the actions of the Sudanese government, sparking an international debate among practitioners and scholars about whether events on the ground in Sudan constituted genocide, and the U.S. House of Representatives voted unanimously that this was the case.[43] The Security Council, with resolution 1564, invited the Secretary-General to create the Independent Commission of Inquiry on Darfur to investigate whether genocide was occurring in Sudan, and while the commission stopped short of calling the violence genocide, it did find that serious crimes were being committed. This eventually led the Security Council to refer the matter to the International Criminal Court (ICC), a remarkable occurrence given the U.S. antagonism to the ICC.[44] The ICC has since issued indictments against two Sudanese officials for their role in the conflict. In 2008, the ICC prosecutor sought an indictment against Sudanese President Omar Hassan al-Bashir, given his noncooperation regarding the first two indictments. The ruling by a panel of judges was likely to add to an already controversial course of action, especially when fuel was added to the fire in March 2009 with an arrest warrant for the sitting president. Some critics question the wisdom of such an indictment when UN and AU officials are seeking more cooperation and consent from Sudan concerning additional security operations in the field. This, of course, has been a common bone of contention since Nuremberg between those who seek to turn a page on conflict and those who view impunity as a longer-run threat to a society. Some even criticized the fact that African states were the main target for the ICC's attention.

In 2005 Security Council resolution 1590 created the United Nations Mission in Sudan (UNMIS) to monitor the Comprehensive Peace Agreement signed between rebel groups and the Sudanese government. The main thrust of the agreement was to end hostilities in southern Sudan, but it was also seen as a framework for ending hostilities throughout Sudan including Darfur. UNMIS was also tasked with providing political and logistical support to the floundering AMIS with the hopes of stabilizing peacekeeping operations.[45] The mandate of UNMIS includes protecting civilians; however, its primary operations are in southern Sudan, where a relative peace prevails and the civilian population is not at risk.

The Security Council was, and remains, deeply divided between members who want to authorize a more forceful UN response and those members, such as Russia and China, who are wary of infringing on Sudanese sovereignty, which is augmented by their desire to protect their commercial (oil and arms) interests. As such, most of the Darfur resolutions passed by the Security Council have been watered down so that a consensus could be reached. Still, the Security Council was able to place limited, but targeted, sanctions on certain individuals and authorize an arms embargo and no-fly zone.[46] The government of Sudan has resisted accepting UN peacekeepers, claiming that the deployment of a peacekeeping force would amount to a Western recolonization of Sudan, an argument that still resonates with many developing countries. As a compromise, Sudan accepted a small, underfunded, and poorly equipped AU mission. UNMIS was accepted later only because its principal task is to monitor the cease-fire created by the Comprehensive Peace Agreement and to "support" AMIS. In 2006, the Security Council, in resolution 1706, in theory expanded the scope, military troop levels, and mandate of UNMIS. The intent was to deploy UN peacekeepers to Darfur; however, in a Security Council compromise, the resolution also called for Sudan's consent. Needless to say, the government of Sudan never gave its consent and limited progress has been made to protect civilians in Darfur.

The UN's supporting role did pave the way for an unprecedented hybrid peacekeeping force between the UN and the African Union. With its July 2007 resolution 1769, the Security Council finally authorized the creation of a more robust peacekeeping force, armed with a mandate to protect civilians. This new peacekeeping operation, called United Nations/African Union Mission in Darfur (UNAMID) involves folding in AMIS forces and beefing up the entire mission to include 26,000 people, most of whom are to be uniformed military and a few thousand police personnel. The resolution authorized the United Nations to assume peacekeeping duties in Darfur on the last day of December. If and when UNAMID reaches full strength, it will be the largest peacekeeping in UN history with a price tag to match. Nearly $1.5 billion was authorized for the one-year period from July 2007 to July 2008. Its existence is seen by some as an early success for Secretary-General Ban Ki-moon, who is largely credited with gaining China's acquiescence to the mission.[47]

Unfortunately, UNAMID did not get off to a good start. Khartoum appointed alleged war criminal Ahmad Harun to coordinate and oversee the deployment of UNAMID, suggesting the government's disdain for international opinion and

Chinese Engineers working for the United Nations/African Union Mission in Darfur (UNAMID) unload their equipment kits upon arrival in Nyala, Sudan. (UN Photo # 190255/Stuart Price)

for a strong UN presence in Darfur. In late 2008 the force was still less than half strength (with 7,000 soldiers coming from the beleaguered AU mission already in Darfur) and without the necessary logistical and communications support. In addition, Sudan also objected to non-Muslim and non-African contingents and kept changing the terms of the mission. UNAMID also came under fire from Sudanese government forces and by various rebel factions. Seven UNAMID peacekeepers were killed in a rebel ambush in July 2008. As a result and after the ICC prosecutor sought the indictment against al-Bashir in August 2008, UNAMID convoys were attacked by government forces. In what many saw as a textbook case for the "responsibility to protect," the new norm seemed very much in question if moral rhetoric and political reality were so distinct.

CONCLUSION: THE RESPONSIBILITY TO PROTECT

The status of the R2P norm eight years after it was unveiled by the ICISS is at best cloudy. The track record of UN security activities in the early part of the twenty-first century confirms this. On the one hand, the UN has fielded significant security operations in some of the world's most troubled hot spots and saved and improved the lives of civilians. Often this has been done with the "coerced consent" of the parties involved—e.g., Serbia in Kosovo and Indonesia in East Timor. At the end of 2008, the United Nations was engaged in sixteen peacekeeping operations and twelve additional peace-related field missions. When already authorized missions have been fully deployed, well over 110,000 uniformed personnel will be in the field from some 120 troop-contributing member states.

On the other hand, important states such as China and Russia, along with many developing countries, have created a backlash against the responsibility to protect, as is clearly evident in the case of Darfur. Despite the norm's approval of paragraphs 138 and 139 of the *World Summit Outcome Document*,[48] evidence of "buyer's remorse" continues to surface in New York, as some of the "usual suspects" who are uneasy with any incursions into human rights are up in arms and trying to argue that the emerging norm is no longer emerging and should not be described as having emerged.[49]

Civil society's norm entrepreneurs can make a difference, which requires R2P supporters to advocate for an alternative vision that is intellectually and doctrinally coherent and clearly expressed. The long-term goal is protecting the essence of the R2P norm such that it triggers effective action to save lives from mass atrocities. The more immediate goal is ensuring that R2P supporters influence the purpose and tenor of any debate on R2P in the General Assembly so that the 2005 agreement is not weakened. The Secretary-General's promising July 2008 speech in Berlin was followed by a disappointing laundry list instead of a strategy in a document to the General Assembly early in 2009.[50] This document was followed by a lengthy debate within the assembly that was postponed several times but finally took place in July 2009. While the usual suspects sought to raise the usual concerns, there was no normative rollback; the agreement from the World Summit remained intact.

The R2P notion is complex and multifaceted. Earlier in discussing the need for conceptual clarity, we saw that some observers hope the responsibility to protect can be a springboard for all international responses to prevent and resolve armed conflicts, while others see it as a framework for international efforts to protect civilians, and still others as a framework for military intervention. Whatever else, R2P is fundamentally about overriding sovereignty when mass atrocities occur, and so the concept will always be contested. Diplomatic efforts to keep all of the countries happy all of the time is a fool's errand.

And so, it is important to place these developments within a historical context.[51] With the possible exception of the prevention of genocide after World War II, no idea has moved faster or farther in the international normative arena than the responsibility to protect. It was not so long ago, in 1995 for example, that the Commission on Global Governance proposed amending the UN Charter to explicitly permit Chapter VII military action with a humanitarian justification.[52] The recommendation was moot, however, as we have seen in the previous chapter and this one. Since the interventions of the 1990s the Security Council has clearly recognized that massive suffering constitutes a sufficient threat to international peace and security to justify forceful action. José Alvarez observes the acceleration in the usual pace for normative development: "Traditional descriptions of the requisites of custom—the need for the passage of a considerable period of time and the accumulation of evidence of the diplomatic practices between sets of states reacting to one another's acts—appear increasingly passé."[53]

At the same time, the Security Council's painful dithering since early 2003 over large-scale murder and massive displacement in Darfur or the collective foot-dragging in the Congo after some 5 million war-related deaths also demonstrates, at the very least, the dramatic disconnect between multilateral rhetoric and reality.[54] However, normative developments and political reality are rarely in synch. Sometimes norm entrepreneurs scramble to keep up with events, and sometimes they are ahead of them.[55] In this case, the humanitarian interventions in northern Iraq in 1991 and Somalia in 1992 were agreed on by the UN before there was any significant discussion of conditioning state sovereignty on human rights. Plotting the growing consensus about R2P on a graph would thus reflect a steady growth since the early 1990s, whereas the operational capacity and political will to engage in humanitarian intervention—like the transformed humanitarian system[56]—would seem to be on a roller coaster. Hence, the 2005 World Summit marked the zenith of international normative consensus about R2P, on the one hand. But the blowback from 9/11 and the war in Iraq, along with the absence of military capacity besides the American one, which is tied down, explains the current nadir in actual humanitarian intervention—the contemporary manifestation of what one of us earlier called "collective spinelessness" in the Balkans.[57] It may turn out to be the case that President George W. Bush was genuinely concerned about Darfur, but being bogged down in both Iraq and Afghanistan, he was unable to exercise the kind of leadership his father had shown regarding Somalia in 1992.

What is perhaps most important is the reconceptualization of state sovereignty—from an absolute barrier to outside action, to the duty to protect human rights and respect human security. After centuries of more or less passive and mindless acceptance of the proposition that state sovereignty was a license to kill and repress, it is now clear that sovereigns have the duty to govern responsibly. We are at the dawn of a new normative era, but in the dusk of the most bullish days of humanitarian intervention. As in other arenas, actions speak louder than words. And in this latter regard, the international response to Burmese policy in the wake of a devastating cyclone in May 2008 can only give pause. That military government was clearly insensitive to the humanitarian needs of many of its coastal citizens who were further impoverished and sometimes displaced by natural disaster, after tens of thousands had been killed. Yet important outsiders like China were not much interested in compelling the government to act on behalf of those in need, so the government's sluggish response continued for some time. This insensitivity involved the refusal to give permission to U.S. Navy vessels and others waiting offshore for permission to provide assistance. The ships eventually sailed away for lack of sovereign consent, although the predicted mass starvation and disease did not transpire.

In short, we can say that the R2P norm has moved quickly but that the concept is young. The Secretary-General's special advisor with an R2P portfolio, Edward Luck, provides a note of caution: "Like most infants, R2P will need to walk before it can run."[58] We see that R2P is an idea, and we should remind ourselves that ideas matter, for good and for ill. Political theorist Daniel Philpott's study of revolutions in sovereignty demonstrates that they are driven primarily by the power of ideas,[59] and we are in the midst of a revolution in which state sovereignty is becoming more contingent on upholding basic human rights values. Gareth Evans encourages us in his new book on the subject: "And for all the difficulties of acceptance and application that lie ahead, there are—I have come optimistically, but firmly, to believe—not many ideas that have the potential to matter more for good, not only in theory but in practice, than that of the responsibility to protect."[60]

NOTES

1. International Commission on Intervention and State Sovereignty, *The Responsibility to Protect: Report* (Ottawa: ICISS, 2001). See also Thomas G. Weiss and Don Hubert, *The Responsibility to Protect: Research, Bibliography, and Background* (Ottawa: ICISS, 2001). For scholarly reviews of the implications, see Adam Roberts, "The Price of Protection," *Survival* 44, no. 4 (2002–2003): 157–161; Joelle Tanguy, "Redefining Sovereignty and Intervention," *Ethics & International Affairs* 17, no. 1 (2003): 141–148; Martha Finnemore, *The Purpose of Intervention: Changing Beliefs about the Use of Force* (Ithaca, N.Y.: Cornell University Press, 2003); Neta Crawford, *Argument and Change in World Politics: Ethics, Decolonization, and Humanitarian Intervention* (New York: Cambridge University Press, 2002); Fernando Tesón, *Humanitarian Intervention: An Inquiry into Law and Morality*, 3rd ed. (Ardsley, N.Y.: Transaction Publishers, 2005); J. L. Holzgrefe and Robert O. Keohane, eds., *Humanitarian Intervention: Ethical, Legal, and Political Dilemmas* (Cambridge: Cambridge University Press, 2003); and Alex Bellamy, *Responsibility to Protect: The Global Effort to End Mass Atrocities* (Cambridge, UK: Polity, 2009). For interpretations by some of the major participants, see Gareth Evans, *The Responsibility to Protect* (Washington, D.C.: Brookings Institution, 2008); Thomas G. Weiss, *Humanitarian Intervention: Ideas in Action* (Cambridge, UK: Polity, 2007); and Ramesh Thakur, *The United Nations, Peace and Security: From Collective Security to the Responsibility to Protect* (Cambridge: Cambridge University Press, 2006).

2. Annan, *Question*, and *"We, the Peoples": The United Nations in the 21st Century* (New York: United Nations, 2000). For a discussion of the controversy surrounding the September 1999 speech, see Thomas G. Weiss, "The Politics of Humanitarian Ideas," *Security Dialogue* 31, no. 1 (2000): 11–23.

3. For an overview, see Mohammed Ayoob, "Humanitarian Intervention and International Society," *Global Governance* 7, no. 3 (2001): 225–230; and Jackson, *The Global Covenant*.

4. Christine Bourloyannis, "The Security Council of the United Nations and the Implementation of International Humanitarian Law," *Denver Journal of International Law and Policy* 20, no. 3 (1993): 43.

5. Th. A. van Baarda, "The Involvement of the Security Council in Maintaining International Law," *Netherlands Quarterly of Human Rights* 12, no. 1 (1994): 140.

6. Annan, *Question*, 39.

7. Inter-Agency Standing Committee, "Working Paper on the Definition of Complex Emergency" (December 1994), in *Humanitarian Report 1997*, by the Department of Humanitarian Affairs, United Nations (New York: United Nations, 1997), 9.

8. Robert D. Kaplan, "The Coming Anarchy," *Atlantic Monthly* 273, no. 2 (1994): 44–76, and *The Ends of the Earth: A Journey at the Dawn of the 21st Century* (New York: Random House, 1996).

9. John Gerard Ruggie, *The United Nations and the Collective Use of Force: Whither? or Whether?* (New York: United Nations Association of the USA, 1996), 1. See also Niels Blokker and Nico Schrijver, eds., *The Security Council and the Use of Force—A Need for Change?* (Leiden, Netherlands: Martinus Nijhoff, 2005).

10. Michael Mandelbaum, "The Reluctance to Intervene," *Foreign Policy* 95 (Summer 1994): 11.

11. Brahimi is the former Algerian foreign minister and experienced UN troubleshooter who ended up as the special representative in Afghanistan to follow up the Bonn agreements.

12. Giandomenico Picco, "The U.N. and the Use of Force," *Foreign Affairs* 73, no. 5 (1994): 15. See also his *Man Without a Gun* (New York: Random House, 1999).

13. Fen Osler Hampson, *Nurturing Peace: Why Peace Settlements Succeed or Fail* (Washington, D.C.: U.S. Institute of Peace Press, 1996), 226. See also William I. Zartman, *Elusive Peace: Negotiating an End to Civil Wars* (Washington, D.C.: Brookings Institution, 1995).

14. James Dobbins, *The UN's Role in Nation-building: From Congo to Iraq* (Santa Monica, Calif.: Rand Corporation, 2005).

15. U Thant, *View from the U.N.* (Garden City, N.Y.: Doubleday, 1978), 32.

16. Ian Johnstone, ed., *Global Peace Operations 2007* (Boulder, Colo.: Lynne Rienner, 2007), 22–232; this publication is now annual.

17. Annan, *Report on the Fall of Srebrenica*, document A54/549, November 15, 1999; *Report of the Independent Inquiry into the Actions of the United Nations During the 1994 Genocide in Rwanda*, document S/1999/1257, December 15, 1999; and *Report of the Panel of Experts on Violations of Security Council Sanctions Against UNITA*, document S/2000/203, March 10, 2000.

18. See Michael Pugh and W. Pal Singh Sidhu, eds., *The United Nations and Regional Security: Europe and Beyond* (Boulder, Colo.: Lynne Rienner, 2003); Thomas G. Weiss, ed., *Beyond UN Subcontracting: Task-Sharing with Regional Security Arrangements and Service-Providing NGOs* (London: Macmillan, 1998); and William B. Tow, *Subregional Security Cooperation in the Third World* (Boulder, Colo.: Lynne Rienner, 1990).

19. Independent Commission on Kosovo, *Kosovo Report: Conflict, International Response, Lessons Learned* (Oxford: Oxford University Press, 2000).

20. *Financial Times*, October 8, 1998.

21. Kofi A. Annan, "Secretary-General's Speech to the 54th Session of the General Assembly," September 20, 1999. This and other speeches on humanitarian intervention are published in *The Question of Intervention: Statements by the Secretary-General* (New York: United Nations, 1999).

22. UN Press Release SG/SM/6878, January 28, 1999.

23. Adam Roberts, "NATO's 'Humanitarian War' in Kosovo," *Survival* 41, no. 3 (1999): 102–123.

24. See the report by Human Rights Watch at www.hrw.org/english/docs/2004/07/27/serbia9136.htm.

25. For a summary of the status of negotiations, see www.un.org/radio/print_all.asp?NewsDate=12/10/2007.

26. The European Union is divided, with Greece, Italy, Cyprus, Romania, and Spain opposing recognition of Kosovo if it issues a unilateral declaration of independence. Moreover, many in Europe see the status of Kosovo as a proxy for U.S.-Russian relations, which may change with new leadership in both countries. For a succinct analysis, see Dan Bilefksy, "Time Is Running Out," *International Herald Tribune*, November 6, 2007, 5.

27. See Neil MacFarquhar, "Serbia Wins Bid to Review Independence of Kosovo," *New York Times*, October 9, 2008.

28. In 1975, the Portuguese government announced it would relinquish its remaining colonies, which included East and West Timor. A civil war broke out and rebels in East Timor declared formal independence. Indonesia, which exercises sovereignty over much of the archipelago, invaded East Timor shortly after the declaration and annexed it as its twenty-seventh province, spurring an armed resistance to Indonesian rule. For an overview of the East Timor crisis, see http://news.bbc.co.uk/go/pr/-/1/hi/world/asia-pacific/country_profiles/1504243.stm.

29. See Michael G. Smith with Moreen Dee, *Peacekeeping in East Timor: The Path to Independence* (Boulder, Colo.: Lynne Rienner, 2003).

30. For an overview of UN peacekeeping in Sierra Leone, see Funmi Olonisakin, *Peacekeeping in Sierra Leone: The Story of UNAMSIL* (Boulder, Colo.: Lynne Rienner, 2008).

31. For an overview of the UK intervention, see http://news.bbc.co.uk/2/hi/africa/country_profiles/1065898.stm.

32. See David Curran and Tom Woodhouse, "Cosmopolitan Peacekeeping and Peacebuilding in Sierra Leone: What Can Africa Contribute?" in *International Affairs* 83, no. 6 (2007): 1055–1070.

33. See Thierry Tardy, "The UN and the Use of Force: A Marriage Against Nature," *Security Dialogue* 38 (March 2007): 49–70.

34. Sandra Whitworth, *Men, Militarism and UN Peacekeeping: A Gendered Analysis* (Boulder: Colo.: Lynne Rienner, 2004).

35. For the full report, see General Assembly document A/61/901 and Security Council S/2007/269 at www.mofa.go.jp/mofaj/gaiko/peace_b/pdfs/sil_070514_missionrep.pdf.

36. Colum Lynch, "France Declines to Contribute Major Force for UN Mission," *Washington Post*, August 16, 2006, available at www.washingtonpost.com/wp-dyn/content/article/2006/08/17/AR2006081700813.html.

37. www.un.org/Depts/dpko/missions/unifil/facts.html.

38. David Axe, "UN Adds Bulk to Peacekeeping Forces in Lebanon," *Aviation Week*, February 7, 2007, available at www.aviationweek.com/aw/generic/story_generic.jsp?channel=dti&id=news/dtLEB0207.xml.

39. Yaakov Yatz, "Israel Fears European Powers Might Downsize from UNIFIL; Troops Are Said to Be Busier Protecting Themselves than Tackling Hizbullah," *Jerusalem Post*, November 9, 2007, 3.

40. For an interesting discussion of the "peacekeeping syndrome," see Andrzej Sitkowski, *UN Peacekeeping: Myth and Reality* (Westport, Conn.: Praeger Security International, 2006).

41. This is the assessment of Secretary-General Kofi Annan and the UN. See "Annan Demands Darfur Resolution" at http://news.bbc.co.uk/2/hi/africa/4327693.stm.

42. The civil war paused between 1979 and 1983.

43. See, for example, Scott Strauss, "Darfur and the Genocide Debate," *Foreign Affairs* 84 (2005): 123–133; Noelle Quenivet, "The Report of the International Commission of Inquiry on Darfur: The Question of Genocide," *Human Rights Review* 7 (July 2006): 38–68; Gerard Prunier, *Darfur: the Ambiguous Genocide* (Ithaca, N.Y.: Cornell University Press, 2007).

44. See Corrina Heyder, "The U.N. Security Council's Referral of the Crimes in Darfur to the International Criminal Court in Light of U.S. Opposition to the Court," *Berkeley Journal of International Law* 24 (2006): 650–671.

45. www.unmis.org/english/Q-A.htm.

46. For an excellent overview of Security Council deliberations, see Alex J. Bellamy and Paul D. Williams, "The UN Security Council and the Question of Humanitarian Intervention in Darfur," *Journal of Military Ethics* 5 (June 2006): 144–160.

47. "The Rewards of Beavering Away," *The Economist*, January 3, 2008, available at www.economist.com/world/international/displaystory.cfm?story_id=10438482.

48. 2005 World Summit Outcome, UN document A/60/1, October 24, 2005, paras. 138–139.

49. This conclusion draws on Thomas G. Weiss, "Political Innovations and the Responsibility to Protect," in *Deeper Causes of Forced Migration and Systemic Response,* ed. David Hollenbach (Washington, D.C.: Georgetown University Press, forthcoming).

50. Ban Ki-moon, "Implementing the Responsibility to Protect, Report from the Secretary-General," UN document A/63/677, January 12, 2009; and Ban, "Address of the Secretary-General, Berlin, 15 July 2008," UN document SG/SM/11701.

51. See Thomas G. Weiss, "R2P after 9/11 and after the World Summit," *Wisconsin International Law Journal* 25, no. 1 (2006): 741–760.

52. Commission on Global Governance, *Our Global Neighbourhood* (Oxford: Oxford University Press, 1995), 90.

53. José E. Alvarez, *International Organizations as Law-makers* (Oxford: Oxford University Press, 2005), 591.

54. Hugo Slim, "Dithering over Darfur? A Preliminary Review of the International Response," *International Affairs* 80, no. 5 (2004): 811–833. See also Cheryl O. Igiri and Princeton N. Lyman, *Giving Meaning to "Never Again": Seeking an Effective Response to the Crisis in Darfur and Beyond* (New York: Council on Foreign Relations, 2004), CFR No. 5.

55. Martha Finnemore and Kathryn Sikkink, "International Norm Dynamics and Political Change," *International Organization* 52, no. 4 (1998): 887–917.

56. Michael Barnett, "Humanitarianism Transformed," *Perspectives on Politics* 3, no. 4 (2005): 723–740. See also Michael Barnett and Thomas G. Weiss, eds., *Humanitarianism in Question: Politics, Power, Ethics* (Ithaca, N.Y.: Cornell University Press, 2008).

57. Thomas G. Weiss, "Collective Spinelessness: U.N. Actions in the Former Yugoslavia," in *The World and Yugoslavia's Wars*, ed. Richard H. Ullman (New York: Council on Foreign Relations, 1996), 59–96.

58. Edward C. Luck, "The United Nations and the Responsibility to Protect," *Policy Analysis Brief* (Muscatine, Iowa: Stanley Foundation, 2008), 8.

59. Daniel Philpott, *Revolutions in Sovereignty: How Ideas Shaped Modern International Relations* (Princeton, N.J.: Princeton University Press, 2001).

60. Evans, *The Responsibility to Protect,* 7.

CHAPTER 5

The Challenges of the Twenty-First Century

I N LOOKING AHEAD to future security operations, we retain our focus on
the political dynamics that have propelled UN activities and will continue to
do so. The political landscape, which reappears in the next two parts of this volume, helps us situate whether and how the world organization can respond to
contemporary security challenges that confront both member states and the secretariat, or what we called at the outset "the two United Nations." We begin with
a lengthy look at September 11 and terrorism, weapons of mass destruction, and
the war against Iraq, crucial events for the world organization, as well as for the
United States.[1]

AFTER SEPTEMBER 11, WHAT'S NEW?

A few days after the tragic attacks on New York and Washington in September
2001, which killed some 3,000 civilians—twice the number of combatants who
died in the Japanese attack on Pearl Harbor in December 1941—Secretary-
General Kofi Annan outlined the relevance of the topic: "Terrorism is a global
menace. It calls for a united, global response. To defeat it, all nations must take
counsel together, and act in unison. That is why we have the United Nations."[2]

In addition to drawing the world's attention to the issue of terrorism, the
events of September 11 brought into sharper focus the post–Cold War world's
problem of disarmament, proliferation, and regulation of weapons of mass destruction (WMD). The possibility that terrorist groups could get their hands on
WMDs emerged as yet another critical security concern on the world body's
agenda. Moreover, the possibility of rogue regimes' allying themselves with terrorist groups—exemplified by the United States' tenuous and ultimately erro-
neous linkage of Saddam Hussein and Al Qaeda—renders the issue of WMDs
even more urgent. The security threats posed by terrorism and WMDs figure
prominently on the radar screens of UN member states.

111

Terrorism

Until the 1990s terrorism was dealt with almost entirely by the General Assembly, which approached the issue as a general problem of international law rather than one relating to specific events or conflicts. The twelve existing UN conventions related to terrorism identify particular forms of outlawed action but contain no definition of terrorism per se.[3] The lack of consensus among member states about the definitional issue exposes a rift in the world organization. It also explains at least in part why the UN has not been central to this problem. The UN can act only when its members allow it to act, on the basis of agreed ends and means.

The struggle over how to define terrorism is affected by many concerns of various states, such as their wanting to protect the option of small-scale and supposedly nonstate violent resistance to foreign occupation, like the French resistance against Nazi Germany in the 1940s. Other states want to protect the option of using small-scale and supposedly nonstate force to harass what they see as unjust domination, as the American colonists did early on against their British masters.

Reaching broad transnational agreement on the definition of terrorism is no easy matter. Some states may find it useful to oppose the terrorism du jour, but they also want to preserve their freedom in choosing force in the future.[4] There always have been two main sticking points: The first was captured by the expression "your terrorist is my freedom fighter"—that is, many developing countries justify armed violence by those fighting for national liberation. The second was whether "state terrorism" should be included in any definition agreed on by the vast majority of member states—some uses of force by Israeli and more recently U.S. forces, resulting in civilian casualties, for many, is mentioned in the same breath as suicide bombers.

Significantly, the UN's High-level Panel on Threats, Challenges and Change confronted head-on these traditional stumbling blocks: "Attacks that specifically target innocent civilians and non-combatants must be condemned clearly and unequivocally by all."[5] The Secretary-General added, "The proposal has clear moral force."[6] While the final text from the 2005 World Summit lacked a clear definition of terrorism, for the first time in UN history the heads of state and government issued an unqualified condemnation. They agreed to "strongly condemn terrorism in all forms and manifestations, committed by whomever, wherever and for whatever purposes."[7] However, the final text also eliminated earlier and clearer language that making targets of civilians could not be justified—even for movements resisting occupation. On balance, the summit added momentum to the Secretary-General's evolving counterterrorism strategy. The summit's clear condemnation of terrorism was a step forward, fully consistent with the laws of war. It has ethical content, contains the basis for a future treaty that would reinforce existing humanitarian law, and places the UN near the center of the fight against terrorism—at least in terms of important norms if not operational decisions.

Several points have become clear over the years. Attacks on civilians who take no active part in hostilities are prohibited by international humanitarian law, specifically the 1949 Geneva Conventions and Additional Protocols of 1977. Various other treaties prohibit attacks on diplomats and the interference with civilian aircraft. Thus, the international community of states can and has reached agreement on prohibited targets of violence, thereby bypassing disagreement on an all-encompassing definition of terrorism.

The Security Council became more focused on terrorism, primarily at the instigation of the United States and in response to events: several aerial incidents in the late 1980s, including the downing of a Pan American flight over Lockerbie, Scotland; the attempted assassination of Egyptian president Hosni Mubarak in 1995; and the bombings of U.S. embassies in East Africa in 1998. In each case, the Security Council responded by imposing sanctions against states like Libya, Sudan, and Afghanistan for refusing to extradite suspects. Sanctions contributed to curbing state terrorism by Libya and Sudan; however, they were ineffective in altering the behavior of the Taliban and Al Qaeda because such groups "situate themselves outside of the international system and reject its institutions and norms."[8]

The Security Council's approach changed in the aftermath of September 11. Whereas states like Israel, Spain, Germany, and others had experienced terrorism in the past, this time the remaining superpower had been attacked. The council acted immediately and endorsed measures ranging from approval of the use of force in self-defense to requiring member states to undertake wide-ranging and comprehensive measures against terrorism. Previously an issue drawing inconsistent attention from both the General Assembly and the Security Council, terrorism quickly became a persistent and systematic focus at the UN.

The council's responses are noteworthy. Resolution 1368, passed the day after the attacks on U.S. territory, recognized "the inherent right of individual or collective self-defense." This was the first time that the right to self-defense was formally recognized as a legitimate response to nonstate violence. A few weeks later, the Security Council passed a comprehensive resolution outlining a series of wide-ranging measures to be undertaken by states to "prevent and suppress" terrorist acts. Resolution 1373 detailed the requirements for member states, including changes to national legislation. The resolution established the Counter-Terrorism Committee (CTC) to monitor member-state implementation of these measures. Once again the council shrunk the domain of purely domestic affairs, in that national legislation involving tax laws for contributions to charities was subjected to international monitoring and mandates. And the Security Council went further in resolution 1540, unsettling some states as well as international lawyers by using Chapter VII to call upon states to enact national legislation

President George W. Bush and Secretary-General Kofi Annan at Ground
Zero in New York City. (UN/DPI photo)

intended to prohibit nonstate actors from acquiring WMDs. Resolution 1540
also mandated that states detail to the Security Council, through a committee,
their legislative and administrative efforts to curb the proliferation of WMDs.

The General Assembly's work in developing international conventions on terrorism, while subsequently overshadowed by the Security Council, remains important. The most significant advantage of the assembly is that it is an inclusive
forum involving all member states. It is also the place where decisions about al-
locating organizational resources are made, thus giving it a direct impact on determining the administrative capability of the world organization to deal with
terrorism. Still, this organizational capacity is greatly affected by the political will
of member states. Thus, codification of emerging norms can perhaps better take
place in a forum that can take a comprehensive, politically informed, and longer-
term view.

The Secretary-General and the Secretariat also play roles. The Secretary-
General has the ability to take a less reactive, more comprehensive approach.
After September 11, Kofi Annan established a Policy Working Group on terrorism to examine how the UN should deal with the phenomenon.[9] In September
2006, the General Assembly agreed to the UN Global Counter-Terrorism Strategy, which enables the UN to take a more coordinated approach to combating
terrorism by building state capacity. Most of the heavy lifting in implementing
the strategy is done by the Counter-Terrorism Task Force, which is chaired by the
Office of the Secretary-General. Ban Ki-moon has made combating terrorism a

priority for his office and, in February 2007, launched an online handbook on counterterrorism to help states, agencies, and regional organizations coordinate operations.[10]

Despite much discourse to the contrary, how the United Nations might have dealt with Iraq was only tangentially connected with Washington's so-called war on terrorism. The U.S. decision to go to war with Iraq in March 2003 related more to regime change, compliance with Security Council resolutions, the question of Iraq's possible possession of WMDs prohibited by the UN, and the demonstration of U.S. military might than to Iraqi terrorism against the United States. The government of Saddam Hussein had undoubtedly supported violence against the state of Israel via groups like Hamas. Yet, no evidence has surfaced linking Iraq to the attacks on New York and Washington, or indicating any substantial links to Al Qaeda. Moreover, the terrorist groups known to exist in Iraq at the time, such as Ansar al-Islam, were Kurdish groups outside the effective control of Hussein and were operating in the American-imposed northern "no-fly zone."

WMDs

The UN's efforts to grapple with the threats to world peace posed by weapons of mass destruction extend back to the founding of the world body. Although absent from the Charter, eliminating atomic weapons arsenals and other weapons adaptable to mass destruction was the centerpiece of the General Assembly's first resolution, passed in 1946.[11] The long-standing efforts of the "two UNs" to regulate WMDs have met varying degrees of success in at least two ways.

First, the UN is a forum for negotiations among states, for example, through the General Assembly and its First Committee, and the Conference on Disarmament, which is not formally part of the UN but reports to the assembly and is staffed by UN officials.[12] Among the major treaties concluded under UN auspices is the 1968 Nuclear Non-Proliferation Treaty (NPT). The only countries that have not joined the regime are India, Pakistan, and Israel, and in 2003 North Korea withdrew. In addition to North Korea, the United States identified Iran and Hussein's Iraq as recalcitrant states—together composing what George W. Bush termed "the axis of evil."

The NPT rests on an asymmetric agreement between nuclear and nonnuclear states, committing the former to complete disarmament and the latter to forgo the acquisition of nuclear weapons capabilities. The lack of progress on the disarmament side of the equation reveals the overall lack of commitment from nuclear powers to eliminate their stockpiles. September 11 generated increased emphasis, especially by the United States, on nonproliferation. In particular, it shined a spotlight on the possibility of "rogue regimes" acquiring nuclear capabilities. At the same time, the Bush administration explored vertical proliferation and new roles for WMD in the fight against terrorism. As Nina Tannenwald has noted, "Arms control, for the time being . . . appears to have trumped disarmament."[13]

In addition to the NPT, other major treaties include the 1972 Biological Toxins and Weapons Convention, the 1993 Chemical Weapons Convention, and the Comprehensive Test Ban Treaty, which the General Assembly adopted in 1996 but has not yet entered into force.

The UN also has a limited role in directly implementing arms control and disarmament. It collaborates with the International Atomic Energy Agency (IAEA), which conducts inspections to verify that nuclear materials and activities are not used for military purposes. As well the UN works with the Organization for the Prohibition of Chemical Weapons and the Preparatory Commission for the Comprehensive Nuclear-Test-Ban Treaty Organization.

The UN has also engaged in coercive disarmament, particularly with regard to Iraq. After the Gulf War of 1990–1991, the Security Council passed resolution 687—requiring Iraq to declare its WMD programs and facilities—imposed sanctions, and established intrusive weapons inspections bodies, such as the UN Special Commission (UNSCOM). UNSCOM uncovered nuclear, chemical, and biological weapons programs and oversaw the destruction of Iraq's chemical weapons and facilities as well as the country's biological weapons industry. UNSCOM's activities, however, were compromised by not only Iraqi deception but also its association with the CIA, which led the Hussein regime to expel the commission and ban IAEA inspections in 1998. This brought to the forefront the issue of the autonomy of multilateral monitoring organizations that lack their own intelligence-gathering capacity. Subsequently the UN Monitoring, Verification, and Inspection Commission (UNMOVIC) was established and began a round of renewed weapons inspections in 2002, after a three-year hiatus.

By the end of 2002, the United States was determined to overthrow Saddam Hussein on the premise that his regime had violated previous council resolutions and was engaging in the development of WMDs—which could potentially fall into the hands of terrorist groups, particularly Al Qaeda. Britain sided with the United States, but France, Russia, and China staunchly opposed the use of force to disarm Iraq without the passage of more time and without an additional resolution from the Security Council.

The debate at the UN about how to deal appropriately with Iraq reflects the nature of power and how it manifests in the world organization—and world politics more generally. In a world where the sole superpower was attacked by a non-state actor, the struggle over resolutions in the Security Council and the publication of a new doctrine of a very broad anticipatory self-defense, or preventive, war (incorrectly, in international legal terms, dubbed "preemption" by U.S. officials),[14] is relevant to assessing the role of international law and the UN. Also relevant is the United States' and Great Britain's taking forceful action without UN authorization and the U.S. declaration of a goal of "regime change" in Iraq. The interplay of law and politics is part and parcel of understanding the UN's role in world affairs.

The U.S. invocation of self-defense against terrorism in response to September 11, and its military campaign in Afghanistan to dislodge a government that was intertwined with a terrorist network, was approved by the council. The U.S. focus on WMDs in Iraq that might be put at the disposal of terrorists was placed within the framework of previous UN resolutions, thus indicating that traditional concerns about state security are by no means incompatible with international law and organization. Up to this point, basic U.S. foreign policy was largely consistent with and supportive of international law and the UN. Moreover, President George W. Bush was persuaded by British Prime Minister Tony Blair and U.S. Secretary of State Colin Powell to return to the council in the fall of 2002, even after the United States had started its military buildup in the Persian Gulf during the summer. These actions indicate that the United Nations still matters and that obtaining international legitimacy through UN endorsement still counts for something, even to the United States, whose government under the George W. Bush administration believed in doctrinaire unilateralism.[15]

The rest of the story about Iraq and the UN in 2003 demonstrates that a fundamental point had not changed since 1945, namely that the members of the Security Council need to be in agreement for it to be effective, diplomatically and militarily.[16] The council was in agreement up to a point, demanding Iraqi compliance with previous disarmament resolutions and stating in resolution 1441 that serious consequences would follow upon further noncompliance. The United States tried to get the council to state that the time for diplomacy had ended and that military responses were in order. But Washington was unable to muster the nine votes for its draft resolution (cosponsored by Britain and Spain), much less counter an expected veto of its proposal by France, Russia, and China. In fact, except for the United States, Britain, Spain, and perhaps Bulgaria, votes for war were hard to find in the council. This was a remarkable development, because in the fall of 2001 the council had endorsed U.S. military strikes on the Taliban government in Afghanistan, which had supported the Al Qaeda network, and in fall 2002, the council had unanimously called for Iraq's rapid disarmament or it would face "serious consequences."

States like France and Russia did not believe that the United States had demonstrated a substantial link between Iraq and the terrorist attacks on New York and the Pentagon. The Bush administration's argument that in the future Saddam Hussein might cooperate with terrorists in some type of attack on the United States seemed too amorphous for many states to justify an invasion of Iraq. These dissenting states were troubled by this new Bush doctrine, namely a broad notion of preventive war. This hesitation is understandable. The Bush administration argued that it alone would determine what government, because of its own actions or through state-supported terrorism, would be targeted by the extremely powerful U.S. military. This was too much for council members like Chile and Mexico, even though their governments were basically friendly toward the United States.

The U.S. stance was controversial and departed from the notion in international law of a limited preemption doctrine that might be appropriate when threats were immediate and overwhelming, leaving no time for further diplomacy. This approach, articulated in the nineteenth century by U.S. Secretary of State Daniel Webster in the *Caroline* affair—when Canadian loyalists to the British crown destroyed a U.S. ship that was being used to supply arms and other provisions to Canadian rebels—was replaced by the Bush administration with the much broader standard of a possible and distant threat. This latter standard was not in line with customary international legal norms and not a doctrine that many states wanted the council to endorse in the Iraqi case.[17] These critical states saw the Bush doctrine of so-called preemption as a large Pandora's box. Would, for example, Russia have the unilateral right to use force in a neighboring state with no role for other states or the UN?

There were other complications. Based on the reasonably successful earlier efforts at monitoring in Iraq,[18] the council had created a new weapons inspection regime centered on UNMOVIC for chemical and biological weapons, and on the IAEA for nuclear weapons. These two UN agencies, one ad hoc and one permanent, had elicited some cooperation from Saddam Hussein—in the context of a U.S. military buildup in the Persian Gulf that eventually reached about 300,000 soldiers. Many states wanted to avoid war by giving these UN inspection teams more time to work, whereas the United States and its allies, especially Britain, felt that Iraq could always evade the more important inspection efforts. Moreover, Washington was concerned that protracted diplomacy would undercut its military pressure. More than one state also thought the United States had always been more interested in removing the Saddam Hussein regime than in making serious arguments about homeland security. Indeed, both Clinton and Bush administration officials had talked of removing that regime even before the 9/11 attacks.

Many subplots were at work to fracture the Security Council over what to do about Iraq. Some observers thought that France was again deliberately taking anti-American positions and demonstrating a persistent effort to play the role of global power despite its limited economic and military capacity. Some thought that Russia was only too happy to make difficulties for a United States that had seemed disdainful of a major Russian role after the Cold War. Moreover, Russia had substantial economic interests both in Iraq and in a continued high price for oil, one of Russia's chief exports. Both France and Russia had businesses that benefited extensively from the $64 billion Oil-for-Food Programme. Germany, then a nonpermanent member, opposed U.S. policy in order to appeal to domestic public opinion and win elections—at least in the view of many commentators. Some thought the Bush administration was never interested in the type of multilateral diplomacy that constrained decision-making in Washington and that the Bush team simply wanted to use its power superiority to take out a "rogue state" and part of "the axis of evil"—even absent any substantial connection to Al Qaeda or any other group interested in attacks on the United States.

After all, most high officials in the Bush administration thought that the United States had lost the war in Southeast Asia (1954–1975) because of a failure to apply its hard power in a determined way. The "Vulcans" or "hawks" or "war cabinet" in the Bush administration were determined not to repeat what they saw as the central mistake of previous administrations.[19]

As on the question of Kosovo in 1999, the Security Council could not present a united front regarding Iraq in 2003. Unlike Kosovo, the United States could not fall back on the collective approval of the liberal democratic states making up NATO, because NATO was also divided over Iraq—as were the members of the European Union. The United States could only seek legitimization through a "coalition of the willing," albeit a less impressive one than had been mobilized in 1991 (to push Iraq from Kuwait) and 1999.[20]

The 2003 U.S. invasion of Iraq raised the question of the continued viability of the United Nations for maintaining or restoring international peace and security. U.S. officials sometimes said that the council had been irresponsible in not maintaining a tough line in keeping with the terms of resolution 1441 on the consequences of Iraq's failure to disarm. French officials sometimes said that a council that only rubber-stamped the dubious arguments of the United States would have no credibility in the eyes of the world. Many Third World countries clamored that the world organization was helpless to stand in the way of the hegemon and its partners. These views overstated the crisis because both with regard to Kosovo in 1999 and earlier with regard to northern Iraq in the spring of 1991, the United States and its allies had used military force without explicit Security Council approval—and the UN had not collapsed. Moreover, there is little or no evidence to indicate that the council's legitimacy was weakened by the stance member states took in March 2003. As one young scholar concluded, "International organisations remain crucial gatekeepers to international legitimacy for interstate military deployments."[21] And the United Nations is the most active, if not the only, such organization and its universal membership provides a unique source of legitimacy.

The question of the collective authorization of force is a perennial one in international relations, especially when an armed attack against a state has not occurred. In the future the council undoubtedly will be seized by similar questions. The Bush doctrine of preventive self-defense, when the alleged threat did not constitute a clear and present danger, is indeed difficult to square with the Charter paradigm for regulating force. In the final analysis, U.S. policy toward Iraq—which was linked to a "war" against terrorism—not UN politics within the Security Council, damaged the world organization and international law.[22] Even so, as the Bush team met serious difficulties in the occupation of Iraq and the follow-on transitional period, it became anxious for UN officials and agencies to reenter the picture in order to execute roles such as supervising elections. So U.S. doctrinaire unilateralism was somewhat tempered by recognition of at least some of the costs from that previous course of action and of the limits of raw military force. In a parallel move, the Bush administration welcomed an ex-panded role for NATO in Afghanistan in late 2005 and 2006, despite having re-jected such a role in late 2001—indeed, by 2008, Washington was complaining that many NATO members were unwilling to pay the price of being a member of the alliance, especially with boots on the ground in dangerous zones.

POLITICAL CHALLENGES

The United Nations faces several daunting political challenges that will deter-mine its effectiveness in the future. The first political challenge is that of leader-ship. U.S. decisions regarding Iraq and President Bush's controversial recess appointment of outspoken UN critic John Bolton in 2005 as the U.S. representa-tive to the UN raised serious questions about Washington's ability to provide constructive leadership at the UN at that critical juncture.[23] Without the support of the sole remaining superpower, the world body faced marginalization on is-sues relating to international security. Such leadership is necessary to build a rel-ative consensus regarding strategies for handling today's security problems: failed states, terrorism by nonstate actors, and secessionist movements dismem-bering existing states. Bolton was forced to leave his position after his recess ap-pointment expired in 2007, and Bush appointed Zalmay Khalilzad to the post. Khalilzad, the former U.S. ambassador to Afghanistan and Iraq, was far more polished and diplomatic than Bolton; however, he hailed from the same neocon-servative school that generally distrusts multilateralism.

The 2008 election of Barack Obama as the forty-forth president renewed hope that Washington would assume a constructive leadership role at the United Nations. President-elect Obama appointed his confidante Susan Rice as the U.S. representative to the UN and elevated that position to cabinet level. Washington may face a residue of bitterness at UN headquarters on First Avenue in Manhat-tan; nonetheless, most member states long for a return to constructive American engagement with the world organization.

The leadership provided by the Secretary-General is also in question.[24] The administrations of Kofi Annan and Boutros Boutros-Ghali came under fire for mismanagement of the Oil-for-Food Programme and the alleged corruption of staff and family members.[25] Although the scale of corruption was extremely lim-ited, the United States has cited the kickbacks and inept oversight as reasons to end the standoff between Iraq and the UN in the lead-up to the 2003 war. A strong and independent Office of the Secretary-General is crucial for UN legiti-macy and for conflict resolution in the future. U.S. efforts to undermine the in-tegrity and independence of the Office of the Secretary-General, coupled with scandal and mismanagement, have done little to strengthen the UN's major rep-resentative to the rest of the world. The five-volume report issued in 2005 by the commission headed by former Federal Reserve chairman Paul A. Volcker made for sober reading and cast a shadow over Kofi Annan.[26] Annan's successor, Ban

Secretary-General Ban Ki-moon addresses the staff members of the United Nations High Commissioner for Refugees. (UN Photo # 201380/Jean-Marc Ferre)

Ki-moon, is a South Korean career diplomat with little experience within the UN itself. The first years of his tenure have yielded a few diplomatic victories, such as Chinese consent to a UN Darfur peacekeeping mission; however, concrete successes are few and far between for a Secretary-General who has far less charisma and visibility than his two immediate predecessors.[27] Time will tell whether Secretary-General Ban's quiet and humble approach—thus far he has singled out global climate change and the responsibility to protect as his signature issues—can successfully lead the world organization's operations and reform efforts.

A second political challenge centers on the safety of UN personnel. Since the 1990s UN workers have been killed, kidnapped, and physically and sexually assaulted in record numbers. United Nations personnel have become targets in Bosnia, Lebanon, Congo, Sudan, Rwanda, Iraq, Afghanistan, Kosovo, Algeria, and Cambodia. The UN must be able to defend itself if it is to continue humanitarian and development operations in challenging and insecure environments. The bombings of the UN headquarters in Iraq in August and September 2003, killing 22 and injuring 162, exacerbated the U.S.-UN relationship, as U.S.

occupying forces were unable to provide a secure environment for UN personnel. According to the *Report of the Independent Panel on the Safety and Security of UN Personnel in Iraq*, the attacks are "signals of the emergence of a new and more difficult era for the UN system."[28] The new security environment involving failed states and terrorism requires that the UN move beyond merely guarding against criminal and opportunistic attacks to develop a comprehensive strategy for protecting personnel in conflict areas. The same security problems confront private relief and development agencies that work in tandem with UN programs. In December 2007, UN and private aid agencies were targeted by terrorists in Algeria. The attack on UN facilities killed forty-one people including seventeen UN personnel. Secretary-General Ban responded by unveiling plans to create another independent panel to investigate the attacks in Algeria and other security threats UN personnel face around the world. Algeria responded negatively, claiming it was not consulted and therefore would not consent to the investigation.

A third political challenge centers on the proliferation of actors, particularly nonstate actors (NSAs).[29] The nature and dynamics of peaceful relationships require that the UN pay more attention to NSAs and differentiate among them based on their importance to the issue at hand, especially in the humanitarian arena. Conflicts have deeper roots than governments or armed opposition groups hoping to assume power. The origins of armed conflicts as well as their mitigation and management must be conceived broadly enough to include a host of such nongovernmental actors as clans, "terrorist groups," and the ICRC. People make war and people respond to it. Experience in Sudan, for example, suggests that the UN as an intergovernmental organization is frequently at a disadvantage in dealing with irregular forces and insurgents.[30] Private relief agencies may be better placed than intergovernmental ones for delivering goods in certain war zones.

A fourth political challenge centers on resources. The UN simply does not have enough money to properly conduct peace operations.[31] It does not have adequate resources to properly fight poverty, promote economic and social development, or protect and promote human rights. Many member states, including the United States, are in arrears of their regular and peacekeeping dues, and the UN peacekeeping coffers were over $1 billion in arrears at the end of 2008. Compared to the annual global defense expenditures of over $1 trillion, the amount contributed to peacekeeping seems almost trivial. If every country devoted 1 percent of its defense budget to UN efforts, $10 billion would be available. Other measures, such as surcharges on the sale of weaponry and on the use of UN-provided services—for example, ensuring the right of passage for ships—could help provide additional income. The solution supported by an independent group of bankers and politicians is that governments must respect their international treaty obligations to pay the bills for UN security operations.[32] The UN's long-standing resource problems are bound to be exacerbated by the global financial and economic crisis, as states are devoting scarce resources to domestic initiatives in order to stave off economic collapse.

INSTITUTIONAL CHALLENGES

In 2003, the UN began in earnest the process of substantive reform. On the management side, staff morale was low as scandals appeared. Moreover, politically everyone was unhappy—the UN could not impede U.S. hegemony, and the UN could not approve requisite action against Saddam Hussein. Secretary-General Annan appointed the High-level Panel on Threats, Challenges and Change (HLP), which consisted of sixteen former government officials, including Brent Scowcroft, the former national security advisor for President George H. W. Bush. The HLP was tasked with identifying the principal threats facing the international community in the twenty-first century and developing proposals to reform the UN to meet its new challenges. The panel issued its final report, *A More Secure World: Our Shared Responsibility,* in December 2004, and the report served as the foundation for the Secretary-General's recommendations, *In Larger Freedom: Towards Development, Security and Human Rights for All.* Both documents, in turn, were used to set the stage for the September 2005 World Summit, dubbed "San Francisco II" for its ambitious task of remaking the UN. The result of the largest-ever gathering of presidents, prime ministers, and monarchs was either summarized pessimistically by the lead editorial from the *New York Times* or somewhat more optimistically by the Secretary-General's op-ed in the *Wall Street Journal.* It was either that a "once-in-a-generation opportunity to reform and revive the United Nations has been squandered"[33] or, alternatively, that the UN's "glass [is] at least half full."[34]

The distance between the two foundational documents and the report on the 2005 World Summit Outcome reflects the difference between the "two United Nations" concerning what knowledgeable government and UN officials deem necessary and what is politically possible among the 192 member states. A great deal of consensus existed on the threats facing the international community of states; however, important political differences centered on definition, priorities, strategies, and implementation. The interplay between the two United Nations illustrates the complexities of governance on international security issues.

The reform proposals discussed below also highlight several operational changes as the UN adapts to new kinds of armed conflict not imagined when the UN Charter was drafted. The world organization and its member states probably will not often face the classic interstate confrontation that precipitated the collective response in the 1991 Persian Gulf War, because such textbook land grabs are rare. The 2003 war on Iraq was what international lawyers call a classic international armed conflict; however, intrastate conflict is replacing interstate conflict as the dominant menace to international peace and security. Fueled by ethnic, economic, and nationalist desires for autonomy inside the borders of existing geographic states, civil war is becoming the most common form of armed conflict. Insurgent groups fight existing governments or sometimes other insurgents either for control or for secession. The Human Security Centre confirms these trends, but it also provides evidence that international involvement and stewardship has made a difference over the past two decades.[35]

This is the case even if the UN's security mechanism was not designed to deal with violence and wars of this kind, and blue helmets have encountered their most significant problems in attempting to quell internal wars. At the end of 2008, more than 2,400 peacekeepers had lost their lives since the inception of peacekeeping in 1948.[36] Although the ideal of collective security could be applied to intrastate activity, the UN Charter was designed to prevent recurrences of World War II—characterized by the invasion of one state by another. The world organization is ill equipped to deal with violent conflicts occurring within internationally recognized borders. Improving its capabilities in this area requires changes in the approach to sovereignty and the operational components of international forces in order to safeguard peace and security.

The extent to which the principle of state sovereignty has been the foundation of the international system should be clear to readers by now. Despite the presence of numerous challenges to their supremacy, states are unwilling as a matter of principle to cede daily sovereignty to improve the functioning of the UN. However, changes in world politics in the past half-century have steadily chipped away at the foundation, and changes since the mid-1980s have created a new potential for multilateral action.[37] Sovereignty, of course, has never been a fixed notion—we earlier cited Stephen Krasner's characterization, "organized hypocrisy." Notwithstanding the observers who see national interests and military power as the only answer to an anarchical international system, recent political changes—the immediate ones after the Cold War and the deeper ones resulting from interdependence—have on occasion and for some countries shifted the balance between the authority of states and the authority of international society.[38]

The United Nations itself reflects an institutional structure created in one historical period that is trying to cope with the challenges of a distinctly different era. A conceptual and operational leap must be made, striking a new balance between state sovereignty and the need for effective UN security operations in the post–Cold War era. A Westphalian vocabulary (territory, authority, independence, and population defining the state) is of doubtful utility for the Somalias, Rwandas, Liberias, Burundis, Timors, and Yugoslavias. A first step would be a straightforward confrontation with the meaning of "consent" when there is no sovereign or when a sovereign acts in an opprobrious way and pursues genocide or crimes against humanity as a policy. If the international community of states is willing through the Security Council to apply, instead of to talk about, the actual use of overwhelming force, then consent is unnecessary. If not, then the consent of powerful local actors remains the sine qua non of successful UN operations.

Many Chapter VII operations have had humanitarian motivations or dimensions. The opening sentence of the report by the International Commission on Intervention and State Sovereignty[39] essentially endorses what Francis M. Deng, from 1992 to 2004 the special representative of the Secretary-General for internally displaced persons and now the special representative for the prevention of genocide, and his colleague Roberta Cohen have called "sovereignty as responsibility."[40] It is primarily state authorities whose citizens are threatened who have the responsibility to protect. Yet, a residual responsibility rests with the larger community of states when an aberrant member misbehaves egregiously or simply implodes. The status of state sovereignty is not challenged per se but rather reinforced. However, if a state is unwilling or unable to exercise its protective responsibilities for the rights of its own citizens, it temporarily forfeits its moral claim to be treated as legitimate. Its sovereignty, as well as its right to nonintervention, is suspended, and the residual responsibility necessitates vigorous action by outsiders to protect populations at risk. In brief, the traditional characteristics of a state in the Westphalian system are supplemented by another, a modicum of respect for human rights.

The HLP report and *In Larger Freedom* identify violence within states, such as civil war, widespread human rights abuses and genocide, and terrorism as clusters of threats. Both reports also reaffirm the principle of the responsibility to protect, and Kofi Annan goes further to argue that the UN embrace the principle as a basis for collective action against genocide, war crimes, ethnic cleansing, and crimes against humanity.[41] In other words, while the Security Council has always been in a position to act in the face of threats to international peace and security, the World Summit agreed that it is now also their responsibility to intervene collectively when national authorities are unwilling or unable to protect their own citizens or are themselves the perpetrators of mass atrocities.[42]

However, conceptual and practical alterations to the UN's military operations need to parallel those made in the domain of sovereignty. How is the United Nations to operate effectively in intrastate conflicts where the consent of warring parties is likely to be less than that found in traditional operations or where consent evaporates after the parties have agreed to stop fighting but find that elections or other events no longer go their way? The world organization requires military teeth when it runs the risk of encountering active and perilous opposition. Future UN security operations need to be better armed and more able to operate like professional armies. But if political will is not present, it is better for the world organization to negotiate with powerful parties and hand serious military efforts over to a coalition of the willing and able. Otherwise, the Security Council discredits itself.

The political will, or more often the lack thereof, behind the responsibility to protect via forceful intervention highlights again the relation between decisions outside and inside the UN. In all member states, including in the Western liberal democracies that pay for and otherwise support most of the UN's operations, there are circles of opinion that are not very interested in spending national blood and treasure for others that do not have the stomach for such sacrifices. One can think not only of many Americans and Belgians in Rwanda in 1994, but of many Dutch and Canadians in southern Afghanistan in 2006. The question is widely heard in Chicago, Brussels, Amsterdam, and Ottawa: Why should our soldiers die in foreign places when our vital interests are not at stake? A UN willingness to override claims to sovereignty and to prepare for the effective use of force starts with responsible national leadership. This means above all that prime ministers and presidents have to lead on these questions, informing legislatures and public opinion about the values and long-term interests at stake.

The world body continues to search for ways and money to upgrade its military capability to meet future needs absent a viable Military Staff Committee or standby military capability. The financing for peacekeeping lags far behind demand. Both Boutros-Ghali and Annan, like their predecessors, have been categorical in this regard. Boutros-Ghali, for example, lamented, "A chasm has developed between the tasks entrusted to this Organization and the financial means provided to it. The truth of the matter is that our vision cannot really extend to the prospects opening before us as long as our financing remains myopic."[43] Despite increased demand and praise, peacekeeping arrears have grown since the Nobel Peace Prize was awarded to UN peacekeeping forces in 1988. They continue in Secretary-General Ban's first term.

UN peace operations, particularly in West Africa, the Congo, and the Balkans, have come under criticism for widespread incidents of sexual abuse by peacekeepers and humanitarian workers against the populations whom they were assigned to protect. The sexual abuse has involved pedophilia, forced prostitution, pornography, and the exchange of humanitarian aid for sexual services. The institutional response of the UN has fallen short as it has no real power to enforce the Code of Conduct for blue helmets. Any disciplinary or prosecutorial action is the responsibility of the troop-contributing state. At best, the UN can recommend the repatriation of peacekeepers for violations; however, the bureaucratic procedures are complicated and cumbersome. In *Larger Freedom* notes that the Secretary-General is "especially troubled by instances in which United Nations peacekeepers are alleged to have sexually exploited minors and other vulnerable people, and I have enacted a policy of 'zero-tolerance' towards such offences that applies to all personnel engaged in United Nations operations. I strongly encourage Member States to do the same with respect to their national contingents."[44]

In addition to correcting flaws in UN peacekeeping, the HLP and the Secretary-General recommended the creation of what is now the Peacebuilding Commission (PBC) to enhance the UN role in post-conflict societies, which was implemented by the General Assembly in December 2005.[45] As the Secretary-General noted, "If we are going to prevent conflict we must ensure that peace agreements are implemented in a sustained and sustainable manner."[46] The PBC is attempting to better coordinate aid and activities among the various actors and agencies involved in post-conflict reconstruction. This reflects the conceptual movement behind the evolution of the notion of post-conflict peacebuilding. The UN's experiences in this regard have been growing, as evidenced most clearly by the operations in Bosnia, Kosovo, East Timor, Afghanistan, and, undoubtedly, sometime in Iraq. Peacebuilding is a work in progress, and Annan was cautious to clarify in his 1997 reform report that, although peacebuilding must be supported by humanitarian and development activities, it also needs to reorient them so that they become politically relevant, serving to reduce the risk of resumed conflict and promote reconciliation and recovery.[47]

It is worth spending a moment on the PBC, which was one of the few concrete steps taken by the September 2005 World Summit, along with the decision to establish its supporting office along with a new fund specifically geared to elicit more coherence from UN partners in their collective efforts to move beyond conflict and begin a process of sustainable development.[48] Trying to restore broken states along this path was clearly a challenge emerging from the UN's main growth industry, and just as clearly the incoherence of UN efforts in picking up the pieces from conflict was no longer desirable.

The decision to establish the PBC in spring 2006 was a step in the right direction toward improving efficiency in UN efforts to prevent conflict relapse in war-torn countries that have just turned a page on armed conflict. Its mandate is to propose integrated strategies for post-conflict peacebuilding; ensure predictable financing for recovery; draw international attention to peacebuilding; provide recommendations and information to improve coordination; and develop best practices requiring the collaboration of a variety of actors.

The PBC has an Organizational Committee, which comprises thirty-one members: seven from the Security Council; seven from the UN Economic and Social Council (ECOSOC); five of the main financial contributors to the United Nations; five of the top military contributors to the world organization's peace operations; and seven elected by the General Assembly to redress geographical imbalances that may result from the other selection criteria. The Peacebuilding Commission also includes country-specific committees, which tailor programs to include country representatives and relevant contributors in each case.

The World Summit Outcome document also requested that the Secretary-General establish a Peacebuilding Support Office (PBSO) within the Secretariat whose staff are to assist and support the PBC as well as advise the Secretary-General. The PBSO also oversees the Peacebuilding Fund (PBF), which Kofi Annan established in 2006 with a target of $250 million. As of March 2009, deposits have reached about $290 million, and its total portfolio is approximately $320 million.

The aim of the fund is to provide initial support for peacebuilding efforts and kick-start donor investment in long-term recovery. If managed effectively, the fund has the potential to reduce the duplication of efforts and waste and enhance coordination among financial sources because the power of the purse is to make decisions centrally. Thus far, it has allocated $35 million to both Burundi and Sierra Leone, the two countries on which the PBC focused attention in its first year of operation. Secretary-General Ban Ki-moon has declared Guinea-Bissau and Comoros eligible to receive assistance, and funding is pending. Additionally, the PBSO has approved emergency funding for urgent peacebuilding activities in Burundi, the Central African Republic, Guinea, Côte d'Ivoire, Haiti, Liberia, and Kenya.

Like all international institutions, however, the PBC is not without shortcomings. It is a subsidiary body of both the General Assembly and the Security Council, which exacerbates reporting problems. Its functioning depends on the cooperation among the main UN organs. Moreover, like most UN entities, it is an advisory body, rather than a decision-making body, and lacks enforcement mechanisms. As one analyst notes, "The advisory nature of the PBC—coupled with the stipulation that it 'shall act in all matters on the basis of consensus of its members'—seems at odds with the very concept of the body assuming the final responsibility for peacebuilding."[49] Moreover, there appears to be some overlap between the PBSO and the activities entrusted to the Department of Political Affairs (DPA) and the Department of Peacekeeping Operations (DPKO), which means that there is potential for turf battles.

Nevertheless, the creation of the PBC, PBSO, and PBF is an important step toward enhancing the coordination, efficiency, and effectiveness of post-conflict peacebuilding efforts financed and supervised by the United Nations. Relevant here is the combination of actors at work in Afghanistan. Enforcement action against the Taliban and Al Qaeda was carried out by a U.S.-led coalition acting with the green light of the Security Council. The UN then sponsored a peace conference that led to the emergence of an interim government under Hamid Karzai. Various NATO members then took the lead in organizing an international military force—the NATO-led International Security Assistance Force (ISAF)—that maintained some security in Kabul initially and in 2005 and 2006 expanded to some 16,000 troops, which allowed the U.S. Operation Enduring Freedom (OEF) to scale down. Granted that, as feared by many observers, all post-conflict operations in Afghanistan suffered from lack of political commitment and resources from UN member states, at least there was a division of labor. The United Nations exercised its diplomatic and legitimating functions but left the heavy lifting of coercive action to states and military organizations like NATO. Not by coincidence, the special representative of the Secretary-General in Afghanistan was Lakhdar Brahimi, who had chaired a panel that in 2000 recommended such an approach to security operations.[50]

The most ambitious reform proposals center on adapting the Security Council to meet new and evolving threats. These reforms involve representational changes and clearly define the circumstances and conditions under which the council will authorize military force. Representational changes involve complicated issues. In the aftermath of the Cold War, and notwithstanding splits in the council over northern Iraq in 1991, Kosovo in 1999, and Iraq in 2003, the Security Council has tried—at least more so than during the Cold War—to fulfill its duties as a guarantor of international peace and security. Permanent-member goodwill manifested itself in the shelving of the veto for three years beginning in May 1990, and there has been only scarce resort to it since.

The clear threat of a veto, however, greatly affected matters both in 1999 and 2003. Changes in the international climate could render the Security Council less able to provide for peace and security. Neither the United States nor France showed much sensitivity to the damage that they were doing to collective security structures during their open disagreement over how to deal with Iraq in 2003, whether one speaks of the UN Security Council, NATO, or the European Union. A particular problem resides in what former French foreign minister Hubert Védrine calls the "hyperpower" (*hyperpuissance*) of the United States. Washington has always had great trouble in accepting a multilateralism that constrains its national power even if it has played a leadership role on numerous occasions—earlier we cited Edward Luck's characterization of "mixed messages."[51]

While the rise of China and India complicate generalizations,[52] nonetheless the United States remains the world's only "superpower," and this accentuates a host of problems.[53] At the onset of the post–Cold War era, bipolarity gave way to what was supposed to be American primacy. But the military prowess in Afghanistan and Iraq—like the conduct of the intervention in Kosovo by NATO in 1999—made crystal clear that "primacy" was a vast understatement. Scholars like Joseph Nye discuss the nuances of economic and cultural leverage resulting from American "soft power,"[54] but there is no debate about the base hard currency of international politics—military might. Washington already spends more on its military than the next fifteen to twenty-five (depending on who is counting) countries. As noted earlier, with additional appropriations for Iraq and Afghanistan, the United States now spends more than the rest of the world's militaries combined.

The collapse of the Soviet Union left the Security Council with a composition that generally was sympathetic to Washington's interests and those of the West more generally.[55] With the Soviet Union no longer acting as a counterbalance to the United States, such states as Japan, Germany, India, Brazil, Nigeria, South Africa, and Egypt believe that they deserve greater say in the council's decision-making. The continuing permanent membership of France and Great Britain, whose international influence has declined significantly since 1945, offends Japan and Germany, whose influence in decision-making is in no way commensurate with their funding of the organization's activities. Countries like Canada that routinely contribute troops to all UN operations complain of being left out of decisions that affect their soldiers.

Reform of the Security Council's permanent membership is seemingly a permanent agenda item in New York, with little likelihood of being resolved anytime soon.[56] Possibilities for long-term reform involve changes in the Security

Council's permanent membership; shorter-term changes involve longer and more frequent terms on the council for influential countries. However, each major structural reform opens another Pandora's box. Which developing countries should be added? Should they be the most powerful or populous? After a civil war, should a splintered state retain its seat? Why should economic powers whose constitutions impede overseas military involvement be given a seat? Should there be three permanent European members? What about the European Union? Which countries should wield vetoes? Should not all regions have at least one permanent member?

The introduction of changes could create additional decision-making problems that could result in stalemates like those the Security Council faced during the Cold War. Precisely how a "rump" General Assembly would facilitate decision-making is unclear. A larger council would still be too small to represent the membership as a whole but too large to act in a businesslike fashion.[57] Assuming the continuation of at least some North-South ideological, political, and economic tensions that reflect growing disparities in wealth, decision-making in the council could become as paralyzed in the future as it was in the past. Instead of an automatic Soviet veto, other effective vetoes from dissenters or foot-draggers could thwart the Security Council's ability to make decisions.

To enhance the decision-making power of the council under these circumstances, reform of the veto system also has been proposed, with equal success—that is, none. This system has always been controversial because the interests or even the whims of a single permanent member can impede effective action when the rest of the international community of states is prepared to act. It is virtually unthinkable that the veto could be eliminated altogether, but proposals have been made to lessen its impact. These include limiting the range of areas in which the veto can be used, allowing it only when an item affects a permanent member's "supreme national interests," which presumably would preclude humanitarian disasters; instituting a system of weighted voting that would allow the council to override a veto; and increasing the total number of negative votes needed to veto a resolution.

The founders made the Charter extremely difficult to amend. Such amendments require a two-thirds vote of the General Assembly, then ratification by two-thirds of the parliaments of member states, including affirmative action by all of the permanent five. Hence, given the controversy surrounding all proposals for reform, formal council restructuring is, at best, a long shot even if increases in membership for both the Security Council and ECOSOC in 1965 were the only previous Charter amendments.

The High-level Panel took that shot in 2004 by proposing two models for Security Council reform.[58] Both models are based on regional representation in that they create new council seats (expanding the council from fifteen to twenty-four members) and distribute them between four major regional areas: Africa, Asia/Pacific, Europe, and the Americas. The models do not expand the veto or change the veto among the existing permanent members. The models also ad-dress several principles designed to avoid many of the issues discussed above. The first principle is that all members of the council have enhanced financial, military, and diplomatic responsibilities to the UN. Second, the models bring more countries, especially countries from the South, into the decision-making process. Third, the models do not impair the council's effectiveness. Finally, both models increase democracy and accountability.

Model A proposed creating six new permanent seats, albeit without the veto, and three new nonpermanent (elected for the usual two-year term, renewable), bringing the total membership to twenty-four. Africa would receive two perma-nent seats and four nonpermanent seats, thereby having six representatives. Asia/Pacific would receive two new permanent and three new nonpermanent seats. Coupled with China's permanent seat with veto, this region would also have six representatives. Europe would receive one new permanent and two non-permanent seats. Coupled with the three existing seats (Great Britain, France, and Russia), Europe would have six seats. The Americas would have one new permanent seat and four nonpermanent seats. With the existing seat held by the United States, the region would have its six representatives.

Model B was similar in terms of making the council more representative; however, rather than creating new permanent seats, it establishes an entirely new category of eight seats that have four-year renewable terms and one new non-permanent seat with a nonrenewable two-year term. In this reform scenario, each region would receive two of the new, four-year renewable seats, and Africa, Asia/Pacific, Europe, and the Americas would each receive four, three, one, and three nonrenewable two-year seats, respectively. Added to the five existing per-manent members, the total membership of the council would be expanded to twenty-four states with each region having six representatives.

The numbers games intensified in the lead-up to the September 2005 gather-ing in New York to mark the sixtieth anniversary of the world organization. We turn to this story, one that continues in 2009.

THE WORLD SUMMIT 2005

The 2005 World Summit celebrated the UN's sixtieth birthday, but, more impor-tant, it was supposed to transform the organization to meet the challenges of the twenty-first century. After years of laying the groundwork through the work of HLP and others, a preliminary draft included several important interconnected reforms that would affect UN security operations: proposals to enlarge the Se-curity Council; new guidelines for authorizing military action (including in-ternational intervention in countries that fail to protect their people against genocide); terrorism; strategies for controlling the proliferation of nuclear weapons; new policies to curb abuses by peacekeepers; and the creation of a new Peacebuilding Commission. These are discussed in turn below while other measures—related to human rights and sustainable development—were also on the table but are discussed later in Parts Two and Three of this book.

Security Council Reform. The HLP was divided and hence proposed two models. The Secretary-General did not express a preference. If sixteen individual members of a panel and the UN's chief could not make a recommendation, how could states come to a consensus? The best member states could muster was to reaffirm their desire to make the council more representative and recommend "that the Security Council continue to adapt its working methods so as to increase the involvement of States not members of the Council in its work, as appropriate, enhance its accountability to the membership and increase the transparency of its work."⁵⁹ At least the verbal jousting and rhetoric over the years had created a permissive environment that helped change these procedures. It facilitated pragmatic modifications in working methods. These have injected more openness, accountability, and diverse inputs into council deliberations and should be expanded.⁶⁰

Authorizing Military Force. The controversial aspects of the debate about under what conditions the UN should authorize military force involve what constitutes an imminent threat to international peace and security and situations where governments are unable or unwilling to protect their citizens against genocide. These issues are very contentious and divisive in the best of times and even more so in the not-so-best of times. An odd alliance emerged between the United States and the many developing countries whereby they would support the status quo by avoiding formal criteria for authorizing force and language that would formally allow for humanitarian intervention in cases of genocide. The former served the interests of the United States, whose use of force in Iraq was still widely criticized long after 2003, and the latter served the interests of many developing countries concerned that any right to humanitarian intervention would threaten their hard-won but shaky sovereignty.

The summit outcome reiterated the prohibition against the use of force in international relations except in self-defense, with no reference as to what constitutes an imminent threat as it relates to self-defense. It also reiterated that the primary responsibility to protect is with states, and that the first duty of the international community is to use appropriate nonviolent means to protect populations. The UN may "take collective action, in a timely and decisive manner, through the Security Council, in accordance with the Charter, including Chapter VII, on a case-by-case basis and in cooperation with relevant regional organizations as appropriate, should peaceful means be inadequate and national authorities are manifestly failing to protect their populations from genocide, war crimes, ethnic cleansing, and crimes against humanity."⁶¹ In diplomatic-speak, the international community of states avoided a formal right to humanitarian intervention, yet left open the possibility that military intervention could be authorized if the Security Council had the political will to determine that such situations constituted a threat to international peace and security.

Terrorism. A clear definition of terrorism eludes the UN and efforts to confront it have lacked coherence. International law and norms clearly prohibit deliberate attacks on civilians, and the HLP reinforces the prohibition by describing terrorism as any act "that is intended to cause death or serious bodily harm to civilians or non-combatants, when the purpose of such act, by its nature or context, is to intimidate a population, or to compel a government or an international organization to do or abstain from doing any act."[62] As discussed earlier, at the World Summit, a formal definition of terrorism could not be adopted for many of the reasons cited above, but the member states did agree to "condemn terrorism in all its forms and manifestations, committed by whomever, wherever, and for whatever purposes, as it constitutes one of the most serious threats to international peace and security."[63] Member states also committed themselves to reach an agreement regarding a comprehensive treaty on international terrorism and to cooperate to fight terrorism in conformity with international law.

The outcome reflects what is politically possible between states that see violence as necessary for national liberation and a superpower that articulates a right to fight terrorism as it sees fit. Although debate was heated and inconclusive to some, it nonetheless was significant that heads of state and government present in New York agreed that terrorism "in all forms" was a common threat to international stability and was to be condemned.[64] In September 2006 Secretary-General Annan unveiled the UN's counterterrorism strategy, which is being implemented under the leadership of Secretary-General Ban; however, the General Assembly has been unable to conclude a comprehensive convention on international terrorism.

Nonproliferation. Perhaps the biggest disappointment at the World Summit was the inability to reach any agreement on the proliferation of WMDs, supposedly one of the main reasons the summit was organized in the first place. In light of the threat such weapons pose in an era of global terrorism in general and the justification of the 2003 Iraq war on the same grounds, member states should have been able to find common ground for controlling these weapons. The HLP and the Secretary-General identified proliferation as one of the more serious threats to international peace and security. The United States blocked the inclusion of nonproliferation in the World Summit document, as many states insisted upon matching nonproliferation measures with steps toward disarmament by existing nuclear states. This is the same dynamic that has characterized virtually all discussions, and so the World Summit's final document is totally silent on disarmament and nonproliferation. This crucial priority for the United States was a victim of last-minute horse-trading—a "disgrace," according to Kofi Annan.[65] Washington has since agreed to provide material and technical atomic assistance to India, a nuclear state outside of the nonproliferation treaty, further undercutting U.S. leadership abilities in this important area. All of this is not lost on Iran, which resents Western pressure to alter its nuclear policies, given that particularly Britain, France, and the United States have not paid much attention to the disarmament called for in the NPT agreement and have not criticized the presumed acquisition of nuclear weapons by Israel.

Sexual Abuse by Peacekeepers. Member states included strong language in the World Summit Outcome document regarding sexual exploitation and abuse by peacekeepers. They urged that UN policies of zero tolerance and zero impunity be implemented without delay. The formal procedures the UN developed to curb sexual abuse represent an important first step in restoring the credibility of UN peacekeeping. However, a formal change in procedures does not translate into a formal change in attitudes. A report issued by Refugees International in October 2005 charges that the procedures are not being implemented because the "boys will be boys" attitude in peacekeeping missions breeds tolerance for exploitation and abuse.[66] Rapes continue to be dismissed as simple acts of prostitution. Anna Shotton, author of the report, does nonetheless argue that progress has been made. In the past, the UN had only occasionally repatriated uniform personnel, but in the twenty months preceding her report the UN had completed 221 investigations that resulted in the firing of ten civilian employees and the repatriation of eighty-eight military personnel, including six commanders.[67] Still, much work remains to be done in prosecuting sex crimes by troop-contributing states and on changing the attitudes among the armed forces involved in peacekeeping.

Peacebuilding. Perhaps the most significant accomplishment of the 2005 World Summit for the security arena was the decision to create a new Peacebuilding Commission. The PBC actually represents a "follow-through," or learning based on previous UN peacekeeping and peacemaking activities in places like Somalia, Sierra Leone, Haiti, Liberia, the Congo, and Rwanda. It is necessary to rebuild state capacity. This is not nostalgia for the national security state of the past, but a clear recognition that a modicum of state capacity is a prerequisite for peace or development.

The initial optimism surrounding the potential of the 2005 UN summit was tempered by the political realities of an international system in an unusual period of transition. The responsibility to protect was reaffirmed, but no right of humanitarian intervention was created. Terrorism in "all its forms" was condemned, but terrorism could not be defined. The summit did reiterate the importance of strengthening the role of the Secretariat in maintaining international peace and security—an issue to which we now turn.

STRENGTHENING THE SECRETARIAT

The 1991 Persian Gulf War represented the first military enforcement action of the post–Cold War era, but the UN Secretary-General and the Secretariat remained virtual outsiders to the process by which the war was waged. This pattern has been repeated, most recently in Afghanistan in 2001 for Operation Enduring Freedom and in NATO's follow-on ISAF. Kosovo in 1999 and Iraq in 2003 are not entirely relevant, since the Security Council did not authorize force in either case, but again it became involved in approving the military forces in subsequent phases in Bosnia, first by NATO, then by the EU, and even in Iraq after the occupation began.

Although Security Council authorizations were politically useful in 1991 and 2001, the coalition forces were not accountable to the world organization. The ability of the Secretariat and thereby of the Security Council to monitor enforcement operations has long been a subject of heated discussions,[68] which has been exacerbated by the occupation in Iraq. The enormous difficulties surrounding the deployment of the first UN troops with Chapter VII provisions under the command and control of the Secretary-General in Somalia serve to highlight the critical nature of this issue. Observers of the United Nations Protection Force in the Balkans, which the council eventually gave a Chapter VII mandate, were struck by the muddled nature of UN command and control over that mostly unhappy experience.

Several proposals have been put forth to increase the Secretary-General's influence over Security Council decision-making and subsequent UN military operations. Article 99 of the Charter already empowers the Secretary-General to bring the council's attention to matters that he believes could threaten international peace and security. Greater use of this article could allow the Secretary-General to place issues on the council's agenda that otherwise might be avoided due to their sensitivity, but a Secretary-General risks alienating states if he goes too far too fast, which explains why this solution is not really a solution. The double standard with which the council has addressed past threats to the peace could be mitigated if the Secretary-General were to use the powers of his office to try to ensure a more consistent consideration of issues even when powerful states might prefer to ignore them. Experience shows, however, beginning with Trygve Lie in the 1950s that the Secretary-General who offends a P-5 member cannot be an effective leader of the UN. Indeed, the potential threat of Article 99 is probably more valuable than its actual use.

The Office of the Secretary-General has asked for a mandate to request advisory opinions from the International Court of Justice (ICJ) under Article 96 of the Charter. Such a course of action could allow the organization's head to help refine the legitimate definitions of those situations that present threats to the peace as well as to provide more concrete policy options that are both politically and legally acceptable. One key to advisory opinions is asking a question and getting a specific-enough response. Like all courts, the ICJ oftentimes avoids the substance of an issue and relies upon procedural interpretations to set aside a case. Time is also a problem because the ICJ never acts quickly, and until recently the court decided only a case or two a year. Moreover, given that the United States has made clear that it does not want the new International Criminal Court second-guessing its decisions about choice of weapons and targets in armed conflict, it is highly doubtful that the United States—or Russia or China—would welcome the Secretary-General's raising similar questions of the ICJ.

Agreement on standards may be increasingly necessary, however. Resolutions are often kept vague to secure intergovernmental assent ("all necessary means" in the war against Iraq created a host of questions about proportionality, and "all measures necessary" was quintessential UN doublespeak that did not permit sufficient action to help Bosnia's Muslims). The language of international decisions is sometimes too elliptical to allow a determination of which concrete actions and procedures would constitute legitimate follow-up. The Secretary-General—and not just the General Assembly, the Security Council, and other UN organs—should be authorized to request advisory opinions from the ICJ to help reduce the criticism of selective application by the Security Council of the principles guiding its decision-making. Although seeking the court's opinion would be harmful in the midst of a crisis, it could be useful in anticipating future contingencies.

As part of the reform process, steps have been taken to enhance the Secretariat's means of fact-finding so that the Secretary-General can improve his access to timely, unbiased, and impartial accounts of dangerous situations. Special units have proliferated that focus exclusively on early warning and prevention. The mandate of these units is to provide greater access to information about potential threats to the peace, thus enhancing the Secretariat's ability to launch preventive diplomacy and possibly to recommend preventive deployment. Of course, much more could be done, and the Secretary-General's office could and should be equipped and staffed to act as an effective crisis-monitoring center for events that threaten the peace.

The end of the Cold War has permitted the world organization to move toward reviving old-fashioned ideals of an objective and competent international civil service, upon which the organization was supposedly founded.[69] The success of the organization's activities begins and ends with the people in its employ. A long-ignored reality is the need to overhaul the international civil service, for which qualifications have long been secondary to geographic and political considerations, and within which women have hardly played a role commensurate with their potential.[70]

This reality became more obvious with the release of the five reports on the Oil-for-Food Programme, whose commission was headed by Paul A. Volcker. Along with the earlier sexual scandals involving peacekeepers, these reports demonstrate serious flaws in management and judgment by the central administration, which is almost universally agreed to be inefficient, politicized, and in desperate need of repair. The preface to the fourth Volcker report contained language that could have been written by an American unilateralist: "The inescapable conclusion from the Committee's work is that the United Nations Organization needs thoroughgoing reform—and it needs it urgently."[71] Nothing has changed since 2005. As we have discovered earlier, "urgent" has an unusual connotation in UN circles that is distinct from any commonsensical definition.

After 1997, when Kofi Annan unveiled his strategy of a "quiet revolution" to reform the world organization, he initiated meaningful steps to make the UN a more effective mechanism for administering and managing peacekeeping operations.[72] The creation and effective implementation of a rationalized cabinet system, consisting of the Senior Management Group (SMG), comprising division heads and an executive committee system, introduced a much greater degree of horizontal cooperation than had been the case before. Senior officials throughout the organization (including those based in Geneva and Vienna through teleconferencing) meet weekly with the Secretary-General. In addition, the executive committee on peace and security, which brings together those senior officials whose units deal with peacekeeping, holds biweekly discussions. This process is supplemented with a number of issue-specific task forces, including special ones for each multidisciplinary peace operation, as well as special meetings involving a much wider set of actors who serve as operational partners in the field, including development and humanitarian agencies and international financial institutions.

In regard to headquarters operations, a division of authority has been worked out between the DPA, the Office for the Coordination of Humanitarian Affairs (OCHA), and the DPKO. The former has primary responsibility for preventive diplomacy and peacemaking, the middle one coordinates assistance, and the latter takes the lead in peacekeeping. Although these changes represent important steps in enhancing interdepartmental cooperation and improving the effectiveness of peace operations, the continued splitting of peacemaking and peacekeeping across separate administrative units serves to limit the overall effectiveness of such activities. The support office for the PBC also needs to become an integral member of this core team over time.

In the field, coordination has been centralized under the special representative of the Secretary-General, who assumes authority over all UN entities in the mission area. In cases where department expertise is especially crucial, such as in the Central African Republic and Liberia, for example, a UNDP resident coordinator (who in peacetime is the UN's point person) may also be appointed to serve as deputy head of mission. Within this structure, special emphasis is placed on working in close cooperation with relevant parties, including NGOs.

As the pool of potential partners grows, so does the necessity for developing systematic criteria for determining partnership acceptability. Of course, not all NGOs and other entities from civil society are necessarily constructive forces for building and sustaining peace. Neither may be all regional security organizations, as demonstrated by the numerous allegations of serious human rights violations by members of the Military Observer Group of the Economic Community of West African States (ECOMOG) force in Liberia and Sierra Leone or earlier allegations about Canadian soldiers abusing Somalis. At the same time, however, a broad conception of partnerships is likely to be even more important in the future than it is now. Given the increasing importance placed on creating the requisite social and economic infrastructures for sustaining peace in conflict-torn regions, new and innovative types of partnerships with the private sector, religious groups, local governmental bodies, labor, and others will certainly be needed.

Determining whether to get involved in political-humanitarian crises requires familiarity with a host of actors besides states. Humanitarian action has made possible new coalitions—the media and the public can demand that something be done, the military can respond, and relief agencies can ask for help because on occasion they recognize both the war-fighting and logistical capacities of the armed forces. Commitments by major powers are greatly affected by their leaders' calculations of domestic costs, benefits, and risks. The arithmetic in part reflects the success of domestic and transnational constituencies in mobilizing support for humanitarian action and in altering conceptions of interests and rewards.

A good example of the importance of numerous actors is the "Ottawa process" on antipersonnel land mines. The dynamics of this case demonstrate how humanitarian values have penetrated the foreign policies of other countries. A transnational coalition successfully imbued the domestic politics of a sufficient number of states with enough humanitarian concern to redefine state interests in a way that led to the treaty.[73] Unlike many cases of transnationalism, this one touches directly on the high politics of military security. Substate and transnational actors are important in influencing, framing, and ultimately redefining state interests.[74] The initial impetus in the anti–land mines campaign was provided by a formidable coalition of civil society organizations. The International Campaign to Ban Land Mines grew out of private advocacy organizations whose main orientation was domestic and public (that is, oriented toward change in state behavior). Its success depended on co-opting states (and notably Canada, the Scandinavian countries, and South Africa) to "determine what states want."[75] Their support depended not only on the moral appeal of the cause but also on the consideration of domestic and international political interests and risks.

State involvement was necessary to translate social pressure into international law. The key to the outcome was to move states and alter definitions of perceived interests by persuading politicians. A basic aspect of the process was to remove land mines from the rarefied realm of technical military strategy and to place the issue firmly in the political realm of domestic constituencies.[76]

Humanitarian values are in the forefront of concerns motivating many societal forces that may inform leaders' perceptions of interest. In commenting on the intervention in Kosovo, journalist Max Frankel concluded, "It's those pictures of almost unfathomable atrocity that once again drive our politics."[77] This is not the place to discuss in depth the so-called CNN effect, which influences both the perception of tragedy and the pace of decision-making. However, the increasing reach and efficiency of international communications, along with the related growing influence of transnational and nongovernmental actors, point toward changing domestic environments and decision-making contexts. Armed with graphic images of suffering, these nonstate actors help shape definitions of state interest. We are witnessing a phenomenon not of receding state authority, but of states being influenced by coalitions of actors with humanitarian values. Their agendas to some extent and in some circumstances become those of their governments.[78]

Member states and peoples across the world are looking toward the United Nations to muster multilateral responses for international and civil strife. Human rights and sustainable development play a much less significant role in the Charter than military security. But these "softer" sides of the UN moved forward during the Cold War while collective-security mechanisms stalled. The end of the Cold War had a decided impact on international efforts to constitute working regimes in these areas, too. Moreover, the meaning of "security" has come into question as issues of human rights, democratization, and sustainable human development have worked their way into global discourse about security matters.

EXPLAINING CHANGE

For the security domain, as will be the case in subsequent chapters for human rights and development, it is not easy to deal with matters of presumed knowledge and learning. What are the proper lessons to be drawn from decades of UN peacekeeping, from various efforts at enforcement, from failures to reach a common approach to Kosovo in 1999 and Iraq in 2003? Do different actors learn different things based on their existing ideologies or mind-sets, indicating an absence of scientific certainty on these matters and the persistent presence of ever-changing policy debates?

Disappointingly, so much UN peacekeeping, even of the traditional type, is still unsystematic, still ad hoc in composition and deployment. Many states have not learned that international peace and security could be improved by concluding Article 43 agreements with the UN, which would provide the Secretary-General with advance notice of what military units would be available for armed interposition under UN aegis. States like Canada certainly recognize that a UN rapid-reaction force could be a significant contribution to stability and humanitarian actions in a world of failed states and small wars. But it seems that many states—including the important ones with the most military wherewithal, such as the United States, China, and Russia—do not want to transfer much hard power to the UN even if under the ultimate authority of the Security Council, where they have a veto.

Thus, the Secretary-General has to go begging and start from scratch if he advocates a multilateral force for places like Liberia or Darfur. Even for the armed observation of cease-fires, which the UN has been doing consistently well and on a fairly large scale since 1956, there is no UN system that can be activated on short notice, ready for rapid deployment. Indeed, deployments were done more quickly in the 1950s and 1960s than now because of the absence of political will in nastier conflicts. The problem is not intellectual but the absence of national and international political will. Important states simply do not wish to commit in advance even small, voluntary parts of their armed forces for deployments determined by the council and managed by the Secretariat. Even for traditional peacekeeping, not to mention the more ambitious and complex type of peace operations, there have not been so much "learning lessons" as "spurning lessons." In short, policy changes to make the whole enterprise more streamlined and effective make good sense, just not political sense to key states.

Enforcement events indicate the same lack of decisive change, the same lack of policy transformation, which would indicate not much learning. Iraq in 2003 demonstrated starkly what Kosovo had already shown in 1999, namely that the permanent members of the Security Council could be as deeply divided after the Cold War as during it. In both of those cases, one saw a determined hyperpower ready to employ its military superiority, even in the face of opposition within the council. Regarding Iraq in 2003, much of the opposition was well considered and well argued, as recent events have borne out, even if some of it stemmed from historic ambitions (for example, France) or domestic political calculation (for example, Germany). Iraq had no substantial links with Al Qaeda nor operational chemical or biological weapons, and it did not present a clear and present danger to U.S. security. The United States, being determined to exploit its power advantage over the Saddam Hussein regime and destroy it, "learned" that the members of the council could not be relied upon to endorse decisive preventive action. Kosovo had already demonstrated that war by multilateral committee was a bad idea. At the same time, what a majority of the council members "learned" about Hussein's Iraq was that diplomacy still had a chance of containing and deterring that regime. So "knowledge" in this case was not a scientific matter but a debatable proposition greatly affected by perceptions of power and norms.

The Security Council, of which ten members are not permanent and serve only two-year terms, may "learn" the benefits of involving the UN in post-combat security measures of occupation, state-building, and nation-building. On the one hand, the United States was encountering many difficulties in trying to transform an occupied Iraq. On the other hand, the UN had demonstrated a certain messy success in administering Bosnia, Kosovo, and East Timor. Afghanistan was a separate case in which the UN was involved immediately after combat in a diplomatic way but did not have major responsibility for security and other measures on the ground for the Hamid Karzai government. Post-combat Afghanistan was a fractured, dangerous, and deadly place, but the UN Assistance Mission for Afghanistan (UNAMA) was part of the picture in support of both NATO's ISAF and the United States' OEF. Over time even if UNAMA grows and takes certain initiatives, it will still require the cooperation of Brussels and Washington.

The fallout from September 11 and the Bush administration's war on terrorism and war in Iraq has had a negative and significant impact on human rights and humanitarian law. With the Obama administration now in place in Washington, it seems likely that the UN will be more central to U.S. foreign policy than it was from 2000 to 2008—it would be difficult to be less. Post-war (if that is the correct term) activities there have demonstrated that recovery, reconstruction, and rebuilding are not U.S. strong suits. Meanwhile, the UN has accumulated substantial experience over several decades, and this comparative advantage makes the PBC a sensible idea. Former U.S. assistant secretary of state James Dobbins and a Rand Corporation evaluation team have argued that the world organization's performance in post-conflict effectiveness is remarkably good in comparison with Washington's—they say that seven of eight UN operations have been successful versus only four out of eight for the United States.[79]

Almost all actors, whether state participants or nonstate observers and experts, had "learned" that the UN was not good at the heavy lifting of combat and that the UN lacked the independent power and management skills to move beyond collective legitimization and the less muscular forms of peacekeeping. There also seemed to be widespread learning regarding "smart" sanctions, which targeted elites rather than the rank-and-file citizen, who often had little control over events.

NOTES

1. This discussion draws on Jane Boulden and Thomas G. Weiss, "Whither Terrorism and the United Nations?" in *Terrorism and the United Nations: Before and After September 11*, eds. Jane Boulden and Thomas G. Weiss (Bloomington: Indiana University Press, 2004), 3–26. See further Thomas G. Weiss, Margaret E. Crahan, and John Goering, eds., *War on Terrorism and Iraq: Human Rights, Unilateralism, and U.S. Foreign Policy* (London: Routledge, 2004).

2. UN Press Release, SG/SM/7962/Rev.1, September 18, 2001.

3. See Adam Roberts, "Terrorism and International Order," in *Terrorism and International Order*, eds. Lawrence Freedman, Christopher Hill, Adam Roberts, R. J. Vincent, Paul Wilkinson, and Philip Windsor (London: Routledge and Kegan Paul/Royal Institute of International Affairs, 1986), 9–10; and M. J. Peterson, "Using the General Assembly," in *Terrorism and the United Nations: Before and After September 11*, eds. Jane Boulden and Thomas G. Weiss (Bloomington: Indiana University Press, 2004), 173–197.

4. Peterson, "Using the General Assembly."

5. United Nations, *Report of the High-level Panel on Threats, Challenges and Change, A More Secure World: Our Shared Responsibility* (New York: United Nations, 2004), para. 161. For discussions of the reform, see Special Section: "The Report of the High-level Panel on Threats, Challenges and Change," *Security Dialogue* 36, no. 3 (2005): 361–394; and Paul Heinbecker and Patricia Goff, eds., *Irrelevant or Indispensable? The United Nations in the 21st Century* (Waterloo, Ontario: Wilfred Laurier University Press, 2005).

6. Kofi Annan, *In Larger Freedom: Towards Development, Security and Human Rights for All*, UN document A/59/2005, March 21, 2005, para. 91.

7. *2005 World Summit Outcome*, UN document A/60/1, October 24, 2005, para. 81.

8. Chantal de Jonge Oudraat, "The Role of the Security Council," in *Terrorism and the UN: Before and After September 11*, eds. Jane Boulden and Thomas G. Weiss (Bloomington: Indiana University Press, 2004), 151–172.

9. *Report of the Policy Working Group on the United Nations and Terrorism*, UN document A/57/273/S/2002/875.

10. See statements by Secretary-General Ban at www.un.org/terrorism/sg.shtml.

11. This discussion of the UN's history in grappling with WMDs relies on the work of Nina Tannenwald, "The UN and Debates Over Weapons of Mass Destruction," in *The United Nations and Global Security*, eds. Richard M. Price and Mark W. Zacher (New York: Palgrave, 2004), 3–20.

12. See Jane Boulden, Ramesh Thakur, and Thomas G. Weiss, eds., *The United Nations and the Nuclear Challenges* (Tokyo: UN University Press, 2009).

13. Tannenwald, "The UN and Debates Over Weapons of Mass Destruction," 6.

14. George W. Bush, in an address to cadets at the U.S. Military Academy (West Point) on June 1, 2002, described the role of preventive war in U.S. foreign policy and national defense, saying that Americans needed "to be ready for preemptive action when necessary to defend our liberty and to defend our lives."

15. For an exposition of doctrinaire unilateralism, compared to occasional and pragmatic unilateralism, see the chapter by John Ruggie in David P. Forsythe, Patrice C. Macmahon, and Andrew Wedeman, eds., *American Foreign Policy in a Globalized World* (New York: Routledge, 2006).

16. See further Rosemary Foot, S. Neil MacFarlane, and Michael Mastanduno, eds., *The United States and Multilateral Organizations* (Oxford: Oxford University Press, 2003).

17. Regarding the *Caroline* case and anticipatory self-defense in international law, see Anthony Clark Arend and Robert J. Beck, *International Law and the Use of Force* (London: Routledge, 1993). On the Bush doctrine as a violation of the UN Charter, see Tom J. Farer, "Beyond the Charter Frame: Unilateralism or Condominium," *American Journal of International Law* 96, no. 2 (2002): 359–364. Israeli scholars, like Yoram Dienstein, in *War, Aggression and Self Defense*, 2nd ed. (Cambridge: Cambridge University Press, 1994), who endorse the notion of anticipatory self-defense as found in Israel's first use of force in 1967, still say that the threat of imminent attack is necessary in exercises of this form of self-defense.

18. See Jean E. Krasno and James R. Sutterlin, *The United Nations and Iraq: Defanging the Viper* (Westport, Conn.: Praeger, 2003).

19. James Mann, *Rise of the Vulcans: The History of Bush's War Cabinet* (London: Penguin, 2004).

20. When the Reagan administration invaded the Caribbean island of Grenada in 1982, it manufactured the collective approval of the Organization of East Caribbean States because any approval by either the UN or OAS was out of the question. So U.S. administrations that believe in doctrinaire unilateralism do understand the desirability of some kind of collective approval, but they are prepared to essentially go it alone while regarding collective approval as a minor matter. After the invasion of Iraq in 2003, the Bush administration made sure to obtain UN approval for the dispatch of UN blue helmets to Haiti.

21. Katharina P. Coleman, *International Organisations and Peace Enforcement: The Politics of International Legitimacy* (Cambridge: Cambridge University Press, 2007), 2.

22. On the great damage that the Bush policy toward Iraq did to the long effort to restrict the first use of force, see especially Michael J. Glennon, "Why the Security Council Failed," *Foreign Affairs* 82, no. 3 (2003): 16–35. On the broad perception that the Iraq war in 2003 weakened the United Nations, see Meg Bortin, "Poll Shows U.S. Isolation," *International Herald Tribune*, June 4, 2003.

23. For his depiction of those years, see John Bolton, *Surrender Is Not an Option: Defending America at the United Nations* (New York: Threshold Editions, Baker & Taylor, 2008).

24. See Bertrand G. Ramcharan, *The UN and Preventive Diplomacy* (Bloomington: Indiana University Press, 2008).

25. For a summary account, see Jeffrey A. Meyer and Mark G. Califano, *Good Intentions Corrupted: The Oil-for-Food Scandal and the Threat to the U.N.* (New York: PublicAffairs, 2006).

26. The complete reports by Paul A. Volcker, Richard J. Goldstone, and Mark Pieth are available at www.iic-offp.org.

27. For an assessment of Ban Ki-Moon's first year as Secretary-General, see "The Rewards of Beavering Away," *The Economist*, January 3, 2008, at www.economist.com/world/international/displaystory.cfm?story_id=10438482.

28. *Report of the Independent Panel on the Safety and Security of UN Personnel in Iraq* (October 20, 2003), available at www.un.org/News/dh/iraq/safety-security-un-personnel-iraq.pdf.

29. See Thomas G. Weiss and Peter J. Hoffman, "Making Humanitarianism Work," in *Making States Work: State Failure and the Crisis of Governance*, eds. Simon Chesterman, Michael Ignatieff, and Ramesh Thakur (Tokyo: UN University Press, 2005), 296–317. See also Michael Barnett and Thomas G. Weiss, eds., *Humanitarianism in Question: Politics, Power, Ethics* (Ithaca, N.Y.: Cornell University Press, 2008).

30. See Larry Minear et al., *Humanitarianism Under Siege: A Critical Review of Operation Lifeline Sudan* (Trenton, N.J.: Red Sea Press, 1991); and Francis M. Deng and Larry Minear, *The Challenge of Famine Relief* (Washington, D.C.: Brookings Institution, 1993).

31. For contemporary challenges, see William J. Durch, ed., *Twenty-First Century Peace Operations* (Washington, D.C.: U.S. Institute of Peace, 2006).

32. For other ideas about financing, see the thoughts of a group of experts under the chairmanship of Paul Volcker and Shijuro Ogata, *Financing an Effective United Nations* (New York: Ford Foundation, 1993).

33. "The Lost U.N. Summit Meeting," *New York Times*, September 14, 2005.

34. Kofi A. Annan, "A Glass at Least Half Full," *Wall Street Journal*, September 19, 2005.

35. Andrew Mack, ed., *Human Security Report 2005* (Vancouver: Human Security Centre, 2005), and in subsequent updated briefings available at www.humansecuritybrief.info. See also Human Security Project Report and World Bank's Mini-atlas of Human Security, available at www.miniatlasofhumansecurity.info.

36. For these and other statistics, see "Fatalities," available at www.un.org/Depts/dpko/fatalities/StatsByYear%201.pdf.

37. See James Rosenau, *The United Nations in a Turbulent World* (Boulder, Colo.: Lynne Rienner, 1992).

38. See the classic treatment by Kenneth Waltz, *Man, the State and War* (New York: Columbia University Press, 1968), in contrast with Philip Allott, *Eunomia: New Order for a New World* (New York: Oxford University Press, 1990).

39. International Commission on Intervention and State Sovereignty, *The Responsibility to Protect* (Ottawa: ICISS, 2001).

40. Francis M. Deng, *Protecting the Dispossessed: A Challenge for the International Community* (Washington, D.C.: Brookings Institution, 1993); Francis M. Deng et al., *Sovereignty as Responsibility* (Washington, D.C.: Brookings Institution, 1995); Francis M. Deng, "Frontiers of Sovereignty," *Leiden Journal of International Law* 8, no. 2 (1995): 249–286; Roberta Cohen and Francis M. Deng, *Masses in Flight: The Global Crisis of Internal Displacement* (Washington, D.C.: Brookings Institution, 1998); Roberta Cohen and Francis M. Deng, eds., *The Forsaken People: Case Studies of the Internally Displaced* (Washington, D.C.: Brookings Institution, 1998); and Francis M. Deng, "Dealing with the Displaced: A Challenge to the International Community," *Global Governance* 1, no. 1 (1995): 45–57. This story is told in detail in Thomas G. Weiss and David A. Korn, *Internal Displacement: Conceptualization and Its Consequences* (London: Routledge, 2006).

41. Annan, *Larger Freedom*, 59.

42. *2005 World Summit Outcome*, paras. 138–139.

43. Boutros-Ghali, *Agenda*, para. 69.

44. Annan, *Larger Freedom*, 31 para. 113.

45. For a discussion of the needs, see Oliver Jütersonke and Rolf Schwarz, eds., *Post-Conflict Peacebuilding: Security, Welfare and Representation*, *Security Dialogue* (special issue) 36, no. 4 (2005); and Mark T. Berger, ed., "From Nation-Building to State-Building," *Third World Quarterly* (special issue) 27, no. 1 (2006).

46. Annan, *Larger Freedom*, 31 para. 114.

47. Kofi Annan, *Renewing the United Nations: A Programme for Reform* (New York: United Nations, 1997).

48. Robert Jenkins, *Peacebuilding and the Peacebuilding Commission* (London: Routledge, forthcoming). On the issue of state-building, there is a burgeoning literature: Graciana del Castillo, *Rebuilding War-Torn States: The Challenges of Post-Conflict Reconstruction* (Oxford: Oxford University Press, 2008); Simon Chesterman, *You, The People: The United Nations, Transitional Administration and State-Building* (Oxford: Oxford University Press, 2004); James Crawford, *The Creation of States in International Law*, 2nd ed. (Oxford: Oxford University Press, 2006); Ralph Wilde, *International Territorial Administration: How Trusteeship and the Civilizing Mission Never Went Away* (Oxford: Oxford University Press, 2008); Mark T. Berger, ed., "From Nation-Building to State-Building," *Third World Quarterly* (special issue) 27, no. 1 (2006); Charles T. Call with Vanessa Hawkins Wyeth, eds., *Building States to Build Peace* (Boulder, Colo.: Lynne Rienner, 2006); Richard Caplan, *International Governance of War-Torn Territories: Rule and Reconstruction* (New York: Oxford University Press, 2005); Simon Chesterman, Michael Ignatieff, and Ramesh Thakur, eds., *State Failure and the Crisis of Governance: Making States Work* (Tokyo: UN University Press, 2005); and Paul Collier et al., *Breaking the Conflict Trap: Civil War and Development Policy* (Washington, D.C.: World Bank, 2003).

49. Alberto Cutillo, "International Assistance to Countries Emerging from Conflict: A Review of Fifteen Years of Interventions and the Future of Peacebuilding," International Peace Academy, The Security-Development Nexus Program, February 2006, 60.

50. *Report of the Panel on United Nations Peace Operations*, UN document A/55/305–5/2000/809, August 21, 2000.

51. See also John Gerard Ruggie, *Winning the Peace: America and World Order in the New Era* (New York: Columbia University Press, 1996).

52. See, for example, Fareed Zakaria, *The Post-American World* (New York: Norton, 2008), and Kishore Mahbubani, *The New Asian Hemisphere: The Irresistible Shift of Power to the East* (New York: PublicAffairs, 2008).

53. For analyses of the implications, see Rosemary Foot, S. Neil MacFarlane, and Michael Mastanduno, eds., *U.S. Hegemony and International Organizations: The United States and Multilateral Organizations* (New York: Oxford University Press, 2003); Stewart Patrick and Shepard Forman, eds., *Multilateralism and U.S. Foreign Policy: Ambivalent Engagement* (Boulder, Colo.: Lynne Rienner, 2002); and David M. Malone and Yuen Foong Khong, eds., *Unilateralism and U.S. Foreign Policy: International Perspectives* (Boulder, Colo.: Lynne Rienner, 2003). See also John Gerard Ruggie, *Multilateralism Matters: The Theory and Praxis of an Institutional Form* (New York: Columbia University Press, 1993).

54. Joseph E. Nye Jr., *Soft Power: The Means to Success in World Politics* (New York: Public Affairs, 2004).

55. For a quantitative and qualitative discussion, see Ernest B. Haas, "Collective Conflict Management: Evidence for a New World Order?" in *Collective Security in a Changing World*, ed. Thomas G. Weiss (Boulder, Colo.: Lynne Rienner, 1993), 63–117.

56. See Edward C. Luck, *Reforming the United Nations: Lessons from a History in Progress* (New Haven, Conn.: ACUNS, 2003), Occasional Paper No. 1: 7–16. See also Brian Urquhart and Erskine Childers, *A World in Need of Leadership: Tomorrow's United Nations—A Fresh Appraisal* (Uppsala, Sweden: Dag Hammarskjöld Foundation, 1996); Commission on Global Governance, *Our Global Neighbourhood* (Oxford: Oxford University Press, 1995); South Centre, *For a Strong and Democratic United Nations: A South Perspective on UN Reform* (Geneva: South Centre, 1995); and Erskine Childers and Brian Urquhart, *Renewing the United Nations System* (Upland, Penn.: Diane Publishing Company, 1999).

57. See Thomas G. Weiss, *Overcoming the Security Council Reform Impasse: The Implausible versus the Plausible* (Berlin: Friedrich Ebert Stiftung, 2005), Occasional Paper No. 14.

58. High-level Panel, *More Secure World*, para. 2497–260.

59. General Assembly, *2005 World Summit Outcome*, para. 154.

60. See Thomas G. Weiss and Karen Young, "Compromise and Credibility: Security Council Reform?" *Security Dialogue* 36, no. 2 (June 2005): 131–154, and Thomas G. Weiss, *Overcoming the Security Council Impasse: Envisioning Reform* (Berlin: Friedrich Ebert Stiftung, 2005), Occasional Paper No. 14.

61. Ibid., para. 139.

62. High-level Panel, *More Secure World*, para. 164(d).

63. General Assembly, *2005 World Summit Outcome*, para. 81.

64. Ibid.

65. Paragraphs 57–64 of the *Draft Outcome Document*, August 5, 2005, were devoted to this topic.

66. For an overview of this report, see Warren Hoge, "Report Finds U.N. Peacekeeping Isn't Moving to End Sex Abuse by Peacekeepers," *New York Times*, October 19, 2005.

67. Ibid.

68. See John Mackinlay, "The Requirement for a Multinational Enforcement Capability," in *Collective Security in a Changing World*, ed. Thomas G. Weiss (Boulder, Colo.: Lynne Rienner, 1993), 139–152.

69. The classic treatment of this subject is by Dag Hammarskjöld, "The International Civil Servant in Law and in Fact," lecture of May 30, 1961 (Oxford: Clarendon Press, 1961). For further information, see Thomas G. Weiss, *What's Wrong with the United Nations and How to Fix It* (Cambridge, UK: Polity, 2009) and *International Bureaucracy* (Lexington, Mass.: Heath, 1975); and Robert S. Jordan, ed., *International Administration: Its Evolution and Contemporary Applications* (New York: Oxford University Press, 1971).

70. For a discussion, see Christine Chinkin and Hilary Charlesworth, *The Boundaries of International Law: A Feminist Analysis* (New York: Juris Publications, 2000).

71. Paul A. Volcker, Richard J. Goldstone, and Mark Pieth, *The Management of the Oil-for-Food Programme*, vol. 1, September 7, 2005, 4, available at www.iic-offp.org.

72. Kofi Annan, "The Quiet Revolution," *Global Governance* 4, no. 2 (1998): 123–138.

73. See Stephen Biddle et al., *The Military Utility of Landmines Implications for Arms Control* (Alexandria, Va.: Institute for Defense Analyses, 1994).

74. See Thomas Risse, Stephen C. Ropp, and Kathryn Sikkink, eds., *The Power of Human Rights: International Norms and Domestic Change* (Cambridge: Cambridge University Press, 1999).

75. Richard Price, "Reversing the Gun Sights: Transnational Civil Society Targets Land Mines," *International Organization* 52, no. 3 (1998): 617.

76. For a comparison across cases of NGOs, IGOs, and governmental partnerships, see Don Hubert, *The Landmine Ban: A Case Study in Humanitarian Advocacy* (Providence, R.I.: Watson Institute, 2000), Occasional Paper No. 42.

77. Max Frankel, "Our Humanity vs. Their Sovereignty," *New York Times Magazine*, May 2, 1999, 36.

78. See S. Neil MacFarlane and Thomas G. Weiss, "Political Interest and Humanitarian Action," *Security Studies* 10, no. 1 (2000): 166–198.

79. James Dobbins et al., *The UN's Role in Nation-Building: From the Congo to Iraq* (New York: Rand Corporation, 2005), xxxvii.

PART TWO

HUMAN RIGHTS AND HUMANITARIAN AFFAIRS

CHAPTER 6

The United Nations, Human Rights, and Humanitarian Affairs

IN 2008, THE WORLD celebrated the sixtieth anniversary of the Universal Declaration of Human Rights (UDHR), which helped focus attention on the important role the United Nations plays in promulgating and promoting international human rights norms and principles. The UDHR reminds the world that the principles espoused in it are an elaboration of the UN Charter, and they place limits on governments' claims to unbridled sovereignty. According to those principles, established standards of civilized conduct apply to all states and manage the relationship between governments and those over whom they rule.

Yet those standards have been challenged in recent years. After the terrorist attacks on September 11, 2001, Alan Dershowitz, a lawyer at Harvard University, openly advocated torture as a legitimate security measure under certain conditions.[1] Another prominent public intellectual, Michael Ignatieff, who directed a human rights center at Harvard before being elected to the Canadian parliament, argued that even liberal democracies could understandably violate even the most basic human rights when faced with major threats to national security.[2] In January 2003, the respected British magazine *The Economist* ran a cover story under the title "Is Torture Ever Justified?" This focus was a follow-up to a *Washington Post* story reporting that in its war on terrorism, the United States was using "stress and duress" interrogation techniques on prisoners detained in Afghanistan and at its detention facility in Guantánamo Bay, Cuba, where more than thirty prisoners had attempted suicide. At the now infamous prison in Iraq, Abu Ghraib, U.S. personnel subjected prisoners to torture and degrading treatment. The United States also transferred certain prisoners to states such as Egypt, Morocco, Jordan, and Syria, where interrogation procedures were, euphemistically speaking, harsh. All of this was coupled with secret CIA detention facilities acknowledged by President George W. Bush, probably in Eastern Europe and elsewhere. The president vetoed a bill that would have required the

CIA, like the military, to avoid torture as well as inhumane and degrading treatment of prisoners. The feelings of insecurity have weakened such human rights norms as the total prohibition of torture and lesser forms of mistreatment in all situations. War and protection of many human rights, like the prohibition of torture, appear to be inversely correlated.[3]

But where does all this fit in the scope of the global human rights regime, and what are likely implications for the future of promoting, maintaining, and expanding human rights around the world? Answering this question is the purpose of this chapter.

THE THEORY

Since 1945 states have used their plenary or constitutive sovereignty and agreed to create international human rights obligations that in turn have restricted their operational sovereignty. The international law of human rights, developed on a global scale mostly at the United Nations, clearly regulates what legal policies states can adopt even within their own territorial jurisdictions. International agreements on human rights norms have been followed at least occasionally by concrete, noteworthy developments showing that international organizations have begun to reach deeply into matters that were once considered the core of national domestic affairs.

Moreover, the process by which a territorial state's assumed sovereignty has given way to shared authority and power between the state and international organizations is not a recent phenomenon. These changes accelerated with the start of the United Nations in 1945, became remarkable from about 1970, and became spasmodically dramatic from about 1991. The UN's role in human rights remains one of the more provocative subjects of the twenty-first century, what Roger Normand and Sarah Zaidi have aptly called "the unfinished revolution."[4]

Acknowledging these historical changes concerning the United Nations and human rights is not the same as being overly optimistic about these developments. Indeed, some UN proceedings on human rights would "depress Dr. Pangloss," the character in Voltaire's *Candide* who believes that all is for the best in this best of all possible worlds.[5] Although noteworthy in historical perspective, UN activity concerning human rights often displays an enormous gap between the law on the books and the law in action. At any given time or on any given issue, state expediency may supersede the application of UN human rights standards. Revolutionary change in a given context may not be institutionalized in UN machinery;[6] similar situations can give rise to different UN roles and different outcomes for human rights. A number of states, some of them with democratic governments, have opposed progressive action for human rights at the United Nations. If the international movement for human rights means separating the individual from full state control, then this movement has not always been well received by those who rule in the name of the state and who may be primarily interested in power, wealth, and independence.

The territorial state remains the most important legal-political entity in the modern world despite the obvious importance of ethnic, religious, and cultural identifications and an increasing number of actors in civil society everywhere. Thus many ethnic and religious groups try to capture control of the government so that they can speak officially for the state. The state constitutes the basic building block of the United Nations. State actors primarily shape the world organization's agenda and action on human rights, although states are pushed and pulled by other actors, such as private human rights groups and UN Secretariat officials. Developments at the UN concerning human rights have sometimes been remarkable. However, in general, state authorities still control the most important final decisions, and traditional national interests still trump individual human rights much of the time in international relations. In the final analysis, states must be the main protectors of human rights, while at the same time—by definition—states are the primary violators of international human rights.

Positive and negative developments concerning the United Nations and human rights were evident at the 1993 World Conference on Human Rights in Vienna.[7] Many states reaffirmed universal human rights, but a small minority of delegations, especially from Asia and the Middle East, argued for cultural relativism in a strong form—namely, that there were few or no universal human rights, mostly only rights specific to various countries, regions, or cultures.[8] Some of the delegates making arguments in favor of strong cultural relativism were representing states that were party to numerous human rights treaties, without reservations.

A large number of NGOs attended the conference and tried to focus on concrete rights violations in specific countries, but most governments wanted to deal with abstract principles, not specific violations. At the same time that the U.S. delegation took a strong stand in favor of internationally recognized human rights in general, the Clinton administration refused to provide military specialists and protective troops to conduct an investigation into war crimes in Serbian-controlled territory in the Balkans. These examples show that a certain diplomatic progress concerning international human rights was accompanied by much controversy and reluctance to act decisively.

A legal distinction exists between human rights and humanitarian affairs. In international law, there are two legislative histories and bodies of law: one for human rights and one for international humanitarian law—the latter pertaining to situations of armed conflict. Increasingly human rights groups like Amnesty International and Human Rights Watch concern themselves with the part of the laws of war pertaining to civilians and detained fighters in war, not just with human rights standards in peace. Human rights law and humanitarian law both focus on protecting human dignity, yet they have separate legislative histories, and humanitarian law applies only to armed conflict.

Actions undertaken because persons have a legal right to them must be distinguished from actions undertaken because they are humane, because in the former, persons are fundamentally entitled to the actions, but in the latter they are not. For example, in the diplomacy of the Conference on Security and Cooperation in Europe during the Cold War, some families divided by the Iron Curtain were reunited in the name of humanitarianism. The objective was to achieve a humane outcome, sidestepping debates about a right to emigrate. Likewise, some foreign assistance is provided for victims of earthquakes and other natural disasters at least in part because of humane considerations, whether or not persons have a legal right to that international assistance.

A great many international actions are undertaken for mixed motives with various justifications. The Security Council authorized the use of force, in effect, to curtail starvation in Somalia. To some, this was a response to the codified human rights to life, adequate nutrition, and health care. To others, this was acting humanely to alleviate suffering. The concept of international security was expanded to include humanitarian threats so that the Security Council could respond with a binding decision. States used the United Nations to improve order and reduce starvation. Whether outside troops went into Somalia for reasons of human rights or humanitarian affairs was a theoretical distinction without operational significance.

In this section we refer mostly to "human rights." Sometimes we note that UN involvement in a situation is oriented toward humane outcomes, whether or not the language of human rights is employed. Internationally recognized human rights have been defined so broadly that one can rationalize almost any action designed to improve the human condition in terms of fundamental rights. Given the extent of violence in the world, those concerned about individuals in dire straits need to be aware of international humanitarian law for armed conflicts and the long effort to create humanitarian space in the midst of what belligerents call "military necessity." As we saw in Part One, other terms have come into play at the United Nations from time to time, such as "human security" and "complex political emergency." Regardless of terminology, the driving force behind many of these developments has been to protect or restore human dignity—meaning the fundamental value and worth of the human person. There is no more fundamental right than to life.

UNDERSTANDING RIGHTS

Human rights are fundamental entitlements of persons, constituting means to the end of minimal human dignity or social justice. If persons have human rights, they are entitled to a fundamental claim that others must do, or refrain from doing, something. Under the Westphalian system of international relations, which the UN modifies but does not fundamentally contradict, states are primarily responsible for order and social justice in their jurisdictions. Their governments are the primary targets of these personal and fundamental claims. If an individual has a right to freedom from torture, governments are obligated to ensure that torture does not occur. If an individual has a right to adequate health care, governments are obligated to ensure that such health care is provided, especially to those who cannot afford it.

The legal system codifies what are recognized as human rights at any point in time. The legal system, of course, recognizes many legal rights. The ones seen as most fundamental to human dignity—that is, a life worthy of being lived—are called human rights. There is a difference between fundamental human rights and other legal rights that are perhaps important but not, relatively speaking, fundamental. This theoretical distinction between fundamental and important rights can and does give rise to debate. Is access to minimal health care fundamental, and thus a human right, as the Canadian legal system guarantees? Or is that access only something that people should have if they can afford it, as the U.S. system implies? Why does the U.S. legal system recognize a patient's legal right to sue a doctor for negligence but not allow that same person access to adequate health care as a human right?

The origin of human rights outside of codification in the legal system is also debated. Legal positivists are content to accept the identification of human rights as found in the legal system. But others, especially philosophers, wish to know what are the "true" or "moral" human rights that exist independently of legal codification. Natural law theorists, for example, believe that human rights exist in natural law as provided by a supreme being. Analytical theorists believe there are moral rights associated inherently with persons; the legal system only indicates a changing view of what these moral rights are.[9] According to Michael Ignatieff, we now have human rights at home and abroad not because of philosophy but because of history. If one reads history and notes the chronic abuse of individuals by public authorities, and if one notes that the societies that accept human rights do a better job of providing for the welfare of their citizens, that is sufficient justification for human rights.[10] Despite the long-standing debate about the ultimate origin of human rights, many societies have come to some agreement about fundamental rights, writing them into national constitutions and other legal instruments. In international society formal agreement exists on what constitutes universal human rights.[11]

International Origins

When important territorial states arose and became consolidated in the middle of the seventeenth century, human rights were treated, if at all, as national rather than international issues. Indeed, the core of the 1648 Peace of Westphalia, designed to end the religious wars of Europe, indicated that the territorial ruler would henceforth determine the territory's religion. In the modern language of rights, freedom of religion, or its absence, was left to the territorial ruler. The dominant international rule was what today we call state sovereignty. Any question of human rights was subsumed under that ordering principle. As "English school" theorists constantly remind us, international order was based on the principle of noninterference in domestic affairs.

Later, the Americans in 1776–1787 decided to recognize human rights, and the French in 1789 attempted to do so, both revolutions referring to such rights as universal. These revolutions had no immediate legal effect, and sometimes no immediate political effect, on other countries. In fact, many non-Western peoples and their rulers were not immediately affected by these two revolutions, oriented as they were to definitions of what were then called "the rights of man." Many non-Western societies, such as China, relied primarily on enlightened leaders for human dignity and social justice. Such leaders might be seen as limited by social or religious principles, but they were not widely seen as limited by personal rights.[12]

During the middle of the nineteenth century, the West was swept by a wave of international sentiment.[13] Growing international concern for the plight of persons without regard to nationality laid the moral foundations for a later resurrection and expansion of the notion of personal rights. Moral concern led eventually to an explosion in human rights developments even if the notion of human rights was not particularly resurrected then.[14] In some ways Marxism was part of this European-based transnational concern for the individual, since Karl Marx focused on the plight of the industrialized worker everywhere under early and crude capitalism. But he was not a persistent or consistent champion of all individual rights, being especially critical of unbridled property rights.

Early Marxism had its moral dimensions about individual suffering. Two other moral or social movements occurred about the same time and are usually cited as the earliest manifestations of internationally recognized human rights. In the 1860s, about the time Marx wrote *Das Kapital,* a Swiss businessman named Henry Dunant started what is now called the International Red Cross and Red Crescent Movement. Dunant was appalled that in the 1859 Battle of Solferino in what is now Italy, which was entangled in the war for the Austrian succession, wounded soldiers were simply left on the battlefield.[15] Armies had no adequate medical corps. European armies had more veterinarians to care for horses than doctors to care for soldiers.[16] Dunant envisioned what became national Red Cross societies, and these putatively private agencies not only geared up for practical action in war but also lobbied governments for new treaties to protect sick and wounded soldiers. In 1864 the first Geneva Convention for Victims of War was concluded, providing legal protection to fighters disabled in international war and the medical personnel who cared for them.[17] Today the International Red Cross and Red Crescent Movement encompasses over 186 national Red Cross or Red Crescent societies, the associated but autonomous International Federation of Red Cross and Red Crescent Societies, and the independent International Committee of the Red Cross.

The antislavery movement was another nineteenth-century effort to identify and correct a problem of human dignity on an international basis. By 1890 in Brussels, all the major Western states finally signed a multilateral treaty prohibiting the African slave trade. This capped a movement that had started about the turn of the nineteenth century in Britain. Just as private Red Cross organizations had pushed for protection and assistance for victims of war, so the London-based Anti-Slavery Society (today, Anti-Slavery International) and other private groups pushed the British government in particular to stop the slave trade. Britain outlawed the trade in the first decade of the nineteenth century; obtained a broader, similar international agreement at the Congress of Vienna in 1815; and thereafter used the British navy to try to enforce its ban on the slave trade.

The early resistance by the United States and other major slave-trading states was overcome by the end of the century. Yet an international agreement on principles and applications, reaching deeply into the European colonies in Africa, was necessary to significantly reduce this long-accepted and lucrative practice. In the twentieth century freedom from slavery, the slave trade, and slavery-like practices came to be accepted as an internationally recognized human right. Its roots lay in the transnational morality of the nineteenth century.

This trend of focusing on human need across national borders increased during the League of Nations era, although most efforts met with less than full success in an era of fascism, militarism, nationalism, racism, and isolationism. The Versailles conference in 1919 represented efforts to write into the League of Nations Covenant rights to religious freedom and racial equality. The British even proposed a right of outside intervention into states to protect religious freedom. These proposals failed largely because of Woodrow Wilson. Despite a Japanese push for the endorsement of racial equality, the U.S. president was so adamantly against any mention of race that U.S. and British proposals on religious freedom were withdrawn.[18] During the 1930s the League's assembly debated the merits of an international agreement on human rights in general, but French and Polish proposals to this effect failed. Some states were opposed in principle, and some did not want to antagonize Nazi Germany, given the prevailing policy of accommodation or appeasement. Nevertheless, the language of universal human rights was appearing more and more in diplomacy.

International efforts to codify and institutionalize labor rights were more successful. The International Labour Organization (ILO) was created and based in Geneva alongside the League. Its tripartite membership consisted of government, labor, and management delegations from each member state. This structure was conducive to the approval of a series of treaties and other agreements recognizing labor rights, as well as to the development of mechanisms to monitor state practice under the treaties. The ILO thus preceded the United Nations but continued after 1945 as a UN specialized agency. It was one of the first international organizations to monitor internationally recognized rights—in this case labor rights—within states.[19]

Although the Covenant of the League of Nations—the equivalent of the UN's Charter—failed to deal with human rights in general, its Article 23 did indicate that the League should be concerned with social justice. In addition to calling for international coordination of labor policy, Article 23 called on member states to take action on such matters as "native inhabitants," "traffic in women and children," "opium and other dangerous drugs," "freedom of communications," and "the prevention and control of disease." Precise standards, however, were decidedly lacking in these issue areas.

The League of Nations was connected to the minority treaties designed for about a dozen states after World War I in an effort to curtail the ethnic passions that had contributed to the outbreak of the Great War in the Balkans. Only a few states were legally obligated to give special rights to minorities. The system of minority treaties did not function very well under the acute nationalist pressures of the 1930s. So dismal was the League record on minority rights that global efforts at minority protection per se were not renewed by the United Nations until the 1980s—a gap of about fifty years. One UN agency carried the name of Sub-Commission on Prevention of Discrimination and Protection of Minorities for a time but did not take up the question of minority protection for some four decades. The minority treaties provided some useful experience. For instance, under certain treaty provisions, individuals could directly petition the League Council, the organization's most important body, for redress of alleged treaty violations. Ironically, in 1933 the Nazis paid some compensation for early anti-Semitism, responding to individual petitions under this system.[20]

Also, the League mandate system sought to protect the welfare of dependent peoples. The Permanent Mandates Commission supervised the European states that controlled certain territories taken from the losing side in World War I. Those European states were theoretically obligated to rule for the welfare of dependent peoples. Peoples in "A" mandates were supposed to be allowed to exercise their collective right to self-determination in the relatively near future. The Permanent Mandates Commission was made up of experts named by the League Council, and it established a reputation for integrity—so much so that the controlling states regarded it as a nuisance. There was some exercise of the right of individual petition, and the commission publicized some of the shortcomings from the policies of mandatory powers.[21]

In other ways, too, the League of Nations tried to promote humane values— a synonym for social justice. It was concerned with human dignity, even if it did not often use the specific language of human rights. In some cases it sought to improve the situation of persons without actually codifying their rights. In so doing it laid the foundation for later rights developments. For example, the League of Nations Refugee Office sought to help refugees, which was useful in 1951 when the UN sponsored a treaty on refugee rights and established the United Nations High Commissioner for Refugees.

The increased interaction among peoples—no doubt produced by changes in travel and communications technology that had also led to the first experiments with international institutions in the nineteenth century[22]—led in time to an increased moral solidarity or concern for human dignity across borders. War victims increasingly were seen as entitled to certain humane treatment regardless of nationality. Slavery and the slave trade were seen to be wrong regardless of what nationalities were involved. Labor was seen as needing protective regulation regardless of where the factory or shop was located. Developed states accepted a vague obligation to the League to rule at least some dependent territories for the good of the inhabitants. Refugees came to be seen as presenting common needs, wherever they might be found.

These and other developments in the late nineteenth and early twentieth centuries expressed "an epochal shift in moral sentiment."[23] The growing "moral interdependence" was to undergird the creation of human rights "regimes" in the UN era.[24] This moral solidarity was not cohesive enough to eradicate many of the ills addressed. How could it be when in the 1930s some major states (Germany, Italy, and Japan) were glorifying brutal power at the service of particular races or nationalities? And one major state (the Soviet Union) had an extensive record of brutal repression and exploitation within its borders? And another major state (the United States) refused to put its putative power at the service of systematic international cooperation? Moreover, the United States engaged in its own version of apartheid (namely, legally sanctioned racial segregation and discrimination) as well as blatantly racist immigration laws. Thus, while a shift occurred toward a cosmopolitan morality that tended to disregard national boundaries and citizenship, a "thick morality" still centered on national communities and was subject to the disease of chauvinistic nationalism. "Thin morality" was left for international society. Prevailing "wisdom" was that governments existed to pursue the national interest, whereas attention to the plight of others abroad was a distinctly secondary consideration.

Legal and organizational developments during the League of Nations era were more important as historical stepping-stones than as durable solutions in and of themselves. International moral solidarity was strong enough to create certain laws, agreements, and organizations, but states lacked sufficient political will to make these legal and organizational arrangements function effectively. Cosmopolitan compassion did not always fit well with traditional raisons d'état.[25]

When the United Nations was created in 1945, a growing corpus of legal and organizational experience existed that the international community could draw on in trying to improve international order and justice. By 1948, conventional wisdom held that internationally recognized human rights would have to be reaffirmed and expanded, not erased. The UN would have to devise better ways of improving human dignity, through both law and organization.

BASIC NORMS IN THE UN ERA

The American and British founders of the UN were determined to include human rights in the Charter. This determination actually preceded widespread knowledge about the extent of the Holocaust and other World War II atrocities.[26] Intellectual opinion in Britain and the United States pushed for an endorsement of human rights as a statement about the rationale for World War II. This could be seen in the Atlantic Charter issued by the United States and Britain early in 1941. Franklin D. Roosevelt stressed the importance of four freedoms, including freedom from "want." A handful of Latin American states joined in this push to emphasize human rights as a statement about civilized nations. Eleanor Roosevelt became an outspoken champion of human rights in general and women's rights in particular. In the UN Human Rights Commission, however, which Eleanor Roosevelt chaired in the 1940s, the most outspoken advocate for women's rights was the Indian representative, Hansa Mehta.

The Truman administration, under pressure from both NGOs and concerned Latin American states, and unlike the Wilson administration in 1919, agreed to a series of statements on human rights in the Charter and successfully lobbied the other victorious great powers. This was not an easy decision for the Truman administration, particularly given the continuation of legally sanctioned and widely supported racial discrimination within the United States. Whether the Truman administration was genuinely and deeply committed to getting human rights into the Charter[27] or whether it was pushed in that direction by others[28] remains a point of historical debate. Franklin D. Roosevelt had become convinced that the origins of World War II lay in the denial of human rights in fascist Europe and imperial Japan, and Harry Truman accepted this interpretation. Various other states and NGOs expanded the references to human rights in the UN Charter, but without changing the U.S. position that this human rights language would remain general and judicially unenforceable.[29]

Why Joseph Stalin accepted these human rights statements is not clear, especially given the widespread political murder and persecution within the Soviet Union in the 1930s and 1940s. Perhaps the USSR saw this human rights language as useful in deflecting criticism of Soviet policies, particularly since the Charter language was vague and not immediately followed by specifics on application. Perhaps Stalin saw the language of rights as useful in his attempt to focus on socialism—that is, one might accept the general wording on rights if one intended to concentrate only on social and economic rights.[30] This would not be the last time the Soviet Union underestimated the influence of language written into international agreements. The 1975 Helsinki Accord, and especially its provisions on human rights and humanitarian affairs, generated pressures that helped weaken European communism. The Soviet Union initially resisted human rights language in the accord, but it eventually accepted that language in the mistaken notion that the codification and dissemination of human rights would not upset totalitarian control.[31]

The United Kingdom accepted the Charter language on human rights with the understanding that it would not be applied in British colonies. For Winston Churchill, who had helped author ringing pronouncements about human rights during the Second World War to highlight enemy atrocities, the British Empire should continue, with all that it implied about an unequal status for nonwhite peoples. In this view, he was not dissimilar from the American Founding Fathers in the eighteenth century, whose proclamations about human rights were not intended for women, slaves, or Native Americans. The 1945 Charter statements on human rights, although more progressive than some had originally wanted, were vague. Nevertheless, they provided the legal cornerstone or foundation for a later legal and diplomatic revolution. The Charter's preamble states that a principal purpose of the UN is "to affirm faith in fundamental human rights." In Article 1, the Charter says that one of the purposes of the organization is to promote and encourage "respect for human rights and for fundamental freedoms for all without distinction as to race, sex, language, or religion." In Article 55, the Charter imposes on states these legal obligations:

With a view to the creation of conditions of stability and well-being which are necessary for peaceful and friendly relations among nations based on respect for the principle of equal rights and self-determination of peoples, the United Nations shall promote:

A. higher standards of living, full employment, and conditions of economic and social progress and development;

B. solutions of international economic, social, health, and related problems; and international cultural and educational cooperation; and

C. universal respect for, and observance of, human rights and fundamental freedoms for all without distinction as to race, sex, language, or religion.

Article 56 states that "all Members pledge themselves to take joint and separate action in cooperation with the Organization for the achievement of the purposes set forth in Article 55."

The language of Article 55 endorses the notion of human rights because they were linked to international peace and security. Western democracies believed that states respecting human rights in the form of civil and political rights would not make war on others. In this view, brutal authoritarian states, those that denied civil and political rights, were inherently aggressive, whereas democracies were inherently peaceful. At the same time, many accepted the notion of human rights by seeing them as a means to human dignity, not necessarily or primarily as a means to ensure international peace.

Both motivations drove the diplomatic process regarding human rights in 1945. Some policymakers genuinely saw human rights as linked to peace, and others may have accepted that rationale as a useful justification while believing that one should promote and protect human rights for reasons of human dignity disconnected from questions of peace and war. Motivation and justification are not the same,[32] but in reality separating the two is difficult. The relationship between human rights and peace has intrinsic importance to world politics. A clear correlation between at least some human rights and peace has importance not only for a direct and "micro" contribution to human dignity but to human dignity in a "macro" sense by enhancing international—and perhaps national—security and stability by eliminating major violence.

The connection between various human rights and international and national peace—with peace defined as the absence of widespread violence between or within countries—has been widely researched. The following five statements summarize some of that voluminous research. First, liberal democratic governments (those that emerge from, and thereafter respect, widespread civil and political rights) tend not to engage in international war with one another.[33] Documenting international war between or among democracies is difficult, and some scholars believe that the absence of war is not because of democracy. The United Kingdom and the United States fought in 1812, but one scholar holds that because of the severely limited franchise, the United States did not become a democracy until the 1820s and Britain not until the 1830s.[34] The debate about threshold conditions for democracy continues today. One view is that the United States did not become a democracy until women, 50 percent of the population, gained the franchise. In the American Civil War, the Union and the Confederacy both had elected presidents, but the Confederacy was not recognized as a separate state by many outsiders, and it also severely restricted the voting franchise. At the start of World War I, Germany manifested a very broad franchise, but its parliament lacked authority and its kaiser went unchecked in making much policy. Even though some scholars think the historical absence of war between democracies is either a statistical accident or explicable by security factors, other scholars continue to insist that consolidated liberal democracies (as compared to transitional democracies and illiberal democracies) do not make war on each other.[35] But as long as scholars cannot explain precisely why the latter is usually true, one must remain cautious about the accuracy and durability of this apparent pattern.

Second, liberal democratic governments have used covert force against other elected governments that are not perceived to be truly in the liberal democratic community. The United States during the Cold War used force to overthrow some elected governments in developing countries—for example, Iran in 1953 (Mohammed Mossadeq was elected by Iran's parliament), Guatemala in 1954 (Jacobo Arbenz Guzmán was genuinely if imperfectly elected in a popular vote), Chile in 1973 (Salvador Allende won a plurality), and Nicaragua after 1984 (some international observers regarded Daniel Ortega as genuinely if imperfectly elected).[36] Several democracies used force to remove the Patrice Lumumba government in the Congo in the 1960s; those elections, too, were imperfect but reflected popular sentiment.[37]

Third, some industrialized liberal democratic governments seem to be war-prone and clearly have initiated force against authoritarian governments. Britain, France, and the United States are among the most war-prone states, owing perhaps to their power and geography. Liberal democratic governments initiated hostilities in the Spanish-American War of 1898 and the Suez crisis of 1956, not to mention U.S. use of force in Grenada and Panama in the 1980s, or in Iraq in 2003.

Fourth, human rights of various types do not correlate clearly and easily with major national violence such as civil wars and rebellions.[38] In some of these situations a particular human rights issue may be important—for example, slavery in the American Civil War, ethnic and religious persecution in the Romanian violence of 1989, and perceived ethnic discrimination in contemporary Sri Lanka. But in other civil wars and similar intranational violence, human rights factors seemed not to be a leading cause—for example, the Russian civil war of 1917 and the Chinese civil war in the 1930s. The Universal Declaration of Human Rights presents itself, in part, as a barrier to national revolution against repression. This follows the Jeffersonian philosophy that if human rights are not respected, revolution may be justified. But this link between human rights violations and national violence is difficult to verify as a prominent and recurring pattern. A number of repressive and exploitative governing arrangements have lasted for a relatively long time. And various rights-protective governments have yielded under violent pressure to more authoritarian elites.

Fifth, armed conflict seems clearly to lead to an increase in human rights violations.[39] If some uncertainty remains about whether liberal democracy at home leads to a certain peace abroad, a reverse pattern does not seem open to debate. When states participate in international and internal armed conflict, there is almost always a rise in violations of rights of personal integrity and an increase in forced disappearance, torture, arbitrary arrest, and other violations of important civil rights. Human rights may or may not lead to peace, but peace is conducive to enhanced human rights.

CORE NORMS BEYOND THE CHARTER

The UN Charter presented the interesting situation of codifying a general commitment to human rights before an international definition or list of human rights was developed. To answer the question of what internationally recognized human rights states are obligated to apply, the United Nations developed the Universal Declaration of Human Rights in an effort to specify Charter principles. On December 10, 1948—December 10 is now recognized as International Human Rights Day—the General Assembly adopted the UDHR without a negative vote (but with eight abstentions: the Soviet Union and its allies, Saudi Arabia,

Eleanor Roosevelt holding a Universal Declaration of Human Rights poster. (UN/DPI Photo 23783)

and South Africa). This resolution, not legally binding at the time of adoption, listed thirty human rights principles covering perhaps sixty rights. They fell into three broad clusters.[40]

First-generation negative rights are the individual civil and political rights that are well-known in the West. They are called "first-generation" because they were the ones first endorsed in national constitutions and called "negative" because civil rights in particular blocked public authority from interfering with the private person in civil society. These were the rights to freedom of thought, speech, religion, privacy, and assembly—plus the right to participate in the making of public policy. In the view of some observers, these are the only true human rights. In the view of others, these are the most important human rights because if one has civil and political rights, one can use them to obtain and apply the others. In the view of still others, these rights are not so important because if one lacks the material basics of life such as food, shelter, health care, and education, then civil and political rights become relatively meaningless.

Second-generation positive rights are socioeconomic rights.[41] They are called "second-generation" because they were associated with various twentieth-century revolutions emphasizing a redistribution of the material benefits of economic growth, and "positive" because they obligate public authority to take positive steps to ensure minimal food, shelter, and health care. European states,

Japan, and Canada have enshrined these rights in their welfare states, and these rights have been rhetorically emphasized in many developing countries. How important these rights are is still a matter of debate. In the United States, the Democratic Carter and Clinton administrations accepted them in theory and gave them some rhetorical attention but never fully embraced them. Republican administrations from Ronald Reagan to George W. Bush rejected them as dangerous to individual responsibility and leading to big government.

Third-generation solidarity rights are the rights emphasized by some contemporary actors. They are called "third-generation" because they followed the other two clusters and also are called "solidarity" because they pertain to collections of persons—for instance, indigenous peoples—rather than to individuals. Later formulations have included claims to a right to peace, development, and a healthy environment as the common heritage of humankind. In some national law, groups receive formal recognition. Some minorities are guaranteed a certain number of seats in Parliament. Other peoples are recognized as holding collective title to land. Whether some of these group arrangements should be called collective human rights of universal validity remains controversial.

One collective right, a people's right to self-determination, has been much discussed, especially since the end of World War II. The principle of national self-determination is recognized as the first article in both the International Covenants on Civil and Political Rights and on Economic, Social and Cultural Rights. Thus the collective right to self-determination is cast in modern times as a human right. It is clear, however, that this general principle has not been translated into specific rules indicating which group is a national people with this right, and which is not. Also lacking is a clear indication of what self-determination means, and the options range from various forms of internal autonomy to full independence. Unfortunately, most claims to self-determination are resolved by politics, including violent politics, rather than peaceful change under judicial supervision.

Parsing rights into several categories or "generations" is perhaps useful to summarize developments, but analytical care is necessary. To apply negative rights, positive action must be taken. States must develop legislation to protect civil and political rights and spend billions each year to see that they are respected. Second-generation socioeconomic rights were emphasized by the Catholic Church as well as by the state of Ireland and various Latin American states relatively early on. Collective rights can also pertain to individuals. Moreover, they are not so new. The right to national self-determination is actually a right of peoples or nations that has been (a vague) part of international law for decades.

A prevalent view, articulated nicely by Mary Robinson, the former president of Ireland who stepped down in September 2002 as the UN high commissioner for human rights, is that all of the generations should be viewed as a "package" of rights.[42] Her position reflected votes in the General Assembly stating that all internationally recognized rights were important and interdependent. At the same time, however, the Security Council created international criminal tribunals for the former Yugoslavia and Rwanda with legal jurisdiction for genocide, war crimes, and crimes against humanity. This suggested that the right to be free from these violations was more important or more basic. UN member states created the International Criminal Court with the same focus. The structure of the International Covenant on Civil and Political Rights suggests that even within that category of rights some rights are core, permitting no violation even in national emergencies, while other rights can be suspended in exceptional times. All of this leads to much debate about whether there should be some prioritizing of rights action.[43]

The United States is an outlier among states that traditionally support human rights. It has not ratified three of seven core treaties—the ones protecting economic, cultural, and social rights, protecting children's rights, and eliminating discrimination against women. Within the Group of 8 (G-8), or the seven most powerful Western democracies (including Japan) and the Russian Federation, the United States is the only country that has not ratified any of these. Moreover, even when ratifying human rights treaties like the Convention on the Prevention and Punishment of the Crime of Genocide and the Covenant on Civil and Political Rights, the United States adds reservations and other statements that prevent the treaties from having domestic effect, which, as a former State Department lawyer noted, makes it very difficult to get international law introduced into courts within the United States.[44]

No state voting for the Universal Declaration of Human Rights has succeeded in meeting all its terms through national legislation and practice. This vote was the homage that vice paid to virtue. This would not be the last time that state diplomacy presented a large measure of hypocrisy. Yet, most contemporary states want to be associated with the notion of human rights. Of 192 member states, 154 had formally accepted the civil-political covenant by May 2007, and 151 the economic-social-cultural covenant.

Since 1948, the Universal Declaration of Human Rights has acquired a status far beyond that of a normal or regular General Assembly recommendation. Some national courts have held that parts of the declaration have passed into customary international law and thus became legally binding (e.g., the declaration's Article 5, prohibiting torture). Some authorities and publicists believe the entire declaration is now legally binding, whereas others say that only parts of it are. The International Court of Justice in The Hague has not rendered an opinion on this question,[45] and so the declaration's overall legal status remains unclear.

Nonetheless, the practical impact of the declaration is considerable. Its principles have been endorsed in numerous national constitutions and other legal and quasi-legal documents. All the new or newly independent European states that once had communist governments accepted its principles in theory in the 1990s. Of the eight states abstaining in 1948, seven had renounced their abstention by 1993. Only Saudi Arabia continued to object openly to the declaration.

Even China, despite its repressive policies and government, issued statements accepting the abstract validity of the universal declaration.

Having adopted the declaration, UN member states turned to an even more specific elaboration of internationally recognized human rights. The decision was made to negotiate two separate core human rights treaties, one on civil and political rights and one on social, economic, and cultural rights. This was not done only, or even primarily, because of theoretical or ideological differences among states. The different types of rights also were seen as requiring different types of follow-up. A widely held view was that civil-political rights could be implemented immediately, given sufficient political will, and were enforceable by judicial proceedings. By comparison, socioeconomic rights were seen as requiring certain policies over time, as greatly affected by economic and social factors, and hence as not subject to immediate enforcement by court order. As mentioned earlier, the more recent approach within the United Nations, in the General Assembly and elsewhere, is to blur distinctions and consider rights comprehensively.

By 1956 two UN covenants, or multilateral treaties, were essentially complete on the two clusters of rights. By 1966 they were formally approved by states voting in the General Assembly, the time lag indicating that not all states were enthusiastic about the emergence of human rights treaties limiting state sovereignty. By 1976 a sufficient number of state adherences had been obtained to bring the treaties into legal force by parties giving their formal consent. Few followed the example of the United States of accepting one but rejecting the other (the United States became a party to the civil-political covenant in 1992, with reservations, but not to the socioeconomic covenant). Most states accepted both covenants.

More than fifty states (not including the United States) have agreed to allow their citizens to petition the UN Human Rights Committee (after exhausting national efforts) alleging a violation of the civil-political covenant by a government. The Human Rights Committee was made up of individual experts, not governmental representatives. It was not a court but a "monitoring mechanism" that could direct negative publicity toward an offending and recalcitrant government. It worked to prod governments toward fulfilling their international commitments. All states that accepted the socioeconomic covenant were automatically supervised by a UN Committee of Experts. After a slow start, that committee, too, began a systematic effort to persuade states to honor their commitments. The mechanisms of both committees are treated below.

These three documents, the 1948 Universal Declaration of Human Rights and the two 1966 UN covenants, make up what was not included in the UN's Charter: an International Bill of Rights, or a core list of internationally recognized human rights that would have similar status to the Bill of Rights in the U.S. Constitution. Most of the treaty provisions are clarifications of, and elaborations on, the thirty norms found in the declaration. There are a few discrepancies. The

The Palais des Nations, UN Office at Geneva. (UN/DPI Photo/P. Klee)

declaration notes a right to private property, but this right was not codified in the two covenants. After the fall of European communism, the General Assembly on several occasions returned to a recognition of property rights. As already noted, there was a broad and formal acceptance of this International Bill of Rights, even though there is no such official label or document. At the same time, a number of governments were tardy in filing reports with both the Human Rights Committee under the civil-political covenant and the Committee of Experts under the socioeconomic covenant. But from either 1966 or 1976, depending on which date is emphasized, there was a core definition of universal human rights in legally binding form with a monitoring process designed to specify what the treaties meant.

SUPPLEMENTING THE CORE

During most of the UN era, states were willing to endorse abstract human rights. But until the 1990s, they were not willing to create specialized human rights courts—or even to make the global treaties enforceable through national courts. In the next chapter we address the establishment of ad hoc international criminal tribunals for the former Yugoslavia and Rwanda and the International Criminal Court with broad jurisdiction, as well as the Pinochet case from Chile involving national action concerning torture and other crimes against humanity. Traditionally, in the absence of dependable adjudication, states tried to reinforce the International Bill of Rights, while protecting their legal independence, by negotiating more human rights treaties. This is a way to bring diplomatic emphasis to a problem, to raise awareness of a problem, or to further specify state obligation in the hopes that specificity will improve behavior. The process is similar to some aspects of national law. In the United States, if the Congress is dissatisfied with executive performance under a law, rather than seek adjudication in the courts, an action that frequently is unproductive, the Congress may pass a more specific follow-up law.[46]

About one hundred international human rights instruments exist. These include conventions, protocols, declarations, codes of conduct, and formal statements of standards and basic principles. Table 6.1 summarizes part of the situation. Despite overlap and duplication, the United Nations has seen the emergence of treaties on racial discrimination, apartheid, political rights of women, discrimination against women, slavery, the slave trade and slavery-like practices, genocide, hostages, torture, the nationality of married women, stateless persons, refugees, marriage, prostitution, children, and discrimination in education. The ILO has sponsored treaties on forced labor, the right to organize, and rights to collective bargaining, among others. A number of supplemental human rights treaties are in varying stages of negotiation at the United Nations, including those on indigenous peoples, forced disappearances, persons with disabilities, and minorities. A collective right to development has been declared by various UN bodies, including the General Assembly, and may become the subject matter of a treaty.

Regional human rights treaties fall outside the domain of the UN, as do some treaties on human rights in armed conflict that are sponsored by the International Committee of the Red Cross and Switzerland, the latter being the official depository for what is called international humanitarian law (IHL). In this regard, diplomatic events that technically fall outside the UN, especially related to IHL, contributed to further specifying international standards on human rights and humanitarian affairs. IHL sought to protect human dignity in armed conflicts, just as human rights law sought to protect human dignity more generally.[47]

In 1949 the international community of states adopted four conventions for victims of war. Initially drafted by the ICRC, the Geneva Conventions of August 1949 sought to codify and improve on the humanitarian practices undertaken during World War II. For the first time in history, a treaty was directed to the rights of civilians in international armed conflict and in occupied territory resulting from armed conflict. Each of the four Geneva Conventions of 1949 contained an article (hence Common Article 3) that extended written humanitarian law into internal armed conflict. The ICRC, although technically a Swiss private association, was given the right in public international law to see detainees resulting from international armed conflict.[48] And for the first time in history, civilians in occupied territory were recognized as having a right to humanitarian assistance.

TABLE 6.1   UN Human Rights Conventions

Convention (grouped by subject)	Year Opened for Ratification	Year Entered into Force	Number of Parties
General Human Rights			
International Covenant on Civil and Political Rights	1966	1976	154
Optional Protocol to the International Covenant on Civil and Political Rights (private petition)	1966	1976	105
Second Optional Protocol to the International Covenant on Civil and Political Rights (abolition of death penalty)	1989	1991	56
International Covenant on Economic, Social and Cultural Rights	1966	1976	151
Racial Discrimination			
International Convention on the Elimination of All Forms of Racial Discrimination	1966	1969	170
International Convention on the Suppression and Punishment of the Crime of Apartheid	1973	1976	106
International Convention Against Apartheid in Sports	1985	1988	59
Rights of Women			
Convention on the Political Rights of Women	1953	1954	115
Convention on the Nationality of Married Women	1957	1958	70
Convention on Consent to Marriage, Minimum Age for Marriage, and Registration of Marriages	1962	1964	49
Convention on the Elimination of All Forms of Discrimination Against Women	1979	1981	180
Optional Protocol to the Convention on the Elimination of All Forms of Discrimination Against Women (communication procedures)	1999	2000	74
Slavery and Related Matters			
Slavery Convention of 1926, as amended in 1953	1953	1955	95
Protocol Amending the 1926 Slavery Convention	1953	1953	59
Supplementary Convention on the Abolition of Slavery, the Slave Trade, and Institutions and Practices Similar to Slavery	1956	1957	119
Convention for the Suppression of the Traffic in Persons and the Exploitation of the Prostitution of Others	1950	1951	74

TABLE 6.1   *(continued)*

Convention (grouped by subject)	Year Opened for Ratification	Year Entered into Force	Number of Parties
Refugees and Stateless Persons			
Convention Relating to the Status of Refugees	1951	1954	140
Protocol Relating to the Status of Refugees (extends time of original convention)	1967	1967	138
Convention Relating to the Status of Stateless Persons	1954	1960	54
Convention on the Reduction of Statelessness	1961	1975	26
Other			
Convention on the Prevention and Punishment of the Crime of Genocide	1948	1951	138
Convention on the International Right of Correction	1952	1962	15
Convention on the Non-Applicability of Statutory Limitations of War Crimes and Crimes Against Humanity	1968	1970	49
Convention Against Torture and Other Cruel, Inhuman, or Degrading Treatment or Punishment	1984	1987	141
Convention on the Rights of the Child	1989	1989	192
Optional Protocol to the Convention on the Rights of the Child (on the Involvement of Children in Armed Conflict)	2000	2002	104
Optional Protocol to the Convention on the Rights of the Child (on the Sale of Children, Child Prostitution, and Child Pornography)	2000	2002	101

This body of humanitarian law, from one point of view the international law for human rights in armed conflict, was further developed in 1977 through two protocols (or additional treaties): Protocol I for international armed conflict and Protocol II for internal armed conflict. Normative standards continued to evolve. For the first time in the history of warfare, Protocol I prohibited the starvation of civilians as a legal means of warfare. Protocol II represented the first separate treaty on victims in internal war. In 2005 Additional Protocol III was added, regulating neutral emblems for aid societies. Among its practical effects was allowing the official Israeli aid society, Magen David Adom (MDA), to be recognized into the International Red Cross and Red Crescent Movement. Before, since MDA used the Red Shield of David as its emblem, it could not be officially recognized by the ICRC or admitted into the Federation of Red Cross and Red Crescent Societies. For many states, what was at issue was indirect recognition of the legitimacy of the state of Israel through accommodation of its official aid society. For that reason, Protocol III was approved not by consensus but by contested vote. The Protocol allowed use of a Red Crystal, in addition to the Red

Cross and Red Crescent, as approved neutral emblems, to which national emblems could be added. Thus MDA could now use the Red Crystal in international operations devoid of religious or historical significance, along with its red six-sided star. Such were the complications when humanitarian considerations collided with state strategic calculation.

Regional human rights developments are noteworthy. A regional human rights regime was created in Western Europe, and it served as an excellent model for the international protection of human rights. The European Convention on Human Rights and Fundamental Freedoms defined a set of civil and political rights. For a time the European Commission on Human Rights served as a collective conciliator, responding to state or private complaints to seek out-of-court settlements. The European Court of Human Rights existed to give binding judgments about the legality of state policies under the European Convention on Human Rights.

All states in the Council of Europe bound themselves to abide by the convention. All governments allowed their citizens to have the right of individual petition to the commission, a body that could then—failing a negotiated agreement—take the petition to the European Court of Human Rights. All states eventually accepted the court's supranational authority. Member states voluntarily complied with its judgments holding state policies illegal. Such was the political consensus in support of human rights within the Council of Europe. This regional international regime for human rights functioned through international agencies made up of uninstructed individuals rather than state officials—although there was also a Committee of Ministers made up of state representatives.

In the mid-1990s, Council of Europe members progressively moved toward giving individuals standing to sue in the European Court of Human Rights without having the commission represent them. Thus an individual would have almost the same legal "personality" or status in the court as a state. Persons came to acquire both substantive and procedural rights of note, a distinctive feature, since formerly it was possible to present a case—or have full "personality," in the language of international lawyers—only as a state.

In fact, the European system for the international protection of civil and political rights under the European Human Rights Convention generated such a large number of cases that, to streamline procedure, the commission was done away with. Individuals were allowed to proceed directly to a lower chamber of the European Court of Human Rights for an initial review of the admissibility of their complaint. If the complaint met procedural requirements, the individual could then move on to the substantive phase, basically on an equal footing with state representatives. (There were other regional human rights regimes in the Western Hemisphere and Africa, but they did not match the West European record in successfully protecting human rights.) The European situation shows that "muscular," supranational, effective protection of human rights is possible in international relations when there is sufficient political will. Unfortunately, the European situation also shows how far the UN system has to go before it can provide the same sort of human rights regime. Popular and state commitment to the serious protection of human rights is much greater in Europe than is true on a global basis. Possibilities at the UN are determined by this factor. In this sense political culture is the independent variable, and institutional authority the dependent variable.

Diplomatic activity concerning setting human rights standards internationally has expanded greatly. A sizable, and still expanding, part of international law deals with human rights. Human rights have been formally accepted as a legitimate part of international relations. Most states do not oppose these normative developments in the abstract—that is, they do not dispute that international law should regulate the rights of persons even when persons are within states in "normal" times. This generalization also pertains to international or internal armed conflict, and to public emergency—although some rights protections can be modified in these exceptional situations. All states are now parties to the 1949 Geneva Conventions. The United Nations clearly is acting within accepted bounds in establishing human rights standards. For ease of reference, Table 6.1 contains a list of human rights that are generally accepted as protected under international law.

One theme that appears in Part Three of this volume is how contemporary globalization represents a powerful challenge to integrating human rights more effectively into efforts to ensure a values-led process. Upon resigning from the UN, former high commissioner for human rights Mary Robinson founded Realizing Rights—Ethical Globalization Initiative to pursue her agenda.[49] The progressive integration of economies and societies, a helpful definition formed by the ILO's World Commission on the Social Dimensions of Globalization,[50] has generated uneven benefits. While an academic debate continues about whether globalization is new,[51] its costs are borne unevenly. Future human rights challenges include the need for global policies to address a host of problems, including human rights, which emerge from such global problems as transnational criminal and terrorist activities, human trafficking, and HIV/AIDS. Secretary-General Kofi Annan launched the Global Compact, an effort to get powerful multinational corporations to pledge to respect human rights along with other standards that pertain to protecting the environment and reducing corruption.

The Permanent Court of International Justice said in the early 1920s that what is international and what is domestic depends on the changing nature of international relations.[52] The UN era has clearly seen the zone of exclusive or essential domestic jurisdiction shrinking. Article 2 (7) mandates that the UN shall not "intervene" in matters "essentially" within the domestic jurisdiction of states. The diplomatic record confirms, however, that most states no longer view many human rights matters as essentially within domestic jurisdiction. Certainly the establishment of international standards on human rights cannot logically be considered an unlawful intrusion into state internal affairs. If the Security Council decides that international peace and security are threatened, even internationally approved "intervention"—in the sense of coercive economic and military action—can be taken to rectify massive human rights violations under the doctrine of "the responsibility to protect."

As the extensive standard-setting activity of the UN has made clear, at least in legal theory, human rights have been internationalized. Beyond setting standards, an answer is emerging to the ancient question: Quis custodiet ipsos custodes? (Who shall guard the guardians?). In the field of human rights, the United Nations will supervise governmental policy against the background of global norms.

NOTES

1. Dana Priest and Barton Gellman, "For CIA Suspects Abroad, Brass-Knuckle Treatment," *Washington Post*, December 27, 2002. This article generated virtually no immediate reaction in official Washington. Compare "Is Torture Ever Justified?," *The Economist*, January 11–17, 2003. Harvard University law professor Alan Dershowitz defended some use of torture in a debate with Kenneth Roth of Human Rights Watch on NBC, *Today Show*, March 4, 2003.

2. Michael Ignatieff, *The Lesser Evil: Political Ethics in an Age of Terror* (Princeton, N.J.: Princeton University Press, 2005).

3. See Kenneth Roth, "Getting Away with Torture," *Global Governance* 11, no. 3 (2005): 389–406. This is an underlying theme in a series of essays in Thomas G. Weiss, Margaret E. Crahan, and John Goering, eds., *Wars on Terrorism and Iraq: Human Rights, Unilateralism, and U.S. Foreign Policy* (London: Routledge, 2004).

4. Roger Normand and Sarah Zaidi, *Human Rights at the UN: The Political History of Universal Justice* (Bloomington: Indiana University Press, 2008).

5. Tom J. Farer, "The UN and Human Rights: More Than a Whimper, Less Than a Roar," in Adam Roberts and Benedict Kingsbury, *United Nations, Divided World*, 2nd ed. (New York: Oxford University Press, Clarendon Paperback, 1993), 129.

6. For an overview, see Julie A. Mertus, *The United Nations and Human Rights*, 2nd ed. (London: Routledge, 2009). See also Martin J. Rochester, *Between Peril and Promise: The Politics of International Law* (Washington, D.C.: CQ Press, 2006); Michael Byers, ed., *The Role of Law in International Politics: Essays in International Relations and International Law* (Oxford: Oxford University Press, 2000).

7. For a discussion of this session in the broader one of such meetings, see Michael G. Schechter, *United Nations Global Conferences* (London: Routledge, 2005), 128–134.

8. This debate often went under the label of "East Asian values." See Joanne R. Bauer and Daniel A. Bell, eds., *The East Asian Challenge for Human Rights* (Cambridge: Cambridge University Press, 1999).

9. Jack Donnelly, *Universal Human Rights in Theory and Practice*, 2nd ed. (Ithaca, N.Y.: Cornell University Press, 2003), 7–21.

10. Michael Ignatieff, *Human Rights As Politics and Idolatry* (Princeton, N.J.: Princeton University Press, 2001).

11. For a good overview, see Stephen James, *Universal Human Rights* (New York: LFB Scholarly Publishing, 2007). See also David P. Forsythe, general ed., *Encyclopedia of Human Rights*, 3rd ed. (New York: Oxford University Press, 2009).

12. The idea of human rights was a Western invention in both theory and practice, but ethical considerations from many cultures affected European and North American thought. See Micheline R. Ishay, *The History of Human Rights: From Ancient Times to the Globalization Era* (Berkeley: University of California Press, 2004).

13. John F. Hutchinson, "Rethinking the Origins of the Red Cross," *Bulletin of Historical Medicine* 63: 557–578. See also his *Champions of Charity: War and the Rise of the Red Cross* (Boulder, Colo.: Westview Press, 1996).

14. Jan Herman Burgers, "The Road to San Francisco: The Revival of the Human Rights Idea in the Twentieth Century," *Human Rights Quarterly* 14, no. 2 (1992): 447–478.

15. For discussion of the ICRC's history and impact, see David P. Forsythe, *The Humanitarians: The International Committee of the Red Cross* (Cambridge: Cambridge University Press, 2005).

16. François Bugnion, *Le Comité International de la Croix-Rouge et la protection des victims de la guerre* (Geneva: ICRC, 1994). An English edition exists. For an overview, see Edwin M. Smith, "The Law of War and Humanitarian War: A Turbulent Vista," *Global Governance* 9, no.1 (2003): 115–134.

17. To be exact, according to a third protocol added to the 1949 Geneva Conventions in December 2005, neutral emblems recognized for certain aid societies in armed conflict are the Red Cross, the Red Crescent, and the Red Crystal. Other neutral emblems are also recognized. See David P. Forsythe and Barbara Ann J. Rieffer, *The International Committee of the Red Cross: A Neutral Humanitarian Actor* (London: Routledge, 2007).

18. Paul Gordon Lauren, *Power and Prejudice: The Politics and Diplomacy of Racial Discrimination* (Boulder, Colo.: Westview Press, 1988), 76–101; Burgers, "Road," 449. As noted earlier, Wilson was not entirely a Wilsonian in terms of consistent approaches to foreign affairs. While he championed the League, he opposed the United States' becoming the day-to-day protector of the Armenians under Turkish/Ottoman rule. Hence, he opposed the daily involvement in international relations that would be necessary to make the League work effectively.

19. Ernst Haas, *Human Rights and International Action* (Stanford, Calif.: Stanford University Press, 1970). See further Hector G. Bartolomei de la Cruz et al., *The International Labor Organization: The International Standards System and Basic Human Rights* (Boulder, Colo.: Westview Press, 1996). For an up-to-date look, see Steve Hughes, *The International Labour Organization* (London: Routledge, 2009).

20. Burgers, "Road," 456.

21. Neta Crawford, *Argument and Change in World Politics: Ethics, Decolonization, and Humanitarian Intervention* (Cambridge: Cambridge University Press, 2002), argues that the League Permanent Mandates Commission was important over time in the effort to discredit colonialism.

22. See Craig N. Murphy, *International Organization and Industrial Change: Global Governance since 1850* (Cambridge, UK: Polity, 1994). See also Michael Barnett and Martha Finnemore, *Rules for the World: International Organization in Global Politics* (Ithaca, N.Y.: Cornell University Press, 2004).

23. Farer, "UN and Human Rights," 97.

24. Jack Donnelly, "International Human Rights: A Regime Analysis," *International Organization* 40, no. 3 (1985), 599–642.

25. Farer, "UN and Human Rights," 98.

26. See Burgers, "Road."

27. Cathal J. Nolan, *Principled Diplomacy: Security and Rights in U.S. Foreign Policy* (Westport, Conn.: Greenwood Press, 1993), 181–202.

28. Burgers, "Road," 475.

29. For a concise statement, see David P. Forsythe, "Human Rights and Peace," in *Encyclopedia of Human Rights* (New York: Oxford University Press, 2009), 187–196.

30. See Nolan, *Principled.*

31. See further Daniel C. Thomas, *The Helsinki Effect: International Norms, Human Rights, and the Demise of Communism* (Princeton, N.J.: Princeton University Press, 2001), and William Korey, *The Promises We Keep: Human Rights, the Helsinki Process, and American Foreign Policy* (New York: St. Martin's Press, 1993).

32. Robert W. Tucker and David C. Hendrickson, *The Imperial Temptation: The New World Order and America's Purpose* (New York: Council on Foreign Relations Press, 1992), 86.

33. See Bruce Russett, "Politics and Alternative Security: Toward a More Democratic, Therefore More Peaceful World," in *Alternative Security: Living Without Nuclear Deterrence,* ed. Burns Weston (Boulder, Colo.: Westview Press, 1990), 107–136.

34. Samuel P. Huntington, *The Third Wave: Democratization in the Late Twentieth Century* (Norman: University of Oklahoma Press, 1991).

35. See especially Bruce M. Russett and John Oneal, *Triangulating Peace* (New York: Norton, 2001). They argue that liberal democracy, free trade, and membership in international organizations have the combined effect of reducing international war. Other factors also come into play, such as the distribution of military power.

36. David P. Forsythe, "Democracy, War, and Covert Action," *Journal of Peace Research* 29, no. 4 (1992): 385–396.

37. David N. Gibbs, *The Political Economy of Third World Intervention: Mines, Money, and U.S. Policy in the Congo Crisis* (Chicago: University of Chicago Press, 1991).

38. David P. Forsythe, *Human Rights and Peace: International and National Dimensions* (Lincoln: University of Nebraska Press, 1993).

39. Steven C. Poe and C. Neal Tate, "Repression of Human Rights to Personal Integrity in the 1980s: A Global Analysis," *American Political Science Review* 88, no. 4 (1994): 853–872.

40. See further Johannes Morsink, *The Universal Declaration of Human Rights: Origins, Drafting and Intent* (Philadelphia: University of Pennsylvania Press, 1999), and Mary Ann Glendon, *A World Made New: Eleanor Roosevelt and the Universal Declaration of Human Rights* (New York: Random House, 2001).

41. For discussions about taking these rights seriously, see William F. Felice, *The Global New Deal: Economic and Social Human Rights in World Politics* (Lanham, Md.: Rowman & Littlefield, 2003), and A. Belden Fields, *Rethinking Human Rights for the New Millennium* (New York: Palgrave, 2003).

42. This is the theme of UNDP, *Human Development Report 2000* (New York: Oxford University Press, 2000).

43. Also, in international law there is the concept of *jus cogens*: fundamental legal rights that can never be abridged, even by other rights developments. There is no definitive list of *jus cogens* approved by states, but a virtually universal view is that some human rights, such

as freedom from genocide and summary execution and torture, are part of *jus cogens*. This consideration again leads to the conclusion that some human rights are more basic than others.

44. John F. Murphy, *The United States and the Rule of Law in International Affairs* (Cambridge: Cambridge University Press, 2004).

45. See Hurst Hannum, "The Status of the Universal Declaration of Human Rights in National and International Law," *Georgia Journal of International and Comparative Law* 25 (1995–1996): 287–397.

46. David P. Forsythe, *Human Rights and U.S. Foreign Policy: Congress Reconsidered* (Gainesville: University Press of Florida, 1988).

47. This is not the place for a technical discussion of the two bodies of law. There is some overlap, because, for example, the core rights of the civil-political covenant, such as the prohibition on torture, are legally valid in armed conflict as well as in other situations.

48. To better establish its independence, the ICRC and the government of Switzerland signed a headquarters agreement protecting its premises and personnel from review or intrusion by Swiss authorities, as if the ICRC were an intergovernmental organization. The ICRC seems neither fully public nor fully private, legally speaking; rather it is sui generis (unique or in a category by itself). See Forsythe, *The Humanitarians*.

49. See www.eginitiative.org.

50. See www.ILO.org/public/english/wcsdg/index.htm.

51. See David Held, Anthony McGrew, David Goldblatt, and Jonathan Perraton, *Global Transformation: Politics, Economics and Culture* (Stanford, Calif.: Stanford University Press, 1999); James P. Muldoon et al., *Multilateral Diplomacy and the United Nations Today* (Boulder, Colo.: Westview Press, 1999); and James Rosenau and Ernst-Otto Czempiel, eds., *Governance Without Government* (Cambridge: Cambridge University Press, 1992).

52. Nationality Decrees in Tunis and Morocco, Permanent Court of International Justice, Series B, no. 4, *World Court Report*: 143.

CHAPTER 7

The United Nations and Applying Human Rights Standards

A VARIETY OF UN ORGANIZATIONS, offices, and agencies help and encourage states to apply the norms of internationally recognized human rights.[1] Through their governmental authorities, states are primarily responsible for promoting and protecting human rights within their territorial jurisdiction, and sometimes beyond. Individuals and private groups may have obligations in the field of human rights, and nongovernmental actors may play a large role at the UN, but under international law, governments are legally obligated to make national law and practice consistent with the international agreements that they have accepted.

Where application of rights means protection, the function of the UN system is usually indirect. This means that UN organizations normally try to encourage, push, prod, and ultimately embarrass states into taking steps to guarantee the proper practice of rights. UN organizations normally begin to seek protection through positive steps of encouragement and then gradually shift to more critical stances. A small human rights assistance program also takes a cooperative approach to improving rights protection. On occasion the Security Council authorizes outside parties to undertake direct protection, and UN officials themselves can engage in direct protection.

The overall UN process of helping to apply international human rights standards is exceedingly broad and complex. The structure of the main organizational components underpinning that process is illustrated in Figure 7.1. Fundamentally, UN diplomacy for human rights involves informal education or socialization, in that the UN seeks to "teach" new attitudes that benefit individuals. Changing attitudes may take quite a long period of time—as it did with slavery and decolonization.[2] As part of this long-term socialization process, the United Nations is extensively engaged in supervising state behavior under international

FIGURE 7.1 UN Human Rights Organizational Structure

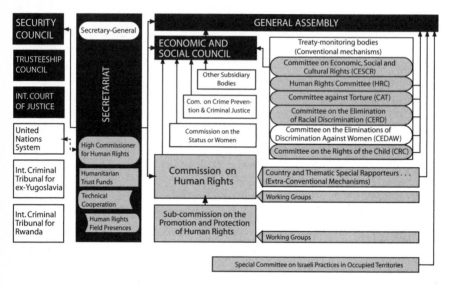

Source: United Nations High Commissioner for Human Rights, website: http://www
.unhchr.ch/hrostr.htm. (The Human Rights Council now replaces the Commission on
Human Rights.)

human right standards. Actors concerned with other aspects of international
relations—for example, sustainable development—are still trying to gain the
same degree of international supervision already achieved in the field of human
rights even if human rights activists lament the feebleness of UN mechanisms.

SECURITY COUNCIL

As we saw in Part One, the Security Council has the authority to declare a situation a threat to or breach of the peace, which enables it to play an important role
in promoting and protecting human rights. It can invoke Chapter VII of the
Charter and reach a "decision" binding on all states. Such decisions can entail
economic or military action. On several occasions the Security Council has
linked an ugly human rights situation to a threat to or breach of the peace, or it
has otherwise reached a legally binding decision declaring that economic or
military steps are needed to correct a human rights problem. With its power of
self-definition—that is, what it declares to be a threat to international peace and
security is a threat to international peace and security—the council often links
human rights to security.

Despite the initial concerns of several states, human rights have been on the
Security Council's agenda as part of an expanded definition of legitimate threats

to international peace and security. A dramatic set of developments in international criminal law followed the decisions about peace operations. The council established the ad hoc international criminal tribunals for the former Yugoslavia in 1993 and Rwanda in 1994 to seek legal justice against those responsible for war crimes, crimes against humanity, and genocide. Subsequently, in 2002 the council convened both a special court and a fact-finding commission in Sierra Leone, in 2003 created a special court in East Timor, and established another hybrid court (part national and part international) in 2005 in Cambodia to try members of the former Khmer Rouge regime who were responsible for the "killing fields."

These binding council decisions under Chapter VII are in addition to the more usual advisory resolutions that, although not directly and legally binding on states, may generate some influence for human rights. In 1989 the council created the UN Transition Assistance Group in Namibia (UNTAG) to oversee the transition to statehood. Among its other duties, UNTAG engaged in verifying free and fair elections, and thus of the human right to participate in governing arrangements. From a legal view, the suggestive council resolutions were not legally binding on states, although they were binding on other UN organs and agencies.

Action by the Security Council under Chapter VII shows the maximum concern for human rights expressed through the United Nations. During the Cold War, only two situations led to the invocation of Chapter VII concerning human rights; both pertained to white-minority rule in southern Africa. We emphasized earlier the coercive aspects of sanctions; here we stress the rationale behind them—namely, the protection of basic human rights.

In 1966 the Security Council voted mandatory economic sanctions on the Ian Smith government of what was then southern Rhodesia. A more comprehensive action in 1968 mentioned the human rights situation as one justification for the sanctions. Another justification addressed illegal secession from the United Kingdom. These sanctions remained in effect until 1979, when majority rule was obtained in the new state of Zimbabwe. Although the sanctions were too gradual and porous to have been the only cause of the fall of white-minority rule in Rhodesia, they were the first attempt at UN collective economic measures—of a mandatory nature—at least partly in the name of human rights. The council, being a political as well as legal body, often uses general language to maximize support for a resolution, even if doing so makes precise legal analysis more difficult.

In 1977 the Security Council voted a mandatory arms embargo on the Republic of South Africa. Human rights were not explicitly mentioned, only "the situation in South Africa," but the basic issues of concern to the international community were apartheid, the denial of a people's right to self-determination, and majority rule—all defined as human rights issues in international law. The arms embargo, although perhaps manifesting some symbolic value, was too limited and again too porous to end apartheid by itself. It was one element among many that led to progressive change in South Africa by the 1990s.

After the end of the Cold War, the Security Council expanded the use of Chapter VII in relation to human rights with mixed results. In 1991, after the first Persian Gulf War, the council declared that the international repercussions of the human rights situation in Iraq, especially pertaining to the Iraqi Kurds, constituted a threat to international peace and security. Iraqi Kurds were fleeing into both Iran and Turkey to escape repression, although international armed conflict among states was not imminent over this migration. This was the council's first explicit declaration that violating human rights created an international security threat since the vague resolutions on both Rhodesia and South Africa.

The Security Council did not expressly authorize the use of force to stop Iraqi repression of its citizens, but several states claimed that the council had implicitly authorized force for that purpose. Led by the United States, they created a protected area for Iraqi Kurds in northern Iraq. Airpower was later used in southern Iraq to protect Iraqi Shiites then being repressed by the government, again with the claim that the council had implicitly approved such force.

Three political factors were crucial in the evolution of events: the overall weakness of the Iraqi government after its widely condemned invasion of Kuwait in 1990, continuing U.S. commitment against the various policies of Saddam Hussein, and deference to the United States as the only global military superpower. The United States was widely seen as being tough on Iraq in the Security Council, but not so tough on some other states, such as Israel, concerning implementation of equally demanding council resolutions linked to human rights and international humanitarian law.

In the Balkans following the breakup of greater Yugoslavia, the Security Council, apart from its other actions, authorized the use of all necessary means for the delivery of humanitarian assistance in Bosnia. The initial UN peacekeeping forces were deployed under Chapter VI; humanitarian assistance was treated under Chapter VII. Once again, the diplomatic language "all necessary means" was a euphemism for authorizing military force.

In spite of this authorizing language, UN member states remained more reluctant to use force in Bosnia than in the Persian Gulf without the expressed consent of the various fighting parties. Member states' officials, including those in the United States, feared a complex and open-ended involvement in the Balkans that might come to resemble the Vietnam War. The cases of Rhodesia, South Africa, and Iraq showed that the council could link human rights violations to international peace and security. Although the Security Council declared the same linkage in Bosnia's case, the council was extremely cautious about implementing what it had declared when the military costs were high. In other words, the costs of enforcement carried weight in considering whether to insist upon respect for agreed-upon standards of human rights.

Likewise, when the council adopted resolutions on the question of Balkan war crimes and related atrocities, the resolutions looked more like diplomatic bluff than strong political will to stop such gross violations of human rights as genocide, political murder, and the use of rape as a weapon of war. Even systematic rape and ethnic cleansing did not motivate the Security Council to decisive action. The council did create "safe areas" but did not provide this UN peace operation with the legal authority to militarily protect the areas. Srebrenica, where some 7,000 Muslim men and boys were massacred by Serb militias in July 1995, serves as a reminder of the disastrous consequences of the council's indecisiveness when the willingness to commit military resources lagged behind its rhetoric. Information was collected for possible war-crimes prosecutions, but initially there was no permanent international criminal court to which that information could be submitted. In early 1993 the Security Council resolved to create such an international court strictly for the armed conflict in the Balkans, but a number of major hurdles remained. The number of suspects was great. The international community of states did not have physical custody of most of them. A paper trail proving violations of international law was needed that would stand up in court. Moreover, parties seeking a negotiated solution to the political and humanitarian problems of the area needed cooperation from some of the persons identified as potential war criminals.[3]

Political factors had encouraged the Security Council to break new ground concerning human rights in Iraq. But different political factors led to the council's caution in dealing with the Balkans. The council endorsed the Dayton agreements, after which NATO initially deployed some 60,000 troops, including approximately 20,000 Americans, to constitute IFOR—the Implementation Force. Although this military deployment helped end the fighting and secured the disengagement of fighting parties, IFOR was reluctant at first to use force to arrest indicted war criminals or to secure the safe return of refugees and displaced persons. Both of these human rights objectives were written into the Dayton accords but were not pursued rigorously.

Initially in Somalia in 1992, in the context of extensive coverage of the situation by the Western communications media, the council authorized all necessary means to create "a secure environment" for the delivery of humanitarian relief. In addition, the council declared that in that "unique" situation—referring to the chaos that constituted the absence of effective government—civilians had a right to humanitarian assistance. Anyone blocking delivery of that assistance would be committing a war crime for which there was individual responsibility. Under this path-breaking resolution, some 37,000 troops—mostly from the United States—were deployed in Somalia to maintain the order necessary to feed starving civilians. As a result of Security Council resolution 814, the United Nations took control of this operation with 28,000 of its own blue helmets in May 1993. This was the first Chapter VII military operation under actual command and control of the United Nations.

The primary political factors encouraging these developments in Somalia were not only media coverage and exhortations from the Secretary-General but also the absence of a national government, which had disintegrated into a multisided civil war. Moreover, the costs of the undertaking were judged by military establishments, perhaps mistakenly, to be reasonable. The international community of states, including developing countries prone to defend the most expansive interpretation of state sovereignty, found it easier to act when there was no national government whose consent was being bypassed. And from the viewpoint of the developed countries, the local armed factions, unlike perhaps in the Balkans, were clearly no match for Western military forces. Some authors believe that the United States—and UN—were more assertive in Somalia than in the Balkans because at the outset of military operations the former looked "more doable" than the latter. Lest anyone forget, power calculation counts.[4]

These events clearly demonstrate that the Security Council can authorize direct protection for persons such as the Kurds in Iraq or millions of civilians in southern Somalia. International peace and security could mean not just the security of states from foreign attack but also the security of persons inside states. Talk of "human security" could often be heard in the UN's corridors and conference rooms. The legality of the council's linkage of human rights and international peace and security has never been reviewed by the International Court of Justice.[5] So the linkage is whatever the council says it is. No agreed-upon criteria exist for authorizing coercion to enforce human rights or humanitarian law; such actions reflect what the international political traffic can bear at a particular moment—borne out at the 2005 World Summit when criteria still were not on the table although the responsibility to protect was. So there still are no precise rules for when military intervention for human protection purposes is appropriate.

In Somalia, the low risk of international violence, or even much international disruption outside the country, did not deter the Security Council from invoking Chapter VII and passing resolution 794 in December 1992, which ordered fighting parties to resolve their differences and permit humanitarian assistance. In reality, the council was applying Chapter VII to an internal conflict with primary emphasis on humanitarian action. This application has led some observers to conclude that the Security Council was developing, after 1990 and especially in Somalia, a doctrine of truly humanitarian intervention apart from issues of international peace and security.[6] Formally, however, the council asserted not a right of forcible humanitarian intervention per se but a right to respond to situations that it said threatened international peace and security. From Somalia some war refugees fled to states like Kenya, but the international implications were not great, relatively speaking.[7] Likewise, the council did not formally elevate the notion of human security inside states to a level equal with traditional interstate security. However, human security, and especially the protection of civilians, informed council decisions.[8]

Likewise in Haiti in 1994, the council labeled the situation a threat to international peace. The situation clearly did not involve a threat of attack on any other state by the weak authoritarian government. Rather, the most pressing interna-

Haitians take to the streets of Port-au-Prince to celebrate Jean-Bertrand Aristide's election in 1990. (UN Photo 177258/M. Grant)

tional issue was the flight of asylum seekers to the United States, stemming from an abusive national regime that also failed to promote sustainable development. Once the council authorized the use of all necessary means to restore democracy, the United States was in a strong position to threaten the use of force. The reactionary rulers eventually agreed to yield peacefully, and migration to the United States was greatly reduced. The UN and a bevy of other agencies subsequently tried to consolidate the fragile democracy in Haiti. The situation by 2008, reinforced by a different UN peacekeeping operation, seems a modest improvement over pre-1994, but many human rights problems remain. The UN has been involved in several firefights with gangs and militias, and kidnapping rates have increased dramatically. In an effort to establish order and stability, the UN has taken a more robust posture by militarily confronting the armed gangs.

The primary external agents of UN protection for Iraq, Somalia, the Balkans, and Haiti, for example, were states, through their military establishments. The Security Council played an authorizing role, but a very minor operational role. The delivery of assistance under the aegis of the International Red Cross and Red Crescent Movement, which was a form of guaranteeing socioeconomic human rights, initially went well in Somalia. But the Balkans showed clearly that some situations did not lend themselves easily to outside intervention, even for those with the purest of motives. People had internationally recognized human rights, in both peace and war. But guaranteeing those rights involved complex calculations about feasibility linked to power.

The Security Council can authorize a member state or regional organization to enforce human rights, or the council itself can manage direct enforcement. For the first time, as already noted, UN personnel in Somalia, beginning in May 1993, directly managed a UN military operation to enforce human rights. What the UN had previously done, in addition to authorizing enforcement by others, was to provide armed observation and reporting elements, usually referred to as peacekeeping forces. In places such as Nicaragua, El Salvador, Namibia, and Cambodia, UN forces managed by UN personnel had mainly observed electoral and other agreements. But in these types of operations UN armed personnel had not tried to enforce human rights standards themselves. They had only observed the situation. UN personnel expected that UN headquarters would take steps with national parties to see that rights were protected. The more frequent UN role was not direct protection through enforcement of human rights norms but indirect protection by prodding others to take action.

Increasingly traditional peacekeeping entailed a human rights element. As Secretary-General Boutros-Ghali wrote in his last annual report in 1996, "The United Nations . . . has moved to integrate, to the extent possible, its human rights and humanitarian efforts with its peace efforts."[9] The first United Nations Angola Verification Mission verified both troop movements and elections in Angola. The same was true of the United Nations Transition Assistance Group in Namibia. The United Nations Protection Force in the Balkans was intended to supervise a cease-fire and deliver humanitarian relief. In Cambodia, in an effort to achieve a national peace, the Khmer Rouge—killers of at least a million persons in the 1970s—were persuaded by UN personnel to sign the Geneva Conventions protecting human rights in armed conflict. In fact, all personnel of the United Nations Transitional Authority in Cambodia were supposed to carry out human rights functions.

Controversy surrounds the question of whether the UN itself should enforce, rather than observe and mediate, human rights standards. In Somalia, military forces under UN command fired on both civilian demonstrators and combatants and launched military operations against one of the major warlords of the country. While the UN was trying to produce national reconciliation and an effective and democratic government, the scores of fatalities and chain reaction of violence led to declining enthusiasm for international involvement.

These events greatly undermined risk-taking in Rwanda during 1994, when approximately 800,000 persons were murdered during a genocide committed by Hutu extremists manipulated by militant Hutu elements within the government against the Tutsi minority and some moderate Hutus as well. The Security Council balked at taking the necessary steps to halt the genocide and actually reduced its presence during the worst of the killing. When the Security Council members agreed to send more troops six weeks after the beginning of the slaughter, the then under-secretary-general for peacekeeping, Kofi Annan, contacted over eighty governments but none were willing to commit troops. Later the Secretary-General contacted a number of states with a view to a military deployment in Burundi, where similar ethnic violence was resulting in the "slow-motion genocide" of perhaps 150,000 persons during a five-year period. Of the fifty states approached, only twenty-one responded. Of these, eleven declined to help; of the remaining ten, only three offered ground troops.[10] The situation did not explode in a Rwanda-like fashion, but the country remained on the brink of a human rights disaster.[11]

The Security Council's response to the evolving humanitarian crisis in Kosovo in 1998–1999 added another twist to the story. Concerned with the increased violence and human rights violations in the territory, the council responded in September 1998 by condemning such acts and calling for an end to all such conflict and terrorism. Yet no concrete preventive or protection action was taken. And when NATO finally acted militarily to deal with the eroding human security situation in March 1999, it did so without explicit UN authorization.

The Security Council's complex and multidimensional operational responses to the crises in East Timor, Sierra Leone, and the Democratic Republic of the Congo similarly demonstrate a growing willingness to incorporate human rights elements, including special attention to children, directly into peacekeeping operations. They also reflect an increased commitment to the concept of comprehensive human security and peacebuilding. At the same time, they also reflect a lack of political will to match rhetoric with operational resources. Expansive words in New York outstripped action in the field.

The operational definition of security the council has employed has evolved in recent years to include a much broader range of human security concerns, not the least of which are actions to stop genocide and other gross violations of human rights. How far council members are willing to go remains to be seen. The Security Council's painful dithering over Darfur, for instance, demonstrates the dramatic disconnect between multilateral rhetoric and reality.[12] As Roméo Dallaire, the Canadian general in charge of the feeble UN force in Rwanda when civil war turned to genocide in 1994, lamented, "Having called what is happening in Darfur genocide and having vowed to stop it, it is time for the West to keep its word."[13] Dallaire was referring to the collective yawn since early 2003 in the face of genocide in Darfur. Could this be even more destructive of the fabric of international law than the 800,000 deaths in Rwanda? At least in 1994 there was an attempt to maintain the fiction that no such horror was under way. No one in the Clinton administration, for instance, dared to use the "G" word, which would have implied the necessity to act.[14]

A decade later, the U.S. Congress condemned Darfur unanimously, voting 422–0 in July 2004 that Khartoum was committing "genocide,"[15] while Secretary of State Colin Powell actually used the dreaded term in a speech in September of that year,[16] coinciding with views from such private groups as Physicians for Human Rights.[17] In September, European Union parliamentarians urged Sudan to end actions that could be "construed as tantamount to genocide."[18] Meanwhile, the African Union sent 7,000 ill-equipped troops to Sudan to protect its sixty monitors although not the Sudanese victims.[19] The repeated failure to come to the rescue mocks the value of the emerging "responsibility to protect" norm and ultimately may further erode public support for the United Nations.

Critics correctly point out that the Security Council still has a long way to go to achieve a balanced and systematic record concerning the protection of human rights, especially under Chapter VII. Many more persons died in Rwanda during 1994 or in the Democratic Republic of the Congo in 2002 than died in Kosovo in 1999. Yet the council, pushed by Western states, had shown far more interest in the human rights violations in the Balkans than in Africa. This double standard stemmed partly from the media coverage of Western-based reporting, partly from the interests of Western governments. Racism may also have been involved. China and Russia, which have less than stellar human rights records themselves, have consistently protected notorious violators of human rights from Security Council scrutiny. In January 2007, China and Russia helped block a council resolution sponsored by the United States and the United Kingdom condemning Myanmar's (formerly Burma) human rights violations and declaring the situation a threat to international peace and security. China and Russia admitted that human rights violations existed but asserted there was no threat to international peace and security. After Myanmar's bloody crackdown on demonstrators in September 2007, China blocked a council resolution calling for sanctions.[20]

GENERAL ASSEMBLY

Beyond standard-setting, the General Assembly indirectly protects human rights in two ways. It passes resolutions to condemn or otherwise draw attention to violations of human rights. It also creates and funds various agencies or meetings to deal with human rights.

About one-third of the General Assembly's resolutions each year deal with human rights, which keeps its main committee—the Third Committee—dealing with social, humanitarian, and cultural affairs quite busy. Many of these resolutions are adopted by consensus and constitute a rough barometer of which rights policies are judged most acceptable or egregious. In 1995, for example, the General Assembly responded to the execution of a Nigerian human rights and environmental activist, Ken Saro-Wiwa, with a resolution condemning that military government. The vote was 101–14, with 47 abstentions (mostly African states). This was one of forty-six human rights resolutions adopted during that session. Other years show the same general pattern. For example, in 2008 the General Assembly adopted a resolution expressing deep concern regarding Iran's human rights practices and adopted fifty-six resolutions dealing with human rights and humanitarian affairs.

When a resolution targets a specific country or violation, evaluating the resolution's effect over time is difficult. The assembly's repeated condemnations of apartheid in South Africa may have had some impact on changing attitudes among South Africans. At the same time, words divorced from coercive power cannot have much effect in the short term. In trying to account for change in South Africa, violence against apartheid, formal economic sanctions, and the shrinking of investments by the international business community all played a role.

Still, General Assembly resolutions on human rights often send important signals, but this observation is difficult if not impossible to measure. The assembly supported the Secretary-General, for example, in his mediation of the civil war in El Salvador, which was tied to a human rights accord. Assembly action sent the signal to both the governmental and the rebel sides that the international community supported a negotiated end to that bloody conflict. This signaling role is shared with other UN agencies such as the Security Council and the former UN Commission on Human Rights (CHR), and its successor, the Human Rights Council (HRC), covered below.[21]

A General Assembly resolution on human rights can also work against the protection of those rights. General Augusto Pinochet in Chile used assembly resolutions to rally nationalistic support for his rule despite the gross violations of basic rights that he was overseeing.[22] The assembly's 1975 declaration that Zionism was a form of racism not only antagonized Israel but alienated some of Israel's supporters from the assembly. The resolution did nothing for the practice of rights in either Israel proper or the occupied territories that Israel controlled militarily. The resolution was repealed in 1991.

The General Assembly has created a segment of the UN Secretariat to deal with Palestinian rights and a committee to oversee Israeli practices pertaining to human rights in the territories militarily occupied since 1967. The assembly also voted to hold the World Conference on Human Rights during June 1993 in Vienna. Sometimes the assembly takes a half-step to help with rights. It created the Fund for Victims of Torture, but it refused to make the fund part of the regular UN budget. The fund relies on voluntary donations. This and other compensatory funds for the victims of human rights violations have been poorly supported.

When decisions are not made by consensus, human rights policies reflect the majority controlling the General Assembly. From 1945 until about 1955, the Western majority was not very sensitive to issues of racial discrimination and tended to focus instead on such issues as forced labor under communism. In the period that followed, the assembly tended to emphasize issues of national self-determination and an end to racial discrimination, reflecting the desires of the developing countries, which had recently become a different "automatic majority" through decolonization. After the end of the Cold War, an intensified North-South conflict dominated human rights proceedings in the assembly.

Manifestations of this North-South conflict were evident. For example, in the late 1980s and 1990s, developing countries successfully reaffirmed the principle of state sovereignty in the face of the industrialized countries' desires to emphasize a right of humanitarian assistance that would supersede state sovereignty. By the early twenty-first century, little had changed in this debate. While the members of the International Commission on Intervention and State Sovereignty could assert "No More Rwandas," states from the global South such as Algeria, despite the terrible violence occurring within it, stressed the supremacy of state sovereignty, as did Zimbabwe's President Robert Mugabe, when criticism arose of his brutal internal crackdown.

While more stable states from the North, such as Sweden, stress the supremacy of the obligation of the international community of states to interfere to protect the interests of the victims of violence or deprivation, many countries from the global South still see the discourse of human rights as menacing their sovereignty. For them, for instance, the responsibility to protect may be seen as a Trojan horse for Western imperialism. In short, no consensus in the assembly existed as to the proper limits of state sovereignty or when the UN was justified in approving action without state consent in the name of human rights.

In other manifestations, the General Assembly was also characterized by fragmented views that shifted from issue to issue. On the question of human rights in Iraq during the 1990s, for example, a number of Islamic states thought that the Security Council had gone too far in restricting Iraqi sovereignty. Yet, on the question of human rights for Muslims in Bosnia, many Islamic states in the assembly wanted the Security Council to go further in challenging Yugoslav and Serbian policies toward Bosnia. Thus, Western states do not have a monopoly on human-rights double standards.

Although developing countries control the majority of votes in the General Assembly, the West has predominant economic and military power. This situation provides the recipe for some accommodation between North and South, especially since the number of developing countries with governments prone to compromise rather than to confrontation had grown substantially since the mid-1980s. Hence, in the assembly in the early 1990s, several resolutions endorsed democracy and the integration of civil and political rights into development decisions.[23] These resolutions of the 1990s were not a radical change from some earlier resolutions endorsing the equal value of all human rights, whether civil-political or socioeconomic. They did emphasize democracy more than did other earlier resolutions. In fact, the General Assembly had more democracies among member states by 2008 than at any other time in the organization's history.

INTERNATIONAL CRIMINAL COURT

After a decade of efforts by the assembly and certain subsidiary bodies, like the International Law Commission, 160 member states met in Rome during June and July 1998 to finalize a treaty on international criminal justice. Against some difficult odds, this United Nations Conference of Plenipotentiaries on the Establishment of an International Criminal Court was successful in doing just that. The resulting Rome Statute entered into force upon ratification by sixty states, which occurred on July 1, 2002. By early 2003, the first set of judges (who sit in their individual capacity rather than as state representatives) had been elected and took up their positions in The Hague. Canada's Philippe Kirsh was the court's first president, and Argentina's Luis Moreno Ocampo was its first chief prosecutor.

By 2007, the governments of Uganda, the Democratic Republic of Congo, and the Central African Republic had authorized the ICC to conduct investigations in their states regarding possible genocide, crimes against humanity, or war crimes. In some matters the prosecutor convened a panel of ICC judges to consider making formal indictments and proceeding with cases against certain individuals. In 2005, the Security Council instructed the prosecutor to inquire into bringing charges against certain individuals in Sudan because of policies in the Darfur region that might constitute one or more of the crimes covered by the ICC's statute. In 2008, Moreno Ocampo sought an indictment of Sudanese President Omar Hassan al-Bashir, along with two of his colleagues in the Sudanese government, and in March 2009 an arrest warrant was issued. Thus, the court was increasingly busy, despite the opposition or tepid support by a number of important states. Indeed, although 20 African countries were among the founders of the ICC and 30 of its 108 members are African, a communiqué from the African Union in 2008 asking the Security Council to suspend the court's proceedings against al-Bashir suggests that the sentiment that some international prosecutions are a Western plot still exists.

The UN had thus helped establish a permanent international criminal court to try individuals for certain egregious human rights violations, the first such court in history.[24] The court's jurisdiction is complementary to states in that, unlike the two ad hoc criminal tribunals for the former Yugoslavia and Rwanda, states retain the primary responsibility to respond to allegations of the stated abuses. Through the independent prosecutor, who, like the judges, is elected by states that have accepted the Rome Statute, the court becomes active only if a state is unwilling or unable to investigate such allegations and, if warranted, prosecute.

The future role of the court is unclear. By the end of 2008 over one hundred states, including most NATO members that did indeed sometimes deploy their military forces abroad, had accepted the Rome Statute and hence the ICC's jurisdiction and authority, which was encouraging for the protection of fundamental human rights. Yet, important states such as the United States, Israel, Russia, China, India, and others rejected the court. The United States led an active opposition for a time, threatening states that accepted the court with dire consequences and concluding new agreements with as many states as possible in which the two states agreed not to turn over the other's citizens to the court. Sometimes, as in Colombia, the United States reduced military assistance to try to pressure a state into noncooperation with the ICC. During 2002 the United States delayed extending deployments of UN blue helmets until the Security Council granted it a one-year renewable extension from the court's jurisdiction. Also in 2002, the U.S. Congress passed legislation, subsequently signed into law by President George W. Bush and dubbed "The Hague Invasion Act," which among other sections authorized the United States to use force to liberate any American citizen detained in relation to the ICC.

The United States claimed that it feared politically motivated and false charges against its citizens by other states, a rogue prosecutor who would engage in the same behavior, and legal exposure to its citizens that was unacceptable given the extensive security operations taken in the name of the UN or NATO. Furthermore, the Rome Statute was vague about the crime of "aggression." Signing onto the court potentially could limit U.S. use of military force without UN authorization. Washington's opposition to the court could also be more ideological than pragmatic. Given that, for example, the prosecutor could not proceed with charges against a U.S. citizen unless such proceedings had been approved by a special panel of judges of the court, it seems that the United States was more interested in defending an absolute conception of state sovereignty and national independence than in resisting potential and unwarranted dangers to its citizens.

The ICC still could come into play when and if the United States were to select targets and weapons that might contradict international humanitarian law and thus constitute war crimes or crimes against humanity. The latter concept pertains to a systematic attack on civilians, whether in peace or war. Such charges about illegal U.S. policies arose with regard to such matters as military attacks on a TV station in Belgrade in 1999 or the use of cluster bombs in civilian areas in Afghanistan in 2001. Such policy decisions pertaining to war were never independently investigated either by the U.S. Congress or the federal courts. It was precisely in such situations that the ICC might become operational with regard to U.S. citizens, if the state in which events occurred was a party to the court's statute.

Either the state where the alleged crime took place or the state of the defendant would have to be a party to the Rome Statute for the ICC to have jurisdiction. Ironically, when the United States engaged in armed conflict in Iraq in 2003, neither U.S. nor Iraqi citizens were subject to the court's jurisdiction since neither state had exercised the necessary consent. But British policymakers and military personnel were. Thus a state such as France could file a complaint in the ICC about systematic policy in Iraq against a British national, but not against an American or an Iraqi.

The court marked a historical milestone in the evolution of efforts to improve the protection of important human rights. The ICC can be "pulled off the shelf" if states do not exercise their responsibility to seriously follow up on allegations of certain major crimes. Whether it will actually play an active and important deterrent or enforcement role in international relations will be determined by future events. While the ICC is accepted by the likes of Britain, France, Italy, and

Canada, it continues to be generally opposed by the United States and other important states such as Russia and China.[25] Indeed, two scholars, albeit of realist orientation, warned that the ICC was an example of "international idealism run amuck."[26]

In 2005, however, the Bush administration allowed to pass without a veto Security Council resolution 1593 authorizing the ICC prosecutor to open an investigation into the criminal liability of certain Sudanese officials for actions in Darfur. The Sudanese government, which had not ratified the Rome Statute, vehemently rejected the ICC's right to proceed. On the basis of this and other evidence, U.S. hostility to the ICC seemed to be weakening, at least in situations where it seemed unlikely that any Americans would wind up being defendants in the court.

OFFICE OF THE SECRETARY-GENERAL

Before the arrival in office of Kofi Annan, UN Secretaries-General did not display a major commitment to human rights.[27] Perhaps they had seen their primary role as producing progress on peace and security. This emphasis was understood to mean that they could not speak out on specific human rights violations. Had Javier Pérez de Cuéllar, for example, made protection of individual human rights his primary concern, his office probably would have been unacceptable as mediator between Iran and Iraq, or between the Salvadoran armed forces and the FMLN, or in the Afghan situation after the Soviet invasion.

Virtually all Secretaries-General have engaged in good offices or quiet mediation for the advancement of human rights.[28] But only Annan systematically, though cautiously, threw the full weight of his office behind human rights protection. The current Secretary-General, Ban Ki-moon, has spoken out on Darfur; but it is too early to determine whether he will make human rights central to his tenure. His nonconfrontational personality and style make him unlikely to use the UN's bully pulpit for human rights to the same extent as his immediate predecessor. Whether one speaks of Dag Hammarskjöld or Kurt Waldheim, however, the point on human rights remains the same. Hammarskjöld, the Swedish economist, was personally not much interested in human rights at the United Nations and concentrated on finding a diplomatic role for the UN in the East-West conflict. Hammarskjöld did find time to take up the case of U.S. airmen detained in China after the Korean War. Waldheim, who served in the German army during World War II, was much less dynamic than Hammarskjöld. Yet he, too, took up human rights or humanitarian questions, such as the situation of refugees in Africa, somewhat ironically, in light of his own isolation following exposure of his Nazi past. Much the same could be said for U Thant from Burma, who was not as personally committed to individual rights as he was to the collective right of peoples to self-determination. But on occasion he, too, engaged in quiet diplomacy for human rights.

As human rights became more institutionalized in UN proceedings, however, Secretaries-General took a higher profile on rights issues. Pérez de Cuéllar is instructive in this regard. A cautious Peruvian diplomat, he entered office showing great deference to states, especially Latin ones. One of his first acts was to not renew the contract of his most senior human rights official, Theo van Boven of the Netherlands. Van Boven had irritated the Argentine junta, then in the process of murdering at least 9,000 Argentines, and its U.S. supporters. By the end of his term, Pérez de Cuéllar had projected the UN, by his own authority, deep into the affairs of both El Salvador and Nicaragua, including deep involvement on human rights issues. In Nicaragua during his tenure, the UN came to oversee a regional peace accord, to supervise national elections for the first time in a sovereign state, and to collect weapons from a disbanding rebel force. He also oversaw human rights observers in Haiti in 1991, the first time UN election verification had taken place in a country not wracked at the time by civil conflict.

When human rights were linked to peace, Pérez de Cuéllar and his office came to be bold and innovative. And the two issues were indeed inseparable in places like El Salvador, Nicaragua, Namibia, Angola, Cambodia, Bosnia, East Timor, and Kosovo. The office of the Secretary-General took initiatives, then obtained the backing of both the General Assembly and the Security Council. Increasingly, the Secretary-General was drawn into rights questions that had previously been considered the domestic affairs of states or seen as in opposition to U.S. desires.

Boutros Boutros-Ghali of Egypt followed in his predecessors' footsteps. Upon becoming Secretary-General in 1992, he seemed uninterested in human rights, even appointing an old friend without a human rights record as head of the UN Centre for Human Rights in Geneva. But within the year, Boutros-Ghali was as deeply involved in human rights issues as Pérez de Cuéllar had been. In El Salvador, for example, Boutros-Ghali was active in supporting President Alfredo Cristiani as he tried to purge the army of most of those who had committed gross violations of internationally recognized human rights. Boutros-Ghali was quite outspoken in promoting democratic or participatory values as part of the quest for economic development. This stand may not have been completely desired by some developing countries, but his speeches and reports in support of democratic development were backed by many donor countries. In the early 1990s the major donor countries pushed for more grassroots participation in the search for sustainable development, whether through bilateral programs, the World Bank, or agencies of the UN. The Secretary-General's position fit nicely within this paradigm shift in favor of the human right to participation in public affairs.

Moreover, Boutros-Ghali appointed the Swedish diplomat who had mediated the Iran-Iraq War, Jan Eliasson, to a new position as emergency relief coordinator (ERC) responsible for pulling together the various parts of the UN system to provide humanitarian assistance. This post evolved toward being a type of general troubleshooter for humanitarian affairs, which were difficult to insulate from wider human rights issues, as discussed below.

Until 1993, the General Assembly had long been unwilling to formally create the post of high commissioner for human rights, largely because of opposition from developing and communist countries. But developing countries tolerated this new post. As human rights became more entrenched in UN proceedings, the UN Secretary-General became more openly active on the issue especially when the human rights issue was integrated with peace and security matters.

Below the highest levels of the Office of the Secretary-General, parts of the Secretariat have often actively tried to improve behavior under human rights norms.[29] Van Boven, who had annoyed the Argentine junta before his "non-renewal" by Pérez de Cuéllar, was the clearest example, but other UN officials also were active, frequently behind the scenes. Nevertheless, the Secretary-General sets the tone on human rights for the Secretariat, and van Boven's fate showed that these officials could do only so much without the support of the Secretary-General at the top.[30]

The UN's seventh Secretary-General, Kofi Annan, was a much more activist human rights leader, including in his priority concerns the encouragement and advocacy of human rights, the rule of law, and the universal values of equality, tolerance, and human dignity as articulated in the UN Charter. One of his most eloquent statements in this regard was the 1998 address to the UNESCO (United Nations Educational, Scientific and Cultural Organization) ceremony marking the fiftieth anniversary of the Universal Declaration of Human Rights. In part he said:

> Our belief in the centrality of human rights to the work and life of the United Nations stems from a simple proposition: that States which respect human rights respect the rules of international society. States which respect human rights are more likely to seek cooperation and not confrontation, tolerance and not violence, moderation and not might, peace and not war. States which treat their own people with fundamental respect are more likely to treat their neighbors with the same respect. From this proposition, it is clear that human rights—in practice, as in principle—can have no walls and no boundaries.[31]

One of Annan's pet projects was to try to galvanize the for-profit sector into a greater interest in human rights, in partnership with the UN. Recognizing the economic power of transnational corporations (TNCs), the Secretary-General tried to get them to take a broad approach to their role in the world, one that reflected more social responsibility. In 1999 the Secretary-General launched the idea of a Global Compact at the World Economic Forum in Davos, Switzerland, which projected certain universal principles relevant to business practices in the areas of human rights and the environment. The four main UN agencies that participated in this venture were the Office of the High Commissioner of Human Rights (OHCHR), the International Labour Organization, the UN Development Programme, and the UN Environment Programme. Hoping to reduce especially what some called economic exploitation of labor (and damage to the environment), Annan worked hard to create this partnership—which had great implications for many human rights, even if much of the discourse was about social responsibility. By 2008 some 3,700 corporations had signed on to this initiative.[32] The efforts of the Secretary-General reflect the growing realization that states are not the only entities that can violate internationally recognized human rights.

Secretary-General Annan also demonstrated the strength of his commitment to internationally recognized human rights by nominating a strong-willed high commissioner for human rights, former president of Ireland Mary Robinson. Such an appointment had its own merits and contrasted sharply with her diplomatic predecessor, Ecuador's José Ayala-Lasso. Robinson was initially welcomed by the United States and certain other Western states, which after the Cold War seemed to want the United Nations to be more assertive in general on human rights issues. Robinson's departure in September 2002 came, to a significant degree, because the United States had become disillusioned with her.[33]

Human rights are important to the eighth Secretary-General, Ban Ki-moon, but also appear to rank below other priorities, such as management reform and global climate change. Secretary-General Ban got off to a rough start when he declined to oppose or criticize the execution of Saddam Hussein despite the UN's long-standing condemnation of the death penalty as a violation of human rights. Moreover, he stated that "the issue of capital punishment is for each and every member state to decide."[34] He later clarified his remarks by acknowledging the growing trend among states to abolish the death penalty; however, concern remains as to whether he will be as powerful a voice for human rights as Annan. In spite of his low-key, nonconfrontational approach, Secretary-General Ban has publically denounced human rights violations in Myanmar, Sudan, and Kenya and on occasion appointed special envoys. This has not, however, translated to improved human rights conditions in these states.

HIGH COMMISSIONER FOR HUMAN RIGHTS

Debate about the need for a UN high commissioner for human rights started in the 1940s. The 1993 UN Vienna conference on human rights recommended that the General Assembly create such a post. After a heavy lobbying campaign by a variety of actors—including many NGOs, the Carter Presidential Center, and the U.S. government—the General Assembly finally created the post that autumn. The office had a vague mandate with weak authority. Secretary-General Boutros-Ghali appointed as the first occupant José Ayala-Lasso of Ecuador, who had held several national diplomatic posts, including foreign minister under a repressive military government. He began his activities in 1994.

The first UN high commissioner for human rights practiced quiet diplomacy out of the limelight rather than being a visible public advocate. This approach helped alleviate some of the developing countries' fears that the post would be used exclusively to emphasize civil and political rights favored by Western states, with developing countries serving as "primary targets." The first high commissioner had met with any number of developing countries with questionable human rights policies; during these visits, those policies presumably had been discussed. Among other activities, Ayala-Lasso had tried to interject more attention to economic and social rights into the work of the UN regional commissions for economic development. This emphasis was continued by his successor.

Beyond making an annual report on international human rights at the UN, probably the most important work of the first high commissioner was to establish human rights field missions inside countries either as part of, or as separate from, UN peacekeeping operations. The first of these missions was established in Rwanda, where the human rights field staff broke new ground in legal and diplomatic theory but achieved little in practical terms during its early deployment. Ayala-Lasso then tried to turn Rwanda into a precedent by creating field missions in other countries, the first of which were Abkhazia, Georgia, Colombia, and Zaire.

By the end of the decade and with Mary Robinson's enthusiastic backing, a UN field presence for human rights had expanded to include Cambodia, the Central African Republic, the Democratic Republic of the Congo (formerly Zaire), El Salvador, Gaza, Guatemala, Indonesia, Liberia, Malawi, Mongolia, Sierra Leone, South Africa, southern Africa, and Southeast Europe. Once more, in the name of universal human rights, the UN was acting on matters that had once been considered fully part of domestic affairs. In addition to debates about human rights in New York and Geneva, the second high commissioner was trying to make a difference "on the ground."[35]

The OHCHR also processed requests from states regarding electoral assistance. By the mid-1990s, it was assisting seventeen states in the quest to hold free and fair elections that were internationally supervised. Regional IGOs and NGOs, along with state delegations, were also active in this regard.

The establishment of this post created some confusion about the overall management and coordination of UN human rights work. Sometimes the high commissioner, the Office of the Secretary-General, and the UN Commission on Human Rights did not seem to be playing from the same page of music; nor was it always clear who, if anyone, was the conductor. The division of labor is in the process of being worked out. In 1997 the Centre for Human Rights was merged with OHCHR; however, the Office of the High Commissioner remained chronically short of staff and funds. And questions remain about the organization and effectiveness of the UN's human rights machinery.

But Robinson increasingly ran afoul of particularly the United States, and in 2002 she stepped down under pressure. Just as the United States had seen to it that Boutros Boutros-Ghali did not continue as Secretary-General, so Washington also made it clear that Robinson's high-profile discussion of human rights violations in such places as China and Israeli-occupied territories did not coincide with U.S. policies. In China, for instance, the United States had adopted a bipartisan policy of engagement with authoritarian Beijing, in which human rights was relegated to quiet diplomacy, not public pressure. Regarding Israel, the United States had long declined to take up seriously Israel's repeated violations of the Fourth Geneva Convention of 1949 regulating occupied territory, as affirmed by various UN agencies as well as the ICRC. Because Robinson was more committed to raising the awareness of human rights, and also human rights violations, than to quiet diplomacy, she became an irritant not only to those states with serious human rights violations, but also to the United States, which had close relations with some of these same states. Robinson also openly criticized U.S. policy regarding interrogation and other treatment of "enemy combatants" after 9/11. The final straw for Washington was the perceived way that Robinson ran the World Conference against Racism, Racial Discrimination, Xenophobia, and Related Intolerance in Durban, South Africa, in September 2001, which featured attacks on Israel and Zionism. She also championed socioeconomic human rights, which the United States rejected.

Secretary-General Annan, whose diplomatic skills were normally commensurate with the demands of his position, then nominated, and the General Assembly approved, Brazil's Sergio Vieira de Mello as high commissioner. He had considerable UN experience in humanitarian and refugee matters—in UNHCR, as emergency relief coordinator, and head of UN operations in Kosovo and East Timor—and he was known as a much more polished diplomat than Robinson. Some private human rights groups thought he might be too polished, at the expense of defending human rights for the sake of getting along with the governments that violate them. His good relations with the George W. Bush administration made him the U.S. choice to be the Secretary-General's representative in post-combat Iraq, where he and twenty-one other colleagues were killed during a suicide bombing of UN headquarters in August 2003. After Vieira de Mello's tragic death, Bertrand Ramcharan of Guyana became acting high commissioner.

In July 2004, Louise Arbour assumed the key human rights post, having been a judge on Canada's Supreme Court and chief prosecutor for the international criminal tribunals for the former Yugoslavia and Rwanda. Arbour had more of a judicial temperament than Robinson. And, given what had happened to both van Boven and Robinson, for a time Arbour took a lower-key approach to her role. But over time, she spoke out more. And like her predecessors, she wound up in public conflict with Washington especially when she took exception to some U.S. policies pertaining to the detention and interrogation of suspected terrorists. Arbour's statements caused her to be publicly rebuked by U.S. permanent representative John Bolton.[36] In 2008, Secretary-General Ban Ki-moon selected a distinguished South African female jurist of South Asian ethnicity, Navanethem Pillay, to succeed Arbour.

States like to be associated with the notion of human rights as a matter of principle, but they often take exception when UN officials criticize their policies or those of their allies. The UN high commissioner for human rights, like the Secretary-General, has found it difficult to be a public advocate for human rights and to satisfy the human rights NGO community, which often demands clear and decisive action, while maintaining the support of member states. Both the Secretary-General and the UN high commissioner for human rights have an impossible job and must walk a diplomatic high wire.

COMMISSION ON HUMAN RIGHTS (1946–2006)

If, when dealing with human rights, the broad and complex UN system is thought of as a wheel, the Commission on Human Rights was the hub from its establishment in 1946 until its abolition in 2006.[37] This commission was eventually made up of fifty-three states elected officially by ECOSOC, and its history reflects in microcosm the legal and diplomatic revolution on human rights. Despite Western domination of the UN during its early years, the commission was content to promote rights by setting standards rather than by trying to protect them, even indirectly, through various forms of diplomatic pressure. The early commission adopted the position that it lacked the authority to inquire into rights behavior in specific states. When private complaints about rights violations came to the UN, the CHR buried them in an elaborate proceeding leading nowhere, one of the most complicated trash baskets ever devised. The early commission, in the words of one careful observer, displayed a "fierce commitment to inoffensiveness."[38]

A North-South compromise, however, opened up new possibilities between 1967 and 1970. The commission began to deal with specific states and began to examine private complaints more seriously. Developing states wanted to focus on Israel and South Africa, but developed states broadened the commission's mandate so that states like Greece under military rule (1967–1974) and Haiti under the Duvalier dynasty (1957–1986) also became targets of commission scrutiny. Moreover, member states of the commission agreed that private petitions could lead, after screening, to quiet diplomacy and even the publication of a "blacklist" of states with a pattern of gross violations of human rights. These private petitions, however, were treated in a confidential process that minimized the negative publicity that could be directed at an offending government. Ironically, a state could minimize public scrutiny of its rights record by responding somewhat to private petitions in the confidential process.

The Commission on Human Rights struggled to find ways of working for human rights in meaningful ways. It created "thematic procedures" to deal with certain violations. That is, it created either working groups of states or special experts, called rapporteurs, to examine more than two dozen issues, such as forced disappearances, arbitrary detention, summary execution, torture, religious discrimination, mercenaries, and deprived or suffering children.[39] Some working groups not only studied problems with reference to specific states but also sent official telegrams to political authorities and in other ways tried to help persons in the short term.

The CHR also dealt in various ways with a series of specific states, both publicly and privately. For a time that list of targeted states seemed more or less balanced. During the waning days of the Cold War, some of these targeted states were aligned with the United States (for example, El Salvador); others were aligned with the Soviet Union (for example, Cuba). Communist China was extensively discussed after the Tiananmen Square massacre, proving that even permanent members of the Security Council are not immune to critical debate. But in 1995 the commission refused, by a one-vote margin, to censure China for its repressive policies. In this same session, however, the commission adopted critical resolutions pertaining to a range of states in the global South, such as Zaire, Sudan, and Afghanistan, along with the former Yugoslavia. This pattern continued into the early twenty-first century, when Russia was censured by the commission for its brutal policies in dealing with secessionist elements in Chechnya. Russia thus became the one P-5 member to be condemned by a vote in the CHR.

The subject of human rights affects crucial questions of governmental power, and thus this intergovernmental commission was highly politicized. Various double standards and inconsistencies are well-documented. The United States at times focused on rights violations in Cuba out of proportion to events there, especially compared to more serious rights violations in allied states like Guatemala and El Salvador.[40] Washington had long used human rights criticism as a political weapon to try to delegitimize the Castro government. During the Cold War, the Soviet Union was openly opportunistic in the commission, using human rights as a weapon against U.S. allies, such as Pinochet's Chile from 1974 to about 1984, but remaining silent about major violations of human rights in communist states. Again, human rights language was put at the service of ideological and strategic calculations. Most of the developing states paid far more attention to rights violations by South Africa and Israel than to egregious ones in Idi Amin's Uganda or Indira Gandhi's India, especially when she declared a national emergency and suspended most constitutional protections of rights.

In 2002 Libya was put forward by the African caucus as president of the commission. Given Libya's poor record on many civil and political rights, the African caucus obviously placed more emphasis on equitable geographical representation and friendly relations than on sterling performance in these human rights matters. Since, according to UN tradition, it was "Africa's turn" to hold the presidency of the commission, Libya was duly elected over the protests of the United States and other Western governments. Adding fuel to the fire, other prominently repressive governments like Cuba and Saudi Arabia were also elected to the commission by their regional caucuses.

This history showed clearly that for many states, especially in the global South, human rights were still not taken seriously; and indeed, election to the commission was a way to avoid criticism. After assuming the presidency, and contrary to promises of balance and integrity, the Libyan representative made polemical speeches. Coming the year after the failure of the United States to be elected, for the first time, to the commission, these developments gave the UN a bad name in the field of human rights, especially in the United States and other Western countries. But the source of the problem lay in the foreign policies of member states, including the United States, which moved time and again to protect its friends, such as the Barr regime in Somalia, from condemnation for rights violations. The Commission on Human Rights was never made up of "a club of the clean" who acted consistently on principle and without regard to strategic calculations.

Moreover, a number of elected governments, such as those in India and the Philippines, opposed certain initiatives designed to help protect human rights.[41] They elevated either solidarity among developing countries or the principle of state sovereignty over rights protection. At times, regional or bloc voting prevailed. A number of Latin American states, including some that were democratic and sensitive to rights at home, tried to shield more repressive Latin American states from the commission's pressure. Again, emphasis on state sovereignty or cultural solidarity superseded UN efforts to protect rights.

For those with a historical perspective, the failure of democratic governments to always rally to UN human rights issues should come as no surprise. At the end of World War II, Winston Churchill's government in London wanted to summarily execute high German officials rather than try them at Nuremberg,[42] and London was not enthusiastic about the UN Charter's language on human rights because it might interfere with the smooth continuation of British colonialism.[43] Developing countries do not have a monopoly on double standards in their foreign human rights policies.

Yet these double standards by states operated side-by-side with the more principled work of human-rights NGOs that participated in commission proceedings. So some procedural progress was made inside the CHR. Indeed, NGOs played a more significant role in Geneva in the CHR than they played on other issues or in UN institutions elsewhere. NGOs focused on the commission and increased their numbers and influence.[44] By the 1990s large numbers of NGOs were active in all phases of the commission's proceedings.[45] The end of East-West conflict meant that a number of former communist states became champions of human rights; they often teamed with NGOs in the commission. Because some states teamed with NGOs in a principled way, the various controversies did not halt the growth and use of thematic procedures and country-specific investigations. The reports from these individuals and groups at least brought some diplomatic pressure to bear on the problems addressed, although decisive and short-term improvement in the practice of rights was rare to nonexistent.

Over time the commission dealt mostly with civil rights such as freedom from racial discrimination, torture, forced disappearances, summary execution, and arbitrary detention. This might be seen as a bias stemming from Western states and NGOs, and from developing countries aligned with the West; however, many of these civil rights are fundamental to protecting personal integrity. The CHR did not deal very frequently or specifically with socioeconomic rights. Developing states spent time debating a right to development, but most concrete efforts regarding socioeconomic rights in the UN system were handled by agencies like UNICEF and the WHO. The commission also devoted little time and attention to political rights associated with democracy. In the early history of the UN, only about one-third of all states had stable liberal democratic governments. Most of the states represented in the commission were listed by Freedom House, a New York–based NGO, as either partly free or un-free.[46] Thus, securing sustained attention to political rights was difficult. Additionally, some democratic governments did not want to emphasize democracy in their foreign policy because they had authoritarian allies. Moreover, many of the authoritarian governments were engaged in brutal repression. These conditions caused the commission to focus on fundamental civil rights such as freedom from torture and summary execution. After the Cold War, the number of democracies increased. This change allowed more attention to democratic or participatory rights within the UN system. But in the CHR democratic states did not always get a seat because of the way regional caucuses operated. Even democratic states did not always elevate human rights over security and economic calculation.

Whether the Commission on Human Rights had a specific and beneficial impact on a situation in the long term is difficult to discern. Charting changing commission procedures and activity is one thing, demonstrating the impact of changes inside the commission on state behavior quite another. The commission wielded few resources besides diplomatic pressure. The Security Council could authorize sanctions. The General Assembly commanded more publicity. However, if a government believed that violation of human rights was necessary for the government's security or the broader national interest, then the words generated by the commission were unlikely to change government policy in the short term.

The obvious shortcomings of the commission figured prominently in the report from the High-level Panel on Threats, Challenges and Change (HLP). Viewed from Washington as well as many other capitals, the performance of the UN's human rights machinery was scandalous. The primary evidence for the travesty was the commission's fifty-three elected members, who in 2005 included Sudan while it was pursuing genocide in Darfur, and Zimbabwe while it was bulldozing the houses of 700,000 opposition supporters and rounding up journalists and other critics. That China and Cuba played prominent roles and that Libya was a former chair of the commission added to the litany of embarrassments. The HLP recognized the "eroding credibility and professionalism" and that "states have sought membership of the Commission not to strengthen human rights but to protect themselves against criticism or to criticize others."[47]

However, the HLP recommendation was counterintuitive: universal membership instead of "only" one-quarter of the members. Advancing serious attention to human rights is not served by having matters discussed by a committee of the whole, in this case 192 state delegations. This idea deservedly found its way to the trash heap of diplomatic history. The Secretary-General, in his only serious dissent from the HLP's recommendations, courageously went out on a limb and proposed that member states "replace the Commission on Human Rights with a smaller standing Human Rights Council."[48] By the 2005 World Summit, the word "discredited" was used in tandem to describe the Commission on Human Rights, and member states agreed to replace it.

Any obituary of the UN Commission on Human Rights should also include its accomplishments. Although it was politicized and prone to double standards and hypocrisy, the commission did target states that were egregious violators of human rights.[49] Commission activities may have had only a limited role in improving human rights conditions in target countries, but they did serve to socialize and educate all states on the importance of human rights over time. The commission also amassed an impressive record of originating and developing human rights instruments.[50] The Commission on Human Rights held its final session in Geneva in March 2006 and was abolished in June 2006. At that final session, then high commissioner Louise Arbour noted, "It would, however, be a distortion of fact, and a gross disservice to this institution, if we failed on this occasion to celebrate the achievements of the Commission even as we, in full knowledge of its flaws, welcome the arrival of its successor." She listed those accomplishments as setting standards, establishing the system of special procedures, considering the situations in specific countries, creating global forums, and nurturing a unique relationship with civil society.[51]

HUMAN RIGHTS COUNCIL (2006–)

The heads of state and government at the 2005 World Summit resolved to create a Human Rights Council as a subsidiary of the General Assembly. The General Assembly was assigned the responsibility for creating it (as Charter Article 22 so provides) and deciding its "mandate, modalities, functions, size, composition, membership, working methods, and procedures."[52] During assembly deliberations, language proposing that membership be subjected to a two-thirds vote of the General Assembly was eliminated as well as the possibility that it might someday be transformed into a principal organ—hence, requiring a formal amendment in the Charter. The U.S. permanent representative to the UN, John

Bolton, who had delegated midlevel staff to represent the United States in these negotiations, had been harshly critical that the old commission too easily enabled states with questionable human rights records, such as China, to be elected to membership. Yet during deliberations over creating the new council, Bolton suggested that China and Russia, along with the United Kingdom, France, and the United States, be granted automatic "permanent" membership on the new Human Rights Council instead of being obliged to rotate off after two consecutive two-year terms. After discovering that this proposal would likely undermine the integrity of the HRC, it was dropped. In March 2006, the General Assembly finally created the Human Rights Council despite the negative U.S. vote and eventual unwillingness to stand as a candidate.

Given the bitter disputes over the shape of the new council, it was surprising the General Assembly came to an agreement at all. Jan Eliasson, the assembly's president, managed to push for a vote on the Human Rights Council with three-year terms with the assent of a simple majority of the General Assembly. Some were disgruntled because the numbers in the new council had decreased only to forty-seven—hardly a big decrease from fifty-three and perhaps still too large to be businesslike. Membership was subject only to a simple majority vote instead of the more stringent two-thirds requirement the Secretary-General proposed and the United States desired. However, membership to the council entails special scrutiny designed to discourage the worst human rights offenders. States sitting on the council are subject to a council review during their first term, forcing such abusers as Libya or Zimbabwe to think twice about candidacy. That the new council would meet for ten weeks at least three times a year was a step in the right direction.

Unfortunately, the first election to the Human Rights Council yielded human rights "stalwarts" such as Algeria, China, Pakistan, Saudi Arabia, and Cuba, confirming U.S. fears that the council was more like "a caterpillar with lipstick on" than a "butterfly"—in Bolton's picturesque imagery, which ignored that even larvae require nourishment to grow. The United States chose not to stand for election; however, given that the United States had always sought a position on the commission, many viewed this stand not as a protest, but as a tactic to avoid embarrassment because it might not have had enough votes to be elected. After all, the Bush administration was flagrantly violating international human rights with regard to its "detainees" in its "war on terrorism."

The Human Rights Council's record during its first years is, as expected, mixed.[53] In terms of promoting and protecting human rights in specific states, the council spent its first year investigating Israel, which was the only state drawing a critical council resolution. On the other hand, Sudan, China, Myanmar, and Zimbabwe were not criticized. By the council's second year, Israel had been criticized fifteen times and Myanmar only once (after its junta's bloody crackdown on monks and demonstrators in September 2007). The council's biased and unbalanced focus on Israel drew a rare rebuke by Secretary-General Ban,

Secretary-General Ban Ki-moon unveils the artistic new ceiling of a conference room of the United Nations Human Rights Council. (UN Photo # 206120/Jean-Marc Ferre)

who stated he was "worried by its disproportionate focus on violations by Israel." The council, he said, "has clearly not justified all the hopes that so many of us placed on it."[54]

On a more positive note, the council has continued the commission's tradition of using special rapporteurs and working groups. In 2007, the council appointed a working group to study the feasibility of individual private petitions under the International Covenant of Economic, Social and Cultural Rights. Such petitions would enhance UN supervision of these often neglected rights. In terms of setting standards, the council has approved a new Convention of Enforced Disappearances, which has been approved by the General Assembly. The council also approved a draft Declaration on the Rights of Indigenous Peoples, and after a year's delay it was passed by the General Assembly over the opposition of the United States, Canada, and Australia. In many respects, the nascent Human Rights Council is very much like its predecessor—politicized and ineffective at tangibly improving human rights conditions in some of the worst offending states. But the glass is perhaps half full when considering the council's standard-setting activities that can help educate and socialize states over the long term.

Most member states of the UN agreed on getting rid of the old Commission on Human Rights, but for different reasons. This same disagreement, essentially a North-South conflict with Russia aligned with the South, implied rough sailing in familiar troubled waters for the new Human Rights Council. At least all UN member states were to be subjected to scrutiny regarding their human rights records under the council's Universal Periodic Review. How rigorous that scrutiny would be was being established as this edition goes to press.

SUPPLEMENTAL HUMAN RIGHTS BODIES

A brief depiction of supplemental human rights bodies is necessary to understand the full panoply of UN machinery.

Sub-Commission. The former UN Sub-Commission on Prevention of Discrimination and Protection of Minorities, then the UN Sub-Commission on the Promotion and Protection of Human Rights, is another all-purpose human rights agency. It is composed of individual experts rather than state or governmental representatives. It screens private petitions before sending them to the Human Rights Council. These private petitions may come from NGOs, not just from victimized individuals. After a dismal start to the petition process, the sub-commission began to display increasing seriousness, but the process generated only weak pressure. The process was confidential, with a minimum of vague publicity through the parent commission.

Much of the sub-commission's other work overlapped with that of the CHR. It manifested considerable dynamism on a number of issues, so much so that its recommendations often were rejected or ignored by government representatives on the commission. At one point during a financial crisis, the sub-commission's sessions were suspended. Many suggested that it be either drastically reformed or dissolved.[55] Now that the UN Human Rights Council has been created, the sub-commission has become a permanent advisory body to that council, with uncertain role and influence.

Human Rights Committee. Not to be confused with the UN Commission on Human Rights, which reported to the General Assembly through ECOSOC, the UN Human Rights Committee was created under the UN Covenant on Civil and Political Rights. It is composed of individual experts, elected by parties to that convention, and functions only in relation to monitoring the implementation of the civil and political rights codified in that treaty. It reports to the General Assembly but is not part of the "regular" UN bureaucracy.

From the late 1970s the Human Rights Committee has processed state reports about implementing the civil-political covenant and handled individual petitions when state parties have allowed their citizens that procedural right. Despite the Cold War, European communist states became parties to the covenant, and the committee managed to question many states objectively about their record on civil and political rights. In a few cases the committee clearly tried to pressure such states as Uruguay to improve their records by using negative publicity. Evidence suggests that because of committee questions and observations, some states have changed their national legislation to conform to the covenant's requirements. In some court cases judges have made explicit reference to the covenant or committee. One student of the process found matters "quietly encouraging."[56]

Many states are lax about reporting, and about fifty have adhered to the covenant but not consented to the right of individual petition. The United States is among this group. Some of the changes made by states after legal adherence have been small and technical. By the early 1990s only eight states had reported court cases that applied the covenant directly.[57] The committee seemed most influential when dealing with states committed to human rights but perhaps needing some prodding to conform to all international obligations.

The United States, having ratified the covenant with significant and debatable reservations, understandings, and declarations imposed by the Senate, found itself embroiled in an acrimonious exchange with the committee. The committee, among other things, questioned whether U.S. reservations were compatible with the spirit and purpose of the covenant, and the U.S. Senate, led by Jesse Helms, then the Republican head of the Foreign Relations Committee, not only questioned the right of such a UN committee to review U.S. actions but also withheld certain appropriations to the UN. Several allies questioned whether the United States could become a legal party to the covenant and still reserve the right not to make any changes in its incompatible national laws.[58] Ironically, the communist states also took a highly restrictive view of the authority of the UN Human Rights Committee during the Cold War, arguing that it had no authority to make general comment on state reports. Yet after the Cold War, because of legislators like Helms and the more conservative views in the Senate, it was the United States that took the lead in challenging the committee's authority.

A second optional protocol prohibits the death penalty for common crime. In 2005, Canada became the fifty-fifth state to accept this international obligation in the field of human rights. Like most other Western democracies, Canada long ago eliminated almost all possibility of using the death penalty in its domestic laws. Still, only 55 of 192 UN member states are parties to this protocol, which has been open for acceptance since 1991. Japan, like the United States, is among the few liberal democracies to maintain the death penalty for common crime. All EU members except France are parties to the protocol.

Committee on Economic, Social and Cultural Rights. The UN Covenant on Economic, Social and Cultural Rights authorized ECOSOC to supervise the application of the treaty. State parties are obligated to submit a report periodically on state action to implement the covenant. This provision allows some members of ECOSOC to comment on state behavior under the treaty, even though the state making the comments is not a party to the treaty. The United States falls into this category.

In 1979, ECOSOC created the Committee of Governmental Experts to process these state reports. Because it was drawn from governments, this committee was unable to encourage serious attention to treaty obligations.[59] In 1985,

ECOSOC replaced it with the Committee of Individual Experts. So, whereas the Commission on Human Rights never had its membership altered from state representatives to individual experts, a situation that also pertains in the Human Rights Council, the monitoring mechanism under the Covenant on Economic, Social and Cultural Rights has been so changed.

Since it first met in 1987, this new committee has proved much more dynamic than its predecessors. Initially taking a cooperative or positive approach toward reporting states, it has tried to get states to establish national guidelines for minimum standards of food, shelter, health care, and the other rights found in the socioeconomic covenant. Thus the supervising committee did not seek at first to establish a global standard, or its standard, for socioeconomic rights. Rather, it prodded states to think seriously about what the covenant meant in their jurisdictions. The focus was on "the extent to which the most disadvantaged individuals in any given society are enjoying a basic minimum level of subsistence rights."[60] The committee sought to establish this by examining not only legislation but also socioeconomic statistics.

Alone among the UN monitoring mechanisms, the Committee of Individual Experts accepts written submissions from NGOs and IGOs. But most human rights NGOs have not been active regarding these socioeconomic rights.[61] Advocacy groups like Amnesty International and Human Rights Watch concentrated primarily on civil and political rights, and only in about 2000 did they write an interest in broader rights into their mandates. Most NGOs working for adequate food, clothing, shelter, and health care conducted humanitarian or development programs rather than human rights campaigns. This meant that NGOs such as Oxfam have been oriented more toward practical results in a country based on humanitarian concerns and less toward lobbying for socioeconomic rights through the Committee of Individual Experts.

Despite praise for its independence, effective procedures, and constructive recommendations, several problems have plagued the committee. It has functioned in a political vacuum, since few powerful actors have wanted to devote diplomatic efforts to helping implement socioeconomic rights internationally. It considers only a few state reports each year because reports are late and are delayed at the request of states. This UN effort to monitor and improve state behavior pertaining to socioeconomic rights is a long-term project.

Other Supervising Committees. Four other human rights treaties create supervising committees of individual experts that function in similar ways: the Committee on the Elimination of Racial Discrimination (CERD), the Committee on the Elimination of Discrimination Against Women (CEDAW), the Committee Against Torture (CAT), and the Committee on the Rights of the Child (CRC). They may have generated some influence on states that are parties to the treaties, but not enough to merit detailed study here.

A few words about CERD and its parent treaty against racial discrimination help outline the gap between normative theory and behavioral reality. More than 130 states are parties to this human rights treaty, and much rhetoric has been expended within the UN system about the evils of racial discrimination. Every four years state parties are required to submit comprehensive reports regarding compliance with treaty provisions, with briefer updating reports due every two years. Such reports serve as the primary input into the committee's work. Yet many states routinely fail to comply, thus making it difficult for the committee to fulfill its mandate. Also, only a few states permit their citizens to bring a private petition to CERD claiming violation of the treaty, as specified under the treaty's Article 14. These kinds of problems are common to the overall monitoring of various human rights treaties. State reports are filed late and are not always serious in substance. Private petitions do not often lead to clear protection of rights within a reasonable time. The media do not often cover proceedings or outcomes. Consequently, various proposals to improve the fractured UN system of monitoring human rights treaties have lacked impact. Given the fragmentation of the system, proposals to merge the supervising committees have not led to significant change, although the committees do now meet to try to coordinate their efforts.[62] They sometimes issue joint reports to try to highlight issues and maximize impact.

UN High Commissioner for Refugees. The Office of the UN High Commissioner for Refugees warrants special mention given the sheer numbers of people falling under the UNHCR's formal and informal mandates.[63] In the past ten years, the number of persons of concern to the UNHCR has ranged between 15 million and 25 million. The UNHCR was created by the General Assembly in 1950 and functions largely under the 1951 Refugee Convention and its 1967 Protocol, providing protection and assistance to refugees and people in refugee-like situations. Originally the UNHCR mandate centered on *de jure* refugees, or "convention refugees," defined by the 1951 Convention/1967 Protocol as those who have crossed an international border because of a well-founded fear of persecution. Over time, the UNHCR's mandate has expanded to include those who are in refugee-like situations, which means the General Assembly has authorized the UNHCR to deal, at least sometimes, with persons displaced within a state—internally displaced persons (IDPs) in official parlance—and with those fleeing war or a breakdown in public order.

States themselves make the final determination of who is a convention refugee and therefore entitled to temporary asylum from persecution. The exact role of the UNHCR in protection can vary according to national law, but in general one of its primary roles is to help states determine who should not be returned to a situation of possible persecution. The agency calls this "legal" or "diplomatic" protection, and it can involve interviewing those who claim to be refugees, advising executive branches of government, and helping legislators draft or submit legal papers in court cases.

Particularly when faced with an influx of unwanted persons, states may show a racial, ideological, or other bias in their procedures to determine who is recognized as a legal refugee—and entitled not to be returned to a dangerous situation. At times the UNHCR will publicly protest what a government is doing. For example, even though the United States is the largest contributor to the agency's voluntary budget, in 1992 the UNHCR officially protested the forced return of Haitians without a proper hearing about their refugee status.

The agency also is involved in assistance. Rather than being an operating agency itself, the UNHCR normally supervises material and medical assistance to refugees, broadly defined, by contracting with NGOs to provide for the delivery of necessary goods and services to both refugees and internally displaced persons. In 2008 the agency had operations in 110 countries with a staff of 6,300 assisting 32.9 million people. About 425 NGOs were implementing partners. Most of the amounts raised through voluntary contributions were devoted to assistance, and most of this was spent in Africa and Asia.

In the 1990s the UNHCR became deeply enmeshed in the Balkans, devoting about a third of its total resources there. In 1994 the agency was responsible for coordinating relief to some 2 million persons who had fled Rwanda. The growing emphasis on assistance has led some observers to criticize the diminishing role of its traditional legal protection in the organization's priorities. A basis for this criticism is that many institutions can provide aid but only the UNHCR can protect refugees. Internally displaced persons are also of concern to the UNHCR as they experience refugee-like situations but have been unwilling or unable to flee their war-torn countries.[64] IDPs have become more numerous than refugees, numbering 25 million to 30 million in 2008, while refugees numbered only around 9 million. When IDPs were first counted in 1982, there were only a million, at which time there were about 10.5 million refugees.[65]

The rapid evolution of measures on behalf of IDPs in the 1990s and the embrace of their plight by IGOs and NGOs demonstrate the increasing weight of human rights in state decision-making. Efforts accelerated as individuals and private institutions pushed governments and intergovernmental organizations to find new ways to deal with the growing problem of internal displacement. Roberta Cohen documents that "as early as 1991, non-governmental organizations (NGOs) began calling for the consolidation into a single document of the different international standards that apply to IDPs."[66] As the numbers of internally displaced victims rose, so did the decibel level within the UN Commission on Human Rights via the voices of such NGOs as the Quakers, the Refugee Policy Group, the World Council of Churches, and Caritas.

In 1992, Secretary-General Boutros-Ghali submitted the first analytical report on IDPs to the UN Commission on Human Rights in Geneva.[67] In its resolution 1992/73, and not without considerable controversy, the commission authorized the Secretary-General to appoint a representative to explore "views and information from all Governments on the human rights issues related to internally displaced persons, including an examination of existing international human rights, humanitarian and refugee law and standards and their applicability to the protection of and relief assistance to internally displaced persons." Shortly thereafter the UN Secretary-General designated Francis M. Deng, a former Sudanese diplomat, as his representative on internally displaced persons. The development of a comprehensive global approach for effective assistance and protection of IDPs was independently formulated and financed. In a number of publications, Deng assumed the continuing centrality of the Westphalian system and sought to reconcile international involvement with the state's traditional prerogatives through "sovereignty as responsibility."[68] To the three characteristics usually considered attributes of a sovereign (territory, a people, and authority), Deng added a fourth (respect for a minimal standard of human rights). Between his appointment in 1992 and his replacement by Swiss jurist Walter Kälin in 2004, Deng's efforts put the issue of IDPs squarely on the international agenda, including the development of "soft law," embodied in the *Guiding Principles of Internal Displacement*.[69] Still, IDPs have no institutional home in the UN system.[70]

Whether for IDPs or refugees, the UNHCR has always found it difficult to negotiate what it calls "durable solutions." The preferred option is repatriation, but this usually entails fundamental political change in the country of origin—something the UNHCR obviously cannot produce. The UNHCR does not deal with Palestinian refugees; they are serviced by the UN Relief and Works Agency (UNRWA).[71] But the fundamental problems remain the same. In the Middle East, at least two generations of refugees have been born in camps; "durable solutions" have proven elusive.

The UNHCR and UNRWA share other frustrations. Both depend on host-state cooperation for security and other policies in refugee camps. For Rwandan refugees in the Democratic Republic of the Congo (formerly Zaire), as for Palestinian refugees in Lebanon or Syria, the host state decides what groups are allowed to have arms or engage in political activity. In both examples, refugees have been active, respectively, in preparing to launch cross-border armed attacks in Rwanda or Israel. UN refugee agencies are caught in these types of political struggles without either the legal authority or the power to make a difference.[72] Because of such considerations in Zaire and Tanzania, some NGOs, or at least some of their national sections such as Doctors Without Borders, refused to service refugee needs, believing the NGO was contributing to a resumption of violence. The UNHCR decided to stay, as it did not want to abandon civilians who had been displaced and really were being held hostage by armed militias. In the view of the UNHCR, the Security Council has the responsibility to provide proper security in refugee camps.

Another durable solution entails resettlement. This option is made difficult because of the very large numbers of people involved in many migrations.

Despite the best efforts of Operation Lifeline Sudan, millions of displaced people endured famine in the country even in areas that did not directly experience military clashes. (UNHCR Photo/E. Dagnino, A. G. L. Ronchi)

Permanent resettlement for most refugees was out of the question as far as host states were concerned. For example, almost 5 million persons, or a third of the population, left Afghanistan during the fighting there in the 1980s. Iran and Pakistan hosted many of these persons. Resettlement was not a serious option given the sheer numbers and the lack of economic infrastructure of the two host states. And most refugees do not want to settle in a strange land if there is any hope of a sufficient change to make their home country safe. Moreover, even smaller numbers of persons may seem too large. Since the 1980s, the United States has tried to exclude as many Haitians as possible from coming to Florida, as many residents do not want to resettle more Haitians. In the 1990s the German government decided it had too many foreigners of all nationalities applying for asylum. The neo-Nazi right wing in Germany carried out a number of violent attacks. Further refugee resettlement, whether temporary or permanent, seemed out of the question to a German government struggling to maintain social peace. In fact, all countries of traditional refugee resettlement, from Canada to Australia, have decided to restrict as many refugees as possible in the post–Cold War era. The attacks of September 11, 2001, have also made governments more wary of accepting refugees for resettlement.

Restricting numbers is relatively easy when a country is one of second asylum, or resettlement. A state party to the 1951 treaty is not obligated to accept any refugees for resettlement. When dealing with refugees from Vietnam who are in

Hong Kong, the United States can select whomever it wishes for entry into the United States. Only a country of first asylum is legally obligated not to return those with a well-founded fear of persecution. Economic migrants can be returned legally, but for genuine refugees under the UN convention of 1951, no ceiling exists on the number entitled to temporary safe haven in the form of asylum. This can be a problem from the point of view of *raisons d'état*. Thus the UNHCR can find itself trying to protect and assist refugees, but in a context in which the host government may have its own reasons for denying safe haven to as many as possible. The UNHCR does not have the legal authority to make the final determination, much less the power to get states to do what it prefers.

In trying to manage large and politically sensitive problems, the UNHCR for a time developed a reputation for effectiveness. In 1981 it was awarded the Nobel Peace Prize. Afterward, however, criticisms increased about its internal management and external influence.[73] One high commissioner, Jean-Pierre Hocké of Switzerland, resigned in the midst of controversy over his spending habits. In 1990 Sadako Ogata of Japan became the first woman to head the agency, and the agency regained some of the previous high ground. But by the end of the 1990s, questions continued about what had become a sizable bureaucracy. Ogata was replaced after two five-year terms by a former Dutch prime minister, Ruud Lubbers. Responding to the desires of the Western states that funded his budget, he instituted a series of cost-cutting measures but then resigned in early 2005 amid allegations of sexual harassment.[74] Antonio Guterres, a former Portuguese prime minister, replaced him. Since taking office, he has focused especially on voluntary repatriation initiatives and the refugee/IDP situation stemming from the violent conflict in the Darfur region of Sudan.

Refugees and those in refugee-like situations usually are fleeing human rights violations. Hence, the root causes of these human flows must be addressed if the preferred durable solution, repatriation, is to be achieved. This requires political commitment by member states. The large number of refugees from Afghanistan, who had taken refuge in neighboring countries, were able to return in safety only when the Taliban government was removed by international armed conflict in 2001, and the new government of Hamid Karzai provided a more welcoming, albeit not problem-free, environment. In the meantime, the UNHCR is left to cope as best it can, which can be especially challenging in the context of the deteriorating humanitarian situation throughout much of Africa. Yet the approach to post-conflict peacebuilding employed under UN aegis in Bosnia, Kosovo, East Timor, and elsewhere provided hope for improved assistance and protection to those forcibly displaced by armed conflict.

HUMAN RIGHTS AND DEVELOPMENT

Despite resolutions from the General Assembly and Commission on Human Rights about socioeconomic rights and a claimed right of development, the first forty-five years of the United Nations witnessed too few concrete efforts to translate this diplomatic rhetoric into policy. For much of the UN's history, government policymakers and decision-makers made little effort to devise programs that promoted economic growth in developing countries while integrating internationally recognized human rights. As a former head of the UN Centre for Human Rights documented, rhetoric about human rights and planning for economic growth were kept in separate compartments at the UN.[75] The UNDP, the World Bank, UNICEF, the WHO, the WFP, and other UN organizations went about their traditional business in developing countries without much regard for the language of rights.

This situation began to change in the late 1980s and early 1990s. Important opinion leaders in developed countries became dissatisfied with the record of attempts to achieve economic growth through authoritarian governments. The record in Africa was especially poor. Political changes, particularly in Latin America but to a lesser extent elsewhere, gave rise to more democratic governments in developing countries. Seeking macro-national economic growth without attention to human rights could lead to marginalization of sectors of society. Even the World Bank, which had long claimed that human rights factors were "political" and therefore not within the Bank's mandate, began to reconsider its stance—albeit with considerable confusion. The Bank, the largest lender to developing countries, began to emphasize what it called "good governance." This could and sometimes did entail attention to civil and political rights, even though competing interpretations abounded. Although the Bank still sought to avoid taking a stand about democracy at the national level, it did endorse participatory development. Within the concept of social assessment, it made judgments about the extent of popular participation in development projects.[76]

As part of this broad shift by various actors toward incorporating human rights considerations into "development," the UNDP created indices trying to measure "human freedom" and "human development" in a socioeconomic context, which are illustrated in Tables 7.1 and 7.2. Now two decades old, the effort began in 1990 under the guidance of the late Pakistani economist Mahbub ul Haq. The annual *Human Development Report*[77] has provoked a storm of controversy, often from developing countries.[78] The UNDP was said to exceed the responsibilities of an international civil service because it touched upon human rights and domestic jurisdiction. Developing countries had long been sensitive to secretariat officials' passing judgment about how states measured up to international standards. But to its credit, the UNDP stood its ground and even devoted an entire issue to human rights in the *Human Development Report 2000: Human Rights and Human Development.* UNDP had abandoned its freedom index, but like the World Bank, the agency talked more about participatory development. It endorsed an active role for citizens' groups in development projects. This approach entailed defense of civil rights such as freedom of speech and freedom of association.

As noted above, from 1987 the expert committee supervising the Covenant on Economic, Social and Cultural Rights became more assertive. This increased activity, too, fed into the increased efforts at the United Nations to link human rights and development. The Commission on Human Rights began to study accurate indicators for social and economic rights. The basic logic of the claimed

TABLE 7.1   Controversial Human Freedom Index

Countries Scoring High	Countries Scoring Low
Perfect = 40	
Sweden, 38	Iraq, 0
Denmark, 38	Libya, 1
Netherlands, 37	Romania, 1
Finland, 36	Ethiopia, 2
New Zealand, 36	China, 2
Austria, 36	South Africa, 3
Norway, 35	USSR, 3
France, 35	Bulgaria, 4
Germany, 35	Zaire, 5
Belgium, 35	Pakistan, 5
Canada, 34	Vietnam, 5
Switzerland, 34	Indonesia, 5
United States, 33	North Korea, 5
Australia, 33	Syria, 5
Japan, 32	Cuba, 5
United Kingdom, 32	Mozambique, 6
Greece, 31	Saudi Arabia, 6
Costa Rica, 31	Czechoslovakia, 6

Source: Based on information in UN Development Programme found at http://hdr.undp.org/en/statistics/.

TABLE 7.2   Human Development Index, 2008

Top Ten	Bottom Ten
Iceland	Chad
Norway	Guinea-Bissau
Canada	Burundi
Australia	Burkina Faso
Ireland	Niger
Netherlands	Mozambique
Sweden	Liberia
Japan	Congo, Dem. Rep.
Luxembourg	Central African Republic
Switzerland	Sierra Leone

Source: Based on information in UN Development Programme found at http://hdr.undp.org/en/statistics/.

right to development—which had been accepted in resolution form by the General Assembly but not turned into a treaty right—was that economic development meant more than economic growth. Development meant economic growth with attention to civil-political and socioeconomic rights.

The logic of the so-called International Bill of Rights—the Universal Declaration and the two 1966 international covenants—is that economic growth is to be pursued primarily according to democratic state capitalism with a welfare state. Political participation, which entails certain civil rights, is part of the policymaking process. The state exercises broad responsibility for the economy and society; private property is respected in principle; and the state guarantees minimal standards of material welfare. In hyperbolic synopsis, the International Bill of Rights calls for Sweden writ large. Whether real life can be breathed into the right to development, especially over the opposition of conservatives in the United States, is not clear. Would the Senate consent to treaties on these subjects, or the Congress provide foreign assistance to fund projects abroad that were directed to minimum standards of food, clothing, shelter, and health care? Although the Bush administration pledged to add $5 billion at the International Conference on Financing for Development in 2002, the United States ranked last among all OECD states in percentage of its gross national product directed to official development assistance. For the United States, as for most other states, rhetoric in favor of human rights exceeds the reality of support for concrete UN human rights action.[79]

EMERGENCY ASSISTANCE

What happens when development (meaning economic growth accompanied by internationally recognized human rights) breaks down because of war, public emergency, or natural disaster (sometimes combined with corruption or incompetence)? Various UN organizations exist either to prepare for these disasters or to respond to them.[80] In 1992 the Department of Humanitarian Affairs, incorporating the UN Disaster Relief Office (UNDRO), was created to coordinate international humanitarian relief. In January 1998, as part of the Secretary-General's reform initiative, the department was restructured and renamed the Office for the Coordination of Humanitarian Affairs. OCHA is headed by an under-secretary-general who serves as emergency relief coordinator (ERC) responsible for coordinating disaster relief both within and outside the UN system. The UNHCR and UNICEF usually play active, and sometimes lead, roles in coordinating international relief. The WFP is usually involved in logistics. The WHO and the Food and Agriculture Organization usually are not far behind. And the UNDP, which is supposed to coordinate all UN activities within a country, is also involved. The ERC has been mandated the responsibility of overseeing the rapid deployment of staff during crisis situations and ensuring that appropriate coordination mechanisms are set up.

Moreover, a galaxy of private relief organizations also is active. The International Federation of Red Cross and Red Crescent Societies, which loosely coordinates about 186 national units, sees natural-disaster work as one of its primary reasons for being. Hundreds of other private agencies, such as Oxfam, Caritas, and Feed the Children, try to respond to natural disasters with emergency assistance. Ian Smillie and Larry Minear, for instance, have calculated that "humanitarianism has become a big business, now involving some $10 billion annually."[81] As a result, critics have pointed out that quest for market share may be assuming more importance for these agencies than saving lives. Although it might or might not be the marketplace that unleashes an "NGO scramble,"[82] there is little question that an environment with scarce resources required for humanitarian organizations to survive and thrive will create a competitive dynamic.

The major problem with all of this international assistance, broadly conceived, is that no one really is in charge. "Coordination" is an oft-used word to describe a loosely knit network of IGOs and NGOs as well as state agencies active in humanitarian relief. Every agency is in favor of coordination in principle, but few wish to be coordinated in practice. UN organizations have been protective of their decentralized independence. Private agencies have resisted coming under the full control of public authorities. As such, agencies compete among themselves for a slice of the action and for credit for whatever accomplishments can be achieved. The result is often confusion and duplication of services.

Still, emergency assistance has been delivered and lives have been saved in a vast number of situations. Host governments have frequently welcomed international help for natural disasters, although some of the less savory governments have diverted sizable chunks of this aid to the pockets of the elite—for example, in Somoza's Nicaragua after a severe earthquake. The General Assembly, mostly reflecting the view of developing countries, has endorsed the idea of international assistance as long as state consent is obtained. Actors like the United States and the European Union have coordinated some of the assistance by providing public money to NGOs (sometimes called PVOs, private voluntary organizations, or VOLAGs, volunteer agencies). At times all of this activity is put under a UN umbrella, as in northern Iraq and the former Yugoslavia. But by and large, coordination in the form of an institutionalized response has been lacking. Coordinated effectiveness has to be constructed almost from scratch for each assistance operation by what Larry Minear has called the "humanitarian enterprise."[83]

The General Assembly in 1991 authorized in resolution 46/182 a new position of under-secretary-general for emergency relief. But this official, however well intentioned and adept, still operates in a milieu in which public and private agencies resist central control over their independence of action and fund-raising. Donor states have expressed growing concern about this "non-system" and in the early 1990s issued a statement saying, "We commit ourselves to making the United Nations stronger, more efficient and more effective in order to protect human rights." At that time they also called for an "improvement in the UN system . . . to meet urgent humanitarian needs in time of crisis."[84] But decisive change for the better has not really materialized; in fact, the changes have been mainly cosmetic.[85]

With the creation of OCHA and the ERC, a step was taken toward a more coherent coordination approach. The ERC chairs an Inter-Agency Standing Committee (IASC), which includes major UN and non-UN humanitarian actors. This body strives to facilitate interagency analysis and decision-making in response to humanitarian emergencies. Also, in his role as a UN under-secretary-general, the head of OCHA serves as convener of the Executive Committee for Humanitarian Affairs (ECHA), a cabinet-level forum for coordinating humanitarian policies within the UN. The relevance of OCHA was demonstrated in the aftermath of the 2004 Southeast Asian tsunami, which killed approximately 275,000 people and left tens of millions homeless and without basic services, such as food, water, housing, and medical care. Under-Secretary-General Jan Egeland prodded many donor countries, which eventually contributed billions of dollars in the largest relief operation in history. OCHA shifted into high gear again to respond to the 2005 earthquake in the Kashmir region, which left approximately 30,000 people dead and millions homeless.

In armed conflicts and public emergencies stemming from so-called human-made disasters, the politics of providing emergency relief to civilians is far more complicated than in natural disasters, and the task of effectively protecting war victims may be impossible depending on the security situation and the stance of a government or political authorities. By law and by tradition, the International Committee of the Red Cross coordinates international relief in international wars on behalf of the International Red Cross and Red Crescent Movement. The 1949 Geneva Conventions for victims of war, and the supplemental 1977 Protocol I, give the ICRC a preferred position for this task, especially since protecting powers (neutral states appointed by the fighting parties for humanitarian tasks) are rarely named anymore. The Security Council has affirmed the rights of civilians to international assistance in such wars, and belligerents have a legal duty to cooperate with neutral relief efforts. Protocol I from 1977 states clearly that starvation of civilians is not legally permitted in warfare and that belligerents are not legally permitted to attack objects vital to the survival of the civilian population.

The ICRC is a private agency whose sources of funds are summarized in Table 7.3. The agency is specifically recognized in public international law and by the General Assembly, which has accorded the ICRC observer status along with the Federation of Red Cross and Red Crescent Societies. For large-scale relief the assembly prefers that UN organizations, along with NGOs, be the primary operational agents of humanitarian assistance and that the ICRC adopt a monitoring role.[86] In Somalia in the early 1990s, the ICRC remained to play a central role in relief, even after the Security Council authorized the use of force to deliver that relief. In other violent situations, as on the Indian subcontinent in

TABLE 7.3 Top Financial Contributors to the International Committee of the Red Cross, 2007

Governments
United States
European Commission
United Kingdom
Switzerland
Sweden
Netherlands
Austria
Denmark
Germany
Canada
Australia
France

Source: Based on information in UN Development Programme found at http://hdr.undp.org/en/statistics/.

1971, the ICRC worked closely with the UN system in monitoring the delivery of food and other socioeconomic relief to East Pakistan/Bangladesh.

Here again the disorganization of the UN system regarding assistance comes into play. No institutionalized UN agency exists to take the system's lead in armed conflicts. The Secretary-General or General Assembly may ask an agency on an ad hoc basis to take the lead—for example, that was the case for the UNHCR in the Balkans during 1992–1995. The under-secretary-general for humanitarian affairs still must negotiate operational details from a welter of options. What is now called the Red Cross and Red Crescent Movement is either disorganized or decentralized; the ICRC does not fully control national Red Cross–Red Crescent units and certainly not their international federation. Suggestions concerning how to improve the broad international response to civilian need in violent situations remain just suggestions.[87]

The situation is even more complicated in internal armed conflict where one or more fighting parties do not represent a widely recognized state and where most of the fighting occurs primarily in the territory of one state.[88] The laws of war (which also are called humanitarian law, the law of armed conflict, or the law for human rights in war) do not create a clear obligation to cooperate with the purveyors of humanitarian assistance. The ICRC does not have the same legal rights in intrastate wars that it does in interstate wars. Moreover, states and other fighting parties frequently disagree on whether an internal armed conflict exists as compared to a rebellion or insurrection falling under national rather than international law. The number of interstate wars has declined since 1945, but the number of violent situations seen by some as "internal wars" has risen, accompanied by great civilian loss of life and other suffering. A series of events since the end of the Cold War—within the former Yugoslavia and Soviet Union and within Somalia, Angola, Afghanistan, Burundi, Rwanda, Liberia, Mozambique, East Timor, and Cambodia—suggests that atrocities and brutality are prevalent features of civil wars. In December 1996 in Chechnya, six Red Cross workers were murdered in their beds.

Neither the UN organization nor NGOs nor the ICRC has had consistent success in delivering humanitarian assistance in complex emergencies because permitting such assistance has limited meaning to parties using starvation as a weapon and who are engaged in ethnic cleansing, genocide, widespread rape, and deliberate attacks on civilians and aid personnel. Child soldiers and ragtag local militias make the inculcation of humanitarian values difficult.[89] Given the difficulties encountered by both the UN and the ICRC in obtaining the consent of fighting parties in internal wars and public emergencies, some NGOs, such as Médecins sans Frontières (Doctors Without Borders), have engaged in "cross-border" operations without consent. Most organizations and agencies are reluctant to do so, however, as their policy guidance and funding come from states. Although they have relatively independent secretariats, they are part of an intergovernmental system whose officials must deal with governments in governing councils as well as in field programs. Executive heads of various UN organizations, and the Office of the Secretary-General, have been creative in trying to cope with famine and disease in places like the southern Sudan and Somalia. But as a practical matter, trying to proceed without the consent of the warring parties can lead—and has led—to attacks on international and local relief personnel. Beyond legal niceties centering on sovereignty, the safety of staff members is of practical concern. Since 1990, more journalists and aid workers have died than peacekeepers. For aid agencies, this kind of insecurity represents a very acute challenge.

In general, international pressure is growing on warring parties in violent situations to permit access to civilians by humanitarian agencies. But UN organizations and the ICRC still have major difficulties in providing relief on neutral or balanced terms. Governmental consent was effectively overlooked in Somalia because there was no central government. Consent was bypassed to provide relief and protection to Iraqi Kurds because the government in Baghdad was an international pariah after its invasion of Kuwait. "Consent" in East Timor from the Indonesian government was more a fiction than a fact because of the extreme pressure placed on Jakarta by Western donors. Situations in Bosnia and the Balkans, Sudan, and old Ethiopia presented a different and more typical picture. The fighting parties regarded food relief as a political factor, and outside states saw very high costs in trying to coerce fighting parties into respecting the rights of civilians to adequate food, clothing, shelter, and health care. Many parties recoil at the paradox of "humanitarian war."[90] NATO's "humanitarian bombing," which many humanitarians judged as an oxymoron, of Kosovo and Serbia in 1999 brought this paradox into bold relief.

Addressing the nationalistic, ethnic, and communal wars and tensions was not only traumatic for states; it was traumatic as well for aid agencies. Until recently, the two most essential humanitarian principles (neutrality and impartiality) had been relatively uncontroversial, along with the key operating procedure of seeking consent from belligerents.[91] These principles, too, became casualties as "these Maginot line principles defending humanitarianism from politics crumbled during the 1990s."[92] A host of factors have challenged the classical posture: the complete disregard for international humanitarian law by war criminals and even by child soldiers; the direct targeting of civilians and relief personnel; the use of foreign aid to fuel conflicts and war economies; and the protracted nature of many so-called emergencies.[93]

In many ways, international humanitarian law seems to have been formulated to deal with a different world—one populated by governments and regular armies whose interests were often served by respecting the laws of war.[94] In writing of old-fashioned humanitarianism, David Rieff has gone so far as to suggest "the death of a good idea."[95] At the end of the day, he came around to the view that traditional, neutral, limited humanitarianism was the right course of action after earlier having been a proponent of armed intervention to halt atrocities.[96]

In spite of these problems—and "identity crisis"[97] is not too strong a term to describe the individual and collective soul-searching by civilian personnel—the preceding pages should have made clear that humanitarian values and expenditures on emergency assistance have expanded substantially. The big business of almost $10 billion a year[98] has led such harsh critics as Mark Duffield to question whether humanitarian assistance has not become a necessity for maintaining Western hegemony.[99] And at a minimum, the marketplace unleashes a "scramble" because an environment of scarce resources creates a competitive dynamic for status, power, and authority among competitive UN agencies and NGOs whose staffs and budgets depend upon expanding resources.[100] "In the 1990s," summarized Adam Roberts, "humanitarian issues have played a historically unprecedented role in international politics."[101] In the dramatic example of the military campaign in Kosovo, Michael Ignatieff noted that "its legitimacy [depends] on what fifty years of human rights has done to our moral instincts, weakening the presumption in favor of state sovereignty, strengthening the presumption in favor of intervention when massacre and deportation become state policy."[102] The NATO bombing of Serbia over Kosovo may have been illegal in international law, in that NATO engaged in the first use of force without Security Council approval, but to many it was legitimate because of the moral argument Ignatieff suggested.

Normative developments and political reality are rarely in sync. The responsibility to protect, for instance, reflects a steady and clear growth since the early 1990s, whereas the operational capacity and political will to engage in humanitarian intervention has been on a roller coaster. The 2005 World Summit marks the zenith of international consensus about R2P, but the blowback from September 11 explains the current nadir with a total absence of political will and meaningful humanitarian intervention in Darfur—the 2005 manifestation of what one of us earlier called "collective spinelessness" instead of collective security.[103]

NOTES

1. In general, see Julie A. Mertus, *The United Nations and Human Rights,* 2nd ed. (London: Routledge, 2009); Philip Alston, ed., *The United Nations and Human Rights,* 2nd ed. (Oxford: Clarendon Press, 1995); David P. Forsythe, "The UN and Human Rights at Fifty," *Global Governance* 1 (1995): 297–318; and *Human Rights in International Relations* (Cambridge: Cambridge University Press, 2000).

2. See Neta C. Crawford, *Argument and Change in World Politics: Ethics, Decolonization and Humanitarian Intervention* (Cambridge: Cambridge University Press, 2002), and Paul Gordon Lauren, *Power and Prejudice: The Politics and Diplomacy of Racial Discrimination,* 2nd ed. (Boulder, Colo.: Westview Press, 1996).

3. Roger S. Clark and Madeleine Sann, eds., *The Prosecution of International Crimes: A Critical Study of the International Tribunal for the Former Yugoslavia* (New Brunswick, N.J.: Transaction, 1996).

4. Jon Western, *Selling Intervention and War* (Baltimore: Johns Hopkins University Press, 2005).

5. The International Court of Justice arguably has the right to review such council determinations in the light of the wording of the Charter and other parts of international law. See Thomas M. Franck, "The 'Powers of Appreciation': Who Is the Ultimate Guardian of UN Legality?" *American Journal of International Law* 86, no. 519 (1992): 519–523.

6. Fernando R. Tesón, "Changing Perceptions of Domestic Jurisdiction and Intervention," in *Beyond Sovereignty: Collectively Defending Democracy in the Americas,* ed. Tom Farer (Baltimore: Johns Hopkins University Press, 1996), 29–51.

7. Over time the absence of government in Somalia created a major international security problem, as pirates operating primarily from lawless Somalia hijacked a number of ships with their crews and demanded ransom. Various states and NATO took military action to counter the threat to merchant shipping.

8. *Report of the Secretary-General to the Security Council on the Protection of Civilians in Armed Conflicts,* March 30, 2001, UN document S/2001/331. The Security Council also adopted resolution 1296 on protecting civilians on April 19, 2000; resolution 1325 on protecting women's rights on October 31, 2000; and resolution 1379 on protecting children's rights on November 20, 2001.

9. *Report of the Secretary on the Work of the Organization,* UN document A/51/1, para. 1132.

10. Barbara Crossette, "UN Asks for Intervention Force as Burundi Nears Collapse," *New York Times,* July 25, 1996.

11. International Crisis Group, "A Framework for Responsible Aid to Burundi," www.intl-crisis-group.org/projects/showreport.cfm?reportid=901.

12. Hugo Slim, "Dithering over Darfur? A Preliminary Review of the International Response," *International Affairs* 80, no. 5 (2004): 811–833. See also Cheryl O. Igiri and Princeton N. Lyman, *Giving Meaning to "Never Again": Seeking an Effective Response to the Crisis in Darfur and Beyond* (New York: Council on Foreign Relations, 2004), CFR No. 5.

13. Roméo Dallaire, "Looking at Darfur, Seeing Rwanda," *New York Times,* October 4, 2004.

14. Samantha Power, *"A Problem from Hell": America and the Age of Genocide* (New York: Basic Books, 2001).

15. UN OCHA, "Sudan: US Congress Unanimously Defines Darfur Violence as 'Genocide,'" July 23, 2004, available at http://www.globalsecurity.org/military/library/news /2004/07/mil-040723-irin03.htm.

16. "The Crisis in Darfur," written remarks before the Senate Foreign Relations Committee, Washington, D.C., September 9, 2004, available at www.state.gov/outofdate/bgn/ s/99318.htm.

17. Physicians for Human Rights, "Call for Intervention to Save Lives in the Sudan: Field Team Compiles Indicators of Genocide," June 23, 2004, available at http://physiciansfor humanrights.org/about/record/pdf/summer04_record.pdf.

18. Agence France-Presse, "EU Lawmakers Call Darfur 'Crisis Genocide,'" September 16, 2004, available at www.middle-east-online.com/english/sudan/?id=11287.

19. See Scott Straus, "Darfur and the Genocide Debate," *Foreign Affairs* 84, no. 1 (2005): 123–133.

20. See David Lague, "China Braces for Prospect of Change," *New York Times*, September 27, 2007.

21. On the UN and El Salvador, and other human rights situations in the Western Hemisphere, see David P. Forsythe, "The United Nations, Democracy, and the Americas," in *Beyond Sovereignty: Collectively Defending Democracy in the Americas*, ed. Tom J. Farer (Baltimore: Johns Hopkins University Press, 1996), 107–131, and WOLA, *Reluctant Reforms: The Cristiani Government and the International Community in the Process of Salvadoran Post-War Reconstruction* (Washington, D.C.: Washington Office on Latin America, 1993).

22. David P. Forsythe, *Human Rights and World Politics*, 2nd ed. (Lincoln: University of Nebraska Press, 1989), chap. 3.

23. John Tessitore and Susan Woolfson, eds., *A Global Agenda: Issues Before the 47th General Assembly of the United Nations* (Lanham, Md.: University Press of America, 1992), 240.

24. For the context, see Richard J. Goldstone and Adam Smith, *International Judicial Institutions: The Architecture of International Justice at Home and Abroad* (London: Routledge, 2008). See also Gary Jonathan Bass, *Stay the Hand of Vengeance: The Politics of War Crimes Tribunals* (Princeton, N.J.: Princeton University Press, 2000); Steven R. Ratner and James L. Bischoff, eds., *International War Crimes Trials: Making a Difference* (Austin: University of Texas Law School, 2004); and Eric Stover and Harvey M. Weinstein, eds., *My Neighbor, My Enemy: Justice and Community in the Aftermath of Mass Atrocity* (New York: Cambridge University Press, 2004).

25. See further David P. Forsythe, "The United States and International Criminal Justice," *Human Rights Quarterly* 24, no. 4 (2002): 974–991.

26. John Goldsmith and Stephen D. Krasner, "The Limits of Idealism," *Dædalus* 132, no.1 (2003): 47–63.

27. David P. Forsythe, "The UN Secretary-General and Human Rights," in *The Challenging Role of the UN Secretary-General*, eds. Benjamin Rivlin and Leon Gordenker (Westport, Conn.: Greenwood Press, 1993), 211–232. See also Kent Kille, ed., *The Moral Authority of the UN Secretary-General* (Washington, D.C.: Georgetown University Press, 2008).

28. See Bertrand G. Ramcharan, *The UN and Preventive Diplomacy* (Bloomington: Indiana University Press, 2008).

29. Early influence by UN staff members on behalf of human rights can be seen in John P. Humphrey, *Human Rights and the United Nations* (New York: Transaction Books, 1984).

30. A joke circulating about the various recent heads of the UN Centre for Human Rights involved these characters: Van Boven was supposedly the most active and committed; his successor, Kurt Herndl, having seen what happened to van Boven, supposedly kept a low profile; his successor, Jan Martenson, was supposedly preoccupied with a public image for himself and his office; his successor, Antoine Blanca, was supposedly an old crony of the Secretary-General who had no interest in human rights. So the joke went like this: Van Boven (in fact) wrote the book *People Matter*; so Herndl supposedly wrote *States Matter*; Martenson, *I Matter*; Blanca, *It Doesn't Matter*.

31. Press Release SG/SM/6825 HR/4391, December 8, 1998.

32. www.unglobalcompact.org.

33. Brian Knowlton, "Rights Chief Talks of U.S. Role in Her Leaving," *International Herald Tribune*, July 31, 2002, 6.

34. See Julia Preston, "New U.N. Chief Invites Controversy by Declining to Oppose Hussein Execution," *New York Times*, January 3, 2007, available at www.nytimes.com/2007/01/03/world/middleeast/03nations.html.

35. Bertrand G. Ramcharan, ed., *Human Rights Protection in the Field* (Leiden, Netherlands: Martinus Nijhoff, 2006).

36. For an overview of this issue, see David P. Forsythe, "U.S. Policy Toward Enemy Detainees," *Human Rights Quarterly* 28, no. 2 (2006). On the conflict between Arbour and Bolton, see "U.S. Attacks UN Official on 'Jails,'" *BBC News*, January 24, 2006.

37. Howard Tolley Jr., *The UN Commission on Human Rights* (Boulder, Colo.: Westview Press, 1987). There has not been a sequel to this thorough study, so we do not have an in-depth scholarly overview of the commission from 1986 to 2006. For a general picture, however, see Roger Normand and Sarah Zaidi, *Human Rights at the UN: The Political History of Universal Justice* (Bloomington: Indiana University Press, 2008). See also James H. Lebovic and Eric Voeten, "The Politics of Shame," *International Studies Quarterly* 50, no. 4 (2006): 861–888.

38. Tom J. Farer, "The UN and Human Rights: More Than a Whimper, Less Than a Roar," in *Human Rights and the World Community: Issues and Action*, 2nd ed., eds. Richard Pierre Claude and Burns H. Weston (Philadelphia: University of Pennsylvania Press, 1992).

39. For a firsthand portrait, see Paulo Sérgio Pinheiro, "Musings of a UN Special Rapporteur on Human Rights," *Global Governance* 9, no. 1 (2003): 1–13.

40. For an example of this American bias, see Morris B. Abram, "Human Rights and the United Nations: Past as Prologue," *Harvard Human Rights Law Journal* 4 (1991): 69–83.

41. Tessitore and Woolfson, *Global*, 236.

42. Telford Taylor, *The Anatomy of the Nuremberg Trials* (New York: Knopf, 1992), 29.

43. Cathal J. Nolan, *Principled Diplomacy: Security and Rights in U.S. Foreign Policy* (Westport, Conn.: Greenwood Press, 1993), chap. 7.

44. Tolley Jr., *Commission*, 179.

45. Joe W. Pitts III and David Weissbrodt, "Major Developments at the UN Commission on Human Rights in 1992," *Human Rights Quarterly* 15, no. 1 (1993): 122–196.

46. Raymond Gastil, ed., *Freedom in the World, 1992* (New York: Freedom House, 1993).

47. HLP, *A More Secure World*, paras. 283 and 285.

48. Annan, *In Larger Freedom*, para. 183.

49. Lebovic and Voeten, "The Politics of Shame."

50. See Thomas Buergenthal, "The Evolving International Human Rights System," *American Journal of International Law* 100 (October 2006): 791.

51. Louise Arbour, "Statement by High Commissioner for Human Rights to Last Meeting of Commission on Human Rights," March 27, 2006, 3–6. See further David P. Forsythe, with Baekkwan Park, "Turbulent Transition," in *The United Nations: Past, Present, and Future*, eds. Alissa Warters and Scott Kaufman (Hauppaugne, N.Y.: Nova Science Publishers, 2009).

52. General Assembly, *2005 World Summit Outcome*, UN document A/60/L.1, September 15, 2005, paras. 157 and 160.

53. See Nico Schrijver, "The UN Human Rights Council: 'A Society of the Committed' or Just Old Wine in New Bottles?" *Leiden Journal of International Law* 20, no. 4 (2007): 809–823, and Yvonne Terlingen, "The Human Rights Council: A New Era in UN Human Rights Work?" *Ethics & International Affairs* 21, no. 2 (2007): 167–178.

54. Quoted in Warren Hoge, "Dismay Over New U.N. Human Rights Council," *New York Times*, March 11, 2007.

55. Karen Reierson and David Weissbrodt, "The Forty-third Session of the UN Sub-Commission on Prevention of Discrimination and Protection of Minorities: The Sub-Commission Under Scrutiny," *Human Rights Quarterly* 14, no. 1 (1992): 271.

56. Cindy A. Cohn, "The Early Harvest: Domestic Legal Changes Related to the Human Rights Committee and the Covenant on Civil and Political Rights," *Human Rights Quarterly* 13, no. 2 (1991): 320–321.

57. Ibid., 321.

58. William Schabas, "Spare the RUD or Spoil the Treaty: United States Challenges the Human Rights Committee on Reservations," in *The United States and Human Rights*, ed. David P. Forsythe (Lincoln: University of Nebraska Press, 2000), 110–125.

59. David Harris, "Commentary by the Rapporteur on the Consideration of States Parties' Reports and International Cooperation" (paper presented at symposium: The Implementation of the International Covenant on Economic, Social and Cultural Rights), *Human Rights Quarterly* 9, no. 1 (1997): 149.

60. Philip Alston and Bruno Simma, "First Session of the UN Committee on Economic, Social and Cultural Rights," *American Journal of International Law* 81, no. 3 (1987): 750.

61. Leckie, "Overview," 566–567.

62. See further Philip Alston and James Crawford, eds., *The Future of UN Human Rights Treaty Monitoring* (Cambridge: Cambridge University Press, 2000), and Anne Bayefsky, *The UN Human Rights Treaty System: Universality at the Crossroads* (Ardsley, N.Y.: Transnational Publishers, 2001).

63. See especially Gil Loescher, *The UNHCR and World Politics: A Perilous Path* (Oxford: Oxford University Press, 2001); Arthur C. Helton, *The Price of Indifference* (Oxford: Oxford University Press, 2002); and Niclaus Steiner, Mark Gibney, and Gil Loescher, eds., *Problems of Protection: The UNHCR, Refugees, and Human Rights* (New York: Routledge, 2003).

64. See Thomas G. Weiss, "Internal Exiles: What Next for Internally Displaced Persons?" *Third World Quarterly* 24, no. 3 (2003): 429–447, and Kathleen Newland with Erin Patrick and Monette Zard, *No Refuge: The Challenge of Internal Displacements* (New York and Geneva: UNOCHA, 2003).

65. The changing numbers of "persons of concern" to the UNHCR can be followed by checking the different editions of *The Refugee Survey Quarterly*, published by the UNHCR,

or by going to www.unhcr.org. For complete statistics on IDPs, see www.idpproject.org, maintained by the Norwegian Refugee Council.

66. Michael Ignatieff, "Human Rights: The Midlife Crisis," *New York Review of Books* 46, no. 9 (1999): 58.

67. Commission on Human Rights, *Analytical Report of the Secretary-General on Internally Displaced Persons*, UN document E/CN.4/1992/23.

68. In addition to earlier citations, see also the publication about research from which the concept emerged in Frances M. Deng et al., *Sovereignty as Responsibility: Conflict Management in Africa* (Washington, D.C.: Brookings Institution, 1996).

69. UN Office of Coordination of Humanitarian Affairs, www.reliefweb.int/ocha_ol/pub/index.html.

70. See Thomas G. Weiss and David A. Korn, *Internal Displacement: Conceptualization and Its Consequences* (London: Routledge, 2006).

71. Benjamin N. Schiff, *Refugees unto the Third Generation: UN Aid to Palestinians* (Syracuse, N.Y.: Syracuse University Press, 1995).

72. See further Fiona Terry, *Condemned to Repeat? The Paradox of Humanitarian Action* (Ithaca, N.Y.: Cornell University Press, 2002).

73. Tessitore and Woolfson, *Global*, 260.

74. UNHCR local staff in East Africa were accused of exchanging services for sexual favors, a controversy that did not enhance the agency's reputation. Loescher found in his 2001 study that parts of the UNHCR headquarters could be insensitive to refugee needs.

75. Theo van Boven, "Human Rights and Development: The UN Experience," in *Human Rights and Development*, ed. David P. Forsythe (London: Macmillan, 1989), 121–135.

76. Internal World Bank documents increasingly dealt with human rights. See, for example, C. Mark Blackden, "Human Rights, Governance, and Development: Issues, Avenues, and Tasks," October 10, 1991, 17 plus attachments. For an overview, see David P. Forsythe, "Human Rights, Development, and the United Nations," *Human Rights Quarterly* 19, no. 2 (1997): 334–349.

77. See Khadija Haq and Richard Ponzio, eds., *Pioneering the Human Development Revolution: An Intellectual Biography of Mahbub ul Haq* (Delhi: Oxford University Press, 2008).

78. Tessitore and Woolfson, *Global*, 245.

79. David P. Forsythe, "Human Rights and U.S. Foreign Policy: Two Levels, Two Worlds," *Political Studies* (special issue) 43 (1995): 111–130.

80. For a discussion of these organizations and the difficulties encountered in crises of the 1990s, see Thomas G. Weiss and Cindy Collins, *Humanitarian Challenges and Intervention*, 2nd ed. (Boulder, Colo.: Westview Press, 2000), and Jonathan Moore, *The UN and Complex Emergencies* (Geneva: UN Research Institute for Social Development, 1996).

81. Ian Smillie and Larry Minear, *The Charity of Nations: Humanitarian Action in a Calculating World* (Bloomfield, Conn.: Kumarian, 2004), 8.

82. Andrew Cooley and James Ron, "The NGO Scramble: Organizational Insecurity and the Political Economy of Transnational Action," *International Security* 27, no. 1 (2002): 5–39.

83. Larry Minear, *The Humanitarian Enterprise: Dilemmas and Discoveries* (Bloomfield, Conn.: Kumarian, 2002).

84. David J. Scheffer, "Challenges Confronting Collective Security: Humanitarian Intervention," in *Three Views on the Issue of Humanitarian Intervention*, ed. U.S. Institute of Peace (Washington, D.C.: U.S. Institute of Peace, 1992), 5.

85. Thomas G. Weiss, "Humanitarian Shell Games: Whither UN Reform?" *Security Dialogue* 29, no. 1 (1998): 9–23.

86. David P. Forsythe, "Choices More Ethical Than Legal: The International Committee of the Red Cross and Human Rights," *Ethics & International Affairs* 7 (1993): 131–152.

87. For a discussion of future possibilities, see a series of essays from practitioners in Thomas G. Weiss and Larry Minear, eds., *Humanitarianism Across Borders: Sustaining Civilians in Times of War* (Boulder, Colo.: Lynne Rienner, 1993).

88. See Peter J. Hoffman and Thomas G. Weiss, *Sword & Salve: Confronting New Wars and Humanitarian Crises* (Lanham, Md.: Rowman & Littlefield, 2006).

89. Simon Chesterman, ed., *Civilians in War* (Boulder, Colo.: Lynne Rienner, 2004); P. W. Singer, *Children at War* (New York: Pantheon, 2005).

90. There is a vast literature on humanitarian intervention. Two scholarly treatments are Nicholas J. Wheeler, *Saving Strangers: Humanitarian Intervention in International Society* (Oxford: Oxford University Press, 2000), and Robert Keohane and J. L. Holzgrefe, eds., *Humanitarian Intervention* (Cambridge: Cambridge University Press, 2003).

91. See Thomas G. Weiss, "Principles, Politics, and Humanitarian Action," *Ethics & International Affairs* 13 (1999): 1–22, as well as "Responses" by Cornelio Sommaruga, Joelle Tanguy, Fiona Terry, and David Rieff on 23–42.

92. Michael Barnett, "Humanitarianism Transformed," *Perspectives on Politics* 3, no. 4 (2005): 724.

93. For more extensive discussions of this landscape, see Michael Maren, *The Road to Hell: The Ravaging Effects of Foreign Aid and International Charity* (New York: Free Press, 1997), and Alex de Waal, *Famine Crimes: Politics and the Disaster Relief Industry in Africa* (Oxford: James Currey, 1997). This debate was initiated by Alex de Waal and Rakiya Omaar, *Humanitarianism Unbound? Current Dilemmas Facing Multi-Mandate Relief Operations in Political Emergencies* (London: African Rights, 1994), Discussion Paper no. 5. For a discussion of the disarray among humanitarians, see, for example, John Borton, "The State of the International Humanitarian System," Overseas Development Institute Briefing Paper no. 1 (March 1998); Myron Wiener, "The Clash of Norms: Dilemmas in Refugee Policies," *Journal of Refugee Studies* 11, no. 4 (1998): 1–21; and Mark Duffield, "NGO Relief in War Zones: Toward an Analysis of the New Aid Paradigm," in *Beyond UN Subcontracting: Task-Sharing with Regional Security Arrangements and Service-Providing NGOs*, ed. Thomas G. Weiss (London: Macmillan, 1998), 139–159. For a look at the political economy of conflict, see, for example, Mark Duffield, "The Political Economy of Internal War: Asset Transfer and the Internationalisation of Public Welfare in the Horn of Africa," in *War and Hunger: Rethinking International Responses to Complex Emergencies*, eds. Joanna Macrae and Anthony Zwi (London: Zed Books, 1994), 5–69; David Keen, *The Economic Functions of Violence in Civil Wars* (Oxford: Oxford University Press, 1998), Adelphi Paper 320; and François Jean and Christophe Rufin, eds., *Economies des guerres civiles* (Paris: Hachette, 1996).

94. See Adam Roberts, "Implementation of the Laws of War in Late 20th Century Conflicts," Parts 1, 2, *Security Dialogue* 29, nos. 2 and 3 (1998): 137–150 and 265–280; and a special issue on "Humanitarian Debate: Law, Policy, Action," *International Review of the Red Cross* 81, no. 833 (1999).

95. David Rieff, "The Death of a Good Idea," *Newsweek*, May 10, 1999, 65.

96. David Rieff, *A Bed for the Night: Humanitarianism in Crisis* (New York: Simon & Schuster, 2002).

97. David Rieff, "Humanitarianism in Crisis," *Foreign Affairs* 81, no. 6 (2002): 111–121. For a recent set of essays on the topic, see Michael Barnett and Thomas G. Weiss, eds., *Humanitarianism in Question: Politics, Power, Ethics* (Ithaca, N.Y.: Cornell University Press, 2008). For a review of this work and a broader essay on humanitarianism, see David P. Forsythe in the *Human Rights Quarterly* 31, no. 1 (2009): 269–277.

98. Development Initiatives, *Global Humanitarian Assistance 2007/2008* (Somerset, UK: Development Initiatives, 2008).

99. Mark Duffield, *Global Governance and the New Wars: The Merging of Development and Security* (London: Zed Books, 2001). See also Philip White, "Complex Political Emergencies—Grasping Contexts, Seizing Opportunities," *Disasters* 24, no. 4 (2000): 288–290, and Des Gasper, "'Drawing a Line'—Ethical and Political Strategies in Complex Emergency Assistance," *European Journal of Development Research* 11, no. 2 (1999): 87–114.

100. Andrew Cooley and James Ron, "The NGO Scramble: Organizational Insecurity and the Political Economy of Transnational Action," *International Security* 27, no. 1 (2002): 5–39.

101. Adam Roberts, "The Role of Humanitarian Issues in International Politics in the 1990s," *International Review of the Red Cross* (1999):19–43.

102. Michael Ignatieff, "Human Rights: The Midlife Crisis," *New York Review of Books* 46, no. 9 (1999): 58.

103. Thomas G. Weiss, "Collective Spinelessness: U.N. Actions in the Former Yugoslavia," in *The World and Yugoslavia's Wars*, ed. Richard H. Ullman (New York: Council on Foreign Relations, 1996), 59–96.

CHAPTER 8

Change,
the United Nations,
and Human Rights

T HE PHRASE "THE UNITED NATIONS" refers more to a framework, a stage, or an institutional setting than to an organization with the capacity for independent action. Although some people, such as those in the Office of the Secretary-General, can take relatively independent action, "the UN" mostly refers to a process in which the most important policy decisions are made by governments representing territorial states. Fundamentally, the UN has become involved in changing policies toward human rights as states have changed their policies. But other actors have been important, too.[1]

The promotion and protection of human rights has become one of the UN's more prominent activities. In the annual United Nations Yearbook, more pages are usually devoted to human rights, by far, than to any other subject matter. Those printed pages accurately reflect the attention given to UN diplomacy on human rights. However, problems continue relating to definition, implementation, and coordination. Below are several ideas to improve on the UN's central role in promoting and protecting human rights through diplomacy:

- The Secretary-General or his representative should present an annual human rights report, similar to his annual report on the work of the organization, to the General Assembly each September in which he draws attention to the most important rights problems. The UN high commissioner for human rights already makes an annual report, but it does not receive the same attention as those from the Secretary-General. The new UN Human Rights Council is moving toward a Universal Periodic Review of member states, but this will take time and be implemented over time. A concentrated Secretary-General report, highlighting major issues, is still desirable.

The Peace Palace, seat of the International Court of Justice. (UN/DPI Photo/A. Brizzi)

- Treaty-monitoring bodies should be allowed to participate in the work of other UN bodies—for example, the Human Rights Council. They should continue to coordinate their activities to fight fragmented efforts and in search of concentrated impact.
- UN programs of technical assistance and education for human rights should be greatly expanded to strengthen national institutions for rights protection and thus to head off major rights problems before they become international crises. There is no substitute for strong commitment to human rights at the national level.
- The Office of the Secretary-General, in conjunction with OHCHR and OCHA, should improve dramatically the UN's early-warning system to predict gross violations of internationally recognized human rights that are likely to lead to mass migration.
- A concerted effort should be made to more extensively integrate human rights considerations into development programs through the UNDP, World Bank, International Monetary Fund (IMF), and UN specialized agencies. Just as there is a new UN body on sustainable development, there should be a coordinating body on human rights in development. These efforts have been grouped under the rubric of "mainstreaming human rights," although change has been more rhetorical than real. Some agencies like UNICEF have a good record in this regard, while the WHO, World Bank, IMF, and WTO have lagged.

- Greater use should be made of preventive diplomacy, such as the systematic dispatch of UN human rights observers in situations of tension, both to deter rights violations and to provide timely reporting to New York.

These "doable" steps could be taken without waiting for a radical alteration in state attitudes. Nevertheless, a meaningful improvement in UN action for human rights depends on further change in state foreign policies. But especially most post-colonial states are very protective about any codification of norms encroaching on conventional notions of state sovereignty. And when it comes to its own sovereignty, the United States is as protective as states in the global South like India or Mexico. The modest reforms approved at the 2005 World Summit reflected this reality. The change from the Human Rights Commission to the Human Rights Council showed above all that many states were not ready for strong enforcement of human rights standards through the new council, preferring to emphasize continuing dialogue over time. Even exceptionally poor human rights situations, as in Darfur, produced only modest responses.

MORE ON *RAISONS D'ÉTAT*

The meaning of national interest is not fixed.[2] "National interest," like "state sovereignty," is a social construct. Humans derive ideas about national interest in a process of change over time. Even for schools of thought like realism that emphasize the concept of national interest as a core component of international relations theory, the concept lacks precise and transcendent meaning. Whether human rights should be, or can be, linked to national interests is a matter of debate. Some say that ideas about human rights constitute intangible national interests.

Many states increasingly have included human rights within the domain of state interests. This can be done for different reasons. The delegations of some states have pursued human rights at the United Nations as a weapon in power struggles. The objective has been to delegitimize a certain government; the means has been to emphasize human rights violations. In the previous chapter we mentioned U.S. policy toward Cuba in the Commission on Human Rights.[3] We are witnessing this with Muslim states targeting Israel in the Human Rights Council.

Some states have adopted a broad definition of their own self-interests. Like Canada or Sweden, they seek not just territorial integrity, political independence, and other goals directly related to the narrow and expedient interests of the state. They also define their interests in terms of an international society in which human dignity is advanced by serious attention to human rights. Just as governments have defined their domestic interests beyond physical security and economic welfare, so have they used their foreign policies to advance human rights and humanitarian goals.

Navanethem Pillay, United Nations high commissioner for human rights, addresses a plenary meeting of the General Assembly on the promotion and protection of human rights, on the sixtieth anniversary of the adoption of the Universal Declaration of Human Rights. (UN Photo # 234409/Paulo Filgueiras)

Some states have adopted a variation on this theme by arguing that the practice of human rights advances not only human dignity but also national security and peace. The lack of major international wars between liberal democracies serves as evidence. Sometimes dealing with human rights violations is requisite for bringing peace to countries like El Salvador or Bosnia.

Some states may even lend support to international action on human rights not because they believe any of the arguments above but simply because they feel pressured or obligated to support such action. Various states will sometimes align with China or the United States on human rights issues not because of the merits, but to curry favor with the powerful.

For all of these reasons, states have brought about a legal and diplomatic revolution with regard to the treatment of human rights at the United Nations. The same process has occurred in such multilateral forums as the Council of Europe, the EU, the CSCE and OSCE, OAS, and to a lesser extent, the African Union and the Arab League. Especially the powerful liberal democracies have a human rights component to their foreign policies, inconsistent and with other defects, to be sure, and this affects the UN.

The link between human rights and *raisons d'état* at least sometimes is a reflection of increasing moral solidarity in international society. Governmental au-

The rubble of United Nations headquarters in Baghdad following a suicide bomber attack on August 19, 2003, that killed twenty-two, including the Secretary-General's special representative for Iraq, Sergio Vieira de Mello. (UN/DPI Photo)

thorities may speak in terms of their interests, but the deeper process may involve a moral stance on the dignity of persons without regard to nationality or borders. John Ruggie has shown that a concern to better the world is deeply ingrained in American culture and history and that this concern has often taken a multilateral form, including great attention to the United Nations, in the twentieth century.[4] Edward Luck, however, has emphasized a fundamental ambivalence in American attitudes toward multilateralism.[5] Clinton officials may have spoken of American strategic interests in a stable, democratic, and prosperous Europe, but the deeper driving force behind Washington's policy may have been moral outrage at atrocities in the Balkans. In Bosnia and other parts of the former Yugoslavia, U.S. policy was intertwined with various multilateral efforts, including those of the United Nations.

Moral and practical components of state foreign policy may also be sufficiently entangled as to be inseparable. The United States in 1999 might have been morally outraged about Kosovo and at the same time may have believed that self-interest dictated not ignoring Serbian atrocities of ethnic cleansing. Not to oppose those human rights violations would have been to encourage more atrocities. Not to act against atrocities might have been to encourage refugee flight that could destabilize friendly states. Not to so act might have entailed loss of reputation, and thus some loss of soft power.

Whether state foreign policies are driven by practical or moral wellsprings, or whether it is even possible to say what is expedience as compared to morality, the cumulative effect of the shifting and complex redefinition of national interests has been to internationalize human rights. State authorities in general consider human rights, even those within a state's territorial boundaries, to be a proper subject for international discussion. They often are willing to engage in a wide range of diplomatic activity to promote and also indirectly to protect those rights. At times states are even willing to engage in economic coercion in the name of rights, and more rarely they at least agree to some type of military action to guarantee such fundamental rights as the access by suffering civilians to international help.

States certainly have not abandoned the principle of state sovereignty or the derivative notion of national interest. Any thought that we are moving toward a world community with consensus about the protection of human rights in complicated and difficult situations is exceedingly optimistic and naive if past is prelude. Sovereignty is often used as a defense against UN action on human rights by different states on different issues at different times. The principle is especially favored by the authorities of weaker and younger developing countries that fear losing status and influence at the hands of more powerful states. Older, more powerful states like the United States also do not hesitate to trot out the tired slogans of state sovereignty when the international community of states, through some UN agency or the European Union, questions American policy toward the treatment of terrorist suspects or the death penalty.

At the same time that the United States was chastising others for politicizing the old UN Human Rights Commission, it was engaged in the forced disappearance and abuse of certain detainees who were terror suspects or insurgent fighters in Afghanistan and Iraq. The United States wanted a more vigorous UN Human Rights Council, but for a time it strongly resisted UN rapporteurs and agencies trying to implement UN standards on torture and mistreatment of prisoners.

Yet over time, the appeal to restrictive notions of state sovereignty and their use have weakened. As a result, UN organizations have expanded their diplomatic activity for human rights across and even within states; they also have occasionally resorted to economic and military sanctions in this area. The UN is now deeply involved in human rights issues to an extent completely unforeseen in 1945.

As noted earlier, states have created UN standards and supervisory procedures that later restricted their operational sovereignty in the field of human rights. In legal theory, states are no longer free to treat even "their own" citizens as they wish. Internationally recognized human rights impose standards that are binding on governments. In political practice, governments may be pressured or coerced because of human rights violations. The process is far from consistent, systematic, reliable, or effective, but it is irreversible.

STATE COALITIONS

In multilateral organizations like the United Nations, many key decisions are taken by voting, so coalitions among states become important. During the early years of the UN, the Western coalition controlled proceedings in the General Assembly and the CHR. The International Bill of Rights was effectively negotiated between 1948 and 1956, and this was an important step in the promotion of internationally recognized human rights. Western states pushed for the Universal Declaration of Human Rights and at least the negotiation of the UN Covenant on Civil and Political Rights and the UN Covenant on Economic, Social and Cultural Rights. The communist coalition played the game of negotiating the treaties and accepting human rights in theory while opposing the implementation of many internationally recognized rights in practice. Yet beyond setting standards, few breakthroughs in UN diplomatic action for protecting human rights followed.

Perhaps most important, Washington exercised little constructive leadership on human rights at the United Nations for several decades after about 1953.[6] The United States was a dominant power and, to some states, a hegemonic power on security and economic issues. But it was neither dominant nor hegemonic on human rights. Human rights issues were a sensitive topic in the United States both because of legally sanctioned racial discrimination and because some members of Congress feared a more powerful executive through the treaty process. So from Dwight D. Eisenhower to Jimmy Carter, no president asked the Senate for advice or consent on the two core UN human rights covenants.

Beyond the United States and the Western coalition of states, the admission of newly independent developing countries from 1955 and the acceleration of this pattern from 1960 drastically changed the voting on human rights at the United Nations. The dynamics were fueled by a dialectical process resulting in a new synthesis. Developing countries sought to use the language of human rights to pressure Israel and South Africa, and the West countered with efforts to broaden those rights-oriented maneuvers. Human rights NGOs helped fashion this North-South compromise. The result was a new diplomatic dynamism in UN attempts to protect certain human rights in certain countries. The Soviet coalition added its own emphases, particularly focusing on rights violations in Augusto Pinochet's Chile after the overthrow of Marxist president Salvador Allende.

This North-South interchange on human rights, with European communist states usually aligned with the South, accounted for many human rights developments at the United Nations from 1970 to 1985. For example, rhetorical interest was taken in a collective right to development after the newly independent states from the South gained membership to the UN General Assembly. This new alignment of states can also explain why efforts to protect human rights did not happen at the UN. The UN was unable to put diplomatic pressure on Idi Amin's brutal government in Uganda because of the shield provided by the solidarity of

At the "Killing Fields" memorial near Phnom Penh, shelves filled with skulls testify to Cambodia's tragic past. (UN Photo 159753/J. Isaac)

many states in the global South. A double standard emerged whereby discrimination by a black government against Asians and white Europeans was not of major concern in the General Assembly. This same anti-colonial shield has so far protected Robert Mugabe's repressive government in Zimbabwe, as South Africa and others avoid publicly criticizing a hero who struggled against white domination and spent eleven years in white prisons for it. A related reaction was an African Union communiqué asking the Security Council to suspend the ICC's proceedings against Sudanese president Omar Hassan al-Bashir.

After the transition period of 1985–1991, during which European communism collapsed, the coalitions shifted. More democratic governments both in the General Assembly and on the CHR meant more attention to human rights and overall collaboration in the Security Council. Yet even democratic governments in the global South like India and Mexico were not always enthusiastic about UN activities regarding protection of human rights. Several developing countries sought to block certain protective attempts by the CHR. Established liberal democracies in the CHR had their own record of double standards and blind spots. Ambivalence on the part of developing countries about international action for human rights and humanitarian affairs was evident. They knew that their sovereignty was at issue. Most developing countries in the General Assembly refused to elevate a right to humanitarian assistance above the right of state sovereignty. Resolutions on this subject in the late 1980s and early 1990s were ambiguous and complex. Although reaffirming the principle of state sovereignty, resolution 46/182 indicated that parties in a "country," but not necessarily only the government of a state, might request international assistance. It also suggested that a state's consent to international humanitarian action might be tacit. In practice, developing countries went along with the Security Council's assertiveness in defeated Iraq after 1991 and in Somalia on behalf of outside action for human rights.

Beyond developing countries, some permanent members of the Security Council also were ambivalent or reluctant about international action for human rights and humanitarian affairs. Russia expressed open reservations about some of the policies being pursued against rights violations by governments in Iraq and Serbia. China did not support international action to protect human rights, but it abstained on most council resolutions rather than vetoing them. The United States usually protected Israel from any condemnation or sanction by the council with regard to its policies in the territories occupied after the 1967 war.

The North-South conflict continues to limit UN efforts to protect human rights, and Russia and China regularly join developing countries in obstructing protective efforts.[7] But Western states like France and the United States blocked UN intervention to stop the genocide in Rwanda. At the 1993 Vienna World Conference on Human Rights, most developing and formerly communist countries reaffirmed the idea of universal human rights. But since 1948 the central problem has not been the abstract codification of norms, but rather marshaling sufficient political will to deal with concrete violations of internationally recognized human rights. The major fault line in negotiations about the new UN Human Rights Council was a North-South conflict, with Russia aligned with most of the South, while Chile and Mexico and a few other developing democracies aligned with the North.

NONSTATE ACTORS

States may be the official building blocks of the United Nations, but nonstate actors have been active and influential in human rights and humanitarian matters. Three types of nonstate actors are discussed here: NGOs, individual experts, and Secretariat personnel. Precision is difficult when gauging the influence generated by NGOs on human rights matters. In a speech at the United Nations just after the adoption of the Universal Declaration in December 1948, Eleanor Roosevelt aptly predicted that "a curious grapevine" would spread the ideas contained in the Declaration far and wide.[8]

The most general analytical problem, then, is that their impact becomes intertwined with governmental and other influences, often making it impossible to say with precision where NGO influence leaves off and governmental influence begins. If Amnesty International lobbies for new standards and monitoring mechanisms concerning torture, and if states in the General Assembly finally approve these ideas in treaty form, it is difficult to pinpoint what has occurred because of Amnesty International's efforts and what has occurred because of governmental policy.[9] The same analytical problem has been recognized in trying to chart the influence of interest groups in domestic politics by comparison to governmental officials. When one finds a transnational network active for human rights and containing both state and nonstate actors, as occurred in movements for the International Criminal Court and for a treaty banning antipersonnel land mines, it is difficult to specify the exact influence of the various actors.

Only a few genuine human rights NGOs are active on a transnational or international basis with a mandate linked to the International Bill of Rights: Amnesty International, the International Commission of Jurists, the International League for Human Rights, Human Rights Watch, Physicians for Human Rights, Doctors Without Borders, and a few others. The ICRC comes close to meeting this definitional test, although its historical mandate is linked more to the laws of war than to the International Bill of Rights. Other broadly oriented NGOs are active on human rights from time to time, but they are linked more to religion or some other normative standard than to the International Bill of Rights. An example is the World Council of Churches.

Moreover, some NGOs with narrower mandates take up particular human rights questions. They have more to do with a particular problem or nationality than with internationally recognized rights per se. Cultural Survival, for example, concentrates on indigenous peoples. Anti-Slavery International focuses on slavery, slave-like practices, and the slave trade. All sorts of nationally-based or nationally-oriented groups take up particular causes while frequently ignoring the human rights situation in other nations.

All of these NGOs have been active on human rights issues at the United Nations. And they certainly have generated influence for the promotion and protection of human rights in the abstract. Their cumulative impact has been such that various states have opposed UN consultative status for some of the more assertive NGOs. In 1991 Cuba and some Arab states temporarily prevented Human Rights Watch, based in New York, from obtaining consultative status via ECOSOC. NGOs want to achieve that status because they gain the right to circulate documents and speak in UN meetings. During the Cold War several human rights NGOs were excluded from consultative status by communist and developing governments, a practice that continues. In 1995 Freedom House, based in New York, was temporarily denied consultative status by a coalition of states including democracies such as India and the Philippines. These states disliked the rating system and other reports authored by Freedom House. Had NGOs generated no influence, certain governments would unlikely try so hard to keep them out of UN proceedings.

Toward the end of 2007 the government of Vladimir Putin was trying to obstruct the activities of a number of Western-based NGOs active on human rights in Russia. Putin has adopted a variety of policies that reduced individual freedom, and his crackdown on human rights NGOs, both domestic and international, was part of that orientation. Had human rights NGOs generated no influence in Russia on behalf of the UN's International Bill of Human Rights, it is unlikely that Putin would have devoted so much effort to harassing them. He also blocked effective election monitoring by the OSCE in 2008.

At the 1993 Vienna World Conference on Human Rights, the tensions between governments and human rights NGOs were very evident. Some governments feared the influence that might be generated by NGOs, perhaps by releasing damaging information to the world press. At the 1968 UN International Conference on Human Rights in Teheran, NGOs participated in the intergovernmental sessions. In Vienna in 1993, governments denied NGO participation in the official meetings but agreed to a separate NGO parallel conference. This formula was followed at the 1995 Beijing Fourth UN World Conference on Women and at the 2002 World Conference against Racism, Racial Discrimination, Xenophobia, and Related Intolerance in Durban, South Africa. On human rights as on many other subjects, states feel they cannot completely suppress NGOs, but many states try to limit NGO influence.

The ICRC is the only nonstate actor working for human rights and humanitarian affairs that has been granted observer status in the General Assembly; it also meets monthly with the president of the Security Council. This came about because of its close work with governments especially in situations of armed conflict and because of its reputation. The ICRC is a quasi-public actor, being explicitly recognized in international public law, such as the 1949 Geneva Conventions for armed conflict. But the ICRC follows a general policy of discretion and therefore does not normally reveal the details of what its delegates have observed inside states. Unlike Human Rights Watch and Amnesty International, for example, the ICRC does not normally rely on detailed public pressure to achieve its objectives. For all these reasons states were prepared to accord to the ICRC a status at the UN "higher" than other private or quasi–private agencies. The International Federation of Red Cross and Red Crescent Societies is also accorded observer status. It normally works in situations of natural and industrial/ technological disasters, but it also works with refugees. The RC Federation is made up of state-sanctioned relief agencies; they are quasi–state agencies.

Large numbers of NGOs had consultative status and participated in meetings of the Commission on Human Rights, which is also true of the new HRC. They submitted private complaints about a pattern of gross violations of human rights to the UN system. Their information is officially used in most of the monitoring agencies of the UN system such as the Human Rights Committee, the Committee on Economic, Social and Cultural Rights, CERD, CEDAW, CAT,

CRC, and others. Some NGOs have played influential roles behind the scenes in the adoption of General Assembly resolutions concerning human rights.

Just as private human rights groups have had an impact on national policies concerning human rights, so have NGOs influenced UN proceedings. A formal UN vote or document, reflecting the policy of a majority of governments, may have started or been advanced by one or more NGOs. Clearly NGOs advanced the UN Declaration on Minorities and the Declaration on Indigenous Peoples, although states voted for it. Some 1,000 NGOs attended the World Conference on Human Rights, conducting their own proceedings and engaging in the specific criticisms that state delegations at the conference had agreed to avoid. Without doubt certain NGOs were influential in the negotiation and adoption of the treaties banning antipersonnel land mines and creating the International Criminal Court.

Just as private groups have teamed with the U.S. Congress to improve human rights reporting by the Department of State,[10] NGOs have teamed with interested governments to improve rights activity through the United Nations. Just as a group of secular and faith-based private groups pressured Congress to do more about the violation of religious freedom in the world, so these and other groups constantly pressure states at the UN to take action for human rights. If human rights NGOs had been absent at the UN during its first half century, it is unlikely that the world organization's record would be as good as it is. The record is not good enough in the view of these same NGOs, but some positive steps have been taken.[11]

Had those NGOs been absent, something would have been done on human rights nevertheless—not only because of states but because of Secretariat personnel. John P. Humphrey of Canada, the first UN director-general of human rights, appears to have had some influence on the content of the Universal Declaration of Human Rights. Other Secretariat personnel have advanced ideas or proposals that eventually were accepted by governments voting in UN bodies. Executive heads of UN agencies like UNICEF, WHO, UNHCR, and ILO have clearly taken action on their own for children's health care, the right to adequate health care in general, refugee rights, and labor rights. All this is apart from the human rights activity of the Office of the Secretary-General itself.

Moreover, the individual experts who have sat on the UN Sub-Commission on Protection of Minorities or who have been rapporteurs or other experts for the Commission on Human Rights have often nudged the process along. Most of the monitoring agencies created by treaty have been staffed by individuals acting in their personal capacity. Many have been truly independent from their governments as well as serious about and dedicated to human rights.

It is worth recalling Samantha Power's argument about how the genocide convention came into being.[12] She greatly credits the tireless effort of one private person, Raphael Lemkin. So in her view, widely shared, individuals can make a difference with regard to human rights over time. She also credits, for instance, the individual efforts of U.S. Sen. William Proxmire for helping get the United States to accept that treaty.

THEORIES OF CHANGE

Can we develop a summary statement that clarifies the dynamics of activity on human rights at the UN? Can we theorize why this activity has been what it has been? And can we project what directions this activity will take in the future?

Two related views are relevant. The first focuses on the notion of knowledge. Ernst Haas argues that if private communities of knowledge come to an agreement on human rights, this agreement eventually will produce a policy consensus in the public sector.[13] When this public consensus emerges, the United Nations and other IGOs become empowered to take important action for human rights. This means complete change in the UN, not just partial change. For example, if most human rights groups could prove that civil and political rights were necessary for economic growth or that socioeconomic rights were necessary for stable democracy, that private agreement would eventually affect public policy through the UN and would lead to dramatic change.

The second and related view emphasizes learning. George Modelski returns to the ideas of Immanuel Kant to suggest that those who speak for states are in the process of learning a commitment to human rights, especially to the civil and political rights making up democracy.[14] In this view, historical evolution shows expanded learning of the benefits of democracy—whether in terms of human dignity or in terms of international peace.

If Haas's view is correct about the state of knowledge in epistemic communities, several generalizations emerge. First, if all or most private groups active on human rights agreed on particulars, this consensus of knowledge should eventually inform public policy in such a way that the United Nations would be mandated by governments to take more authoritative and effective action for human rights. We may be seeing a paradigm shift. Even the World Bank, which long sought to avoid the "political" matter of human rights, now says that economic growth should be pursued with attention to "good governance." The Bank and its supporters have concluded—at least for now—that at least some authoritarian models of economic growth do not work very well. In fact, good governance— rule of law, transparency, market-oriented policies—has essentially been defined as the opposite of what authoritarian Third World and Soviet bloc countries did in the 1960s, 1970s, and 1980s. Clearly, these approaches have substantial and positive human rights dimensions.

Knowledge about human rights is not so much scientific knowledge, however, as moral judgment. Achieving widespread agreement on morality is far more difficult than on hard data. Even within one nation with a dominant culture, private groups differ over such human rights issues as abortion, the death penalty, health care, and adequate nutrition.

Getting private groups to agree that children are better off if vaccinated is not so difficult, as many do not disagree with a vaccination program. Opinion is based on irrefutable scientific knowledge. Getting private circles of opinion to agree that internationally recognized human rights should be applied in all cultures and situations is far more difficult. Not all medical experts agree that health care should be treated as a human right. Not all medical personnel agree that abortion should be legal. They may agree on the technical process of how to perform an abortion, for that is based on science. But they disagree on whether abortion should be legal, for that is based on moral judgment. Moral judgment is greatly affected by varieties of opinion because moral argument cannot be easily proved or disproved.

Not everyone will always, everywhere be better off if rights are applied. If repressive governments respect civil and political rights, many if not most of them will lose power. This may usher in a period of disorder and economic decline. The former Soviet Union is a clear example, at least in the short run. In repressive China, many persons have been advancing economically, since macroeconomic growth as stimulated by an expanding private sector was around 10 percent per year in the early 1990s. In private circles of opinion, many do not believe that rights, especially political rights, would do anything but interrupt this beneficial process in China. Spectacular economic growth has been achieved in Singapore since the 1970s, but without full civil and political rights. Important religious circles in Islamic nations believe freedom of religion and gender equality would hurt society.

Even actors that generally seek to protect rights do not insist on the application of rights in every situation. Many Western private groups do not press the issue of the practice of human rights in Saudi Arabia. They also defer to a military coup in Algeria that prevented the election of a fundamentalist Islamic party. Some of these groups believe on moral grounds that Western access to oil or blocking fundamentalist Islam justifies repressive governments. We know for sure that elections in places such as Sri Lanka have led to illiberal governments that discriminate against minorities and commit other rights violations. So a commitment to human rights such as democratic political participation is less a matter of scientific proof of inherent progress and more a matter of moral and political choice in context.

Beyond the essential distinction between scientific knowledge and moral judgment in private networks, the public policy consensus across governments at the UN concerning human rights is incomplete, to say the least. The formal consensus is broad, but the real consensus is weak. In other words, human rights treaties are widely accepted in law and widely violated in practice. Learning of "correct" policies has been more formal than substantive.

As long as actual consensus remains weak, human rights activity will not lead to systematic and authoritative protection by the United Nations. New and potentially important steps may happen spasmodically, but these steps will fall short of full change leading to systematic and effective protection. Inconsistency is the hallmark of international organization. The Security Council may authorize humanitarian intervention in Somalia, but at roughly the same time it will fail to sponsor decisive action in similar situations in Liberia or Sudan, Rwanda or Burundi. The council may set the stage for the use of force in Iraq, at least partially in the name of persecuted civilians, but it will be lethargic about similarly appalling conditions in the Democratic Republic of the Congo. Greater legal authority and financial resources were not provided to the CHR and have not been transferred to the OHCHR. The Human Rights Council is not significantly different from its predecessor. The latter partial change shows clearly that UN member states disagree on how to evaluate the preceding sixty years of proceedings by the Commission on Human Rights.

Knowledge, Learning, and Courts

The issue of the UN and international courts provides a good test of the Haas theory of change, linked to knowledge, and the Modelski theory of change, linked to learning.[15] Under the Modelski theory the question is raised whether states, acting through the world organization, have shown a propensity to learn that international relations must be governed by a humane rule of law. Are states learning that they will be more secure, and their citizens better off, if there is either a permanent UN criminal court or a series of ad hoc criminal courts to deal with particular situations? To use semantics from the Haas theory, have private groups used their knowledge to push states into agreement on the demonstrable truth that just as all national societies have institutionalized procedures for criminal cases, so international relations should, too? Or are states just muddling through on this issue with incomplete agreement leading to the piling up of actions at the UN without any clear and firm overall position on authoritative and effective criminal courts?

Such learning—to the extent that it occurred—was clearly not universal. Some states, especially those that contemplate use of their militaries in armed conflict, are reluctant to create a judicial organ to which they might, as a last step under the principle of complementarity, have to turn over their citizens to face the ICC—for example, for charges of violations of the laws of war. Neither George W. Bush nor the Congress was generally supportive of the ICC. The United States has not "learned" the advantages of having a permanent mechanism for international criminal prosecution; nor is it clear that "knowledge" compels movement in this direction. Emotive or romantic nationalism may trump expert knowledge about the benefits of international criminal justice. So may tough-minded realism. In the name of national interest, the Bush administration authorized as policy the forced disappearance and abuse of certain prisoners taken in its "war on terrorism." The last thing these officials wanted was an international criminal court looking at the question of whether war crimes had been committed.

In general, state learning pertaining to international criminal law showed differences and inconsistencies. States approved ad hoc criminal courts now and then, but at the end of 2007 only some one hundred countries were parties to the Rome Statute of the International Criminal Court. Optimists were buoyed by the extent of state support while pessimists pointed out that about half of the UN members were not sure they wanted to be under the jurisdiction of a UN standing criminal court. States might feel the need to show a response to atrocities by creating ad hoc courts, but some of the same states might still eschew the costs of a decisive involvement that would curtail the atrocities and punish those responsible. States might agree in theory that individual punishment for atrocities is a good idea, but in particular situations they might like the freedom to negotiate and strike deals with war criminals and the like. In 2003, in the context of an impending war in Iraq, there was much discussion of the wisdom of offering Saddam Hussein amnesty and impunity for past atrocities, because such a process would avoid much destruction and bloodshed involved in his forceful removal and possible trial. His eventual capture, trial, and execution within Iraq had no discernible impact on anything.

Peace and justice can be sought through both diplomacy and criminal proceedings. In places like Yugoslavia in 1995 and immediately thereafter, it was not clear that one could follow both avenues at once. If various political leaders had not been defeated and had retained power, and if one then had to include them in negotiations aimed at stopping the fighting and curtailing human rights violations, pursuing them as international criminals might not be the wisest course of action.

This type of analysis pertained to criminal leaders like Slobodan Miloševíc in 1995 and Charles Taylor in Liberia in 2003, as well as Mohammed Farah Aideed in Somalia in 1993. In the Balkans, trying to prosecute Miloševíc in 1995–1996 was neither wise nor possible, but by 2002 he was on trial. After four years on trial, he may have cheated justice by dying before a judgment was made, but at least he died in a cell rather than enjoying a comfortable exile or exercising power in Serbia. Charles Taylor agreed finally in August 2003 to go into exile in Nigeria after having wreaked havoc in West Africa, which resulted in his being indicted by the special court in Sierra Leone for war crimes and crimes against humanity. He was apprehended trying to flee Nigeria after the new Liberian president, Ellen Johnson-Sirleaf, requested his extradition. To avoid further disorder by his followers in both Liberia and Sierra Leone, Taylor is being tried in The Hague.

In writing the rules for the operation of international courts, humane progress through political choice and diplomacy needs to be allowed. "Learning" on these matters is an imprecise and complicated matter.[16] Scientific evidence about the correct way to proceed is hard to come by. Many "experts" support different policies in different situations.

Equally complex is the question of whether criminal proceedings contribute to or impede national reconciliation after armed conflict.[17] The theory behind criminal courts, national or international, is that license to commit atrocities has to end in order to "clear the air," provide catharsis to the victims and their families, and deter future violations of rights. But one could certainly question whether criminal trials of Hutus in Rwanda while a Tutsi-dominated government controlled the country would achieve the desired objectives. And in many places, from South Africa to El Salvador, national and international officials concluded that the way to advance national reconciliation after brutal internal war was to avoid criminal proceedings as much as possible. A country might utilize truth commissions to establish facts, but only in a few places, such as South Korea, Ethiopia, and Germany, did trials proceed against former repressive rulers. Whether such national trials were, on balance, a good thing is difficult to determine. After dictatorship ended, Spain and Portugal moved toward stable liberal democracy by avoiding both trials and truth commissions. Acquiring human rights knowledge is a complicated affair about which reasonable persons can differ, and the UN's forays into international criminal justice have been carried out in the context of a lack of clear consensus and firm commitment about the "legalization" of the response to gross violations of human rights.[18]

Summary, with Reference to Democracy

The relation between knowledge, learning, and UN human rights activity can be summarized by acknowledging the difficulty in achieving a broad consensus about human rights among private networks because the issue deals more with morality than with science. Without this NGO and "expert" agreement about human rights specifics, the consensus among governments on human rights and public policy will remain incomplete. The situation is one of varied learning and incomplete change. The UN acts more for human rights now than before, but it still falls short of being fully systematic and institutionalized as well as authoritative and effective.

For example, it is illustrative to examine the question of whether states are learning, on the basis of cumulative knowledge, a commitment to liberal democracy (meaning elected governments that are rights-protective). The UN certainly now advocates democratic development. Some evidence seems encouraging. Immanuel Kant suggested that over time liberal democracies would become more numerous. A wave of democratization from about the mid-1970s to the early 1990s seemed to verify that Kantian view from the eighteenth century. Francis Fukuyama argued in the early 1990s that right-thinking persons had to necessarily conclude that liberal democracy was the best way to respect individuals and limit governmental power. Thus, the development of the norms of liberal democracy represented the "end of history," at least in political theory, and a liberal democrat became the last "political man."[19] Within the empirical democratic trend, however, there are illiberal democracies that are genuinely supported by majority opinion but are not rights-protective. Yugoslavia under Slobodan Miloševíc and Croatia under Franjo Tudjman were clear examples. If it holds, a historical trend toward liberal democracy would suggest a growing acceptance not only of civil and political rights but of economic and social ones as well. Almost all democracies, except the United States, endorse the latter rights as well as the former. Thus most liberal democracies are also social democracies that recognize a human right to basic health care and other socioeconomic public goods as provided by the state.[20]

But we should be wary. No more than about one-third of the states in the world have been truly stable or consolidated liberal democracies at any given time. Moreover, earlier waves of democracy suffered setbacks or reverse waves, and this could happen again. Many states with elected governments still have strong militaries not fully controlled by elected leaders. And the results of elections in some former Soviet republics, as in other parts of the world, might even suggest nostalgia for enlightened authoritarian government.

Over a rather long time, the advantages of liberal democratic government have received increased recognition. Respect for civil and political rights has grown, albeit in a zigzag rather than a linear progression. This learning had been enhanced, at least temporarily, by the various failures of authoritarian communism in Europe and authoritarian models among developing countries.

But in many countries ruled by newly democratic governments, major obstacles to the consolidation—meaning stabilization and maturation—of democracy remain. To state the obvious, elections do not a democracy make, and long-term commitments are necessary to consolidate fledgling states.[21] Perhaps most important, economic growth was slow or nonexistent, and the benefits of the economic system were widely perceived as inequitable. New democratic governments, confronted with particularly daunting economic problems, continue to struggle to create the socioeconomic context that would sustain a new and fragile democracy. Particularly in Latin America, but elsewhere as well, democracy has been created but not necessarily consolidated. Indeed, as Thomas Carothers argues, "Of the nearly 100 countries considered as 'transitional' in recent years, only a relatively small number—probably fewer than 20—are clearly en route to becoming successful, well-functioning democracies or at least have made some democratic progress and still enjoy a positive dynamic of democratization."[22] In a number of countries, something of a hybrid regime—combining democratic practices with enduring authoritarian institutions—has emerged and often appears as quite stable.[23] Were civil and political rights being learned systematically, or was democratic learning frequently followed by a relearning of the advantages of authoritarianism?

Moreover, not all democratic governments at the UN have fully supported its human rights program. U.S. authorities have at times tried to suppress diplomatic pressure on authoritarian friends. British officials have opposed all sorts of human rights initiatives.[24] The Indian government has at times elevated the principle of state sovereignty above UN pressure for human rights concerning itself and other developing countries.

A Web of Norms Resulting in Change?

Most situations in which human rights are respected are produced by national conditions—with only secondary influence from international factors.[25] This axiom contains considerable truth but can be overstated. The relaxation of the Soviet grip on Eastern Europe in the late 1980s was the key factor in unleashing local human rights forces. By 1996, more IGO, NGO, and state policies operated in support of international human rights than ever before. In some cases, as in Haiti in 1994, international factors were decisive—at least in the short run. The international normative context for human rights had definitely changed for the better.

A theory of transnational change and human rights is relevant to our discussion here. According to the book *The Power of Human Rights*, a transnational advocacy network, made up of both private and public actors, can definitely bring about progressive change with regard to rights of personal integrity.[26] A merger of international and national actors can, over time, institutionalize human rights norms pertaining to summary execution, torture and mistreatment, and other fundamental civil rights referred to collectively as rights of personal integrity. Hence in this view, domestic private groups, acting in tandem with foreign actors of various sorts, can bring effective pressure for rights-protective change on repressive governments. In this theory, UN norms and UN actors play important roles. In fact, this theory allows for considerable variation in which actors in the transnational coalition exert the most influence on behalf of human rights— international NGOs, domestic private groups, officials of international organizations, officials of states. The sum total of the efforts of these various and shifting actors accounts for progressive change.

Furthermore, this hopeful theory of change in the domain of human rights pertains not only to rights of personal integrity in repressive non-Western countries. Some research suggests that the same analytical perspective, originally developed to explain change regarding rights of personal integrity in repressive non-Western states, might also be helpful in understanding change on minority rights in emerging liberal democratic states in Eastern Europe.[27] In this view, the Czech Republic has come to better protect the rights of the Roma, and Romania has come to better protect the rights of its ethnic Hungarian minority, because of a transnational advocacy process that has grown steadily. In these two cases, it may have been the Council of Europe and the European Union, more than the United Nations, that largely accounted for pulling these governments into practicing what they had promised on minority rights. But in other cases, as in El Salvador in the late 1980s and early 1990s, UN officials like the Secretary-General play central roles.

This theory about the importance of human rights norms and discourse over time, as linked to transnational pressure, which eventually traps states in their own stated commitments to human rights, can incorporate incidental knowledge about human rights and change. For example, UN sanctions against both Rhodesia and South Africa in the 1960s and 1970s did not create the resistance to white-minority rule. But these international actions helped to empower local citizens to confront the policies of governments based on racial discrimination. The Guatemalan ambassador to the United States had it exactly right when describing the democratic resistance to an authoritarian coup in 1993: It was the Guatemalan people, local human rights groups, national business elements, and even sectors of the military that demanded a return to democracy as a human right; the role of the international community was important but secondary.[28] The United Nations then accelerated its efforts in Guatemala, negotiating human rights agreements and mediating conflicts. The role of the world organization was to facilitate local trends toward liberal democracy, which by definition encompasses the protection of many human rights. A transnational focus remains necessary to encompass the totality of change pertaining to human rights.

FINAL THOUGHTS

The lip service paid to human rights at the UN is not always backed by serious commitment. Early innovations to meet the human rights challenges in the former Yugoslavia in the early 1990s received so little financial and political support that they were mere tokens. Still, the UN has taken innovative steps including the first emergency session convened by the Commission on Human Rights; the first deployment of field monitors by the UN Centre for Human Rights (now OHCHR); the appointment of a special rapporteur to report to the Security Council on human rights abuses and of a Commission of Experts to report on breaches of the Geneva Conventions; the assignment of human rights responsibilities to UNHCR protection officers in the field; and, most significant, the establishment of international war-crimes tribunals and the ICC. But the credibility of these initiatives was undermined to the extent that they were not matched by the resources and leadership to make them work—indeed, many were hurt by foot-dragging, or worse, from one or more of the great powers. Ineffectiveness is distressing enough for the victims in the former Yugoslavia and Rwanda. But perhaps even more important is the potential negative impact that weakness and failure will have for future violators of human rights, where effective international action will obviously be necessary.

At the UN, disagreements about human rights protection abound. We are dealing with moral and political matters more than with scientific knowledge, and particularly states have "learned" a variety of things from past experience. Given the legal starting point of state sovereignty, the international community of states has come a long way in generating respect for the idea of human rights.

If we compare international action on human rights at the League of Nations and at the United Nations, the latter changes seem revolutionary. But all three UNs—states, staff, and relevant nonstate actors—still have a long way to go before achieving the systematic observance of human rights as called for in the Charter "without distinction as to race or nationality, sex, language or religion."[29]

Three analysts have put forward an image that may help readers understand the disconnect between rhetoric and reality in the human rights arena. There is a disparity between the normative and "operating" systems.[30] The UN's operating system is not the basic equivalent of a computer operating system (for example, Microsoft Windows) that functions to allow the use of spreadsheets or word processing. Even when functioning well, the international human rights operating system requires consensus, effort, intense diplomacy, and much luck to produce what are, at best, modest results—more akin to scribbles in pencil on the back of an envelope than a computer-generated image. All of this is shown clearly in the modest change from the UN Human Rights Commission to the Council on Human Rights.

NOTES

1. Marina Ottaway and Thomas Carothers, eds., *Funding Virtue: Civil Society Aid and Democracy Promotion* (Washington, D.C.: Carnegie Endowment, 2000).

2. See further David P. Forsythe, ed., *Human Rights and Comparative Foreign Policy* (Tokyo: United Nations University Press, 2000).

3. On the use of human rights by governments that primarily has to do with their strategic or other expediential interests, see Kirsten Sellars, *The Rise and Rise of Human Rights* (Phoenix Mill, UK: Sutton Publishing, 2002).

4. John Gerard Ruggie, *Winning the Peace: America and World Order in the New Era* (New York: Columbia University Press, 1996).

5. Edward C. Luck, *Mixed Messages: American Politics and International Organization 1919–1999* (Washington, D.C.: Brookings Institution, 1999).

6. Tony Evans, *U.S. Hegemony and the Project of Universal Human Rights* (London: Macmillan, 1996).

7. On voting at the UN and the North-South conflict in particular, see Soo Yeon Kim and Bruce Russett, "New UN Voting Alignments," *International Organization* 50, no. 4 (1996): 629–652.

8. Quoted in William Korey, *NGOs and the Universal Declaration of Human Rights: "A Curious Grapevine"* (New York: St. Martin's Press, 1998), 9.

9. For a detailed case study of Amnesty International's role in developing the UN treaty against torture, see Peter R. Baehr, "The General Assembly: Negotiating the Convention on Torture," in *The United Nations in the World Political Economy*, ed. David P. Forsythe (London: Macmillan, 1989), 36–53.

10. David P. Forsythe, *Human Rights and U.S. Foreign Policy: Congress Reconsidered* (Gainesville: University Press of Florida, 1988).

11. Rodney Bruce Hall and Thomas J. Biersteker, *The Emergence of Private Authority in Global Governance* (Cambridge: Cambridge University Press, 2002).

12. Samantha Power, *"A Problem from Hell": America and the Age of Genocide* (New York: Basic Books, 2002).

13. Ernst B. Haas, *When Knowledge Is Power: Three Models of Change in International Organizations* (Berkeley: University of California Press, 1990).

14. George Modelski, "Is World Politics Evolutionary Learning?" *International Organization* 44 (Winter 1990): 1–24.

15. On international courts and international criminal justice, see Steven R. Ratner and Jason S. Abrams, *Accountability for Human Rights Atrocities in International Law: Beyond the Nuremberg Legacy* (Oxford: Clarendon Press, 1997); Aryeh Neier, *War Crimes: Brutality, Genocide, Terror, and the Struggle for Justice* (New York: Times Books, 1998); and Sarah B. Sewall and Carl Kaysen, eds., *The United States and the International Criminal Court: National Security and International Law* (Lanham, Md.: Rowman & Littlefield, 2000).

16. Martha Minow makes clear that no one response to atrocities is right in every situation; see *Between Vengeance and Forgiveness: Facing History After Genocide and Mass Violence* (Boston: Beacon Press, 1998). There is now a very large literature on "transitional justice." See, for example, Ruti G. Teitel, *Transitional Justice* (New York: Oxford University Press, 2000).

17. See Rama Mani, *Beyond Retribution: Seeking Justice in the Shadows of War* (Cambridge, UK: Polity, 2002). And see Patrice C. McMahon and David P. Forsythe, "Judicial Romanticism meets Network Politics," *Human Rights Quarterly* (May 2008), for a study showing the lack of positive influence by the ICTY on Serbian and Balkan politics. Particularly in Serbia, the ICTY would have been ignored had not a transnational network led by the European Union and the United States compelled Serb attention to the court.

18. For an overview of the "legalization" of international relations, see the special issue of *International Organization* (Summer 2000). This issue traces the growing demand for specific international law that is adjudicated.

19. Francis Fukuyama, *The End of History and the Last Man* (New York: Free Press, 1992).

20. For arguments in favor of a broad conception of freedom and human rights, including especially rights to education, health care, and minimum wage and social security, see Amartya Sen, *Development As Freedom* (New York: Knopf, 1999), and Cass R. Sunstein, *The Second Bill of Rights: FDR's Unfinished Revolution and Why We Need It More Than Ever* (New York: Basic Books, 2004).

21. See Paul Collier, *Wars, Guns, and Votes: Democracy in Dangerous Places* (New York: HarperCollins, 2009), and Roland Paris, *At War's End: Building Peace after Civil Conflict* (Cambridge: Cambridge University Press, 2004).

22. Thomas Carothers, "The End of the Transition Paradigm," *Journal of Democracy* 13, no. 1 (2002): 9.

23. See also Terry Lynn Karl, "The Hybrid Regimes of Central America," *Journal of Democracy* 6, no. 3 (1995): 73–86; David Collier and Steven Levitsky, "Democracy with Adjectives: Conceptual Innovation in Comparative Research," *World Politics* 49, no. 3 (1997): 434–435; and Larry Diamond, "Thinking about Hybrid Regimes," *Journal of Democracy* 13, no. 2 (2002): 21–35.

24. Tom J. Farer, "The United Nations and Human Rights: More Than a Whimper, Less Than a Roar," in *Human Rights in the World Community: Issues and Action*, 2nd ed., eds. Richard Pierre Claude and Burns H. Weston (Philadelphia: University of Pennsylvania Press, 1992), 227–244.

25. See, for example, Jack Donnelly, "Human Rights in the New World Order: Implications for Europe," in *Human Rights in the New Europe*, ed. David P. Forsythe (Lincoln: University of Nebraska Press, 1994), 7–35.

26. Thomas Risse, Stephen C. Ropp, and Kathryn Sikkink, eds., *The Power of Human Rights: International Norms and Domestic Change* (Cambridge: Cambridge University Press, 1999).

27. Safia Swimmelar, "The Making of Minority Rights and the Return to Europe: International Norms and Transnational Actors in the Czech Republic and Romania" (PhD diss., University of Nebraska–Lincoln, 2003).

28. Edmond Mulet, "The Palace Coup That Failed," *New York Times*, June 22, 1993.

29. See further David P. Forsythe, *Human Rights in International Relations* (Cambridge: Cambridge University Press, 2000), chap. 3.

30. See Paul E. Diehl, Charlotte Ku, and Daniel Zamora, "The Dynamics of International Law: The Intervention of Normative and Operating Systems," *International Organization* 57, no. 3 (2003): 43–75.

PART THREE

SUSTAINABLE HUMAN DEVELOPMENT

CHAPTER 9

Theories of Development
at the United Nations

POVERTY PLAGUES A substantial portion of humankind, and the international community of states has come to embrace poverty eradication as a leading priority—at least in theory. Over a billion people are going hungry today, and half the population in the global South is undernourished. Nearly 3 billion people struggle to survive on less than $2 a day, not to mention the nearly 1 billion who have less than $1. The numbers have not appreciably changed since the World Bank made the first calculations in 1990, which is appalling on the face of it.[1] Thus, any priority given to poverty eradication should be easy to understand on moral grounds alone.[2] At the same time, however, there are signs of hope. The 2007 Millennium Development Goals Report indicates that for the first time the statistics indicate clear progress toward reducing poverty. Between 1990 and 2005 the proportion of people living below the poverty line (now calculated at $1.25/day) fell from 41.7 percent to 25.7 percent. Yet abject poverty persists on a broad basis, and the governments of countries in which so many citizens live in chronic poverty emphasize development as a value in and of itself. At the same time, development has a broader importance even to those in the advanced industrialized states, as a pragmatic link exists between poverty in the global South and important economic and security interests as defined by the global North.

THE POLITICS OF CHANGING THEORIES

"Development" has long dominated much of discourse and practice throughout the UN system.[3] The notion of development, however, means different things to different people and is contested on many levels.[4] Development may mean economic growth defined in macroeconomic terms as increases in gross domestic product (GDP), import-export figures, and levels of industrialization. Development may include a human element such as humans' ability to meet their basic human needs through their own initiative. Development may also mean to others sustainability in that economic growth and the ability of human beings to meet their basic needs should not deplete natural resources to the extent that those resources become unavailable for future generations. Since development has many contested conceptions, the international community is indeed challenged to successfully arrive at strategies for pursuing development. There is also the question of the link between development and the sizable list of human rights found in the International Bill of Rights, especially economic, social, and cultural rights. The UN role in promoting economic and social development has evolved to include forging compromises, setting agendas, creating norms, and building relative consensus among diverse constituencies. After all, none of these conceptions or definitions of development is mutually exclusive. A certain amount of prosperity is inherent to economic development in macroeconomic terms and necessary for individuals to achieve housing, food, health care, and a basic education. At the same time, healthy and educated individuals are necessary to achieve macroeconomic growth. Table 9.1 highlights UN development milestones between 1948 and 1980.

In this chapter we review how the complex, changing, and controversial definitions have been mirrored in UN approaches to development. Moreover, the UN organs and agencies dealing with the issue also have different conceptions of development (and, therefore, different approaches) that are not necessarily shared in other parts of the UN system. We begin by reviewing the historical evolution of the UN's development work in the context of changing theories of development. As Kenneth Dadzie suggests, the world organization has gone through four phases in dealing with the issue of development.[5] In essence, the UN has tried four theories or general approaches to development that reflect the evolution of economic thought since World War II. The transition from one phase to another represents an intellectual shift as to the causes of underdevelopment and the appropriate policies for combating poverty and allowing individuals to fulfill their full potential.

Phase One: National State Capitalism (1945–1962)

Development at the inception of the UN system focused on reconstruction and development after World War II. The concept of development, as it has come to be embraced in UN discourse and practice over the past sixty years, has entered through the back door. Yet it entered quite quickly nonetheless in the form of national economic development. National economic growth was endorsed by the UN through state-centered economic liberalism. This position was informed by the economist John Maynard Keynes; in this view states would pursue a large private for-profit sector based on extensive property rights while the government would manage the economy at the macro level. This approach recognized the dangers of unregulated capitalism that gave rise to harsh living conditions everywhere under industrialized capitalism, not to mention the indignities during the Great Depression, and, at the same time, recognized the benefits generated by

TABLE 9.1   UN Development Milestones with a Strong Economic Flavor, 1943–1980

1943	United Nations Relief and Rehabilitation Administration (UNRRA)[a]
1947	Economic Commission for Asia and the Far East (ECAFE)[a]
1948	Economic Commission for Latin America (ECLA)[a]
1950	Expanded Program of Technical Assistance[a]
1955	Afro-Asian Conference in Bandung/Nonaligned Movement[a]
1956	International Finance Corporation[a]
1958	UN Special Fund[a]
	Economic Commission for Africa (ECA)[a]
1960	First UN Development Decade[a]
	Declaration on the Granting of Independence to Colonial Countries and Peoples
	International Development Association[a]
1964	United Nations Conference on Trade and Development (UNCTAD I)[a]
	Group of 77[a]
1965	United Nations Development Programme (UNDP)[a]
	United Nations Industrial Development Organisation (UNIDO)[a]
1973	OPEC Price Increase
1974	Sixth Special Session of UN General Assembly
	Declaration and Programme of Action on the Establishment of a New International Economic Order (NIEO)
	World Population Conference
	Food Conference
	Economic and Social Commission for Western Asia (ESCWA)[a]
1975	Seventh Special Session of UN General Assembly
	UN World Conference of the International Women's Year
	UN Development Fund for Women (UNIFEM)[a]
1975–1977	Conference on International Economic Co-operation
1976	UNCTAD IV
	UN Conference on Human Settlements (HABITAT)
	UN Decade for Women
1979	OPEC Price Increase
	UN Conference on Science and Technology for Development
1980	Independent Commission on International Development Issues (Brandt Commission) Report
	UN World Conference of the Mid-Decade for Women

[a] Denotes the establishment of the body or commencement of the activity

markets and capitalism. It also realized that the immediate post-war world economy was in shambles and that a certain amount of multilateral management was needed to restore stability. This Keynesian synthesis sought to harness markets to the development interests of states while acknowledging the state's role in promoting economic growth and full employment—but with social protections. This synthesis reflected the initial dominance of Western capitalist states in the world organization and the weakness of communist states in voting and other UN arrangements. Most of the global South still existed as colonies and were subject to the choices made by imperial governments in the West.

Development was thus thought of primarily in national economic terms and the emphasis was on lending through the World Bank and other types of foreign assistance (either through state bilateral policies or the UN Expanded Programme of Technical Assistance, or EPTA). The goal was to create national infrastructures that would provide the basis for economic growth led by the private for-profit sector. Although the EPTA was symbolically important for establishing a role for the UN in the development area, its expenditures were nominal. Beginning with an initial operating fund of $20 million in 1951, the program grew only moderately over the next decade. The United States reduced its contribution from 60 percent downward over the years, and other rich countries failed to take up the slack.[6]

At the UN the global economic situation, at least in the Western world, was seen as neutral or benign, although prone to periodic instability. If proper national decisions were taken, then national macroeconomic growth would eventually occur over time. The role of international organizations centered on international infrastructure, such as agreements on monetary exchange rates, communications, and the like. States were obligated by the UN Charter to cooperate internationally on development matters and to report to the United Nations. But the principal UN organs, including ECOSOC, were not seen as having a major operational role in advancing development. ECOSOC and the General Assembly were seen as legitimating and coordinating mechanisms. In part this approach reflected the wariness of the rich Western capitalist states in affording too great a role to UN organizations characterized by broad membership and majority voting.

From the very beginning of the UN, important donor governments preferred the Bretton Woods institutions.[7] The differences in resources give the reader an idea of this preference. While in recent years the rest of the UN system spent some $12 billion to $15 billion annually, the World Bank Group in 2008 managed a loan portfolio totaling well over $200 billion and committed $38.2 billion in loans, grants, equity investments, and guarantees to over eighty countries.

The World Bank (or simply the Bank) and the International Monetary Fund (or simply the Fund, or IMF) were created prior to the United Nations proper at a conference in Bretton Woods, New Hampshire, in 1944 by the members of the U.S.-led United Nations alliance.[8] These agencies, although officially or technically part of the UN system, by design take their decisions entirely independently from ECOSOC and the General Assembly, with proportional voting as determined by funding provided mostly by member states. This arrangement has given the United States and other wealthy states not only control over decisions taken in the name of the Bank and the Fund but also significant influence in selecting the executive heads of these two agencies. The president of the Bank has always been American and the managing director of the IMF has always been European.[9] The extent of government ownership of economic enterprises and regulations of the economy has varied. For example, the United States is much less Keynesian than states in Europe; however, most developed countries believe in the core virtues of markets, entrepreneurship, and private property. This was and is true even in Scandinavian states that also believe in extensive economic regulation, with much emphasis on community objectives in addition to personal freedoms.

Among many decisions at the Bank, the major donor countries agreed in 1960 to create the International Development Association (IDA), the so-called soft loan window for developing countries. In large part this was a response to an early 1950s initiative by developing countries, which had used their growing numbers to vote into being the Special United Nations Fund for Economic Development (SUNFED) to augment technical assistance activities with long-term low-interest loans aimed at building infrastructure. The word "special" was added after officials recognized that without it the acronym was UNFED (which actually would have been more accurate since Western donors never put resources into it). The move to create such a fund was opposed by major donors. Washington first objected on grounds that the American people could not support such a capital fund while underwriting a war in Korea. Besides, the United States had just pumped over $13 billion—approximately $130 billion in 2006 dollars—into sixteen European countries under the Marshall Plan. But even after 1953 and the end of the Korean War, the United States continued its opposition. In the last analysis, SUNFED was stillborn for lack of resources. Developing countries demonstrated that their increasing numbers at the UN could be translated into General Assembly and ECOSOC resolutions, but such initiatives amounted to little without financial resources.

The United States did not trust international agencies that it did not control or heavily influence. The United States and other major donor governments hesitated or refused to contribute significantly to development programs guided by majority voting in a one-state-one-vote system that had always been the UN's operating style because Charter Article 2 (1) speaks of the sovereign equality of members.

Almost from the beginning, the UN created regional development bodies to encourage economic growth and different approaches in the different geographical areas of the world: the economic commissions for Europe (ECE in 1947); for Asia and the Far East (ECAFE in 1947, which later became ESCAP for "Asia and the Pacific"); for Latin America (ECLA, created in 1948, which later became ECLAC to include the Caribbean); for Africa (ECA in 1958); and for Western Asia (ESCWA, in 1973).[10] Some of these came to be quite important in the evolution of ideas and norms, as was true of ECLA in the Western Hemisphere. Some of these commissions never achieved their promise, and the one in Europe was eclipsed by other regional economic arrangements such as the European Community (EC), which evolved into the European Union. These regional commissions were created within ECOSOC, which had been mandated the responsibility of coordinating the social and economic work of the UN itself and the specialized agencies.

Coordination was vexing, however, as specialized agencies were set up as autonomous organizations, and many preceded the founding of the UN proper.

The International Labour Organization, for example, had been carried over from the League of Nations. Others like the World Meteorological Organization (WMO), the International Telecommunications Union (ITU), and the Universal Postal Union (UPU) were even older. But then a host of new agencies, such as the World Health Organization, the Food and Agriculture Organization, the UN Educational, Scientific and Cultural Organization, as well as the Bretton Woods institutions, were also created as part of the post-war UN system. While *de jure* part of that system, the Bretton Woods agencies are *de facto* autonomous. These and other agencies each had their own chartering legal instrument, assessed dues system for funding, executive head, and normally a separate headquarters building if not location.

States could join or withdraw from them independently of their membership in the United Nations itself. At one point, for example, the United States withdrew from both the ILO and UNESCO to protest certain policies and for ideological reasons in the case of UNESCO.[11] Such withdrawal did not affect its membership in the UN or U.S. voting in the Security Council and General Assembly. Although ECOSOC was nominally to be the coordinator of all UN economic and social organizations, their legal and financial arrangements ensured their independence. Specialized agencies report to the General Assembly through ECOSOC, but the UN's six principal organs do not really control the specialized agencies.[12] So from the beginning, the way the UN was set up ensured a shotgun approach to development. The primary idea (promoting national economic liberalism with minimal international involvement beyond basic infrastructure) was to be accomplished collectively through the work of a constellation of agencies.

Moreover, numerous UN specialized agencies indicated a "theory within a theory." Beyond the UN's central idea of encouraging states to make the "right" decisions to achieve economic growth, the theory of functionalism explained how to achieve international peace. Functionalism, as developed by David Mitrany, was purported to lead to world peace not by a frontal assault on aggression and other "political" questions, but by sidestepping these issues and concentrating on the separate elements of development.[13] A functional approach to development—concentrating on labor issues, children's issues, science, education, culture, agriculture, and so on—would not only advance economic and social development but also build strong operational networks so that states would learn cooperation in these functional areas. This functional cooperation would eventually spill over into other areas, even "political" ones, thereby allowing international agreement on aggression, self-defense, intervention, and the other subjects entailed in international peace and security.

So in this early UN approach to development, the Keynesian theory of economic growth through state-regulated capitalism and international economic liberalism gave guidance on economic and social matters, while the theory of functionalism explained how international state capitalism could contribute to peace. Actual attempts to apply the theory of functionalism, and its variant neofunctionalism, to development, particularly in Europe, led to reconsideration of functionalism as a path to peace.[14] First, development proved to be as political and contentious as any other issue. Building infrastructure through specialized agencies involved both governmental decisions and controversy. Second, "spillback" as well as "spillover" could occur. The controversies over monetary policy and other technical issues led to such intergovernmental conflict that further advances of an "economic" nature could be halted or even set back for a time. Third, "political" issues beyond the immediate development process intruded on policymaking. In Western Europe during the Cold War, considerations spawned by power struggles between the North Atlantic Treaty Organization and Warsaw Pact countries affected decisions about building Europe. Policy decisions about what would become the European Union were not well explained by a functionalist theory that posited regional technical issues as dominant. Global great-power struggles proved as important, or more important, than functionalist theory applied regionally.

The early UN approach to poverty and economic development in many countries was to reiterate for the globe the standard recipe of economic liberalism understood as national state-capitalism informed by the Keynsian compromise. The need for some international institutions did not detract from the central propositions of capitalist theory, namely that the role of public agencies was mainly to provide the infrastructure for private entrepreneurship and manage the economy using regulation and macroeconomic policies.

Phase Two: International Affirmative Action (1962–1981)

By 1961, the United Nations had 104 member states, more than double the original 51 members in 1945. The increase in membership mostly was due to the decolonization process that took place, at least in part, under the auspices of the Trusteeship Council, one of the UN's six principal organs. One consequence of decolonization was that the new majority of UN members, almost all of whom found themselves confronted with a very unequal global economic playing field, preferred more transnational public regulation of private economic activity. This regulation was intended to benefit the poorer countries by redressing global imbalances and evening that playing field. Even the World Bank, which did not completely share the new orientation to development by the General Assembly and ECOSOC, began to rethink the causes of underdevelopment and poverty. The automatic nature of development through traditional capitalist recipes and national economic liberalism was questioned.

The turning point was the beginning of the preparations for the UN Conference on Trade and Development (UNCTAD).[15] Beginning in the mid-1960s, UN development activity focused on persistent income inequalities between the rich North and the poor South, between developed and developing countries, between industrialized nations and the Third World. The 1960s were also designated the first UN Development Decade.[16] The origins of this reorientation lay

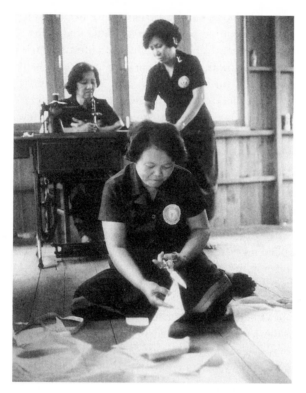

Housewives cut and sew traditional farmers' cotton shirts to
be sold in local markets and the women's cooperative shop
in Mung Mo, Thailand. (UN Photo 150947/C. Redenius)

primarily in the thinking of Raúl Prebisch and his colleagues in ECLA, who argued that the international capitalist system was stacked against poorer countries. Their economic world view, which is often mistakenly perceived to have
been based in Marxian critiques of capitalism, focused on the structural depen-
dence created and reinforced by the unequal playing field between grossly unequal participants in the capitalist world system. Thus, whereas the Bretton
Woods agencies were based on the view that economics and economic development could be largely separated from "politics," the post-colonial states saw their
economic condition as the product of the colonial policies of the past and the
power politics of the present that created an uneven economic playing field.
The charters of the Bank and Fund say they are to be nonpolitical, but the new
developing countries saw them as inherently political, as would any student of
political science.

On the basis of their experience mainly in the Western Hemisphere, Prebisch
and his colleagues saw the countries of the "periphery" trapped in relationships

of dependency with regard to the "center"—namely, the wealthy developed countries at the center of world trade and finance. Since, for example, the price of finished goods exported by the rich continued to rise while the price of most raw materials (including oil at the time, but that would change a decade later) exported by the poor fluctuated greatly and tended to decline over time, the global terms of trade were inimical to the interests of most countries in the global South. Those societies caught in conditions of dependency could not accumulate capital and grow without external infusions of capital from the North. This view supposedly explained the growing gap between the rich and poor countries.

The General Agreement on Tariffs and Trade (GATT) governed an inherently discriminatory trading system that helped make the rich richer and the poor poorer. The GATT was geared toward liberalizing trade in manufactured goods (exports from the core) but did little to liberalize trade in primary products and agricultural products (exports from the periphery). Developing states were placed at a structural disadvantage as their exports were discriminated against while at the same time they were forced to abide by liberal trade rules for manufactured goods. This led to deteriorating terms of trade, poverty, and debt—in a word, dependency.

The many variants of "dependency theory"[17] proved attractive, not only to Latin Americans, but especially to the growing number of newly independent and former colonial territories who attributed underdevelopment to the legacy of colonialism and the structure of the capitalist system. In 1964, the General Assembly created UNCTAD as a permanent "voice" of the Third World within the UN system. With Prebisch as its first secretary-general, it advocated a restructuring of global economic relations to the advantage of the poorer countries. The views UNCTAD championed were largely synonymous with the views of the Group of 77 (the major UN caucus of developing countries, which over time has grown to some 130 members but maintains its original label because of its historic significance).[18]

During a series of conferences in the mid-1970s, the G77 formulated its agenda for restructuring the global political economy. The main thrust came during the Sixth Special Session of the General Assembly in late spring 1974, at which the Declaration and Programme of Action on the Establishment of a New International Economic Order was adopted, but with significant reservations by many Western countries and the United States in particular. The demands of the declaration were wide-ranging but can be classified into four broad themes: economic sovereignty, trade, aid, and participation.[19] These issues were raised time and again in various ways and in various settings during the remainder of the decade. The North-South battle lines quickly became unambiguously drawn. A number of "global ad hoc conferences"[20] focusing on specific issues, such as population and food, and the more broad-based Conference on International Economic Co-operation, which met in December 1975 and June 1977 under the auspices of the French government, provided additional forums for expanding at the global level what some called "dialogue" between North and South but would more accurately be labeled "invective" or perhaps "dialogue of the deaf." Neither side seemed willing to listen to, and neither could hear what the other was trying to say.

The General Assembly majority presented a demand for a New International Economic Order (NIEO) intended to modify the fabric of economic relations between the global North and South. The NIEO was supposed to be made up of a series of treaties that would greatly regulate transnational economics and redistribute power and wealth. Specific measures on trade, investment, transnational corporations, and official development assistance were informed by the notion that wealth and resources should be authoritatively redistributed rather than allowing the "invisible hand" of the market determine that distribution. Markets were seen as inherently biased toward and too easily manipulated by the wealthy and the powerful.

The fate of the NIEO was sealed by the changing political and economic environment. The majority of states at the UN might call special sessions of the General Assembly and have the votes to create revolutionary new schemes on paper to alter the distribution of economic power. But even with the newly found (and temporary) power of the Organization of Petroleum Exporting Countries (OPEC), the South was unable to persuade the North of the wisdom of such economic restructuring. In the wake of the 1973 war in the Middle East between Israel and principally Egypt, OPEC was able to implement for a time an oil embargo (to several countries) and a more general slowdown in oil deliveries (to the rest of the oil-importing countries). But in the last analysis OPEC was not able to force the United States and other Western countries to alter their support for Israel, and OPEC was not able to maintain its unity. More generally, OPEC was unable for long to use oil as a weapon in the larger struggle to compel rich countries to radically transform international economics so as to close the gap between the developed and developing countries. On balance, OPEC's actions had an impact more profound in the South, which depended heavily on petroleum to fuel its agricultural and industrial development, than the North. The major international oil companies took advantage of the situation to greatly enhance their wealth, and the United States and the rest of the West maintained the power to resist demands for an NIEO and adjusted to the new economic reality.

All the same, the UN increased technical assistance to the poorer countries through the new UN Development Programme, created in 1965. The UNDP reflected a merger of the earlier EPTA and the stillborn SUNFED. Still, the UNDP and other agencies refused to yield their independence. The so-called Jackson report of 1969, named after its primary drafter, Sir Robert Jackson, called for more centralization of development efforts in the UN system but fell mostly on deaf ears.[21] Funding for the new UNDP was an important factor for improved development in many countries, but its resources remained decidedly meager. With less than $1 billion, its focus is on technical assistance and preinvestment studies,

TABLE 9.2   UN Development Milestones with a Strong Ecological Flavor, 1948–1982

1948	International Union for the Conservation of Nature and National Resources (IUCN)[a]
1964	International Biological Program[a]
1968	Intergovernmental Conference on Biosphere[a]
1970	Scientific Committee on Problems of the Environment (SCOPE)/ICSU[a]
1972	UN Conference on the Human Environment (UNCHE) Environmental Forum
	Limits to Growth published by the Club of Rome UN Environment Programme (UNEP)[a]
1973	Convention for the Prevention of Pollution by Ships (MARPOL)
1974–1981	UN Conference on the Law of the Sea
1976	UN Conference on Human Settlements (HABITAT)
1979	World Climate Conference
	Convention on Long-Range Transboundary Air Pollution
1980	Committee of International Development Institutions on the Environment (CIDIE)[a]
	World Conservation Strategy (ICSN/UNEP)
	Convention on Conservation of the Arctic Living Resources
1982	Convention on the Law of the Seas

[a] Denotes the establishment of the body or commencement of the activity

because donor countries preferred the World Bank and the IMF as the main vehicles for multilateral development finance.

In a significant change, the UN increased its activities on behalf of the environment as indicated in Table 9.2. In 1972 the UN sponsored a global ad hoc United Nations Conference on the Human Environment (UNCHE) in Stockholm out of which was born UNEP, the United Nations Environment Programme.[22] This was largely a new initiative from certain developed countries, mostly European, concerned that the pursuit of economic growth was causing fundamental harm to the environment. This "green movement" was not always welcomed by poorer countries. Many saw a focus on the environment as interfering with their development. As such, the environmental movement was often viewed in the global South as a form of neocolonialism because industrialized countries had grown rich without much consideration to environmental destruction, whereas developing countries were supposed to face a different cost structure in pursuing growth while protecting the environment. Thus, some states in the global South did not see environmental protection as an inherent part of development but rather as an impediment to a development defined in strictly economic terms. Leaders of the G77, such as China and India, did not lead on development-related issues, unless by "leadership" one means leading the opposition. These states saw environmental damage as being caused primarily by the capitalist development of just seven countries (G7)—and now these same countries were trying to pass the cost of their development on to the South. In other words, the G7 caused most of the damage and, therefore, should pay for environmental protection. These and other developing countries could be brought on board only for certain green treaties, such as the 1987 Montreal Protocol on protection of the ozone, with the carrots of compensatory financing.[23]

Meanwhile, the IMF and the World Bank were stymied by the lack of rapid economic progress according to prevailing doctrines in many parts of the South. The Bank continued to emphasize export-led development, meaning precisely the emphasis on participation in the world economy that Prebisch and UNCTAD thought so detrimental to the developing countries under the rules of the game established by GATT. So the Bank, in particular, was not on the same page of music as UNCTAD and the UN's other major development organizations. A number of Asian states, dubbed at the time the "East Asian Tigers," began to make rapid economic gains through, among other policies, emphasis on investment and trade. Singapore, for example, in a period of about twenty years, surpassed Britain, its former colonial master, in per capita income. But these tigers, such as South Korea, also continued various forms of "statism," similar to how agriculture was treated in the rich countries, by protecting key national industries from full global competition. States like Japan had already proved successful at export-led economic growth through an industrial policy that amounted to state subsidies for, and other benefits to, selected national industries. There was extensive trade, but it was not free trade in the sense of pure economic competition. Clearly East Asia was not Latin America. A certain type of authoritarian development worked well in places like China, Singapore, Malaysia, South Korea, and Taiwan—at least in the short and intermediate term. In the latter two cases, authoritarian development gradually became more democratic.

The East Asian Tigers notwithstanding, the World Bank and the IMF, given the low rates of economic growth in Africa and some other parts of the South, continued to press for policy changes in developing countries. Increasingly the World Bank was concerned about how noneconomic factors like corruption and cronyism could affect rates of economic growth. According to its charter, as noted, the Bank was a nonpolitical organization, but it came to adopt the policy that it should take into account factors that might not be strictly economic but that did affect economic growth.

Especially after Robert McNamara, former U.S. secretary of defense and head of the Ford Motor Company, became its president in 1967, the World Bank began to target poverty within developing countries. McNamara was committed to increasing dramatically the resources available for fighting poverty. Between 1969 and 1973, the Bank provided twice as much assistance as in the previous five years. The Bank's poorest members were given special consideration, and the Bank began to make loans with a view to changing things at the grassroots. Under his leadership, development became more than just economic growth. Agriculture, population planning, water supply, pollution control, nutrition, and

A slum in São Paulo, Brazil, illustrates the shortage of adequate housing as rural settlements are abandoned by people moving to the cities. (UN Photo 155212/C. Edinger)

other problems took center stage on the agenda. By June 1972, lending for agriculture became the single leading sector of the Bank's lending. In his thirteen-year tenure as president, McNamara increased World Bank Group lending twelvefold, from $1 billion to $12 billion.

The World Bank still undertook projects designed to promote macro national economic growth. Some of these projects, such as funding for large hydroelectric dams, proved enormously controversial given the displacement of people and destruction of the environment that often occurred. But increasingly the Bank focused on pockets of poverty rather than macroeconomic growth pure and simple. The Bank pursued its own version of international affirmative action, but not by focusing on terms of trade and other issues championed by UNCTAD. The Bank made loans at very low interest rates to the poorest of the poor. It made loans, and even grants, to, for example, poor families in South Asia so that their children could attend schools rather than work as child laborers. Thus, much of the UN system along with the World Bank rethought the prevailing wisdom about economic development—even if they did not necessarily adopt precisely the same revisions. The UN's emphasis was on the overall international economic environment, while the Bank focused more on domestic policies. While the Bank's changing views were often seen as progressive, because of the broader focus on social if not political factors, it was still criticized for a top-down approach and for not consulting enough with the persons affected by its policies.

Phase Three: Return to Neoliberalism (1981–1989)

The economic thinking and political development in the West that contributed to the rise of Margaret Thatcher in Britain and Ronald Reagan in the United States led to changes in Western foreign economic policy. Thatcher and Reagan were adherents of the writings of Frederich von Hayek, an Austrian economist who stressed individual freedom and markets as the path to economic prosperity. An intellectual rival to Keynes, Hayek stressed government regulation and management of the economy as causes of economic stagnation and high inflation. The Keynesian compromise that dominated much of the post–World War II era was replaced with a return to a relatively more *laissez-faire*, free market capitalist approach first articulated by Adam Smith, the father of capitalism. Given the power of Britain and the United States in the world and in the UN system, they also led a return to classical economic thinking within the world organization. For example, during the 1980s, the United States insisted that the IMF and the World Bank implement structural adjustment programs, conditioning loans on the willingness of developing states to prune back public spending and other public involvement in economic matters. Structural adjustment became code for implementing market reforms and economic liberalization in developing countries seeking multilateral development assistance.

The fall of the Berlin Wall in 1989 and the end of the Cold War meant that socialism as practiced by the Soviet Union and its allies was exposed as a bankrupt approach. The United States and other Western governments had mostly resisted but on occasion been obliged to accommodate Third World economic demands during the Cold War; but after its end there was no viable alternative to Western views on global capitalism—and no political reason for the West to compromise. Thus, a new packaging of an old vision took place, what World Bank economist John Williamson called the "Washington consensus."[24] The IMF, the World Bank, and the U.S. government—hence, the "Washington consensus" although it also could have been called the "Brussels consensus" since many Europeans were also on board even if "consensus" was absent in much of the global South— stressed again the role of private markets rather than governmental policies that intruded into those markets. Just as Ronald Reagan was dismantling Franklin Roosevelt's New Deal in the United States, so the new orthodoxy in international economics represented a return to minimal regulation and maximum private entrepreneurship. This time around, the IMF, the World Bank, and the development agencies of the UN system, at least for a while, were mostly in agreement.

The global South was in a weakened position both economically and politically. Not only had they already demonstrated the inability to force the idea of an NIEO, but suddenly the Soviet Union disintegrated as an ideological partner. The G77 fragmented as an effective political force. So the return of neoliberal economics was complete. After a long silence and toward the end of the period, some UN organizations began to criticize the impact on societies of economic liberalization—the most notable being UNICEF's concern with the impact on children and ECA's with the devastating impact on Africa.[25]

Over the first three UN Development Decades—1960s, 1970s, and 1980s—development thus had taken on various meanings as the global political context shifted. In the early years, development was defined largely in terms of national economic growth as measured in aggregate and per capita income. It also meant seeking national self-reliance for Third World countries. Slowly the added, and somewhat different, value of satisfying people's basic needs came into mainstream thinking in the 1970s. This definition slowly yielded ground to the incorporation of popular participation and local self-reliance in the satisfaction of basic needs. In this way, development discourse has come to embrace simultaneously three widely shared global values: peace, human security (including human rights), and sustainable human development.

Phase Four: Sustainable Development (1989–present)

The need to simultaneously foster economic development and ensure the availability of resources for future generations, or "sustainable development," was framed by a commission headed by then Norwegian prime minister Gro Harlem Brundtland, who later headed WHO.[26] The dialectical interchange between those stressing the role of markets and free trade versus those emphasizing public regulation and assistance for both social and economic reasons has yet to yield a new synthesis. These tensions have continued but abated somewhat as the UN shifted its attention to the idea of sustainable development. In 1994 Secretary-General Boutros Boutros-Ghali presented the General Assembly with *An Agenda for Development*.[27] Declaring development to be a fundamental human right, he presented a framework within which he highlighted the interdependence of peace, economy, civil society, democracy, social justice, and environment as an indispensable component of the development process. In this regard, he pointed to the special position, role, and responsibility of the United Nations in promoting development in all its aspects but with specific regard to setting priorities and facilitating cooperation and coordination.

The election of George H. W. Bush and then Bill Clinton to the White House had much to do with the evolving state of affairs. Both were less ideological, in devotion to free market orthodoxy, than the Reagan administration had been. The demise of communism and the increase in pragmatism by the global South also contributed. Still, the tension between regulation, either at the state or international level, and market-oriented approaches plagued international efforts to promote sustainable development. For example, strategies for protecting the environment while achieving economic development can involve market-based solutions. Markets use resources more efficiently and generate the kind of wealth and technologies that in theory could allow societies to concentrate more on environmental protection. From the neoliberal perspective, markets are the solution to environmental problems. From a Keynesian perspective, both government regulations and markets should be brought to bear on environmental problems. From a more engaged "pro-green" environmentalist perspective, unregulated capitalism is the cause of environmental degradation, and the economy must be thoroughly regulated to protect against environmental damage. These competing world views about the causes and the solutions to international problems complicate international negotiations and make compromise difficult.

Nevertheless, the intensive series of international conferences in the 1990s led to a reasonably coherent framework of development goals, objectives, and sectoral policies. That framework formed the foundation for the Millennium Declaration and was couched in the language of shared fundamental values—freedom, equality, solidarity, tolerance, respect for nature, shared responsibility. For those who read it even casually, Secretary-General Annan's Millennium Report was reminiscent of U.S. President Franklin D. Roosevelt's "Four Freedoms" speech.[28] The UN's foundations in liberal capitalist ideology appear not only to be still firmly in place but greatly strengthened by the absence of any potential significant challengers. Like Roosevelt's New Deal, the new international agreement contained elements of social democracy. All of this was entirely consistent with the International Bill of Rights. We have argued that the 1948 Universal Declaration of Human Rights, and the two core covenants, one on civil and political rights, and the other on economic, social, and cultural rights, cumulatively add up to social democracy.

Also in the 1990s, the UN and its associated agencies began to pay more attention to the role of women and gender in development.[29] Building on the work of feminist economists, UN agencies such as UNCTAD, UNDP, UNICEF, and the United Nations Development Fund for Women (UNIFEM) as well as the World Bank and the IMF began to research how men and women are positioned differently in the world economy and in poverty. Under particular scrutiny were the structural adjustment programs on women in countries experiencing economic crises. By examining how the policies of governments and multilateral institutions affect the everyday lives of women, strategies could be developed to avoid the ill effects or unintended consequences. For example, the World Bank and the IMF have modified their policies such that structural adjustment loans can now be used, in part, for the alleviation of poverty and not just for market reforms. Furthermore, the World Bank now considers gender equality as fundamental to economic development. While the inclusion of women and gender issues on the development agenda has obvious benefits, it also complicates North-South relations in that their respective conceptions regarding the status of women and women's rights are markedly different.

In 2001, both the North and South agreed at a conference in Monterrey, Mexico, that governments of developing countries had an obligation to reform themselves for the purpose of economic efficiency, while those in developed countries had an obligation to provide meaningful assistance for that improved process of development. Termed the "Monterrey consensus," this approach attempted to

UNICEF supplies the Zarghuna Girls School with educational supplies, provides teachers' training, and assists in repairing the infrastructure. (UN/DPI Photo/E. Debebe)

reconcile the need for structural/market reforms and the need to authoritatively redistribute some wealth of the rich North to the impoverished South.

The George W. Bush administration followed with an announcement of a new Millennium Challenge Account (MCA) of foreign assistance to the poorest countries. Recipient countries would have to meet certain criteria dealing both with economic effectiveness and good governance. The MCA would not be a multilateral arrangement, but rather would be administered by an independent corporation—the Millennium Challenge Corporation—of the United States. Congressional appropriations for the MCA, however, have consistently fallen short by about half of the administration's budgetary requests. Given the restrictive nature of funding criteria, very few of the world's poorest countries are able to qualify for assistance. Moreover, as illustrated with regard to the February 2006 $11 million Threshold Program to Tanzania to fight corruption, it is not always clear that the MCA guidelines are being implemented according to established criteria.[30] Given U.S. budget deficits and pressing problems both at home and abroad, by 2008 many observers thought the future of the MCA looked anything but rosy, given that foreign assistance had for a long time not been very popular in Washington. The Bush administration also initiated the President's Emergency Plan for AIDS Relief (PEPFAR) in 2003, which committed $15 billion over five years to combat HIV/AIDS. Nearly all of the funds were tied to bilateral aid programs in fifteen countries, and of the $1 billion available for multilateral assistance, a substantial portion was restricted to abstinence education. It was estimated that PEPFAR provided antiretroviral therapy to over 1.9 million people, and the program was renewed by Congress in 2008 and increased to $48 billion over the following two years.

The tension between proponents of rather pure liberal capitalism and of rather extensive public regulation account for the discontinuities in contemporary approaches to development through multilateral institutions. Chief among them is the lack of coordination between the World Trade Organization and IMF on the one hand, and agencies representing ecological and human rights concerns on the other. In 1995 GATT was transformed into the WTO, whose rules endorse free trade and minimal social regulation—whether that regulation is to protect the environment, human rights, or any other concern. So single-minded was the WTO's focus on strictly economic matters that U.S. national legislation to protect endangered sea turtles from certain fishing nets was struck down by a WTO dispute settlement panel as an inappropriate restraint on free trade.[31]

Given the numbers of persons—in industrialized as well as developing countries—left behind by the forces of globalization, the unalloyed advantages of freer markets and technologically led specialization were less than obvious. This particular tide did not lift all boats. Globalization signaled new wealth and freedom for some, but to others the process seemed uninvited and cruel. It brought a cornucopia of benefits to many in developed countries, but its wake brought inequality unprecedented in human history.[32] Given such rules, decisions, and emphases within the WTO, its policies received broad and intense negative reactions. The "battle of Seattle" was a highly visible reminder of this reaction, as violent street demonstrations and civil disobedience accompanied the WTO meeting in that city in late 1999. And other kinds of civil disobedience have come to be a feature of other WTO and Group of 8 (G8) meetings. An important multilateral agency was approaching development in an exceedingly narrow way, as if trade or development were only purely economic processes in which human rights and ecology and culture did not matter. The WTO, for example, said nothing about labor rights.

The creation of the WTO certainly did not mean that UNEP went out of business, any more than the emphasis on free trade meant that the ILO went out of business. But the continuing Washington consensus clearly left unresolved the relationship between trade and other strictly economic processes, on the one hand, and matters like ecology and labor rights that had increasingly been considered part of a broader and legitimate conception of development, on the other hand. To date, no formal link has been established between the WTO, the ILO and other human rights agencies, and the UNEP and other environmental agencies. It is as if at the WTO one had reverted to the 1940s and the view that development was an economic and nonpolitical matter.

At the World Bank, however, protecting the environment was increasingly seen as a legitimate part of its approach to investing in development. The Bank joined with UNEP and UNDP to create the Global Environment Facility (GEF), through which Bank funding was combined with UNEP and UNDP programming. Thus, the Bank's operations were much more intertwined with parts of the UN system, even if key decision-making remained fragmented. Although underfunded, the GEF represented a clear recognition of the relationship between development and the environment. Moreover, in 1992 at the UN Conference on Environment and Development (UNCED) in Rio de Janeiro, states voted into being a new UN coordinating organ, the Commission on Sustainable Development (CSD), which clearly incorporated ecological concerns and sustainability. This CSD was weak in legal authority, and hence weak in practical coordination, but even its name had symbolic importance. Over time, however, its specific accomplishments have been difficult to establish.

Market emphases notwithstanding, the new broadly shared conception of sustainable human development became the central component in the UNDP's *Human Development Reports*.[33] Started in 1990 by a prominent Pakistani economist, Mahbub ul Haq, then carried on by Richard Jolly of the United Kingdom and others, the annual reports analyzed international cooperation for development in a broad, multifaceted way. The annual report sometimes stressed human rights, sometimes women, sometimes ecology. It ranked countries not just by GDP per capita, but by a more complex formula attempting to measure quality of life. Wealth and prosperity loomed large, of course, but so did education and medical care. Various indices sought to measure discrimination against women, not only legally and politically but also in terms of basic health and education. In its approach to development, the UNDP dovetailed with the Overseas Development Council (ODC), a private group based in the United States that had pioneered in creating the Physical Quality of Life Index, which sought to measure the quality of all countries according to wealth, medical care, and education.

The Human Development Report and the ODC Physical Quality of Life Index both treated development in the broad fashion intended by the UN's approach to development in the fourth phase. The controversial nature of the *Human Development Report* stemmed from several factors. First, a United Nations agency "rated" countries according to subjective criteria—and states on the bottom disliked the publicity, while states not quite at the top, including the United States, grumbled. Second, many governments resented the fact that poorer neighbors got higher ratings because they were better at making decisions about priorities, having devoted more of their limited resources to education and health instead of spending them on weapons. Third, sometimes the methodology the UNDP used to establish its comparative ratings was, in fact, open to serious criticism, as in the 2000 volume stressing human rights. Accurate statistics are difficult to come by in many countries; moreover, given the subjectivity involved in choosing measures of human development, debates raged about what to include in the HDI as well as how the variables were weighted.

In 2000, member states at the Millennium Summit endorsed human security—the elimination of poverty and the promotion of sustainable development—as the world organization's highest priority. In doing so, member states recognized the link between the UN's work in economic and social domains and the world organization's mandate for international peace and security, which emphasizes the argument that promoting social and economic development and protecting human rights are indirect approaches to "peace." Economic equity, the pursuit of economic growth, and the satisfaction of basic human needs could do more than just improve the material quality of life. They could reduce the likelihood of violent conflict. The causes of violence between and within states could be decreased by reducing gross social and economic inequalities and deprivations. In the oft-cited *An Agenda for Peace*, Secretary-General Boutros-Ghali highlighted this link between the UN's work in the social and economic realm and the promotion of international security. He placed economic despair, social injustice, and political oppression among the "deepest causes of conflict."[34] The international community of states has more or less come to embrace the proposition that "the concept of security must change—from an exclusive stress on national security to a much greater stress on people's security, from security through armaments to security through human development, from territorial security to food, employment, and environmental security."[35]

Creating the foundation for sustainable human security entails empowering individuals, groups, and communities to become engaged constructively and effectively in satisfying their own needs, values, and interests, thereby providing them with a genuine sense of control over their futures. This was given an additional boost with a report from an eminent group of persons headed by former UN high commissioner for refugees Sadako Ogata and Nobel laureate in economics Amartya Sen, which focuses on "shielding people from acute threats and empowering them to take charge of their own lives."[36] Sen was certainly interested in development, but along with that focus he was also interested in various "unfreedoms," like lack of education and health care.

The 2000 summit's final document reiterated the Millennium Development Goals (discussed in detail in Chapter 11), which formed the foundation for the United Nations Millennium Declaration.[37] MDGs are eight main development goals and eighteen related targets that guide development policies and assess progress toward poverty reduction and sustainable human development. As such, the MDG process represents a larger strategic vision for mobilizing the international community for action. At the 2005 World Summit, heads of state and governments met in New York to review progress toward achieving the MDGs and to endeavor to agree on reforms to enhance the capacity and effectiveness of the world organization.

The diplomats negotiating the final summit outcome agreement in August 2005 were initially stunned when the U.S. permanent representative to the UN, John Bolton, suddenly proposed removing all references to the goals by name and substituting only broad support for development objectives in general. There was a predictable uproar among other UN member states. Within days, Bolton had reversed course and allowed specific references to the MDGs—given their worldwide profile and acceptance—to go back into the final agreement, albeit with language that permitted Washington to maintain a distinction between what states had agreed on in 2000 and the specifics attached afterward by the UN Secretariat. To cap the partial change of heart, credited to the intercession of Secretary of State Condoleezza Rice and Under Secretary Nicholas Burns, President Bush's address to the summit on September 14, 2005, included this unexpectedly categorical statement: "We are committed to the Millennium Development Goals."[38] Beyond restoring the goals by name, the United States also backed away from other proposed deletions on subjects such as the Kyoto agreement on climate change, which was only slightly fuzzed in the final document to indicate there was not universal agreement.[39] We will see, however, that state fidelity to the MDGs is anything but certain.

By 2005 the UN had, after a long and torturous process, evolved a broad notion of development. In some ways the United States, the most powerful state, had finally been brought into the global consensus. The United States agreed that it and the other developed countries had an obligation to increase assistance to poorer countries, although Washington emphasized bilateral rather than multilateral arrangements. Furthermore, U.S. officials have continually refused to agree to any specific target level for such assistance.

The links between poverty and underdevelopment and violent conflict are hard to ignore even if the causal link is empirically hard to prove. The poverty and human rights abuses in Afghanistan undoubtedly permitted the growth of Al Qaeda. This terrorist organization, or at least its leader in the form of Osama bin Laden, had also found refuge in a Sudan that was both poor and repressive. Islamic extremism and virulent nationalism have at least some roots in economic deprivation and the problems of persistent poverty, even if some leaders like bin Laden are wealthy.[40] Leaders from the upper classes often mobilize followers who are frustrated by poverty and unemployment. According to Thomas Friedman, columnist from the *New York Times*, it is often the "stand around guys" from the unemployed ranks who turn out to be suicide bombers and other terrorists. As Nobel Laureate Amartya Sen stated: "Even though definitive empirical work on the causal linkages between political turmoil and economic deprivations may be rare, the basic presumption that the two phenomena have firm causal links is widespread. . . . Of course, avoidance of war and eradication of destitution are both important ends, and it is quite plausible that each feeds the other."[41] Discourse and practice among developed and developing countries in the UN in 2008 continue to reflect the importance of this development-conflict nexus. What is very clear is that lack of development under the Karzai government in Afghanistan, for example, was one of the major factors that allowed the radical Taliban to make a comeback there. When citizens are disenchanted with

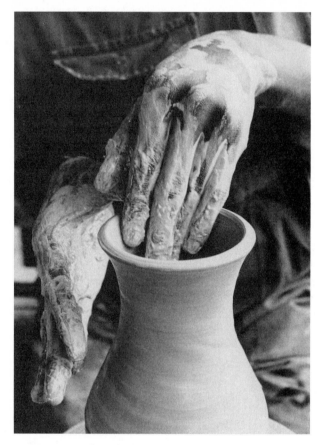

With UNDP and ILO support, the Rural Artisan Training
Centre in Dakar, Senegal, instructs rural artisans, such as this
potter. (UN/DPI Photo/Y. Nagara)

poverty and corruption, they become willing to look favorably on even extrem-
ist alternatives.

   With this overview of changing development thinking in mind, we now
turn to the UN and international cooperation for development at a more specific level. We look at the record of UN bodies in advancing development and
assess the value they add to the development process. We also examine the role
of the UN in the creation or development of "norms" and the extent to which
development efforts respect a right of participation by the stakeholders in the
process. We also explore how the UN has pursued sustainable development in
the real world of national interests, humanitarian crises, and environmental
degradation.

NOTES

1. See World Bank, *World Development Report 1990* (Oxford: Oxford University Press, 1990).

2. Food and Agriculture Organization, *State of Food Insecurity in the World 1999* (Rome: FAO, 1999), and UN Development Programme, *Human Development Report 2002* (New York: Oxford University Press, 2002), table 3.

3. Development is a contested notion because of the implications that it implies progress and other advances that some critics see as dubious. We do not continue using scare quotes around the term but are aware of the problems associated with its use.

4. For a review of the primary documents, see Mahfuzur Rahman, *World Economic Issues at the United Nations: Half a Century of Debate* (Dordrecht, Netherlands: Kluwer, 2002). For an analytical overview of the period, see Louis Emmerij, Richard Jolly, and Thomas G. Weiss, *Ahead of the Curve? UN Ideas and Global Challenges* (Bloomington: Indiana University Press, 2001), and Richard Jolly, Louis Emmerij, Dharam Ghai, and Frédéric Lapeyre, *UN Contributions to Development Theory and Practice* (Bloomington: Indiana University Press, 2004). These books are part of a multivolume series from the United Nations Intellectual History Project, an attempt to map economic and social ideas. For details, see www.unhistory.org.

5. Kenneth Dadzie, "The UN and the Problem of Economic Development," in *United Nations, Divided World: The UN's Roles in International Relations*, 2nd ed., eds. Adam Roberts and Benedict Kingsbury (Oxford: Clarendon Press, 1995), 297–326.

6. See Olav Stokke, *International Development Assistance: The UN Contribution* (Bloomington: Indiana University Press, 2007).

7. For an overview of the World Bank, see Devesh Kapur, John P. Lewis, and Richard Webb, *The World Bank: Its First Half Century*, vol. 1, "History" (Washington, D.C.: Brookings Institution, 1997) and vol. 2, "Perspectives." The previous history was written by Edward Mason and Robert Asher, *The World Bank Since Bretton Woods* (Washington, D.C.: Brookings Institution, 1973). For the IMF, see, for example, Margaret G. de Vries, *The International Monetary Fund, 1945–1965: The Twenty Years of International Monetary Cooperation* (Washington, D.C.: IMF, 1969), *The International Monetary Fund, 1966–1971: The System Under Stress* (Washington, D.C.: IMF, 1976), and *The International Monetary Fund, 1972–1978: Cooperation on Trial* (Washington, D.C.: IMF, 1985); and James Boughton, *Silent Revolution: The International Monetary Fund, 1979–1989* (Washington, D.C.: IMF, 2001). See also Norman K. Humphreys, ed., *Historical Dictionary of the IMF* (Washington, D.C.: IMF, 2000); Ngaire Woods, *The Globalizers: The IMF, the World Bank, and Their Borrowers* (Ithaca, N.Y.: Cornell University Press, 2006); Ariel Buira, ed., *Reforming the Governance of the IMF and World Bank* (London: Anthem Press 2005); and Nancy Birdsall and John Williamson, *Delivering on Debt Relief: From IMF Gold to a New Aid Architecture* (Washington, D.C.: Institute of International Economics, 2002).

8. See James Raymond Vreeland, *The International Monetary Fund: Politics of Conditional Lending* (London: Routledge, 2007), and Katherine Marshall, *The World Bank: From Reconstruction to Development to Equity* (London: Routledge, 2008).

9. The Clinton administration angered the Europeans by vetoing their preferred choice for head of the IMF. From the European view, such a decision was theirs alone. But as a reflection of U.S. hyperpower status after the Cold War, the Clinton team felt that the German national nominated was not an appropriate choice. The Europeans then proceeded to their

second preference, with considerable hard feelings toward the United States. The rest of the world had no say in such matters.

10. For a discussion, see Yves Berthelot, ed., *Unity and Diversity in Development Ideas: Perspectives from the UN Regional Commissions* (Bloomington: Indiana University Press, 2004).

11. Roger A. Coate, *Unilateralism, Ideology, and U.S. Foreign Policy: The United States In and Out of UNESCO* (Boulder, Colo.: Lynne Rienner Publishers, 1988).

12. See Erskine Childers with Brian Urquhart, *Renewing the United Nations System* (Uppsala, Sweden: Dag Hammarskjöld Foundation, 1994).

13. David Mitrany, *A Working Peace System* (Chicago: Quadrangle Books, 1966), and *The Progress of International Government* (New Haven, Conn.: Yale University Press, 1933). Later, a "neofunctionalist" school formed around such ideas linked to European integration, including Ernst B. Haas, *Beyond the Nation State* (Stanford, Calif.: Stanford University Press, 1964).

14. For an overview of much of the functionalist and neofunctionalist literature applied to Europe, see Robert O. Keohane and Stanley Hoffmann, eds., *The New European Community: Decisionmaking and Institutional Change* (Boulder, Colo.: Westview Press, 1991). Certainly in the North Atlantic area, various functionalist theories have faded with time.

15. See Ian Taylor, *UN Conference on Trade and Development* (London: Routledge, 2007); John Toye and Richard Toye, *The UN and Global Political Economy: Trade, Finance, and Development* (Bloomington: Indiana University Press, 2004); and Thomas G. Weiss, *Multilateral Development Diplomacy in UNCTAD, 1964–84* (London: Macmillan, 1986).

16. For a fuller discussion of the development decades, see Jolly, Emmerij, Ghai, and Lapeyre, *UN Contributions*.

17. The two main schools were a more radical version proposed by André Gunder Frank in *Development and Underdevelopment in Latin America* (New York: Monthly Review Press, 1967), and a subtler version by Fernando Henrique Cardoso, *Dependency and Development in Latin America* (Berkeley: University of California Press, 1979).

18. For more information, see www.g77.org.

19. See Robert S. Jordan, "Why an NIEO? The View from the Third World," in *The Emerging International Economic Order: Dynamic Processes, Constraints and Opportunities*, eds. Harold K. Jacobson and Dusam Aidjanski (Beverly Hills, Calif.: Sage, 1982), 59–80.

20. See Thomas G. Weiss and Robert S. Jordan, *The World Food Conference and Global Problem Solving* (New York: Praeger, 1976). For an overview, see Michael Schechter, ed., *United Nations-sponsored World Conferences* (Tokyo: UN University Press, 2001); and Michael G. Schechter, *United Nations Global Conferences* (London: Routledge, 2005).

21. *A Study of the Capacity of the United Nations Development System* (Geneva: UN, 1969), document DP/5.

22. See Elizabeth DeSombre, *Global Environmental Institutions* (London: Routledge, 2006).

23. Richard Benedick, *Ozone Diplomacy: New Directions in Safeguarding the Planet*, 2nd ed. (Cambridge, Mass.: Harvard University Press, 1998). This is the definitive if overly detailed account of how developing countries were enticed into concrete measures to protect the ozone. It is also an account of how pragmatic diplomats and business leaders were able to get the Reagan administration, with its free market and anti-regulation ideology, to support international law to protect the environment.

24. See John Williamson, ed., *Latin America Adjustment: How Much Has Happened?* (Washington, D.C.: Institute for International Economics, 1990); and John Williamson, "The Washington Consensus Revisited," in *Economic and Social Development in the 21st Century*, ed. Louis Emmerij (Baltimore: Johns Hopkins University Press, 1997), 48–61.

25. See Giovanni A. Cornia, Richard Jolly, and Frances Stewart, eds., *Adjustment with a Human Face: Country Case Studies* (Oxford: Oxford University Press, 1992).

26. World Commission on Environment and Development, *Our Common Future* (Oxford: Clarendon Press, 1987).

27. Boutros Boutros-Ghali, *An Agenda for Development* (New York: United Nations, 1995).

28. Kofi A. Annan, *"We the Peoples": The United Nations in the 21st Century* (New York: UN, 2000).

29. See Devaki Jain, *Women, Development, and the UN: A Sixty-Year Quest for Equality and Justice* (Bloomington: Indiana University Press, 2005); Lourdes Benería, *Gender, Development and Globalization: Economics As If All People Mattered* (New York: Routledge, 2003); Hilkka Pietila, *Engendering the Global Agenda: The Story of Women and the United Nations* (New York: UN Non-governmental Liaison Service, 2002); Suzanne Bergeron, *Fragments of Development: Nation, Gender and the Space of Modernity* (Ann Arbor: University of Michigan Press, 2006); and Jael Silliman and Ynestra King, *Dangerous Intersections: Feminist Perspectives on Population, Environment and Development* (Cambridge, Mass.: South End Press, 1999).

30. Center for Global Development, MCA Monitor Blog, February 2, 2006, http://blogs .cgdev.org/mca-monitor/archives/2006/02/foreign_aid_to.php.

31. See Bernard M. Hoekman and Petros C. Mavroidis, *The World Trade Organization: Law, Economics, and Politics* (London: Routledge, 2007).

32. See Anthony Giddens, *Runaway World: How Globalization Is Reshaping Our Lives* (New York: Routledge, 2000); David Held, Anthony McGrew, David Goldblatt, and Jonathan Perraton, *Global Transformations: Politics, Economics, and Culture* (Stanford, Calif.: Stanford University Press, 1999); Joseph Stiglitz, *Globalization and Its Discontents* (New York: Norton, 2002); and James H. Mittelman, *Globalization: Critical Reflections* (Boulder, Colo.: Lynne Rienner, 1996), *The Globalization Syndrome* (Princeton, N.J.: Princeton University Press, 2000), and *Whither Globalization? The Vortex of Knowledge and Ideology* (London: Routledge, 2004).

33. This is an important part of the discussion by Craig Murphy, *The United Nations Development Programme: A Better Way?* (Cambridge: Cambridge University Press, 2006). See also Khadija Haq and Richard Ponzio, eds., *Pioneering the Human Development Revolution: An Intellectual Biography of Mahbub ul Haq* (Delhi: Oxford University Press, 2008).

34. Boutros Boutros-Ghali, *An Agenda for Peace: Preventive Diplomacy, Peacemaking and Peace-keeping* (New York: United Nations, 1992), para. 15.

35. UNDP, *Human Development Report 1993* (New York: Oxford University Press, 1993), 5.

36. Commission on Human Security, *Human Security Now* (New York: Commission on Human Security, 2003), iv.

37. For an overview of their importance, see Sakiko Fukada-Parr, "Millennium Development Goals: Why They Matter," *Global Governance* 10, no. 4 (2004): 395–402, and *Millennium Development Goals* (London: Routledge, forthcoming).

38. "Statement of H.E. George W. Bush, President of the United States of America, 2005 World Summit, High Level Plenary Meeting, September 14, 2005," available at www.un .org/webcast/summit2005/statements/usa050914.pdf.

39. For details, see Thomas G. Weiss and Barbara Crossette, "United Nations: Post-Summit Outlook," in *Great Decisions 2006* (New York: Foreign Policy Association, 2006), 9–20.

40. While the foot soldiers of Islamic terrorism may come out of poverty and/or blocked socioeconomic mobility, bin Laden was partially affected by the fact that the government of Saudi Arabia chose the United States, not him, to eject Saddam Hussein's forces from Kuwait in 1990–1991. See Steve Coll, *Ghost Wars: The Secret History of the CIA, Afghanistan, and bin Laden, from the Soviet Invasion to September 10, 2001* (New York: Penguin, 2004). In short, the top leadership of Al Qaeda is not easily explained by simple reference to poverty and lack of development.

41. Amartya Sen, "Global Inequality and Persistent Conflicts," paper presented at the Nobel Awards Conference 2002, reprinted in Commission on Human Security, *Human Security Now* (New York: Commission on Human Security, 2003), 132.

CHAPTER 10

Sustainable Development as Process: UN Organizations and Norms

THE WORK OF the United Nations in the development field was born decentralized and has reached advanced middle age in essentially the same state. At the same time, however, what began largely as an implicit and secondary goal has evolved into one of the world organization's primary activities. Over the decades, scores of development-related agencies, funds, programs, commissions, and committees have continued to spring up, thereby creating an ever more complex institutional web (see Appendix A). "Unpacking" the complex structure of UN development reveals three main clusters of somewhat autonomous activity. The first cluster centers on the United Nations proper—the relevant principal organs, regional commissions, and central parts that are not specialized agencies (especially UNDP, UNICEF, and UNCTAD) but that operate more or less in tandem with the specialized agencies and are as important to the development efforts of the system as a whole. The second cluster focuses on the specialized agencies themselves, especially the IMF and the World Bank—which, as mentioned, often go their own way although *de jure* are parts of the UN system. The third is trade related and centers on the activities of the WTO.[1] With the issue of development we once again meet the "two United Nations"—one of states and one of international civil servants—as these organizations are composed of their governing bodies and their secretariats. As was the case for earlier discussions of security and human rights, these organizations are also complemented by a third United Nations comprising NGOs and experts.

We start by reviewing some recent efforts at improving coordination of the many moving parts of the UN's institutional machinery. Then we look at particular agencies and programs in order to address the question of what individual UN organizations contribute to sustainable human development. Of course we cannot be comprehensive in this regard, but we use a representative sample to provide an introduction and "feel" for the system's operations. Some observers use the term "UN family" instead of "system," which has the advantage of associating the adjective "dysfunctional" to describe the kinds of routine battles and quarrels that occur between and among agencies themselves and between agencies and the member states that compose them.

Next, and most important, we suggest that beyond the particular contributions of individual institutions, the UN system's collective contribution to development is more notable for nurturing agreement about ideas and principles for sustainable human development—also known as human security—than for its operational impact. We explore this in the specific context of discourse and practice surrounding the concept of "eco-development," as it has evolved over the decades. Secretary-General Boutros Boutros-Ghali wrote in 1998, "The United Nations is the mechanism in place and is best prepared to facilitate the work of achieving a new development rationale."[2] He stressed ideas and not field operations. Particularly in a world in which states and their preferred organizations beyond the UN (narrowly defined) still control many of the resources that contribute to development, such as money and terms of trade, we should not overlook the important role of ideas—development rationales—that shape how resources are employed. After all, much of international relations is about ideas and changing ideas.[3] Our hope is that by the end of the chapter the reader will be familiar with the various moving parts of the UN system and how they contribute to the idea of sustainable human development.

UNDERSTANDING THE ORGANIZATIONAL CHART: COORDINATION, AGAIN

The UN—even for seasoned observers—is a bewildering alphabet soup of semi-autonomous programs, funds, committees, commissions, and agencies; and this reality is most striking in the development arena. At the core of this system is the General Assembly, whose agenda grows longer from year to year.[4] Its influence, however, may be the inverse. Most development issues are dealt with in the assembly's Second Committee (Economic and Financial), which is made up of representatives of all member states (in UN parlance, "a committee of the whole"). The General Assembly, for example, voted in 1983 to create what came to be called the Brundtland Commission, which was an important milestone in changing ideas about development by fusing the seemingly clashing perspectives about economic growth versus environmental protection. Over the years, however, the assembly's most important work in the development field generally has taken place in special sessions or in global, ad hoc conferences convened to consider specific issues or topics, such as women, population, development financing, and HIV/AIDS. Normally the assembly deals with substantive ideas, or the big picture, rather than the details of management, administration, and coordination.

A female work crew builds a road in Lesotho, 1969. (UN/DPI Photo by K. Muldoon)

The assembly elects fifty-four of its member states to sit on the Economic and Social Council, which under Article 55 of the Charter is the principal organ mandated with the responsibility for promoting development and coordinating UN activities. The General Assembly, ECOSOC, and other UN governing bodies are composed of states but rely on the UN's administrative branch—the Secretariat—for staffing and support.

ECOSOC is made up of five regional and ten functional commissions that cover the gambit of development issues and concerns. It officially coordinates the work of fourteen specialized agencies and eleven UN funds and programs. Over the years, some of the five regional economic commissions have been instrumental in establishing international development financial institutions and other development infrastructures within their respective regions, as noted in the previous chapter. Prominent people and ideas from ECLAC also served as the catalyst for the creation of UNCTAD, and many of the ideas that became manifest in the call to establish a New International Economic Order. The commissions reflect varying perspectives from each of the world's major geographic regions relating to such issues as the status of women, population and development, social development, science and technology for development, and sustainable development.[5]

The alphabet soup thickens when considering the numerous UN development-related bodies for which ECOSOC oversees coordination. These UN bodies include several abbreviations that we have encountered throughout this book: UNDP, UNICEF, UNCTAD, UNFPA, UNHCR, OHCHR, UNEP, and WFP. These UN bodies are also only part of the much larger UN system for which ECOSOC is responsible for facilitating cooperation and coordination. The mandates and work programs of these various agencies overlap, which has made the job of coordination daunting. In an interdependent world, analysts and decision-makers see how difficult it is to separate functional specialization. But the UN system reflects exactly that functional specialization.

The UN continuously encounters the challenges of coordination. In reality, ECOSOC is something of a mailbox between the General Assembly and the rest of the socioeconomic agencies involved in development. As such, ECOSOC—meaning the states that have representatives there—has had to develop supplemental coordinating arrangements.

Boutros Boutros-Ghali had focused attention on the role of the United Nations in promoting development in his 1994 *An Agenda for Development*. Yet the world organization was found inadequate for the task. Kofi Annan was elected in December 1996, and in January 1997 when he assumed his duties he was the first person to hold the office of Secretary-General who had spent virtually his entire professional career as an international civil servant—nearly three decades working his way up through the ranks and being exposed to the best and the worst of the organization. Upon arriving in office, he committed himself and the world organization to a reform process.[6] This subject was also important for the United States, because the largest donor to both the regular and voluntary UN budgets had long been pressing for administrative and structural reform. According to one of the chief critics of the UN, U.S. senator Jesse Helms, the "literally hundreds of UN agencies, commissions, committees, and subcommittees [that] have proliferated" since 1945 are one of the chief problems of the organization. Thus, Helms argued that either the Secretary-General should lead a drastic reform effort or the UN could not be saved.[7] So Annan knew the organization from the inside and was aware of pressures for administrative reform from the outside. As we have seen earlier, the same necessities for adaptation and change existed at the end of his second term. But as he himself said, "Reform is not an event; it is a process."[8] John Bolton put it more picturesquely: "Reform is not a one-night stand."[9] Annan, perhaps much more so than Bolton, understood that reform is not an objective process of building a leaner, meaner, and more effective organization; it is above all a political process, and a highly contested one at that.

At the heart of Annan's reform program was the reorientation and reorganization of the UN's administration and management. More change has actually taken place than is customarily appreciated. In his effort to bring unity of purpose to the diverse activities of the UN and provide clear lines of responsibility, in 1997 he created—for the first time in the UN's half-century—a cabinet structure. This Senior Management Group (SMG) is made up of the various under-secretaries-general, the heads of UN funds and programs, and the deputy-secretary-general, a post created in 1998 to oversee the reform process and coordinate development activities. Similarly, four thematic executive committees (Peace and Security, Humanitarian Affairs, Economic and Social Affairs, and UN Development Group) were created and charged with overseeing the coordination of policy development, management, and decision-making. The conveners of each of these committees sit on the SMG.

Two of these executive committees are of particular importance for development. The Economic and Social Affairs Executive Committee (EC-ESA) is convened by the under-secretary-general for economic and social affairs and comprises representatives from eighteen UN bodies. Like all the other executive committees, the EC-ESA serves as a consultative body for facilitating decision-making, policy development and coordination, and better management.

The United Nations Development Group Executive Committee is convened by the administrator of UNDP and includes the UNFPA, UNICEF, and WFP. This body also serves as the secretariat for the United Nations Development Group (UNDG), which also was created in 1997 to provide better coordination among the numerous UN funds, programs, and other bodies that have proliferated over the years in the development area. The UNDG consists of twenty-eight member agencies plus five observers. In addition to its own operational activities, the UNDP administers several special-purpose funds and programs, including the UN Capital Development Fund (UNCDF). And in cooperation with the World Bank and UNEP, the UNDP serves as an implementing agency for Global Environment Facility (GEF), which provides concessional funding and grants for certain environmentally sound development projects.

UN development activities have benefited from enhanced coordination via the Office of the Secretary-General and UNDP. Given that states vote to create all sorts of UN development institutions, it falls to these two parts of the UN system to bring as much order as possible to a multifaceted process. States get the kind of UN for which they vote and otherwise support. Unfortunately, all too often, member states vote for or against a particular UN organization or one of its activities as a diplomatic concession to some domestic group or as part of a compromise with other states. The public display of affection or disgruntlement may or may not have a concrete follow-on in the form of necessary diplomatic and economic support. As such, the UN record for success in promoting sustainable development is mixed at best.

PARTICULAR CONTRIBUTIONS TO
SUSTAINABLE DEVELOPMENT

Many UN agencies and bodies working for sustainable development were given unrealistic mandates, and many overlap with other parts of the UN system. Member states voted to create them but provided them neither with the necessary resources nor sufficient political will to make them effective. Nevertheless, these agencies and bodies play important roles by pushing states to live up to their obligations or develop new ones. They participate in joint efforts that have discernible impacts in setting and advancing development goals. They also bring a modicum of order to what we have already called a shotgun approach to development.

UNDP

The UNDP's annual sponsorship of the *Human Development Report* is an important avocation, but its main purpose is development work in the field. In January 2008, it was actively engaged in 166 countries. Its most senior official in developing countries, the UNDP resident representative, also acts as the resident coordinator for the UN system. As the primary unit devoted to capacity building for social and economic development, the program was created in 1965 to take the lead in providing technical assistance.[10] In this regard, it works with other UN units in a wide variety of thematic contexts. For example, it provides assistance to the Department of Economic and Social Affairs (DESA) in support of the UN's standard-setting and normative work in developing countries and provides integrated follow-up to the UN's global conferences of the 1990s. It works in the security realm to support elections, demobilization and reconciliation initiatives, and human rights. In the humanitarian field, the agency provides support for disaster prevention, mitigation, and preparedness; the reintegration into society of refugees, former combatants, and internally displaced persons; and the implementation of post-disaster national plans for reintegration, reconstruction, and recovery.

UNDP is also the administering agency for a number of special development-related funds and programs, including UNIFEM. This particular agency was created in 1975 by the General Assembly with a mandate to support initiatives that benefit women and to bring women into mainstream development activities. Specifically, UNIFEM has focused its activities on reducing feminized poverty and violence; reversing the spread of HIV/AIDS among women and girls; and achieving gender equality in democratic governance.[11] UNIFEM has served as a catalyst for coordinating gender development issues among the various development agencies.[12]

The UNDP has prioritized its program activities around four interrelated themes: advocacy, advice, pilot projects, and partnerships. Priority action areas in 2008 include democratic governance, poverty reduction, crisis prevention and recovery, energy and environment, and HIV/AIDS. Now a minister with a portfolio covering Africa, Asia, and the United Nations, Mark Malloch Brown was UNDP administrator until 2005, and he argued that the program's annual *Human Development Report* gives the agency a "special voice and pulpit and authority to develop alternative ideas," a view also favored by his immediate successor, Kemal Derviç,[13] as it undoubtedly will be by his successor, Helen Clark. The advisory function focuses on building capacity in a variety of areas, including legal, political, and regulatory frameworks as well as infrastructure for basic social and economic development. Given the agency's limited budget, it concentrates on doing things that can serve as catalysts for mainstreaming particular policy agendas as opposed to taking on expensive large-scale projects. Technical assistance and pre-investment studies have been its portfolio since operations began in 1966.

The UNDP's partnership function is wide-ranging, focusing on integrating diverse elements of society and the private sector into development. The agency sees promoting sustainable development as requiring new forms of cooperation and involving complex interventions from a wide variety of actors—governments at all levels, NGOs, private business enterprises, and local community groups. The focus is on empowering people and creating the conditions necessary for "people-centered" development. The guiding philosophy is that "people should guide both the state and the market, which need to work in tandem, with people sufficiently empowered to exert a more effective influence over both."[14] In brief, the UNDP's underlying theme is getting the product to the poor and empowering them with the capacity for good governance. Priority is placed on democratization and empowerment through participation. This means, among other things, that the UNDP has "mainstreamed" human rights considerations into its development work.

Of course, empowerment, like most development activities, requires resources, especially financial resources and a commitment from the central government. In this regard, the UNDP, working with the UNCDF, has undertaken an initiative to provide what is called microfinance—providing financial services to the poor at the local level. Its Special Unit for Microfinance is devoted to supporting the creation of start-up micro-financial institutions in rural areas in the poorest countries. The underlying philosophy is simple: "The program is predicated on the concept that most donor support has been so far directed towards large and successful organizations, and that small amounts of capital (up to $150,000) invested primarily in recipient organizations displaying vision, commitment and competence, can help widen tomorrow's market of successful micro-financial institutions."[15]

In the context of the shrinking financial resources for multilateral development assistance over the past two decades, the UNDP clearly adds value to the overall development process. Even though the UNDP's core operating budget and the size of its headquarters staff has been cut, it remains at the forefront of promoting sustainable human development through its fieldwork and by build-ing cooperative relationships. Reflecting on his first years in office, Malloch Brown opined: "When I took office the agenda was clear: Reform of UNDP. . . . The message was close to reform or die."[16] By the time he left the agency to be-come chief of staff for the Secretary-General, and then the deputy secretary-general, the UNDP was at the forefront of the MDG process. But as Malloch Brown has acknowledged, "In the final analysis, we cannot judge our reform by its impact on UNDP alone, but rather on how we help strengthen the critical role of the United Nations system as a whole in all aspects of development coopera-tion."[17] The UN has fostered international cooperation by creating and building consensus around the idea that development means human development. What was once a counter-discourse to the Bretton Woods notion of development de-fined as increases in GDP is now a mainstream concept with widespread global agreement.[18] If the UNDP is supposed to assist in the creation of successful market democracies, then democracy and human rights are as important as ef-ficient markets.

UNCTAD

This institution began in 1964 as a debating forum and think tank for develop-ing countries (G-77) and their advocates who sought a counter-forum to the General Agreement on Tariffs and Trade. For most of its existence, it largely served that function. The conference itself meets in formal session every four years, but its Trade and Development Board (TDB) meets annually, and the sec-retariat in Geneva operates continuously. UNCTAD served as the focal point for formulating and articulating NIEO ideas. However, the end of the Cold War brought with it hard times. After the creation of the WTO, UNCTAD adopted a more conciliatory tone by seeking finally to end impediments to trade in agri-cultural products.[19] UNCTAD remains an important forum in that it continues to articulate the unintended consequences of trade liberalization on develop-ment in the global South. It highlights alternative theories that may be more suitable for impoverished states as they pursue development in a globalized world.[20] UNCTAD is also instrumental in exposing how certain trade rules are biased against developing states especially as it relates to the agricultural subsi-dies in the global North.

UNCTAD is also part of former Secretary-General Kofi Annan's initiative of forging innovative partnerships with other international organizations, local governments, NGOs, the private sector, and civil society. UNCTAD's role has taken a wide variety of forms and complexions. In 1999, for example, UNCTAD, along with UNDP and Habitat, initiated a global partnership—World Alliance of Cities Against Poverty (WACAP)—with civil society, the private sector, and local governments to carry out the goals of the 1995 World Summit for Social Devel-opment in Copenhagen. This alliance quickly became formalized and has grown substantially. It seeks to strengthen networks among cities around the world.

During the Third UN Conference on Least Developed Countries in Brussels in 2001, for instance, WACAP organized a parallel "Mayors Meeting," bringing together representatives from 216 cities around the world. The primary purpose of this conference was action. A "city-to-city solidarity market" was held in which requests of assistance were matched with offers. On the spot, twelve formal agreements of cooperation were concluded between cities in Belgium and cities in Africa, Asia, and Latin America. The requests of 120 other cities from developing regions were tendered and are currently either under consideration or being related to cities throughout the world through the numerous global, regional, and national city networks that also participated at the meeting.[21] At a conference in São Paulo in 2004, UNCTAD member states agreed to better integrate the work of civil society, the private sector, and academia into its work.[22] The theme of the 2008 session of UNCTAD XII was globalization and the challenges it poses to trade and development. This builds on its partnership role with civil society, which seeks to capture the benefits of globalization through the "new regionalism" that emerged as a result of the WTO's failure to successfully negotiate further trade liberalization at the global level.[23] UNCTAD sees opportunities for regional trading arrangements to negotiate better rules and terms of trade for poor and impoverished countries.

UNICEF

The UN Children's Fund is often called and is actually better known by its acronym, and its work ranges from child and maternal health care and basic education to water and sanitation.[24] UNICEF has special initiatives dealing with HIV/AIDS, participation and rights of adolescent girls, tobacco-free youth, adolescent health and development, and school health, hygiene, and nutrition. It also initiates specific appeals to meet challenging crises. In 2003, for example, UNICEF undertook an appeal to deal with a series of overlapping and overwhelming crises in six southern African countries. Extreme poverty, a severe drought, HIV/AIDS, and an educational crisis have put more than 2.4 million children under the age of five and their more than 10 million family members in imminent risk of dying.

The reference to "family members" means that UNICEF focuses as much on women and mothers as on children. Underdevelopment is gendered in that females bear the brunt of poverty, according to UN and other statistics.[25] They are often denied adequate education and health care and are victims of various forms of discrimination. The exclusion of women from key decision-making positions and their lower political and social status have meant that women in underdeveloped countries constitute a "new global underclass."[26] UNICEF is confronting and trying to change this reality.

UNICEF is a full and active partner in the UN's sustainable human development efforts. A key focus in this regard is girls' education in the context of "education for every child," especially the "girl child." Education is seen as the path to empowerment. The agency's executive director has argued forcefully that "there can be no significant or sustainable transformation in societies and no significant reduction in poverty until girls receive the quality basic education they need to take their rightful place as equal partners in development."[27]

UNICEF led preparations for the 2002 UN General Assembly Special Session on Children, where member states adopted the Declaration and Plan of Action, "A World Fit for Children." It was intended to commit governments to a specific set of goals for youth and an associated timetable for achieving them. In May 2003, UNICEF issued its first report card on attaining those commitments. In the report, *The United Nations Special Session on Children: A First Anniversary Report on Follow-up*, the authors noted that "the world's attention and resources have been diverted to crises and war while pressing yet hidden challenges facing humankind—fighting HIV/AIDS, child illness and malnutrition, illiteracy and child abuse—have been sidelined." In 2003 when much of the world was focused on "regime change" in Iraq, UNICEF Executive Director Carol Bellamy voiced this criticism:

> The children of Iraq are important, but there are 2.1 billion children in this world, half of them living in abject poverty, 150 million who are malnourished, 120 million who never go to school, and 11 million who die from totally preventable causes every year. These are the things that governments must focus on with consistency and rigor.[28]

In the domain of child welfare, once again states endorse worthy goals and reiterate them, but they do not always follow up on the ground. As Bellamy said in 2003, "The global follow-up to last year's commitments has gone forward."[29] Yet, UNICEF reported that "most countries have barely begun to implement the targets, with only half of the world's governments even taking the first step of developing an action plan."[30] More promising is UNICEF's partnership work. In September 2007, the International Health Partnership was formed with six European states, UNICEF, the World Bank, and several other UN agencies to improve the delivery of health care to the neediest countries in Africa and Asia to help them meet the MDGs. This partnership promises to streamline the delivery of several complementary initiatives and encourage the efficient use of resources.[31]

More than most UN agencies reviewed here, UNICEF has sought to "mainstream" human rights considerations into its operations, tying itself increasingly to the Convention on the Rights of the Child. Whereas the agency used to see itself as a development and then also an emergency relief agency, it now sees itself as a human rights agency. The assumption is that using the discourse on children's rights will garner more support, and hence effectiveness, for its operations.[32]

Commission on Sustainable Development

Growing out of the Earth Summit in Rio de Janeiro in 1992, the CSD was given dual responsibilities for overseeing the implementation of the provisions of Agenda 21, the policy blueprint for the environment, and coordinating the sustainable development activities of the various organizations within the UN system.[33] Agreement did not readily follow, however, over many important details about how this new commission was to be empowered to fulfill its mandate effectively. Although CSD was assigned the role of being the primary mechanism within the UN system for coordinating sustainable development, its relationship to UNEP, the World Bank, and other intergovernmental entities was vaguely defined.

The CSD also has a mandate to strengthen and integrate the role of major societal groups and civic actors as effective participants in sustainable development decision-making at all levels. The text of Agenda 21 specifically addressed the roles of ten major groups: NGOs, indigenous peoples, local governments, workers, businesses, scientific communities, farmers, women, children, and youth. Exactly how this mandate for mainstreaming was to be institutionalized in practice, however, was left undefined. Only 18 NGOs were represented at the first CSD meeting, although ECOSOC had authorized the CSD to consider including all 1,400 NGOs represented at the Earth Summit. As recognized in both Agenda 21 and the Rio Declaration, fulfilling this mandate effectively is the fundamental cornerstone for successfully implementing sustainable development programs and practices. The mandate poses a challenge for the CSD as well as for the UN system and multilateral organizations more generally. Establishing an effective relationship between the sovereignty-based world of states and intergovernmental organizations with global civil society within which that interstate order exists was an elusive quest during the first sixty years of the UN's existence.[34]

Yet the CSD has served as a focal point for reviewing and assessing progress toward fulfilling Agenda 21 goals and objectives. In May 2003, the CSD decided to organize its multiyear program of work around two-year "implementation cycles," beginning in 2004–2005 and running to 2016–2017. Each work cycle is to focus on a specific cluster of topics and cross-cutting issues. For 2004–2005, for example, the thematic cluster included water, sanitation, and human settlements with a dozen cross-cutting issues: poverty eradication, changing unsustainable patterns of production and consumption, protecting and managing the natural resource base of economic and social development, sustainable development in a globalizing world, health and sustainable development, sustainable development of small island developing states (SIDS), sustainable development of Africa, other regional initiatives, means of implementation, institutional framework for sustainable development, gender equality, and education. The second two-year cycle focuses on energy, industrial development, air pollution, and climate change, with the same cross-cutting issues. Each two-year implementation

290 SUSTAINABLE HUMAN DEVELOPMENT

cycle includes a "Review Year," during which time progress toward implementing sustainable development goals will be assessed, and a "Policy Year," in which decisions will be made about how to speed up implementation and mobilize additional support.

The efficacy of the CSD remains an open question. The fifteenth session of the CSD in May 2007 proved contentious as delegates were unable to reach an agreement for implementing commitments, including target dates for increased energy efficiency and reducing air pollution. This session ended with no final outcome agreement as the compromise document was ultimately rejected by the European Union.[35] To complicate matters, CSD members elected Zimbabwe, an environmental and development disaster, to chair the commission for 2008, when its official inflation rate reached 100,000 percent. Viewed in a pessimistic light, Zimbabwe's election illustrates the hollow and hypocritical nature of the CSD. But, as *The Economist* rather cheekily noted, this odd choice might not necessarily be a bad thing. After all, "few things are more dull than a worthy cause run by a do-gooding country. It is a fair bet that if, say, Sweden or Canada were chairing the commission no one outside the aid industry would hear a squeak about its doings over the next year. Zimbabwe's stewardship, by contrast, will attract much scrutiny."[36] The principal goals behind creating the CSD were to enhance the integration of environment and development, to raise awareness, and to promote dialogue among the major actors.[37] Perhaps with Zimbabwe as chair, CSD activities will come under greater media attention, thereby raising awareness and perhaps even socialize egregious offenders to international norms regarding sustainable development.

UNEP

The UN Environment Programme was created in 1973 to serve as the UN's main mechanism for "policy review and coordination" on environmental issues, including those associated with development. Its Governing Council consists of fifty-eight members elected by the General Assembly, and it meets biennially and reports to the General Assembly through ECOSOC. Its main mandate is to encourage and coordinate environmental activities within the UN system. The work of the program is carried out through a modest secretariat headed by an executive director. The agency is based in Nairobi, Kenya, and is financed through the UN regular budget.

The UNEP, like the CSD, was assigned the function of forging interagency cooperation throughout the UN system to promote environmental protection. Since environmental concerns cut across virtually every conceivable area of human economic activity, this was indeed a broad mandate. The problem was, however, that neither UNEP nor CSD was given primary responsibility to take on operational functions that might interfere with the work of other organizations.

At the same time, both UNEP and CSD were superimposed on existing interorganizational systems. When UNEP was created, a number of UN agencies—

including UNESCO, FAO, WHO, and WMO—were already engaged in environmental work. In addition, several UNESCO-related scientific programs—including the International Oceanographic Commission, the International Hydrological Program, and the intergovernmental Man and the Biosphere project—either were functioning or were in the early stages of development. The CSD was dropped into an even more complex and somewhat chaotic multiorganizational system. Although it possessed the potential to serve as a complement to the coordination work of UNEP, the history of international organizations would seem to suggest that CSD was just as likely to act as a fierce competitor.

The process of system-wide interagency coordination in eco-development evolved slowly through trial and error. In UNEP's early years, a comprehensive procedure for system-wide review, called joint programming, was adopted. Interagency discussions focused on selected environmental topics, the objective of which was to identify gaps in existing knowledge and practices and to design strategies to fill them. Over the years, these exercises expanded from bilateral to multilateral thematic programming.

Perhaps UNEP's most important role is generating international norms and setting standards to protect the human environment rather than concrete projects to help improve air quality or protect forests or enforce norms on the books. The agency has played an instrumental role in the negotiation and adoption of a number of major international environmental conventions, including the Vienna Convention for the Protection of the Ozone Layer, the Convention on Climate Change, and the Convention on Biodiversity. More recently, UNEP consultations in Nairobi cautioned that biofuels, such as corn-based ethanol, were not a panacea for climate change and oil scarcity and could actually exacerbate food insecurity while not significantly reducing greenhouse gas emissions or energy costs.[38] Although UNEP does administer certain environmental projects, it is not primarily a project-executing agency in the sense of most other UN specialized agencies. Also, UNEP is not a source of financing—unlike UNDP, the World Bank group, and other multilateral funding agencies. It does, however, disperse modest funds through its Environment Fund. However, the waters surrounding its somewhat confused mandate have been muddied further with the creation of the CSD and still more overlapping functions.

Effective project implementation requires coordination at the operational level in the field. Although UNEP itself does not execute country programs, it cooperates with numerous other organizations in overseeing the implementation of projects that are supported by the UNEP Environment Fund. Many of these projects are executed by "cooperating agencies" (that is, UN system agencies and bodies), primarily FAO, UNESCO, WHO, WMO, and UNCHS (UN Center for Human Settlements, or Habitat). Other resources from this fund support project implementation by other intergovernmental organizations, NGOs, research institutions, and other civic-based bodies (referred to in UNEP as supporting organizations). When projects also include UNDP sources, the resident coordinator in the country serves as the primary point person for orchestrating the UN system's environmental activities in the field. Still, according to the UN Panel on System-Wide Coherence, UNEP relations with other UN agencies, especially UNDP, remain chaotic, which further complicates efforts to improve UNEP's country-level integration without duplicating UNDP fieldwork.[39]

This overlapping jurisdiction on coordination adds a significant degree of complexity and ambiguity to UNEP's functions. The trend toward greater decentralization, regionalism, and involvement of civic-based entities in global governance complicates the already problematic task of making the UN function coherently, for the environment as for other substantive areas. In addition to dwindling funds, a number of major donor governments, including the United States, preferred to bypass UNEP regarding financial matters. In such a position, UNEP remains a technical agency concentrating largely on environmental monitoring and assessment. The importance of this role is seen with UNEP's coordination of scientific information on ozone depletion effectively becoming an expert lobby backing up diplomatic efforts to produce broad and binding agreement.[40]

So what can UNEP reasonably be expected to accomplish? The short answer is very little, certainly in comparison with the sweeping challenges of its mandate. The task of coordinating the environmental activities of the diverse array of institutional actors and arrangements is a conundrum. Many UN bodies are legally and practically autonomous; many of them were active in environmental work before the formation of UNEP and have access to far more significant technical and financial resources. Once again, the UN appears as the logical choice for coordination, but UNEP has neither the authority nor the organizational wherewithal to coordinate the globe's network of institutions. An important role that UNEP fills in the development area is to remind us that over the years the concepts of development and environment became fused in the global development debate into "eco-development," which provides important insight on UN agencies' approaches to sustainable human development. Moreover, as a kind of global "lobbyist," its role has been substantial in helping to move states toward acceptance of important treaties, such as the Montreal Protocol to the Vienna Convention for the protection of the ozone. In an attempt to capture more of a leadership role, in October 2008 UNEP called for a "Global Green New Deal" and launched the Green Economic Initiative (GEI). Secretary-General Ban Ki-moon reiterated the call at the UN Climate Change Conference in Poznan, Poland, in December 2008. GEI is a medium- to long-term strategy to deal with environmental problems and promote sustainable development. An interesting element of GEI is the Green Jobs Initiative, which is a partnership program in cooperation with the ILO, the International Trade Union Confederation (ITUC), and the International Organization of Employers to create jobs that reduce carbon emissions.

Other UN Agencies and Their Roles in Eco-Development

UNESCO began in the 1960s with a wide variety of other environmental concerns that cut across its main areas of competence—science, education, culture, and communications. Of course, these areas are very much key to development, however defined. In 1965, a ten-year program, the International Hydrological Decade, was launched to promote the study of hydrological resources, including water pollution. This early environmental focus was strengthened with the hosting of the Biosphere Conference, the 1970 Helsinki Interdisciplinary Symposium on Man's Role in Changing His Environment, and the 1972 Convention Concerning the Protection of the World Cultural and Natural Heritage. UNESCO has been responsible for creating a number of affiliated bodies, such as the International Oceanographic Commission (IOC). This particular body has been important in promoting international marine scientific research with special emphasis on pollution prevention. Since the late 1980s, the UNESCO secretariat in Paris has emphasized coordination of the environmentally related activities and programs within its various divisions. It has been actively involved in follow-up activities to the 1992 UNCED and the implementation of a variety of related agreements.

For many years, UNESCO has had a special relationship with the International Council of Scientific Unions (ICSU) and with its member unions in the environmental area. The ICSU is an NGO comprising scientific academies, research councils, and scientific unions. It facilitates and coordinates the work of large international research programs, such as the International Biological Programme (IBP) and the International Geosphere-Biosphere Programme (IGBP). In 1969 the Scientific Committee on Problems of the Environment (SCOPE) was established within the ICSU. This committee has been responsible for reviewing information on the implications of human-induced environmental change. Two decades later, in 1989, the Advisory Committee on the Environment was created to provide counsel to the ICSU Executive Board on all ICSU activities related to the environment and global climate change and to provide a link with external bodies in this regard.

In addition to UNESCO, most other agencies within the UN system have operational mandates linked to eco-development. The environmental relationships of some of these bodies are more obvious and more direct than others. Most, if not all, of the work of the World Meteorological Organization, for instance, focuses on eco-development. Its broad, heavily scientific mandate includes atmospheric pollution, meteorological aspects of water pollution, climate change, the effects of pollution on climate change and vegetation, and the relationship between climate, weather, and agricultural practices. Along with the IOC and ICSU, the WMO cosponsors the World Climate Research Programme (WCRP). This joint initiative examines the dynamic aspects of the earth's climate system and stands as a counterpart to the IGBP, which studies biological and chemical aspects of global change.

The work of the World Health Organization, at its Geneva headquarters and in the field, focuses broadly on the relationship between human beings and their environments with regard to their health ramifications.[41] This institution is concerned with controlling environmental pollution in all forms as well as all other environmental factors that affect health. The agency undertakes pollution surveys and initiates programs for improving methods for measuring pollution and for designing programs for pollution abatement and control. Just as UNICEF has taken more of a human rights approach to its concern for children around the world, so WHO has been trying to get states to view adequate health and health care as a human right. WHO has undertaken a major effort to reduce the use of tobacco in its various forms and has come close to facilitating in many countries a ban similar to those in effect in Europe and many U.S. states. Here again we see part of the UN system collecting and disseminating scientific information, then trying to advance ideas based on that knowledge—in this case to improve health. WHO has led the international community frontline response to emerging deadly diseases such as SARS, a rare but deadly respiratory disease, the avian (bird) flu, and the H1N1 flu virus (a form of the swine flu). The avian flu is of particular concern because it has a high mortality rate when it infects humans. Fearing a worldwide pandemic, WHO has been instrumental in tracking and isolating the deadly virus and in educating governments about it. Similarly, WHO has taken the lead in addressing the H1N1 flu, declaring a pandemic in June 2009. While the initial outbreak has proven relatively mild to those infected, WHO and governments are coordinating national and international responses should the H1N1 virus become more lethal.

The FAO has an array of activities on eco-development based both at its headquarters in Rome and in its operational projects. They include sustainable water management through water harvesting, agriculture investment, radioactive contamination, contamination of food by pesticides, and marine pollution related to fisheries. The agency works to establish criteria for water quality management, soil and water resource management, pesticide control, fisheries management, and general control of pollution. Several important environmental conventions fall under FAO auspices, including the International Convention for the Conservation of Atlantic Tunas, the FAO International Code of Conduct on the Distribution and Use of Pesticides, and the Code of Conduct for Responsible Fisheries.

Marine pollution is important to the work of the International Maritime Organization (IMO), established in 1948 as the Intergovernmental Maritime Consultative Organization. At the heart of this agency's work in London are concerns about legal liability and the rights of parties to seek redress from pollution by ships and equipment operating in marine areas, as well as how to prevent such pollution. Over the years, the agency has promoted more than two dozen international conventions and protocols, ranging from the International Convention for the Prevention of Pollution at Sea by Oil in 1959 to the International Convention on Oil Pollution Preparedness Response and Cooperation in 1990. In fulfilling its environment-related mandate, the IMO has maintained close working relations with UNEP, FAO, ILO, the United Nations Commission on International Trade Law, UNCTAD, and WHO, as well as the International Union for the Conservation of Nature and National Resources (IUCN, also known as the World Conservation Union), the International Chamber of Shipping, and various other nongovernmental organizations.

The eco-development work of some UN agencies often may not be obvious. The International Civil Aviation Organization, for example, deals with aircraft noise pollution from its headquarters in Montreal. The ILO has an interest in the impact of various forms of pollution on the working environment. Of course the ILO, as noted in Chapter 6, tries to ensure that the pursuit of economic growth is accompanied by attention to labor rights. Environmental concerns related to the peaceful uses of nuclear energy, such as radioactive waste management, fall within the realm of the International Atomic Energy Agency.

One of the most important international environmental organizations is the hybrid IUCN. It comprises states, governmental agencies, and international and national NGOs. Although possessing only a small secretariat, it conducts a remarkably wide range of activities through numerous standing commissions and committees. The IUCN helped forge the conceptual link between development and environment. With the World Wide Fund for Nature and UNEP, and in association with FAO and UNESCO, the IUCN launched the World Conservation Strategy in 1980. As a precursor to sustainable development, this initiative set forth principles promoting the sustainable use of the earth's living resources.

Global environmental norms have spread through international conventions and declarations.[42] An extensive codification of international environmental law dealing with marine pollution, for example, has come about in this way since the late 1960s. As discussed, the IMO has played an instrumental role in developing an international maritime pollution regime, with important contributions also coming from UNEP and the multiyear negotiations of the Third United Nations Conference on the Law of the Sea.

Additionally, the Global Environmental Facility provides grants to developing countries for environment-related projects and facilitates networking and cooperation among donors. It operates in four main issue areas—protection of the ozone layer, international waters, biodiversity, and climate change—and is charged with working with other UN agencies, regional development banks, and bilateral donors in integrated technical assistance and investment projects. This limited coordination role has been complemented in recent years by the work of the Joint Consultative Group on Policy. This body has organized collaborative efforts among five other UN agencies: UNDP, UNFPA, UNICEF, WFP, and the International Fund for Agricultural Development. Despite such attempts to engender cooperation and undertake coordination within and among the diverse field of actors in this issue arena, fragmentation abounds.

Yet the quest for interorganizational coherence continues. In October 2007, the UN Chief Executives Board initiated the UN Climate Neutral Strategy, which is a system-wide effort to diminish each organization's greenhouse gas emissions. Under this initiative, UN agencies are required to adopt an integrated and comprehensive environmental management approach; implement measures to reduce greenhouse gas emissions; prepare and communicate regular reports of their emissions inventory, together with any targets or goals for emissions reductions; and document initiatives, data, lessons learned, and best practices. The aim of the strategy is to lead by example and create a new pro-green organizational culture. It covers procurement, renovation, construction, facilities management, and field operations. It encompasses five focus areas (reducing emissions from deforestation and forest degradation, technology transfer, finance, capacity building, and adaptation) and four cross-cutting areas (scientific assessment, monitoring, and warning; support of global, regional, and national action; public awareness; and a climate-neutral UN).

The UN Climate Neutral Strategy illustrates how important it is to understand what happens in the formal structures and informal behavior of individual UN organizations. A proper evaluation of particular UN actors requires that we broaden our focus to acknowledge a cumulative impact through joint undertakings. As Robert Keohane, who some believe is the world's most influential international relations scholar, has concluded, it is very difficult to say with precision why any particular international organization succeeds or fails.[43] In the final analysis, what is important is the collective impact of the UN system in promoting sustainable human development and human security. In this regard, the story is not complete without incorporating the work of the World Bank, the IMF, and the WTO.

THE WORLD BANK, IMF, AND WTO

For most of the UN's existence the Washington-based international financial institutions functioned almost completely autonomously from the UN proper, as noted above. In many depictions of the so-called UN system, including in Appendix A, dotted lines connected to the World Bank and International Monetary Fund suggesting their independent status. The Geneva-based WTO is vaguely designated a "related" UN organization and does not even have a dotted line. In terms of resources, however, these organizations are the vehicles through which member states have chosen to pursue development defined as increases in GDP, imports-exports, and industrialization. Hence, the bulk of their financing for development is largely geared toward promoting macro-economic growth, albeit with the assumption that such market-oriented growth can enhance the ability of individuals to meet their basic human needs and promote the efficient use of resources, thereby protecting the environment. In this section, we briefly review the development strategies of the World Bank, IMF, and WTO and conclude with the international efforts to coordinate the work of the UN proper with these very important vehicles for pursuing sustainable human development.

The World Bank

The World Bank comprises the International Bank for Reconstruction and Development (IBRD) and four associated agencies or affiliates: IFC, IDA, MIGA, and ICSID.[44] The IBRD functions like a traditional bank and was created at the 1944 conference at the Bretton Woods resort in New Hampshire to help rebuild Europe after World War II. Its funding comes from states as well as financing raised on open capital markets. The first affiliate, the International Finance Corporation (IFC), was created in 1956 to encourage private investment in developing countries. Its principal strategy centers on providing seed money for business ventures and domestic infrastructure, which can then attract domestic investment and foreign direct investment by multinational corporations. The IFC also created its own International Securities Group (ISG) to advise developing states on creating a domestic stock market and helping local businesses to issue stock and list their stock on the major exchanges. The IBRD and the IFC are clearly wedded to economic development in a neoliberal sense; however, they also consider environmental impacts of proposed projects and assist states in preparing loan requests with an eye toward sustainable development.

In 1960, the International Development Agency (IDA) was created to help alleviate poverty by providing soft loans to the poorest of the poor. Soft loans are loans that are made at cost, at extremely low interest rates, and have an unusually long repayment period. In 1988, the Multilateral Investment Guarantee Agency (MIGA) was created to help war-torn and/or extremely impoverished states, not by making loans or investments, but by insuring private investors against loss. Through this insurance program, private investment in high-risk states can be encouraged. Finally, the International Centre for Settlement of Investment Disputes (ICSID) was created by treaty in 1965. It serves as an impartial forum for resolving international investment disputes among its 143 members. These latter affiliates demonstrate that the Bank is aware of the special situation of extremely poor and post-conflict societies; however, the Bank still prefers to devote a significant portion of its resources to encourage market-based, private solutions.

The World Bank experienced a crisis of leadership in the first decade of the twenty-first century. President Paul Wolfowitz, a former Pentagon neoconservative supported by the Bush administration, left office in 2007 under a cloud of nepotistic allegations relating to his companion's employment at the World Bank. Since anticorruption is a cornerstone of World Bank lending, this made its work more difficult under the current president, Robert Zoellick, the former U.S. trade representative to the WTO. A special commission headed by Paul Volcker, the former head of the U.S. Federal Reserve, recommended that the World Bank work on improving its relations with developing countries and examine its own corruption before pushing its anticorruption agenda on developing states. Thus, the multilateral institution that receives and distributes the lion's share of multilateral development assistance was put on the defensive.

Although Zoellick began his tenure under the cloud of his predecessor, governments were more than willing to move ahead quickly and put the divisiveness and bitterness of the Wolfowitz years behind them. Under Zoellick, the World Bank has improved its relations with many members of the global South through a number of measures. It defended the eligibility of middle-income states, such as India and China, to development loans. The Bank also provided assistance to developing countries experiencing food shortages because of the global spike in commodity prices in 2007–2008, partially reflecting the fact that land was being diverted for crops that could be used for biofuels (competitive because of increasing oil prices). The World Bank began stressing development programs that would help states achieve a measure of domestic food security even if it was cheaper and more efficient to import food in the long run.

The IMF

The IMF was also created at the Bretton Woods conference to handle the UN system of national accounts and help attenuate currency fluctuations and balance-of-payments problems in the international monetary system based on fixed exchange rates (which in part explains its de facto independence from the UN).[45] Over time, and with the collapse of the fixed exchange rate system in the 1970s, the IMF reinvented itself as the "lender of last resort." This means that the IMF's role in development has been that of a crisis troubleshooter because it provides financial assistance to otherwise un-creditworthy states. Such states usually experience an economic crisis that also involves a run on their currency, greatly reducing its value. During these kinds of crises, the IMF will work with states and the World Bank to put together loan packages designed to stabilize currency values and stave off economic catastrophe. However, the loan packages come with strings attached, namely conditions designed to fundamentally change the underlying conditions that, in theory, gave rise to the crisis in the first place. These structural adjustment loans involve requiring states to implement market reforms, privatize government-owned industries, and reduce government deficits.

The IMF and its structural adjustment loans have other critics, on the Left and the right. On the left, critics claim that structural adjustment loans increase poverty and the costs of restructuring the economy are borne by the poor, especially poor women. These critics also claim that Bank and IMF SAPs (structural adjustment programs) reinforce authoritarian government, in that only repressive governments can carry out the unpopular cost-cutting programs. For instance, Naomi Klein argues that much structural reform had nothing to do with the origins of some economic problems but was an attempt to advance the ideology of market capitalism.[46] On the right, the IMF is interventionist, bailing out states and investors making high-risk and, ultimately, poor choices. Bailouts like the national ones begun in 2008–2009 could have the effect of rewarding bad behavior, and the same type of reasoning applies internationally. At the same time, governments cannot sit idly by while an economy crashes or the financial system implodes. Most governments and international financial institutions (IFIs) tend to be pragmatic rather than dogmatic in selecting economic policy tools.

Regardless of the criticism, the IMF remains the only mechanism to coordinate multilateral responses to monetary crises. In an interesting twist of fortune, both the IMF and, to a lesser extent, the World Bank are facing an identity crisis.[47] According to the IMF's managing director, Dominique Strauss-Khan, "What might be at stake today is the very existence of the I.M.F. as a major institution providing financial stability to the world, a global public good. . . . In sum, the two main issues are relevance and legitimacy."[48] With globalization and massive financial transfers occurring daily, the IMF can no longer handle a financial crisis like that in Asia in the late 1990s or Argentina at the start of the twenty-first century, let alone the one under way in 2009; and the states it assisted in the 1990s have, for the most, only partially repaid loans. However, relations between those states have soured given the heavy-handed approach of IMF structural adjustment programs. Former managing director Rodrigo de Rato argues that the IMF should promote transparency, monitor currency manipulations, and otherwise monitor the global economy as well as provide technical assistance in monetary matters.[49] Moreover, the IMF, like the other development-related agencies, is also facing staff and budget cuts.

The IMF and the World Bank are significantly challenged by the ongoing global financial crisis. In November 2008, European leaders sought to hold a major conference seen by many as "Bretton Woods II" whereby the IMF and World Bank would be reformed to address the financial challenges of the twenty-first century. The Bush administration resisted any initiative that would lead to a global financial management scheme but then called a meeting of the G20 in Washington because the smaller G7 or G8 did not include either the largest potential creditors or sources of possible growth. At the end of 2008, states were addressing the financial crisis unilaterally with very limited multilateral coordination anywhere, even in Europe. As such, the World Bank and the IMF basically watched from the sidelines, doing little other than issuing alarming indicators of the world economy's future performance.

The WTO

Trade and development are linked in that trade brings the goods, services, and technology necessary for economic growth and increased standards of living. Moreover, trade promotes the efficient use of resources contributing to sustainability. The development success stories are those of trade-related, export-led growth. In 1995, the WTO was created, as the last order of business of the

Uruguay round of the GATT to help overcome several problematic trade issues. While the GATT had been quite successful at reducing tariffs, duties, and quotas on manufactured goods, it could not deal with emerging new protectionist measures (known as nontariff barriers or NTBs) and had little success in liberalizing the agricultural and services sectors of the world economy. Also important to many trading states was the Agreement on Trade-Related Aspects of Intellectual Property Rights (TRIPS) and rules regarding trade-related investment measure (TRIMS). The WTO was created to help member states overcome their differences on these issues through consensus-based rule-making and the Dispute Settlement Panel (DSP), a mechanism through which disputes can be authoritatively decided (by neutral trade experts) and trade rules enforced. While DSPs stipulate what trade practices are in accord with WTO rules (or not), it is states that decide whether to impose sanctions—ironically such as higher tariffs—against those whole policies have been held to violate the rules.

The differences among member states on trade issues are real and sometimes intractable because free trade may bring many benefits that are distributed unevenly between and within societies. Free trade also brings many problems as local businesses and industries can be threatened and workers can be displaced. This makes it very difficult for states in the global South, and to a lesser extent the global North, to ensure the basic human needs of their people and stable sustainable economic growth. Hence, reaching consensus on trade rules has proven difficult and contentious. The 1999 anti-globalization protests at the ministerial meeting in Seattle in part was about the WTO making trade rules without the input of environmental, labor, and human rights groups and the concern that state regulations protecting the environment, labor, and human rights would be undermined by WTO decisions. And as we discuss in Chapter 11, the most recent round of WTO trade negotiations, called the Doha Round, has yet to yield any significant trade agreements because of the North-South divide on trade priorities and rules.

Building Bridges

The World Bank, the IMF, and the WTO, on the one hand, and the UN proper, on the other hand, are supposed to be promoting sustainable human development, albeit using different rationales and means. This represents a change over time and under pressure,[50] and critics still have their doubts as to the exact impact.[51]

Needless to say, coordination among these different development mechanisms is not all it could be. Kofi Annan's "Quiet Revolution" sought to redress this situation and bring the UN, the international financial institutions, and the WTO into closer working relations.[52] The subject is immensely important, beyond just budgets and finances. A greater integration of the IFIs, the WTO, and the UN proper is necessary for policy coherence. The World Bank, especially in regard to a narrow and rather technical approach to economic growth, leaves out many important human aspects of the development process.[53] At the same time, the UN system manifests a broader and coherent development rationale through the MDGs. The IMF may use structural adjustment programs to reform a state's economy, but UNICEF knows how to put a human face on such conditionality.[54]

One important initiative for improving cooperation, communication, and coordination has been the revitalization of the Administrative Committee on Coordination by transforming it into a Chief Executive Board for Coordination. Beginning in 1998, a new spirit of cooperation emerged between the United Nations and the Bretton Woods institutions under the leadership of Secretary-General Kofi Annan and then World Bank president James Wolfensohn.[55] Given the history of noncooperation between the IFIs and the UN system, this was quite extraordinary. In 2002, the General Assembly decided to host a special high-level meeting among representatives of the World Bank, IMF, WTO, and civil society to evaluate progress made since the International Conference on Financing Development, held earlier that year in Monterrey, Mexico.[56] In April 2003, ECOSOC convened another high-level meeting to discuss policy coherence in implementing the Monterrey Commitments. For the first time, the WTO was participating as an active partner.

In this context, the director of the WTO, managing director of the IMF, and president of the World Bank made a joint plea to the Group of 8. The G8, or the "club" of the richest seven industrialized countries in the West, were formerly known as the G7 but were joined by Russia beginning in mid-2003.[57] Since then, the need to include such other important players as China and India increases the number after the "G," with the current next likely figure being the G20, which met in Washington in late 2008 and in London in 2009.

Earlier, these international officials called upon the industrialized countries to provide the political guidance and follow-through on commitments that are needed to move trade negotiations and the development agenda forward.[58] So far, however, the G8 has demonstrated little collective leadership and guidance in this regard. And voices have been raised in some important circles arguing that the Bank now has such a broad agenda that its programs are unwieldy; consequently, so the argument runs, the Bank should get back to basics.[59]

Despite promising steps toward integration and cooperation and despite rhetoric coming from Washington about the need for greater attention to the "softer" sides of development, the UN, the IFIs, and the WTO still primarily reflect different views as to the causes of underdevelopment and poverty and the appropriate strategy for tackling these difficult issues. The United Nations tends to have a Keynesian approach that requires a relatively strong role for the state in promoting development and eliminating poverty, while the IMF/World Bank tends to be more skeptical of state solutions, opting for markets and private initiatives instead. Given the nature of the largely unilateral U.S. response to the global economic and financial crisis that began in 2008, which has injected the state deeply into the economy, it will be interesting to observe the effects that this approach to the ongoing crisis may have on the Bank and the Fund.

What is important to remember here is that the UN has been instrumental in developing a reasonably coherent framework to fight poverty and promote human development through its agenda-setting and coordination activities. Perhaps most important is its role in creating norms and developing ideas that actors can agree upon (relatively speaking) given competing world views about the causes of, and therefore the solutions to, poverty and underdevelopment.

NORM CREATION AND COHERENCE: A HISTORY OF IDEAS

The consensual framework of sustainable human development is the product of extensive multilateral development diplomacy and related institutional processes of recent decades and especially the global, ad hoc conferences of the 1990s that are chronicled in Table 10.1. Building on the activities of the UN's first three development decades (1960–1989), international conversations since the end of the Cold War have transformed the global development debate and UN discourse in general. The 2000 Millennium Summit and the 2005 World Summit represent just two—albeit two very important—links in a growing chain of multilateral global conferences and activities focusing on development-related issues and problems.[60]

Capacity building, good governance, and popular participation are all essential ingredients for promoting sustainability. The MDGs lie at the center of this global development agenda. They have been commonly accepted throughout the UN system, and by the IFIs, as a framework for guiding development policies and assessing progress. They are viewed as being mutually reinforcing with the overarching objective being the reduction of poverty and encouragement of sustainable human development. In the following section we review how the international community has arrived at the current synthesis of understanding "development" as sustainable human development.

From Stockholm to Rio de Janeiro

The process of norm creation began three decades ago in Stockholm with the United Nations Conference on the Human Environment. During the preparations for this conference, experts in Founex, Switzerland, led by then-UNCHE secretary-general Maurice Strong probed the concept of eco-development, thereby integrating development and the environment. The Club of Rome and others had also put forward similar notions, although these largely intellectual exercises did not carry the same force or impact as the Founex report.[61] Under Strong's leadership, the participants were able to bridge some important political divides, in particular the clash of priorities between developing countries in pursuit of economic growth and developed countries concerned about conservation of natural resources. The clash was captured by India's prime minister, Indira Gandhi, who opened the Stockholm conference by arguing that in developing countries "poverty is the greatest polluter."[62] By arguing that long-term development was necessary to combat the poverty that contributed to pollution but that such growth also depended on dealing with shorter-term environmental problems, Strong was able to bridge the divergent North-South divide. He also suggested that the governments of industrialized countries help defray the costs of environmental protection that developing countries would be forced to bear. The concept of "additionality," meaning to increase resources in order to apply them to a new problem rather than to subtract them from another use, helped overcome skepticism in the South over global economic inequities.[63]

Two decades later, the issues were revisited. In 1987, the Brundtland Commission, created by the General Assembly in 1983 to intellectually bridge the divide between economic growth and environmental protection, reframed the solution to the conflict as "sustainable development." This in turn fed into the preparations for and activities surrounding the 1992 UN Conference on Environment and Development (UNCED), also known as the Earth Summit, to be held in Rio de Janeiro. The Earth Summit far exceeded almost all normal conceptions of a conference, as did the extensive documentation.[64] The Rio process was massive. In addition to the intergovernmental conference, which incorporated a summit meeting of heads of state or government during its final days, the Rio gathering included a series of related events, unparalleled in scope and sponsored by civic-based entities that together were referred to as the Global Forum. These parallel activities drew tens of thousands of participants and an estimated 200,000 onlookers. A record number of national governmental delegations attended the Earth Summit, and some 1,400 NGOs with approximately 18,000 participants were at the parallel Global Forum.

The "road to Rio," then, was arduous.[65] Participants were engaged in the preparatory process almost continuously for three years. Maurice Strong, who after twenty years was selected to serve again as secretary-general of the conference secretariat, repeated what he had said about UNCHE, namely that in many important respects "the process was the policy."[66] The process of building consensus was regarded by many participants as being just as important an outcome of UNCED as any set of declarations, treaties, or other specific products. However, that process was not always an easy one, and the end products were not satisfactory to a majority of the participants. After three years of laborious and often tedious negotiations, for example, the specification of timetables, qualitative and quantitative targets, and acceptable limits still eluded negotiators as they rushed to finalize agreement on the conventions, statements of principles, and plan of action.

The North-South tensions so evident in many aspects of UN diplomacy were, not surprisingly, evident in the sustainability debated and continue today. Southern governments were skeptical of the Northern push to impose ecological imperatives on the global development agenda. From their perspective, ozone depletion, hazardous waste pollution, and global climate change were products

Brazilian president Collor de Mello acknowledges the applause of world leaders
after he formally closes the UN Conference on Environment and Development in
June 1992. (UN Photo 180108/T. Prendergast)

of industrialization and overconsumption in the North, but suddenly the new
priority to protect the environment was to come at the expense of development
in the South. Cooperation from developing countries was conditioned on the
North's willingness to pay the bill for at least part of its past environmental sins.
If the North wants the active partnership of the South in redressing these problems, Northern donor governments should make available additional financial
and technical resources.

These North-South tensions were brought into particularly sharp focus during the debate over deforestation. Southern negotiators, led by the Brazilians, In-
dians, and Malaysians—in an echo of what we heard earlier when sovereignty
was under siege in the security and human rights arenas—forcefully resisted any
incursion into the principle of sovereignty over natural resources. Similarly, tensions prevailed in drafting the Rio Declaration, which was to guide governments
and nongovernmental actors in implementing the many provisions of Agenda
21. With its unmistakable flavor of compromise between negotiators from industrialized countries and developing ones, this declaration integrated many of
the most important elements of the development and environment perspectives
of both sides. Even as the rights to exploit resources within a state's geographical
boundaries were reaffirmed, the responsibility of states to exercise control over
environmentally damaging activities within their boundaries also was pro-

claimed. In addition, among the twenty-seven principles embodied in the declaration was one stating that the cost of pollution should be borne at the source and should be reflected in product cost at all stages of production.

Two legally binding international conventions—on biodiversity and on climate change—were incorporated as part of the larger Rio process. The Convention on Biodiversity requires signatories to pursue economic development in such a way as to preserve existing species and ecosystems. The Convention on Climate Change embodies a general set of principles and obligations aimed at reducing greenhouse gases. Due largely to the intransigent position of the first Bush administration during the negotiation process, formal intergovernmental negotiations over the creation of these two legal conventions proved to be difficult to finalize. The final documents emerging from the Earth Summit represented "framework conventions." Although these conventions designated general principles and obligations, specific timetables and targets were left unspecified and subject to future negotiations over protocols—that is, additional treaties.

Agenda 21 comprised more than six hundred pages and covered a large gamut of issues. Although most of this text was agreed to before UNCED, a number of contentious items were carried to the Earth Summit itself. In keeping with the general tenor of debates, problems included issues related to biodiversity, biotechnology, deforestation, and institutional and procedural issues involving financing, technology transfer, and institutional arrangements for carrying out the elements of the action agenda.

A number of these issues proved to be intractable and remained unresolved at the close of UNCED. Foremost among them was how to generate the financial resources needed to implement the program of action and associated activities. Estimates varied; the calculations made by the UNCED secretariat put the price tag at well over $100 billion per year for the first decade alone. These figures reflected the massive scope of the components inherent in the marriage between development and environment as they had come together within the Rio process.

Linked to the issue of financing was governance. At the core is the question: Who decides when and how such resources are to be spent? As the negotiations during the Rio process clearly revealed, some minimal basic agreement about governance is a prerequisite for agreement over financing. Again, North-South tensions fueled the debate. The northern negotiators, led by Washington, pressed to have all such financing channeled through the World Bank Group. In that setting, the locus of control would be well established, with the G8 possessing effective veto power. Also, the World Bank and the IMF tended to approach environmental protection through markets. The Global Environment Facility was in place and might be expanded to encompass a broader mandate.

This proposed solution, however, was not acceptable to most southern participants, who preferred what they called a "more democratic" arrangement. These governments proposed the creation of a new "green fund," which would operate on more egalitarian voting principles. Most major northern donors found this proposal wholly unacceptable. For them to commit significant levels of funding, some guarantee of control was required. A compromise was achieved to enhance the South's participation while retaining for donor states elements of control. Interim financing for Agenda 21 implementation would be provided under the aegis of the World Bank Group. The GEF would be expanded and its rules altered to provide for decision-making by consensus among equally represented groupings of donors and recipients. The governance issue has, at least temporarily, been put to rest. But the matter of securing the requisite financial resources remains problematic, with only a very small fraction of the necessary funds actually committed to date.

Beyond Rio

In the years immediately following the Earth Summit, two overriding challenges arose. The first was how to generate and sustain effective cooperation. This problem had both horizontal and vertical dimensions. Effective cooperation would be required horizontally across different autonomous organizational domains, legal jurisdictions, and sectors of society as well as vertically across different levels of social aggregation, from individuals in their roles in groups and communities to representative governance in international forums.

The second challenge was how to reorient UN discourse and practice to overcome the constraints inherent in the organization's legal foundations in state sovereignty. The UN's involvement in eco-development rejoins our earlier treatment of its activities in international peace and security and human rights matters. They all highlight the limits of working with a system circumscribed by the concept of sovereignty. The foundations of the UN Charter, especially Article 2 (7), and the institutional structures and practices of multilateral diplomacy, constrain attempts to incorporate nonstate and market actors into a full partnership in global policy processes.

These challenges seem forbidding, but as the heads of government at Rio pointed out, the costs of not rising to the challenge could be perilous. As they warned in the preamble of Agenda 21, "Humanity stands at a defining moment in history. We are confronted with a perpetuation of disparities between and within nations, a worsening of poverty, hunger, ill health and illiteracy, and the continuing deterioration of the ecosystems on which we depend for our well-being." The Agenda 21 text argues that only by creating global partnerships and involving all sectors of world society can the world's peoples expect "the fulfillment of basic needs, improved living standards for all, better-protected and better-managed ecosystems and a safer, more prosperous future." Creating the necessary global partnerships on an unprecedented scale will, in turn, require meeting the twin challenges of cooperating effectively and moving beyond the confines of sovereignty. Before exploring the nature and scope of those challenges, however, we need a better understanding of the dynamic interplay of the forces and tensions that have given shape to the contemporary discourse and practice of sustainable development.

The debate over sustainable development places people-centered development at the core of the UN's work—even if the Bank, the Fund, and the WTO are generally thought to contribute less to this concept than they should.[67] This was also the case in respect to issues such as population, human settlements, health, food, and women. This shifting focus was captured in the names of special organizational campaigns, programmatic slogans, and conference titles reflected in Table 10.1. This evolving emphasis on people-centered development was given enhanced visibility through the reports of a series of special high-level, independent global commissions comprising eminent persons, which had begun with the Pearson Commission in 1969 but shifted away from an almost exclusive focus on governments and economic development toward engaging other actors in the work of the world organization. We have spoken about the three most prominent recent ones—on global governance (1995), intervention and state sovereignty (2001), and human security (2003)—as essential contributions to the normative climate, and in each of them the third UN played an essential role.[68]

The role sustainable development played in traversing the turf and ideological divide that otherwise separates actors in the global arena provides insight about the future of the UN's development work. In the Rio process and beyond, sustainability has served as an important bridge in institutional bargaining. The associated political processes have been characterized by bargaining among autonomous and self-interested participants striving for consensus. Operating under a veil of uncertainty about the likely effects of their alternative choices, participants engage in transnational alliance formation and politics that link issues. Many may be associated with specific communities of knowledge, but the political process is a pluralistic one in which groups of participants perceive and act on differing perceptions of problems, values, interests, and stakes.

Despite numerous difficulties, the general ideas articulated at Rio on behalf of sustainable development increasingly took hold. In the mid-1990s the UNDP/UNFPA Executive Board decision 94/14 adopted "sustainable human development" as a new mission for technical assistance. Like other development concepts before it, sustainable human development was viewed as a prerequisite for creating and maintaining a secure and peaceful world order. The barrage of political discourse over development in the 1990s led most member states to expect the UN to play a meaningful role in realizing such a goal.

The decade of the 1990s witnessed an almost continuous negotiating process. As is obvious from Table 10.1, member states were constantly involved in, preparing for, or actually attending a major international social-economic gathering. And this became especially the case when planning follow-up sessions at five- and ten-year intervals. But conferencing was not the only significant process. In the early years of his administration, Secretary-General Boutros Boutros-Ghali and his top staff argued that the UN should concentrate on issues in which it had the comparative advantage. From this perspective, development assistance, which is much broader than critical-aid programs and which substitutes environmentally degrading practices for sustainable ones, should be left to the

308

TABLE 10.1   Chronology of Selected Development-Related Conferences,
1990–2005

1990 — World Summit for Children (WSC)
Second World Climate Conference
World Conference on Education for All
Second UN Conference on the Least Developed Countries

1992 — UN Conference on Environment and Development (UNCED)
International Conference on Nutrition

1993 — UNCTAD VIII: Eighth Session of the Conference on Trade and Development

1994 — Global Conference on Sustainable Development of Small Island Developing States
International Conference on Population and Development (ICPD)
World Conference on Natural Disaster Reduction

1995 — UN Fourth World Conference on Women
World Summit for Social Development

1996 — Second United Nations Conference on Human Settlements (HABITAT II)
World Food Summit
UNCTAD IX: Ninth Session of the Conference on Trade and Development

1997 — Special Session of UN General Assembly on Sustainable Development

1998 — World Conference of Ministers Responsible for Youth

1999 — Special Session of UN General Assembly on Small Island Developing States
Special Session of UN General Assembly on Population and Development

2000 — UNCTAD X: Tenth Session of the Conference on Trade and Development
Special Session of the UN General Assembly on World Summit for Social
Development and Beyond: Achieving Social Development for All in a
Globalised World
World Education Forum
Millennium Summit

2001 — Third United Nations Conference on the Least Developed Countries
Special Session of UN General Assembly on the Problem of Human
Immunodeficiency Virus/Acquired Immunodeficiency Syndrome (HIV/AIDS)
in All its Aspects
International Conference on Fresh Water
First Session of the UN Forum on Forests
Special Session of the UN General Assembly on Human Settlement in the New
Millennium

2002 — International Conference of Financing for Development
Special Session of UN General Assembly on Children
World Food Summit: Five Years Later
World Summit on Sustainable Development
Second World Assembly on Aging

2003 — World Summit on the Information Society: the First Phase
International Ministerial Conference on Landlocked and Transit Developing
Countries and Donors

TABLE 10.1   *(continued)*

2004— Session of the Commission on Population and Development

2005— World Conference on Disaster Reduction

World Summit on the Information Society: the Second Phase

Session of the Commission on the Status of Women

Session of the Commission for Social Development

World Summit

International Meeting for the Sustainable Development of Small Island
Developing States

multilateral development banks and other funding institutions that are presumably far better endowed and equipped for such activities.

In 1994, as previously noted, Boutros-Ghali declared development a human right.[69] In his shared view, "development" meant something much broader than simply economic growth. Development increasingly came to be viewed in human, as opposed to exclusively national economic, terms. Reality always lags rhetoric, but UN documents now clearly indicate that "development" signifies not only improved material welfare with adequate attention to sustainability but also improved human rights and social justice. As always, practice lags far behind rhetoric.

In a related fashion, the concept of "good governance" came into common use within UN developmental circles in the 1980s and 1990s. The emergence of the idea of good governance can be traced to international concerns with state-dominated models of economic and social development so prevalent throughout the socialist bloc and much of the Third World in the 1950s, 1960s, and 1970s. International efforts, especially since the 1980s, have emphasized support for political democratization (including elections, accountability, and human rights) and economic liberalization.

In its *Human Development Report 1994*, the UNDP provided a basic framework for focusing discourse. It suggested that the UN's development work should be based on at least five "new pillars": new concepts of human security, new models of sustainable human development, new partnerships between states and markets, new patterns of national and global governance, and new forms of international cooperation. Each subsequent *Human Development Report* has served to elaborate, extend, and clarify specific aspects of the development–human security nexus: funding priorities (1991); global markets (1992); democracy (1993); environment (1994); gender (1995); growth (1996); poverty (1997); consumption patterns (1998); globalization (1999); human rights (2000); sustainable livelihoods (2001); democracy (2002); millennium development goals (2003); cultural liberty (2004); international cooperation (2005); water resources (2006); and climate change (2007).

Scene at the Non-Governmental Organizations Forum held in Huairou, China, as part of the Fourth UN World Conference on Women held in Beijing, September 4–15, 1995. (UN/DPI Photo/M. Grant)

Participation and empowerment have been two of the priority themes running throughout these annual reports. Placing the emphasis on people, rather than states and macro-level growth, was an important rhetorical and actual advance, in particular for the most marginalized elements of society. The emphasis also helped incorporate civil society and the for-profit sector as central elements of the development equation. The way to eradicate poverty, the UNDP reports have argued, is to empower the poor and marginalized elements of society to provide for the satisfaction of their own basic needs and values. The notion of popular sovereignty has come to eclipse older conceptions of state sovereignty (that is, sovereignty of the people, not of the sovereign).

In attempting to correct the euphoria that had surrounded the so-called Washington consensus of the 1980s and early 1990s, arguments within the UN often have sought to counterbalance or dilute the approaches in vogue since the Reagan and Thatcher administrations—namely, that anything the government can do, the private sector can do better, and that more open markets, free trade, and capital flows are necessarily beneficial to everyone, everywhere. This revisionist view took on added strength after the 2008 economic and financial meltdown, which started with poor decisions in the financial (especially mortgage) private sector. And poor supervision and regulation from the public sector also became evident.

Refugees returning to Cambodia in 1992 under the oversight of the UN Transitional Authority in Cambodia were offered different forms of UNHCR assistance, including a house plot and house kit. (UNCHR Photo/K. Gooi)

In a departure from its previous orthodoxy and as a sign of the pendulum's swing, the World Bank's *World Development Report 1997* emphasized that the state is capable of, and should perform the role of, producing welfare-enhancing outcomes.[70] The report's subtitle, *The State in a Changing World*, was indicative of a reversal led by Joseph Stiglitz, then controversial chief economist and senior vice president of the Bank.[71] Essentially, in contrast to the wave of economic liberalization programs of the 1980s, various political liberalization efforts of the 1990s gradually came to place a greater emphasis on good government, human rights, the role of law and individual access to justice, and basic freedoms. Stiglitz won the 2001 Nobel Prize for Economic Science while at Columbia University, shortly after his resignation from the World Bank over substantive differences. After his resignation, one of his contributions was to demonstrate the real, long-term, high cost of wars such as the 2003 invasion of Iraq.[72]

Good Governance

Today's discussions about good governance stress improving the leadership and management of democracies, including the "deepening" of democracy and more active roles for nonstate actors. Yet, the thinking about new patterns of governance remained rather vague and unspecified. Decentralization of power is lauded as one of the best ways to bring about the empowerment of people, but decentralization at whatever level—local, state, national, and global—can result in empowering elites even more rather than empowering people in the sense of popular participation. New participants may lack the time, motivation, and skills to participate, leaving entrenched elites with unchallenged power. This point is important because sustainable growth and development require the active participation of people at all levels of governance. With regard to UN structure, the most difficult choice may be between the traditional focus on the specialized agencies and the growing need to raise environmental concerns in broader, cross-cutting arenas and in interagency settings in which turf consciousness usually outweighs cooperative instincts. In the post-UNCED era, the discourse of environmentalism is clearly moving in the direction of cross-cutting themes. The traditional eco-systemic focus on air, land, water, and species is giving way to a social-systems focus on international trade, global finance, sovereignty, development, and other key processes and institutions. The old focus was consistent with the UN's functional organization into specialized agencies and bodies. While there are calls to dismantle the world organization, most observers call for renewing the United Nations or establishing new forums to address the new focus.[73]

In this regard, the special initiatives with system-wide coordination and partnership building discussed above have tended to reinforce the evolving consensus over the UN system development strategy. At both the Ministerial Conference of the WTO held in Doha, Qatar, in September 2001 and the summit-level UN-sponsored Conference on Financing for Development in Monterrey, Mexico, in March 2002, for example, donor countries expressed an increased commitment to fighting poverty. In addition to the new spirit of cooperation between the UN and the IFIs noted earlier, the Monterrey gathering for the first time brought together stakeholders representing governments, business, civil society, and international institutions for a formal exchange of views. The "Monterrey Consensus," as that conference's outcome document was called, recognized the need to increase official development significantly in order to meet the MDGs.[74]

The 2002 World Summit on Sustainable Development held in Johannesburg attempted to reinvigorate the sustainable development activities in the wake of deepening poverty and environmental degradation. New targets were set, timetables established, and commitments agreed on. Yet, as the UN Web site for Johannesburg Summit 2002 made clear, "there were no silver bullet solutions . . . no magic and no miracle—only the realization that practical and sustained steps were needed to address many of the world's most pressing problems." The summit reflected a new approach to conferencing and to sustainable development more generally. It was a dialogue among major stakeholders from governments, civil society, and the private sector. Instead of concentrating primarily on producing treaties and other outcome documents, participants focused on creating new partnerships to bring additional resources to bear for sustainable development initiatives.

Secretary-General Annan and core administrative staff in the UNDP continued to aggressively build an array of partnerships with civil society and the private sector. Predictably, these activities—most especially through the Global
Compact with business—have brought with them another dimension of the
challenge to sovereignty debate.[75] The notion of the Global Compact is predicated
on the assumption that development, especially for poorer developing countries,
cannot occur through governmental or intergovernmental means alone, even
when augmented by assistance from the multitude of nongovernmental development assistance organizations. Neither can it occur through unbridled market
forces alone. Creating local, national, and international enabling environments
is essential, and a broad-based partnership involving all relevant "stakeholders"
is required.

Of course, this may be deemed inappropriate or unacceptable for some—
often of quite diverse and even opposing ideological perspectives—that see various
particular types of stakeholders as being unacceptable or illegitimate partners.[76]
Nonetheless, the Global Compact has been steadily expanding. In late 2007,
nearly 2,900 corporate partners had joined the agreement. One of the principles
that underpins the Global Compact is that UN organizations should "undertake
a deeper examination of issues related to corporate governance" in the context of
developing countries' specific legal, social, and cultural environments "to develop and implement international accounting, reporting and auditing standards." While encouraging information sharing about potential investment
opportunities, the UN development framework cautions that "international institutions involved in supporting FDI [foreign direct investment] flows should
evaluate the development impact of investment flows in recipient countries, including social development concerns."[77] Similarly, by joining the Global Compact, businesses recognize that they have a responsibility for helping the
international community meet the MDGs.[78]

The Global Compact represents only one dimension of the UN system's
evolving partnership with the private sector. With the UNDP's reprioritized
functions around the four themes of advocacy, advice, pilot projects, and partnerships, its partnership function is wide-ranging. It begins with the UN and the
IFIs, but it expands far beyond the intergovernmental system. It entails building
and expanding constructive partnerships with civil society, the private sector,
and local authorities. Underpinning this strategy is the belief that "people should
guide both the state and the market, which need to work together in tandem,
with people sufficiently empowered to exert a more effective influence over
both."[79] Critical to this endeavor is creating in these varied constituencies an
identity of being "stakeholders."

Within the developing world this initiative to forge new partnerships has taken
a variety of complexions. The UNDP and other UN agencies have strengthened
their direct involvement with diverse elements of society—including NGOs, the

A visiting foreign official inspects a solar cooker at a research facility in Gansu Province in China. The Natural Energy Research Institute focuses on new forms of energy-producing products. (UN Photo 150767/D. Lovejoy)

private sector, and civil society organizations. Similar efforts have also been made in the IFIs. While active engagement with NGOs has been widely recognized for some time as an essential input into the development process, cooperation with private sector entities at the country level has been less widely publicized. However, these measures are not without controversy. Yet, in a world with scarce and dwindling financial resources and limited access to technology, the prospects of gaining greater access is difficult to resist, despite many potential stumbling blocks and drawbacks.

THE UN'S SUSTAINABLE HUMAN DEVELOPMENT MODEL

Sustainable human development is part of an overall human security framework that has been in the making since the early 1990s—although many could argue that the combination of security, human rights, and sustainable development in separate streams has constituted the history of international organization.[80] In this regard, UNDP's *Human Development Report 1994* provides a useful point of departure.[81] Making human beings secure, the approach argues, means more than protecting them from armed violence and alleviating their suffering. If international organizations are to contribute meaningfully to the promotion of human security, security needs to be defined in much broader terms than protection from threats to physical well-being from military violence. It is worth

A water pump powered by solar energy at Thies, Senegal. (UN Photo 150182/S. Sprague)

noting, as we did in the first two parts of this volume, that protecting civilians in war zones or from thuggish repression is itself far from guaranteed. Doing both simultaneously, as the human security concept proposes, is logical but hardly easy. The *Human Development Report 1994* was a precursor to one a decade later from the Commission on Human Security in that both agreed this concept "must stress the security of people, not only of nations."[82] Thus, the way that citizens and their governments, and also scholars and international officials, think about security would be altered: People and their needs would trump such calculations as bombs and bullets, and considerations like access to food would be as important as military budgets. Thus sustainable human development can be viewed as a process of improving and sustaining human security.

Sustainable development, like human security, is a qualitative condition that entails individual and collective perceptions of low threats to physical and psychological well-being from all agents and forces that could degrade lives, values, and property. At a minimum, people may be considered secure if they are protected from the threat of the physical destruction of their lives or property as a result of assault from others. At the opposite extreme, maximum human security can be imagined in a totally threat-free environment where human beings are protected against all threats to their lives, values, and property. Various qualities of human security can be imagined depending on the relative ordering of the priorities that people place on the satisfaction of various needs, values, and interests.

Human security bridges the traditional divisions of international organizational agendas, where questions of war and peace have been separated from economic and social ones. According to this new conceptualization, peace as the lack of direct violence is only one attribute of a secure environment, and international organizational action is the means of establishing this peace. Further, the notion of human security focuses the attention of international organizations directly on individuals and their circumstances, thereby constituting a subtle challenge to state sovereignty. Making people psychologically secure may, under some circumstances, be the antithesis of making the governments of states and their territorial boundaries physically secure, especially when states themselves are the perpetrators of individual insecurities. Pressing international organizations into the service of individually focused human security could therefore constitute an incremental step toward circumventing or marginalizing states and legitimizing supranational governance.

Most important, conceptualizing the mission of multilateral organizations as one of comprehensively promoting human security rather than separately promoting economic and social development, sustainable development, military security, human rights, and a variety of other goals frees the policy imagination to contemplate holistically the nature and variety of threats to individual environments. Although critics rightly point out that such a blanket concept can lead to fuzzy thinking with little intellectual traction,[83] human security can free the policy imagination to consider how such threats may be removed and to formulate policy prescriptions for how international organizations might contribute to removing them.[84] Because the sources of human insecurity vary from region to region, so, too, will the definition of human security and the missions of international organizations. It may be that in many, if not most, cases multilateral agencies are not very appropriate, efficient, or effective mechanisms for transferring material development assistance. They appear to be relatively better suited to promoting and enhancing human security via policies, programs, and activities that focus on nonmaterial resource transfers and exchanges, including training and the exchange of ideas and information. But such a shift of institutional focus requires rethinking the nature and meaning of sustainable human development.

The foundations for sustainable human development require individuals, groups, and communities to take charge of their own destinies. They thereby themselves become engaged significantly in the satisfaction of their own needs, values, and interests. In short, they control their own futures. "Human development is development of the people for the people by the people. . . . Development for the people means ensuring that the economic growth they generate is distributed widely and fairly. . . . Development by the people [means] giving everyone a chance to participate."[85] Yet the concept of popular participation has proven to be woolly and the debate about its meaning unfocused. In the World Bank, for example, popular participation has at various times and in various contexts been articulated as and associated with the "empowerment" of NGOs and the enhancement of their involvement in making Bank policy; increased bank accountability and control of the Bank's programs, projects, and activities by "domestic" actors; and the active engagement in project planning of previously excluded individuals and groups with an emphasis on the importance of local knowledge and the satisfaction of local needs.

These aspects of participation are important, but this discourse has so far done little to change the essential course of the Bank's policy so as to enhance its role in promoting human security or to construct new models of development focusing on the satisfaction of basic human needs and values. Development models and institutional policies that fail to take adequate account of human needs may actually work to erode human security and inhibit sustainable human development.

In the next chapter, this new global development agenda is examined in the context of the Millennium Development Goals and the challenges posed by globalization. Most world leaders acknowledge that "security" in the twenty-first century includes "human security" and that the UN's development agenda is a necessary component. However, is there sufficient international political will to move fast enough to confront and manage the ill effects of HIV/AIDS, extreme poverty, and other social maladies?

NOTES

1. The WTO is not formally part of the UN system but is considered a UN-related organization. See Bernard M. Hoekman and Petros C. Mavroidis, *The World Trade Organization: Law, Economics, and Politics* (London: Routledge, 2007), and Rorden Wilkinson, *The WTO: Crisis and the Governance of Global Trade* (London: Routledge, 2006).

2. Boutros Boutros-Ghali, "A New Departure on Development," *Foreign Policy* no. 98 (1995): 47. This is the working assumption behind the United Nations Intellectual History Project, which is producing fourteen volumes and an oral history around this theme. For details, see www.unhistory.org.

3. See especially John Mueller, *Quiet Cataclysm: Reflections on the Recent Transformation of World Politics* (New York: HarperCollins, 1995).

4. For a brief and complete introduction, see M. J. Peterson, *The UN General Assembly* (London: Routledge, 2005). Each year the UN Association of the United States publishes an introduction to key issues. For example, see the one for the sixtieth anniversary by Angela Drakulich, ed., *A Global Agenda: Issues Before the 60th General Assembly of the United Nations* (New York: UNA-USA, 2005).

5. See Gert Rosenthal, *The Economic and Social Council of the United Nations*, Occasional Paper no. 15 (Berlin, Friedrich-Ebert-Stiftung, 2005); Yves Berthelot, "Unity and Diversity of Development: The Regional Commissions' Experience," in *Unity and Diversity in Development Ideas: Perspectives from the Regional Commissions*, ed. Yves Berthelot (Bloomington: Indiana University Press, 2004), 1–50.

6. Kofi A. Annan, *Renewing the United Nations: A Programme for Reform* (New York: UN, 1997).

7. Jesse Helms, "Saving the U.N.: A Challenge to the Next Secretary General," *Foreign Affairs* 75, no. 5 (1996): 2–7, at 5.

8. Kofi Annan, *Renewing the United Nations: A Programme for Reform*, UN document A/51/950, July 14, 1997, para. 25.

9. Quoted by Warren Hoge, "Envoys Reach Compromise on Scaled-Back U.N. Reform Plans," *New York Times*, September 13, 2005.

10. For an overview of the first forty years, see Crain N. Murphy, *United Nations Development Programme: A Better Way?* (Cambridge: Cambridge University Press, 2006).

11. UNIFEM, www.unifem.org.

12. Devaki Jain, *Women, Development, and the UN: A Sixty-Year Quest for Equality and Justice* (Bloomington: Indiana University Press, 2005); Peggy Antrobus, *The Global Women's Movement: Origins, Issues and Strategies* (London: Zed Books, 2004); and Rosalind Petchesky, *Global Prescriptions: Gendering Health and Human Rights* (London: Zed Books, 2003).

13. UNDP, Annual Report of the Administrator, June 19, 2003. *The Journal of Human Development: Alternative Economics in Action* has been published three times a year since 2000.

14. UNDP, *Human Development Report 1993* (New York: Oxford University Press, 1993).

15. www.uncdf.org/sum/index.html.

16. Mark Malloch Brown, "Opening Statement at the UNDP/UNFPA Executive Board," New York, June 10, 2003, 1.

17. Ibid., 11.

18. Desmond McNeill, "Human Development: The Power of the Idea," *Journal of Human Development* 8 (March 2007): 5–23; see also Desmond McNeill and Asunción Lera St. Clair, *Global Poverty: Ethics and Human Rights: The Role of Multilateral Organisations* (London: Routledge, 2009).

19. See Ian Taylor, *UN Conference on Trade and Development* (London: Routledge, 2007), and John Toye and Richard Toye, *The UN and Global Political Economy: Trade, Finance, and Development* (Bloomington: Indiana University Press, 2004).

20. See, for example, Charles Gore, "Which Growth Theory Is Good for the Poor?" *European Journal of Development Research* 19 (March 2007): 30–48.

21. UNCTAD-UNDP-HABITAT, Press Release, May 16, 2001.

22. UNCTAD, UNCTAD and Civil Society, available at: www.unctad.org/Templates/StartPage.asp?intItemID=3455&lang=1.

23. UNCTAD, Press Release, "Trade and Development Board Holds Annual Hearing with Civil Society," www.unctad.org/Templates/webflyer.asp?docidID=9241&intlItem=16348&&lang=1.

24. See Yves Beigbeder, *New Challenges for UNICEF: Children, Women, and Human Rights* (New York: Palgrave, 2001).

25. See Jain, *Women, Development, and the UN*.

26. See further Mayra Buvnic, "Women in Poverty: A New Global Underclass," *Foreign Policy* no. 108 (1997): 38–54.

27. www.unicef.org/programme/girlseducation/25_2005/index.htm.

28. UNICEF Press Release, May 8, 2003.

29. UNICEF, *The United Nations Special Session on Children: A First Anniversary Report on Follow-up*, May 8, 2003.

30. UN News Centre, "Countries Slow to Act on 2002 Summit Goals to Better Children's Lives—UNICEF," May 27, 2003.

31. Owen Dyer, "New Partnership Is Set Up to Improve Aid," *British Journal of Medicine* 335 (September 15, 2007): 532.

32. Joel Ostreich, *Power and Principle* (Washington, D.C.: Georgetown University Press, 2007).

33. For an overview of the CSD and other institutions, see Elizabeth R. DeSombre, *Global Environmental Institutions* (London: Routledge, 2006).

34. For an overview, see Helmut Anheier, Marlies Glasius, and Mark Kaldor, *Global Civil Society 2001* (Oxford: Oxford University Press, 2001).

35. Elsa Tsioumani, "CSD-15 Concludes with No Final Outcome Adopted," in *Environmental Policy and Law* 37 (2007): 288–289.

36. "Hot Seats," *The Economist*, May 19, 2007, 19.

37. See Stine Madland Kaasa, "The UN Commission on Sustainable Development: Which Mechanisms Explain Its Accomplishments," *Global Environmental Politics* 25 (August 2007): 107–129.

38. "Africa: Nairobi Meeting Wars of Biofuel Dangers," *Earth Island Journal* 22 (Spring 2007): 4–5.

39. Soledad Aguilar and Elisa Morgera, "Delivering as One for the Environment," *Environmental Policy and Law* (2007): 274–280.

40. See further Richard Benedick, *Ozone Diplomacy: New Directions in Safeguarding the Planet* (Cambridge, Mass.: Harvard University Press, 1998). Benedick shows that UNEP, especially through the activity of its executive director, Mostafa Tolba, was an important player in diplomatic proceedings.

41. For further discussion on the WHO, see Gian Luca Burci and Claude-Henri Vignes, *World Health Organization* (The Hague: Kluwer Law International, 2004).

42. See, for example, Norman J. Vig and Regina S. Axelrod, eds., *The Global Environment: Institutions, Law, and Policy* (Washington, D.C.: CQ Press, 1999).

43. Robert O. Keohane, "International Institutions: Can Interdependence Work?" *Foreign Policy* (special edition) (Spring 1998): 82–96.

44. See Edward Mason and Robert Asher, *The World Bank since Bretton Woods* (Washington, D.C.: Brookings Institution, 1973), and Devesh Kapur, John P. Lewis, and Richard Webb, *The World Bank: Its First Half Century*, vol. 1, "History" (Washington, D.C.: Brookings Institution, 1997). Morten Bøås and Desmond McNeill, *Global Institutions and Development: Framing the World?* (London: Routledge, 2004).

45. See, for example, Margaret G. de Vries, *The International Monetary Fund, 1945–1965: The Twenty Years of International Monetary Cooperation* (Washington, D.C.: IMF, 1969), *The International Monetary Fund, 1966–1971: The System Under Stress* (Washington, D.C.: IMF, 1976), and *The International Monetary Fund, 1972–1978: Cooperation on Trial* (Washington, D.C.: IMF, 1985). See also Norman K. Humphreys, ed., *Historical Dictionary of the IMF* (Washington, D.C.: IMF, 2000).

46. See Naomi Klein, *The Shock Doctrine: The Rise of Disaster Capitalism* (London: Macmillan, 2007).

47. Steven Weisman, "I.M.F. Faces a Question of Identity," *New York Times*, September 28, 2007.

48. Ibid.

49. Ibid.

50. The impact of critics on early Bank policy can be found in Robert Wade, "Greening the Bank: The Struggle over the Environment," in *The World Bank: Its First Half Century*,

eds. Devesh Kapur, John P. Lewis, and Richard Webb, vol. 1 (Washington, D.C.: Brookings, 1997), 611–734.

51. Richard Peet, *Unholy Trinity: The IMF, World Bank and WTO* (London: Zed Books, 2003).

52. Kofi Annan, "The Quiet Revolution," *Global Governance* 4, no. 2 (1998): 123–138.

53. See, for example, Jonathan Pincus et al., *Reinventing the World Bank* (Ithaca, N.Y.: Cornell University Press, 2002). As for the IMF, see Devesh Kapur, "The IMF: A Cure or a Curse?" *Foreign Policy* no. 111 (Summer 1998): 114–131. In general, see Graham Bird and Joseph P. Joyce, "Remodeling the Multilateral Financial Institutions," *Global Governance* 7, no. 1 (2001): 75–94.

54. See the now famous UNICEF report, "Structural Adjustment with a Human Face." This was the first report by a UN agency challenging IMF conditionality on the grounds that such loans unnecessarily increased human suffering.

55. For overviews, see Katherine Marshall, *The World Bank: From Reconstruction to Development to Equity* (London: Routledge, 2007); James Vreeland, *The International Monetary Fund* (London: Routledge, 2007); and Hoekman and Mavroidis, *The World Trade Organization*. See also Ariel Buira, ed., *Reforming the Governance of the IMF and World Bank* (London: Anthem Press, 2005), and Paul Blustein, *The Chastening: Inside the Crisis That Rocked the Global Financial System and Humbled the IMF* (New York: Public Affairs, 2001).

56. *United Nations Chronicle* (online edition), issue 1, 2003.

57. See Hugo Dobson, *The Group of 7/8* (London: Routledge, 2006); John J. Kirton and Takase Junichi, eds., *New Directions in Global Political Governance: The G8 and International Order in the Twenty-First Century* (Aldershot, UK: Ashgate, 2002); and Nicholas Bayne, *Hanging In There: The G7 and G8 Summit in Maturity and Renewal* (Aldershot, UK: Ashgate, 2000) and *Staying Together: The G8 Summit Confronts the 21st Century* (Aldershot, UK: Ashgate, 2005).

58. IMF Press Release no. 03/68.

59. Jessica Einhorn, "The World Bank's Mission Creep," *Foreign Affairs* 80, no. 5 (2001): 22–35.

60. For a discussion on global conferences, see Michael G. Schechter, *United Nations Global Conferences* (London: Routledge, 2005).

61. UNEP, "Development and Environment: The Founex Report: In Defense of the Earth," *The Basic Texts on Environment*, UNEP Executive Series 1, Nairobi, 1981.

62. Quoted by Maurice Strong, "Policy Lessons Learned in a Thirty Years' Perspective," Ministry of the Environment, *Stockholm Thirty Years On* (Stockholm: Ministry of the Environment, 2002), 18. The essays in this volume provide an interesting historical overview.

63. Branislav Gosovic, *The Quest for World Environmental Cooperation: The Case of the UN Global Environment Monitoring System* (London: Routledge, 1992). See also, Regina S. Axelrod, David Leonard Downie, and Norman J. Vig, eds., *The Global Environment: Institutions, Law and Policy* (Washington, D.C.: CQ Press, 2005); Frank Biermann and Steffen Bauer, eds., *A World Environment Organization* (Aldershot, UK: Ashgate, 2005); W. Bradnee Chambers and Jessica F. Green, eds., *Reforming International Environmental Governance: From Institutional Limits to Innovative Reforms* (Tokyo: UN University Press, 2005); Pamela S. Chasek, David L. Downie, and Janet Welsh Brown, *Global Environmental Politics*, 4th ed. (Boulder: Colo.: Westview Press, 2006); Pamela S. Chasek, *Earth Negotiations: Analyzing Thirty Years of Environmental Diplomacy* (Tokyo: UN University Press, 2001).

64. For a review of the documentation, see Shanna Halpren, *The United Nations Conference on Environment and Development: Process and Documentation* (Providence, R.I.: Academic Council on the United Nations System, 1992).

65. For a discussion, see Michael McCoy and Patrick McCully, *The Road from Rio: An NGO Guide to Environment and Development* (Amsterdam: International Books, 1993). For a more general discussion, see Kerstin Martens, *NGOs and the United Nations* (New York: Palgrave, 2006). See also the three reports in 2001, 2002, and 2003 by Helmut Anheier, Marlies Glasius, and Mary Kaldor, eds., *Global Civil Society* (Oxford: Oxford University Press, 2001, 2002, and 2003).

66. For this and other stories, see Maurice Strong, *Where On Earth Are We Going?* (New York: Norton, 2001).

67. See Richard Jolly, Louis Emmerij, and Thomas G. Weiss, *The Power of UN Ideas: Lessons from the First Sixty Years* (New York: United Nations Intellectual History Project, 2005), and *UN Ideas That Changed the World* (Bloomington: Indiana University Press, 2009).

68. Commission on International Development, *Partners in Development* (New York: Praeger, 1969); Commission on Global Governance, *Our Global Neighbourhood* (Oxford: Oxford University Press, 1995); International Commission on Intervention and State Sovereignty, *The Responsibility to Protect* (Ottawa: ICISS, 2001); and Commission on Human Security, *Human Security Now* (New York: Commission on Human Security, 2003). This was also a view expressed in oral histories from some of the main participants in Thomas G. Weiss, Tatiana Carayannis, Louis Emmerij, and Richard Jolly, *UN Voices: The Challenge of Development and Social Justice* (Bloomington: Indiana University Press, 2005), part three; for the complete transcripts, see the CD-ROM, *The Complete Oral History Transcripts from "UN Voices"* (New York: United Nations Intellectual History Project, 2006).

69. Boutros Boutros-Ghali, *An Agenda for Development* (New York: United Nations, 1995).

70. World Bank, *World Development Report 1997: The State in a Changing World* (New York: Oxford University Press, 1997).

71. See, for example, Joseph Stiglitz, "Redefining the Role of the State: What Should It Do? How Should It Do It? And How Should These Decisions Be Made?" www.world bank.org. See also his *Globalization and Its Discontents* (New York: Norton, 2002).

72. See Joseph Stiglitz and Linda Bilmes, *The Three Trillion Dollar War: The True Cost of the Iraq Conflict* (New York: Norton, 2008).

73. Craig Murphy, "Global Institutions and the Pursuit of Human Needs," in *The Power of Human Needs in World Society*, eds. Roger A. Coate and Jerel A. Rosati (Boulder, Colo.: Lynne Rienner, 1988), 217.

74. Barry Herman, "Civil Society and the Financing for Development Initiative at the United Nations," in *Civil Society and Global Finance*, eds. Jan Aart Scholte and Albrecht Schabel (London: Routledge, 2002), 162–177.

75. See John Gerard Ruggie, "global_governance.net: The Global Compact as Learning Network," *Global Governance* 7, no. 4 (2001): 371–378, and Jean-Philippe Thérien and Vincent Pouliot, "The Global Compact: Shifting the Politics of International Development?" *Global Governance* 12, no. 1 (2006): 55–75.

76. Ellen Paine, "The Road to the Global Compact: Corporate Power and the Battle Over Global Public Policy at the United Nations," www.igloo.org/library/edocuments?id =%7b64DA8794-1BC3-4DAF-9FD3-6F0C2840C5C7%7d.

77. UN document A/AC.257/12.

78. See www.unglobalcompact.org.

79. UNDP, *Human Development Report 1993* (New York: Oxford University Press, 1993).

80. See Fen Hampson and Christopher Penny, "Human Security," in *The Oxford Handbook on the United Nations*, eds. Thomas G. Weiss and Sam Daws (Oxford: Oxford University Press, 2007), 539–557.

81. Ken Conca, "Greening the UN: Environmental Organizations and the UN System," in *NGOs, the UN, and Global Governance*, eds. Thomas G. Weiss and Leon Gordenker (Boulder, Colo.: Lynne Rienner, 1996), 114–115.

82. UNDP, *Human Development 1993*, 2.

83. See S. Neil MacFarlane and Yuen Foong Khong, *The UN and Human Security: A Critical History* (Bloomington: Indiana University Press, 2005), and Roland Paris, "Peacebuilding and the Limits of International Liberalism," *International Security* 22 (Fall 1997): 54–89.

84. Fen Osler Hampson et al., *Madness in the Multitude: Human Security and World Disorder* (Toronto: Oxford University Press, 2001).

85. UNDP, *Human Development 1993*, 2.

CHAPTER 11

The UN, Development, and Globalization

GLOBALIZATION, WHICH HAS economic, social, and political dimensions, is not a new phenomenon. Yet the forces and processes associated with it, as well as opportunities and challenges, are ever more apparent in a post–September 11 world. While economic globalization yields many benefits, especially to those in wealthier countries, or perhaps for many in the upper classes of all countries, it also has brought in its wake unprecedented inequality. Former Secretary-General Kofi Annan reflected on this problem in his report *"We the Peoples": The Role of the United Nations in the 21st Century*, in which he wrote: "The benefits of globalization are plain to see: faster economic growth, higher living standards, accelerated innovation and diffusion of technology and management skills, new economic opportunities for individuals and countries alike." Yet these benefits are distributed very unequally and inequitably. They are "highly concentrated among a relatively small number of countries and are spread unevenly within them."[1]

The impact of globalization varies dramatically from region to region and case to case. As underscored in an earlier report by Annan, the "actual experience of globalization, to a great degree, varied with the level of development at which a country experienced it."[2] In some cases, where national economies were well positioned in terms of capacity and economic orientation, rapid economic growth has ensued. Elsewhere the result has been much less positive, contributing to increased poverty, inequality, marginalization, and human insecurity—particularly through unemployment. In some places globalization may actually undermine many of the development efforts by UN agencies.

The Millennium Declaration identified challenges related to globalization as the key issue confronting the international community of states. UN member states accordingly pledged to act "to ensure that globalization becomes a positive force for all the world's people."[3] But what is globalization? How should we assess the UN system's responses to it? How does globalization affect the MDGs and the recurring tension between state and market-driven efforts to promote sustainable human development and human security? Answers to these questions are at the center of this chapter.

GLOBALIZATION AND GLOBAL GOVERNANCE

A cottage industry has developed for books on "globalization."[4] On one hand, globalization as a concept is useful for understanding contemporary world affairs. On the other hand, it has no widely accepted definition. At its core globalization refers to the movement of goods, services, ideas, and people across national borders. In this sense it is related to internationalization, interconnectedness, interdependence.[5] At the beginning of this century, global transactions in foreign exchange markets had reached a level nearly eighty times larger than world trade. The growth in foreign direct investment and portfolio capital flows in developing countries has also outpaced international trade. The expansion of global markets and production and other aspects of the worldwide diffusion of capitalism, however, is only one dimension of the social transformations involved in globalization.

Ngaire Woods suggests three core elements of globalization: the expansion of markets, challenges to the state and institutions, and the rise of new social and political movements.[6] While the economic core entails the proliferation of production, trade, and financial activity spurred by technological change and governmental deregulation, the second core element focuses on the emergence of a new form of global politics enabled and necessitated by the first. Also, Woods argues that society and culture themselves are being transformed, which brings reactions, resistance, and even rebellions. As the financial and economic collapse in the United States made clear, globalization also means that serious economic problems in the world's largest economy cause serious economic problems in many other parts of the world.

Jan Aart Scholte, an observer of global social transformation, identifies production, governance, and culture as main areas underlying the globalization debates. To these, he adds a fourth: modernity and post-modernity. He adds at least five broad definitions of the globalization concept.[7] First, globalization is often treated as being synonymous with internationalization—the spread of cross-border relations and activities—and growing interdependence. Second, the concept is frequently used to imply the opening up or liberalization of intersocietal relations. In this context, the removal of governmental restrictions on trade and other social exchanges is seen to be yielding a more borderless world.

The third view holds that globalization is profoundly changing the face of world politics and the nature of human social interaction and existence. The nature, structure, geographical pattern, and magnitude of world trade and investment, for example, are in transformation, and these changes have had an especially hard impact on poor developing countries in terms of growth, poverty, and income inequality. Economic liberalization has fostered the diffusion of multinational production networks, capital mobility, and new technologies, which has tended in many cases to place downward pressures on wages and working conditions and otherwise make labor in developing societies increasingly susceptible to global forces. The development of financial markets and institutions, along with the tremendous growth in foreign direct investment, short-term portfolio investment, and other transnational capital flows in developing regions, has dramatically transformed the political economic climate there.[8]

The fourth take on globalization concentrates on the worldwide syntheses of values and cultures. This view is not neutral, as it equates globalization with the Westernization or even Americanization of the world's cultures. "Following this idea globalization is a dynamic whereby the social structures of modernity (capitalism, rationalism, industrialism, bureaucratism, etc.) are spread the world over, normally destroying preexisting cultures and local self-determination in the process."[9] Scholte refers to these conceptualizations as "redundant."

The fifth conceptualization is the idea that globalization focuses on the reconfiguration of social space beyond traditional conceptions of territorial boundaries. Like David Held and collaborators, Scholte structures his interpretations and understandings of processes of globalization on the basis of this fifth conceptualization.[10] We too concentrate here on those processes that reconfigure and transform the organization of social relations and transactions in social space and in the minds of social actors.

This reconfiguration finds current concepts and conventional language insufficient to portray their intended meanings, resulting in a stultifying vocabulary. Words like "globality," "deterritorialization," "supraterritorial relations,"[11] "unbundled territoriality,"[12] and "hyper-globalism"[13] are offered as central organizing concepts. Turgid language or not, the intent is to portray a set or sets of social processes that are transforming both the world and how human beings think about it and behave within it. As stressed by Manuel Castells, Ankie Hoogvelt, and others, at the core of this transformation is the ascendancy of "real time virtual reality" over physical time and space.[14] They argue that the distinguishing characteristic of contemporary globalization is not to be found in the widening—that is, the global geographic spread—of human social relations of production, consumption, and so on, but rather in the deepening and intensification of "capitalist integration" and global consciousness. Some talk of global villages, others about the emergence of global civil society, and still others about a global informational network society.[15]

This kind of theorizing provides a context within which to frame and understand issues and challenges of global governance and assess the work of international institutions in fulfilling their mandates in promoting human security and sustainable human development. Perhaps more than any other analyst, James Mittelman provides concrete insight in this regard. In his discussion of "captors" and "captives" of globalization, he considers the dialectic of inclusion and exclusion that result from the complex forces and tensions at play.[16] He suggests that to create adequate governance responses, three very "vexing" aspects must be dealt with: control, autonomy, and agency. In other words, we need to understand not only globalization processes but also how different communities respond to them and benefit or suffer deprivations from them. Globalization is a contested process in which there is no predetermined outcome. At the same time, control and power structures are very uneven, and that fact greatly influences outcomes. Participants' needs, values, and interests all play critical roles.

The central challenge facing the United Nations is to find ways to use the opportunities inherent in globalization to help people everywhere better cope with its undesirable side effects. Opportunities are related to increased access to new-age information and communications technology, greater public exposure to and awareness of their interdependence and vulnerabilities, and "real-time" social exchanges. The strategy for implementing the MDGs illustrates both the opportunities and the challenges globalization presents for achieving sustainable human development and security.

THE MDG STRATEGY

International gatherings over the past two decades have resulted in a largely consensual strategy for assessing progress toward dealing with the negative impacts of globalization and eradicating poverty. At the same time, these gatherings reflected a tension between states favoring a more authoritative and regulative approach to promoting development and those seeking to harness market forces to this end. This tension has resulted in an ambiguous compromise whereby both strategies are pursued, albeit with asymmetrical resources. The consensual strategy is organized around eight main development goals, the MDGs, and eighteen related targets. Each target has a specific time frame and aim and one or more indicators to be monitored to assess movement toward achievement. The Millennium Development Goals are enumerated in Table 11.1.

Seven of the eight main goals focus on substantive objectives. The eighth MDG deals with creating the capacity to achieve the other seven. Cumulatively, the MDGs can be seen as both mutually reinforcing and intertwined. Eradicating extreme poverty, for example, would most likely drastically reduce infant mortality, improve maternal health, and better ensure environmental sustainability. Similarly, achieving universal primary education, promoting gender equality, empowering women, and combating HIV/AIDS, malaria, and other diseases would undoubtedly move forward progress toward eradicating poverty.

A UN system-wide strategy has been designed for mobilizing support and monitoring progress toward achieving the MDGs. The strategy has four main components: Millennium Project, Millennium Campaign, Millennium Reports, and country-level monitoring and operational country-level activities. The Millennium Project sought to mobilize scholars from around the world and focus

TABLE 11.1   Millennium Development Goals and Targets

Goal 1: Eradicate extreme poverty and hunger
Target 1   Halve, between 1990 and 2015, the proportion of people whose income is less than $1 a day
Target 2   Halve, between 1990 and 2015, the proportion of people who suffer from hunger

Goal 2: Achieve universal primary education
Target 3   Ensure that, by 2015, children everywhere, boys and girls alike, will be able to complete a full course of primary schooling

Goal 3: Promote gender equality and empower women
Target 4   Eliminate gender disparity in primary and secondary education, preferably by 2005, and to all levels of education no later than 2015

Goal 4: Reduce child mortality
Target 5   Reduce by two-thirds, between 1990 and 2015, the under-five mortality rate

Goal 5: Improve maternal health
Target 6   Reduce by three-quarters, between 1990 and 2015, the maternal mortality ratio

Goal 6: Combat HIV/AIDS, malaria, and other diseases
Target 7   Have halted by 2015 and begun to reverse the spread of HIV/AIDS
Target 8   Have halted by 2015 and begun to reverse the incidence of malaria and other major diseases

Goal 7: Ensure environmental sustainability
Target 9   Integrate the principles of sustainable development into country policies and programs and reverse the loss of environmental resources
Target 10 Halve, by 2015, the proportion of people without sustainable access to safe drinking water
Target 11 By 2020, achieve significant improvement in the lives of at least 100 million slum dwellers

Goal 8: Develop a global partnership for development
Target 12 Develop further an open, rule-based, predictable, nondiscriminatory trading and financial system (Includes a commitment to good governance, development, and poverty reduction—both nationally and internationally)
Target 13 Address the special needs of the least developed countries (Includes tariff- and quota-free access for LDC exports; enhanced program of debt relief for HIPC and cancellation of official bilateral debt; and more generous ODA for countries committed to poverty reduction)
Target 14 Address the special needs of landlocked countries and small island developing states (through the Program of Action for the Sustainable Development of Small Island Developing States and the outcome of the twenty-second special session of the General Assembly)
Target 15 Deal comprehensively with the debt problems of developing countries through national and international measures in order to make debt sustainable in the long term

TABLE 11.1   (*continued*)

Target 16 In cooperation with developing countries, develop and implement strategies for decent and productive work for youth

Target 17 In cooperation with pharmaceutical companies, provide access to affordable, essential drugs in developing countries

Target 18 In cooperation with the private sector, make available the benefits of new technologies, especially information and communications

Source: http://www.unmillenniumproject.org/goals/gti.htm#goal1

their collective wisdom and research efforts on achieving the MDGs. The purpose of this initiative was to help member states and agencies develop implementation strategies for accomplishing the MDGs. It endeavored to identify priorities, implementation strategies, and financing means. At its inception, the project was directed by Columbia University's Jeffrey Sachs, who served as special adviser to the Secretary-General. Ten expert task forces were set up to carry out the needed research and report their findings to the Secretary-General and the UNDP administrator. Each task force focused on a specific set of MDG targets. Part of the process was the Human Development Report 2003 that focused on the MDGs.[17] Also, the campaign seeks to promote and reinforce cooperation among UN agencies, the IMF/World Bank, and the WTO.

The final summary report by Sachs's team, *Investing in Development,* was published in March 2005 as background for the World Summit and noted that the development aid system is still not MDG-based and lacks a coherent approach to poverty. The ten accompanying reports provided statistical backup in some depth for the argument. Although some low-level coordination has taken place, the IMF, the World Bank, and the regional development banks still are not well linked to UN agencies for local projects.[18] In 2006, MDG Support replaced the Millennium Project and works with countries to develop and implement their national development strategies. Two advisory groups have been established to assist in implementing the project. The first is the UN Experts Group, consisting of senior representatives from UN agencies to ensure that the ten task forces have access to and fully utilize the relevant knowledge, experience, and capacities of the UN system. The second is an International Advisory Panel of experts in the respective areas of concern.

The Millennium Campaign was designed to mobilize support for the MDGs. This entailed coaching member states to comply with the commitments already made and convincing them that greater consistency across trade, finance, education, health, development, and other ministries is crucial to MDG success. At least one positive outcome of the campaign at the 2005 World Summit was to garner U.S. support for the MDGs.

Millennium Reports constitute the third pillar of the strategy. The reports are in essence individual country report cards. Country-level monitoring entails col-

Miguel d'Escoto Brockmann, president of the sixty-third session of the General Assembly, joined by Secretary-General Ban Ki-moon, addresses a high-level event of world leaders, private sector representatives, and civil society partners to discuss specific ways to energize collaboration to achieve the Millennium Development Goals (MDGs). (UN Photo 196894/Marco Castro)

lecting and analyzing data on progress toward achieving individual MDGs. UN teams assist countries in designing and implementing policies necessary for successful progress. As of January 2008, 140 countries had completed Millennium Reports. Halfway through the MDG process, only three dozen or so countries are on track for meeting the 2015 MDGs.[19]

The UN's Non-Governmental Liaison Service (NGLS) reported, "The Millennium Development Goals, over a relatively short period of time, have gained tremendous currency, primarily in development circles but increasingly in related trade and finance circles. Many actors are now counting on the goals . . . to galvanize disparate and sometimes competing development agendas and are imagining how they might become a powerful political tool to hold governments and international institutions accountable."[20] The MDGs provide a widely used framework for examining the work of the UN system in response to globalization.

IMPLEMENTING THE MDGS

Poverty eradication lies at the core of the MDGs and the UN's sustainable development efforts. The world organization measures extreme poverty by determining the number of people living on less than $1.25 a day (previously the level was $1.00 a day). Given this measure, poverty rates have declined in most regions since 1990, with the notable exception of Western Asia. According to the *Millennium Development Goals Report 2008* (MDGR 2008), the proportion of people living below the poverty threshold fell from 41.7 percent in 1990 to 25.7 percent in 2005.[21] Although extreme poverty worldwide is in decline, the benefits of growth measures by overall statistics disguise the fact that such benefits are not distributed evenly. China continues to make impressive progress—and along with India is statistically responsible for progress measured globally because the two account for a third of the world's population. China is distinctive in having made tremendous strides during the 1990s in reducing the number of extremely poor. This Chinese success correlates highly with its unprecedented economic growth during the same time period, which has accelerated in the twenty-first century. A number of other East Asian and Pacific countries made impressive gains too—cutting by half the number of extremely poor in the region as a whole.[22] The international community overall is on track to meet target 1 in 2015; however, sub-Saharan Africa and South Asia are not and remain a concern for all of the MDG targets. The absolute number of people in sub-Saharan Africa living in extreme poverty, for example, increased by 100 million between 1990 and 2005 and the poverty rate there remains around 50 percent, with the average individual living on 70 cents a day.

Achieving full and productive employment for all is one of the targets of MDG 1 (see Table 11.1). However, half of the world's labor force still works in insecure and unstable jobs. In search of strategies for getting countries on track for meeting MDG 1, the United Nations points to microfinance, which provides loans to over 113 million clients worldwide. The Grameen Bank of Bangladesh, with over 7.5 million borrowers, Latin America's ACCION International, and the Self-Employed Women's Association Bank in India represent several of the most successful microfinance efforts that could be replicated elsewhere.

Hunger

Hunger and malnutrition are highly correlated with poverty. The specific target is to halve the proportion of people who suffer from hunger between 1990 and 2015. In 1997, the number of chronically hungry people stood at 791 million, which represented a dramatic reduction from 1970, when the figure was 959 million. Yet, in the late 1990s a strong reversal occurred, and by 2002 the number had risen to 852 million. In 2002, the MDG hunger target was being met in only 3 percent of the countries and only 46 percent were on track. Of the remaining 51 percent, about half (24 percent of the total) were lagging far behind. On a somewhat more positive note, child hunger is declining in most regions. FAO data indicate that over one-third of the people living in least developed countries (LDCs) and 17 percent of people in the developing world as a whole are undernourished, and the rate of reduction reflects that the situation is getting worse, not better in recent years.[23] According the MDGR 2007, "Globally, the proportion of children under five who are underweight declined by one fifth over the period 1990–2005. Eastern Asia showed the greatest improvement and is surpassing the MDG target, largely due to the nutritional advances of China, where child malnutrition was cut in half between 1990 and 2006."[24]

Predictably, Southern Asia and sub-Saharan Africa, while improving somewhat, are still at unacceptable levels. Yet there are positive stories even there. Faced with famine and the opposition of some of its international donors, for example, the Malawi government in 2005 instituted an aggressive subsidization program for 1 million smallholder maize farmers. This program has yielded significant results. Not only has the country diverted famine but now even exports maize to neighboring countries. As such, and if current trends continue or are worsened by the global recession, the MDG hunger target will remain elusive. The global spike in commodity prices including food in 2007–2008 exacerbated hunger not only in Southern Asia and sub-Saharan Africa but also in places like Thailand, Malaysia, and Vietnam. For many developing countries, the food crisis was more unsettling than the global economic and financial crisis. By the end of 2008, it was estimated that 1 billion people lacked access to adequate food supplies and that over half of the developing world's population was undernourished.

Education

The education target (MDG 2) is to ensure that by 2015 "children everywhere, boys and girls alike, will be able to complete a full course of primary education." The record to date, however, indicates lackluster results toward achieving MDG 2. Developing-country primary-school completion rates average 83 percent. Much progress has been made in many parts of the developing world, including Asian CIS, East Asia, Latin America and the Caribbean, and North Africa. Also, there has been progress toward reducing gender disparities in many regions. Yet 121 million children are being left behind, especially in sub-Saharan Africa, South Asia, Oceania, West Asia, and European CIS countries. With completion rates of around 50 percent, sub-Saharan Africa is at the bottom of the list, followed by South Asia, which stands at around 70 percent. Well over half of the children out of school are girls.[25]

On balance, the world is far off target for meeting this MDG. Only 37 countries thus far have achieved universal primary education, with only an additional 32 of the more than 150 developing and transitional countries likely to achieve the goal by 2015. At least 86 countries are at risk of missing the 2015 mark, and 27 are seriously off track.[26] Poverty aggravates gender disparities as well as dropout rates. The poorest elements of the population, those living in rural areas, ethnic minorities, the disabled, and children living in conflict or post-conflict situations are disproportionately excluded. The education-income gap is greatest in South Asia, and in Central and Western Africa the median grade completion level for the poorest 40 percent of the population is zero.

At the 2005 World Summit, the heads of state and government present in New York reaffirmed this commitment "that all children have access to and complete free and compulsory primary education of good quality, to eliminate gender inequality and imbalance and to renew efforts to improve girls' education."[27] Moreover, member states committed themselves to support national efforts to implement the Education for All initiatives. But lofty words have been heard before; time will tell whether words will translate to meaningful action.

Population growth plays a major role in facilitating or constraining a country's ability to move ahead. In certain regions, such as East Asia and the Pacific, where the school-age population is projected to decline by some 22 million in the next decade, providing universal education is not as daunting as in other developing regions. On the other hand, in sub-Saharan Africa the primary-school-age population is projected to grow by over 34 million, adding yet more stress to already overburdened educational infrastructures.[28] Accordingly, sub-Saharan Africa lags well behind the other regions. A large part of that region is unlikely to come anywhere close to reaching the MDG education goal.

To spearhead the drive for universal literacy, the General Assembly has declared 2003–2012 as "The UN Literacy Decade." This UN system-wide effort, coordinated by UNESCO, focuses on extending literacy to all who are not currently literate—children and adults alike. Thus, the poorest and marginalized population segments are key targets for the campaign, which is being conducted under the banner of "Literacy for All: Voice for All, Learning for All." Creating sustainable local "literacy environments" is a primary objective of the initiative.[29]

The International Plan of Action for the Literacy Decade outlines six primary avenues of effort. First, policy change is required in most countries to provide a framework for increased local participation in literacy programs. Second, literacy programs need to be flexible, use appropriate and culturally relevant materials, respect the needs of learners, and use appropriate languages. Third, attention needs to be paid to capacity building and training literacy facilitators. Fourth, policies and policy actions need to be grounded in sound empirical research. Fifth, broad-based community participation is required to build a sense of community "ownership" over the literacy programs. Finally, effective indicators of progress are needed, as are enhanced systems for monitoring and evaluation.

Various UN agencies have been attempting to bolster the global effort to achieve MDG 2. For example, there is a UN system-wide initiative, the United Nations Girls' Education Initiative, to assist governments in eliminating gender disparities. The ILO has placed special focus on promoting free and universally accessible education. Member states are being called upon to enforce compulsory schooling up to a minimum age for employment. The FAO and UNESCO have spearheaded a partnership—Education for Rural People—with other international agencies, governments, and civil society to reduce rural-urban disparities and improve the quality of rural education. UNESCO, UNICEF, WHO, the

World Bank, and Education International have launched a program: Focusing Resources on Effective School Health.

UN agencies, individually and collectively, can do only so much. Real and sustainable progress depends on commitment and follow-through at the national and international levels. Here the picture is not very bright. As highlighted above, the international community of states has repeatedly set and failed to attain goals for providing universal primary education. The Education for All Fast Track Initiative was launched in 2002 in an attempt to mobilize external funding for educational development assistance. It is a compact between donors and developing countries that requires recipient governments to commit to far-reaching reforms of their educational systems in line with MDG 2, and in turn, donors pledged to provide the necessary funding. A dozen developing countries submitted and negotiated such plans to accommodate donors' demands. However, the donors failed to follow through and reciprocal funding has never materialized. Again, the talk was cheap.

One of the keys to increasing school enrollment has been abolishing school fees, which has been especially critical in Africa. In one year alone, between 2004 and 2005, public school enrollment in Ghana's most deprived districts increased from 4.2 million to 5.4 million. In Kenya the change was even more dramatic, because from 2003 to 2004 primary school enrollment vaulted from 1.3 million to just over 6 million. Other African countries, including Burundi, Democratic Republic of the Congo, Ethiopia, Malawi, Mozambique, Tanzania, and Uganda, have experienced significant, albeit much less dramatic, results.

Women in Development

Poor women are the most marginalized of social groups who do not benefit from globalization. MDG 3 focuses on gender inequality and empowering women for development. While promoting gender equality is an important objective in itself, enhancing the status of women in society is also important for a variety of reasons. Reducing gender differences in education may lead to other positive effects, such as increased creation of sustainable livelihoods and increases in productivity, improved maternal health, reduced fertility rates, and higher primary school retention. As Malloch Brown argues, "Empowering women is not just one of the goals; it plays a critical role in the achievement of the other seven as well." He continues, "Women are the poorest of the poor: disproportionately, women lack access to land, water, and sources of energy; women lack access to education and other social services; and too often women are absent from decision-making, not only at the national, regional, or local level, but even within their own families."[30]

The main target specified for this goal is to eliminate gender disparity in primary and secondary education, preferably by 2005, and in all levels of education no later than 2015. A large number of countries appear to be on track. In East

334 SUSTAINABLE HUMAN DEVELOPMENT

and Southeast Asia, Latin America, the Caribbean, and the CIS, basic parity has been attained; and despite problems, much progress has been made in South Asia. However, substantial disparities persist in sub-Saharan Africa, North Africa, the Middle East, and West Asia. By 2005, 113 countries had failed to achieve parity in primary and secondary education, and at current rates only 18 of these will achieve the target by 2015. The situation with regard to secondary education is bleaker. Only about one-third of the developing countries have attained parity in secondary education.

The World Bank's Millennium Goal Web site points out that "differences persist everywhere in legal rights, labor market opportunities, and the ability to participate in public life and decision making."[31] Women lag far behind men in terms of wage employment in the nonagricultural sector. Despite the fact that women account for half the hours worked worldwide, only about 30 percent of their work is paid, compared to 75 percent for men. Among the notable efforts to reverse the situation has been the UNDP's partnering with the Bill and Melinda Gates Foundation to use low-cost technology to enhance women's productivity and income levels in Burkina Faso, Mali, and Senegal. After just two years, women in the program have tripled their incomes and evidence suggests that the program has also dramatically improved literacy levels among women. One area in which women hold the dubious honor of being far ahead of men is HIV/AIDS. In sub-Saharan Africa, HIV-positive women outnumber HIV-positive men three to one.

A May 2003 UNIFEM report, *Progress of the World's Women 2002: Gender Equality and the Millennium Development Goals*, discloses that "although women have progressed relatively slowly in the last two years in the areas of education, literacy and employment, there have been encouraging signs of improvement in women's legislative representation." The report points out that this MDG indicator is the only gender inequality indicator that is not linked to poverty and disparities between rich and poor countries. "The United States, France and Japan, where women's share of parliamentary seats is 12 percent, 11.8 percent and 10 percent respectively, lag behind 13 developing countries in sub-Saharan Africa, which is experiencing the greatest regional poverty in the world. In South Africa and Mozambique, women's share of seats is 30 percent, while Rwanda and Uganda have 25.7 percent and 24.7 percent respectively."[32] As the MDGR 2007 notes, the existence of a government-required quota system makes all the difference. In a quota system, women's inclusion in politics is authoritatively mandated by setting aside seats in legislatures and positions in government specifically for women. In 2003, for example, Rwanda adopted a new constitution that mandates a minimum of 30 percent of parliamentary seats go to women. As a result, Rwanda now has the largest proportion of women in parliament in the world.

Underlying the UN's work in this area for the past two and a half decades has been the Convention on the Elimination of All Forms of Discrimination against Women. The convention binds acceding states to several important obligations.

State parties agree to incorporate the principles of equality of men and women in their legal system, abolish all discriminatory laws, and adopt appropriate ones prohibiting discrimination against women; establish tribunals and other public institutions to ensure the effective protection of women against discrimination; and ensure elimination of all acts of discrimination against women by persons, organizations, or enterprises.[33] Although the United States is a signatory, it has never ratified the convention. Some 170 other countries have ratified it.

UN member states' collective commitment to the rights of women was reinforced at the Fourth UN World Conference on Women in Beijing in 1995, twenty years after the issue was officially and visibly placed on the international agenda at a first global conference on women in Mexico City. The UN's Commission on Human Rights has been another important forum for promoting women's rights. A focal point of the 2003 commission proceedings was an open debate on "integration of the human rights of women and a gender perspective." Commission members addressed a number of critical issues, including eradicating violence against women.[34]

UNIFEM plays a key advocacy role in promoting women's rights and the implementation of the convention against the discrimination of women. UNIFEM is committed to working to eliminate violence against women and girls, such as "trafficking in persons." Here women and girls are most vulnerable to systematic exploitation. Article 3, paragraph (a) of the Protocol to Prevent, Suppress and Punish Trafficking in Persons defines the legal concept as follows:

> ... the recruitment, transportation, transfer, harbouring or receipt of persons, by means of the threat or use of force or other forms of coercion, of abduction, of fraud, of deception, of the abuse of power or of a position of vulnerability or of the giving or receiving of payments or benefits to achieve the consent of a person having control over another person, for the purpose of exploitation. Exploitation shall include, at a minimum, the exploitation of the prostitution of others or other forms of sexual exploitation, forced labour or services, slavery or practices similar to slavery, servitude, or the removal of organs.[35]

While trafficking in persons is not new, trafficking especially in women and girls is the fastest-growing area of organized crime.[36] In 2000, the General Assembly adopted the UN Convention against Transnational Organized Crime and the associated Protocol against the Smuggling of Migrants by Land, Sea or Air and the Protocol to Prevent, Suppress and Punish Trafficking in Persons, especially Women and Children. As of December 2007, 147 member states had signed the convention, and 117 had ratified the protocol.[37] In 2002 the HRC announced the "establishment of the Intergovernmental Organization Contact Group on Trafficking and Migrant Smuggling, under the coordination of the Office of the High Commissioner for Human Rights and cochaired by the United Nations

High Commissioner for Refugees and the International Labour Organization. This brings together representatives of the major Geneva-based intergovernmental organizations working on trafficking, as well as relevant nongovernmental organizations, for collaboration and cooperation on the issue of trafficking."[38] The issue was also the focal point of the UN Commission on Crime Prevention and Criminal Justice in Vienna in May 2003.

Beyond legal norms and diplomatic statements, however, the UN has had to confront this issue of trafficking in its own field operations. Some military and civilian personnel in UN peace operations and other missions related to conflict (for example, civilian police) have been involved in certain aspects of the organized traffic in women, as in the Balkans. The Secretary-General has implemented a zero-tolerance policy, and the climate itself led to the much publicized departure of the UN's most senior refugee official and former Dutch prime minister, Ruud Lubbers, under allegations of sexual harassment. However, since trafficking in women is so closely tied to a legal or quasi-legal sex industry, discerning between permissible and impermissible behavior is difficult. Moreover, as Secretary-General Ban Ki-moon reminded the world on International Women's Day 2007, violence toward women and girls persists in many countries, despite the fact that their national laws prohibit such atrocities, precisely because it is tolerated under the guise of local cultural norms and practices—cultural relativity.

Transnational Public Health

Three MDGs deal with various health-related topics: reducing child mortality; improving maternal health; and combating HIV/AIDS, malaria, and other diseases. In addition, one of the targets for the eighth MDG calls for a global partnership with pharmaceutical companies to provide access to affordable, essential drugs in developing countries. All of these health-related goals are mutually reinforcing and are highly associated with the overall goal of poverty reduction. Disease and poor health provide a drag on economic growth and development. HIV/AIDS is particularly acute in this regard and threatens to undermine the development efforts of the entire sub-Saharan African region.

The issue of the role of child mortality in development is complex, and reducing infant and child mortality is problematic because of the lack of adequate medical treatment and immunization, unsafe drinking water, poor sanitation, civil strife, endemic disease, and malnutrition. Approximately 70 percent of child deaths are associated with some combination of disease and/or malnutrition, with pneumonia being the leading cause of death. "Rapid improvements before 1990 gave hope that mortality rates of children under five could be cut by two-thirds in the following 25 years. But progress slowed almost everywhere in the 1990s, and in parts of Africa infant mortality rates increased."[39] The situation with regard to progress toward achieving the MDG child mortality goal is bleak. Only thirty-six developing countries are on target for reducing under-five child mortality to a third of its 1990 level by 2015. Moreover, 94 percent of child deaths take place in sixty countries, and some African countries are lagging behind by a century and, at current rates, will not reach the MDG 4 target level until 2115. More children die from disease and malnutrition than the total number of adults who die from the three great endemic killer diseases: HIV/AIDS, malaria, and tuberculosis.

Malnutrition is a leading cause of child death, and poor rural areas have a disproportionate number of deaths regardless of geographical location. Malaria and other diseases are also leading causes. In this regard, the "Nothing but Nets" campaign to provide insecticide-treated bed nets in malaria-prone countries has made a real difference. In Kenya, for example, there was a 44 percent reduction in child deaths among those sleeping under insecticide-treated nets compared with children who were not. Measles is another child killer, which strikes some 30 million to 40 million children each year and kills nearly half a million. The Global Measles Initiative to vaccinate children was launched in 2001 and represents another success story—measles mortality declined by 68 percent between 2000 and 2006. In sub-Saharan Africa the results have been even more dramatic, with a 91 percent reduction in child measles deaths. Bangladesh's measles eradication program gained world attention in 2006 when 33.5 million children were vaccinated in twenty days.

At its 2003 annual meeting, the World Health Assembly adopted a new strategic initiative to deal with child and youth health care. WHO's governing body thus identifies and targets seven priority areas for the future: maternal health, nutrition, prevention of communicable diseases, injuries, physical environment, psychosocial development and mental health, and children in difficult circumstances. In the context of this new strategy, WHO family and community health executive director Tomris Turmen offers that "the improvement of child and adolescent health should be the easiest of the Millennium Development Goals to achieve. . . . The strategy shows the way."[40] The MDGR 2007 points out that child mortality has declined globally in large part by interventions as simple as vaccinations for measles and other known child-killers. The continued success of such interventions requires enhanced resources and commitment, not only in delivery but also in educating children's caregivers about the necessity of childhood vaccinations.

MDG 5 centers on improving maternal health care. The target for this goal is to reduce by three-quarters, between 1990 and 2015, the maternal mortality ratio. Maternal health problems are the leading cause of death of women of reproductive age, and every minute a woman dies of complications of pregnancy or childbirth. Nearly all maternal-related deaths occur in developing countries, and most are preventable. Inadequate delivery services and prenatal and postnatal care as well as unsafe abortions account for a large number of such deaths. For every woman who dies during childbirth, twenty more sustain debilitating pregnancy-related injuries. In the context of high-income countries the answer seems simple: adequate pre- and postnatal maternal health care, family planning, skilled birth attendants, clean birthing facilities with adequate and safe blood supplies, and prevention of unsafe abortions. Unfortunately, in poor countries such luxuries simply are often not available, especially to the poor. Progress toward achieving the MDG target for maternal health is mixed and, in parts of Asia and nearly all of sub-Saharan Africa, very disappointing. In sub-Saharan Africa, for example, a woman has a 1 in 16 chance of dying during pregnancy and childbirth, compared with a 1 in 2,800 chance in developed countries. Adolescent fertility has increased in sub-Saharan Africa in recent years, which in itself represents another problem because girls ten to fourteen years of age are five times more likely to die in pregnancy and childbirth than women ages twenty to twenty-four. Part of the challenge is that "no single intervention can address the multiple causes of maternal deaths."[41]

Adequately measuring and assessing maternal mortality is difficult. Most countries do not have good vital registration systems, and underreporting is acute in situations where a skilled health attendant is absent. The proportion of births attended by skilled health personnel is used as an important indicator because of the high correlation between maternal mortality and the absence of skilled personnel. Within countries, great gaps exist. In India, for example, the rich are seven times more likely than the poor to have access to a skilled attendant, and in Ethiopia the ratio is 28 to 1. The United Nations Population Fund (UNFPA) initiated a Campaign to End Fistula in 2006. Obstetric fistula afflicts many women in developing countries and is highly correlated with maternal death. Obstetric fistula is a complication of pregnancy in high-risk areas whereby the excretory organs attach to the reproductive organs, poisoning the woman. Even if death does not result, the woman often faces incontinence and an inability to control bowel movements. The program operates in forty countries in sub-Saharan Africa, South Asia, and the Arab states; in late 2008, significant progress was reported in twenty-five of those countries. Also, in sub-Saharan Africa, maternal mortality is linked to HIV/AIDS, malaria, and other endemic diseases—or MDG 6.

HIV/AIDS is currently the most devastating health pandemic of our time—or, for that matter, any time in history—that challenges international cooperation.[42] HIV/AIDS has become the fourth-largest cause of death in the world. The MDG target related to AIDS is to have halted and begun to reverse the spread of HIV/AIDS by 2015. Yet this task seems daunting, especially in Africa and other low-income countries.

Approximately 33 million people have been infected with HIV and more than 5,700 people a day die from AIDS-related conditions.[43] Every day approximately 6,800 new cases of HIV infection are diagnosed. On a positive note, the number of people newly infected fell from 3 million in 2001 to 2.7 million in 2007. AIDS-related deaths similarly declined from 2.2 million in 2005 to 2 million in 2007.

Sub-Saharan Africa is home to the largest number of AIDS cases, with some 22.5 million people living with HIV/AIDS, followed by Asia, with 4.7 million cases. As might be expected, sub-Saharan Africa has suffered significant setbacks in life expectancy. In nearly two dozen countries, life expectancy has fallen over the past decade and a half. In six—Botswana, Burundi, Namibia, Rwanda, Zambia, and Zimbabwe—the decline has been more than seven years. In Botswana, Malawi, Mozambique, and Swaziland life expectancy is now less than forty years. Instead of a theoretical average life expectancy of sixty-two years in the absence of HIV/AIDS, sub-Saharan Africa's is only forty-seven years.[44] In the face of this overwhelming health crisis, Africa is experiencing a profound shortage of personnel in the health care sector.[45]

Between 1998 and 2007, there was a tenfold increase in funding for anti-HIV/AIDS programs globally. This amount, however, represented less than half of what is estimated to be necessary annually to make headway in the fight against the disease. Largely as a result of increased funding from the Global Fund to Fight AIDS, Tuberculosis and Malaria (Global Fund), in 2007 there was a 42 percent increase in access to anti-retroviral therapy. Despite the increase, less than one-third of those needing treatment had access.

The relationship between HIV/AIDS and humanitarian crises in Africa is particularly acute as extremely high levels of HIV coexist with a severe food crisis. Over 14 million persons are on the verge of starvation in six southern African countries, including Lesotho, Swaziland, and Zimbabwe, where adult HIV prevalence exceeds 30 percent. "Long-standing, severe epidemics are plunging millions of people deeper into destitution and desperation as their labour power weakens, incomes dwindle, assets shrink and households disintegrate."[46]

The situation in Africa clearly illustrates how the implications of AIDS for development go far beyond economic factors. One of the most significant impacts has been on educational systems. In the most highly infected countries, "HIV/AIDS kills teachers faster than they can be trained, makes orphans of students, and threatens to derail efforts . . . to get all boys and girls into primary school by 2015." Moreover, AIDS has resulted in a widening gender gap. In addition to being more susceptible to infection than boys, girls are more prone to dropping out of school to care for sick family members.[47]

The Sachs Millennium Project report and the HLP report on threats, challenges, and change both stressed the need to commit the resources required to deal effectively and quickly with AIDS. Nearly all the AIDS-related recommendations in these reports found their way into the Secretary-General's 2008 report to the General Assembly on Progress Made in the Implementation of the Declaration of Commitment on HIV/AIDS. One of the Secretary-General's key recommendations focused on the need to mobilize the financial resources required to fund a comprehensive response to the pandemic. He argued that an estimated $18 billion above what was currently pledged would be required to fund worldwide HIV/AIDS efforts over the next three years, including treatment, care, and prevention.

In his State of the Union address in 2003, President George W. Bush announced launching the President's Emergency Plan for AIDS Relief (PEPFAR) to provide $15 billion over five years. Congress responded positively to the plan, yet the White House consistently under-requested the level of funding needed to fulfill the promise. Also, even if fully funded, all but $1 billion of the $15 billion pledged is to be spent on bilateral programs in only fifteen targeted countries. Of the $1 billion pledged for the Global Fund to Fight AIDS, Tuberculosis and Malaria (a health funding partnership between governments, civil society, the private sector, and affected communities), only 20 percent may be used for HIV prevention, and of that amount a minimum of one-third must be spent on abstinence education. In 2008, Congress increased the PEPFAR program to $48 billion and broadened its mandate.

The lower status of women has led to the "feminization" of HIV/AIDS. Married women are contracting the disease from their partners and often are not in a position to question their partner's multiple sexual encounters or insist on condom use. As such, women are contracting the disease at a higher rate than men. Compounding the problem is the care of so-called AIDS orphans. As the MDGR 2007 highlights, "The care of orphans is an enormous social problem, which will only get worse as more parents die of AIDS."[48] The UN estimates that by 2010 over 20 million will have lost one or both of their parents to AIDS, the vast majority of them in sub-Saharan Africa.[49] Clearly this will challenge local, national, and global efforts to reduce childhood poverty and hunger, as well as providing primary and secondary education.

The second target for MDG 6 is to have halted by 2015 and begun to reverse the incidence of malaria and other major diseases. Malaria is the most prevalent tropical disease in the world with between 350 million and 500 million cases a year, resulting in over 1 million deaths. Although malaria is found in 109 countries, approximately 90 percent of the cases are located in sub-Saharan Africa with other pockets of prevalence in tropical climates. The death rate from malaria in sub-Saharan Africa is truly staggering. About 90 percent of those deaths are children under the age of five—nearly 800 per 100,000 children. This statistic is even more staggering when one considers that malaria deaths of young children in the region nearly doubled between 1990 and 1998 in comparison to the previous decade. Northern Africa has the second-highest death rate, at 47, followed by western Asia at 26 per 100,000.[50] But again, the core of the disease resides in sub-Saharan Africa, where malaria accounts for over one-fifth of all child deaths and places a tremendous strain on health-care facilities and systems.[51] The UN has pursued a variety of prophylactic measures,[52] the most promising of which is the use of insecticide-treated bed nets. The UN goal is to increase the coverage of people using these nets to 80 percent by 2010. As of 2007, net usage has yet to be quantified, but predictably, coverage in sub-Saharan Africa is trailing other regions. So, while progress is being made, no region is on track for achieving the target of halting or reversing the spread of malaria by 2015. The UN estimates that $3 billion is needed for malaria prevention and treatment, but the latest figures suggest that only $600 million is currently available.[53]

One-third of the world's population—over 2 billion people—is infected with tuberculosis (TB). Luckily, most such individuals, especially in more affluent countries, will never develop active TB. The developing world is home to about 90 percent of all active cases. In terms of impact, TB is the single most devastating disease among adults in the developing world, and sub-Saharan Africa and South Asia are the most affected regions. TB and HIV/AIDS are highly associated diseases. In sub-Saharan Africa, three-quarters of those infected with HIV/AIDS develop active TB. No region is on track for achieving the MDG target for TB. It is estimated that between 2000 and 2010 nearly a billion new infections will have occurred. Of those billion new infections, about 200 million persons will become sick and 35 million of those will die.[54]

At the same time, one of the success stories in international health has been the battle against polio. Only a few small pockets of the disease persist. Of all remaining cases, 99 percent are located in three countries—India, Nigeria, and Pakistan—with most of the remaining 1 percent located in just four additional countries. WHO, UNICEF, the U.S. Centers for Disease Control and Prevention, and Rotary International announced the new Global Polio Eradication Initiative in 2003. This program focuses its efforts in these seven most affected countries and in six others where there exists significant risk of re-infection.[55]

New on the scene in 2003 was SARS (severe acute respiratory syndrome), a powerful reminder, if one was needed, of how globalization has enabled disease to spread as easily as tourists and financial flows. In fact, SARS was the first new major communicable disease to emerge in the twenty-first century, with the first case identified in February 2003 in Hanoi, Vietnam. The disease is suspected to have originated in China except it was identified as an atypical respiratory disease. WHO was quick to act and in mid-March 2003 issued a global alert about mysterious cases of a severe atypical pneumonia with unknown etiology. Two days later, Canadian health authorities reported two deaths from a similar phenomenon. The following day, WHO elevated its alert as cases were being reported in Singapore and elsewhere. Within weeks the situation worsened in Hong Kong, and mainland China and WHO took the unprecedented step of issuing travel advisories for Beijing, Hong Kong, Guangdong Province, Shanxi Province, and Toronto (the site of a North American outbreak).

The global response to SARS illustrates how effective international cooperation can be in response to a crisis and how important international organizations and their leadership can be. In this case, WHO under the leadership of Gro Harlem Brundtland did not hesitate to confront both a great power (China) and a traditional organizational supporter (Canada). The level of cooperation was unprecedented. While not yet fully contained everywhere, the potentially rapid spread of the lethal disease (an estimated 8–10 percent of cases) does appear to have been checked.[56] WHO is currently leading the world's response to the avian influenza (A/(H5N1)), which, if it mutates so that it can be passed from human to human, threatens to be a worldwide pandemic that could kill tens of millions of people, because about half of those infected to date have died. As of December 2007, the disease had largely been contained, with two-thirds of all human cases in one country, Indonesia.

Ensuring Environmental Sustainability

The MDG goal of ensuring environmental sustainability centers on integrating the principles of sustainable development in development efforts and reversing the loss of environmental resources. The list of environmental problems plaguing the world's poor is daunting, including access to safe water and sanitation, modern energy supplies, deforestation, and desertification. Global climate change has emerged as a major environmental problem facing the international community. As articulated by the Intergovernmental Panel on Climate Change (IPCC), climate change is primarily caused by the burning of fossil fuels, which contributes to the buildup of "greenhouse gases" such as carbon dioxide and methane in the atmosphere. Climate change is also exacerbated by other environmental problems such as deforestation and desertification. In 1989, the UN held a conference in the Netherlands to map out a strategy for tackling climate change. The three-part strategy that emerged centered on first getting all states to commit to stabilizing and reducing carbon dioxide emissions by a fixed date. Second, only the advanced industrialized states should have binding targets and should pay for new environmentally friendly technologies to be used by developing countries to help them reduce their emissions without compromising their economic development. The third part was to conduct more research to reach a scientific consensus as to the causes and effects of climate change. This strategy served as the basis for the 1992 Earth Summit in Rio de Janeiro, which resulted in the 1992 Framework Convention on Climate Change and the follow-up treaty, the 1997 Kyoto Protocol.

The Kyoto Protocol was innovative in many respects. First, it set binding reductions on greenhouse-gas emissions on developed states whereby the European Union, the United States, and Japan agreed to reduce their emissions by 8 percent, 7 percent, and 6 percent below 1990 levels, respectively. To encourage efficiency and encourage growth, Kyoto also included transferable emissions permits that would allow states to buy and sell the right to pollute. This works by assigning each country a certain amount of emitting rights, determined by their contribution to world GDP and other considerations, and placing a cap on overall global emissions. For example, China, which is experiencing tremendous economic development (and emitting more greenhouse gases as a result), should not have to sacrifice economic growth because it has exceeded its emissions limit. Rather, China could buy the pollution rights of a sub-Saharan African country, which probably emits very little. Under this kind of "cap and trade" arrangement, China wins because it can continue its economic development without externalizing the costs and the sub-Saharan country earns money that can be used to achieve its own development goals. The main drawback of the Kyoto Protocol resulted from a negotiating concession, namely that developing countries only had "voluntary" reduction targets. Despite the drawbacks, the Clinton administration agreed to the Protocol but did not submit it to the U.S. Senate, as the prospects for passage were slim. In 2001, the Bush administration rejected the protocol.

With the world's largest greenhouse-gas emitter on the sidelines, the international community struggled along with a series of conferences in Marrakech (2001) and Montreal (2005). The United States participated in these conferences but only as a nonbinding member. In November 2006, a framework for UN collaboration in assisting countries to develop the capacity to respond effectively to climate change—the Nairobi Framework—grew out of a climate change conference in that city. In 2007, the theme of the annual opening of the General Assembly was climate change. Bolstered by the Academy Award–winning film by former U.S. Vice President Al Gore, *An Inconvenient Truth*, and the awarding of the Nobel Prize for Peace to Gore and the IPCC, global warming and climate change are now front and center of the international agenda. Once contested, global warming and climate change are now almost universally regarded as a central problem facing humanity. Prior to leaving office, George W. Bush also recognized the seriousness of global warming, though he sought to approach it in his own way, as evidenced by his decision to skip the 2007 UN meetings on the subject in New York and instead hold his own conference at the same time.[57]

Further multilateral progress on addressing climate change was suspended until after the 2008 U.S. presidential elections, as China has linked its cooperation for binding reductions on developing countries to binding U.S. participation.[58] As the MDGR 2007 warns, the science is now unequivocal, and climate change now threatens all human beings. The place of "green" politics in Barack Obama's campaign led many to think optimistically about a possible change in U.S. policy during his administration. Within weeks of taking office, his administration had dramatically altered the calculations for the possibilities of the UN conference in Copenhagen in December 2009. The chief climate negotiator, Todd Stern, raised hopes that an international accord might be possible when he stated that the United States would be involved in the negotiations in Denmark "in a robust way."[59]

Closely linked to climate change are deforestation and biodiversity loss. The world's forests serve as "sinks," absorbing carbon dioxide and conserving water and soil resources. Between 1990 and 2005, there was a 3 percent reduction in global forest coverage, with Latin America and sub-Saharan Africa losing 7 percent and 9 percent of their total forest lands, respectively. In twenty-five countries entire forest systems have disappeared, and in twenty-nine others they have been reduced by 90 percent. Such deforestation threatens biodiversity and is a significant factor in worsening climate change.

Over 60 percent of the world's ecosystems are damaged or being degraded, and biodiversity loss is on the rise. Although in 2002 the World Summit on Sustainable

Development pledged to significantly reduce biodiversity loss by 2010, loss continues unabated, and over 10,000 species are under threat of extinction. In the marine environment, for example, commercially targeted fish species have declined by 90 percent since 1960.

Although climate change and biodiversity loss loom and receive the lion's share of environmental attention, of much greater immediate concern for the overwhelming number of humanity are the scarcity of fresh water and a lack of sanitation. Worldwide over 2.8 billion people, or about 40 percent of the world's population, are experiencing either physical or economic water shortages. Over 1 billion do not have access to safe drinking water. WHO estimates that half the world's hospital beds are occupied by patients suffering from water-related diseases, and nearly 2 million people die from diarrhea and other water-borne diseases each year. One quarter of the people in the developing world use no form of sanitation, and an additional 15 percent use sanitation facilities that bring humans into direct contact with human waste. To focus global attention on the situation, the United Nations declared 2008 the International Year of Sanitation.

A GLOBAL PARTNERSHIP FOR DEVELOPMENT

The focus of MDG 8 is on building a global partnership for sustainable human development. In essence, it addresses the steps that the international community needs to take to attain the other seven goals. This goal specifies seven targets: developing an open, rule-based, predictable, and nondiscriminatory trading and financial system; addressing the special needs of least developed countries, including better access to developed country markets, increased aid, enhanced debt relief, and cancellation of official bilateral debt; addressing the needs of landlocked countries and small island states; increasing development assistance; dealing effectively and comprehensively with debt sustainability problems; developing and implementing strategies for youth employment; providing access to affordable essential drugs; and making certain that the benefits of new technologies are available to all. To meet these targets, new forms of cooperation and partnerships are needed among states, markets, the private sector, voluntary and civic organizations, local communities, and other stakeholders. This was noted especially regarding human rights and humanitarian affairs, where the role of NGOs and transnational corporations was discussed. The effort to forge new partnerships for sustainable human development or human security has taken a variety of forms and complexions. In general there has been a move to strengthen UN agencies' direct involvement with diverse elements of society, including NGOs, the private sector, and many other types of civil society organizations. Similar efforts have also been made by the Bretton Woods institutions. UN cooperation with other actors varies from issue to issue, with some examples of close cooperation and some examples of the opposite.

Business in General

UN partnership activities with for-profit actors—most especially through the Global Compact—have involved innovative thinking and actions. The main assumption underlying the Global Compact, which we analyzed in detail earlier, is that development cannot occur exclusively through governmental, intergovernmental, and nongovernmental organizations, nor can it be based on unbridled market forces alone. Creating local, national, and international enabling environments is essential, and a broad-based partnership involving all relevant stakeholders thus seems desirable.

However, bringing the private sector into the United Nations has brought with it some concerns and opposition. Many governments still hang tenaciously to the tenets of sovereignty and resent actions by multilateral agencies that do not respect the sanctity of that norm. Other governments, including China as the most notable and economically successful, have come to embrace this notion of multi-stakeholder partnerships. Corporations may also be part of the problem in that their activities may contribute to environmental degradation and underdevelopment. Corporations can also violate human rights or work in concert with genocidal regimes. In the view of some critics, the Global Compact is too weak to adequately address these issues and may even help gloss over poor corporate behavior. On the other hand, sustainable development cannot rely solely on foreign assistance and loans; it requires substantial financial investment from the private sector—local and international. Moreover, in the wake of the current global economic crisis, it would seem likely that overseas development assistance (ODA) will not significantly increase any time soon and is likely to continue its downward trend. Public-private partnerships thus may be one of the "evils" required to get necessary investment and liquidity into poorer economies.

Trade and Finance

The first target under MDG 8 is to "develop further an open, rule-based, predictable, nondiscriminatory trading and financial system." This goal inherently includes a commitment to good governance, development, and poverty reduction—both nationally and internationally. However, one of the major problems confronting the UN system almost since its inception has been that the management of trade and finance has seldom, if ever, functioned as the broad and coherent system that appears on paper. As stressed many times above, the United Nations system is but one of a group of interrelated international institutions designed to work toward achieving a set of common ends related to promoting and ensuring international peace, security, and human well-being. Thus, the UN system was designed to function as a norm- and rule-based system of institutions. A liberal, open, rule-based, predictable, nondiscriminatory trading and financial system served as the foundation of this new order. The Cold War and other factors, such as rich-country distrust of majority voting, intervened to frustrate the grand design. As the Cold War wound down and neoliberal economic ideas prevailed, political space opened for the further globalization of the capitalist world economy. For half a century, trade and financial liberalization had primarily affected the governments of advanced market economies. Now, pressure for change arose as global inequalities grew and extreme poverty persisted in large pockets around the globe. The North and South at least professed that the time had come to move toward a more equitable capitalist world order.

In recent years and despite significant inertia, the Washington-based IFIs, the WTO, and the UN system have come closer together. Progress could hardly be made in meeting such goals as target 12 on trade and finance without such collaboration. What has happened? The Millennium Project reports that part of the answer lies in the global economy. Since the successful conclusion in 1994 of the Uruguay Round of trade negotiations, the average tariffs for agricultural products and textiles and clothing have been reduced. However, such tariff and quota reductions do not benefit LDCs much. It is estimated, for example, that even if tariff protection on such products was reduced by half, only a little over 1 percent of the expected $200 billion gain by 2015 would go to sub-Saharan Africa, and only an additional $3.3 billion to South Asia outside of India. Moreover, while tariffs have been reduced, the agricultural sector remains heavily subsidized and these subsidies are more of a barrier to trade than tariffs.

The latest set of trade talks in the WTO is the most complex ever. This so-called Doha Development Agenda round of talks, launched in 2001 in Doha, Qatar, has taken up many of the items that were left unsettled by the Uruguay Round, such as agricultural subsidies, special less stringent adherence to trade rules for poor countries, and access to vital medicines and treatments. Although originally scheduled for completion in January 2005, the negotiations have dragged on and on. The main stumbling block for negotiations centers on a split between North and South regarding trade priorities. Developed countries want greater liberalization of financial and other services as well as an agreement involving trade-related investments (TRIMS). Developing countries, on the other hand, clearly linked agreement in those areas to the reduction of agricultural subsidies in the developed countries, especially Europe, whose position has proven intractable. For example, subsidies to farmers in Organisation for Economic Co-operation and Development (OECD) countries in 2003 totaled more than $349 billion. As David Lynch reminds us, "This is nearly $1 billion per day and is approximately the same amount as the combined annual GDP of all Sub-Saharan Africa."[60] In 2009, with the global financial crisis triggering protectionist policies, Doha seemed to be moribund. In 2004, the World Bank proposed a "trade for aid" initiative to help incorporate trade into development and poverty reduction. "To make trade an effective source of growth, developing countries need to increase the efficiency of their producers, shippers, freight handlers, and customs services—their capacity to trade. Rich countries can help by providing 'aid for trade' and sharing knowledge needed to establish competitive export industries."[61] At the 2005 WTO Ministry Meeting in Hong Kong, this initiative was adopted and was officially placed on the WTO agenda in 2007. However, the timing has raised questions among many developing states. According to WTO Director-General Pascal Lamy, "aid for trade" is designed to "break the shackles that have been holding back the trade potential of many poor countries, such as substandard infrastructure, lack of modern technology and inadequate financing."[62] Yet, developing countries see this as the WTO waving carrots in front of them to get them to make trade concessions on services and TRIMS without corresponding concessions related to reducing agricultural subsidies in the advanced industrialized countries.[63] A brief glimmer of hope emerged in June 2007, when trade talks resumed and the "G4"—Brazil, the European Union, India, and the United States—attempted to hammer out closure on critical issues, but again talks broke down and agreement failed. The North-South divide, thus, continues to frustrate global trade relations and increasingly states are turning to bilateral and regional trading agreements as vehicles for liberalizing trade and achieving more favorable terms of trade.

Development Assistance

Making sustainable human development a reality requires resources, especially financial resources. The governments meeting at the 2002 International Conference on Financing for Development in Monterrey recognized this and struck a bargain in this regard—the "Monterrey consensus." Developing-country governments agreed that sustainable development requires good governance, rule of law, sound government policies, and the mobilization of domestic resources; they committed to implement the reforms necessary to attain such conditions. The global North, on the other side, consented to increase official development assistance and to take concrete steps to increase ODA and move toward the target of 0.7 percent of GNP.

After nearly two decades of decline, development assistance reached a low point in 1997. But then it turned around and for eight straight years increased until it reached a new high in 2005 of $106.8 billion. In 2006, a downturn again set in, and ODA declined by 5.1 percent, and 2007 continued this pattern with an 8.4 percent drop. Although the G8 had committed in 2005 to double aid to Africa by 2010, ODA to the region (excluding debt relief to Nigeria) increased only 2 percent between 2005 and 2006. Only five donor countries—Denmark, Luxembourg, the Netherlands, Norway, and Sweden—have reached the 0.7 percent of GNP target. The United States falls at the bottom of the OECD Development Assistance Committee (DAC) list and devotes a mere 0.16 percent of its GDP to development assistance. The European Union collectively provides 54 percent of all ODA, and EU members have pledged to allocate 0.51 percent of GNP to ODA by 2010 and 0.7 percent by 2015. Unfortunately, these statistics are not likely to improve in the face of the ongoing global economic and financial crisis and economic recession. ODA is a tough sell to domestic constituencies in the best of times and even tougher when citizens are suffering at home.

Debt Relief

More concrete action is to be found in the area of debt relief. A vexing issue for many developing countries is making their debt burden sustainable. In 1996 the World Bank and IMF launched a plan to provide debt relief for the world's poorest, most heavily indebted countries. Under this Heavily Indebted Poor Countries (HIPC) initiative, creditors collectively move to provide exceptional assistance aimed at bringing the debtor country into a position of debt sustainability. As of December 2005, debt-reduction programs had been approved for twenty-eight of the forty-one eligible countries. The total collective debt reduction as of that date was $33 billion with the possibility of a cumulative total of $61 billion, should the remaining thirteen countries reach their decision points for receiving relief. About half comes from bilateral lenders and the remainder from IFIs.[64]

At the July 2005 G8 meeting, heads of government proposed a new Multilateral Debt Relief Initiative to supplement HIPC. Under this plan, three IFIs—the IMF, World Bank (specifically the IDA), and African Development Bank—would be allowed to provide 100 percent debt relief for countries completing the HIPC process.[65] According to the MDGR 2007, "By April 2007, 22 of the 40 HIPC countries had fulfilled all conditions and had been granted debt relief; eight had completed the first stage of the process and received debt relief on a provisional basis."[66] For the eligible countries, 90 percent of their external debt will be canceled. So important progress has been made, but there is a lot more work to go. Ten HIPC countries are still eligible but need help with the process while eleven others remain ineligible because of violent conflict and corruption. Indicating the significance of this problem, more than fifty countries spend more on debt servicing than on public health.

Geographically Challenged

The MDG strategy also places special emphasis on the situation of landlocked developing countries (LLDCs) and small island developing states (SIDS). These two groups are challenged by the particularities of their geographical situations and have attracted international attention beginning in the 1970s but especially since the early 1990s. The UN has summarized the special situation of landlocked countries concisely:

> Lack of territorial access to the sea, remoteness and isolation from world markets and high transit costs continue to impose serious constraints on the overall socio-economic development of landlocked developing countries. . . . Landlocked developing countries are generally among the poorest of the developing countries, with the weakest growth rates, and are typically heavily dependent on a very limited number of commodities for their export

earnings. . . . The lack of territorial access to the sea, remoteness and isolation from world markets appear to be the primary cause of their relative poverty.[67]

A few statistics provide some perspective on the situation. The distance to seaports and world trade routes is in many cases extreme. Six LLDCs, for example, are located more than 2,000 kilometers from the nearest sea, with Kazakhstan being situated 3,750 kilometers from the sea.[68] Also, over half of the LLDCs are least developed countries, adding a further dimension to their plight, as discussed earlier.

In 2001 General Assembly resolution 56/180 convened the International Ministerial Conference of Landlocked and Transit Developing States. In preparation for the August 2003 conference in Almaty, Kazakstan, the Secretary-General issued a report in August 2002 to the General Assembly. He summarized six objectives of the LLDCs with respect to their transit needs: secure unfettered access to the sea, reduce transportation costs and improve services to increase competitiveness, reduce delivery costs of imports, clear trade routes from delays, lessen deterioration and loss of goods during transit, and provide mechanisms for expanding trade.[69]

In comparison, small island developing states tend to have small resource bases, be highly subject to climatic conditions and natural and environmental disasters and deterioration, have limited freshwater resources, depend on conventional energy resources, and have small domestic markets and small populations with rapid growth rates. The situation confronting SIDS was addressed at the Earth Summit in Rio in 1992 and has been an issue continuously before the Commission on Sustainable Development since its creation.

The big push for an international agenda for dealing with SIDS, however, began with the Global Conference on the Sustainable Development of Small Island Developing States, held in Bridgetown, Barbados, during April and May 1994. The conference adopted the Barbados Programme of Action, which set forth specific recommendations and actions for promoting the sustainable development of SIDS.[70] Five years later, at the twenty-second special session of the General Assembly, the UN member states carried out an assessment of the implementation of the action program and called for more concerted action to carry it out. The 2002 World Summit on Sustainable Development recommitted member states to dealing with the special conditions confronting SIDS, and the Johannesburg Plan of Action resulting from the summit called for a ten-year comprehensive review of the Barbados Programme of Action at a high-level international conference. That meeting was held in Mauritius in January 2005, and the assembled member states unanimously adopted a political declaration, the Mauritius Declaration, and a revised plan, the Mauritius Strategy, for further implementing the Barbados Plan of Action.[71] Despite these promises, most landlocked and small island states (72 percent and 80 percent, respectively) received less ODA in 2004 than a decade earlier.

Access to Affordable, Essential Drugs

A key to dealing with endemic diseases like HIV/AIDS, malaria, and TB is providing affordable access to medicines and treatments. Although the situation in the developed world is far from perfect, access to affordable drugs on a sustainable basis is not available to over one-third of the developing world's population. In developing countries, only 35 percent of drugs classified as "essential" are available through the public sector. In both sub-Saharan Africa and South-Central Asia, less than 50 percent have such access. Of course, the situation is far worse for the extremely poor and marginalized parts of these populations.

Solving this problem is challenging because any solution is bundled with a variety of economic, political, legal, and moral issues. Access to medicines to treat those afflicted with HIV/AIDS has sparked a heated debate between developing and the most developed countries. As discussed above, over 90 percent of the 42 million persons currently living with HIV/AIDS live in the developing world. Yet nearly all the drugs that have been developed to treat the disease and its symptoms are produced and controlled under license by pharmaceutical companies in the developed world.

At the center of the controversy over the access issue in recent years has been the Agreement on Trade-Related Aspects of Intellectual Property Rights (TRIPS). Negotiated in the context of WTO, TRIPS represented an attempt to strike a balance between protecting the property rights of the inventory and providing access to the consumer. Article 7 of TRIPS recognizes that the protection of intellectual property contributes to the promotion of technological innovation and to the transfer and dissemination of technology, to the mutual advantage of users and producers of technological knowledge. At the same time, TRIPS attempts to balance the social and human needs of poor countries. TRIPS emerged from a genuine negotiating process where the need for balance was very much to the fore.[72]

The TRIPS agreement has three main aspects. First, the agreement sets minimum standards of protection and obligations for each member country. Second, it specifies general principles that must be followed in all intellectual property rights enforcement procedures. Finally, all disputes under it are subject to WTO dispute settlement procedures. In the context of international health, TRIPS has meant trying to find a balance between the interests of pharmaceutical companies and their home states, and non–technologically advanced countries that desire greater access to drugs that are essential for public health reasons. Under Article 31 of the TRIPS agreement, members are allowed to exercise "compulsory licensing" without the authorization of the property-right holder under certain conditions, such as public health necessities. However, the nature of this right is ambiguous and subject to dispute. Moreover, many developing countries do not have adequate manufacturing capabilities in pharmaceuticals to enable them even to make effective use of compulsory licensing.

At the WTO Ministerial Conference in Doha in November 2001, this issue came to a head. Developing-country governments, seeking greater access to drugs for treating HIV/AIDS, tuberculosis, and other endemic diseases, were able to get member states to agree to a compromise. In adopting the Doha Declaration on the TRIPS Agreement and Public Health, the member states affirmed that "the TRIPS Agreement does not and should not prevent members from taking measures to protect public health. Accordingly, while reiterating our commitment to the TRIPS Agreement, we affirm that the Agreement can and should be interpreted and implemented in a manner supportive of WTO members' right to protect public health and, in particular, to promote access to medicines for all."[73]

The declaration specified that the least developed countries would be given until January 2016 before being required to implement or enforce the TRIPS agreement with regard to pharmaceutical products. The declaration, however, still left unresolved the issue of how to deal with those countries that do not have sufficient manufacturing capabilities in pharmaceuticals to enable them even to make effective use of compulsory licensing. In July 2007, Rwanda became the first country to announce that, because of the lack of local production capacity, it would import cheaper generic drugs made elsewhere under compulsory licensing.

This issue, however, remains contested, with the WTO Council on TRIPS attempting to forge a compromise between the United States and other technologically advanced countries as well as those less technologically advanced member states that are demanding more flexible patent rules for cases of national public health exigencies. The shortage in Europe and the United States of a patented drug that treats the symptoms of avian flu in humans has prompted many in the advanced industrialized countries to rethink primacy of intellectual property rights in the face of an epidemic.

Information/Communication Technology

Globalization is fueled, in large part, by the continuing revolution of information and communication technologies (ICTs).[74] The challenge centers on making the benefits of ICTs available to all, especially given the inequalities inherent in the present information order—the so-called digital divide. According the UN:

> By the end of 2005, just over 15 percent of the world's population was using the internet. However, the proportions are skewed in favour of richer countries. Over half of the population in developed regions was using the internet in 2005, compared to 9 percent in developing regions and 1 percent in the 50 least developed countries.[75]

At the beginning of 2009, 77 percent of those residing in developing countries had possible access to cellular telephone signals. At the same time, however, more than 30 percent of the people in the global South still did not have access to electricity, with the percentage in sub-Saharan Africa being 74 percent.

With regard to promoting human development, ICT has a larger context. As suggested in the final report of the UNDP's Digital Opportunity Initiative, "Used in the right way and for the right purposes, ICT can have a dramatic impact on achieving specific social and economic development goals as well as play a key role in broader national development strategies."[76] Indeed, "ICT provides developing nations with an unprecedented opportunity to meet vital development goals such as poverty reduction, basic health care, and education far more effectively than before."[77] In the highly globalized information age, development cannot occur without such social and economic networks. The UN system has in many ways been energized by the possibilities that ICT presents for promoting human development and achieving the MDGs. As witnessed during the two-year process surrounding the World Summit on the Information Society, many prickly political problems plague the path to creating a common global vision of the norms and principles underlying the information society.[78]

For some years now, the UNDP has been working with member states and other agencies to make ICT an integral part of development strategies and policies. Much of this work has focused on helping countries integrate and prioritize ICT planning in their policy frameworks and Poverty Reduction Strategy Papers. Also, UNDP places emphasis on using ICT to improve governance and the capacity of governments to more effectively achieve the MDGs and to help them foster greater participation by civil society and the private sector.

The creation of effective ICT-related partnerships among international institutions, governments, civil society, and the private sector has increased. Some of these partnerships have been initiated by UN agencies. For example, the UN Information and Communications Task Force (ICT Task Force) was established by the Secretary-General in response to a March 2001 request from ECOSOC. The ICT Task Force was given the task of providing overall leadership to the UN and forging strategic partnerships with private industry, foundations, donors, and other relevant stakeholders. The ICT Task Force works in close cooperation with a growing number of other UN-system networking and capacity-building ICT initiatives, including the Digital Opportunity Initiative (launched by the UNDP, World Bank, Accenture, and Markle Foundation), the Network Readiness and Resource Initiative (UN Foundation, IBM, Markle Foundation, World Economic Forum, Harvard University, and other partners), the UN Volunteers program's United Nations Information Technology Service, WHO's Health InterNetwork, and Netaid.org. The list alone connotes how wide a net must be cast routinely even to form a task force with relevant expertise and outreach.

Some ICT-related partnerships have been initiated by civil society. A noteworthy one is the "$100 laptop," which was started by MIT professor Nicholas Negroponte and his new NGO called One Laptop Per Child (OLPC.org). The idea is that a partnership between the UN, open-source programmers, Google, media mogul Rupert Murdoch, governments, and MIT could create and deliver cheap, yet rugged, battery-driven computers suitable for children in the developing world. The computers could be used in areas where electricity is spotty so students can continue their education by using their battery-powered computers. Negroponte and MIT agreed to build the prototype if governments agreed to buy them in large numbers (to keep the price down) for distribution in developing countries. The UN would assist in distribution and in providing technical assistance. In 2005, the prototype computer made its debut at the UN World Summit on the Information Society in Tunis and by 2007 was in final testing. Although the price is more like $200 a computer, *New York Times* technology reporter David Pogue says the laptop (called the XO) "is absolutely amazing and in my limited tests, a total kid magnet. Both the hardware and the software exhibit breakthrough after breakthrough, some of them not available on any other laptop for $400 or $4000."[79] The computer is predicted to be in demand for children in the North as well as the South. Mass production began in 2008 and OLPC.org has started a new program called "Give 1, Get 1," where the computers will be available to those in developed countries for $400.[80] When someone purchases the XO for a child in the North, a child in the South will receive one as well. Coupled with governments that have already agreed to purchase millions of the machines, this initiative promises to be an important bridge of the technological divide.

EXPLAINING CHANGE

The formal consensus about MDGs, as evidenced by the 2005 World Summit, is not universal. But a generally shared orientation, underpinned by shared meanings and shared values, appears to be present.[81] Disagreements center on strategy and commitments. Governments in Zimbabwe or Burma may vote for the MDGs in New York. But their policies at home reflect anything but a deep commitment to doing what is necessary to enhance human security. Governments in Washington and Paris may also vote for the MDGs, but whether they are prepared to increase their development assistance and make meaningful trade concessions to developing countries is not always evident. The European Union continues to protect European agricultural producers to the detriment of poor countries attempting to sell their exports in Europe, and despite verbal commitments, ODA by the North continues to decline.

Progress toward achieving the MDGs is mixed. Speaking before the 2002 World Economic Forum in New York, Kofi Annan designated poverty as a major threat to global security. In his first annual report on how member states have followed up the Millennium Declaration, he reflected disappointingly that "the world is falling short. If we carry on the way we are, most of the pledges are not going to be fulfilled." He referred to MDG progress as being a mixed record, with significant differences across the world's regions.[82] The series of reports from the team led by Jeffrey Sachs for the 2005 World Summit also emphasized that the glass was not even half full. The MDGR 2007 continued with the "mixed" theme. The successes and failures in reaching MDG goals and associated targets will lead to new goals, new thinking, and new strategies. As a guide for thinking and policy, the concept of sustainable human development will continue to evolve. Students of international organization should struggle to understand how and why processes and structures evolved at the United Nations and should consider what directions development activities might take in the future. In this context, a dispassionate assessment can be made of what the world organization can and cannot reasonably be expected to accomplish.

A traditional starting point for such an assessment is to examine sustainable development activities in the context of functionalism. Proponents argue that "growth of technology and spread and intensification of the desire for higher standards of material welfare" lead to greater international cooperation in search of expanded political authority.[83] Functionalists suggest that popular interest in sustainable development results from expanded technical cooperation in developmental and environmental concerns. Accordingly, technical cooperation for development has spilled over into the environmental area, and technical cooperation on ecological concerns has come to encompass development issues. The interplay between the two has thus become so pervasive that environment and development are no longer separate concepts.

Proponents of this line of reasoning point to the evolving process, beginning around the time of the Stockholm conference, whereby the concept of eco-development came onto the global agenda. In attempting to lay the foundations of a global plan of action for dealing with environmental issues, Maurice Strong and other UN officials quickly came to perceive the inseparability of the two previously separate issues. This orientation evolved over later decades as the environmental science community, development assistance practitioners and scholars, international financiers, government officials, and many others came to see their own work to be achievable only in the context of a more holistic eco-development world view.

Our two explanations for the spread of cooperation in the human rights arena—that is, consensual-knowledge communities and social learning—grow out of this more general functionalist perspective. The first explanation suggests that the convergence of development and environment into sustainable development and the subsequent convergence of sustainable development and human development and human security into sustainable human development on the global public policy agenda grow from agreement over eco-development in private communities of knowledge. The second explanation emphasizes the importance of institutional learning and argues that the normative convergence is a product of a process in which state actors have recognized (or "learned") the inherent inseparability of the two issues.

Proponents of the consensual-knowledge approach point to the growth and involvement, at least of Northern civic actors, in sustainable development politics at the global intergovernmental level. They also point to the evolution of the role of NGOs since Stockholm, to the activities of NGOs in the Rio and subsequent conference processes, and to the influence of knowledge communities on issues such as protection of the ozone layer as evidence that this approach is valid.[84] The same can be applied to global warming and climate change.

The nature of the evolution of NGO involvement in the sustainable human development arena, however, casts some doubt on the validity of this view. There are thousands of opinion communities concerned with sustainable development. Yet the diversity and often outright antagonisms among these communities challenge the notion that some dominant consensual body of knowledge underlies events within global sustainable development processes. The windows broken and the stores looted in such cities as Seattle, Genoa, Montreal, Evian, and Hong Kong (the sites of G8 or WTO summits) attest to this reality.[85] This is not to suggest the absence of a convergence of interests over sustainability issues. Indeed, the concept has come to dominate much of the debate over both development and environment.

Although growing consensus can be observed within specific areas of environmental concern, that consensus has yet to be translated into a coherent global scientific consensus about sustainable development. Moreover, a large gulf still separates basic and applied scientists over many eco-development issues. The notion that some coherent and identifiable social learning process underpins global sustainable development activities is suspect yet may hold somewhat more promise for the future. The idea of sustainable development has served as a common denominator, helping to bridge the turf and ideological divides that otherwise separate the IFIs from other members of the UN family.[86]

In global debates, delegates from the global North usually define sustainability rather narrowly as environmental protection and resource conservation. Southerners normally define the concept with specific reference to meeting basic human needs and reducing poverty. The focus here is on people, on promoting economic growth that produces employment and encourages the wider participation of people in economic processes.[87] Economists have their own definition. They say sustainable development is "an economic process in which the quantity and quality of our stocks of natural resources (like forests) and the integrity of biogeochemical cycles (like climate) are sustained and passed on to the future generations unimpaired."[88] The feedback from seemingly endless conferences and the ever-evolving closer relationship among previously discordant agencies—especially the Bretton Woods institutions and other members of the UN system—may have well served to create a genuine learning environment. Equally important, the Global Compact (GC) was from its origins a normative exercise designed to create social learning. One of its architects, John Ruggie, pointed out:

Companies submit case studies of what they have done to translate their commitment to the GC principles into concrete corporate practices. This occasions a dialogue among GC participants from all sectors—the UN, labor, and civil society organizations. . . . A research network, led by the Corporate Citizenship Unit of Warwick University, facilitates the dialogue. Its aim is to reach broader consensus-based definitions of what constitutes good practices than any of the parties could achieve alone. Those definitions, together with illustrative case studies, are then publicized in an on-line learning bank, which will become a standard reference source for corporate social responsibility.[89]

These examples do not provide concrete proof of an effective learning process. However, they do point to the possibility that organizational learning may well be occurring and help to explain the growing convergence around the MDG consensual framework.

Given limited resources and lack of real sustained leadership on the part of its more powerful members, the United Nations nonetheless has done some remarkable things. The world organization has improved the lives of hundreds of millions of people and launched a host of ideas that have changed the world.[90] The world is far better off with the United Nations than without it. But the world body could do so much more. Some observers and scholars of international relations have argued that the UN must be at the center of global governance in that it is the only organization uniquely positioned to respond to and manage the forces of globalization.[91] Yet, the UN cannot change the priorities of member states so that states also put the UN at the center of global governance. The world organization can suggest priorities, seek commitments, coordinate action, and attempt to bridge divides through norm creation. But ultimately the governments of member-states must choose to work through, and with, the UN to manage pressing global problems such as disease, extreme poverty, and environment degradation. States invest scarce resources into priorities they value, and clearly they continue to value military hardware, subsidies to domestic farmers and industries, and welfare for their own people. Resources provided for the UN in general, and the MDGs in particular, show that the UN and MDGs still do not rate high on the list. Until the priorities of member states change, the UN role in promoting sustainable human development will be, at best, modest.

A recurring problem is that when states become great powers, they think that they have enough economic and military power that they do not need muscular international law and organization. In that sense, great powers usually make bad multilateralists, as they usually have strong unilateralist tendencies and some capacity to pursue an agenda without other countries. It is more the middle and smaller powers that tend to be the greatest supporters of multilateral institutions, but of course they lack the political power to bring about what they want. The United States after World War II led in the creation of international organizations like the UN and the World Bank, but on condition that it have the veto in the Security Council and strong voting rights in the Bank. The WTO is a very interesting contemporary example in that the United States was willing to join the WTO without a veto, or special voting rights, and thus it subjected itself to the authority of the Dispute Resolution Panels. But it is state members, not any WTO body, that decide on sanctions when trade policies are held to violate WTO rules. An intriguing question is whether socioeconomic globalization, combined with the declining utility of great-power war among themselves, can produce a different dynamic that favors the growth of authoritative international organizations like the UN.

There are some signs of partial change in multilateral governance. The G8, for example, has moved to institutionalize (at least for now) an initiative begun by French President Jacques Chirac at the group's annual meeting in Evian in 2003, inviting leaders of select developing countries to participate. Although U.S. President George W. Bush refused to follow suit the following year, Britain's Tony Blair continued the practice at the G8 Summit in Scotland's Gleneagles in 2005. He invited the leaders of Brazil, China, India, Mexico, and South Africa—known as the "Outreach 5" or O5. The O5 leaders were again invited to participate in St. Petersburg, Russia, in 2006, and in 2007 in Germany the process was formalized into the so-called Heiligendamm Process. This process provides for a formalized dialogue among the G8 and O5 countries on the key issues of innovation, freedom of investment, development in Africa, and energy efficiency. At the 2007 parley in Heiligendamm, G8 leaders also pledged to provide $60 billion in assistance for combating HIV/AIDS and other infectious diseases in Africa. The jury is still out, however, on follow-through, the durability of this institutional "change," and implications for global governance and the role of the UN in global governance processes. This example suggests that the world will continue to be characterized by multiple regimes and a variety of governance mechanisms, rather than any simple arrangement that looks like world government.

NOTES

1. Kofi A. Annan, *"We the Peoples": The Role of the United Nations in the 21st Century* (New York: United Nations, 2000), 9–10. Also available at www.un.org/millennium/sg/report/.

2. UN document A.AC.253/25, March 22, 2000.

3. UN document A/RES/55/2, September 18, 2000.

4. See, for instance, David Held and Anthony McGrew, eds., *Governing Globalization: Power, Authority and Global Governance* (Cambridge, UK: Polity Press, 2002); James H. Mittelman, *Whither Globalization? The Vortex of Knowledge and Ideology* (London: Routledge, 2004); Volker Rittberger, ed., *Global Governance and the United Nations System* (Tokyo: United Nations University Press, 2002); Rorden Wilkinson and Steve Hughes, eds., *Global Governance: Critical Perspectives* (London: Routledge, 2002); Esref Aksu and Joseph A. Camilleri, eds., *Democratizing Global Governance* (New York: Palgrave, 2002); Paul Kennedy,

Dirk Messner, and Franz Nuscheler, *Global Trends and Global Governance* (London: Pluto, 2002); Andrew F. Cooper, John English, and Ramesh Thakur, eds., *Enhancing Global Governance: Towards a New Diplomacy* (Tokyo: UN University Press, 2002); Anthony Giddens, *Runaway World: How Globalization Is Reshaping Our Lives* (New York: Routledge, 2000); David P. Forsythe, Patrice C. McMahon, and Andrew Wedeman, eds., *American Foreign Policy in a Globalized World* (New York: Routledge, 2006); John H. Dunning, ed., *Making Globalization Good: The Moral Challenge of Global Capitalism* (Oxford: Oxford University Press, 2003); Rodney Bruce Hall and Thomas J. Biersteker, eds., *The Emergence of Private Authority in Global Governance* (Cambridge: Cambridge University Press, 2002); and Tagi Sagafinejad with John Dunning, *The UN and Transnational Corporations: From Code of Conduct to Global Compact* (Bloomington: Indiana University Press, 2008).

5. For an example of this type of analysis, see especially the chapters by John Ruggie, Edward C. Luck, and Karen Mingst for attention to the UN in the context of an interdependent world in *American Foreign Policy*.

6. Ngaire Woods, "The Political Economy of Globalization," in *The Political Economy of Globalization*, ed. Ngaire Woods (New York: St. Martin's Press, 2000), 1–19.

7. Jan Aart Scholte, *Globalization: A Critical Introduction* (New York: St. Martin's Press, 2000), 13–40.

8. "Impact of Globalization on Social Development," UN document A.AC.253/25, March 12, 2000, 3–8.

9. Jan Aart Scholte, "Globalization: Governance and Corporate Citizenship," Remarks to the Third Annual Warwick Corporate Citizenship Unit Conference, Scarman House, Warwick, England, July 10, 2000, 4.

10. David Held, Anthony McGrew, David Goldblatt, and Jonathan Perraton, *Global Transformations: Politics, Economics and Culture* (Cambridge, UK: Polity Press, 1999), and Scholte, *Critical Introduction*.

11. Scholte, *Critical Introduction*.

12. John Gerard Ruggie, "Territoriality and Beyond: Problematizing Modernity in International Relations," *International Organization* 47, no. 1 (1993): 139–174.

13. For an examination of these issues, see Held et al., *Global Transformations*.

14. Ankie Hoogvelt, *Globalization and the Postcolonial World*, 2nd ed. (Baltimore: Johns Hopkins University Press, 2001), and Manuel Castells, *The Rise of the Network Society* (Cambridge: Oxford University Press, 1996). For an introduction, see Stanley Wasserman and Katherine Faust, *Social Network Analysis: Methods and Applications* (Cambridge: Cambridge University Press, 1994).

15. See Hoogvelt's review of the writings of Roland Robertson, David Harvey, Anthony Giddens, and Manuel Castells in this regard in *Globalization and the Postcolonial World*, 120–143.

16. James H. Mittelman and Norani Othman, *Capturing Globalization* (London: Routledge, 2001).

17. UNDP, *Human Development Report 2003* (New York: Oxford University Press, 2003).

18. See Millennium Development Project, *Investing in Development: A Practical Plan to Achieve the Millennium Development Goals* (New York: UNDP, 2005).

19. World Bank, *World Development Indicators 2006* (Washington, D.C.: International Bank for Reconstruction and Development/World Bank 2006).

20. NGLS Roundup, "MDGs: Moving Forward the Millennium Development Goals," November 2002.

21. *The Millennium Development Goals Report 2008* (New York: United Nations, 2008).

22. Millennium Project, *Investing in Development: A Practical Plan to Achieve the Millennium Development Goals* (New York: UNDP, 2005), also called "Sachs report," 13–14. See "Millennium Indicators Data Base," UN Statistics Division Web site, 2005, and www.develop mentgoals.org/Poverty.htm; and Jeffrey Sachs, *The End of Poverty: Economic Possibilities for Our Time* (New York: Penguin Books, 2005).

23. FAO, *The State of Food and Agriculture 2007*, Rome, November 15, 2007, 130–134.

24. *Millennium Development Goals Report 2007*, 8.

25. Millennium Project, *Investing in Development*, 13–14.

26. Ibid.

27. United Nations General Assembly 2005 World Summit Outcome A/59/2005, para 44; www.un-ngls.org/orf/UN-Summit-SG-Report-Implementation-N0554506.pdf.

28. Paris21, 2000, A Better World for All, "Education," www.paris21.org/betterworld/ education.htm.

29. See, for example, UNESCO, "Literacy," http://portal.unesco.org/education/en/ev .php-URL_ID=40338&URL_DO=DO_TOPIC&URL_SECTION=201.html.

30. Mark Malloch Brown, "World's Top Goals Require Women's Empowerment," March 8, 2003.

31. World Bank, "Millennium Development Goals, Promote Gender Equality and Empower Women," http://ddp-ext.worldbank.org/ext/GMIS/gdmis.do?siteId=2&goalId= 7&menuId=LNAV01GOAL3.

32. UNIFEM Press Release, May 1, 2003.

33. UN, Division for the Advancement of Women, "Convention on the Elimination of All Forms of Discrimination against Women," www.un.org/womenwatch/daw/cedaw/.

34. UN Commission on Human Rights Press Release, April 9, 2003.

35. UN Office on Drugs and Crime, "Trafficking in Human Beings," www.unodc.org/ unodc/en/trafficking_human_beings.html.

36. Ibid. On the topic of crime more broadly, see also Mark Findlay, *The Globalisation of Crime* (Cambridge: Cambridge University Press, 1999); Robin Thomas Naylor, *Wages of Crime: Black Markets, Illegal Finance, and the Underworld Economy* (Ithaca, N.Y.: Cornell University Press, 2002).

37. www.unodc.org/unodc/en/treaties/CTOC/signatures.html. Two other protocols exist: *Protocol to Prevent, Suppress and Punish Trafficking in Persons, Especially Women and Children*, supplementing the United Nations Convention against Transnational Organized Crime; and *Protocol against the Illicit Manufacturing of and Trafficking in Firearms, Their Parts and Components and Ammunition*, supplementing the United Nations Convention against Transnational Organized Crime.

38. UN document E/CN.4/2002/L.63, para. 19.

39. World Bank, "Millennium Development Goals Promote Gender Equality."

40. WHO Press Release, May 26, 2003.

41. *Millennium Development Goals Report 2007*, 17.

42. See Leon Gordenker, Roger A. Coate, Christer Jönsson, and Peter Söderholm, *International Cooperation in Response to AIDS* (London: Pinter, 1995), and Peter Söderholm, *Global Governance of AIDS: Partnerships with Civil Society* (Lund, Sweden: Lund University Press, 1997).

43. In 2007, UNAIDS revised its initial HIV/AIDS figures downward by approximately 12 percent using a more statistically sound methodology. Hence, the figures presented here are significantly lower than in previous editions of this book.

44. UNAIDS, AIDS Epidemic Update, December 2001.

45. WHO Press Release/ReliefWeb, February 1, 2002.

46. Ibid.

47. World Bank, *Education and HIV/AIDS: A Window of Hope*, available at www .worldbank.org/developmentnews/stories/html/050802a.htm.

48. Ibid., 20.

49. Ibid.

50. Global Fund Against AIDS, Tuberculosis and Malaria, "Malaria," www.the globalfund.org/documents/publications/diseasereport/disease_report_malaria_en.pdf; also, http://millenniumindicators.un.org/unsd/mi/mi_worldregn.asp.

51. WHO, *Africa Malaria Report 2003*, available at www.rbm.who.int/amd2003/ amr2003/.

52. *Millennium Development Goals Report 2007*, 20.

53. Ibid.

54. Global Fund Against AIDS, Tuberculosis and Malaria, "Tuberculosis," www.theglobal fund.org.

55. UNICEF Press Release, May 13, 2003.

56. WHO Press Release, May 22, 2003.

57. Steven Lee Meyers, "Bush to Skip U.N. Talks on Global Warming," *New York Times*, September 24, 2007.

58. "Beijing Signals Plan to Reject Emissions Caps," *Bangkok Post*, November 10, 2007, 4.

59. Quoted by Elisabeth Rosenthal, "Obama's Backing Increases Hopes for Climate Pact," *New York Times*, March 1, 2009.

60. David Lynch, "Negotiating Between and Across Borders," in *A Global Agenda: Issues Before the 60th General Assembly of the United Nations*, ed. Angela Drakulich (New York: UNA-USA, 2005), 225.

61. World Bank, "Millennium Development Goals: Building a Global Partnership for Development," http://ddp-ext.worldbank.org/ext/GMIS/gdmis.do?siteId=2&goalId=12& menuId=LNAV01GOAL8.

62. "WTO Places Aid for Trade on Its Agenda," *Bangkok Post*, November 16, 2007, B7.

63. Ibid.

64. IMF, Fact Sheet: "Debt Relief Under the Heavily Indebted Poor Countries (HIPC) Initiative," December 2005, www.imf.org/external/np/exr/facts/hipc.htm.

65. IMF, Fact Sheet: "The Multilateral Debt Relief Initiative (MDRI)," December 2005, www.imf.org/external/np/exr/facts/mdri.htm.

66. *Millennium Development Goals Report 2007*, 30.

67. UN Office of the High Representative for the Least Developed Countries, Landlocked Developing Countries and the Small Island Developing States (UN-OHRLLS), "Landlocked Developing Countries," at www.un.org/special-rep/ohrlls/lldc/default.htm.

68. UN document A/57/340, August 23, 2002.

69. Ibid.

70. UN document A/CONF.167/9, part I, Annex I (1994).

71. UN document A/S–22/9/Rev.1 and Supplement no. 3 (A/S–22/9/Rev.1), and UN Department for Economic and Social Affairs, Division for Sustainable Development, "Small Island Developing States (SIDS)," www.un.org/esa/sustdev/sids/sids.htm.

72. WTO, "Pharmaceutical Patents and the TRIPS Agreement," www.wto.org/english/ tratop_e/trips_e/pharma_ato186_e.htm.

73. WTO, "Doha WTO Ministerial 2001: Ministerial Declaration," www.wto.org/english/thewto_e/minist_e/min01_e/mindecl_e.htm.

74. See John Mathiason, *Internet Governance* (London: Routledge, 2009).

75. *Millennium Development Goals Report 2007*, 20.

76. Digital Opportunity Initiative, "Creating a Development Dynamic: Final Report of the Digital Opportunity Initiative," www.opt-init.org/framework/pages/es.html.

77. UNDP Fast Facts: "Driving."

78. See Andrew Chadwick, *Internet Politics: States, Citizens, and New Communication Technologies* (New York: Oxford University Press, 2006).

79. David Pogue, "Laptop with a Mission Widens its Audience," *New York Times*, October 4, 2007.

80. Ibid.

81. David Held, "Toward a New Consensus: Answering the Dangers of Globalization," *Harvard International Review* 27 (Summer 2005): 14–17.

82. United Nations, "Report of the Secretary-General on the Implementation of the Millennium Declaration," September 2003.

83. Harold Jacobson, *Networks of Interdependence* (New York: Knopf, 1984), 62–63.

84. See, for example, Peter Haas, "Banning Chlorofluorocarbons: Epistemic Community Efforts to Protect Stratospheric Ozone," *International Organization* 46, no. 1 (1992): 187–224.

85. For a more optimistic view, see Michael Edwards, *Future Positive: International Cooperation in the 21st Century* (London: Earthscan, 2000), and *NGO Rights and Responsibilities: A New Deal for Global Governance* (London: Foreign Policy Centre, 2000).

86. For an overview of the evolution of eco-development politics, see Lynton K. Caldwell, *International Environmental Policy: Emergence and Dimensions*, 2nd ed. (Durham, N.C.: Duke University Press, 1991), 81.

87. Alvaro de Soto, "The Global Environment: A Southern Perspective," *International Journal* 15, no. 8 (1992): 679–705, and UNDP, *Human Development Report 1993* (New York: Oxford University Press, 1993). This theme reappears in all subsequent annual reports.

88. Anil Agarwal, "What Is Sustainable Development?" *Concordare* (Spring 1993): 2.

89. John Gerard Ruggie, "Global_governance.net: The Global Compact As Learning Network," *Global Governance* 7, no. 4 (2001): 372–373.

90. See Richard Jolly, Louis Emmerij, and Thomas G. Weiss, *UN Ideas That Changed the World* (Bloomington: Indiana University Press, 2009).

91. See, for example, Yannis A Stivactis, ed., *International Order in Globalizing World* (Burlington, Vt.: Ashgate, 2007), and Joseph E. Stiglitz, *Making Globalization Work* (New York: W. W. Norton, 2006).

Conclusion:
Learning from Change

In a time when winds of change are blowing very strong, we must rest content with knowing that foresight is always imperfect and that choices must always be made in ignorance of their full consequences. That is the price we pay for being able to make the world over by changing our own behavior, individually and collectively, in response to cherished hopes and shared purposes, framed in words. Our capacity to err is our capacity to learn and thereby achieve partial and imperfect, but real, improvement in the conditions of human life.

—William H. McNeill[1]

FROM THE OUTSET, we have portrayed the United Nations and the broader UN system as highly interdependent with their political contexts. The dynamic interplay of interstate politics is the primary force determining the evolution of the UN system. With Cold War blinders removed, even in a world of clear U.S. military primacy, it is evident that multilateral organizations can influence the course of world politics—especially when viewed from a longer-run perspective. For the United Nations to become the centerpiece of global governance, as envisioned by some of its proponents, states would need to transfer much more loyalty, power, and authority to the world body so that it could control more of its surroundings rather than the reverse. But such a radical change is still distant.

Yet world politics continues to evolve, and the need to manage transnational problems remains pressing.[2] Analyzing the UN and charting its future would be easier if we had a surer grasp of the nature of world politics in the twenty-first century. In William McNeill's words, it would certainly be nice to know in which direction the winds of change are blowing. Alas, this is not easy. The initial

363

euphoria about the end of the Cold War and optimism about possibilities for democratization have given way to a more realistic, and perhaps normal, caution. The winds of hypernationalism and unilateralism that blew from the George W. Bush administration led to the November 2008 elections that brought to power the Obama administration, which will likely be more friendly to multilateralism. Stay tuned.

MEASURING CHANGE

A first analytical concern regards defining what constitutes "change."[3] Kal Holsti's *Taming the Sovereigns* probes the concept of change and ways of measuring it: "These include change as novelty or replacement, change as addition or subtraction, increased complexity, transformation, reversion, and obsolescence."[4] Qualitative change can be defined as difference in kind. Novelty and replacement are types of qualitative change. The presumption is of rupture, or a clear break between what once was and what currently is.[5] To that extent, we are looking for discontinuities, when new forms replace old ones, which is pretty much the story of the United Nations—including, for instance, the creation of peacekeeping and the return to peace enforcement; the introduction of gender and other types of human rights mainstreaming; the change from protecting the environment to sustainable development.

Holsti notes that change is quite different for someone playing today's stock market or for those of us trying to understand it in international relations, where recent events are not of interest unless they have a demonstrable effect on how diplomatic, military, or humanitarian work is actually done. "This is the Hegelian and Marxist problem: at what point," he asks, "does quantitative change lead to qualitative consequences?"[6] In other words, we can also characterize as "new" a tipping point at which quantitative change is so substantial that it constitutes something qualitatively "new."[7]

Many of the arguments about the shifts that have occurred over the past twenty years about the nature of humanitarian agencies, for example, are claims that the environment, the relationships among actors, and the process of delivery of relief itself have become more complex. In many respects, the sum of such changes in quantitative trends has combined in such a way as to have "system effects," the equivalent of qualitative change.[8] The growing involvement of states, for instance, has had a series of important consequences on the organization of humanitarian action. The use of the military for human protection purposes is undoubtedly the clearest example.[9]

In many instances, the contemporary international order is in turmoil. The mere quantity of developments may strike readers—it certainly does the authors—as the equivalent of qualitative change. In presenting his proposal to the General Assembly in March 2006, Secretary-General Kofi Annan summarized: "Today's United Nations is vastly different from the Organization that emerged from the San Francisco conference more than 60 years ago."[10] In short, he was pointing to the obvious, namely that a significant shake-up in the way the UN does business is essential to keep pace with the significantly altered circumstances six decades after its founding.

What exactly did he mean? UN security operations increased rapidly beginning in 1988 and then declined, then underwent renewed growth. The notion of security has been broadened incrementally, albeit inconsistently, to encompass the idea of human security—a still evolving concept. The requirements for global action in the humanitarian affairs and human rights arenas have been expanding. Discourse certainly has changed, and advances in humanitarian delivery and prevention are evident. Yet the world organization's capacity to respond has not kept pace. Budgetary shortfalls hinder effective responses, and the absence of political will is demonstrated by lack of appropriate response to major tragedies in Darfur and the Democratic Republic of the Congo. Moreover, some challenges to the predominance of liberal democracy seem to be gaining strength, as we see especially in fundamental political Islamic circles. On the human development front, the world is becoming ever more polarized between the rich and poor, with some of the poorest—in sub-Saharan Africa especially—losing absolute as well as relative ground. Yet we have also seen growing formal consensus, in the form of the MDGs, about what should be done to advance sustainable human development. The formal consensus in support of the MDGs, however, is rather like the formal consensus on the International Bill of Rights—namely, the consensus on norms is not followed by fully effective implementation.

James Rosenau provides us perhaps with a better image when he tells us that world politics is characterized by "turbulence," in which basic patterns are not clear and thus that change is difficult to seize.[11] In this view, world politics can be conceptualized as having "macro" and "micro" dimensions, with "macro" covering the world of states and IGOs and "micro" covering the world of individuals, local communities, and other elements of civil society. Both are in such turmoil at the beginning of the twenty-first century that one can only project alternative scenarios for the future, not specifically describe the likely structure or basic features of world politics. Yet in today's turbulent world political climate and the increasingly nonstate character of threats to global, regional, and local peace, there are mounting pressures to think in terms of human security—as opposed to state security—and a need to integrate elements and dimensions of civil society into the security sphere.

During the United Nations' first sixty years, the density of politics covering individuals and NGOs—what we have referred to as the "third UN"[12]—was different in the three parts of the book. In the security arena, where states historically have presumably had a monopoly on force—except over insurgents and terrorists—considerably fewer nongovernmental organizations have dealt with large-scale force than with human rights or sustainable development.[13] The rise of private security firms, however, may be changing this. In the human rights and sustainable development arenas, NGOs are active in analysis, lobbying, and operations. Hence, the UN of states and of secretariats would not be the same—in either normative or operational terms—without this third United Nations.

Some scholars attempt to deal with such turbulence by focusing on the importance of competing forces in shaping world politics and international organization. Some frame their analyses in terms of simultaneous forces of integration and disintegration. For example, many European states formed the European Union, which transcends the territorial state in some ways, creating a supranational authority for some issues. At the same time, some political movements—such as the Basque separatists in Spain—are seeking smaller political-legal units.[14] The Czechs and Slovaks also split up in the recent past, only to turn around and then join the Council of Europe and European Union, which reduced their national independence. Belgium, which hosts the EU capital in Brussels, was without a functioning government for more than a year circa 2007 and speculation abounds about a formal split between the Flemish-speaking north and the French-speaking south.

For an example of competing forces within a single country, some circles of opinion in the United States want more multilateral diplomacy; others insist that the United States should withdraw from most IGOs and pursue a unilateral foreign policy that is driven strictly by narrow American interests. The vacillation between these positions could hardly have been starker than the successive administrations of George W. Bush and Barack Obama. Competing centripetal and centrifugal forces are integral to the clash between globalism and localism highlighted in the preceding pages and will remain so in the foreseeable future.[15]

In world politics after the Cold War, and after September 11 as well, the United Nations is caught in a political transition. The old patterns of interaction have broken down or changed significantly, but new patterns have not yet crystallized. Many old norms—such as nonintervention in domestic affairs—are under challenge, but new ones—such as the responsibility to protect—have not yet been formally codified. Old ways of doing things may prove insufficient for new problems, yet new ways may be characterized by mistakes. States may be dissatisfied with the record of the old United Nations, but they may not yet have reached the point of providing the political will and material resources necessary for a new third generation of world organization to manage world politics.[16] This reality is regularly on display, as it was at the largest-ever gathering of heads of state and government at the 2005 World Summit. Two years earlier, at the opening of the 2003 General Assembly as preparations began for the sixtieth anniversary, the Secretary-General began his campaign for reform with a rhetorical flourish, pointing to "a fork in the road."[17] In actuality, the 2005 Summit, once seen as a window of opportunity to revisit the United Nations in light of changes in world politics since San Francisco, instead exposed the debilitating political and bureaucratic conflicts that regularly paralyzed the organization in the past.

LEARNING LESSONS?

If gauging change is problematic, what about learning? The lessons of UN history in some ways can be helpful in charting the future direction of the world organization. But history can be misinterpreted and misused as a guide for political choice.[18] For example, many U.S. policymakers misused the "lesson of Munich" in fashioning policy for Southeast Asia in the 1960s and 1970s. Believing that in 1938 the Western states whetted Adolf Hitler's aggressive appetite by appeasing him through the "giveaway" of Czechoslovakia in negotiations at Munich, these policymakers were determined not to "give away" South Vietnam to the communists. This, it was thought, would only whet the aggressive appetite of other communist leaders in Hanoi, Beijing, and Moscow. Yet the eventual creation of a communist Vietnam in 1975 did not lead to falling dominoes throughout Asia and the world. Indeed, by the late 1980s communism itself was retreating virtually everywhere, and in 1991 the "evil empire" itself imploded. Even governments that called themselves "communist," as in China and Vietnam, used increasingly capitalist policies in their pursuit of economic growth. The United States lost more than 55,000 of its own military personnel in Southeast Asia and killed as many as 3 million Asians by using a myth as a guide. The intentions may have been noble to the extent that U.S. policymakers believed they were fighting for freedom,[19] but the results were disastrous for almost everyone involved. And then the pattern of misusing historical lessons continued. George W. Bush's war cabinet, believing that the problem in Vietnam was an insufficiently robust use of U.S. hard power, plunged into Iraq in 2003 without UN approval and against much political opposition in the world. They clearly misread the difficulties in Iraq, especially the extent to which U.S. intervention and occupation would be opposed by a wide variety of Iraqi elements.[20]

One can try to be careful and systematic in wrestling with the lessons of history.[21] One can try to separate what is known from what is unknown or just presumed. In using historical analogies, one can try to be precise about the similarities to, or differences from, a current situation. One can delve into the details of history, clarify current options, guard against presumptions, and avoid stereotypes. When many policymakers look at a contemporary problem, they draw on historical evidence. The ones who do not even try are justly criticized for this deficiency. In the 1990s the UN Secretariat was fairly criticized for not having a policy-planning group able to draw historical lessons from past use of UN force. Certain state bureaucracies, and many academics, were prepared to evaluate UN peacekeeping against the historical background of what had gone wrong with ONUC in the Belgian Congo from 1960 to 1964, or what had gone right in Central America regarding ONUSAL and ONUCA.

The next time the UN takes enforcement action inside a country, whether to deliver humanitarian relief or to disarm belligerents, it will be only natural to try to draw historical lessons from events in northern Iraq, Somalia, Bosnia, Rwanda, Haiti, Kosovo, or Timor. The next time the Security Council authorizes the use of force in response to aggression, many policymakers will draw comparisons with the historical lessons from the events of 1990–1991 in Iraq and Kuwait. The temporary decline in UN peacekeepers after the mid-1990s should not have lessened the need for organizational learning. Experience in Kosovo and Timor in 1999 indicated that there would be cases in which peacekeeping and enforcement actions would be deemed necessary in the twenty-first century. By 2005 with large operations in West Africa and in the Democratic Republic of the Congo, for example, UN soldiers were once again almost back to the previous deployment highs of the mid-1990s, and in 2007–2008 were at record levels. The lessons from Afghanistan and the 2003 war in Iraq are beginning to emerge as we continue to face challenges of terrorism and WMDs. These lessons include the usefulness of UN diplomacy and inspections and the need for multilateral stabilization efforts. The political and financial costs of "going it alone" have affected the United States, which is once again considering more multilateral diplomacy to manage potential crises with Syria, Iran, and North Korea.

The task of learning is complicated by the pace of change and the culture of the UN bureaucracy. As Shashi Tharoor, then UN under-secretary-general in charge of the Department of Public Information, put it, we "too often find ourselves steering a rattling vehicle that is moving at breakneck speed, without an up-to-date roadmap, while trying to fix the engine at the same time."[22] Learning lessons is different from adapting, because adapting is more reactive and less comprehensive and is represented by incremental and often ambiguous institutional change. As two of the foremost analysts of institutional learning, Peter and Ernst Haas, have written, "Organizations characterized by irreconcilable disagreements over desirable world orders or ineptitude may not even be made capable of learning to manage interdependence rather than merely adapting to it."[23]

The United Nations still has to make a substantial effort to digest the lessons from the recent past in order to formulate a workable strategy for the future.[24] The establishment of lessons-learned units in the Department of Peacekeeping Operations, Department of Political Affairs, and Office for the Coordination of Humanitarian Affairs is not necessarily evidence of progress. These units were established in the 1990s as attempts to understand change within the "two United Nations"—not only the politics of the arenas where governments meet and make decisions but also the operational responses by various secretariats, officials, and soldiers who implement these decisions. There appears to be a growing thirst for independent research and knowledge.[25]

In drawing historical lessons, three fundamental political tasks are characteristic of policymaking and problem solving: articulating interests and consolidating interest groups, making rules, and applying those rules.[26] We conclude this analysis of the first sixty years of the United Nations with our evaluation of what has been learned along these lines. We chart change at the UN before and after the Cold War, and we suggest what these changes portend for an uncertain post–September 11 world.

ARTICULATION AND AGGREGATION OF INTERESTS

Governments of states have learned that they need the United Nations. After the Cold War many new states wanted to join the UN; none of the old members wanted to get out. Since 1945 only one state, Indonesia, has withdrawn even temporarily from the world organization, and its quixotic attempt to create a rival organization soon collapsed. The delegation from South Africa was barred for a time, during part of the apartheid era, from participating in the General Assembly, but the state was still a member of the organization. Even in the doldrums of the 1960s when the Soviet Union proposed replacing the Secretary-General with a troika, or the twenty-first century when some Washington insiders advocated replacing the UN with a league of democracies, states recognize that they need the universal world organization to build diplomatic coalitions, make rules, and monitor adherence to and enforce those rules. Simply put, the old adage still applies: If the UN did not exist, it would have to be invented. As noted earlier, the United Nations may be in perpetual crisis, but it is very much in demand and needs to be fixed.[27]

In our introduction we noted the importance of how states define their national interests, and how these definitions affect the UN's evolution. We noted the crucial nature of short-term and narrow interests. As a general rule, "the United Nations is successful over the long haul only if it helps to uncover or develop genuinely shared interests."[28] A dominant state or coalition can control policy for a time, but the UN is likely to be more effective if it is used in pursuit of widely shared interests.

After the Cold War, the United States was the most important state in the United Nations. It was the only state capable of projecting military power everywhere in the world, it had the world's largest economy, and at least since 1941 it had periodically played a leadership role in world politics. The United States had always been the UN's most important member state. The UN had never undertaken the use of force, for either peacekeeping or enforcement, without genuine U.S. support. The UN had attempted human rights and economic programs in opposition to U.S. policy, but these programs had not achieved much. The rejection of SUNFED and the fate of the NIEO are good examples of the futility of attempting a major program or initiative without U.S. support. However, the survival of the ICC, and even its advancement, in the face of U.S. opposition demonstrates the difficulty of sure generalizations.

To be sure, many UN members were not altogether happy with U.S. domination of the UN in the early twenty-first century. At one point the General Assembly passed a resolution criticizing the United States for continuing its economic pressures against Cuba, and in 2002 the United States failed to be given a seat on the Commission on Human Rights for the first time since its creation, as earlier had been the case on the Administrative Committee on Administrative and Budgetary Questions. These were viable manifestations of resentment against U.S. power. The lack of U.S. support for the Convention on the Rights of the Child, the treaty to ban land mines, the Kyoto Protocol to slow global climate change, the diplomacy to restrict the introduction of light arms into conflict zones, and the International Criminal Court led to much criticism of U.S. unilateralism.[29] This criticism became a torrent after the United States led an invasion of Iraq in 2003 without Security Council authorization. Efforts to control U.S. actions often resemble the Roman Senate's attempts to control the emperor. UN diplomats almost unanimously described the debate surrounding the resolution withdrawn on the eve of the war in Iraq as "a referendum not on the means of disarming Iraq but on the American use of power,"[30] wrote James Traub in the *New York Times Magazine.*

While noting U.S. unilateralism, we can recall issues at the UN for which there was genuine shared interest among UN members. Most states were opposed to Iraqi aggression in 1991. Most states were appalled at human suffering in Somalia in 1992. Most states were in favor of at least diplomatic support for human rights. Most states recognized the need to promote sustainable development. Most states were opposed to Taliban rule and its support for Al Qaeda.

World politics can be thought of as a multilevel game. On the military level, the United States clearly is preponderant, spending more than the rest of the world's militaries combined. But on the economic level, the expanding European Union and the cumulative weight of Asia mean that the United States, while very important with close to a quarter of the world's GDP, does not dictate with the same authority as in the military arena. The UNDP's *Human Development Report 1996* argued that if the past quarter century of economic growth rates were any indication of things to come, the next century may be an Asian, not U.S.- or Europe-centered, one: "The more than 7% average annual per capita income growth rate of East Asia in the 1970s and 1980s is the most sustained and widespread development miracle of the twentieth century, perhaps of all history."[31] An additional political leverage comes from economic and cultural leverage in the international system resulting from U.S. "soft power," but in any case "the world's only superpower can't go it alone."[32] By 2008 a weak dollar in international currency trading and a downturn in the national economy weakened the U.S. economic position further. Some widely read authors such as Kishore Mahbubani and Fareed Zakaria were already talking about the rise of Asia and the nature of a post-American world.[33]

Beyond the military and economic levels of world politics, the more general diplomatic level reveals many more multilateral elements and the need for compromise. For instance, the United States could not block the land-mine treaty or the treaty creating an International Criminal Court. Washington's short list for the UN should include not only post-conflict reconstruction in Afghanistan and Iraq but also fighting terrorism (sharing information and the fight against money laundering), confronting infectious diseases, pursuing environmental sustainability, monitoring human rights, providing humanitarian aid, rescheduling debt, and fostering trade. Indeed, these very items figured in Bush's opening address to the World Summit on September 14, 2005.[34] Whatever the rhetoric, it is hard to imagine that the United Nations will not become more, not less, appealing over the years. Indeed, the former head of the National Security Council for George H. W. Bush, Richard Haass, has put it well: "[F]or all its power, there is virtually nothing the United States can do better without others. The United States needs partners; unilateralism is rarely a viable option."[35]

By naming his confidante Susan Rice as ambassador to the United Nations and restoring the post's cabinet status, Barack Obama enunciated his "belief that the UN is an indispensable—and imperfect—forum."[36] He not only announced that the United States had rejoined the world and was ready to re-engage with all member states, but also that the United Nations would be essential to U.S. foreign policy during his administration. Obama also acknowledged what is evident to most people who were not in the ideological bubble of the Bush administration, namely "that the global challenges we face demand global institutions that work."[37] The UN's universal membership provides legitimacy and is a unique asset that, according to Rice in her confirmation hearing, should "enhance—not diminish—our influence and bring more security to our country and the world."[38]

The complexity of world politics, the difficulties of extracting precise lessons of history, and the challenge of knowing which way the winds of change are blowing serve as appropriate background. We now provide a final overview of learning for our three main issue areas.

Security Issues

In the 1990s the United States was the primary player or moving force in the UN campaign to repel Iraqi aggression against Kuwait, to pressure Iraq to comply with various UN resolutions after Desert Storm, to deliver humanitarian relief in Somalia, and to make other UN security operations succeed. In a continuation of past patterns and in light of the veto and military muscle, no UN security operation was undertaken against the wishes of the United States. When the UN was less than fully effective in some security matters, as early on in Bosnia or Haiti, it was largely a reflection of the unwillingness of the United States to engage fully.

Other states were also important in UN security affairs. The British and French deployed relatively large numbers of peacekeeping troops in the Balkans. The French mounted operations in Rwanda and the eastern Congo, as did the British in Sierra Leone, and the Australians led the UN force in East Timor. The Russians kept the lid on violence in Georgia, at least until the summer of 2008, and Nigeria spearheaded two ECOWAS missions in West Africa—while Brazil took the lead in Haiti. And the European Union took over military responsibilities in Bosnia from NATO, which remained on the ground in Kosovo and Afghanistan.

Indeed, all the permanent members of the Security Council have to at least avoid using their veto for UN decisions in peace and security matters to be made. Apart from permanent Security Council members, numerous states have supported UN peace and security efforts. Japan played a very large role in UNTAC's efforts to stabilize and democratize Cambodia. Canada and Norway and some other states are stalwart supporters of UN peacekeeping. Costa Rica and other Spanish-speaking states played important roles in supporting mediation by the Secretary-General in Central America in the 1980s.

The first term of the Reagan administration aside, the United States wants at least the UN's collective approval, and sometimes the UN's more direct help, in managing international peace and security. The George W. Bush administration took its concerns about Iraq to the Security Council in 2002, but then it attacked Iraq in 2003 without UN blessing and without a persuasive case for self-defense. Nonetheless, the Bush administration went back to the council for approval of its plans for occupation and reconstruction of Iraq. The early occupation was directed by the United States, but as difficulties mounted, it seemed the Bush team was more amenable to UN involvement. The UN helped in the transfer of authority to an interim Iraqi government in June 2005 and has helped administer elections at several junctures. Perhaps because the Bush team recognized, albeit belatedly, some of the difficulties of an essentially unilateral foreign policy, it was careful after 2003 to place the use of force in nearby Haiti under a Security Council mandate. The same was true regarding a projected UN force in Darfur.

Despite U.S. unilateral use of force in places such as Grenada (1983), Panama (1989), and Iraq (2003)—along with its almost total exclusion of the UN from the negotiations leading to the Dayton Peace Accord (1995) for the former Yugoslavia—the dominant trend among all states, including the United States, is to involve the UN in managing military security problems. One reason to rely on the UN for the collective management of security issues is that most other regional options offer little prospect of success. At a minimum, the world organization is required to be associated with security efforts to make subcontracted states and coalitions more accountable for actions undertaken in the name of the larger community of states. For instance, when Nigeria became bogged down in trying to pacify Liberia and Sierra Leone through the use of ECOWAS, this had the effect of increasing, not lessening, demands that the UN become more involved, which in fact is what actually transpired.

It will be interesting to observe developments in efforts to halt mass atrocities with a change of U.S. administration. As seen earlier, we have witnessed a values breakthrough of sorts: The responsibility to protect qualifies as emerging customary law after centuries of more or less passive and mindless acceptance of the proposition that state sovereignty was a license to kill. And Susan Rice, who took part in the Clinton administration's lamentable decision to keep the United States out of Rwanda in 1994, has expressed clearly the need for Washington not to repeat that mistake and to take the lead in conscience-shocking situations. With the leading candidates being Darfur, the Democratic Republic of the Congo, and Zimbabwe, John Prendergast of the "Enough" project that campaigns to prevent genocide calls the combination of the African specialist Rice along with Secretary of State Hillary Clinton and National Security Advisor General James Jones a "dream team."[39] Then-candidate Obama earlier ruminated in *Foreign Affairs* about the importance of "military force in circumstances beyond self-defense" when he specifically listed the need to "confront mass atrocities."[40]

Overall, both great and small powers have sought to confer on the UN an enhanced security role after the Cold War. The articulation of interests and aggregation of interest groups have varied from issue to issue. And states have not always provided sufficient political and material support to enable UN forces and representatives to succeed. Nevertheless, most states seem to have learned that major problems are hardly avoided by the pursuit of unilateral action. Apart from direct threats to a state's existence, multilateral security diplomacy has been a preferable option by most states on numerous occasions.

The U.S.- and UK-led attack on Iraq in 2003 greatly affected perceptions of the United Nations. Virtually everyone was dismayed at the UN's inability to impede U.S. aggression, while the United States was frustrated by the slow progress of the UN's weapons inspections. From 1919, there had been a major international effort to restrict the first use of force; U.S. policy undermined this historic effort—in a brazen way. Council debates were well publicized. The United States resorted to first use of force when a majority in the council, not just a few dissidents, believed that the use of force was not then justified or diplomatic options were not exhausted. But to dismiss the role of the council in the future is premature.[41] In the winter of 2005–2006, the council played a crucial role investigating Syrian actions in Lebanon and may yet play a role in the brewing trouble over Iran's nuclear ambitions. First, the use of force without council authorization cannot be ruled out, as was the case in Kosovo and in the 2003 Iraq war, but the historical trend to restrict the first use of force will continue, and the UN will be the central forum in this regard.

Human Rights Interests

The United States has been much less of a dominant or hegemonic leader in human rights than in security and economic affairs.[42] Donald Puchala argues that leverage in this arena and others is not merely American: "The hegemony that prevails today over the workings of major international organizations, including the United Nations, is not the imposed will of 'the only remaining superpower' but more precisely the imposed will of the historical bloc herein identified as the West."[43] A historic bloc refers to a configuration of social forces and ideas that transcend national boundaries.

The articulation of human rights interests and the aggregation of human rights interest groups, principally through the Commission on Human Rights, came about less because of the United States and more because of a series of compromises among a large number of states, mostly Western in their orientation. At the 1993 World Conference on Human Rights, U.S. delegates played the leading role in pushing for reaffirmation of universal human rights. Ironically, UN norms codify economic and social human rights, which Washington in fact rejects. At one point the U.S. delegates circulated an informal list of states dragging their diplomatic feet. The United States was initially supportive of the idea of creating a more businesslike Human Rights Council to restore legitimacy to international efforts to protect and promote human rights; but it then voted against its creation in March 2006, arguing that it was not sufficiently changed from its predecessor, the CHR. Washington has, however, promised to work closely with the new body. And when it came to the matter of delivering humanitarian assistance in situations of armed conflict, the UN took the most decisive steps in northern Iraq and Somalia, precisely where the United States displayed the most interest and commitment.

Just as most states sought to involve the UN in the management of security issues, so most states sought to use the world organization to promote human rights through international standards and to give at least some attention to their implementation—mostly by diplomacy at least until 1993. Particularly after the Cold War, human rights were vigorously articulated by many democratic governments that had succeeded authoritarian ones—whether communist or otherwise. The Czech Republic and Uruguay are just two examples of governments that sought extensive UN action on human rights as a result of their own previous and traumatic experience with the denial of most internationally recognized rights.

Some states—for example, Burma, China, Cuba, Iraq under Saddam Hussein, Sudan, Syria, Vietnam, Zimbabwe—resisted this dominant trend. Others, such as Saudi Arabia, Algeria, and various states throughout the Middle East, also opposed UN action on human rights—especially concerning women's reproductive rights and homosexuality—but they found it politically prudent to keep a low profile.

Most governmental officials have articulated either a moral or an expediential interest in internationally recognized human rights. They have learned that the advancement of such rights is conducive to human dignity or that such rights have politically desirable consequences—for example, international peace, domestic tranquility, and uninterrupted foreign assistance. States have little choice but to use the United Nations for the articulation and aggregation of universal human rights interests. In theory universal human rights standards could be developed outside the UN much in the same way that international humanitarian law was developed for human rights in armed conflicts. However, international society needs the United Nations to articulate and aggregate global human rights interests. This is represented by the UN debates about the wisdom of various types of international criminal courts.

Whether states have now learned the wisdom of developing international courts so as to enforce certain human rights standards (including international humanitarian law in armed conflict), diplomatic and judicial uncertainty remains. Can the community of states move from the two primary ad hoc tribunals for former Yugoslavia and Rwanda to an important ICC? Will other partially international courts, such as those for Cambodia or Sierra Leone, advance the role of international courts in international human rights and humanitarian matters?[44] Is international criminal justice always the correct response after atrocities, compared to other forms of traditional justice such as truth commissions and apologies? The answers to these questions will go a long way in assessing the extent of state learning in this arena.

Ironically, the United States, which for a time led a determined opposition to the ICC, is the locus of much litigation over internationally recognized human rights in its own courts. Under national legislation dating from the eighteenth century, private parties can bring legal claims against other private parties for violating international law. There have been many court cases in the United States dealing with such internationally recognized human rights violations as torture, forced labor, and rape. Private individuals and corporations, of various nationalities, have been defendants. So while the United States bitterly opposed a Belgian law concerning universal jurisdiction, leading to legal charges against various national leaders, including some Americans, U.S. law itself shows that individuals and human rights NGOs are pushing for more judicial protection of human rights and humanitarian standards, whether in international or national courts.[45] Legal challenges are under way in U.S. courts regarding the detention and treatment of "enemy combatants" in the "war on terrorism." UN norms on human rights have at least an indirect impact on national policies and adjudication.

Sustainable Development

We have shown how the UN has been a central forum for the articulation and aggregation of interests regarding sustainable human development—"human security." We pointed out how the adoption of the Millennium Development Goals and their restatement at the World Summit in September 2005 represents a culmination of this long process, which has taken some six decades.

The UN network was used mostly by developing countries to articulate, as an aggregate, their views of what should be done about poverty in particular and underdevelopment in general. Some of their demands, such as for SUNFED and the NIEO, did not lead to "planetary bargains" between North and South, but major compromises have been struck with various UN agencies and personalities playing important roles in facilitating agreements. At the risk of overgeneralization, over time the industrialized countries have come around to the view that UN agencies have important roles to play in bridging the North-South divide, and that private markets alone cannot provide all that is necessary to overcome underdevelopment in all its forms. Of course, Scandinavians and Canadians have been believers for decades while the United States still expresses more faith in markets than its partners.

Ecological protection is very much part of the quest for sustainable human development. The 1992 Rio conference, where the lengthy Agenda 21 was hammered out and articulated as a policy guideline for the twenty-first century, and where treaties on biodiversity and rain forests were negotiated, remains part of the basic road map. The processes of negotiation represent important steps in interest-group aggregation and articulation in the eco-development arena. Therefore, Agenda 21 and various conventions and declarations that emerged from the Rio process are perhaps best seen as snapshots of an evolving political process, not as static political outcomes. The Commission on Sustainable Development, like UNEP itself twenty years earlier, was the result of a compromise among states about what the United Nations could do to interject environmental protection into efforts to produce economic growth.

The world organization has not exercised a monopoly over efforts to articulate interests related to sustainable development. All developed countries, and many developing ones as well, have individual programs for environmental protection. Regional organizations such as the European Union also have environmental programs that, when added to efforts to ensure economic growth, produce a combined policy on sustainable development. But as with security and human rights issues, the UN has been used by various actors to articulate a vision of how economic growth can be combined with protection of the environment.

Naturally on such a complex matter as eco-development or sustainable human development or human security, different views persist. Should UN agencies and the World Bank continue to support massive dam projects that displace many? Should the Kyoto Protocol be central to efforts to combat global climate change? What is a reasonable economic cost to pay for enhanced ecological measures? We noted with regard to security and human rights issues that there were long-term trends toward multilateral management of many particular issues in that domain. The same seems to hold for development, with general agreement often accompanied by particular disagreement.

RULE-MAKING

Every society requires a collective procedure to establish rules that differentiate permissible from impermissible behavior. The United Nations plays a central role in this essential rule-making for international society—largely through the Security Council, General Assembly, and associated world conferences—but other mechanisms in international society also create rules. Some treaties are made outside the UN system, and regional organizations also make rules. The murky institution of customary international law, which is greatly affected by the behavior of powerful states, also plays a role. As José Alvarez tells us, "Like the Pope, whose historical influence on states has obviously exceeded the Vatican's military or economic capabilities, IOs' [international organizations'] impact on international law-making actors results from, in substantial part, the moral suasion they exert and not from the law-making powers explicitly."[46] In the final analysis, the UN has a major role in rule-making for world politics regarding all three of our major issues. We now attempt to appreciate what has been learned about rule-making in the past six decades.

Security Rules

Many security rules for world politics have been vague. Neither the International Court of Justice nor the Security Council has specified the distinction between a breach of the peace and outright aggression. Moreover, the term "intervention" has never been authoritatively specified; despite a 1974 General Assembly attempt to define aggression, many ambiguities remain. The 1998 Rome Statute for the International Criminal Court recognizes this problem, indicating that no charges can be brought against individuals for aggression (a crime against peace) until that concept is better specified in international law. Moreover, are reprisals legal in peacetime given that the UN Charter has outlawed the threat or use of force in the absence of an armed attack? Can force be used to implement legal rights? Can a regional organization employ force without prior authorization from the Security Council? These and other questions about security rules could benefit from clearer answers.

Since the end of the Cold War, the Security Council in particular has made a number of decisions that clarify at least some questions about security rule-making. The council is sharpening security rules far more than the ICJ. The latter does not normally get the opportunity to pronounce on legal issues related to armed conflict. Most states have regarded security rules as too important to be turned over to fifteen jurists. Therefore, they have not given consent to the court to rule on these matters. The 1986 judgment in the case of *Nicaragua v. United States* is an exception that proves the general rule (and the wisdom of that judgment was extensively debated—especially by the United States, which, having lost the case, refused to implement the judgment). If international security law is to be clarified, it is primarily the Security Council that will do it.

The Security Council in the 1990s gave a very broad interpretation to the scope of Chapter VII of the Charter pertaining to enforcement action in response to threats to and breaches of the peace and acts of aggression. It has determined that peace and security issues may arise from human-rights, economic, and ecological situations—and even from HIV/AIDS in Africa—not just from the use of force across borders by states. It has even said that humanitarian conditions within a state, even those that do not seem to generate external material effects, may constitute a threat to international peace and security and merit an enforcement action under Chapter VII. It has decided to authorize such action to restore an elected government overthrown by military force. Along the way, the Security Council has specified that individuals in zones of armed conflict have a right to humanitarian assistance, and that to interfere with that right is a war crime for which there can be individual prosecution. The council has also authorized member states to seize the property of a state (Iraq) in order to assist in the implementation of binding sanctions. Under Chapter VII the council has created a war-crimes tribunal for the former Yugoslavia and for Rwanda. These are just a few of the decisions about security rules the council made under Chapter VII.

International security rules are likely to remain vague because the competing claims of states are rarely authoritatively reviewed by the Security Council or the World Court. While inconsistency may be the hobgoblin of little minds, world politics is about case-by-case decision-making and double standards, about major powers having a louder and more important voice than middle and small powers. Efforts to clearly delineate the conditions under which force may be authorized stalled at the 2005 World Summit. Nevertheless, the council continues to try to distinguish aggression from self-defense and make use of Chapter VII to organize a legally binding response to threats to and breaches of the peace.

Interestingly, when Israel in 2007 destroyed a Syrian facility suspected of being linked to the quest for nuclear weapons, Israel made no legal claims pertaining to permissibility; and none of the P-5 wanted to deal with the issue—which was never addressed in the Security Council. Unlike the Bush administration in 2003 when invading Iraq, the Israelis made no claim about a doctrine of unilateral preemption and how such an idea should be a permissible pillar of world order (or disorder). So some security issues seemed too complex for formal rule-making and were simply swept under the carpet. It might have been, especially in the wake of the U.S. invasion of Iraq, that most states did not want to endorse unilateral preemption, but did not like the possibility of Syria developing nuclear weapons.

Human Rights Rules

The UN has been codifying rules on internationally recognized human rights since 1948, when the General Assembly adopted the Universal Declaration of Human Rights and also approved the treaty on genocide. Since then, there has been sufficient formal or informal consensus (reflecting an aggregation of interests) to produce numerous treaties, declarations, and resolutions.

Several new developments have happened within the United Nations regarding human rights rules since the end of the Cold War. The Security Council has merged human rights and security rules to a great extent, making decisions under Chapter VII pertaining to peace and security that involved such fundamental rights as the one to adequate nutrition (for example, in Somalia) and freedom from repression (for example, in Iraq). In fact, Stanley Hoffmann has described "international peace and security" as an "all-purpose parachute."[47] In Haiti, the council voted a binding and comprehensive economic embargo on the country during summer 1993 after military elements deposed an elected civilian president. Moreover, the Commission on Human Rights expanded its rule-making even beyond the several dozen treaties and declarations already adopted. The commission took on the complex subjects of the rights of minorities and indigenous peoples. The follow-on Human Rights Council adopted new standards on enforced disappearances and indigenous peoples.

The 1993 Vienna conference witnessed tremendous NGO pressure on all states to continue with UN rule-making on human rights. At Vienna there was especially strong demand for further attention to rules on women's rights. Even states not genuinely committed to personal rights found it difficult to withstand combined NGO and state pressure in support of expanded UN rule-making. The political situation was such that it was easier for these dissenting states to formally accept rules that they did not really support than to stand up and try to oppose them directly. The Vienna process also indicated clearly that established principles of human rights might not be as universally accepted as many UN and human rights observers had previously thought. The debates in Vienna brought out significant challenges to what in some corners are perceived to be Anglo-Saxon–dominated international norms. Although these challenges were kept at bay in Vienna, they have persisted and are not likely to go away given the turbulent nature of the post–Cold War world order.

Since Vienna, as before, there is ample evidence that a plethora of UN rules on human rights is marked also by remarkable state hypocrisy about those rules. The UN treaty monitoring system is plagued by late and superficial reports, not to mention lack of adequate funding to ensure their timely review. The systematic election of rights-violating states to the CHR indicated that many states gave preference to traditional bargaining and geographical considerations rather than to serious respect for the rules. This has yet to change with the new Human Rights Council even though all members are elected by a majority vote of the General Assembly and are subject to having their human rights performance reviewed. The human rights domain at the UN is characterized by extensive codification and other norm development that reflects a formal statement of interests and/or values, but human rights NGOs remain skeptical about state sincerity. This concern remains valid as the new Human Rights Council to date seems little more than old wine in a new bottle.

Rules for Sustainable Development

The Millennium Development Goals are more or less the equivalent of the Universal Declaration of Human Rights with specific reference to development. These core principles include a focus on poverty and hunger, education, gender equality, children's and maternal welfare, good health and especially the threat of HIV/AIDS, and such general matters as sustainable ecology and broad partnership for development. The MDGs also contain relatively specific targets for advancement toward human security.

Whether the MDGs constitute a real road map for development or just another set of pious statements that states do not take seriously remains to be seen. An encouraging sign at the 2005 World Summit was the recommitment by member states, including a recalcitrant United States, to the MDGs. The history of human rights treaties indicates the gap that can exist between normative theory and behavioral reality.

UN organizations and international civil servants along with a phalanx of NGOs, however, will be pressing states to take the MDGs seriously. Just as human rights NGOs lobby for attention to the international rules in the domain of human rights and humanitarian affairs, so there will be nonstate actors of various types seeking to follow up the new rules for development, to help make states accountable for their commitments.

RULE ENFORCEMENT

What is perhaps most striking about the UN system amidst changing world politics is the extent to which judgments are made about the behavior of states under UN-sponsored rules, which themselves reflect interests articulated and aggregated through UN channels. The past six decades reveal important lessons for UN rule enforcement within our three thematic areas.

Enforcing Security Rules

The Security Council has clearly eclipsed the General Assembly in the security area, as the Charter originally intended. In the 1990s the locus of supervisory activity concerning state use of force and other security policies was in the council. In one respect matters have not changed since 1945. The Security Council cannot be expected to override the permanent members in any vigorous or rigorous way. Each still possesses the veto, which guarantees council paralysis when a permanent member's policy is challenged. This is the result not of poor drafting by the Charter's framers but of clear drafting to recognize the realities of power. No coalition of states could hope militarily to coerce the United States into changing its policies; it is doubtful that any coalition could do likewise against Britain, France, Russia, or China without enormous disruption to world politics. Avoiding such a major confrontation was a justification for the UN in the first place.

In spring 2003, most of the members of the council were trying to offset U.S. military power, then focused on Iraq, with diplomatic and legal arguments. In a sense this was classic balance-of-power politics, in that France, Russia, Germany, China, and others tried to restrain the United States (and Britain and Spain) with diplomatic and legal measures. This balancing failed in the short run, in the sense that the United States and a coalition of willing partners were not deterred in their use of force against Iraq. Indeed, given the preponderance of American power, it is difficult to see how such a diplomatic *démarche* could effectively constitute a real balance. In the long run, U.S. difficulties in Iraq may make the hyperpower more cautious about unilateralism in the future, or at least to better appreciate the limits of military power and the advantages of diplomacy.

The United States aside, never before in world history has an IGO sought to pass judgment on states' security policies to the extent that the Security Council has. In historical perspective, this was a major experiment and the outcome was mixed. Working closely with the Secretary-General, the council could count a number of successes in supervising various policies in places such as South-West Africa/Namibia and Central America in the late 1980s and early 1990s. The result was both independence for Namibia and significant steps toward regional peace and national reconciliation in El Salvador and Nicaragua.

From August 1990 the council successfully countered various Iraqi policies that violated international law, primarily because the United States took a very strong interest in resisting aggression against Kuwait and in seeing that council follow-up resolutions were enforced. The council was also successful in ameliorating disorder and starvation in Somalia in 1992 and early 1993, again because the United States decided, for whatever reason, that the situation was intolerable.

At the same time, the Security Council passed numerous resolutions pertaining to the former Yugoslavia that were not implemented. The state members of the council were diplomatically engaged in supervising the policies of the various parties engaged in armed conflict—Serbians, Croats, Bosnians, Bosnian Serbs, Bosnian Croats, and Bosnian Muslims. Those same council members, however, lacked the will to see that the necessary political and material resources were made available to UN forces and representatives in the field. Multilateral diplomacy was divorced from the threat to use power or the effective use of power, with predictably disappointing results. Serbia's original war aims ended up being the negotiated final solution. Nevertheless, the UN did commendable work in trying circumstances by providing humanitarian relief to many thousands of persons.

In Somalia from May 1993, the council and its field representatives through UNOSOM II tried to accomplish what U.S. forces had been unwilling to do under UNITAF—namely, to disarm the internal factions that had been threatening civilian life and to protect relief officials. But this task proved difficult given the inadequate training, coordination, equipment, and overall force levels of UN military contingents. Calling the effort an enforcement operation under Chapter VII did not resolve problems in the field, and the UN had difficulty in suppressing factions that had long used force to gain their political objectives.

The situation was similar for UNTAC in Cambodia. General elections were supervised in May 1993, but the Security Council found it difficult to fashion a policy that would control the Khmer Rouge while helping competing domestic factions that supported national reconciliation. The United Nations also found itself only nominally in control of key departments in the central government, with much power being exercised apart from UN supervision. The four leading Cambodian factions found it difficult to proceed without UN approval, but the world organization found itself facing great difficulties in making its supervision effective. But even those critical of the UN in Cambodia did not seem to have other viable options, and the largest UN operation to that time completed its withdrawal in November 1993 without full peace for Cambodia.

The delayed reactions to genocide in Rwanda and to the ouster of the elected government in Haiti also tarnished the UN's reputation. But in these and other security situations, state members of the council tended to pass resolutions that they were not committed to implementing unless the costs were deemed to be reasonable and the length of the time of an operation short. For example, the council's credibility was damaged when it declared "safe areas" for civilians in the former Yugoslavia, only to have the fighting parties mock them with impunity—including the murder of some 7,000 men and boys in one of them (Srebrenica). The UN was hurt when the council created a war-crimes tribunal for the former Yugoslavia but did not provide adequate staffing for the preliminary investigations or empower IFOR to pursue indicted criminals. The world organization got the criticism, but the real problem was state foreign policy channeled through the United Nations.

Nevertheless, a nonpermanent member contemplating action that could be found to be a threat to or breach of the peace had to deal with the possibility that the Security Council would find its action in violation of international law and therefore launch some coercive response. The UN's probability of firm reaction was in almost direct proportion to the interest that the United States took in the situation and its willingness to act. This state of affairs was markedly different from the Cold War period, when great-power disagreement guaranteed the lack of a firm council response to peace and security issues, with the partial exception of white-minority rule in Africa (Rhodesia and South Africa).

To be effective, peace operations of all varieties should be based on unambiguous operational guidelines and procedures. In this regard, the Security Council moved in 1994 to articulate criteria for a variety of important aspects of operational activities, including the initial deployment of forces, ongoing operational reviews, training, command and control, and financing. In addition, effective rule enforcement entails an adequate capacity to act. In the context of the multitude of security-related activities in which the organization is engaged, the United Nations simply does not possess this capacity. The world organization's military capacity is always on loan; furthermore, it is perpetually drained and strained financially to the limits, as new tasks are added without the requisite addition of new financial and other resources. In the late 1990s, cumulative debts and arrears hovered around $3.5 billion, or about three times the regular annual budget.

As demonstrated in the case of dealing with the crisis in the former Yugoslavia, U.S. officials have shown increasing willingness to "let the UN do it" or to "do it in the name of the UN" but displayed an equally determined commitment to make certain that the required funds were less than forthcoming. In his 1993 address to the General Assembly, President Bill Clinton cautioned that the UN must know when to say no. At that time, as well as during the second Clinton administration and at other times, the United States must also know when to say yes. Despite a "deal" to pay U.S. arrears in December 1999 that narrowly avoided the loss of the U.S. vote in the General Assembly and a much-publicized visit by the Senate's Foreign Relations Committee to the United Nations in January 2000, the future of the UN's capacity to enforce security rules is far from certain.

This uncertainty is reflected in two events that occurred in 1999 and 2000. The crisis in Kosovo was the first, and it showed the old problem that when the P-5 are divided, the Security Council cannot be directly or explicitly involved in security operations. Thus the United States led NATO to use military force in modern Yugoslavia outside the council, because Russia and China were not prepared to support such action against Serbia's persecution of Albanian Kosovars. Russia saw itself as the historical protector of the Serbs, and China was worried about UN approval of strong action against a government's treatment of its own citizens. In the second crisis, however, that pertaining to East Timor and Indonesia, the council was able to authorize a deployment of force to ease the transition problems as East Timor moved from unstable internal status to national independence. Russia expressed no opposition, China was willing to defer, and the United States was content with developments since Australia agreed to take the lead on the ground. Facilitating the entire process was political change in Indonesia, which finally (after much destruction and many deaths) led to considerable cooperation between Jakarta and the UN-approved military force. So in the first instance, the P-5 were not in agreement, and in the second, they were. In the first, the target government (Belgrade) did not give its consent to what was being discussed in the council, and in the second, Jakarta finally did.

Enforcing Human Rights Rules

Since about 1970 the United Nations, principally via the Commission on Human Rights, has been more or less systematically using embarrassment to pressure states violating UN human rights rules to behave. But here, as elsewhere, double standards prevail. Before 1970 the UN sporadically supervised rights performance, but only after 1970 did the world organization make this supervision a regular feature of its actions. The realm of domestic jurisdiction has shrunk progressively, and the realm of international supervision has expanded.

Small and weak developing countries were the most likely targets of UN human rights supervision, but no state could be guaranteed immunity from diplomatic pressure. The Expert Committee supervising the UN Covenant on Economic, Social and Cultural Rights took on the Dominican Republic; the UN Committee on Human Rights supervising the UN Covenant on Civil and Political Rights confronted Uruguay; and the Commission on Human Rights broke new diplomatic ground in supervising Guinea-Bissau. More important states such as China, Iran, Iraq, and Israel were sometimes targeted for diplomatic supervision. Russia has been the only permanent member of the council officially condemned by the CHR; that occurred because of its heavy-handed policies in the breakaway republic of Chechnya. China has intensely lobbied to avoid censure in that commission by the narrowest of votes.

By the 1990s many states could not be sure that the Security Council would not declare a particular human rights situation a threat to international peace and engage in enforcement. Iraq, Somalia, and Haiti had been so targeted. Bosnia was a case in which human rights violations were intertwined with aggression, in the view of the council, and Chapter VII was invoked to deal with both types of issues.

Power greatly affects human rights issues at the United Nations. The United States and Japan were not as likely as Israel to be pressured about racial discrimination. Haiti was more likely to be coercively pressured about the denial of political rights than Myanmar (formerly Burma). China could avoid the issue of suppression of Tibetan rights at the Vienna conference, whereas Israel could not so easily avoid the issue of Palestinian rights to self-determination. Various double standards had impaired the reputation of the Commission on Human Rights over time, not to mention the election to that commission of states known for systematically violating important human rights, or even the election of Libya as chair in 2003. Many are hoping for improvement with the new Human Rights Council, which had its first session in June 2006 and meets three times a year rather than the CHR's annual gathering. "There has been a quiet revolution in human rights in recent months, which has culminated in the creation of the Council," said Louise Arbour, high commissioner for human rights, at the final session of the CHR in March 2006. "Nothing should be taken for granted. . . . There is no guarantee that the Council will fully realize the goals for which it was created."[48]

Nevertheless, as a historical trend, the United Nations is supervising more rights in more states through more intrusive measures than ever before. Although the world organization's record on supervising human rights paled in comparison with the Council of Europe's, the UN might in some respects approximate the Organization of American States; and the UN did not fare so badly in comparisons with the former Organization of African Unity and the Arab League. Many, if not most, states had apparently learned the necessity, if not the benefit, of the UN's passing judgment on their human rights performances.

In recent years member states created special tribunals to deal with genocide and other human rights atrocities in particular places like Rwanda and Yugoslavia, and then they created the ICC. There remained, however, considerable disagreement about enforcing some human rights via international criminal courts. The renaissance of international criminal justice since 1993 is a major development in international relations, and the UN has played a central role in this, even if the ICC is largely (but not entirely) independent of the United Nations. International criminal justice is not a panacea, but the judicial enforcement of major human rights violations is not the moribund subject it was some decades ago.

Enforcing Rules on Sustainable Human Development

The UN's record on supervision is exceedingly complex regarding sustainable human development. The MDGs only generated general policy statements, not precise rules enforceable in a judicial sense. The ILO monitored labor conditions (usually treated as a human rights question), WHO watched over health conditions (also treated by some as a human rights issue), and UNESCO kept an eye on educational issues. But on many core issues of sustainable development, the basic rules, as well as the very meaning of the concept, have only recently met with relative consensus. And deciding what specific data will be used is hardly uncontroversial—readers need only recall the typical reaction to the Human Development Report by the winners and losers to get a sense of reporting problems. Moreover, some sustainable development concerns are treated outside the official framework of the United Nations. For example, the Montreal Protocol on the ozone and related agreements have been negotiated outside the UN, but with some participation by UNEP.

The UN has never played as definitive and large a role in monitoring state economic and ecological policies as it has in supervising security and human rights policies. International supervision of economics has been performed more by the World Bank and the International Monetary Fund. Since 1995, the World Trade Organization, of course, has handled disputes about trading rules. Given the wide range of indicators for MDGs, various UN agencies will engage in "naming and shaming" in an effort to prod states into meeting stated targets. But the more persistent role for UN organizations will be helping states meet the targets.

Just how the Security Council, the General Assembly, or some other centralized UN body could impose itself on a fragmented UN system, and how such a centralized entity would link to the World Bank and its billions in loan funds, is unclear. There undoubtedly will be more cries in the wilderness by visible economists like Jeffrey Sachs and celebrities like U2's Bono before we reach 2015, the target date for the MDGs.[49] Furthermore and as the Millennium Assembly indicated, sustainable development entails processes and conditions that lie well outside the scope and domain of interstate relations. Sustainable development calls for popular participation in decision-making processes and project implementation. It reaches to the lowest level of social aggregation—local communities, social groups, and individuals. These are elements of sustainable human development and of human security that do not fit well with inter-governmentalism, UN style, and associated assumptions of national state sovereignty and noninterference in domestic affairs. Indeed, in many ways the world views underlying interstate relations, on the one hand, and sustainable development, on the other, do not portray the real world at all. The turbulence that characterizes post–Cold War world politics in this regard will need to be addressed if the CSD is to effectively carry out its various mandates. This task and the way it is handled will foretell much about the future of the United Nations in social and economic areas. Bridging the gap between micro- and macro phenomena is a key to coping with turbulence and for promoting human as well as global security.

SOME FINAL THOUGHTS

Earlier we discussed the appearance of "good governance" at the national level as a topic for the UN system. At the international level, another concept has emerged, "global governance," whose origins can be traced to a growing dissatisfaction among students of international relations with the realist and liberal-institutionalist theories that had dominated the study of international organization since World War II. In particular, these traditional perspectives failed to capture adequately the vast increase, in both numbers and influence, of nonstate actors and the implications of technology in an age of globalization.[50] We have emphasized in previous chapters the growing network of actors circumscribing the UN's role in all major activities and the critical importance of working toward—in the words of UNDP administrator Kemal Derviç—"a better globalization."[51] Thus we conclude with a discussion of the significance of global governance for the twenty-first century, a subject of growing interest among scholars and practitioners.[52]

The journey to explore the concept has barely begun, and so readers will not be surprised to learn that the nature of global governance is more inchoate than the nature of governance within countries. At the same time that part of Europe adopts a common currency and tries to move toward a common defense and security policy, for instance, how can the former Yugoslavia implode? James Rosenau, the American academic most closely associated with the notion of global governance, invented the term "fragmegration" to capture the simultaneous integration and fragmentation of societal interactions and authority patterns.[53] Moreover, burgeoning information, communication, market, finance, networking, and business activities are producing a world in which patterns are difficult to discern.

Larry Finkelstein has gone so far as to quip that "we say 'governance' because we don't really know what to call what is going on."[54] In short, analysts are understandably uncomfortable with the traditional frameworks and vocabulary used to describe international relations. However, the nomenclature of "global governance" can be compared to "post–Cold War," which signifies that one period has ended but that we do not as yet have an accurate shorthand to depict the essential dynamics of the new epoch.

In spite of vagueness in ongoing scholarly and policy debates, the application of the notion of governance to the globe was the natural result of mounting evidence that the international system was no longer composed simply of states, but that the world was undergoing fundamental changes. Although such actors as the Catholic Church, General Motors, and the International Committee of the

Red Cross are hardly new to the Westphalian system, the proliferation of nonstate actors and their growing importance and power are a distinctive feature of contemporary world affairs.[55]

Global governance invokes the shifting location of authority. The implications for international action jump from the title of Rosenau's edited volume, with Ernst-Otto Czempiel, *Governance without Government*. Mobilizing support from the bottom up involves increasing the skills and capacities of individuals and altering the horizons of identification in patterns of global life. Elsewhere, Rosenau characterizes global governance as "systems of rule at all levels of human activity—from the family to the international organization—in which the pursuit of goals through the exercise of control has transnational repercussions."[56]

Globalization is neither uniform nor homogeneous, but it is indisputably accelerating the pace and intensity of economic and social interactions at all levels. Although the history is long,[57] its present manifestation is fundamentally different in scale, intensity, and form from what went before. As Jan Aart Scholte reminds us, "If globalization is understood as the spread of transplanetary and supraterritorial relations, then the trend has mainly unfolded in the past half-century."[58] Or as David Held and others have put it, "Contemporary globalization represents the beginning of a new epoch in human affairs [causing] as profound an impact as the Industrial Revolution and the global empires of the nineteenth century."[59]

Students and professors, policy analysts, and practitioners should not feel uncomfortable about admitting their uneasiness and ignorance about understanding the details of the contemporary political economy, and especially about not knowing the best way to address a bewildering array of global problems. As CNN's founder, media mogul Ted Turner aptly summarized that "globalization is in fast-forward, and the world's ability to understand and react to it is in slow motion."[60]

The logical link between the patterns of governance at the national and global levels lies in solving the collective action puzzle in order to provide public goods. "In both modern domestic political systems and the modern international system, the state has been the key structural arena within which collective action has been situated and undertaken," observes Philip Cerny. And as a result of a multiplicity of interactions, "the authority, legitimacy, policymaking capacity, and policy-implementing effectiveness of the state will be eroded and undermined both within and without."[61] Mark Zacher has summarized the nature of the modest order in today's international economic system in the following way: "In short, without these and other regimes and public goods generated by the UN system, it would truly be 'a jungle out there.'"[62]

But governments and their intergovernmental creations are inadequate. Cerny argues that, as market activity intensifies and economic organization becomes increasingly complex, the institutional scale of political structures is no longer capable of providing a suitable range of public goods. In effect, economic globalization is undermining the effectiveness of state-based collective action. Although the state remains a cultural force, its effectiveness as a civil association has declined significantly. The result may be a crisis of legitimacy. This is not to say that state-based collective action has reached its end, but it is significantly different from what it was in the past.

And at the global level, collective action is still more elusive. Although realists and idealists who analyze international organizations disagree about many issues, they agree that the state system is anarchic. Whatever the framers of the UN Charter had in mind and whatever John Maynard Keynes and his colleagues imagined at Bretton Woods, nothing like an overarching authority for either the high politics of international peace and security or the low politics of economic and social development has emerged.

In one crucial aspect then, "global governance" is distinct from good or bad governance at the national level. At the country level, a "good" (that is, account-able, efficient, lawful, representative, and transparent) government usually leads to the development of a complementary level of good governance, whereas bad governance is correlated with conspicuously bad government. At the national and local levels then, governance is "government plus." Although the merits of more or less interventionist stances by states can be debated, there is a primary and identifiable sovereign agent at the helm. Prescriptions to improve policy- and decision-making flow naturally, albeit controversially, from adjusting the potential contribution of the state as agent.

At the global level, in contrast, we need a term to signify the reality that there has never been a world government, and there undoubtedly will not be one during our lifetime. Hence, at the global level, governance is "government minus." Finkelstein, for instance, sees global governance as "doing internationally what governments do at home."[63] But his formulation fails to specify the agencies that are supposed to accomplish globally the numerous tasks that governments do nationally. Thus, at both the country and the global levels, governance encompasses more than government. But as there is no government at the global level, of what utility is the notion of global governance? Is it, as Brian Urquhart once quipped, like the grinning but bodiless Cheshire cat in *Alice in Wonderland*, an agreeable notion because it is without substance?

For us, global governance is most usefully seen as a heuristic device to capture and describe the seemingly ever-accelerating transformation of world order and the international systems within which the United Nations operates. Governments representing states are central players and will remain the most essential units of decision-making, but their authority is eroding on the margins. The world is more or less well ordered despite the lack of coordination between and among states. This order is provided by global markets and a variety of other systems and broad-based institutions within which states must operate.

State creations, intergovernmental organizations, are no more in control than they ever were. Local and international NGOs are proliferating and gaining visibility and resources. And technological developments are increasing the wherewithal of corporations and criminal groups. Within this context, collective action problems associated with the provision of global public goods have become still more intractable than is their provision in the national setting.[64]

The subtext, here and in the analyses of most proponents, is that multilateral institutions, both universal and regional, should be strengthened. The longing for a monolithic and top-down view of government for the globe is understandable but seems misplaced in an increasingly decentralized world. At a time when both problems and solutions transcend national borders and there is no likelihood of a central sovereign, the visceral calls from internationalists to strengthen intergovernmental institutions are comprehensible but appear wistful. There perhaps would be more payoff from thinking creatively about ways to pool the collective strengths and avoid the collective weaknesses of governments, intergovernmental organizations, NGOs, and global civil society. Without denying the need for enhanced IGOs, ironically, this is the conceptual and operational challenge for supporters of the United Nations in the face of changing world politics.

Indeed, this was the organizing principle behind the September 2000 Millennium Summit, when close to 140 heads of government participated in an intense series of private and public sessions. But New York's traffic was congested by more than government limousines because of Secretary-General Kofi Annan's effort to reflect the diverse reality of problem-solving in the contemporary world with a "global compact" between the United Nations and representatives of NGOs and businesses as well as of governments.[65]

While Singapore ambassador to the UN Kishore Mahbubani had called it "the mother of all summits," the record for summits was broken for the September 2005 gathering of 153 presidents, prime ministers, and princes who showed up at the UN's New York headquarters on the eve of the world organization's sixtieth anniversary. We return to the two views that emerged about the results, which we cited earlier. "A once-in-a-generation opportunity to reform and revive the United Nations has been squandered," said the lead editorial from the *New York Times*. Secretary-General Annan, writing in the *Wall Street Journal*, acknowledged in an understatement that his original bold reform plan had been "watered down" but that "a glass [was] at least half-full."[66] Cynics responded that at least there was a glass. We have argued that the creation of the Peacebuilding Commission and of the Human Rights Council appear to be helpful steps, as was the agreement about the responsibility to protect.

In conclusion, we need to reflect again on the primary raison d'être of the United Nations, which is the promotion and maintenance of peace and security and—most especially as we move further into the new millennium—human security. In this regard, we need to stress the inherent and inextricably linked nature of human security, democratization and human rights, and sustainable human development. The latter is aimed at cumulatively improving and sustaining human security and reducing perceived and actual threats to physical and

A group photo of the High-level Plenary Meeting of the sixtieth session of the General Assembly (2005 World Summit). (UN Photo/Eskinder Debebe)

psychological well-being from all manner of agents and forces that could degrade lives, values, and property. Both sustainable human security and sustainable human development require democracy and the protection of fundamental human rights. In short, enhancing human security is what both development and democracy are about. Nothing could be clearer in the post-9/11 world.

The United Nations has always blended ideals and reality. Its Charter represents the idealistic goals of international society, a world of peace and justice. Its operation represents the reality of state foreign policies mediated by the views of nonstate parties such as NGOs and independent international civil servants. The UN thus represents both the striving for a better world—more peaceful, with more human dignity and equitable and sustainable prosperity—and the failure to achieve those goals.

The end of the Cold War provided an opportunity for states to cooperate more through the United Nations. The debilitating competition between the United States and the Soviet Union, between NATO and the Warsaw Pact, between capitalist democracies and authoritarian or socialist states, disappeared along with the Berlin Wall. States have learned from this post–Cold War opportunity how to cooperate within the security realm (for instance, in the 1991 Gulf War and Somalia), the human rights arena (for instance, in Haiti and El Salvador), and the field of sustainable development (for instance, in the Commission on Sustainable Development).

But interstate cooperation via the United Nations clearly has its limits. States learned conflicting lessons about the wisdom of projecting the UN into armed conflict in places like the former Yugoslavia or into the human rights situation in places like China, and how to handle sustainable development in both the North and the South. How effective UN efforts will be in helping to reconstitute Afghanistan and Iraq is as unknown as the effectiveness of the U.S.-led war on terrorism and regime change in Iraq.

In evaluating the successes and failures attributed to the United Nations, we can take a maximalist or minimalist position. If we compare the real record of achievement to the lofty goals stated in the Charter, the world organization's record is bound to be the subject of criticism or even derision. If we recognize that UN actions depend heavily on state foreign policies, which are ever sensitive to calculations about narrowly conceived national interests, and that much of the time the UN is given the difficult problems that states have not been able to solve on their own, then criticism is moderated.

In this respect we may do well to conclude with words attributed to Secretary-General Dag Hammarskjöld: "The purpose of the UN is not to get us to heaven but to save us from hell."

NOTES

1. In the "Winds of Change," *Foreign Affairs* 69, no. 4 (1995): 162–172.

2. See further J. Martin Rochester, *Waiting for the Millennium: The United Nations and the Future of World Order* (Columbia: University of South Carolina Press, 1993); Michael Barnett and Martha Finnemore, *Rules for the World: International Organizations in Global Politics* (Ithaca, N.Y.: Cornell University Press, 2005); and Dennis Dijkzeul and Yves Beigbeder, *Rethinking International Organizations* (New York: Berghahn Books, 2003).

3. This discussion draws on Michael Barnett and Thomas G. Weiss, "Humanitarianism: A Brief History of the Present," *Humanitarianism in Question: Politics, Power, Ethics* (Ithaca, N.Y.: Cornell University Press, 2008), 1–48.

4. Kalevi J. Holsti, *Taming the Sovereigns: Institutional Change in International Politics* (Cambridge: Cambridge University Press, 2004), 12–13.

5. The related distinction between evolutionary and revolutionary change also is germane, as is the analytical distinction between punctuated equilibrium and evolution. See John Campbell, *Institutional Change and Globalization* (Princeton, N.J.: Princeton University Press, 2004), 34.

6. Holsti, *Taming the Sovereigns*, 8.

7. Malcolm Gladwell, *The Tipping Point: How Little Things Can Make a Big Difference* (Boston: Little Brown, 2002).

8. Robert Jervis, *System Effects: Complexity in Political and Social Life* (Princeton, N.J.: Princeton University Press, 1999).

9. Thomas G. Weiss, *Civilian-Military Interactions: Humanitarian Crises and the Responsibility to Protect*, 2nd ed. (Lanham, Md.: Rowman & Littlefield, 2004).

10. Kofi A. Annan, *Investing in the United Nations: For a Stronger Organization Worldwide*, UN document A/60/692, March 7, 2006, 1.

11. James N. Rosenau, *Turbulence in World Politics: A Theory of Change and Continuity* (Princeton, N.J.: Princeton University Press, 1990). The implications of this view for the United Nations are found in his *The United Nations in a Turbulent World* (Boulder, Colo.: Lynne Rienner, 1992).

12. This is more fully developed in Thomas G. Weiss, Tatiana Carayannis, and Richard Jolly, "The 'Third' United Nations," *Global Governance* 15, no. 1 (2009): 123–42.

13. At the same time, probably never before in world history have major states "outsourced" so much of their military operations to private parties. The United States in Iraq has relied heavily on private security firms and other firms for protection of high U.S. officials, interrogation of prisoners, delivery of basic goods and support services for military forces, etc. See further Peter Singer, *Corporate Warriors: The Rise of the Privatized Military Industry* (Ithaca, N.Y.: Cornell University Press, 2003).

14. It is true that in 2005 both France and the Netherlands held referenda that turned down the new EU constitution. But this still left an integrated and supranational European Union that was superior in these respects to all other regional organizations. Moreover, in the past, a crisis in European affairs had usually preceded a further movement toward increased regional integration.

15. The clash between the new global forces and the traditional local forces has been popularly treated by Thomas L. Friedman, *The Lexus and the Olive Tree* (New York: HarperCollins, 1999), and by Benjamin R. Barber, *Jihad vs. McWorld* (New York: Ballantine Books, 1995).

16. For ruminations on this issue, see Thomas G. Weiss, "What Happened to the Idea of World Government?" *International Studies Quarterly* 53, no. 2 (2009): 253–271.

17. "Secretary-General Address to the General Assembly given September 23, 2003," available at www.un.org/webcast/ga/58/statements/sg2eng030923.htm.

18. Ernest R. May, *"Lessons" of the Past: The Use and Misuse of History in American Foreign Policy* (New York: Oxford University Press, 1975).

19. See, for example, Robert S. McNamara, James G. Blight, and Robert K. Brigham, *Argument without End: In Search of Answers to the Vietnam Tragedy* (New York: Public Affairs, 1999).

20. See further James Mann, *Rise of the Vulcans: The History of Bush's War Cabinet* (New York: Viking, 2004).

21. See further Richard E. Neustadt and Ernest R. May, *Thinking in Time: The Uses of History for Decision Makers* (New York: Free Press, 1986).

22. Shashi Tharoor, "Foreword," in *Beyond Traditional Peacekeeping*, eds. Donald C. F. Daniel and Bradd C. Hayes (London: Macmillan, 1995), xviii.

23. Peter M. Haas and Ernst B. Haas, "Learning to Learn: Improving International Governance," *Global Governance* 1, no. 3 (1995): 255–285, quote at 278.

24. See Cindy Collins and Thomas G. Weiss, *Review of the Peacekeeping Literature, 1990–1996* (Providence, R.I.: Watson Institute, 1997).

25. See Michael Barnett, "Humanitarianism as a Scholarly Vocation," and Peter J. Hoffman and Thomas G. Weiss, "Humanitarianism and Practitioners: Social Science Matters," in *Humanitarianism in Question*, chapters 10 and 11.

26. For an example of this approach applied to international organizations, see Harold K. Jacobson, *Networks of Interdependence: International Organizations and the Global Political System* (New York: Knopf, 1979).

27. See Thomas G. Weiss, *What's Wrong with the United Nations and How to Fix It* (London: Polity, 2009).

28. Robert E. Riggs, *US/UN: Foreign Policy and International Organization* (New York: Appleton-Century-Crofts, 1971), 298.

29. From a wealth of sources see Clyde Prestowitz, *Rogue Nation: American Unilateralism and the Failure of Good Intentions* (New York: Basic Books, 2003), and David M. Malone and Yuen Foong Khong, eds., *Unilateralism and U.S. Foreign Policy: International Perspectives* (Boulder, Colo.: Lynne Rienner, 2003).

30. James Traub, "The Next Resolution," *New York Times Magazine*, April 13, 2003.

31. UNDP, *Human Development Report 1996* (New York: United Nations, 1996), 12.

32. See Joseph E. Nye Jr., *The Paradox of American Power: Why the World's Only Superpower Can't Go It Alone* (Oxford and New York: Oxford University Press, 2002).

33. See Kishore Mahbubani, *The New Asian Hemisphere: The Irresistible Shift of Global Power to the East* (New York: PublicAffairs, 2008), and Fareed Zakaria, *The Post-American World* (New York: Norton, 2008).

34. "Statement of H.E. George W. Bush, President of the United States of America, 2005 World Summit, High Level Plenary Meeting, September 14, 2005," www.un.org/webcast/summit2005/statements14.html.

35. Richard N. Haass, *The Opportunity: America's Chance to Change the World* (New York: PublicAffairs, 2005), 199. For an argument that American doctrinal unilateralism, for all of Washington's hard power, is unsustainable in an interdependent world, see David P. Forsythe, Patrice C. McMahon, and Andrew Wedeman, *American Foreign Policy in a Globalized World* (New York: Routledge, 2006).

36. For a discussion, see Thomas G. Weiss, "Toward a Third Generation of International Institutions: Obama's UN Policy," *Washington Quarterly* 32, no. 3 (2009): 343–364.

37. "Announcement of National Security Team," December 1, 2008, http://change.gov/newsroom/entry/the_national_security_team/.

38. "Susan Rice's Testimony at Her U.N. Ambassador Hearing, January 15, 2009," available at www.realclearpolitics.com/articles/2009/01/susan_rices_testimony_at_her_u.html. Other quotations are from this testimony as well.

39. Quoted in *The Economist*, December 13, 2008, 43.

40. Barack Obama, "Renewing American Leadership," *Foreign Affairs* 87, no. 4 (2007): 3.

41. See the views of Joseph P. Nye, Edward C. Luck, Anne-Marie Slaughter, and Ian Hurd in *Foreign Affairs* 82, no. 3 (2003). See also Mats Berdal, "The UN Security Council: Ineffective but Indispensable," *Survival* 45, no. 2 (2003): 7–30. These views were representative of a larger slice of expert commentary.

42. See especially Tony Evans, *U.S. Hegemony and the Project of Universal Human Rights* (New York: St. Martin's Press, 1996), and David P. Forsythe, *Human Rights in International Relations* (Cambridge: Cambridge University Press, 2000).

43. Donald J. Puchala, "World Hegemony and the United Nations," *International Studies Review* 7, no. 4 (2005): 581.

44. From many sources see Sarah B. Sewall and Carl Kaysen, eds., *The United States and the International Criminal Court* (Lanham, Md.: Rowman & Littlefield, 2000).

45. See further Aryeh Neier, *War Crimes: Brutality, Genocide, Terror, and the Struggle for Justice* (New York: Times Books, 1998), and Steven R. Ratner and Jason S. Abrams, *Accountability for Human Rights Atrocities in International Law: Beyond the Nuremberg Legacy* (Oxford: Clarendon Press, 1997).

46. José E. Alvarez, *International Organizations as Law-makers* (Oxford: Oxford University Press, 2005), 626.

47. Remarks made at a symposium on collective responses to common threats, Oslo, Norway, June 22–23, 1993.

48. Louise Arbour, "Statement by High Commissioner for Human Rights to Last Meeting of Commission on Human Rights," March 27, 2006, 1–2.

49. Millennium Project, *Investing in Development: A Practical Plan to Achieve the Millennium Development Goals* (New York: UNDP, 2005), and Jeffrey Sachs, *The End of Poverty:*

Economic Possibilities for Our Time (New York: Penguin Books, 2005), which has a foreword by Bono.

50. See, for example, Andrew Chadwick, *Internet Politics: States, Citizens, and New Communications Technologies* (New York: Oxford University Press, 2006), and Mark D. Alleyne, *Global Lies? Propaganda, the UN and World Order* (Houndmills, Basingstoke, UK: Palgrave Macmillan, 2003).

51. Kemal Derviş with Ceren Özer, *A Better Globalization: Legitimacy, Governance, and Reform* (Washington, D.C.: Center for Global Development, 2005).

52. Since 1995 Lynne Rienner Publishers has, in cooperation with the Academic Council on the United Nations System, published the quarterly journal *Global Governance*. The origins and itinerary of this concept are found in Ramesh Thakur and Thomas G. Weiss, *The UN and Global Governance: An Unfinished Journey* (Bloomington: Indiana University Press, 2009).

53. James N. Rosenau, "'Fragmegrative' Challenges to National Security," *Understanding U.S. Strategy: A Reader*, ed. Terry Hens (Washington, D.C.: National Defense University, 1983), 65–82.

54. Lawrence S. Finkelstein, "What Is Global Governance?" *Global Governance* 1, no. 3 (1995): 368.

55. For a persuasive discussion, see David Held and Anthony McGrew, with David Goldblatt and Jonathan Peraton, *Global Transformations: Politics, Economics, and Culture* (Stanford, Calif.: Stanford University Press, 1999).

56. James N. Rosenau, "Governance in the Twenty-first Century," *Global Governance* 1, no. 1 (1995): 13.

57. Emma Rothschild, "Globalization and the Return of History," *Foreign Policy* 115 (Summer 1999): 106–116.

58. Jan Aart Scholte, *Globalization: A Critical Introduction*, 2nd ed. (New York: Palgrave, 2005), 3.

59. David Held and Anthony McGrew, with David Goldblatt and Jonathan Peraton, "Globalization," *Global Governance* 5, no. 4 (1999): 494.

60. UNDP, *Human Development Report 1999* (New York: Oxford University Press, 1999), 100.

61. Philip G. Cerny, "Globalization and the Changing Logic of Collective Action," *International Organization* 49, no. 4 (1995): 595, 621.

62. Mark W. Zacher, *The United Nations and Global Commerce* (New York: United Nations, 1999), 5.

63. Finkelstein, "What Is Global Governance?" 369.

64. Inge Kaul, Isabelle Grunberg, and Marc A. Stern, *Global Public Goods: International Cooperation in the 21st Century* (New York: Oxford University Press, 1999).

65. Kofi Annan, *"We the Peoples": The United Nations in the 21st Century* (New York: United Nations, 2000). For an analysis, see John Gerard Ruggie, "global_governance.net: The Global Compact as Learning Network," *Global Governance* 7, no. 4 (2001): 371–378.

66. "The Lost U.N. Summit Meeting," *New York Times*, September 14, 2005, and Kofi Annan, "A Glass At Least Half-Full," *Wall Street Journal*, September 19, 2005.

Appendix A:
The United Nations System

The UNITED NATIONS system

PRINCIPAL ORGANS OF THE UNITED NATIONS

| INTERNATIONAL COURT OF JUSTICE | SECURITY COUNCIL | GENERAL ASSEMBLY | ECONOMIC AND SOCIAL COUNCIL | TRUSTEESHIP COUNCIL | SECRETARIAT |

UNITED NATIONS

INTERNATIONAL COURT OF JUSTICE

- Military Staff Committee
- Standing Committee and ad hoc bodies
- International Criminal Tribunal for the Former Yugoslavia
- International Criminal Tribunal for Rwanda
- UN Monitoring, Verification and Inspection Commission (Iraq)
- United Nations Compensation Commission
- Peacekeeping Operations and Missions

GENERAL ASSEMBLY

- Main committees
- Other sessional committees
- Standing committees and ad hoc bodies
- Other subsidiary organs

PROGRAMMES AND FUNDS

UNCTAD
United Nations Conference on Trade and Development

　ITC
　International Trade Centre (UNCTAD/WTO)

UNDCP
United Nations Drug Control Programme

UNEP
United Nations Environment Programme

UNHSP
United Nations Human Settlements Programme (UN-Habitat)

UNDP
United Nations Development Programme

　UNIFEM
　United Nations Development Fund for Women

　UNV
　United Nations Volunteers

UNFPA
United Nations Population Fund

UNHCR
Office of the United Nations High Commissioner for Refugees

UNICEF
United Nations Children's Fund

WFP
World Food Programme

UNRWA**
United Nations Relief and Works Agency for Palestine Refugees in the Near East

UNAIDS
Joint United Nations Programme on HIV/AIDS

OTHER UN ENTITIES

OHCHR
Office of the United Nations High Commissioner for Human Rights

UNOPS
United Nations Office for Project Services

UNU
United Nations University

UNSSC
United Nations System Staff College

RESEARCH AND TRAINING INSTITUTES

INSTRAW
International Research and Training Institute for the Advancement of Women

UNICRI
United Nations Interregional Crime and Justice Research Institute

UNITAR
United Nations Institute for Training and Research

UNRISD
United Nations Research Institute for Social Development

UNIDIR**
United Nations Institute for Disarmament Research

ECONOMIC AND SOCIAL COUNCIL

FUNCTIONAL COMMISSIONS

- Commission for Social Development
- Commission on Human Rights
- Commission on Narcotic Drugs
- Commission on Crime Prevention and Criminal Justice
- Commission on Science and Technology for Development
- Commission on Sustainable Development
- Commission on the Status of Women
- Commission on Population and Development
- Statistical Commission

REGIONAL COMMISSIONS

- Economic Commission for Africa (ECA)
- Economic Commission for Europe (ECE)
- Economic Commission for Latin America and the Caribbean (ECLAC)
- Economic and Social Commission for Asia and the Pacific (ESCAP)
- Economic and Social Commission for Western Asia (ESCWA)
- United Nations Forum on Forests
- Sessional and Standing Committees
- Expert, ad hoc and related bodies

RELATED ORGANIZATIONS

IAEA
International Atomic Energy Agency

WTO (trade)
World Trade Organization

WTO (tourism)
World Tourism Organization

CTBTO Prep.com
PrepCom for the Nuclear-Test-Ban-Treaty Organization

OPCW
Organization for the Prohibition of Chemical Weapons

TRUSTEESHIP COUNCIL

SPECIALIZED AGENCIES*

ILO
International Labour Organization

FAO
Food and Agriculture Organization of the United Nations

UNESCO
United Nations Educational, Scientific and Cultural Organization

WHO
World Health Organization

WORLD BANK GROUP
- **IBRD** International Bank for Reconstruction and Development
- **IDA** International Development Association
- **IFC** International Finance Corporation
- **MIGA** Multilateral Investment Guarantee Agency
- **ICSID** International Centre for Settlement of Investment Disputes

IMF
International Monetary Fund

ICAO
International Civil Aviation Organization

IMO
International Maritime Organization

ITU
International Telecommunication Union

UPU
Universal Postal Union

WMO
World Meteorological Organization

WIPO
World Intellectual Property Organization

IFAD
International Fund for Agricultural Development

UNIDO
United Nations Industrial Development Organization

SECRETARIAT

OSG
Office of the Secretary-General

OIOS
Office of Internal Oversight Services

OLA
Office of Legal Affairs

DPA
Department of Political Affairs

DDA
Department for Disarmament Affairs

DPKO
Department of Peacekeeping Operations

OCHA
Office for the Coordination of Humanitarian Affairs

DESA
Department of Economic and Social Affairs

DGACM
Department of General Assembly and Conference Management

DPI
Department of Public Information

DM
Department of Management

OIP
Office of the Iraq Programme

UNSECOORD
Office of the United Nations Security Coordinator

OHRLLS
Office of the High Representative for the Least Developed Countries, Landlocked Developing Countries and Small Island Developing States

ODC
Office on Drugs and Crime

UNOG
UN Office at Geneva

UNOV
UN Office at Vienna

UNON
UN Office at Nairobi

---

*Autonomous organizations working with the United Nations and each other through the coordinating machinery of the Economic and Social Council.

**Report only to the General Assembly.

Published by the United Nations Department of Public Information
DPI/2299 - February 2003

Appendix B: Concise List of Internet Sites Relevant to the United Nations

General Information on International Relations with Frequent Attention to the UN

Council on Foreign Relations and *Foreign Affairs* magazine: www.cfr.org
Carnegie Council on Ethics: www.carnegiecouncil.org
Foreign Policy Magazine: www.foreignpolicy.com
International Crisis Group: www.intl-crisis-grp.org
General Information on the UN and the UN System
The United Nations Homepage*: www.un.org
The United Nations University: www.unu.edu
UN Wire: www.unwire.org
Academic Council on the UN System (ACUNS): www.acuns.org
UN Association of the USA: www.unausa.org
UN Chronicle magazine: www.un.org/Pubs/chronicle

Security Issues

International Security Magazine: www.harvard.edarticle 545u/publications/cfm
International Institute for Strategic Studies and Survival Magazine: www.iiss.org
Center for Strategic and International Studies: www.csis.org
Women in International Security: www.wiis.org
Security Council Report: www.securitycouncilreport.org
Human Rights and Humanitarian Affairs
International Committee of the Red Cross: www.icrc.org
Amnesty International: www.amnesty.org
Human Rights Watch: www.hrw.org
Coalition for International Justice: www.cij.org
Freedom House: www.freedomhouse.org
Sustainable Human Development
World Bank: www.worldbank.org
Overseas Development Council: www.odc.org
Organization for Economic Cooperation and Development: www.oecd.org
US Agency for International Development: www.usaid.gov
Center for International Development: www.cid.harvard.edu

*All of the websites of the agencies, bodies, programs, and funds of the UN system can be accessed through this site. They are not repeated under substantive headings.

Appendix C:
Charter of the United Nations

Preamble

We the Peoples of the United Nations Determined

to save succeeding generations from the scourge of war, which twice in our lifetime has brought untold sorrow to mankind, and

to reaffirm faith in fundamental human rights, in the dignity and worth of the human person, in the equal rights of men and women and of nations large and small, and

to establish conditions under which justice and respect for the obligations arising from treaties and other sources of international law can be maintained, and

to promote social progress and better standards of life in larger freedom,

And for these Ends

to practice tolerance and live together in peace with one another as good neighbors, and

to unite our strength to maintain international peace and security, and

to ensure by the acceptance of principles and the institution of methods, that armed force shall not be used, save in the common interest, and

to employ international machinery for the promotion of the economic and social advancement of all peoples,

Have Resolved to Combine our Efforts to Accomplish these Aims

Accordingly, our respective Governments, through representatives assembled in the city of San Francisco, who have exhibited their full powers found to be in good and due form, have agreed to the present Charter of the United Nations and do hereby establish an international organization to be known as the United Nations.

CHAPTER I PURPOSES AND PRINCIPLES

Article 1

The Purposes of the United Nations are:

1. To maintain international peace and security, and to that end: to take effective collective measures for the prevention and removal of threats to the peace, and for the suppression of acts of aggression or other breaches of the peace, and to bring about by peaceful means, and in conformity with the principles of justice and international law, adjustment or settlement of international disputes or situations which might lead to a breach of the peace;
2. To develop friendly relations among nations based on respect for the principle of equal rights and self-determination of peoples, and to take other appropriate measures to strengthen universal peace;
3. To achieve international cooperation in solving international problems of an economic, social, cultural, or humanitarian character, and in promoting and encouraging respect for

human rights and for fundamental freedoms for all without distinction as to race, sex, language, or religion; and

4. To be a center for harmonizing the actions of nations in the attainment of these common ends.

Article 2

The Organization and its Members, in pursuit of the Purposes stated in Article 1, shall act in accordance with the following Principles.

1. The Organization is based on the principle of the sovereign equality of all its Members.
2. All Members, in order to ensure to all of them the rights and benefits resulting from membership, shall fulfill in good faith the obligations assumed by them in accordance with the present Charter.
3. All Members shall settle their international disputes by peaceful means in such a manner that international peace and security, and justice, are not endangered.
4. All Members shall refrain in their international relations from the threat or use of force against the territorial integrity or political independence of any state, or in any other manner inconsistent with the Purposes of the United Nations.
5. All Members shall give the United Nations every assistance in any action it takes in accordance with the present Charter, and shall refrain from giving assistance to any state against which the United Nations is taking preventive or enforcement action.
6. The Organization shall ensure that states which are not Members of the United Nations act in accordance with these Principles so far as may be necessary for the maintenance of international peace and security.
7. Nothing contained in the present Charter shall authorize the United Nations to intervene in matters which are essentially within the domestic jurisdiction of any state or shall require the Members to submit such matters to settlement under the present Charter; but this principle shall not prejudice the application of enforcement measures under Chapter VII.

CHAPTER II MEMBERSHIP

Article 3

The original Members of the United Nations shall be the states which, having participated in the United Nations Conference on International Organization at San Francisco, or having previously signed the Declaration by United Nations of January 1, 1942, sign the present Charter and ratify it in accordance with Article 110.

Article 4

1. Membership in the United Nations is open to all other peace-loving states which accept the obligations contained in the present Charter and, in the judgment of the Organization, are able and willing to carry out these obligations.
2. The admission of any such state to membership in the United Nations will be effected by a decision of the General Assembly upon the recommendation of the Security Council.

Article 5

A member of the United Nations against which preventive or enforcement action has been taken by the Security Council may be suspended from the exercise of the rights and privileges of membership by the General Assembly upon the recommendation of the Security Council. The exercise of these rights and privileges may be restored by the Security Council.

Article 6

A Member of the United Nations which has persistently violated the Principles contained in the present Charter may be expelled from the Organization by the General Assembly upon the recommendation of the Security Council.

CHAPTER III ORGANS
Article 7
1. There are established as the principal organs of the United Nations: a General Assembly, a Security Council, an Economic and Social Council, a Trusteeship Council, an International Court of Justice, and a Secretariat.
2. Such subsidiary organs as may be found necessary may be established in accordance with the present Charter.

Article 8
The United Nations shall place no restrictions on the eligibility of men and women to participate in any capacity and under conditions of equality in its principal and subsidiary organs.

CHAPTER IV THE GENERAL ASSEMBLY
COMPOSITION
Article 9
1. The General Assembly shall consist of all the Members of the United Nations.
2. Each member shall have not more than five representatives in the General Assembly.

FUNCTIONS AND POWERS
Article 10
The General Assembly may discuss any questions or any matters within the scope of the present Charter or relating to the powers and functions of any organs provided for in the present Charter, and, except as provided in Article 12, may make recommendations to the Members of the United Nations or to the Security Council or to both on any such questions or matters.

Article 11
1. The General Assembly may consider the general principles of cooperation in the maintenance of international peace and security, including the principles governing disarmament and the regulation of armaments, and may make recommendations with regard to such principles to the Members or to the Security Council or to both.
2. The General Assembly may discuss any questions relating to the maintenance of international peace and security brought before it by any Member of the United Nations, or by the Security Council, or by a state which is not a Member of the United Nations in accordance with Article 35, paragraph 2, and, except as provided in Article 12, may make recommendations with regard to any such questions to the state or states concerned or to the Security Council or to both. Any such question on which action is necessary shall be referred to the Security Council by the General Assembly either before or after discussion.
3. The General Assembly may call the attention of the Security Council to situations which are likely to endanger international peace and security.
4. The powers of the General Assembly set forth in this Article shall not limit the general scope of Article 10.

Article 12
1. While the Security Council is exercising in respect of any dispute or situation the functions assigned to it in the present Charter, the General Assembly shall not make any recommendation with regard to that dispute or situation unless the Security Council so requests.
2. The Secretary-General, with the consent of the Security Council, shall notify the General Assembly at each session of any matters relative to the maintenance of international peace and security which are being dealt with by the Security Council and shall similarly notify the General Assembly, or the Members of the United Nations if the General Assembly is not in session, immediately the Security Council ceases to deal with such matters.

Article 13

1. 1. The General Assembly shall initiate studies and make recommendations for the purpose of:
    A. promoting international cooperation in the political field and encouraging the progressive development of international law and its codification;
    B. promoting international cooperation in the economic, social, cultural, educational, and health fields, and assisting in the realization of human rights and fundamental freedoms for all without distinction as to race, sex, language, or religion.
2. The further responsibilities, functions, and powers of the General Assembly with respect to matters mentioned in paragraph 1(b) above are set forth in Chapters IX and X.

Article 14

Subject to the provisions of Article 12, the General Assembly may recommend measures for the peaceful adjustment of any situation, regardless of origin, which it deems likely to impair the general welfare or friendly relations among nations, including situations resulting from a violation of the provisions of the present Charter setting forth the Purposes and Principles of the United Nations.

Article 15

1. The General Assembly shall receive and consider annual and special reports from the Security Council; these reports shall include an account of the measures that the Security Council has decided upon or taken to maintain international peace and security.
2. The General Assembly shall receive and consider reports from the other organs of the United Nations.

Article 16

The General Assembly shall perform such functions with respect to the international trusteeship system as are assigned to it under Chapters XII and XIII, including the approval of the trusteeship agreements for areas not designated as strategic.

Article 17

1. The General Assembly shall consider and approve the budget of the Organization.
2. The expenses of the Organization shall be borne by the Members as apportioned by the General Assembly.
3. The General Assembly shall consider and approve any financial and budgetary arrangements with specialized agencies referred to in Article 57 and shall examine the administrative budgets of such specialized agencies with a view to making recommendations to the agencies concerned.

VOTING
Article 18

1. Each member of the General Assembly shall have one vote.
2. Decisions of the General Assembly on important questions shall be made by a two-thirds majority of the members present and voting. These questions shall include: recommendations with respect to the maintenance of international peace and security, the election of the non-permanent members of the Security Council, the election of the members of the Economic and Social Council, the election of members of the Trusteeship Council in accordance with paragraph 1(c) of Article 86, the admission of new Members to the United Nations, the suspension of the rights and privileges of membership, the expulsion of Members, questions relating to the operation of the trusteeship system, and budgetary questions.
3. Decisions on other questions, including the determination of additional categories of questions to be decided by a two-thirds majority, shall be made by a majority of the members present and voting.

Article 19

A Member of the United Nations which is in arrears in the payment of its financial contributions to the Organization shall have no vote in the General Assembly if the amount of its arrears equals or exceeds the amount of the contributions due from it for the preceding two full years. The General Assembly may, nevertheless, permit such a Member to vote if it is satisfied that the failure to pay is due to conditions beyond the control of the Member.

PROCEDURE
Article 20

The General Assembly shall meet in regular annual sessions and in such special sessions as occasion may require. Special sessions shall be convoked by the Secretary-General at the request of the Security Council or of a majority of the Members of the United Nations.

Article 21

The General Assembly shall adopt its own rules of procedure. It shall elect its President for each session.

Article 22

The General Assembly may establish such subsidiary organs as it deems necessary for the performance of its functions.

CHAPTER V THE SECURITY COUNCIL
Article 23

1. The Security Council shall consist of fifteen Members of the United Nations. The Republic of China, France, the Union of Soviet Socialist Republics, the United Kingdom of Great Britain and Northern Ireland, and the United States of America shall be permanent members of the Security Council. The General Assembly shall elect ten other Members of the United Nations to be non-permanent members of the Security Council, due regard being specially paid, in the first instance to the contribution of Members of the United Nations to the maintenance of international peace and security and to the other purposes of the Organization, and also to equitable geographical distribution.
2. The non-permanent members of the Security Council shall be elected for a term of two years. In the first election of the non-permanent members after the increase of the membership of the Security Council from eleven to fifteen, two of the four additional members shall be chosen for a term of one year. A retiring member shall not be eligible for immediate re-election.
3. Each member of the Security Council shall have one representative.

FUNCTIONS AND POWERS
Article 24

1. In order to ensure prompt and effective action by the United Nations, its Members confer on the Security Council primary responsibility for the maintenance of international peace and security, and agree that in carrying out its duties under this responsibility the Security Council acts on their behalf.
2. In discharging these duties the Security Council shall act in accordance with the Purposes and Principles of the United Nations. The specific powers granted to the Security Council for the discharge of these duties are laid down in Chapters VI, VII, VIII, and XII.
3. The Security Council shall submit annual and, when necessary, special reports to the General Assembly for its consideration.

Article 25

The Members of the United Nations agree to accept and carry out the decisions of the Security Council in accordance with the present Charter.

Article 26

In order to promote the establishment and maintenance of international peace and security with the least diversion for armaments of the world's human and economic resources, the Security Council shall be responsible for formulating, with the assistance of the Military Staff Committee referred to in Article 47, plans to be submitted to the Members of the United Nations for the establishment of a system for the regulation of armaments.

VOTING
Article 27

1. Each member of the Security Council shall have one vote.
2. Decisions of the Security Council on procedural matters shall be made by an affirmative vote of nine members.
3. Decisions of the Security Council on all other matters shall be made by an affirmative vote of nine members including the concurring votes of the permanent members; provided that, in decisions under Chapter VI, and under paragraph 3 of Article 52, a party to a dispute shall abstain from voting.

PROCEDURE
Article 28

1. The Security Council shall be so organized as to be able to function continuously. Each member of the Security Council shall for this purpose be represented at all times at the seat of the Organization.
2. The Security Council shall hold periodic meetings at which each of its members may, if it so desires, be represented by a member of the government or by some other specially designated representative.
3. The Security Council may hold meetings at such places other than the seat of the Organization as in its judgment will best facilitate its work.

Article 29

The Security Council may establish such subsidiary organs as it deems necessary for the performance of its functions.

Article 30

The Security Council shall adopt its own rules of procedure, including the method of selecting its President.

Article 31

Any Member of the United Nations which is not a member of the Security Council may participate, without vote, in the discussion of any question brought before the Security Council whenever the latter considers that the interests of that Member are specially affected.

Article 32

Any Member of the United Nations which is not a member of the Security Council or any state which is not a Member of the United Nations, if it is a party to a dispute under consideration by the Security Council, shall be invited to participate, without vote, in the discussion relating to the dispute. The Security Council shall lay down such conditions as it deems just for the participation of a state which is not a Member of the United Nations.

CHAPTER VI PACIFIC SETTLEMENT OF DISPUTES
Article 33

1. The parties to any dispute, the continuance of which is likely to endanger the maintenance of international peace and security, shall, first of all, seek a solution by negotiation, enquiry,

mediation, conciliation, arbitration, judicial settlement, resort to regional agencies or arrangements, or other peaceful means of their own choice.

2. The Security Council shall, when it deems necessary, call upon the parties to settle their dispute by such means.

Article 34

The Security Council may investigate any dispute, or any situation which might lead to international friction or give rise to a dispute, in order to determine whether the continuance of the dispute or situation is likely to endanger the maintenance of international peace and security.

Article 35

1. Any Member of the United Nations may bring any dispute, or any situation of the nature referred to in Article 34, to the attention of the Security Council or of the General Assembly.
2. A state which is not a Member of the United Nations may bring to the attention of the Security Council or of the General Assembly any dispute to which it is a party if it accepts in advance, for the purposes of the dispute, the obligations of pacific settlement provided in the present Charter.
3. The proceedings of the General Assembly in respect of matters brought to its attention under this Article will be subject to the provisions of Articles 11 and 12.

Article 36

1. The Security Council may, at any stage of a dispute of the nature referred to in Article 33 or of a situation of like nature, recommend appropriate procedures or methods of adjustment.
2. The Security Council should take into consideration any procedures for the settlement of the dispute which have already been adopted by the parties.
3. In making recommendations under this Article the Security Council should also take into consideration that legal disputes should as a general rule be referred by the parties to the International Court of Justice in accordance with the provisions of the Statute of the Court.

Article 37

1. Should the parties to a dispute of the nature referred to in Article 33 fail to settle it by the means indicated in that Article, they shall refer it to the Security Council.
2. If the Security Council deems that the continuance of the dispute is in fact likely to endanger the maintenance of international peace and security, it shall decide whether to take action under Article 36 or to recommend such terms of settlement as it may consider appropriate.

Article 38

Without prejudice to the provisions of Articles 33 to 37, the Security Council may, if all the parties to any dispute so request, make recommendations to the parties with a view to a pacific settlement of the dispute.

CHAPTER VII ACTION WITH RESPECT TO THREATS TO THE PEACE, BREACHES OF THE PEACE, AND ACTS OF AGGRESSION

Article 39

The Security Council shall determine the existence of any threat to the peace, breach of the peace, or act of aggression and shall make recommendations, or decide what measures shall be taken in accordance with Articles 41 and 42, to maintain or restore international peace and security.

Article 40

In order to prevent an aggravation of the situation, the Security Council may, before making the recommendations or deciding upon the measures provided for in Article 39, call upon the parties concerned to comply with such provisional measures as it deems necessary or desirable. Such provisional measures shall be without prejudice to the rights, claims, or position of the parties concerned. The Security Council shall duly take account of failure to comply with such provisional measures.

Article 41

The Security Council may decide what measures not involving the use of armed force are to be employed to give effect to its decisions, and it may call upon the Members of the United Nations to apply such measures. These may include complete or partial interruption of economic relations and of rail, sea, air, postal, telegraphic, radio, and other means of communication, and the severance of diplomatic relations.

Article 42

Should the Security Council consider that measures provided for in Article 41 would be inadequate or have proved to be inadequate, it may take such action by air, sea, or land forces as may be necessary to maintain or restore international peace and security. Such action may include demonstrations, blockade, and other operations by air, sea, or land forces of Members of the United Nations.

Article 43

1. All Members of the United Nations, in order to contribute to the maintenance of international peace and security, undertake to make available to the Security Council, on its call and in accordance with a special agreement or agreements, armed forces, assistance, and facilities, including rights of passage, necessary for the purpose of maintaining international peace and security.
2. Such agreement or agreements shall govern the numbers and types of forces, their degree of readiness and general location, and the nature of the facilities and assistance to be provided.
3. The agreement or agreements shall be negotiated as soon as possible on the initiative of the Security Council. They shall be concluded between the Security Council and Members or between the Security Council and groups of Members and shall be subject to ratification by the signatory states in accordance with their respective constitutional processes.

Article 44

When the Security Council has decided to use force it shall, before calling upon a Member not represented on it to provide armed forces in fulfillment of the obligations assumed under Article 43, invite that Member, if the Member so desires, to participate in the decisions of the Security Council concerning the employment of contingents of that Member's armed forces.

Article 45

In order to enable the United Nations to take urgent military measures Members shall hold immediately available national air-force contingents for combined international enforcement action. The strength and degree of readiness of these contingents and plans for their combined action shall be determined, within the limits laid down in the special agreement or agreements referred to in Article 43, by the Security Council with the assistance of the Military Staff Committee.

Article 46

Plans for the application of armed force shall be made by the Security Council with the assistance of the Military Staff Committee.

Article 47

1. There shall be established a Military Staff Committee to advise and assist the Security Council on all questions relating to the Security Council's military requirements for the maintenance of international peace and security, the employment and command of forces placed at its disposal, the regulation of armaments, and possible disarmament.
2. The Military Staff Committee shall consist of the Chiefs of Staff of the permanent members of the Security Council or their representatives. Any Member of the United Nations not permanently represented on the Committee shall be invited by the Committee to be asso-

ciated with it when the efficient discharge of the Committee's responsibilities requires the participation of that Member in its work.

3. The Military Staff Committee shall be responsible under the Security Council for the strategic direction of any armed forces placed at the disposal of the Security Council. Questions relating to the command of such forces shall be worked out subsequently.

4. The Military Staff Committee, with the authorization of the Security Council and after consultation with appropriate regional agencies, may establish regional subcommittees.

Article 48

1. The action required to carry out the decisions of the Security Council for the maintenance of international peace and security shall be taken by all the Members of the United Nations or by some of them, as the Security Council may determine.

2. Such decisions shall be carried out by the Members of the United Nations directly and through their action in the appropriate international agencies of which they are members.

Article 49

The Members of the United Nations shall join in affording mutual assistance in carrying out the measures decided upon by the Security Council.

Article 50

If preventive or enforcement measures against any state are taken by the Security Council, any other state, whether a Member of the United Nations or not, which finds itself confronted with special economic problems arising from the carrying out of those measures shall have the right to consult the Security Council with regard to a solution of those problems.

Article 51

Nothing in the present Charter shall impair the inherent right of individual or collective self-defense if an armed attack occurs against a Member of the United Nations, until the Security Council has taken measures necessary to maintain international peace and security. Measures taken by Members in the exercise of this right of self-defense shall be immediately reported to the Security Council and shall not in any way affect the authority and responsibility of the Security Council under the present Charter to take at any time such action as it deems necessary in order to maintain or restore international peace and security.

CHAPTER VIII REGIONAL ARRANGEMENTS

Article 52

1. Nothing in the present Charter precludes the existence of regional arrangements or agencies for dealing with such matters relating to the maintenance of international peace and security as are appropriate for regional action, provided that such arrangements or agencies and their activities are consistent with the Purposes and Principles of the United Nations.

2. The Members of the United Nations entering into such arrangements or constituting such agencies shall make every effort to achieve pacific settlement of local disputes through such regional arrangements or by such regional agencies before referring them to the Security Council.

3. The Security Council shall encourage the development of pacific settlement of local disputes through such regional arrangements or by such regional agencies either on the initiative of the states concerned or by reference from the Security Council.

4. This Article in no way impairs the application of Articles 34 and 35.

Article 53

1. The Security Council shall, where appropriate, utilize such regional arrangements or agencies for enforcement action under its authority. But no enforcement action shall be taken under

regional arrangements or by regional agencies without the authorization of the Security Council, with the exception of measures against any enemy state, as defined in paragraph 2 of this Article, provided for pursuant to Article 107 or in regional arrangements directed against renewal of aggressive policy on the part of any such state, until such time as the Organization may, on request of the Governments concerned, be charged with the responsibility for preventing further aggression by such a state.

2. The term enemy state as used in paragraph 1 of this Article applies to any state which during the Second World War has been an enemy of any signatory of the present Charter.

Article 54

The Security Council shall at all times be kept fully informed of activities undertaken or in contemplation under regional arrangements or by regional agencies for the maintenance of international peace and security.

CHAPTER IX INTERNATIONAL ECONOMIC AND SOCIAL CO-OPERATION

Article 55

With a view to the creation of conditions of stability and well-being which are necessary for peaceful and friendly relations among nations based on respect for the principle of equal rights and self-determination of peoples, the United Nations shall promote:

higher standards of living, full employment, and conditions of economic and social progress and development;

solutions of international economic, social, health, and related problems; and international cultural and educational co-operation; and

universal respect for, and observance of, human rights and fundamental freedoms for all without distinction as to race, sex, language, or religion.

Article 56

All Members pledge themselves to take joint and separate action in cooperation with the Organization for the achievement of the purposes set forth in Article 55.

Article 57

1. The various specialized agencies, established by intergovernmental agreement and having wide international responsibilities, as defined in their basic instruments, in economic, social, cultural, educational, health, and related fields, shall be brought into relationship with the United Nations in accordance with the provisions of Article 63.

2. Such agencies thus brought into relationship with the United Nations are hereinafter referred to as specialized agencies.

Article 58

The Organization shall make recommendations for the coordination of the policies and activities of the specialized agencies.

Article 59

The Organization shall, where appropriate, initiate negotiations among the states concerned for the creation of any new specialized agencies required for the accomplishment of the purposes set forth in Article 55.

Article 60

Responsibility for the discharge of the functions of the Organization set forth in this Chapter shall be vested in the General Assembly and, under the authority of the General Assembly, in the Economic and Social Council, which shall have for this purpose the powers set forth in Chapter X.

CHAPTER X THE ECONOMIC AND SOCIAL COUNCIL
COMPOSITION
Article 61

1. The Economic and Social Council shall consist of fifty-four Members of the United Nations elected by the General Assembly.
2. Subject to the provisions of paragraph 3, eighteen members of the Economic and Social Council shall be elected each year for a term of three years. A retiring member shall be eligible for immediate re-election.
3. At the first election after the increase in the membership of the Economic and Social Council from twenty-seven to fifty-four members, in addition to the members elected in place of the nine members whose term of office expires at the end of that year, twenty-seven additional members shall be elected. Of these twenty-seven additional members, the term of office of nine members so elected shall expire at the end of one year, and of nine other members at the end of two years, in accordance with arrangements made by the General Assembly.
4. Each member of the Economic and Social Council shall have one representative.

FUNCTIONS AND POWERS
Article 62

1. The Economic and Social Council may make or initiate studies and reports with respect to international economic, social, cultural, educational, health, and related matters and may make recommendations with respect to any such matters to the General Assembly, to the Members of the United Nations, and to the specialized agencies concerned.
2. It may make recommendations for the purpose of promoting respect for, and observance of, human rights and fundamental freedoms for all.
3. It may prepare draft conventions for submission to the General Assembly, with respect to matters falling within its competence.
4. It may call, in accordance with the rules prescribed by the United Nations, international conferences on matters falling within its competence.

Article 63

1. The Economic and Social Council may enter into agreements with any of the agencies referred to in Article 57, defining the terms on which the agency concerned shall be brought into relationship with the United Nations. Such agreements shall be subject to approval by the General Assembly.
2. It may coordinate the activities of the specialized agencies through consultation with and recommendations to such agencies and through recommendations to the General Assembly and to the Members of the United Nations.

Article 64

1. The Economic and Social Council may take appropriate steps to obtain regular reports from the specialized agencies. It may make arrangements with the Members of the United Nations and with the specialized agencies to obtain reports on the steps taken to give effect to its own recommendations and to recommendations on matters falling within its competence made by the General Assembly.
2. It may communicate its observations on these reports to the General Assembly.

Article 65

The Economic and Social Council may furnish information to the Security Council and shall assist the Security Council upon its request.

Article 66

1. The Economic and Social Council shall perform such functions as fall within its competence in connection with the carrying out of the recommendations of the General Assembly.

2. It may, with the approval of the General Assembly, perform services at the request of Members of the United Nations and at the request of specialized agencies.
3. It shall perform such other functions as are specified elsewhere in the present Charter or as may be assigned to it by the General Assembly.

Article 67

1. Each member of the Economic and Social Council shall have one vote.
2. Decisions of the Economic and Social Council shall be made by a majority of the members present and voting.

PROCEDURE

Article 68

The Economic and Social Council shall set up commissions in economic and social fields and for the promotion of human rights, and such other commissions as may be required for the performance of its functions.

Article 69

The Economic and Social Council shall invite any Member of the United Nations to participate, without vote, in its deliberations on any matter of particular concern to that Member.

Article 70

The Economic and Social Council may make arrangements for representatives of the specialized agencies to participate, without vote, in its deliberations and in those of the commissions established by it, and for its representatives to participate in the deliberations of the specialized agencies.

Article 71

The Economic and Social Council may make suitable arrangements for consultation with non-governmental organizations which are concerned with matters within its competence. Such arrangements may be made with international organizations and, where appropriate, with national organizations after consultation with the Member of the United Nations concerned.

Article 72

1. The Economic and Social Council shall adopt its own rules of procedure, including the method of selecting its President.
2. The Economic and Social Council shall meet as required in accordance with its rules, which shall include provision for the convening of meetings on the request of a majority of its members.

CHAPTER XI DECLARATION REGARDING NON-SELF-GOVERNING TERRITORIES

Article 73

Members of the United Nations which have or assume responsibilities for the administration of territories whose peoples have not yet attained a full measure of self-government recognize the principle that the interests of the inhabitants of these territories are paramount, and accept as a sacred trust the obligation to promote to the utmost, within the system of international peace and security established by the present Charter, the well-being of the inhabitants of these territories, and, to this end:

to ensure, with due respect for the culture of the peoples concerned, their political, economic, social, and educational advancement, their just treatment, and their protection against abuses;
to develop self-government, to take due account of the political aspirations of the peoples, and to assist them in the progressive development of their free political institutions, according

to the particular circumstances of each territory and its peoples and their varying stages of advancement;

to further international peace and security;

to promote constructive measures of development, to encourage research, and to cooperate with one another and, when and where appropriate, with specialized international bodies with a view to the practical achievement of the social, economic, and scientific purposes set forth in this Article; and

to transmit regularly to the Secretary-General for information purposes, subject to such limitation as security and constitutional considerations may require, statistical and other information of a technical nature relating to economic, social, and educational conditions in the territories for which they are respectively responsible other than those territories to which Chapters XII and XIII apply.

Article 74

Members of the United Nations also agree that their policy in respect of the territories to which this Chapter applies, no less than in respect of their metropolitan areas, must be based on the general principle of good-neighborliness, due account being taken of the interests and well-being of the rest of the world, in social, economic, and commercial matters.

CHAPTER XII INTERNATIONAL TRUSTEESHIP SYSTEM

Article 75

The United Nations shall establish under its authority an international trusteeship system for the administration and supervision of such territories as may be placed thereunder by subsequent individual agreements. These territories are hereinafter referred to as trust territories.

Article 76

The basic objectives of the trusteeship system, in accordance with the Purposes of the United Nations laid down in Article 1 of the present Charter, shall be:

to further international peace and security;

to promote the political, economic, social, and educational advancement of the inhabitants of the trust territories, and their progressive development towards self-government or independence as may be appropriate to the particular circumstances of each territory and its peoples and the freely expressed wishes of the peoples concerned, and as may be provided by the terms of each trusteeship agreement;

to encourage respect for human rights and for fundamental freedoms for all without distinction as to race, sex, language, or religion, and to encourage recognition of the interdependence of the peoples of the world; and

to ensure equal treatment in social, economic, and commercial matters for all Members of the United Nations and their nationals and also equal treatment for the latter in the administration of justice without prejudice to the attainment of the foregoing objectives and subject to the provisions of Article 80.

Article 77

1. The trusteeship system shall apply to such territories in the following categories as may be placed thereunder by means of trusteeship agreements:

   A. territories now held under mandate;

   B. territories which may be detached from enemy states as a result of the Second World War, and

   C. territories voluntarily placed under the system by states responsible for their administration.

2. It will be a matter for subsequent agreement as to which territories in the foregoing categories will be brought under the trusteeship system and upon what terms.

Article 78

The trusteeship system shall not apply to territories which have become Members of the United Nations, relationship among which shall be based on respect for the principle of sovereign equality.

Article 79

The terms of trusteeship for each territory to be placed under the trusteeship system, including any alteration or amendment, shall be agreed upon by the states directly concerned, including the mandatory power in the case of territories held under mandate by a Member of the United Nations, and shall be approved as provided for in Articles 83 and 85.

Article 80

1. Except as may be agreed upon in individual trusteeship agreements, made under Articles 77, 79, and 81, placing each territory under the trusteeship system, and until such agreements have been concluded, nothing in this Chapter shall be construed in or of itself to alter in any manner the rights whatsoever of any states or any peoples or the terms of existing international instruments to which Members of the United Nations may respectively be parties.
2. Paragraph 1 of this Article shall not be interpreted as giving grounds for delay or postponement of the negotiation and conclusion of agreements for placing mandated and other territories under the trusteeship system as provided for in Article 77.

Article 81

The trusteeship agreement shall in each case include the terms under which the trust territory will be administered and designate the authority which will exercise the administration of the trust territory. Such authority, hereinafter called the administering authority, may be one or more states or the Organization itself.

Article 82

There may be designated, in any trusteeship agreement, a strategic area or areas which may include part or all of the trust territory to which the agreement applies, without prejudice to any special agreement or agreements made under Article 43.

Article 83

1. All functions of the United Nations relating to strategic areas, including the approval of the terms of the trusteeship agreements and of their alteration or amendment, shall be exercised by the Security Council.
2. The basic objectives set forth in Article 76 shall be applicable to the people of each strategic area.
3. The Security Council shall, subject to the provisions of the trusteeship agreements and without prejudice to security considerations, avail itself of the assistance of the Trusteeship Council to perform those functions of the United Nations under the trusteeship system relating to political, economic, social, and educational matters in the strategic areas.

Article 84

It shall be the duty of the administering authority to ensure that the trust territory shall play its part in the maintenance of international peace and security. To this end the administering authority may make use of volunteer forces, facilities, and assistance from the trust territory in carrying out the obligations towards the Security Council undertaken in this regard by the administering authority, as well as for local defense and the maintenance of law and order within the trust territory.

Article 85

1. The functions of the United Nations with regard to trusteeship agreements for all areas not designated as strategic, including the approval of the terms of the trusteeship agreements and of their alteration or amendment, shall be exercised by the General Assembly.

2. The Trusteeship Council, operating under the authority of the General Assembly, shall assist the General Assembly in carrying out these functions.

CHAPTER XIII THE TRUSTEESHIP COUNCIL
COMPOSITION
Article 86

1. The Trusteeship Council shall consist of the following Members of the United Nations:
   A. those Members administering trust territories;
   B. such of those Members mentioned by name in Article 23 as are not administering trust territories; and
   C. as many other Members elected for three-year terms by the General Assembly as may be necessary to ensure that the total number of members of the Trusteeship Council is equally divided between those Members of the United Nations which administer trust territories and those which do not.
2. Each member of the Trusteeship Council shall designate one specially qualified person to represent it therein.

FUNCTIONS AND POWERS
Article 87

The General Assembly and, under its authority, the Trusteeship Council, in carrying out their functions, may:

consider reports submitted by the administering authority;
accept petitions and examine them in consultation with the administering authority;
provide for periodic visits to the respective trust territories at times agreed upon with the administering authority; and
take these and other actions in conformity with the terms of the trusteeship agreements.

Article 88

The Trusteeship Council shall formulate a questionnaire on the political, economic, social, and educational advancement of the inhabitants of each trust territory, and the administering authority for each trust territory within the competence of the General Assembly shall make an annual report to the General Assembly upon the basis of such questionnaire.

VOTING
Article 89

1. Each member of the Trusteeship Council shall have one vote.
2. Decisions of the Trusteeship Council shall be made by a majority of the members present and voting.

PROCEDURE
Article 90

1. The Trusteeship Council shall adopt its own rules of procedure, including the method of selecting its President.
2. The Trusteeship Council shall meet as required in accordance with its rules, which shall include provision for the convening of meetings on the request of a majority of its members.

Article 91

The Trusteeship Council shall, when appropriate, avail itself of the assistance of the Economic and Social Council and of the specialized agencies in regard to matters with which they are respectively concerned.

CHAPTER XIV THE INTERNATIONAL COURT OF JUSTICE

Article 92

The International Court of Justice shall be the principal judicial organ of the United Nations. It shall function in accordance with the annexed Statute which is based upon the Statute of the Permanent Court of International Justice and forms an integral part of the present Charter.

Article 93

1. All Members of the United Nations are ipso facto parties to the Statute of the International Court of Justice.
2. A state which is not a Member of the United Nations may become a party to the Statute of the International Court of Justice on conditions to be determined in each case by the General Assembly upon the recommendation of the Security Council.

Article 94

1. Each Member of the United Nations undertakes to comply with the decision of the International Court of Justice in any case to which it is a party.
2. If any party to a case fails to perform the obligations incumbent upon it under a judgment rendered by the Court, the other party may have recourse to the Security Council, which may, if it deems necessary, make recommendations or decide upon measures to be taken to give effect to the judgment.

Article 95

Nothing in the present Charter shall prevent Members of the United Nations from entrusting the solution of their differences to other tribunals by virtue of agreements already in existence or which may be concluded in the future.

Article 96

1. The General Assembly or the Security Council may request the International Court of Justice to give an advisory opinion on any legal question.
2. Other organs of the United Nations and specialized agencies, which may at any time be so authorized by the General Assembly, may also request advisory opinions of the Court on legal questions arising within the scope of their activities.

CHAPTER XV THE SECRETARIAT

Article 97

The Secretariat shall comprise a Secretary-General and such staff as the Organization may require. The Secretary-General shall be appointed by the General Assembly upon the recommendation of the Security Council. He shall be the chief administrative officer of the Organization.

Article 98

The Secretary-General shall act in that capacity in all meetings of the General Assembly, of the Security Council, of the Economic and Social Council, and of the Trusteeship Council, and shall perform such other functions as are entrusted to him by these organs. The Secretary-General shall make an annual report to the General Assembly on the work of the Organization.

Article 99

The Secretary-General may bring to the attention of the Security Council any matter which in his opinion may threaten the maintenance of international peace and security.

Article 100

1. In the performance of their duties the Secretary-General and the staff shall not seek or receive instructions from any government or from any other authority external to the

Organization. They shall refrain from any action which might reflect on their position as international officials responsible only to the Organization.

2. Each Member of the United Nations undertakes to respect the exclusively international character of the responsibilities of the Secretary-General and the staff and not to seek to influence them in the discharge of their responsibilities.

Article 101

1. The staff shall be appointed by the Secretary-General under regulations established by the General Assembly.
2. Appropriate staffs shall be permanently assigned to the Economic and Social Council, the Trusteeship Council, and, as required, to other organs of the United Nations. These staffs shall form a part of the Secretariat.
3. The paramount consideration in the employment of the staff and in the determination of the conditions of service shall be the necessity of securing the highest standards of efficiency, competence, and integrity. Due regard shall be paid to the importance of recruiting the staff on as wide a geographical basis as possible.

CHAPTER XVI MISCELLANEOUS PROVISIONS

Article 102

1. Every treaty and every international agreement entered into by any Member of the United Nations after the present Charter comes into force shall as soon as possible be registered with the Secretariat and published by it.
2. No party to any such treaty or international agreement which has not been registered in accordance with the provisions of paragraph I of this Article may invoke that treaty or agreement before any organ of the United Nations.

Article 103

In the event of a conflict between the obligations of the Members of the United Nations under the present Charter and their obligations under any other international agreement, their obligations under the present Charter shall prevail.

Article 104

The Organization shall enjoy in the territory of each of its Members such legal capacity as may be necessary for the exercise of its functions and the fulfillment of its purposes.

Article 105

1. The Organization shall enjoy in the territory of each of its Members such privileges and immunities as are necessary for the fulfillment of its purposes.
2. Representatives of the Members of the United Nations and officials of the Organization shall similarly enjoy such privileges and immunities as are necessary for the independent exercise of their functions in connection with the Organization.
3. The General Assembly may make recommendations with a view to determining the details of the application of paragraphs 1 and 2 of this Article or may propose conventions to the Members of the United Nations for this purpose.

CHAPTER XVII TRANSITIONAL SECURITY ARRANGEMENTS

Article 106

Pending the coming into force of such special agreements referred to in Article 43 as in the opinion of the Security Council enable it to begin the exercise of its responsibilities under Article 42, the parties to the Four-Nation Declaration, signed at Moscow October 30, 1943, and France, shall, in accordance with the provisions of paragraph 5 of that Declaration, consult with one another and as occasion requires with other Members of the United Nations with a view to such joint action on behalf of the Organization as may be necessary for the purpose of maintaining international peace and security.

Article 107

Nothing in the present Charter shall invalidate or preclude action, in relation to any state which during the Second World War has been an enemy of any signatory to the present Charter, taken or authorized as a result of that war by the Governments having responsibility for such action.

CHAPTER XVIII AMENDMENTS

Article 108

Amendments to the present Charter shall come into force for all Members of the United Nations when they have been adopted by a vote of two thirds of the members of the General Assembly and ratified in accordance with their respective constitutional processes by two thirds of the Members of the United Nations, including all the permanent members of the Security Council.

Article 109

1. A General Conference of the Members of the United Nations for the purpose of reviewing the present Charter may be held at a date and place to be fixed by a two-thirds vote of the members of the General Assembly and by a vote of any seven members of the Security Council. Each Member of the United Nations shall have one vote in the conference.
2. Any alteration of the present Charter recommended by a two-thirds vote of the conference shall take effect when ratified in accordance with their respective constitutional processes by two-thirds of the Members of the United Nations including all the permanent members of the Security Council.
3. If such a conference has not been held before the tenth annual session of the General Assembly following the coming into force of the present Charter, the proposal to call such a conference shall be placed on the agenda of that session of the General Assembly, and the conference shall be held if so decided by a majority vote of the members of the General Assembly and by a vote of any seven members of the Security Council.

CHAPTER XIX RATIFICATION AND SIGNATURE

Article 110

1. The present Charter shall be ratified by the signatory states in accordance with their respective constitutional processes.
2. The ratifications shall be deposited with the Government of the United States of America, which shall notify all the signatory states of each deposit as well as the Secretary-General of the Organization when he has been appointed.
3. The present Charter shall come into force upon the deposit of ratifications by the Republic of China, France, the Union of Soviet Socialist Republics, the United Kingdom of Great Britain and Northern Ireland, and the United States of America, and by a majority of the other signatory states. A protocol of the ratifications deposited shall thereupon be drawn up by the Government of the United States of America which shall communicate copies thereof to all the signatory states.
4. The states signatory to the present Charter which ratify it after it has come into force will become original Members of the United Nations on the date of the deposit of their respective ratifications.

Article 111

The present Charter, of which the Chinese, French, Russian, English, and Spanish texts are equally authentic, shall remain deposited in the archives of the Government of the United States of America. Duly certified copies thereof shall be transmitted by that Government to the Governments of the other signatory states.

IN FAITH WHEREOF the representatives of the Governments of the United Nations have signed the present Charter.

DONE at the city of San Francisco the twenty-sixth day of June, one thousand nine hundred and forty-five.

Appendix D: United Nations Universal Declaration of Human Rights

Adopted and proclaimed by General Assembly Resolution 217 A (III) of 10 December 1948

On December 10, 1948, the General Assembly of the United Nations adopted and proclaimed the Universal Declaration of Human Rights the full text of which appears in the following pages. Following this historic act the Assembly called upon all Member countries to publicize the text of the Declaration and "to cause it to be disseminated, displayed, read and expounded principally in schools and other educational institutions, without distinction based on the political status of countries or territories."

Preamble

Whereas recognition of the inherent dignity and of the equal and inalienable rights of all members of the human family is the foundation of freedom, justice and peace in the world,

Whereas disregard and contempt for human rights have resulted in barbarous acts which have outraged the conscience of mankind, and the advent of a world in which human beings shall enjoy freedom of speech and belief and freedom from fear and want has been proclaimed as the highest aspiration of the common people,

Whereas it is essential, if man is not to be compelled to have recourse, as a last resort, to rebellion against tyranny and oppression, that human rights should be protected by the rule of law,

Whereas it is essential to promote the development of friendly relations between nations,

Whereas the peoples of the United Nations have in the Charter reaffirmed their faith in fundamental human rights, in the dignity and worth of the human person and in the equal rights of men and women and have determined to promote social progress and better standards of life in larger freedom,

Whereas Member States have pledged themselves to achieve, in co-operation with the United Nations, the promotion of universal respect for and observance of human rights and fundamental freedoms,

Whereas a common understanding of these rights and freedoms is of the greatest importance for the full realization of this pledge,

Now, Therefore THE GENERAL ASSEMBLY proclaims THIS UNIVERSAL DECLARATION OF HUMAN RIGHTS as a common standard of achievement for all peoples and all nations, to the end that every individual and every organ of society, keeping this Declaration constantly in mind, shall strive by teaching and education to promote respect for these rights and freedoms and by progressive measures, national and international, to secure their universal and effective recognition and observance, both among the peoples of Member States themselves and among the peoples of territories under their jurisdiction.

Article 1

All human beings are born free and equal in dignity and rights. They are endowed with reason and conscience and should act towards one another in a spirit of brotherhood.

Article 2

Everyone is entitled to all the rights and freedoms set forth in this Declaration, without distinction of any kind, such as race, colour, sex, language, religion, political or other opinion, national or social origin, property, birth or other status. Furthermore, no distinction shall be made on the basis of the political, jurisdictional or international status of the country or territory to which a person belongs, whether it be independent, trust, non-self-governing or under any other limitation of sovereignty.

Article 3

Everyone has the right to life, liberty and security of person.

Article 4

No one shall be held in slavery or servitude; slavery and the slave trade shall be prohibited in all their forms.

Article 5

No one shall be subjected to torture or to cruel, inhuman or degrading treatment or punishment.

Article 6

Everyone has the right to recognition everywhere as a person before the law.

Article 7

All are equal before the law and are entitled without any discrimination to equal protection of the law. All are entitled to equal protection against any discrimination in violation of this Declaration and against any incitement to such discrimination.

Article 8

Everyone has the right to an effective remedy by the competent national tribunals for acts violating the fundamental rights granted him by the constitution or by law.

Article 9

No one shall be subjected to arbitrary arrest, detention or exile.

Article 10

Everyone is entitled in full equality to a fair and public hearing by an independent and impartial tribunal, in the determination of his rights and obligations and of any criminal charge against him.

Article 11

1. Everyone charged with a penal offence has the right to be presumed innocent until proved guilty according to law in a public trial at which he has had all the guarantees necessary for his defence.
2. No one shall be held guilty of any penal offence on account of any act or omission which did not constitute a penal offence, under national or international law, at the time when it was committed. Nor shall a heavier penalty be imposed than the one that was applicable at the time the penal offence was committed.

Article 12

No one shall be subjected to arbitrary interference with his privacy, family, home or correspondence, nor to attacks upon his honour and reputation. Everyone has the right to the protection of the law against such interference or attacks.

Article 13

1. Everyone has the right to freedom of movement and residence within the borders of each state.
2. Everyone has the right to leave any country, including his own, and to return to his country.

Article 14

1. Everyone has the right to seek and to enjoy in other countries asylum from persecution.
2. This right may not be invoked in the case of prosecutions genuinely arising from non-political crimes or from acts contrary to the purposes and principles of the United Nations.

Article 15

1. Everyone has the right to a nationality.
2. No one shall be arbitrarily deprived of his nationality nor denied the right to change his nationality.

Article 16

1. Men and women of full age, without any limitation due to race, nationality or religion, have the right to marry and to found a family. They are entitled to equal rights as to marriage, during marriage and at its dissolution.
2. Marriage shall be entered into only with the free and full consent of the intending spouses.
3. The family is the natural and fundamental group unit of society and is entitled to protection by society and the State.

Article 17

1. Everyone has the right to own property alone as well as in association with others.
2. No one shall be arbitrarily deprived of his property.

Article 18

Everyone has the right to freedom of thought, conscience and religion; this right includes freedom to change his religion or belief, and freedom, either alone or in community with others and in public or private, to manifest his religion or belief in teaching, practice, worship and observance.

Article 19

Everyone has the right to freedom of opinion and expression; this right includes freedom to hold opinions without interference and to seek, receive and impart information and ideas through any media and regardless of frontiers.

Article 20

1. Everyone has the right to freedom of peaceful assembly and association.
2. No one may be compelled to belong to an association.

Article 21

1. Everyone has the right to take part in the government of his country, directly or through freely chosen representatives.
2. Everyone has the right of equal access to public service in his country.
3. The will of the people shall be the basis of the authority of government; this will shall be expressed in periodic and genuine elections which shall be by universal and equal suffrage and shall be held by secret vote or by equivalent free voting procedures.

Article 22

Everyone, as a member of society, has the right to social security and is entitled to realization, through national effort and international co-operation and in accordance with the organization and resources of each State, of the economic, social and cultural rights indispensable for his dignity and the free development of his personality.

Article 23

1. Everyone has the right to work, to free choice of employment, to just and favourable conditions of work and to protection against unemployment.

2. Everyone, without any discrimination, has the right to equal pay for equal work.
3. Everyone who works has the right to just and favourable remuneration ensuring for himself and his family an existence worthy of human dignity, and supplemented, if necessary, by other means of social protection.
4. Everyone has the right to form and to join trade unions for the protection of his interests.

Article 24
Everyone has the right to rest and leisure, including reasonable limitation of working hours and periodic holidays with pay.

Article 25
1. Everyone has the right to a standard of living adequate for the health and well-being of himself and of his family, including food, clothing, housing and medical care and necessary social services, and the right to security in the event of unemployment, sickness, disability, widowhood, old age or other lack of livelihood in circumstances beyond his control.
2. Motherhood and childhood are entitled to special care and assistance. All children, whether born in or out of wedlock, shall enjoy the same social protection.

Article 26
1. Everyone has the right to education. Education shall be free, at least in the elementary and fundamental stages. Elementary education shall be compulsory. Technical and professional education shall be made generally available and higher education shall be equally accessible to all on the basis of merit.
2. Education shall be directed to the full development of the human personality and to the strengthening of respect for human rights and fundamental freedoms. It shall promote understanding, tolerance and friendship among all nations, racial or religious groups, and shall further the activities of the United Nations for the maintenance of peace.
3. Parents have a prior right to choose the kind of education that shall be given to their children.

Article 27
1. Everyone has the right freely to participate in the cultural life of the community, to enjoy the arts and to share in scientific advancement and its benefits.
2. Everyone has the right to the protection of the moral and material interests resulting from any scientific, literary or artistic production of which he is the author.

Article 28
Everyone is entitled to a social and international order in which the rights and freedoms set forth in this Declaration can be fully realized.

Article 29
1. Everyone has duties to the community in which alone the free and full development of his personality is possible.
2. In the exercise of his rights and freedoms, everyone shall be subject only to such limitations as are determined by law solely for the purpose of securing due recognition and respect for the rights and freedoms of others and of meeting the just requirements of morality, public order and the general welfare in a democratic society.
3. These rights and freedoms may in no case be exercised contrary to the purposes and principles of the United Nations.

Article 30
Nothing in this Declaration may be interpreted as implying for any State, group or person any right to engage in any activity or to perform any act aimed at the destruction of any of the rights and freedoms set forth herein.

About the Book and Authors

Heated debates on Iraq in the Security Council. The September 2005 World Summit accompanied by the Oil-for-Food scandal. Resolutions on terrorism. Ongoing peacekeeping in the Congo and the Balkans. Gulf War coalition-building. Humanitarian intervention in Somalia, Kosovo, and East Timor. War-crimes tribunals in the former Yugoslavia and Rwanda. International Criminal Court. A Nobel Peace Prize for the Secretary-General and the world organization. Development debates in Beijing, Cairo, and beyond. Environmental regime-building in and after Rio. New attention to women in development. After decades of neglect—and at times ridicule—the United Nations is back, reflecting a multilateral approach to major issues in international relations, despite much talk about U.S. hegemony and a long-lasting unilateral "moment."

In this thematic and synthetic text, the authors bring to life the alphabet soup of the United Nations, moving from its historical foundations to its day-to-day expanding role in an as-yet-unconsolidated new world order. Students at all levels will learn what the UN is, how it operates, and what its relationships are with the universe of external actors and institutions, from sovereign states to the plethora of nongovernmental and intergovernmental organizations now playing important roles in world politics.

The authors, all of whom have practical as well as academic experience with the UN, show how it has exerted operational and normative influence on issues in three key areas—security, human rights, and sustainable development—even as they make recommendations for improved UN performance in the future.

Well documented and well illustrated, this substantially revised and updated edition includes the UN Charter and organizational schema, extensive suggested readings through expanded reference notes, and photos of UN activities. *The United Nations and Changing World Politics* is essential to a comprehensive and contemporary understanding of the world's leading intergovernmental organization—one that, in the words of Dag Hammarskjöld, may not get us to heaven but could save us from hell.

THOMAS G. WEISS is Presidential Professor and Director of the Ralph Bunche Institute for International Studies at The Graduate Center of The City University of New York, where he is co-director of the UN Intellectual History Project. Previously, he was research professor and director of the Global Security Program at Brown University's Watson Institute for International Studies. He has also held a number of UN posts (at UNCTAD, the UN Commission for Namibia, UNITAR, and ILO) and served as research director of the International Commission on Intervention and State Sovereignty, editor of the journal *Global Governance,* and executive director of both the International Peace Academy and the Academic Council on the United Nations System. He has written or edited some thirty-five books about international organization related to North-South relations, peacekeeping, economic and social development, and humanitarian action.

DAVID P. FORSYTHE is University Professor and Charles J. Mach Distinguished Professor of Political Science at the University of Nebraska–Lincoln. His research interests include international law, organization, and human rights. His research in those areas led to the 2003 Quincy Wright Distinguished Scholar Award given by the Midwest Section of the International Studies Association. He is the author or editor of numerous publications including recently *The Humanitarians*; *Human Rights and Diversity* (with Patrice C. McMahon); *Human Rights in International Relations; Human Rights and Comparative Foreign Policy*; and *The US and Human Rights*. Among other consultancies, he has worked for the International Red Cross and Red Crescent movement and the Office of the United Nations High Commissioner for Refugees.

ROGER A. COATE is a professor of international organization at the University of South Carolina and has taught at Arizona State University. He has worked in the UN Centre for Human Rights, as a consultant to the U.S. National Commission for UNESCO and the Bureau of International Organization Affairs of the U.S. Department of State, as a member of the HABITAT II Secretary-General's Advisory Panel on Housing Rights, and as head of the International Organization Section of the International Studies Association. His most recent books include *United Nations Politics: International Organization in a Divided World* (with Donald Puchala and Katie Laatikainen), *International Cooperation in Response to AIDS* (with Leon Gordenker, Christer Jönsson, and Peter Söderholm), and *United States Policy and the Future of the United Nations*. He was founding coeditor of the journal *Global Governance: A Review of Multilateralism and International Organizations*. He currently directs a large transnational collaborative research and professional development program in partnership with the Executive Office of the UN Secretary-General and the United National University.

KELLY-KATE PEASE is professor of international relations at Webster University and has been a visiting professor at Samara State University School of Law in Samara, Russia. She has taught at Webster University's campuses in London, England; Leiden, the Netherlands; and Cha-Am, Thailand. She was also the director of international relations for Webster University world-wide. She is author of *International Organizations: Perspectives on Governance in the Twenty-First Century* as well as articles and book chapters centering on human rights, humanitarian intervention, economic rights, and moral hazard.

Index

Affirmative action, international,
  259–265
Afghanistan, 48, 120, 128, 129, 140–141
  and Al Qaeda, 273
  and Soviet Union, 50
  See also Taliban
African Union (AU), 21, 23
  and Darfur, Sudan, 100–101, 102, 103
  and human rights, 186
African Union Mission in Sudan (AMIS), 101,
  102
Ahtisaari, Marti, 92
Aideed, Mohammed Farah, 68, 69, 242
Akashi, Yasushi, 62
Al Qaeda, 113, 118, 128, 273
  and Saddam Hussein, 111, 115, 116
  and Taliban, 3, 50, 117, 128, 370
Al-Bashir, Omar Hassan, 101, 103, 189, 234
Allende, Salvador, 160, 233
Alvarez, José, lx, 195, 376–377
Amin, Idi, 233–234
AMIS. *See* African Union Mission in Sudan
Amnesty International, 151, 236
Angola, 48, 51, 61
Annan, Kofi, 11, 85, 86, 90, 94, 120, 123, 389
  and Bosnia, 91
  and change, 364–365
  and counterterrorism, 112, 133
  and Darfur, Sudan, 101
  and development, 268
  and finance, 126
  and globalization, 323
  and human rights, 171, 191, 193–194, 196,
  201
  and Millennium Development Goals, 353
  and nonproliferation, 133–134
  and Peacebuilding Fund, 127

  and responsibility to protect, 125
  and Rwanda, 71–72, 184–185
  and state sovereignty, 16–17
  and sustainable development, 282–283,
  286, 300, 301, 313
  and terrorism, 111, 112, 114
  and UN reform, 137
Antislavery movement, 155
Arab League, 22
Arbenz Guzmán, Jacobo, 160
Arbour, Louise, 196–197, 201
Aristide, Jean-Bertrand, 54, 72, 73–74
ASEAN. *See* Association of Southeast Asian
  Nations
Association of Southeast Asian Nations
  (ASEAN), 21, 22
Atlantic Charter, 158
AU. *See* African Union
Autonomy, 84–85
Ayala-Lasso, José, 194–195

Balkans, 180–181, 183, 195
Ban Ki-moon, 11–12, 126, 128, 197
  and counterterrorism, 114–115, 133
  and Darfur, Sudan, 102
  and human rights, 191, 194, 202–203
  and leadership, 120–121
  and personnel, safety of, 121
  and responsibility to protect, 104, 106
  and terrorism, 114–115
  and women, in development, 336
Bin Laden, Osama, 273
Biological Toxins and Weapons Convention,
  116
Blair, Tony, 117, 357
Bodin, Jean, lii
Bolton, John, 197, 201–202, 272–273, 282

Bosnia, 61, 64–65, 66–67, 93
    and human rights, 180, 188
Boutros-Ghali, Boutros, 11, 58, 64, 120, 194,
    196
    and development, 267, 272, 282–283
    and economic sanctions, 74
    and finance, 126
    and human rights, 184, 192
    and internally displaced persons, 208–209
    and peacekeeping, 35
    and state sovereignty, 16
    and sustainable development, 280, 282,
        307, 309
Brahimi, Lakhdar, 75, 85
Breach of peace, 13–14
Bretton Woods institutions, 256, 258
Briquemont, Francis, 66
Brundtland, Gro Harlem, 267, 341
Burns, Nicholas, 273
Burundi, 97, 185
Bush, George H. W., xlviii, 47, 52, 68, 267
Bush, George W., xlix, l, 74–75, 115, 117, 118,
    120, 195, 196, 364
    and development, 273
    and global governance, 357
    and International Criminal Court, 190, 241
    and public health, 339–340
    and sustainable development, 269–270
    and torture, 149–150
    and unilateralism, 366
    and war on terror, 115, 141
Bush doctrine, 117–118, 119

Cambodia, 61, 62, 179, 184
Capitalism, 254–259
Carlsson, Ingmar, 86
Carter, Jimmy, 53
Castells, Manuel, 325
Castro, Fidel, lvii
Castro, Raúl, lvii
CAT. See Committee Against Torture
CEDAW. See Committee on the Elimination
    of Discrimination Against Women
Cédras, Raoul, 71
Central African Republic, 189
Central America, 21–22, 52–54
Central Intelligence Agency (CIA), 116, 149
Centre for Human Rights, 195
CERD. See Committee on the Elimination of
    Racial Discrimination

Cerny, Philip, 387
Change, 364–366
Chemical Weapons Convention, 116
Chile, 187, 198, 233
China, 90, 92, 93, 104
    and human rights, 186, 196, 198, 201
Chirac, Jacques, 357
Chopra, Jarat, xlix
CHR. See Commission on Human Rights
Churchill, Winston, 159
CIA. See Central Intelligence Agency
CIS. See Commonwealth of Independent
    States
Civil rights, 162, 200
Civil war, 124, 161
Clark, Helen, 285
Climate change, 342–344
Clinton, Bill, 267
Clinton administration, 69, 118, 185
Cohen, Roberta, 125
Cold War, 47, 160
    peacekeeping during, 34–35, 35–37, 37
        (table)
Collective rights, 163
Collective security, 3–7
    and General Assembly, 9–10
    and regional organizations, 18–24
    and Secretary-General, 10–12
    and Security Council, 7–9
    and UN Charter, 12–18
Commission on Global Governance, 104
Commission on Human Rights (CHR), 187,
    197–201, 203, 206
Commission on Sustainable Development
    (CSD), 271, 289–290
Commitment, and collective security, 7
Committee Against Torture (CAT), 206
Committee of Governmental Experts, 205–206
Committee of Individual Experts, 206
Committee on Economic, Social and Cultural
    Rights, 205–206
Committee on the Elimination of
    Discrimination Against Women
    (CEDAW), 206
Committee on the Elimination of Racial
    Discrimination (CERD), 206, 207
Committee on the Rights of the Child (CRC),
    206
Commonwealth of Independent States (CIS),
    23

Communication. *See* Information and communication technologies
Comprehensive Peace Agreement in Sudan, 101–102
Comprehensive Test Ban Treaty, 116
Conference on International Economic Co-operation, 261–262
Conference on Security and Co-operation in Europe (CSCE), 23, 152
Conflict management, 18–24
Congo, 33–34, 86, 185, 186, 189, 195
Consensual-knowledge, 354–355
Consensus, 7, 240–241, 243
Consent, 38, 84, 124
Convention of Enforced Disappearances, 203
Convention on the Prevention and Punishment of the Crime of Genocide, 164
Cordovez, Diego, 50
Cortright, David, 56
Council of Europe, 170, 366
Council of Freely Elected Heads of Government, 53
Counterterrorism, 112, 133. *See also* Terrorism
Counter-Terrorism Committee (CTC), 113
Counter-Terrorism Task Force, 114
Covenant of the League of Nations, 18, 155, 156
CRC. *See* Committee on the Rights of the Child
Croatia, 61, 64, 65, 66
CSCE. *See* Conference on Security and Co-operation in Europe
CSD. *See* Commission on Sustainable Development
CTC. *See* Counter-Terrorism Committee
Cuba, 198, 201
Cyprus, 38

Dallaire, Roméo, 72, 185
Darfur, Sudan, 100–103, 185–186, 189, 191, 195. *See also* Sudan
Dayton Peace Accord, 67
Debt relief, 348
Declaration and Programme of Action on the Establishment of a New International Order, 261
Declaration on the Rights of Indigenous Peoples, 203
Democracy, 160–161, 243–245

Democratic Republic of the Congo (MONUC), 86. *See also* Congo
Democratization, 389–390
Deng, Francis M., 125, 209
Department of Humanitarian Affairs, 214
Department of Peacekeeping Operations (DPKO), 137
Dependency theory, 261
Dershowitz, Alan, 149
Derviç, Kemal, 285, 386
Development, 253–254, 279–280
  and capitalism, 254–259
  and human rights, 211–214
  and international affirmative action, 259–265
  milestones, 1943–1980, 255 (table)
  milestones, 1948–1982, 263 (table)
  and neoliberalism, 266–267
  women in, 268, 333–336
  See also Eco-development; Millennium Development Goals; Sustainable development; Sustainable human development
Disarmament, 115–116. *See also* Nonproliferation
Dispute resolution, 14
Dobbins, James, 141
Domestic jurisdiction, 15–17, 171–172
DPKO. *See* Department of Peacekeeping Operations
Drugs, 350–351. *See also* Public health
Dunant Henry, 154

East Timor, 21, 94–95, 179, 185
EC. *See* European Community
ECA. *See* Economic Commission for Africa
ECAFE. *See* Economic Commission for Asia and the Far East
ECE. *See* Economic Commission for Europe
ECHA. *See* Executive Committee for Humanitarian Affairs
ECLA. *See* Economic Commission for Latin America
ECLAC. *See* Economic Commission for Latin America and the Caribbean
Eco-development, 280, 293–296, 354. *See also* Development
ECOMOG. *See* Military Observer Group of the Economic Community of West African States

Economic and Social Affairs Executive Committee (EC-ESA), 283
Economic and Social Commission for Asia and the Pacific (ESCAP), 257
Economic and Social Commission for Western Asia (ESCWA), 257
Economic and Social Council (ECOSOC), 127, 205–206, 256, 257, 258, 259
and sustainable development, 281–282
Economic Commission for Africa (ECA), 267
Economic Commission for Asia and the Far East (ECAFE), 257
Economic Commission for Europe (ECE), 257
Economic Commission for Latin America and the Caribbean (ECLAC), 257
Economic Commission for Latin America (ECLA), 257, 260
Economic Community of West African States (ECOWAS), 23
Economic sanctions, 14, 42–44, 74, 179
and collective security, 5
and Gulf War (1991), 59
and human rights, 58–61
and military force, 60–61
and terrorism, 113
See also Peacekeeping
ECOSOC. See Economic and Social Council
ECOWAS. See Economic Community of West African States
Education, 331–333
Egeland, Jan, 216
Eisenhower, Dwight D., 33
El Salvador, 52, 54, 184, 187
Eliasson, Jan, 192, 202
Emergency assistance, 214–220
Emergency relief coordinator (ERC), 214, 216
Enforcement, 54–55, 57–58, 140
and Gulf War (1991), 55–58
and human rights, 59–60
See also Peacekeeping
Environment, 355, 342–344
EPTA. See UN Expanded Programme of Technical Assistance
ERC. See Emergency relief coordinator
ESA. See Economic and Social Affairs Executive Committee
ESCAP. See Economic and Social Commission for Asia and the Pacific
ESCWA. See Economic and Social Commission for Western Asia
Esquipulas II agreements, 52–53

EU. See European Union
European Commission on Human Rights, 170
European Community (EC), 21–22, 257
European Convention on Human Rights and Fundamental Freedoms, 170
European Court of Human Rights, 170
European Union (EU), 21–22, 23, 92–93, 185, 366
Evans, Gareth, lvi
Executive Committee for Humanitarian Affairs (ECHA), 216

FAO. See Food and Agriculture Organization
Farabundo Martí National Liberation Front. See FMLN
Finance, 122–123, 126, 345–347, 347–348
Finkelstein, Larry, 386
FMLN (Farabundo Martí National Liberation Front), 54
Food and Agriculture Organization (FAO), 214, 258
Fowler, Robert, 86
France, 70, 118
Frankel, Max, 139
Functionalism, 258–259, 354
Fund for Victims of Torture, 187

GATT. See General Agreement on Tariffs and Trade
GCC. See Gulf Cooperation Council
GEF. See Global Environment Facility
General Agreement on Tariffs and Trade (GATT), 261, 264, 270
General Assembly, 9–10
and human rights, 186–188
and sustainable development, 280–281
and terrorism, 114
Geneva Conventions, 113, 154, 167, 171, 184
Genocide, 185–186
in Darfur, Sudan, 101
in Rwanda, 70–72, 184–185
Germany, 118
Ghandi, Indira, 302–303
Global Compact, 171, 193–194, 313, 389
Global Environment Facility (GEF), 271
Global governance, 325–326, 357, 363, 386–388. See also Governance
Global warming, 342–344
Globalization, 270, 323–324, 387
concepts of, 324–326
definition of, 324

Globalization *(continued)*
  and human rights, 171
  and sustainable development, 344–353
Goldsmith, Jack, liv
Good governance, 212, 239, 388
  and sustainable development, 309, 311–314
  See also Governance
Gorbachev, Mikhail, xlviii, 47, 50, 52
Gore, Al, 343
Goulding, Marrack, 35
Governance, 386–387. *See also* Global
    governance; Good governance
Great Britain, 116, 199
Greece, 197
Gulf Cooperation Council (GCC), 22
Gulf War (1991), 23, 55–58, 123
  and economic sanctions, 59–60
Guterres, Antonio, 211

Haas, Ernst, 368
Haas, Peter, 368
Haass, Richard, liv, 371
Haddad, Saad, 40
Haiti, 54, 59, 61, 182–183, 197
Hammarskjöld, Dag, xlvii, 11, 32, 33–34, 35,
    191, 391
Hampson, Fen, 86
Haq, Mahbub ul, 271
Hariri, Rafik, 100
Harun, Ahmad, 102
Hayek, Frederick von, 266
Health. *See* Public health
Held, David, 325
Helms, Jesse, 205, 282
Helsinki Accord (1975), 158
Herzegovina, 61, 64–65
Hezbollah, 97–100
High-level Panel on Threats, Challenges and
    Change (HLP), 17, 112, 123, 125, 130,
    200–201
Hitler, Adolf, 4, 367
HLP. *See* High-level Panel on Threats,
    Challenges and Change
Hocké, Jean-Pierre, 211
Holbrooke, Richard, 67, 86
Holocaust, 158
Holsti, Kal, 364
Hoogvelt, Ankie, 325
Human rights, 152–153, 166–172, 246–247,
    354, 389–390
  bodies, 204–211 *(see also individual bodies)*
  and change, 239–246, 365–366
  and consensus, 240–241, 243
  and democracy, 243–245
  and development, 211–214
  and economic sanctions, 59–61
  and emergency assistance, 214–220
  and enforcement, 59–60
  and General Assembly, 186–188
  improvement in promotion of,
      227–229
  instruments, 167
  and International Criminal Court,
      188–191, 241–243
  and Iraq, 58
  and just-war doctrine, 82–83
  and knowledge, 239–240, 241–243
  and learning, 239–240, 241–243, 373–375
  and military intervention, 81, 82–84
  and nonstate actors, 235–239
  organizational structure, 178 (figure)
  origins of, 153–157
  and peace, 160
  and *raisons d'état*, 229–232
  and responsibility to protect, 82
  rules, 378–379, 383–384
  and Secretary-General, 191–194
  and Security Council, 178–186
  and state coalitions, 233–235
  and state sovereignty, 105–106, 232
  and torture, 149–150
  and UN Charter, 158–161
  See also Commission on Human Rights;
      Human Rights Council; UN High
      Commissioner for Human Rights;
      Universal Declaration of Human Rights
Human Rights Committee, 204–205
Human Rights Conventions, 168–169 (table)
Human Rights Council (HRC), 187, 201–204,
    206
Human rights courts, 166–167
Human rights law, 151
Human rights standards, 171, 177–178
Human rights treaties, 167
Human Rights Watch, 151
Human security, 272, 314–317, 389–390. *See
    also* Security
Humanitarian affairs, 151–152
Hunger, 330–331

IAEA. *See* International Atomic Energy
    Agency
IASC. *See* Inter-Agency Standing Committee
ICC. *See* International Criminal Court

ICISS. *See* International Commission on Intervention and State Sovereignty

ICJ. *See* International Court of Justice

ICRC. *See* International Committee of the Red Cross

ICTs. *See* Information and communication technologies

IDA. *See* International Development Association

IDPs. *See* Internally displaced persons

IFOR. *See* Implementation Force

Ignatieff, Michael, 149

IHL. *See* International humanitarian law

Ikenberry, John, 1

ILO. *See* International Labour Organization

IMF. *See* International Monetary Fund

Implementation Force (IFOR), 181

In Larger Freedom: Towards Development, Security and Human Rights for All, 123, 125

Independent Commission on Kosovo, 90

India, 38, 135, 198, 199

Indonesia, 94

Indonesian People's Consultative Assembly, 94

Information and communication technologies (ICTs), 351–353

Inter-Agency Standing Committee (IASC), 216

INTERFET. *See* International Force in East Timor

Internally displaced persons (IDPs), 207–209

International affirmative action, 259–265

International Atomic Energy Agency (IAEA), 116, 118

International Bill of Rights, 165–166, 167, 214, 233

International Campaign to Ban Land Mines, 138

International Commission on Intervention and State Sovereignty (ICISS), 81, 82–83, 188

International Committee of the Red Cross (ICRC), 59, 65, 83, 154, 167, 169–170, 216–218, 236, 237

financial contributors to, 217 (table)

International Committee on Intervention and State Sovereignty (ICISS), 125

International Court of Justice (ICJ), 93, 135–136

International Covenant on Civil and Political Rights, 163

International Covenant on Economic, Social and Cultural Rights, 163, 203

International Criminal Court (ICC), 101, 164, 241–243, 375

and human rights, 188–191

International Development Association (IDA), 257

International Federation of Red Cross Society, 154, 215

International Force in East Timor (INTERFET), 21

International Human Rights Day, 161

International human rights standards, 171, 177–178

International humanitarian law (IHL), 113, 150–152, 167, 169, 219

International jurisdiction, 15

International Labour Organization (ILO), 155, 167, 171, 194, 258, 270

International Law Commission, 188

International Monetary Fund (IMF), 10–11, 256, 264, 266, 268, 270

and sustainable development, 296–297, 298–299, 300–302

International Security Assistance Force (ISAF), 128, 141

International Telecommunications Union (ITU), 258

Interstate conflict, 123

Intrastate conflict, 123–126

Iran, 48, 50–51, 100, 135

Iraq, 48, 50–51, 116–120, 129, 195

and Gulf War (1991), 23, 55–58, 59–60, 123

and human rights, 58–59, 180, 181, 183

and International Criminal Court, 190

and Iraq war (2003), 119, 123, 140, 141

and Kuwait, 55, 180

and terrorism, 115

and weapons of mass destruction, 116

ISAF. *See* International Security Assistance Force

Israel, 169–170, 187

and Hezbollah, 97–98, 99–100

and human rights, 196, 197, 198

ITU. *See* International Telecommunications Union

Jackson, Sir Robert, 262

Japan, 62

Johnson-Sirleaf, Ellen, 242

Jolly, Richard, 271

Justice Equality Movement, 100

Just-war doctrine, 82–83

Kälin, Walter, 209
Kant, Immanuel, 239, 243
Kaplan, Robert, 83
Karzai, Hamid, 128, 141
Kellogg-Briand Pact, 4
Keynes, John Maynard, 254, 388
Keynesian theory, 254–255, 258–259
Khalilzad, Zalmay, 120
Kirsh, Philippe, 189
Klein, Naomi, 298–299
Knowledge, 239–240, 241–243, 354–355
Korea, 30–32
Kosovo, 90–93, 119, 129, 139, 140
    and human rights, 81, 185, 186
Kuwait, 55, 180
Kyoto Protocol, 342–343

Labor rights, 155
Landlocked developing countries (LLDCs),
    348–349
Latin America, 199
Leadership, 120–121
League of Nations, 4, 155, 157
League of Nations Refugee Office, 156
Learning, 239–240, 241–243, 354, 355–356,
    367–369, 373–376
Lebanon, 38, 39, 40, 97–100
Legal rights, 153
Lemkin, Raphael, 238
Liberal democracies, 160–161, 243–244
Libya, 198–199, 201
Lichenstein, Charles, xlvii
Lie, Trygve, 11, 12, 31
LLDCs. See Landlocked developing countries
Lomé Peace Agreement, 96
Lopez, George, 56
Lubbers, Ruud, 211, 336
Luck, Edward, liv, 106, 129
Lumumba, Patrice, 160–161

Magen David Adom (MDA), 169–170
Mahbubani, Kishore, 389
Malloch Brown, Mark, 285, 286
Mandelbaum, Michael, 85
Martens, Kerstin, lix
Marx, Karl, 154
MCA. See Millennium Challenge Account
McNamara, Robert, 264–265
McNeill, William, 363
MDA. See Magen David Adom
MDGs. See Millennium Development Goals

Mehta, Hansa, 158
Military force, 39–40, 60–61, 132–133
Military intervention, 81, 82–84, 84–87
Military Observer Group of the Economic
    Community of West African States
    (ECOMOG), 138
Military Staff Committee (MSC), 17
Millennium Challenge Account (MCA), 269
Millennium Challenge Corporation, 269
Millennium Declaration, 268, 272, 323, 353
Millennium Development Goals (MDGs),
    272–273, 344–353, 353–357
    implementation of, 329–344
    strategy, 326–329, 327–328 (table)
    See also Sustainable development
Milošević, Slobodan, 91, 242, 244
Minority rights, 156
MINUSTAH. See UN Stabilization Mission in
    Haiti
Mitrany, David, 258
Modelski, George, 239
Monterrey consensus, 268–269, 347
MONUC. See Democratic Republic of the
    Congo
Moravcsik, Andrew, 23
A More Secure World: Our Shared
    Responsibility (HLP), 123, 125
Moreno Ocampo, Luis, 189
Mossadeq, Mohammed, 160
MSC. See Military Staff Committee
Mubarak, Hosni, 113
Mugabe, Robert, 23, 188, 234
Multilateral governance. See Global
    governance
Multilateralism, 364, 366
Murdoch, Rupert, 353

Namibia, 48, 51–52, 179, 184
Nasser, Gamel Abdel, 32
National interest, lvi, 369–370. See also
    Raisons d'état
National state capitalism, 254–259
Neoliberalism, 266–267
Neutrality, 85–86
New International Economic Order (NIEO),
    262, 266
New wars, 15
NGOs. See Nongovernmental organizations
Nicaragua, 52, 53–54, 184
NIEO. See New International Economic Order
Nigeria, 186

Nobel, Alfred, 35
Nongovernmental organizations (NGOs),
　137–138, 139, 235–237, 237–238
　and human rights, 151, 199–200
Nonproliferation, 115–116, 133–134
Nonstate actors (NSAs), 122, 235–239
Normand, Roger, 150
NPT. *See* Nuclear Non-Proliferation Treaty
NSAs. *See* Nonstate actors
Nuclear Non-Proliferation Treaty (NPT), 115.
　See also Nonproliferation
Nujoma, Sam, 52
Nye, Joseph, xlix, 129

OAS. *See* Organization of American States
OAU. *See* Organization of African Unity
Obama, Barack, 20, 115, 120, 141, 371
　and multilateralism, 364, 366
OCHA. *See* Office for the Coordination of
　Humanitarian Affairs
ODC. *See* Overseas Development Council
OEF. *See* Operation Enduring Freedom
Office for the Coordination of Humanitarian
　Affairs (OCHA), 137, 214, 216
Office of the High Commissioner of Human
　Rights (OHCHR), 194, 195
Ogata, Sadako, 65, 211, 272
OHCHR. *See* Office of the High
　Commissioner of Human Rights
Oil-for-Food Programme, 118, 136–137
ONUC. *See* UN Operation in the Congo
ONUCA. *See* UN Observer Group in Central
　America
ONUSAL. *See* UN Observer Mission in El
　Salvador
ONUVEH. *See* UN Observer Mission to
　Verify the Electoral Process in Haiti
ONUVEN. *See* UN Observer Mission to
　Verify the Electoral Process in
　Nicaragua
OPEC. *See* Organization of Petroleum
　Exporting Countries
Operation Enduring Freedom (OEF), 128,
　141
Operation Restore Hope, 68, 69–70
Operation Support Hope, 70
Opération Turquoise, 70–71
Operation Uphold Democracy, 72
Organization, and collective security, 7
Organization for the Prohibition of Chemical
　Weapons, 116

Organization of African Unity (OAU), 21, 22
Organization of American States (OAS),
　21–22, 53
Organization of Petroleum Exporting
　Countries (OPEC), 262
Organization on Security and Co-operation
　in Europe (OSCE), 23
Ortega, Daniel, 160
OSCE. *See* Organization on Security and Co-
　operation in Europe
Ottawa process, 138
Overseas Development Council (ODC), 271
Owen, David, 65

Pakistan, 38, 48, 50
Palestine, 29–30
PBC. *See* Peacebuilding Commission
PBF. *See* Peacebuilding Fund (PBF)
PBSO. *See* Peacebuilding Support Office
Peacebuilding, 134
Peacebuilding Commission (PBC), 97,
　126–128, 134, 141
Peacebuilding Fund (PBF), 97, 127–128
Peacebuilding Support Office (PBSO), 127,
　128
Peacekeepers, 32–33
　sexual abuse by, 126, 134
Peacekeeping, 24, 48–52, 52–54, 75–76
　characteristics of, 37–40
　during Cold War, 34–35, 35–37, 37 (table)
　definition of, 35
　1978–1988, 41–42
　and Security Council, 38–39
　See also Economic sanctions; Enforcement;
　　Peacekeeping operations
Peacekeeping operations, 88–90 (table), 104
　1988–2000, 49 (table)
　1999–present, 87 (table)
PEPFAR. *See* President's Emergency Plan for
　AIDS Relief
Pérez de Cuéllar, Javier, 11, 51–52, 54
　and human rights, 191, 192, 193
Permanent Court of International Justice, 15,
　171
Permanent Mandates Commission, 156
Persian Gulf War. *See* Gulf War
Peterson, Lester B., 35
Philippines, 199
Philpott, Daniel, 106
Picco, Giandomenico, 85
Pillay, Navanethem, 197

Pinochet, Augusto, 187, 198, 233
Political rights, 162
Portugal, 94
Poverty, 253, 273–274, 329–330
Powell, Colin, 21, 101, 185
Power, 5–6, 356–357
Power, Samantha, 238–239
Prebisch, Raúl, 260–261, 264
Preparatory Commission for the
    Comprehensive Nuclear-Test Ban Treaty
    Organization, 116
President's Emergency Plan for AIDS Relief
    (PEPFAR), 269–270
Prestowitz, Clyde, xlix
Private sector, 345
Proxmire, William, 239
Public health, 336–342. *See also* Drugs
Puchala, Donald, 373
Putin, Vladimir, 237

Raisons d'état, lvi–lviii, 229–232, 389–390. *See
    also* National interest
Ramcharan, Bertrand, 196
Rand Corporation, 86, 141
Rato, Rodrigo de, 299
Reagan, Ronald, xlvii, xlviii, 47, 52, 266, 267
Realizing Rights–Ethical Globalization
    Initiative, 171
Red Crescent Movement, 154, 169–170
Red Crescent Society, 154, 215
Refugee rights, 156
Refugees International, 134
Regional organizations, 18–24
Resolutions, 136
Responsibility to protect (R2P), 82, 103–106,
    125–126, 172
Revolutionary United Front (RUF), 96
Rhodesia, 42–43, 179, 180
Rice, Condoleezza, 273
Rice, Susan, 120, 371
Rieff, David, 61
Robinson, Mary, 163, 171, 194, 195–196
Rome Statute, 189, 190, 191
Roosevelt, Eleanor, 235
Roosevelt, Franklin D., xlvii, 158, 266, 268
Rosenau, James, 365
R2P. *See* Responsibility to protect
RUF. *See* Revolutionary United Front
Ruggie, John, 355–356
Rules, 376–380, 380–386
Russia, 92, 93, 118

and human rights, 186, 198
and responsibility to protect, 104
Rwanda, 61, 70–72, 189
and human rights, 81, 83, 179, 184–185,
    186

SAARC. *See* South Asian Association for
    Regional Cooperation
Sachs, Jeffrey, 328, 354
Saddam Hussein, xlix, 16, 117, 118, 123, 140,
    180
and Al Qaeda, 111, 115, 116
execution of, 194
Sarajevo, 60
Saro-Wiwa, Ken, 186
Scholte, Jan Aart, 324, 325, 387
Scientific knowledge, 239–240. *See also*
    Knowledge
Scowcroft, Brent, 123
Secretariat
reform of, 135–139
and terrorism, 114
Secretary-General, 10–12
and Article 99, 11, 135
authority of, 135–136
and human rights, 191–194
and neutrality, 85–86
reform of, 135–136
and terrorism, 114
Security, 371–373
rules, 377–378, 380–383
See also Human security
Security Council, 7–9
and human rights, 178–186
and peacekeeping, 38–39
and permanent membership, 7–9, 129–130
and presidency, 9
reform of, 129–131, 132, 140–141
and terrorism, 113–114
and veto power, 8–9, 130–131, 372, 380
and voting process, 9, 130–131
Self-defense, 12–13, 113
Self-determination, 163
Sen, Amartya, 272, 273
Senior Management Group (SMG), 283
September 11, 2001 attack, 111, 141
Serbia, 64, 65, 66, 92–93
Sexual abuse, 126, 134
Shotton, Anna, 134
SIDS. *See* Small island developing states
Sierra Leone, 95–97, 179, 185

Sihanouk, Norodom, 63
Slave trade, 155
Small island developing states (SIDS), 348–349
SMG. *See* Senior Management Group
Smith, Adam, 266
Smith, Ian, 43, 179
Social justice, 156
Social learning, 354, 355–356
Socioeconomic rights, 162–163
Solana, Javier, 90
Solferino, Battle of, 154
Solidarity rights, 163
Somalia, 61, 67–70, 181–182, 183, 184, 195
South Africa, 43, 51–52
    and human rights, 179, 180, 187, 197, 198
South Asia, 21
South Asian Association for Regional Cooperation (SAARC), 21
South-West Africa People's Organization (SWAPO), 51–52
Sovereignty, l–li. *See also* State sovereignty
Soviet republics, 22, 23
Soviet Union, 47, 50, 129, 157, 158, 198
Special UN Fund for Economic Development (SUNFED), 257
Stalin, Joseph, 158
Standards, 136, 171, 177–178
State coalitions, 233–235
State sovereignty, li–lvi, 16–17, 124–125, 232
    and human rights, 105–106, 153
    and responsibility to protect, 82
    See also Sovereignty
State terrorism, 112
Stoltenberg, Thorvald, 65
Strauss-Khan, Dominique, 299
Strong, Maurice, 302, 303
Sub-Commission on Prevention of Discrimination and Protection of Minorities, 156
Subcontracting, 23
Sudan, 100, 101–102
    and human rights, 185–186, 200–201
    and International Criminal Court, 189, 191
    See also Darfur, Sudan
Suez, 32–33
SUNFED. *See* Special UN Fund for Economic Development
Sustainable development, 267–274, 280–283, 284–292, 354–356
    and change, 365–366

conferences, 1990–2005, 308–309 (table)
    and finance, 347–348
    and globalization, 344–353
    and good governance, 309, 311–314
    and International Monetary Fund, 296–297, 298–299, 300–302
    and learning, 375–376
    and norm creation, 302–314
    organizations, 279–280
    rules for, 379–380, 385–386
    and World Bank, 296–297, 297–298, 300–302
    and World Trade Organization, 296–297, 299–300, 300–302
    See also Development; Millennium Development Goals
Sustainable human development, 314–317, 354–355, 389–390
SWAPO. *See* South-West Africa People's Organization
Switzerland, 167
Syria, 100

Taliban, xlix, 59, 113, 211, 273–274
    and Al Qaeda, 3, 50, 117, 128, 370
Taylor, Charles, 242
Technology. *See* Information and communication technologies
Terrorism, 112–115
    definition of, 112–113, 133
    and weapons of mass destruction, 111, 114, 115–120, 133–134
    See also Al Qaeda
Thant, U., 11, 191
Tharoor, Shashi, 368
Thatcher, Margaret, 266
Thornburgh, Richard, 62
Threat or use of force, and UN Charter, 12–13
Timor-Leste, 94–95. *See also* East Timor
TNCs. *See* Transnational corporations
Torture, 149–150
Trade, 345–347
Trade-Related Aspects of Intellectual Property Rights (TRIPS), 350–351
Trafficking in persons, 335–336
Transnational corporations (TNCs), 193–194
TRIPS. *See* Trade-Related Aspects of Intellectual Property Rights
Truman, Harry, 158
Tudjman, Franjo, 244
Turmen, Tomris, 337

UDHR. *See* Universal Declaration of Human Rights
Uganda, 189, 198
UN Angola Verification Mission (UNAVEM), 48, 51, 61
UN Assistance Mission for Afghanistan (UNAMA), 141
UN Assistance Mission in Rwanda (UNAMIR), 61, 70–72
UN Charter, 3–4, 12–18, 19, 44, 130
    and human rights, 158–161
UN Children's Fund (UNICEF), 59, 214, 267, 268, 287–288
UN Committee of Experts, 165, 166
UN Conference on Environment and Development (UNCED), 271
UN Conference on International Organization, 4
UN Conference on Plenipotentiaries on the Establishment of an International Criminal Court, 188–189
UN Conference on Trade and Development (UNCTAD), 259, 261, 264, 265, 268, 286–287
UN Covenant on Civil and Political Rights, 164, 233
UN Covenant on Economic, Social and Cultural Rights, 205–206, 233
UN Development Fund for Women (UNIFEM), 268
UN Development Group Executive Committee (UNDG), 283
UN Development Programme (UNDP), 194, 214, 262–263, 268, 271, 284–286
    human freedom and human development indices, 212, 213 (table)
UN Disaster Relief Office (UNDRO), 214
UN Disengagement Observer Force (UNDOF), 36–37, 38
UN Educational, Scientific and Cultural Organization (UNESCO), 258
UN Emergency Force I (UNEF I), 32–33
UN Emergency Force II (UNEF II), 34
UN Environment Programme (UNEP), 194, 263, 270, 290–292
UN Expanded Programme of Technical Assistance (EPTA), 256
UN Global Counter-Terrorism Strategy, 114
UN Good Offices Mission in Afghanistan and Pakistan (UNGOMAP), 48, 50
UN High Commissioner for Human Rights, 194–197

UN High Commissioner for Refugees (UNHCR), 60, 70, 71, 156, 207–211, 214
UN Human Rights Commission, 158, 232
UN Human Rights Committee, 165, 166
UN Integrated Mission in Timor-Leste (UNMIT), 95
UN Interim Administration Mission in Kosovo (UNMIK), 91–92
UN Interim Force in Lebanon (UNIFIL), 38, 39, 40, 98–99
UN Iran-Iraq Military Observer Group (UNIIMOG), 48, 50–51
UN Military Observer Group in Indian and Pakistan (UNMOGIP), 38
UN Millennium Declaration, 268, 272, 323, 353
UN Mission for Sierra Leone (UNAMSIL), 96
UN Mission in East Timor (UNAMET), 94
UN Mission in Haiti (UNMIH), 61, 72–75
UN Mission in Sudan (UNMIS), 101–102
UN Monitoring, Verification, and Inspection Commission (UNMOVIC), 116, 118
UN Nations Conference on the Human Environment (UNCHE), 263
UN Observer Group in Central America (ONUCA), 52–53
UN Observer Mission in El Salvador (ONUSAL), 52, 54
UN Observer Mission in Sierra Leone (UNOMSIL), 96
UN Observer Mission to Verify the Electoral Process in Haiti (ONUVEH), 54
UN Observer Mission to Verify the Electoral Process in Nicaragua (ONUVEN), 52, 53–54
UN Operation in Somalia (UNOSOM), 61, 67–70
UN Operation in the Congo (ONUC), 33
UN Peacekeeping Force in Cyprus (UNFICYP), 38
UN Protection Force in former Yugoslavia (UNPROFOR), 61, 63–67
UN Protection Force in the Balkans, 184
UN Relief and Works Agency (UNRWA), 209
UN Special Commission (UNSCOM), 116
UN Stabilization Mission in Haiti (MINUSTAH), 72–73
UN Sub-Commission on Prevention of Discrimination and Protection of Minorities, 204
UN Sub-Commission on the Promotion and Protection of Human Rights, 204

UN Support Mission in Haiti (UNSMIH), 73

UN Transition Assistance Group in Namibia (UNTAG), 48, 51–52, 179, 184

UN Transitional Administration in East Timor (UNTAET), 94

UN Transitional Authority in Cambodia (UNTAC), 61, 62, 184

UN Truce Supervision Organization (UNTSO), 29–30

UN/African Union Mission in Darfur (UNAMID), 102–103

UNAMET. See UN Mission in East Timor

UNAMID. See UN/African Union Mission in Darfur

UNAMIR. See UN Assistance Mission in Rwanda

UNAMSIL. See UN Mission for Sierra Leone

UNAVEM. See UN Angola Verification Mission

UNCED. See UN Conference on Environment and Development

UNCHE. See UN Nations Conference on the Human Environment

UNCTAD. See UN Conference on Trade and Development

UNDG. See UN Development Group Executive Committee

UNDOF. See UN Disengagement Observer Force

UNDP. See UN Development Programme

UNDRO. See UN Disaster Relief Office

UNEP. See UN Environment Programme

UNESCO. See UN Educational, Scientific and Cultural Organization

UNFICYP. See UN Peacekeeping Force in Cyprus

UNGOMAP. See UN Good Offices Mission in Afghanistan and Pakistan

UNHCR. See UN High Commissioner for Refugees

UNICEF. See UN Children's Fund

UNIFEM. See UN Development Fund for Women

Unified Task Force (UNITAF), 68

UNIFIL. See UN Interim Force in Lebanon

UNIIMOG. See UN Iran-Iraq Military Observer Group

Unilateralism, 117, 364, 366, 370–371

UNITAF. See Unified Task Force

United Kingdom, 96–97, 159, 179

United Nations
  as actor, lviii–lxii
  annual budget, 61–62

brief history of, xlvi–l
creation of, 3–4
as institutional framework, lviii–lxii
and institutional reform, 123–131
and personnel, safety of, 121–122
and political reform, 120–123
and reform, 120–141
and Secretariat, reform of (see under Secretariat)
and Secretary-General, reform of (see under Secretary-General)
and Security Council, reform of (see under Security Council)
See also General Assembly; Secretariat; Secretary-General; Security Council; UN Charter

United Nations Organization (UNO), 3–4

United States, 64–65, 67–68, 72–74, 92–93, 157
and Afghanistan, 117, 120
criticism of, 369–371
and development, 257
and global warming, 343
and Gulf War (1991), 55–57
and human rights, 157, 164, 165, 196, 198, 232, 233
and International Criminal Court, 189–190, 191, 241
and Iraq, 116–120, 119, 180
and Millennium Development Goals, 356–357
and torture, 149–150
and unilateralism, 370–371
and Universal Declaration of Human Rights, 163
and war on terrorism, 115

Uniting for Peace Resolution, 9–10, 32

Universal Declaration of Human Rights (UDHR), 149, 161–166, 233, 235
and first-generation negative rights, 162
impact of, 164–165
and second-generation positive rights, 162–163
and third-generation solidarity rights, 163

Universal Postal Union (UPU), 258

UNMIH. See UN Mission in Haiti

UNMIK. See UN Interim Administration Mission in Kosovo

UNMIS. See UN Mission in Sudan

UNMIT. See UN Integrated Mission in Timor-Leste (UNMIT)

UNMOGIP. See UN Military Observer Group in Indian and Pakistan

UNMOVIC. *See* UN Monitoring, Verification, and Inspection Commission
UNO. *See* United Nations Organization
UNOMSIL. *See* UN Observer Mission in Sierra Leone
UNOSOM. *See* UN Operation in Somalia
UNPROFOR. *See* UN Protection Force in former Yugoslavia
UNRWA. *See* UN Relief and Works Agency
UNSCOM. *See* UN Special Commission
UNSMIH. *See* UN Support Mission in Haiti
UNTAC. *See* UN Transitional Authority in Cambodia
UNTAET. *See* UN Transitional Administration in East Timor
UNTAG. *See* UN Transition Assistance Group in Namibia
UNTSO. *See* UN Truce Supervision Organization
UPU. *See* Universal Postal Union
Urquhart, Sir Brian, 37, 388

Van Boven, Theo, 192
Vance, Cyrus, 65
Védrine, Hubert, 129
Versailles conference (1919), 155
Vieira de Mello, Sergio, 196
Volcker, Paul, 120, 136–137, 297–298

Waldheim, Kurt, 191
War, 160–161
War on terrorism, 115, 141
Washington consensus, 266, 270, 310
Weapons of mass destruction (WMDs), 111, 114, 115–120, 133–134
Webster, Daniel, 118
Western Europe, 157, 170–171
WFP. *See* World Food Programme
WHO. *See* World Health Organization
Williamson, John, 266
Wilson, Woodrow, 155, 158

WMDs. *See* Weapons of mass destruction
WMO. *See* World Meteorological Organization
Wolfensohn, James, 301
Wolfowitz, Paul, 297
Women
in development, 268, 333–336
and women's rights, 158
World Bank, 11, 256–257, 264–265, 266, 268, 270–271
and sustainable development, 296–297, 297–298, 300–302
World Commission on the Social Dimensions of Globalization, 171
World Conference against Racism, Racial Discrimination, Xenophobia, and Related Intolerance in Durban, South Africa, 196
World Conference on Human Rights, 151, 187
World Food Programme (WFP), 60, 214
World Health Organization (WHO), 60, 214, 258
World Meteorological Organization (WMO), 258
World Summit Outcome Document, 104
World Summit (September 2005), 123, 127, 131–134
World Trade Organization (WTO), 270, 346–347
and sustainable development, 296–297, 299–300, 300–302
World War II, 158
WTO. *See* World Trade Organization

Yugoslavia (former), 61, 63–67, 179, 189

Zacher, Mark, 387
Zaidi, Sarah, 150
Zimbabwe, 179, 200–201
Zoellick, Robert, 297, 298